Reader's Digest

Pies, Tarts & Puddings

Reader's Digest

Pies, Tarts & Puddings

Published by The Reader's Digest Association Limited
London • New York • Sydney • Montreal

Pies, Tarts & Puddings is part of a series of cookery books called **Eat Well Live Well** and was created by Amazon Publishing Limited.

Series Editor *Norma MacMillan*
Volume Editor *Maggie Pannell*
Art Director *Ruth Prentice*
Photographic Direction *Ruth Prentice, Alison Shackleton*
DTP *Claire Graham*
Editorial Assistant *Elizabeth Woodland*
Nutritionist *Jane Griffin, BSc (Nutri.), SRD*

Contributors
Writers *Catherine Atkinson, Sara Buenfeld, Linda Collister, Christine France, Angela Nilsen, Maggie Pannell, Anne Sheasby, Susanna Tee*
Recipe Testers *Catherine Atkinson, Juliet Barker, Bridget Jones, Jane Middleton, Maggie Pannell, Susanna Tee*
Photographers *Martin Brigdale, Gus Filgate, William Lingwood*
Stylist *Helen Trent*
Home Economists *Julz Beresford, Lucy McKelvie, Bridget Sargeson, Linda Tubby, Sunil Vijayakar*

For Reader's Digest
Project Editor *Rachel Warren Chadd*
Project Art Editor *Louise Turpin*
Pre-press Accounts Manager *Penny Grose*

Reader's Digest General Books
Editorial Director *Cortina Butler*
Art Director *Nick Clark*
Series Editor *Christine Noble*

Paperback edition 2004
Paperback Art Editor *Jane McKenna*

ISBN 0 276 42802 1

Notes for the reader

- Use all metric or all imperial measures when preparing a recipe, as the two sets of measurements are not exact equivalents.
- Recipes were tested using metric measures and conventional (not fan-assisted) ovens. Medium eggs were used, unless otherwise specified.
- Can sizes are approximate, as weights can vary slightly according to the manufacturer.
- Preparation and cooking times are only intended as a guide.

The nutritional information in this book is for reference only. The editors urge anyone with continuing medical problems or symptoms to consult a doctor.

Contents

56 Simple Family Meals

82 Savoury Dishes for Entertaining

104 Sweet Pies and Tarts

128 Sweet Puddings

Eating well to live well

Eating a healthy diet can help you look good, feel great and have lots of energy. Nutrition fads come and go, but the simple keys to eating well remain the same: enjoy a variety of food – no single food contains all the vitamins, minerals, fibre and other essential components you need for health and vitality – and get the balance right by looking at the proportions of the different foods you eat. Add some regular exercise too – at least 30 minutes a day, 3 times a week – and you'll be helping yourself to live well and make the most of your true potential.

Getting it into proportion

Current guidelines are that most people in the UK should eat more starchy foods, more fruit and vegetables, and less fat, meat products and sugary foods. It is almost impossible to give exact amounts that you should eat, as every single person's requirements vary, depending on size, age and the amount of energy expended during the day. However, nutrition experts have suggested an ideal balance of the different foods that provide us with energy (calories) and the nutrients needed for health. The number of daily portions of each of the food groups will vary from person to person – for example, an active teenager might need to eat up to 14 portions of starchy carbohydrates every day, whereas a sedentary adult would only require 6 or 7 portions – but the proportions of the food groups in relation to each other should ideally stay the same.

More detailed explanations of food groups and nutritional terms can be found on pages 156–158, together with brief guidelines on amounts which can be used in conjunction with the nutritional analyses of the recipes. A simple way to get the balance right, however, is to imagine a daily 'plate' divided into the different food groups. On the imaginary 'plate', starchy carbohydrates fill at least one-third of the space, thus constituting the main part of your meals. Fruit and vegetables fill the same amount of space. The remaining third of the 'plate' is divided mainly between protein foods and dairy foods, with just a little space allowed for foods containing fat and sugar. These are the proportions to aim for.

It isn't essential to eat the ideal proportions on the 'plate' at every meal, or even every day – balancing them over a week or two is just as good. The healthiest diet for you and your family is one that is generally balanced and sustainable in the long term.

Our daily plate

Starchy carbohydrate foods: eat 6–14 portions a day

At least 50% of the calories in a healthy diet should come from carbohydrates, and most of that from starchy foods – bread, potatoes and other starchy vegetables, pasta, rice and cereals. For most people in the UK this means doubling current intake. Starchy carbohydrates are the best foods for energy. They also provide protein and essential vitamins and minerals, particularly those from the B group. Eat a variety of starchy foods, choosing wholemeal or wholegrain types whenever possible, because the fibre they contain helps to prevent constipation, bowel disease, heart disease and other health problems.

What is a portion of starchy foods?

Some examples are: 3 tbsp breakfast cereal • 2 tbsp muesli • 1 slice of bread or toast • 1 bread roll, bap or bun • 1 small pitta bread, naan bread or chapatti • 3 crackers or crispbreads • 1 medium-sized potato • 1 medium-sized plantain or small sweet potato • 2 heaped tbsp boiled rice • 2 heaped tbsp boiled pasta.

Fruit and vegetables: eat at least 5 portions a day

Nutrition experts are unanimous that we would all benefit from eating more fruit and vegetables each day – a total of at least 400 g (14 oz) of fruit and vegetables (edible part) is the target. Fruit and vegetables provide vitamin C for immunity and healing, and other 'antioxidant' vitamins and minerals for protection against cardiovascular disease and cancer. They also offer several 'phytochemicals' that help protect against cancer, and B vitamins, especially folate, which is important for women planning a pregnancy, to prevent birth defects. All of these, plus other nutrients, work together to boost well-being.

Antioxidant nutrients (e.g. vitamins C and beta-carotene, which are mainly derived from fruit and vegetables) and vitamin E help to prevent harmful free radicals in the body initiating or accelerating cancer, heart disease, cataracts, arthritis, general ageing, sun damage to skin, and damage to sperm. Free radicals occur naturally as a by-product of normal cell function, but are also caused by pollutants such as tobacco smoke and over-exposure to sunlight.

What is a portion of fruit or vegetables?

Some examples are: 1 medium-sized portion of vegetables or salad • 1 medium-sized piece of fresh fruit • 6 tbsp (about 140 g/5 oz) stewed or canned fruit • 1 small glass (100 ml/3½ fl oz) fruit juice.

Dairy foods: eat 2–3 portions a day

Dairy foods, such as milk, cheese, yogurt and fromage frais, are the best source of calcium for strong bones and teeth, and important for the nervous system. They also provide some protein for growth and repair, vitamin B_{12}, and vitamin A for healthy eyes. They are particularly valuable foods for young children, who need full-fat versions at least up to age 2. Dairy foods are also especially important for adolescent girls to prevent the development of osteoporosis later in life, and for women throughout life generally.

To limit fat intake, wherever possible adults should choose lower-fat dairy foods, such as semi-skimmed milk and low-fat yogurt.

What is a portion of dairy foods?

Some examples are: 1 medium-sized glass (200 ml/7 fl oz) milk • 1 matchbox-sized piece (40 g/1½ oz) Cheddar cheese • 1 small pot of yogurt • 125 g (4½ oz) cottage cheese or fromage frais.

Protein foods: eat 2–4 portions a day

Lean meat, fish, eggs and vegetarian alternatives provide protein for growth and cell repair, as well as iron to prevent anaemia. Meat also provides B vitamins for healthy nerves and digestion, especially vitamin B_{12}, and zinc for growth and healthy bones and skin. Only moderate amounts of these protein-rich foods are required. An adult woman needs about 45 g of protein a day and an adult man 55 g, which constitutes about 11% of a day's calories. This is less than the current average intake. For optimum health, we need to eat some protein every day.

What is a portion of protein-rich food?

Some examples are: 3 slices (85–100 g/3–3½ oz) of roast beef, pork, ham, lamb or chicken • about 100 g (3½ oz) grilled offal • 115–140 g (4–5 oz) cooked fillet of white or oily fish (not fried in batter) • 3 fish fingers • 2 eggs (up to 7 a week) • about 140 g/5 oz baked beans • 60 g (2¼ oz) nuts, peanut butter or other nut products.

Foods containing fat: 1–5 portions a day

Unlike fruit, vegetables and starchy carbohydrates, which can be eaten in abundance, fatty foods should not exceed 33% of the day's calories in a balanced diet, and only 10% of this should be from saturated fat. This quantity of fat may seem a lot, but it isn't – fat contains more than twice as many calories per gram as either carbohydrate or protein.

Overconsumption of fat is a major cause of weight and health problems. A healthy diet must contain a certain amount of fat to provide fat-soluble vitamins and essential fatty acids, needed for the development and function of the brain, eyes and nervous system, but we only need a small amount each day – just 25 g is required, which is much less than we consume in our Western diet. The current recommendations from the Department of Health are a maximum of 71 g fat (of this, 21.5 g saturated) for women each day and 93.5 g fat (28.5 g saturated) for men. The best sources of the essential fatty acids are natural fish oils and pure vegetable oils.

What is a portion of fatty foods?

Some examples are: 1 tsp butter or margarine • 2 tsp low-fat spread • 1 tsp cooking oil • 1 tbsp mayonnaise or vinaigrette (salad dressing) • 1 tbsp cream • 1 individual packet of crisps.

Foods containing sugar: 0–2 portions a day

Although many foods naturally contain sugars (e.g. fruit contains fructose, milk lactose), health experts recommend that we limit 'added' sugars. Added sugars, such as table sugar, provide only calories – they contain no vitamins, minerals or fibre to contribute to health, and it is not necessary to eat them at all. But, as the old adage goes, 'a little of what you fancy does you good' and sugar is no exception. Denial of foods, or using them as rewards or punishment, is not a healthy attitude to eating, and can lead to cravings, binges and yo-yo dieting. Sweet foods are a pleasurable part of a well-balanced diet, but added sugars should account for no more than 11% of the total daily carbohydrate intake.

In assessing how much sugar you consume, don't forget that it is a major ingredient of many processed and ready-prepared foods.

What is a portion of sugary foods?

Some examples are: 3 tsp sugar • 1 heaped tsp jam or honey • 2 biscuits • half a slice of cake • 1 doughnut • 1 Danish pastry • 1 small bar of chocolate • 1 small tube or bag of sweets.

Too salty

Salt (sodium chloride) is essential for a variety of body functions, but we tend to eat too much through consumption of salty processed foods, 'fast' foods and ready-prepared foods, and by adding salt in cooking and at the table. The end result can be rising blood pressure as we get older, which puts us at higher risk of heart disease and stroke. Eating more vegetables and fruit increases potassium intake, which can help to counteract the damaging effects of salt.

Alcohol in a healthy diet

In recent research, moderate drinking of alcohol has been linked with a reduced risk of heart disease and stroke among men and women over 45. However, because of other risks associated with alcohol, particularly in excessive quantities, no doctor would recommend taking up drinking if you are teetotal. The healthiest pattern of drinking is to enjoy small amounts of alcohol with food, to have alcohol-free days and always to avoid getting drunk. A well-balanced diet is vital because nutrients from food (vitamins and minerals) are needed to detoxify the alcohol.

Water – the best choice

Drinking plenty of non-alcoholic liquid each day is an often overlooked part of a well-balanced diet. A minimum of 8 glasses (which is about 2 litres/3½ pints) is the ideal. If possible, these should not all be tea or coffee, as these are stimulants and diuretics, which cause the body to lose liquids, taking with them water-soluble vitamins. Water is the best choice. Other good choices are fruit or herb teas or tisanes, fruit juices – diluted with water, if preferred – or semi-skimmed milk (full-fat milk for very young children). Fizzy sugary or acidic drinks such as cola are more likely to damage tooth enamel than other drinks.

As a guide to the vitamin and mineral content of foods and recipes in the book, we have used the following terms and symbols, based on the percentage of the daily RNI provided by one serving for the average adult man or woman aged 19–49 years (see also pages 156–158):

✓✓✓	*or* excellent	at least 50% (half)
✓✓	*or* good	25–50% (one-quarter to one-half)
✓	*or* useful	10–25% (one-tenth to one-quarter)

Note that recipes contribute other nutrients, but the analyses only include those that provide at least 10% RNI per portion. Vitamins and minerals where deficiencies are rare are not included.

Ⓥ denotes that a recipe is suitable for vegetarians.

Wonderful Pies, Tarts and Puddings

A wide choice, both sweet and savoury

The cook who brings a pastry dish or pudding to the table will always be greeted with delight. There is something about these comforting dishes that whets the appetite and makes mealtimes so enjoyable. They can fit perfectly into a healthy diet too, because they incorporate such a wide variety of nutrient-rich ingredients, from protein foods, dairy products, grains and other starchy carbohydrates, to nuts and seeds, and fruit and vegetables. You'll be inspired to create starters, snacks, main dishes and desserts that are both nutritious and delicious.

Healthy pies, tarts and puddings

Fillings wrapped in or topped with pastry, and sweet and savoury puddings may not spring to mind as being the healthiest of dishes, but in fact pies, tarts and puddings can be very nutritious and fit well into healthy eating guidelines. With such a wide variety of appetising recipes, friends and family will be able to tuck in with relish.

Food that really satisfies

Pies, tarts and puddings have been popular since medieval times. Like many traditional dishes, they were developed to meet both practical and nutritional needs, as well as to celebrate special occasions. The pie – a filling encased in an edible crust – was the original convenience food, easy to transport and eat without cutlery. And puddings, both sweet and savoury, were satisfying, warming body and soul. The modern versions show that these homely dishes still have plenty to offer, and can be enjoyed as part of a healthy diet.

Pies to please

A pie consists of a sweet or savoury filling covered with a crust or with a crust both on top and at the bottom. The possibilities for tasty fillings are almost endless. And the choice of crust can be deliciously varied, from pastry, bread and scone dough to polenta, rice, tortillas, sliced or cubed bread, and mashed potatoes and other vegetables. Pies can be made in many shapes and sizes, and can be finished with a glaze, a sprinkle of nuts or cheese, or a pastry decoration.

Pies can be plain and simple, making the most of seasonal produce and turning everyday ingredients into tasty dishes for the family, or more exotic and adventurous ones for a special occasion. And from the point of view of healthy eating, one of the merits of a pie is that a nourishing combination of ingredients can be cooked together in their own juices, retaining maximum flavour and goodness.

Tempting tarts

A tart is usually understood to be an open case filled with a sweet or savoury mixture. It may also be called a quiche, which is traditionally filled with a bacon and Gruyère cheese custard, or a flan. Small individual tarts are usually called tartlets.

The fat issue

Many pies and tarts are made with pastry, which is basically a combination of fat and flour bound with water or other liquid to make a dough. It is the fat that provides texture and flavour. Certain pastries, such as puff and flaky, contain a high proportion of fat to flour and cannot be made successfully by altering the balance of ingredients. Others, such as filo and scone pastry, contain very little fat. Shortcrust pastry, which is the most widely used, can be enjoyed in a healthy diet, but to keep the total fat content down it is best to roll out the pastry thinly and to use it only as a single crust, either as a container for the filling or covering it. Shortcrust can also be made successfully with unsaturated fats such as olive or sunflower oil, rather than butter. With a filling that includes a variety of lean and nutritious ingredients, a pie or tart can make a tasty contribution to healthy family eating or be a special meal for guests.

Tart cases can be made from pastry – most commonly shortcrust or crisp and flaky filo – or from other mixtures such as polenta, yeasted bread dough, bread slices or biscuit crumbs.

Comforting puddings

The word pudding is used to describe a number of different kinds of dishes. Thus a pudding can be a savoury recipe, usually served hot and often made in a pudding basin or other mould, or it can be a sweet dish served at the end of a meal. Sweet puddings may be hot or cold, although cold sweet dishes are often called desserts.

The range of sweet and savoury puddings is wide, from Yorkshire puddings, rice puddings, and sponge puddings to classic family favourites such as crumbles and custards.

► Use deliciously crisp, low-fat filo pastry for Oriental crab, corn and asparagus tartlets (see Some more ideas, page 35)

▼ Try Spiced lamb pie, made with lean lamb and lots of nutritious vegetables and covered with a coriander mash (see Some more ideas, page 87)

▲ Make an apple and blackberry pie full of juicy, healthy fruit and topped with a shortcrust pastry lid (see Some more ideas, page 126)

◄ For a vitamin-C boost, layer fresh raspberries with crunchy amaretti and a creamy yogurt custard (see Some more ideas, page 133)

What pies, tarts and puddings have to offer

With such a wonderful variety of pie, tart and pudding recipes, using ingredients from all the different food groups, it is possible to benefit from just about every nutrient needed for good health and wellbeing.

Dairy foods

Milk, yogurt and cream enrich and moisten puddings and fillings for pies and tarts, while cheeses add flavour. Dairy foods are an excellent source of calcium and phosphorus, both needed for strong teeth and bones. Dairy foods also provide protein, other minerals and a variety of vitamins, including A, B-group and D. Full-fat dairy products can be high in saturated fat, but there are many lower-fat versions that work well in cooking. You can also mix high and lower-fat dairy ingredients or, in the case of cheese, choose those strong in flavour so less is needed for maximum taste impact.

Eggs

Eggs, which add flavour, colour and lightness of texture to many puddings and to pie and tart fillings, are nutrient-rich, providing high-quality protein, useful amounts of vitamins A, B_2, B_{12}, E and niacin, and plenty of minerals.

Fats

Fats help to provide taste and texture in pastry and in fillings for pies, tarts and puddings, making them satisfying to eat, as well as improving their keeping qualities. Fats provide fat-soluble vitamins as well as the essential fatty acids, omega-3 and omega-6. Butter, a pure natural fat, is a particularly good source of vitamins A and D, while oils pressed from fruit, vegetables, nuts and seeds contain beneficial phytochemicals and other nutrients such as the antioxidant vitamin E, which can help to prevent heart disease. Although healthy eating guidelines recommend cutting down on fat intake, particularly the saturated type, some fat is necessary for good health and for good eating.

Flour

The flours used for making pastry, bread doughs, sponges and scones consist mainly of valuable starchy carbohydrate. Flour can also be a good low-fat source of vegetable protein, and of B vitamins, minerals and dietary fibre.

Fruit and vegetables

Including vegetables in savoury pie fillings and puddings, and fruit in sweet pies and puddings, boosts their nutritional content, and is an easy way to help meet the 5-a-day target. Whether fresh, frozen, dried or canned, fruit and vegetables are an important part of a healthy diet, providing a range of valuable minerals, vitamins and other beneficial compounds as well as dietary fibre, essential for a healthy digestion. Some vegetables also supply starchy carbohydrate.

Meat, poultry and fish

Protein foods such as meat, poultry and fish turn savoury pies and puddings into satisfying main dishes. Apart from supplying excellent amounts of high-quality protein, they offer many other nutrients. Red meat is a particularly rich source of zinc, several B-group vitamins (especially vitamin B_{12}, which is principally found in animal foods) and iron. Poultry supplies B vitamins and many essential minerals including iron and zinc. Fish and other seafood provide important minerals such as the powerful antioxidant selenium and iodine. Oily fish also supplies the heart-healthy omega-3 fatty acids.

► Fruit and vegetables are the best food sources of valuable antioxidants such as vitamin C and beta-carotene, and also offer disease-fighting phytochemicals

▼ Lean meat and skinless poultry are first-class protein foods and also provide iron and zinc

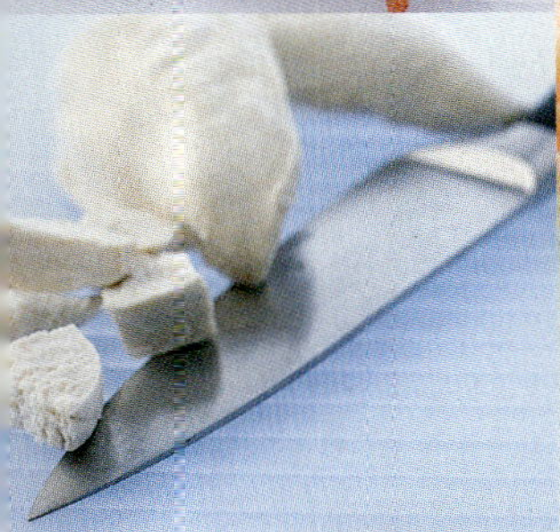

▲ Fish is low in saturated fat, but often high in other beneficial fats, and shellfish is the most reliable natural source of iodine

◄ Pulses and grains supply starchy carbohydrates, the foundation of a healthy, well-balanced diet

Nuts and seeds

Nuts and seeds add crunchy texture to pastries as well as to fillings for pies, tarts and puddings. They also contribute protein (a good source for vegetarians), vitamins, minerals and fibre. Nuts and seeds are high in fat, but (with the exception of coconut) this is mostly in the form of the healthier monounsaturated and polyunsaturated fats.

Pulses

Pulses can add important nutrients to savoury pies and puddings, being good sources of vegetable protein and starchy carbohydrate. They also supply B vitamins (including folate), iron, zinc and dietary fibre. Soya beans are especially nourishing, in that they provide high-quality protein, with all 8 amino acids, just like meat, as well as omega-3 fatty acids, most of the B vitamins, vitamin E and a wide range of minerals. Soya products such as tofu also make a superb nutritional contribution to a pie filling.

Rice and other grains

Grains are the basis of wonderful puddings, both sweet and savoury, and add substance to fillings for pies and tarts. In addition to starchy carbohydrate, they offer some protein, several of the B vitamins, many minerals and dietary fibre. Wholegrains (those which retain the bran and germ) are the most nutritious choice. Rice and grains such as buckwheat, maize, millet and quinoa are gluten-free and so useful for those who suffer from coeliac disease.

Pastry variety

Pastry can be wonderfully varied. By using different fats and flours, changing their proportion to each other and how they're combined, or by adding other ingredients, you can create a range of differently textured and flavoured crusts for pies and tarts that will perfectly complement both sweet and savoury fillings.

Healthy pastry

You may be surprised to see the variety of pastries that can be enjoyed as part of a healthy, well-balanced diet, even those pastries thought of as very high in fat.

Choux pastry Although called a pastry, choux is actually a smooth paste. It is made by melting fat with water and then beating in flour and eggs. It is piped or spooned into shape – for profiteroles, éclairs and so on – and then baked to puff it up. The air trapped inside forms a hollow that can be filled with delicious sweet or savoury mixtures.

Filo pastry The wafer-thin sheets of this low-fat pastry (also called strudel pastry) are brushed sparingly with melted butter or oil and then layered up, to be wrapped, rolled or folded around a sweet or savoury filling, used for delicate pastry cases or scrunched over the top of a pie. During baking the pastry becomes crisp and golden brown. While filo can be made at home, it is labour-intensive, so most cooks prefer to use good-quality chilled or frozen filo.

Hot-water crust This is made with just a small amount of fat (traditionally lard), which is melted with boiling water and then mixed with flour to produce a stiff dough. It needs to be shaped while still warm. It is the classic pastry for 'raised' pies, as it bakes into a firm crust, but also makes a good lower-fat topping for a savoury meat pie.

Scone pastry With a texture that is like a cross between a cake and pastry, scone pastry makes an excellent tart case or top crust for a pie, either sweet or savoury. It is lower in fat than shortcrust, but made in the same way – by rubbing fat into flour and binding with liquid, usually milk. A beaten egg can replace part of the milk for extra nutritional value, and sugar, grated cheese, herbs or spices can be added for flavour.

Suetcrust Quick and easy suetcrust is made with shredded suet and self-raising flour (or plain flour with baking powder). Fresh breadcrumbs can replace part of the flour for a lighter texture, and flavourings such as herbs, grated cheese or nuts can be added for extra taste. Suetcrust is used for pies and for puddings, both sweet and savoury, and is traditionally steamed for a moist texture, although it can also be baked. It should be cooked straight away, as the raising agent in the flour will have started to work as soon as the liquid for binding was added.

Shortcrust pastry The most popular and versatile of pastries, with a delightfully crumbly texture, shortcrust is used for all kinds of sweet and savoury pies and tarts. The fat is usually a hard one such as butter, although oil can be substituted, and it is made by the rubbing-in method. Many other ingredients, such as eggs, oats, sugar, nuts, cheese, citrus zest and spices, can be added to provide exciting flavour variations and additional nutrients. You can also make a lower-fat yeasted version, which has a light 'bready' texture.

Fat contents of different pastries

(based on 100 g/3½ oz uncooked weight of the basic pastry doughs on pages 22–24, and bought filo pastry)

	total fat (g)	saturated fat (g)
filo	4.1	
scone	8.5	5.3
potato	9.9	6.4
choux	14.7	8.4
hot-water crust	16.5	6.6
shortcrust, sweet	22.8	14.0
suetcrust	22.9	12.9
shortcrust, savoury	23.9	15.6

choux pastry

filo pastry

hot-water crust

scone pastry

suetcrust

shortcrust pastry

Ingredients for good pastry

Making the right choice of ingredients is all important for achieving perfect results, and it is also the key to making the healthiest and most nutritious pastry.

Flour

Plain flour is best for most pastries, the exceptions being suetcrust and scone pastry, where a raising agent is needed to produce their characteristic finish. For these, self-raising flour (or plain flour with baking powder) is used. Some cooks also like to use self-raising flour for shortcrust pastry, for a crumblier, more cake-like texture. Strong (bread) flour is unsuitable for short pastries, as the results would be tough, but it can be used for choux pastry and for yeasted pastries.

Both white and wholemeal flours can be used for making pastry. Wholemeal flour contains the whole of the grain and therefore retains most of its nutrients, which means it has more vitamins, minerals, fibre and protein than white flour. Pastries made with wholemeal flour alone have an excellent, almost nutty flavour but a heavier texture. A good compromise is to use half white and half wholemeal flour. In addition, you can use brown flour (also called wheatmeal) or Granary flour.

Flour should be sifted to incorporate air and to mix it with other dry ingredients such as raising agents, salt and spices. After sifting wholemeal flour, tip in the bran left in the sieve.

How do fats compare (per 100 g/3½ oz)?

	total fat*	saturates	polyunsats	monounsats
butter	82 g	54 g	3 g	20 g
margarine (hard)	82 g	31 g	11 g	37 g
suet	87 g	48 g	2 g	32 g
lard	99 g	41 g	10 g	44 g
olive oil	100 g	14 g	11 g	70 g
sunflower oil	100 g	12 g	63 g	20 g

*The total fat figure includes fatty compounds and other fatty acids in addition to saturates and mono and polyunsaturates.

For light-textured pastry, always sift the flour to help to aerate it

Fat

Butter, lard and hard margarines are the fats generally chosen for making pastry, with shredded suet used for suetcrust. Butter gives a lovely short, crumbly texture and the best flavour of all the fats. Lard, which is purified and clarified pork fat, is mild in flavour and gives a good tender texture to pastry, while suet, processed from the crisp white fat surrounding lamb's or beef kidneys, gives suetcrust and suet puddings a melting lightness. (Vegetarians may prefer to use vegetable suet, which is produced from hydrogenated vegetable oils.) Margarine has the same characteristics as butter in pastry-making, but lacks the all-important flavour.

Margarine and other fats produced by hydrogenating vegetable oils, which turns them from liquids into solid fat, contain a high proportion of trans fatty acids. These fats are now thought to be more harmful to health than saturated fat, in increasing the risk of heart disease. For this reason, and because of its superior flavour, butter is recommended for most of the pastries in this book. If you prefer to use margarine, choose one high in monounsaturates, usually made from olive oil, or one labelled 'free from hydrogenated oils' or 'low in trans fats'.

Oils can also be used for making delicious shortcrust pastry. Olive oil has a rich flavour, so is better suited to savoury pies and tarts, whereas oils with a mild flavour, such as sunflower, safflower and corn, can be used for both sweet and savoury shortcrust pastries.

Soft tub margarines and low-fat spreads are not suitable for traditional pastry-making as they have a different composition and a high water content. They should only be used in recipes specially developed for them.

The liquid element

During baking, the liquid in pastry turns to steam, which can help the pastry to rise and to lighten its texture. The amount of liquid given in a recipe can only be approximate as more or less may be needed, depending on the flour used and the humidity in the kitchen. Pastry made with wholemeal flour needs a little more liquid than one made with white flour.

- Egg or egg yolk, often combined with a little milk or water, enriches pastry. It makes shortcrust shorter in texture, with a lovely golden-coloured crust; in choux pastry, beaten egg creates lightness and volume. Egg also provides additional binding and helps to give a sharp edge to a shortcrust tart case.
- Milk will make a slightly softer pastry than egg. Or you can use plain low-fat yogurt for a pleasant tangy flavour.
- Water is the liquid most commonly used for binding pastry ingredients. If it is very cold, it will help to keep the pastry cool while you work with it. Fruit juice is another option.

Why not try fruit juice, such as orange, apple or lemon, instead of water for binding pastry ingredients together? The juice will add a subtle flavour. As with water, add only enough juice to moisten the ingredients so they can be gathered together into a ball

Interesting extras

Lots of other ingredients can be added to pastry to ring the changes with interesting flavours and textures, as well as to help to boost the nutritional value.

- Cheese makes a tasty addition to savoury pastries and is also good for an apple pie. Hard cheeses such as mature Cheddar and Parmesan are high in fat, but you don't need to add very much as they have a strong flavour. Grate the cheese finely and stir in just before adding the liquid. Add a pinch of cayenne pepper or a little dry mustard too, to help to bring out the cheese flavour. Another idea is to replace some of the butter or other fat with reduced-fat soft cheese or a crumbly cheese like feta.
- Citrus zest, particularly lemon and orange zest, adds a delicious flavour to sweet pastries and to some savoury ones. If liked, the fruit's juice can be used in place of some or all of the water to bind the dough together.
- Ground nuts, such as hazelnuts, almonds and walnuts, can be used in short pastries in place of some of the flour, enriching and adding texture.
- Herbs are delicious in pastry for savoury pies and tarts, and give it pretty green specks. Use 1–2 tbsp chopped fresh herbs or 1–2 tsp dried. Good choices include chives, parsley, sage, thyme, coriander, tarragon and basil, depending on the filling.
- Oats and oatmeal can replace some of the flour in short pastry, adding a lovely rough texture and subtle nutty flavour. Oaty shortcrust is good for both sweet and savoury pies and tarts, and works particularly well with fresh and dried fruit, cheese and vegetable fillings.
- Spices of all kinds can be sifted with the flour. Chilli and curry powders are great in pastry for spicy meat or vegetable fillings, and sweet spices such as ground cinnamon, nutmeg, allspice or mixed spice are perfect for fruit pies and tarts. Use 1–2 tsp of the spice, according to the strength required. For an attractive and tasty finish, you can sprinkle seeds such as fennel, cumin or caraway over the top crust of pies before baking.
- Sugar adds sweetness to pastries. Caster sugar is the one most often used, as it has fine grains that dissolve easily. Sifted icing sugar is also suitable.

The art of pastry-making

Master the skills of pastry-making and you'll rapidly gain yourself a reputation for being a brilliant cook! There's nothing particularly difficult to learn, just some basic techniques that, if followed, will guarantee successful results. Don't let lack of time be an excuse for not making your own pastry, as most are really quick and easy.

Rubbing in

This is the method used to combine fat and flour for shortcrust and scone pastries. The fat should be cool, but not straight from the fridge, when it would be very hard and would take longer to rub in.

Use just your fingertips to blend the diced fat with the sifted flour. Lift the mixture from the bowl as you rub in, to incorporate air. When the mixture is in fine crumbs, like breadcrumbs, bind it together with a little cold water (or other liquid). Add the liquid slowly, as too much will result in a sticky dough that will shrink during baking and turn out hard and tough. Conversely, if the dough is too dry, it will crack when rolled out and be difficult to handle, will crumble after baking and be dry to eat.

You can also make rubbed-in pastries very successfully in a food processor fitted with a metal blade or a special pastry-making attachment. In this case, the fat should be very cold and firm, straight from the fridge, and cut into small pieces. Add it to the sifted flour in the processor bowl and mix or pulse for about 3 seconds or until the mixture resembles breadcrumbs. Gradually pour in about two-thirds of the cold liquid through the feed tube, with the motor running, and whizz for a further few seconds, just until a ball of dough is formed. Turn off immediately or the pastry will be over-mixed and difficult to handle. Only add the remaining liquid if the dough doesn't bind together. With a food processor, slightly less liquid is needed as the action of the blades tends to make the dough a little more sticky.

When rubbing in (left), use your fingertips only, to prevent the heat of your hands softening the fat. Add the liquid gradually (above), mixing it in with a table knife. Add just enough liquid to bind the rubbed-in mixture into a dough (right)

► To line a flan tin, drape the rolled-out dough over the tin (near right), gently ease it in (middle right) and then neatly trim off the excess dough (far right)

▼ For baking blind (below), prick the pastry case with a fork, then line with paper and fill with baking beans

Lining a flan tin

When making a tart case, you can use either a metal flan tin, preferably loose-bottomed so it will be easy to remove the baked pastry case, or a flan ring placed on a baking sheet. China flan dishes look attractive, but do not conduct the heat effectively, so the pastry base can turn out a little soggy.

Roll out the pastry dough to a shape about 5 cm (2 in) larger than the flan tin. Lift the dough carefully by draping it over the rolling pin – it's less likely to tear and easier to position this way – and lay it centrally over the tin. Starting from the middle and working out to the sides, carefully ease the dough into the tin without pulling or stretching, then press it gently against the bottom and sides of the tin. If the dough cracks or tears, simply press it back together. When it is neatly lining the tin, fold the excess dough back over the rim of the tin and roll the rolling pin across to trim off the excess. Prick the bottom lightly all over with a fork to release trapped air (this could cause the pastry to rise during baking).

Baking blind

Tart cases are often baked before the filling is added, either partially, just to set and dry the pastry, or completely. To bake unfilled, or 'blind', first line the pastry case with a sheet of greaseproof paper or foil, pressing it neatly into the corners, then weigh the paper down with dried beans or special ceramic baking beans. This will prevent the pastry from rising and losing its shape during baking.

Bake in a preheated hot oven for about 15 minutes, or according to the recipe, then lift out the paper or foil and beans. Return the pastry case to the oven to bake for a further 5 minutes to dry out, or 15 more minutes to cook the pastry case completely (follow individual recipe instructions).

For tartlet cases to be baked blind, it is not necessary to use the paper and beans. Just prick the bottoms well all over with a fork before baking.

Getting ahead

Having pastry on hand is a boon for a busy cook, so why not make a batch when you have some spare time. The rubbed-in mixture can be kept in an airtight container in the fridge for up to 2 weeks, needing only a little liquid to be added to bind it. Pastry dough, wrapped tightly in cling film or greaseproof paper, will keep for 2–3 days in the fridge, or it can be frozen for up to 3 months. Another idea is to freeze pastry cases, in the tin. Bake from frozen, allowing an extra 5–10 minutes, without the paper and beans.

Tips for success

• **Keep everything cool.** Coldness is essential for good pastry and that means keeping the equipment and ingredients cool, as well as your hands. If you have 'hot hands', rinse them under a cold tap to cool them down before starting. In warm weather make your pastry early in the morning while the kitchen is still cool. Once made, shortcrust and scone pastries should be chilled for at least 30 minutes before rolling out. This allows the pastry to firm up, making it easier to roll. Chilling also removes the elasticity that can cause shrinkage during baking. If time allows, the pastry should also be chilled for 10–15 minutes after it has been rolled. During this time you could make the pie or tart filling.

• **Roll out thinly.** Use the minimum amount of pastry to line a tin or cover a pie. Not only is thinner pastry lighter to eat, but the fat content per serving will be less. When rolling, sprinkle the surface very lightly with flour to prevent the dough from sticking – if too much flour is incorporated into the pastry dough during rolling, the finished texture will be dry and heavy. Roll lightly but firmly in one direction only, then lift the dough, turn and roll again. A marble slab is ideal for rolling out as it helps to keep the pastry cool.

• **Handle with care**. Excessive handling and over-stretching the pastry dough will cause it to shrink on baking, as will adding too much liquid when mixing. So make and roll out the pastry with the minimum of handling, and take care not to stretch it when lining the tin.

• **Prevent soggy pastry.** Always place flan tins on a hot baking sheet in a preheated oven. The baking sheet will help to conduct heat to the base of the pastry case and ensure that it is crisp. Baking blind also helps to prevent soggy pastry. An extra precaution is to brush the bottom of the pastry case with a little beaten egg after removing the beans and paper. When the pastry case is returned to the oven for further baking, the egg will cook and seal the surface. For a top crust pie, let the filling cool before covering with the pastry, and make a small hole in the pastry lid to allow steam from the filling to escape.

Good equipment for healthy baking

Kitchen shops, department stores and large supermarkets now sell a wide range of good-quality tins and baking sheets.

• A heavy rolling pin of a good size will make it easy to roll out pastry thinly and evenly.

• Non-stick tins are ideal for healthy baking as they eliminate the need for greasing with fat. Alternatively, you can line tins or baking sheets with non-stick baking parchment.

• Deep tins allow room for plenty of filling in proportion to the amount of pastry used. It is the filling that provides most of the valuable nutrients in a pie or tart.

• A pastry brush is essential for lightly glazing the tops of pies with milk or beaten egg, and for brushing melted butter or oil sparingly on sheets of filo pastry.

Pie and tart finishes

There are many ways of enhancing the appearance of pies and tarts, making them all the more appetising and good to eat. And some finishes add nutritional benefits too.

• **To 'knock up' the edges of a top crust**, hold a sharp knife horizontally to the side of the pastry edge and make shallow cuts all the way round, while pressing down lightly on the top of the pastry with your other forefinger.

• **To flute or scallop the edge**, press your thumb onto the edge of the crust and, at the same time, draw the back of a knife next to your thumb from the edge towards the centre of the pie. Continue round the pie at 2.5 cm (1 in) intervals.

Alternatives to pastry

There are many foods you can use for pie cases and top crusts other than pastry. They will add further interest and variety to pies and tarts, both sweet and savoury, and they'll supply nutrients vital for good health. In addition, most are lower in fat than pastry. Some of these pastry alternatives will be familiar, but others are a little more unusual. Do try them to make new and exciting dishes.

- **Biscuit crumbs** can be used as the base for sweet and savoury tarts, usually combined with melted fat. For a lower-fat version, simply sprinkle crushed crumbs over a lightly buttered tin. Ginger or oaty biscuits and Italian amaretti work particularly well for sweet tarts, and water biscuits can be used for savoury ones. Another good idea is to combine biscuit crumbs with enough beaten egg white to bind, press over the bottom and sides of a non-stick tin, and bake until set.
- **Bread**, an excellent source of starchy carbohydrate plus many vitamins and minerals, can be sliced, cubed or turned into crumbs for a pie topping, or slices can be rolled out thinly and used to line little tins for savoury tarts. All kinds of bread are suitable, from white and wholemeal to oat, Granary, ciabatta, challah, sourdough, rye and so on.
- **Bread and pizza doughs** make a good low-fat case for a tart. Flavour the dough with a little freshly grated Parmesan cheese, if you like. Good fillings include those ingredients typically suited to pizza toppings, such as tomatoes, mushrooms, olives, anchovies and seafood.
- **Polenta (maize or cornmeal)** is a good gluten-free source of starchy carbohydrates. It can be cooked and left to cool, then rolled out and used to line a flan tin or to make a top crust. Use stock instead of water and add chopped fresh herbs or a little finely grated cheese for extra flavour.
- **Rice**, another gluten-free starchy carbohydrate, makes a delicious tart case. Risotto rice works particularly well as it is creamy when cooked (rice that keeps its grains separate, such as basmati, is not suitable). Let the rice cool, then press into the tin and bake. A beaten egg added to the rice will help to bind the mixture together. Couscous bound with egg is another imaginative possibility.
- **Sponge mixtures** made from a whisked eggs and sugar with flour folded in, are almost fat-free. Bake in a sponge flan tin for a fruit filling.
- **Tortillas and pancakes** make a novel tart case, or they can be layered up with a cooked filling to make a pie. Soft flour tortillas (wraps) and corn tortillas, both good sources of starchy carbohydrates, work well with spicy minced meat or vegetable fillings and make well-balanced pies. Pancakes offer protein and calcium too.
- **Vegetables** such as potatoes, swede, winter squashes, parsnips, carrots and sweet potatoes make delicious and colourful toppings for pies, and add valuable vitamins, minerals and fibre. Some supply starchy carbohydrates too. Use 1 vegetable alone, or combine 2 or more. Mash or roughly crush the vegetables, or slice or cube them. Flavour mash with chopped fresh herbs, pesto, garlic, sun-dried tomatoes, mustard, citrus zest or cheese, or mix with chopped watercress, or steamed shredded greens, cabbage or leeks.

Puddings for all occasions

Traditional British cooking is famous for its wonderful puddings, both savoury and sweet. Those rich with meat and vegetables make substantial and nourishing main dishes, while sweet ones, filled with fresh or dried fruit and nuts, are for many the high point of a meal. Puddings can make a great contribution to a well-balanced diet.

Batter puddings

A simple mixture of eggs, flour and milk can be turned into so many puddings, from pancakes and Yorkshire puddings to toad-in-the-hole and the French classic, clafoutis. The combination of the 3 key ingredients provides useful amounts of protein, starchy carbohydrate and calcium, as well as many other nutrients, making batter puddings very nutritious.

- Use half milk and half water for a lighter result.
- Whisk batters for baked puddings well to incorporate the air needed for a good rise.
- Bake in a tin rather than an ovenproof dish, as metal is a better conductor of heat and will produce a crisper result.
- Serve baked batter puddings immediately, while they are still puffed and risen.

Bread puddings

Bread puddings have long been popular as a good way to use up slightly stale bread, and as an economical and filling sweet course. Today, new bread puddings are being devised, both sweet and savoury, with exciting twists on traditional recipes. The bread can be whatever you fancy – all kinds supply essential starchy carbohydrates.

- Layer slices or cubes of bread with lots of vegetables, then pour over a savoury egg custard and bake.
- Add dried fruits and nuts to sweet bread puddings, or base them on fruited loaves, teabreads or brioche.
- Make a glorious summer pudding, by lining a basin with slices of bread, challah or brioche and filling with soft summer fruits. A variation with autumn fruits is equally good.
- Try a charlotte: line a deep tin with bread, fill with stewed fruit and bake.
- Top a savoury mixture with breadcrumbs tossed with melted butter, oil or grated cheese, then bake or grill until crisp.

Crumbles and cobblers

A crumble is simply a shortcrust pastry mixture, rubbed-in to the 'breadcrumb' stage, that is sprinkled over the top of a fruit, vegetable or other filling and then baked. A cobbler uses scone pastry to cover the filling. For a sweet dish, the crumble mixture or scone dough usually includes a little sugar. With a generous amount of fruit, a sweet crumble or cobbler can be a very healthy and nutritious pudding. Savoury crumbles and cobblers make well-balanced main dishes.

- Add ingredients such as nuts, oats, seeds, muesli, chopped herbs or grated cheese to crumble mixtures and scone doughs, to boost the nutritional value.
- Roll out scone dough and lay it in a sheet over the filling. Or, cut it into shapes, or into strips to be laid as a lattice.

Rice puddings

Although sometimes dismissed as nursery food, rice puddings can have a lot of appeal, particularly the innovative modern versions. And they are full of good things such as eggs, milk and rice, which are very nourishing. Short-grain or pudding rice is generally the best type to use for sweet puddings, as the short, plump grains cook to a creamy consistency. Risotto rice is a good choice for savoury rice puddings.

- Flavour sweet rice puddings with lemon zest, pure vanilla extract, almond essence, bay leaf, saffron, grated nutmeg, cinnamon sticks, cardamom seeds or rosewater.
- Add dried fruits such as cherries, cranberries and blueberries or chopped nuts.
- Pack lots of vegetables into savoury rice puddings and enrich them with grated cheese.
- Stir in some fromage frais or Greek-style yogurt just before serving, to add creaminess without a lot of fat.
- Serve sweet rice puddings with a fruit compote or purée.

◄ Top a cannellini bean and mixed vegetable stew with a cheese and oat crumble mixture (see Some more ideas, page 75) for a nourishing vegetarian main dish

▼ Make a savoury rice pudding by cooking rice in tomato juice and mixing it with antioxidant-rich peppers and tomatoes (see Some more ideas, page 79)

▲ Brown lean and meaty venison sausages in the oven, then surround with a fresh herb-flavoured batter for an unusual toad-in-the-hole (see Some more ideas, page 61)

► Spread slices of fruit loaf with orange marmalade, layer with dried peaches and pour over a brandy custard to make an extra-fruity bread pudding (see Some more ideas, page 130)

Use a big spoon to fold whisked egg whites into the soufflé base

Soufflés

A light, fluffy soufflé can be sweet or savoury, hot or cold, and is quick and easy to make. A hot soufflé is traditionally based on a thick white sauce called a panada, which can be thickened with cornflour for a very low-fat result. Egg yolks are beaten into the panada, and then stiffly whisked egg whites are folded in just before baking. Hot soufflés can be based on a thick purée of fruit or vegetables rather than a panada. Cold soufflés are set with gelatine.

- Whisk egg whites in a clean, dry bowl until they will hold stiff peaks, then fold them immediately into the soufflé base. Stir about one-quarter of the whites in first, to lighten the base, then gently fold in the rest. This will retain the air beaten into the whites.
- Be sure the dish for a hot soufflé is evenly buttered, so the mixture will rise up straight and tall during baking.
- Serve hot soufflés straight from the oven, as they will start to deflate within 1–2 minutes.

Sponge puddings

A whisked sponge, used for Swiss rolls, is a light, almost fatless mixture made by whisking eggs with sugar until they are thick and frothy, and then folding in flour. Melted butter can be added, which will help to keep the sponge moist for longer. Another kind of sponge, used for steamed or baked puddings, is based on a creamed butter and sugar mixture, to which eggs and flour are added. A quick all-in-one version can be made with softened butter, eggs, sugar and self-raising flour, beaten together with an electric mixer.

- For a chocolate sponge, a little of the flour can be replaced with cocoa powder. This adds a rich chocolate flavour without the fat of chocolate.
- Fresh or dried fruit in a sponge pudding adds sweetness, so the amount of sugar can be reduced.
- Use sunflower or other oil instead of butter, for a pudding lower in saturated fat.

Bake fresh plums in a sponge mixture flavoured with ginger (see Some more ideas, page 138) for a zesty, fibre-rich pudding

- When whisking eggs with sugar, if not using an electric mixer, set the bowl over a pan of hot, almost boiling water. This will help the mixture increase in volume.
- For a lighter baked or steamed sponge pudding, replace part of the flour with fresh breadcrumbs.
- Roll the sponge for a Swiss roll while it is warm, otherwise it will crack.

Custards

Egg custards are real comfort food, whether in the form of a pouring sauce or as a sweet or savoury pudding baked in a mould until softly set. Powdered custard mixes are quick and foolproof, but they are made just with cornflour, flavouring and colouring and so do not have the same nutritional benefits as a real egg custard.

- Bake custard puddings gently by setting the mould in a bain-marie (a roasting tin of water). This will protect the custard from overheating, which can spoil its texture.
- Cook custard sauces in a heavy-based saucepan, without letting them boil. If the custard does start to curdle or become lumpy, a quick rescue remedy is to pour it into a blender or food processor, add an ice cube and blend until smooth.

Steamed pudding know-how

Puddings cooked in the steam and heat from boiling liquid have a wonderfully light and moist texture. The true, natural flavours of the ingredients are preserved and, as the pudding doesn't come into direct contact with the liquid, water-soluble vitamins are not lost. You can steam a pudding set on a rack over boiling water in a steamer or immersed in boiling water in a saucepan. Steamed puddings can also be cooked in a pressure cooker or microwave, following the manufacturer's instructions.

- When covering the pudding basin, tie on the foil or greaseproof paper securely with string so the covering cannot slip off. Make a loop with the string to act as a handle so the basin can be lifted out of the steamer or pan (see below).
- Be sure the lid of the steamer or pan fits tightly so that steam cannot escape.
- The water level in a saucepan should be about halfway up the side of the basin. Once the water is boiling and the steam circulating, reduce the heat slightly so that the water remains at a constant boil but does not bubble up and get into the pudding.
- Top up with more boiling water as it evaporates.

Real egg custard

Custard, or crème anglaise (English cream), is the most delicious accompaniment for sweet pies, tarts and puddings. Made with egg yolks and vanilla, it tastes just wonderful. Adding a little cornflour helps to stabilise the mixture and prevent it from curdling.

Serves 4

300 ml (10 fl oz) semi-skimmed milk
1 vanilla pod, split lengthways
3 egg yolks
1 tbsp caster sugar
1 tsp cornflour

Preparation and cooking time: about 25 minutes

1 Put the milk and vanilla pod into a heavy-based saucepan and heat until just starting to simmer. Remove the pan from the heat and leave to infuse for 10 minutes.
2 Meanwhile, mix together the egg yolks, sugar and cornflour to a smooth paste in a mixing bowl or jug.
3 Remove the vanilla pod from the milk. If liked, scrape the seeds into the milk for a stronger vanilla flavour. Pour the warm milk onto the egg mixture, stirring.
4 Pour back into the pan and cook gently over a low heat, stirring constantly with a wooden spoon, until thick enough to coat the back of the spoon in a thin layer. Do not allow the custard to boil, and remove from the heat as soon as it has thickened. Serve the custard hot or cool.

Some more ideas

- If you don't have a vanilla pod, you can use vanilla caster sugar or add 1 tsp pure vanilla extract to the cooked custard.
- Instead of flavouring the custard with vanilla, infuse the milk with a strip of lemon, orange or lime zest. Or, add 2 tsp instant coffee powder or 30 g (1 oz) grated dark chocolate to the warm milk. Another idea is to stir 1 tbsp liqueur into the cooked custard.
- To make crème pâtissière, increase the sugar to 25 g (scant 1 oz) and the cornflour to 1½ tbsp. This makes a thick custard that can be used as a filling for sweet tarts. Use when cold.

Little Pies and Tarts

Savoury bites for snacks, starters and lunches

Filo is ideal for little pies and tarts as it is so adaptable – layered into cases for Oriental stir-fried prawns or wrapped into dainty parcels round a tuna filling. Other pastries work beautifully too. Choux puffs up into spectacular buns that are perfect cases for a creamy guacamole, shortcrust makes pretty tartlets, and easy scone dough can be fashioned into stylish French 'galettes'. Pies and tarts need not always be made with pastry, though. Among the tempting variety of little bites here, you'll find bread dough used for spicy Mexican-style turkey pasties, as well as crisp-baked bread cases filled with a piquant mackerel and red pepper mixture.

Tomato and basil galettes

Galette is the French term for a flat, round pastry or cake. The galettes here are made from wholemeal scone dough flavoured with a little Parmesan cheese. They make a delicious base for a tomato, basil and pine nut topping. Serve as a snack or starter, or as a light lunch with a mixed leaf salad. They're also good cold.

Serves 6

Parmesan scone dough
115 g (4 oz) self-raising white flour
85 g (3 oz) self-raising wholemeal flour
1 tsp baking powder
pinch of salt
30 g (1 oz) cool butter, diced
25 g (scant 1 oz) Parmesan cheese, freshly grated
120 ml (4 fl oz) semi-skimmed milk

Tomato and basil topping
3 tsp extra virgin olive oil
1 garlic clove, crushed
3 tbsp sun-dried tomato paste
3 tbsp shredded fresh basil leaves
3 large plum tomatoes, thinly sliced
30 g (1 oz) pine nuts
fresh basil leaves to garnish

Preparation time: 20 minutes
Cooking time: 10–12 minutes

Each serving provides

kcal 240, **protein** 7 g, **fat** 12 g (of which saturated fat 4 g), **carbohydrate** 28 g (of which sugars 4.5 g), **fibre** 3 g

✓✓ copper

✓ A, B_1, E, niacin, calcium, iron, potassium, selenium, zinc

1 Preheat the oven to 220ºC (425ºF, gas mark 7). Sift the white and wholemeal flours, baking powder and salt into a bowl, tipping in the bran left in the sieve. Rub in the butter until the mixture resembles fine breadcrumbs. Stir in the Parmesan cheese.

2 Make a well in the middle and pour in the milk. Mix together to make a fairly soft dough. Knead lightly for a few seconds or until smooth.

3 Roll out the dough on a lightly floured surface to 5 mm (¼ in) thickness. Cut out 6 rounds about 10 cm (4 in) in diameter. You will need to re-roll the trimmings to cut out the last round. Transfer the rounds to a non-stick baking sheet, spacing well apart. Mark the edges with a fork, if liked.

4 Brush the tops with 2 tsp of the olive oil. Mix the remaining 1 tsp oil with the garlic, tomato paste and basil, and spread thinly over the rounds, leaving a border of about 5 mm (¼ in) clear. Arrange the tomato slices on top, overlapping them slightly and covering all of the basil topping.

5 Bake for 7 minutes, then scatter the pine nuts over the tomatoes. Return to the oven and bake for 3–5 minutes or until the galettes are risen and the edges are golden brown. Serve hot, garnished with basil leaves.

Another idea

- For caramelised onion galettes, cook 500 g (1 lb 2 oz) thinly sliced red onions in 1½ tbsp extra virgin olive oil over a low heat, partly covered and stirring occasionally, for about 10 minutes. Add 2 tsp balsamic vinegar and 1 tsp soft light brown sugar. Gently cook for a further 4–5 minutes, stirring frequently, until very soft. Remove from the heat and stir in 30 g (1 oz) chopped dry-packed sun-dried tomatoes. Season with pepper to taste. Make the galette bases, adding 2 tsp chopped fresh thyme to the dry ingredients, and rubbing in only 15 g (d oz) butter and 55 g (2 oz) crumbled feta cheese; omit the Parmesan cheese. Spoon the onion mixture on top of the galettes and bake in a preheated 220ºC (425ºF, gas mark 7) oven for 10–12 minutes or until risen and golden brown.

Plus points

- Wholemeal flour contains more B vitamins, iron, selenium and zinc than white flour, but used on its own makes heavy pastry and scone mixtures. Mixing wholemeal and white flour produces a lighter result.
- Apart from its culinary uses, basil is prescribed by herbalists as a natural tranquilliser and to help relieve cramps, upset stomachs and flatulence.

Oriental prawn tartlets

These pretty little tartlets, filled with stir-fried prawns and a mixture of crisp, colourful vegetables, make a really unusual light snack or a starter for an Asian meal. The filo tartlet cases can be made ahead, but they are best filled just before serving, so the pastry remains crisp.

Serves 4 (makes 12 tartlets)

1 tbsp sunflower oil
1 tsp toasted sesame oil
3 sheets filo pastry, 30 x 50 cm (12 x 20 in) each, about 90 g (3¼ oz) in total
1 garlic clove, crushed
3 spring onions, thinly sliced
1 tbsp finely chopped fresh root ginger
1 carrot, cut into fine julienne strips
300 g (10½ oz) peeled raw tiger prawns
75 g (2½ oz) mange-tout, sliced diagonally
1 small head pak choy, about 85 g (3 oz), sliced
75 g (2½ oz) bean sprouts
1 tbsp light soy sauce
sprigs of fresh coriander to garnish

Preparation and cooking time: 35–45 minutes

Each serving provides

kcal 183, **protein** 18 g, **fat** 5 g (of which saturated fat 1 g), **carbohydrate** 18 g (of which sugars 3 g), **fibre** 2 g

✓✓✓	B_{12}
✓✓	A, E
✓	C, niacin, calcium, copper, iron, potassium, selenium, zinc

1 Preheat the oven to 200°C (400°F, gas mark 6). Mix together the sunflower and sesame oils. Lay the filo pastry sheets out, one on top of the other. Trim the stacked pastry to make a 30 x 40 cm (12 x 16 in) rectangle (discard the excess pastry). Cut it lengthways into 3 and then across into 4, making 10 cm (4 in) squares. You will have 36 squares of filo.

2 Place 1 filo square in each of the 12 hollows in a non-stick bun tin. Brush very lightly with a little of the oil mixture. Place another square of filo on top, arranging it so the corners are not directly on top of those beneath. Brush with a little more oil, then place a third filo square on top, again with the corners offset. Bake the pastry cases for 5–7 minutes or until they are golden brown and crisp.

3 Meanwhile, heat the remaining oil mixture in a wok or large frying pan. Add the garlic, spring onions and ginger, and stir-fry over a moderate heat for about 30 seconds. Add the carrot and stir-fry for 2 minutes, then add the prawns and stir-fry for 2 more minutes or until they turn pink.

4 Add the mange-tout, pak choy and bean sprouts. Stir-fry over a high heat for 2–3 minutes or until all the vegetables are just tender and the mixture is piping hot. Sprinkle with the soy sauce and toss to mix.

5 Spoon the prawn and vegetable mixture into the filo pastry cases and serve immediately, garnished with sprigs of coriander.

Plus points

- Filo pastry has a lower fat content than other pastries. For example, there are 2 g fat and 275 kcal in 100 g (3½ oz) filo pastry compared to 29 g fat and 449 kcal in the same weight of shortcrust pastry.
- Prawns are a good source of low-fat protein and the antioxidant mineral selenium as well as an excellent source of vitamin B_{12}.
- Mange-tout contain more vitamin C than ordinary garden peas. This is because the pods, which as the name implies are eaten too ('mange-tout' means 'eat all'), make an additional contribution.

Some more ideas

• Use peeled prawns instead of tiger prawns. If the prawns are already cooked, add them after stir-frying the vegetables in step 4, and just heat through for 1 minute or so.

• For a vegetarian version, replace the prawns with 300 g (10½ oz) chilled, drained tofu, cut into small cubes. Add at the end of step 3 and stir-fry for 2–3 minutes.

• Replace the pak choy with other leafy greens such as baby spinach leaves or shredded Chinese leaves.

• Try Oriental crab, corn and asparagus tartlets. Instead of sesame oil, mix the sunflower oil with ½ tsp chilli paste. When making the pastry cases, sprinkle lightly between the layered filo squares with 25 g (scant 1 oz) finely chopped peanuts. To make the filling, stir-fry 1 crushed garlic clove, 2 finely chopped shallots and a seeded and finely chopped small hot red chilli in the remaining oil mixture. Stir in 170 g (6 oz) chopped fine asparagus and 100 g (3½ oz) sliced baby corn, and stir-fry for 3–4 minutes or until softened. Add 150 g (5½ oz) fresh or drained, canned white crabmeat and the juice of 1 lime, and stir-fry until hot. Finish by stirring in 2 tbsp chopped fresh coriander.

Puttanesca pizzinis

Home-made mini pizzas topped with a rich tomato, chilli, olive, caper and artichoke mixture will spoil you for anything less. Some crumbled Gorgonzola cheese melted over the top makes a change from the usual mozzarella, and gives these pizzinis a fabulous flavour. Serve with a mixed leaf salad for a delightful lunch or snack.

Serves 6

Oregano pizza dough

450 g (1 lb) strong white (bread) flour
1 tsp dried oregano
1 sachet easy-blend dried yeast, about 7 g
250 ml (8½ fl oz) tepid water, or as needed

Puttanesca topping

1 tbsp extra virgin olive oil
1 red onion, finely chopped
4 garlic cloves, crushed
500 g (1 lb 2 oz) ripe tomatoes, diced
1 fresh red chilli, seeded and finely chopped
50 g (1¾ oz) stoned black and green olives, roughly chopped
1 tbsp capers
1 can artichoke hearts, about 400 g, drained and quartered
100 g (3½ oz) Gorgonzola cheese, crumbled
salt and pepper

Preparation time: 1¾ hours (including rising)
Cooking time: 15 minutes

Each serving provides (V)

kcal 388, **protein** 14 g, **fat** 9.5 g (of which saturated fat 4 g), **carbohydrate** 66 g (of which sugars 6 g), **fibre** 5 g

✓✓✓	selenium
✓✓	B_1, calcium, copper
✓	A, B_6, C, E, folate, niacin, iron, potassium, zinc

1 First make the pizza dough. Sift the flour and ½ tsp salt into a large mixing bowl, and stir in the oregano and yeast. Make a well in the centre and pour in the water. Gradually work the flour mixture into the water to make a soft dough. If it feels too dry, work in a little more water; if the dough sticks to your hand, add a little more flour.

2 Turn out the dough onto a lightly floured work surface and knead for about 10 minutes or until smooth and elastic. Return the dough to the bowl, cover it with a damp tea towel or cling film, and leave to rise in a warm place for 1 hour or until doubled in size.

3 Meanwhile, make the topping. Heat the oil in a medium-sized, heavy-based saucepan and add the onion and garlic. Cook over a low heat for about 10 minutes or until softened, stirring occasionally. Add the tomatoes and chilli, and stir to mix. Cook over a moderate heat for about 25 minutes, stirring occasionally, until very thick.

4 Remove the pan from the heat. Add the olives and capers, and season with salt and pepper to taste. Leave to cool while shaping the pizza bases.

5 Turn out the risen dough onto the lightly floured surface and knock it back. Knead it very lightly, then divide into 6 equal portions. Shape each into a ball, then pat or roll out to a neat disc measuring about 12.5 cm (5 in) across. Arrange the discs, spaced slightly apart, on 2 lightly greased baking trays.

6 Spread the tomato topping evenly over the discs of dough, leaving a 5 mm (¼ in) border clear. Top with the quartered artichokes, then scatter over the Gorgonzola. Leave to rise in a warm place for 15 minutes.

7 Preheat the oven to 230°C (450°F, gas mark 8). Bake the pizzinis for 15 minutes or until the edges of the crust are golden brown and the cheese has melted. Serve hot.

Plus points

- The fat content of olives is relatively high compared to other fruit and vegetables. However, the fat is predominantly unsaturated which is believed to be healthier than the saturated form.
- Artichoke hearts contain a particular type of dietary fibre, called fructoligosaccarides, which encourages the growth of friendly bacteria in the gut.

Some more ideas

• To serve as a starter, divide the dough into 8 equal pieces and shape each into a 10 cm (4 in) diameter disc.

• These pizzinis are equally delicious served cold, to take on a picnic or to include in a packed lunch.

• Replace 50 g (1¾ oz) of the white flour with rye flour or Granary (malted brown bread) flour.

• To make an aubergine pizza tart, press out the risen dough in a Swiss roll tin that measures 22 x 30 cm (8½ x 12 in). Spread over the chilli tomato sauce. Instead of the artichokes, use 1 large aubergine, cut into 1 cm (½ in) dice and tossed with 1 tbsp extra virgin olive oil, 1 tbsp chopped fresh thyme or marjoram and seasoning to taste. Scatter over the tomato sauce and top with 100 g (3½ oz) diced mozzarella. Leave to rise for 15 minutes, then bake for 20–25 minutes or until the edges of the crust are golden brown and the topping is bubbling and golden. Cool for 2 minutes, then cut into 6 squares or 12 slices and serve, garnished with fresh basil leaves.

Smoked mackerel, roasted pepper and horseradish croustades

Slices of bread, lightly brushed with butter and then baked in bun tins, make perfect little 'cups' for a piquant red pepper and mackerel filling. Served with rocket tossed in a lemon vinaigrette, they make a very appealing starter. The bread cases and filling can be made ahead, then assembled just before serving.

Serves 6 (makes 12 croustades)

1 red pepper, halved and seeded
3 large slices of oatmeal bread
15 g (½ oz) butter, melted
150 g (5½ oz) reduced-fat soft cheese
1 tbsp hot horseradish sauce
75 g (2½ oz) skinless smoked mackerel fillet, flaked into large pieces
salt and pepper
fresh dill sprigs or snipped chives to garnish

Rocket salad
2 tbsp extra virgin olive oil
juice of ½ lemon
½ tsp Dijon mustard
pinch of caster sugar
125 g (4½ oz) rocket leaves

Preparation and cooking time: 40–45 minutes

Each serving provides

kcal 219, **protein** 8 g, **fat** 14 g (of which saturated fat 5 g), **carbohydrate** 16 g (of which sugars 4 g), **fibre** 2 g

✓✓✓	C
✓✓	A, B_{12}
✓	B_6, folate, niacin

1 Preheat the oven to 190°C (375°F, gas mark 5). Place the pepper cut side down on a baking sheet and roast in the oven for 15 minutes. Put the pepper into a polythene bag and set aside for 15 minutes or until it is cool enough to handle.

2 Meanwhile, trim the crusts thinly from the bread and discard, then roll over the bread slices with a rolling pin to flatten them. Using a fluted 7.5 cm (3 in) round biscuit cutter, cut out 2 rounds from each slice.

3 Lightly grease the 12 hollows of a deep bun tin using a little of the melted butter. Brush the remaining butter over one side of each bread round and press it into a hollow in the tin, buttered side up. Bake the bread cases for about 12 minutes or until crisp and golden. Leave to cool.

4 Peel the pepper and finely chop the flesh. Mix with the soft cheese and horseradish sauce. Season with salt and pepper to taste. Set aside.

5 For the salad, whisk together the olive oil, lemon juice, mustard, sugar, and seasoning to taste in a mixing bowl. Add the rocket and toss, then arrange on serving plates.

6 Spoon the cheese mixture into the bread cases and top each one with flakes of mackerel. Set 2 croustades on each plate. Garnish with dill or chives and serve immediately.

Another idea

- Make smoked salmon and goat's cheese croustades, using soft-grain bread for the cases. For the filling, coarsely grate 100 g (3½ oz) cucumber and squeeze thoroughly in your hands to remove excess juice. Beat the cucumber into 170 g (6 oz) soft goat's cheese together with 2 tsp chopped capers, 1 tbsp snipped fresh chives, and salt and pepper to taste. Pile the filling into the bread cases, top with 75 g (2½ oz) smoked salmon strips and garnish with chives.

Plus points

- Mackerel is very nutritious, providing vitamins B_2, B_6, D and niacin as well as iodine and potassium. These nutrients are not destroyed by the smoking process.
- Horseradish is used in herbal medicine as an aid to digestion.

Souffléd salmon and dill tartlets

Individual tartlets served with a salad garnish make a very appealing starter. This fish filling is wonderfully light as it's made with a cornflour-thickened sauce, without the addition of fat, and whisked egg whites are folded in for an airy soufflé-like texture. Serve straight from the oven to really impress.

Serves 6

Shortcrust pastry

115 g (4 oz) plain flour
55 g (2 oz) cool butter, diced

Salmon filling

25 g (scant 1 oz) cornflour
150 ml (5 fl oz) semi-skimmed milk
1 can skinless, boneless pink salmon, about 180 g, drained and flaked
2 tbsp chopped fresh dill
2 tbsp snipped fresh chives
2 eggs, separated
salt and pepper

To serve

150 g (5½ oz) mixed salad leaves, such as frisée and rocket
1 red pepper, seeded and cut into thin strips

Preparation time: 40 minutes, plus at least 30 minutes chilling
Cooking time: 15 minutes

Each serving provides

kcal 236, **protein** 11 g, **fat** 12 g (of which saturated fat 6 g), **carbohydrate** 22 g (of which sugars 4 g), **fibre** 1 g

✓✓✓ A, B_{12}, C
✓ E, niacin, calcium, selenium, zinc

1 To make the pastry, sift the flour and a pinch of salt into a large bowl. Rub in the butter until the mixture resembles breadcrumbs. Sprinkle with 2 tbsp cold water and mix with a round-bladed knife to form a dough. Gather the dough into a smooth ball, then wrap in greaseproof paper or cling film and chill for at least 30 minutes. Meanwhile, start preparing the filling.

2 Blend the cornflour with 2 tbsp of the milk to make a smooth paste. Heat the remaining milk in a saucepan to boiling point. Pour a little of the hot milk into the cornflour mixture, stirring. Return this to the milk in the saucepan. Bring to the boil, stirring until the sauce thickens, then reduce the heat and simmer gently for 2 minutes.

3 Remove the pan from the heat. Stir in the salmon, dill, chives, and salt and pepper to taste. Mix in the egg yolks. Set aside.

4 Preheat the oven to 200°C (400°F, gas mark 6). Cut the pastry dough into 6 pieces. Roll out each thinly and use to line 6 individual, loose-bottomed, non-stick tartlet tins 9 cm (3½ in) in diameter and 2.5 cm (1 in) deep.

5 Prick the tartlet cases, then place on a baking sheet. Bake 'blind' (see page 19) for 10 minutes. Remove the paper and beans, and bake for a further 5 minutes or until lightly golden. Allow to cool, then carefully remove the tartlet cases from the tins and set them back on the baking sheet.

6 Whisk the egg whites until stiff, then fold into the salmon mixture. Pile the mixture into the tartlet cases and bake for 15 minutes or until well risen and golden. Serve immediately on individual plates, garnished with the salad leaves and strips of pepper.

Plus points

- Like other oily fish, salmon is a good source of omega-3 fatty acids, which can help to protect against heart disease and strokes.
- The thick sauce (panada) used as the base for the soufflé filling is thickened with cornflour rather than the classic butter and flour roux, and so is much lower in fat.
- Dill has been used for its soothing and sedative properties since Egyptian times. It became known in America as 'meeting house seeds', as dill seeds were chewed by early settlers to prevent tummy rumbles when sermons went on too long.

Some more ideas

• Instead of salmon, use canned tuna in spring water, well drained.

• Serve the tartlets cold. They will not have a soufflé appearance, but will still be delicious.

• For souff éd spinach and Pamesan tartlets, cook 125 g (4½ oz) frozen spinach over a low heat for 2 minutes or until thawed. Squeeze out excess moisture, then add to the sauce together with ½ tsp grated nutmeg; omit the salmon, dill and chives. Mix in the egg yolks and 30 g (1 oz) freshly grated Parmesan cheese. Fold in the egg whites, then bake as in the main recipe. Serve garnished with salad leaves, cherry tomatoes and spring onions.

Spicy filo triangles

Here's a quick version of the popular Indian samosas, baked rather than deep-fried for a healthy, light result. The crisp filo pastry parcels contain a curry-spiced vegetable filling, and they are served hot from the oven with a fresh mango and ginger salsa to make a scrumptious starter or light snack.

Serves 4 (makes 12 triangles)

2 sheets filo pastry, 30 x 50 cm (12 x 20 in) each, about 60 g (2¼ oz) in total
1 tbsp sunflower oil
½ tsp coriander seeds, coarsely crushed

Vegetable filling

1 potato, about 170 g (6 oz), peeled and diced
1 small carrot, peeled and diced
55 g (2 oz) frozen peas
1 tbsp curry paste
1 tbsp chopped fresh coriander
pinch of salt

Mango and ginger salsa

1 ripe but firm mango
½ tsp grated fresh root ginger
1 tsp lemon juice
1 tsp caster sugar
¼ tsp crushed dried chillies
1 tsp sunflower oil

Preparation time: 35 minutes
Cooking time: about 15 minutes

Each serving provides (V)

kcal 156, **protein** 4 g, **fat** 5 g (of which saturated fat 0.5 g), **carbohydrate** 25.5 g (of which sugars 8 g), **fibre** 3 g

✓✓✓ A
✓✓ C
✓ B_1, B_6, E

1 To make the filling, cook the diced potato and carrot in a saucepan of boiling water for 5 minutes. Add the peas and cook for a further 2 minutes. Drain well and tip the vegetables into a bowl. Stir in the curry paste, coriander and salt, mashing the mixture very slightly to combine. Leave to cool.

2 Preheat the oven to 200°C (400°F, gas mark 6). Taking one sheet of filo pastry at a time (keeping the other sheet covered to prevent it from drying out), cut it widthways into 6 strips, each 30 cm (12 in) long. Brush them with a little of the oil.

3 Lay one of the pastry strips lengthways in front of you and put a rounded tbsp of the filling in the middle of the end nearest to you. Pick up one end corner and fold it diagonally over the filling to make a triangular shape, flattening the filling slightly. Continue folding the strip over in a triangular shape until you come almost to the end. Trim off excess pastry from the end. Repeat with the remaining filo pastry and filling to make 12 triangles in all.

4 Place the filo triangles on a non-stick baking sheet, brush the tops with the remaining oil and scatter over the crushed coriander seeds. Bake for 10–15 minutes or until golden.

5 Meanwhile, make the salsa. Cut the mango flesh from both sides of the flat central stone, then peel the flesh and cut into small dice. Mix in a bowl with the ginger, lemon juice, sugar, chillies and oil. Serve the salsa with the hot filo triangles.

Plus points

- Using vegetables in novel and tasty ways, such as in this filling for crisp savoury pastries, can help to boost intake so that the recommended 5 portions of fruit and vegetables a day can easily be achieved.
- Fresh mangoes are an excellent source of beta-carotene, which the body can convert into vitamin A. Beta-carotene also acts as a powerful antioxidant, helping to protect the body from heart disease and cancer.
- Frozen peas are likely to be more nutritious than fresh peas, as they are frozen straight after picking and podding. In particular, their vitamin C content is higher.

Some more ideas

- Serve the triangles as party food. They can be made ahead and then reheated in a 190°C (375°F, gas mark 5) oven for 10 minutes.
- For Thai-style chicken curry spring rolls, cook the potato and peas (omit the carrot), then mix with 115 g (4 oz) cooked skinless, boneless chicken, finely chopped, 2 chopped spring onions, 1 tbsp Thai green curry paste and a pinch of salt. Cut the filo pastry sheets in half lengthways, then into 4 crossways to make sixteen 12.5 x 15 cm (5 x 6 in) pieces. Brush lightly with sunflower oil. For each roll, spread a tbsp of the filling along a short side of a piece of filo to make a plump sausage shape. Fold over the long sides by 1 cm (½ in), then roll up like a cigar. Set the rolls join side down on a baking sheet. Brush with oil, sprinkle with the coriander seeds and bake as in the main recipe. Serve 4 rolls each with a plum dipping sauce: dissolve 30 g (1 oz) sugar in 3 tbsp water, then add 3 large, ripe, red-skinned plums, chopped. Bring to the boil and bubble for 5 minutes or until very soft, stirring often. Press the mixture through a sieve. Stir in 1 tbsp cider or white wine vinegar, then return to the pan and boil for 2 minutes. Cool before serving.

Guacamole choux buns

Savoury choux buns look spectacular, yet are easy to make. Here they are filled with a creamy mixture of avocado, tomato, cucumber and cannellini beans flavoured with lime juice, fresh coriander and a touch of garlic. They make an appealing and well-balanced lunch dish, delightful with a glass of fruity white wine.

Serves 5

1 quantity Choux pastry (see page 23)
2 Little Gem lettuces, separated into leaves

Guacamole and bean filling

1 can cannellini beans, about 410 g, drained and rinsed
2 small avocados
juice of 1 lime
1 large tomato, seeded and finely diced
½ red onion, finely chopped
12.5 cm (5 in) piece of cucumber, finely diced
1 garlic clove, crushed
2 tbsp chopped fresh coriander
salt
cayenne pepper

Preparation time: 40 minutes (including making the pastry)
Cooking time: about 25 minutes

Each serving provides (V)

kcal 313, **protein** 10 g, **fat** 20 g (of which saturated fat 8.5 g), **carbohydrate** 24 g (of which sugars 5 g), **fibre** 6 g

✓✓ A, E

✓ B_1, B_2, B_6, B_{12}, C, folate, calcium, copper, iron, potassium, selenium, zinc

1 Preheat the oven to 220°C (425°F, gas mark 7). Spoon the choux pastry in 5 equal mounds on a large greased baking tray, spacing the mounds well apart. Use the spoon to make the mounds about 7.5 cm (3 in) across and 3 cm (1¼ in) high. Bake them for 18–20 minutes or until well risen and golden brown.

2 Remove the baking tray from the oven. Make a small hole in the side of each bun, using a skewer or the point of a small knife, then return to the oven. Bake for a further 5 minutes. Transfer the buns to a wire rack to cool.

3 Meanwhile, make the filling. Tip the beans into a mixing bowl and mash with a potato masher until quite smooth. Cut the avocados in half, remove the stones and scoop out the flesh into another bowl. Mash the flesh fairly roughly using a fork, then stir into the beans together with the lime juice.

4 Add the tomato, onion, cucumber, garlic and chopped coriander to the bean and avocado mixture. Season with salt and cayenne pepper to taste. Mix together well.

5 Just before serving, split open the choux buns and fill with the guacamole and bean mixture. Place them on individual serving plates garnished with lettuce leaves.

Another idea

• To make crunchy hummus-filled choux buns, purée 1 can of chickpeas, about 410 g, drained and rinsed, in a food processor or blender with 1 tbsp tahini, 1 crushed garlic clove and the juice of 1 lemon. Stir in a 10 cm (4 in) piece of cucumber, finely diced, 1 grated carrot, 2 finely chopped spring onions and 1 seeded and finely diced red pepper. Season with ½ tsp ground cumin, and salt and pepper to taste. Spoon into the choux buns. Garnish with radicchio leaves and serve with a tomato salad.

Plus points

• Cannellini beans, like other pulses, are an excellent source of protein and starchy carbohydrate, while being low in fat.

• Avocados are unusual in that they are fruits that contain a large amount of fat. The fat is predominantly monounsaturated, however, particularly in the form of oleic acid. This can help to lower levels of the harmful LDL cholesterol while raising levels of the beneficial HDL cholesterol.

• Lime juice contains vitamin C, which will help to improve the absorption of iron from the cannellini beans.

Turkey empanadas

There are lots of different variations on these savoury Mexican pastries, which are similar to Cornish pasties. The filling here is a blend of lean turkey and vegetables, subtly flavoured with spices, nuts and dried fruit.

Serves 5

175 ml (6 fl oz) warm water
1 packet white bread or pizza dough mix, about 250 g
1 small egg, beaten
¼ tsp paprika

Spicy turkey filling

1 tbsp sunflower oil
1 onion, thinly sliced
1 garlic clove, crushed
1 fresh green or red chilli, seeded and finely chopped
250 g (8½ oz) minced turkey
300 g (10½ oz) potatoes, peeled and cut into 1 cm (½ in) dice
½ tsp ground cinnamon
½ tsp ground coriander
½ tsp ground cumin
4 tbsp dry sherry or white wine
1 large carrot, coarsely grated
45 g (1½ oz) raisins
30 g (1 oz) blanched almonds, toasted and roughly chopped
2 tbsp tomato purée
2 tbsp chopped fresh coriander
salt and pepper

Preparation time: about 30 minutes, plus 10–15 minutes rising
Cooking time: 25 minutes

1 First make the filling. Heat the oil in a frying pan and cook the onion, garlic and chilli on a fairly high heat for 2–3 minutes, stirring, until softened and lightly browned. Add the turkey mince and stir for a further 4–5 minutes.

2 Meanwhile, part-cook the diced potatoes in a saucepan of boiling water for 5 minutes. Drain well.

3 Stir the cinnamon, coriander and cumin into the turkey mixture and cook for 30 seconds. Add the sherry or wine and simmer for 2–3 minutes or until most of the liquid has evaporated.

4 Stir in the potatoes, carrot, raisins, almonds, tomato purée, chopped coriander, and salt and pepper to taste. Remove from the heat.

5 Stir the water into the bread mix and knead for 2 minutes or until smooth. Cover and leave to rest for 5 minutes, then divide into 5 equal pieces. Roll out each piece on a lightly floured surface to a 20 cm (8 in) round.

6 Preheat the oven to 220°C (425°F, gas mark 7). Divide the filling among the dough rounds, spooning it into the centre. Brush the edge of each round with beaten egg, then fold over into a half-moon shape. Press the edges together and roll over to seal. Place on a non-stick baking sheet, cover with oiled cling film and leave in a warm place for 10–15 minutes or until slightly risen.

7 Uncover the empanadas, glaze them with the rest of the beaten egg and sprinkle with the paprika. Bake for 10 minutes, then reduce the temperature to 180°C (350°F, gas mark 4) and bake for a further 15 minutes. Serve hot or at room temperature.

Plus points

- Turkey mince contains less fat than beef or lamb mince and even less fat than chicken, making it one of the lowest fat meats available.
- White bread and pizza dough are both good sources of starchy carbohydrate. Recommendations are that at least half the calories in a healthy diet should come from starchy foods.
- Raisins, like other dried fruits, are very good sources of dietary fibre. They are also virtually fat-free and provide useful amounts of iron.

Each serving provides

kcal 424, **protein** 24 g, **fat** 10 g (of which saturated fat 2 g), **carbohydrate** 58 g (of which sugars 12 g), **fibre** 5 g

✓✓✓ A, copper, selenium
✓✓ B_1, B_6, B_{12}, E, niacin, zinc
✓ B_2, C, folate, calcium, iron, potassium

Some more ideas

• Sprinkle the empanadas with poppy seeds instead of paprika.

• Make a large pie instead of pasties. Roll out about two-thirds of the dough and use to line a greased 23 cm (9 in) shallow pie dish. Add the filling, smoothing the surface evenly. Moisten the edges with beaten egg. Roll out the remaining dough and use to cover the pie, sealing the edges firmly. Make a steam hole in the centre of the dough lid. Allow to rise in a warm place for 10–15 minutes, then glaze with beaten egg. Bake for 10 minutes. Reduce the heat and bake for a further 20–25 minutes. Serve cut in slices.

• For red bean and pepper empanadas cook 1 thinly sliced onion in 1 tbsp extra virgin olive oil for 2 minutes. Stir in 1 seeded and finely chopped fresh red chilli, 1 seeded and diced red pepper and 1 seeded and diced yellow pepper. Cook on a moderate heat for 4–5 minutes. Add 1 diced courgette and cook for 2–3 minutes to soften. Stir in 2 diced tomatoes, 1 can red kidney beans, about 410 g, drained and rinsed, 1 tsp fennel seeds, 2 tbsp chopped fresh basil, and salt and pepper to taste. Use to fill the empanadas and bake as in the main recipe.

Polenta and mushroom grills

Cooked and cooled polenta can be cut into shapes and grilled to make an excellent base for a tempting topping. Here the polenta is flavoured with Gruyère cheese, and the topping is a savoury mixture of mushrooms, walnuts and herbs. Serve as a sophisticated starter, with a few mixed salad leaves if you like.

Serves 6 (makes 12 polenta grills)
750 ml (1¼ pints) vegetable stock
170 g (6 oz) instant polenta
85 g (3 oz) Gruyère cheese, grated
15 g (½ oz) dried porcini mushrooms
3 tbsp extra virgin olive oil
225 g (8 oz) chestnut mushrooms, sliced
3 tbsp dry sherry
2 tbsp chopped fresh flat-leaf parsley, plus extra to garnish
2 tsp chopped fresh rosemary
30 g (1 oz) walnuts, finely chopped
salt and pepper

Preparation and cooking time: 45 minutes, plus 1 hour cooling

Each serving provides

kcal 203, **protein** 4 g, **fat** 9 g (of which saturated fat 1 g), **carbohydrate** 23.5 g (of which sugars 0.5 g), **fibre** 3 g

✓✓✓ copper

✓ selenium

1 Bring the stock to the boil in a large saucepan. Pour in the polenta in a steady stream, stirring with a wooden spoon to prevent lumps from forming. Cook over a low heat, stirring constantly, for about 5 minutes or until the mixture thickens and pulls away from the sides of the pan. Remove from the heat and stir in the Gruyère cheese. Season with salt and pepper to taste.

2 Pour the polenta onto a damp baking tray and spread out into a rectangle measuring about 20 x 18 cm (8 x 7 in) and about 1 cm (½ in) thick. Leave to cool for 1 hour or until set.

3 Meanwhile, put the dried porcini mushrooms in a bowl and cover with boiling water. Leave to soak for 20 minutes. Drain, reserving 2 tbsp of the soaking liquid. Finely chop the mushrooms.

4 Preheat the grill to moderately hot. Lightly brush the polenta rectangle all over with 1 tbsp of the oil. Cut into 12 fingers, each measuring 5 x 6 cm (2 x 2½ in), trimming the edges to straighten them. Place oiled side up on the rack in the grill pan, and grill for 5 minutes or until lightly browned.

5 Turn the polenta slices over and grill for a further 2–3 minutes or until lightly browned. Remove from the grill and keep hot.

6 Heat the remaining 2 tbsp oil in a frying pan. Add the soaked dried mushrooms and the sliced chestnut mushrooms, and sauté over a fairly high heat for 3–4 minutes or until softened.

7 Add the sherry and the reserved mushroom soaking liquid. Cook over a high heat for 1–2 minutes, stirring, until most of the liquid has evaporated. Add the parsley, rosemary, walnuts, and salt and pepper to taste.

8 Spoon the mushroom mixture on top of the warm polenta fingers. Garnish with a little chopped parsley and serve immediately.

Plus points

- Polenta is fine corn or maize meal. It provides a starchy carbohydrate alternative for those who need to avoid wheat or gluten in their diet.
- All mushrooms are a good source of copper, a mineral with many functions but particularly needed for the maintenance of healthy bones.
- Walnuts are a good source of many of the antioxidant nutrients, including selenium, zinc, copper and vitamin E.

Some more ideas

- Add 2–3 tbsp crème fraîche to the mushroom mixture with the herbs and walnuts, and heat.
- Replace 150 ml (5 fl oz) of the stock with dry white wine.
- Add 1 tsp chilli powder or cayenne pepper to the cooked polenta at the end of step 2.
- Cut the cooled and set polenta into smaller shapes and serve as tasty party nibbles.
- Make polenta and tapenade squares. Cut the cooled and set polenta into squares (or other shapes) and grill as in the main recipe. For the tapenade topping, blend together 85 g (3 oz) stoned black olives, 2 tbsp capers, 30 g (1 oz) sun-dried tomatoes packed in oil, well drained, 1 crushed garlic clove, 3 tbsp extra virgin olive oil, 2 tbsp chopped fresh flat-leaf parsley, and salt and pepper to taste in a food processor. Alternatively, finely chop the olives, capers and tomatoes, and mix with the garlic, oil, parsley and seasoning.

Tunisian tuna and egg briks

These dainty pastry parcels are traditionally made with a special pastry called malsouka and deep-fried, but baked filo pastry gives very good results and is much lower in fat. With a tomato and cucumber salad, and some fruit chutney alongside, they make a really delicious lunch.

Serves 4 (makes 8 briks)

2½ tbsp extra virgin olive oil
8 spring onions, thinly sliced
200 g (7 oz) baby spinach leaves, roughly torn
4 sheets filo pastry, 30 x 50 cm (12 x 20 in) each, about 120 g (4¼ oz) in total
1 can tuna in spring water, about 200 g, drained and flaked
2 eggs, hard-boiled and finely chopped
dash of hot pepper sauce
salt and pepper

To serve

4 ripe tomatoes, chopped
½ cucumber, chopped
1 tbsp lemon juice
4 tbsp mango or apricot chutney

Preparation time: 30 minutes
Cooking time: 12–15 minutes

Each serving provides

kcal 339, **protein** 21 g, **fat** 12 g (of which saturated fat 2 g), **carbohydrate** 39 g (of which sugars 20 g), **fibre** 3 g

✓✓✓	A, B_{12}, selenium
✓✓	C, E, folate, niacin
✓	B_1, B_2, B_6, calcium, iron, potassium, zinc

1 Heat 2 tsp of the oil in a large saucepan and cook the spring onions over a low heat for 3 minutes or until beginning to soften. Add the spinach, cover with a tight-fitting lid and cook for a further 2–3 minutes or until tender and wilted, stirring once or twice. Tip the mixture into a sieve or colander and leave to drain and cool.

2 Using a saucer as a guide, cut out 24 rounds about 12.5 cm (5 in) in diameter from the filo pastry, cutting 6 rounds from each sheet. Stack the filo rounds in a pile, then cover with cling film to prevent them from drying out.

3 When the spinach mixture is cool, squeeze out as much excess liquid as possible, then transfer to a bowl. Add the tuna, eggs, hot pepper sauce, and salt and pepper to taste. Mix well.

4 Preheat the oven to 200°C (400°F, gas mark 6). Take one filo round and very lightly brush with some of the remaining oil. Top with a second round and brush with a little oil, then place a third round on top and brush with oil.

5 Place a heaped tbsp of the filling in the middle of the round, then fold the pastry over to make a half-moon shape. Fold in the edges, twisting them to seal, and place on a non-stick baking sheet. Repeat with the remaining pastry and filling to make 8 briks in all.

6 Lightly brush the briks with the remaining oil. Bake for 12–15 minutes or until the pastry is crisp and golden brown.

7 Meanwhile, combine the tomatoes and cucumber in a bowl and sprinkle with the lemon juice and seasoning to taste. Serve the briks hot with this salad and the chutney.

Some more ideas

- Serve with plain low-fat yogurt rather than fruit chutney.
- For Turkish boreks with feta and tomato, cut the filo pastry into twenty-four 12.5 cm (5 in) squares. For the filling, crumble 200 g (7 oz) feta cheese and mix with 3 seeded and chopped plum tomatoes, 30 g (1 oz) toasted flaked almonds, 2 tbsp chopped fresh coriander, 2 tsp chopped fresh mint and seasoning to taste. For each borek, layer 3 pastry squares, brushing each with a little oil, add a spoonful of filling, and bring the 4 corners together over the top, pinching to seal. Brush with the remaining oil and bake as in the main recipe.

Plus point

- Using tuna canned in spring water, rather than in oil, helps to keep the fat content of the dish healthily low.

Goat's cheese, cranberry and oatmeal tartlets

Adding rolled oats to shortcrust pastry not only makes it more nutritious, it also gives it more texture. The little pastry cases have a delectable tart-sweet filling of cranberry sauce, goat's cheese and a yogurt custard. They make a fine lunch dish. Serve with a crisp mixed leaf salad.

Serves 6

1 quantity Oatmeal shortcrust pastry (see Some more ideas, page 22), chilled for at least 30 minutes

Filling

3 large eggs
120 ml (4 fl oz) plain low-fat yogurt
300 ml (10 fl oz) semi-skimmed milk
4 tbsp cranberry sauce
3 tbsp snipped fresh chives
85 g (3 oz) goat's cheese, crumbled
salt and pepper

Preparation time: 45 minutes (including making the pastry), plus at least 30 minutes chilling
Cooking time: 25–30 minutes

Each serving provides

kcal 363, **protein** 13 g, **fat** 20 g (of which saturated fat 11 g), **carbohydrate** 36 g (of which sugars 15 g), **fibre** 1 g

✓✓	A, B_{12}, calcium
✓	B_1, B_2, E, folate, niacin, copper, zinc

1 Preheat the oven to 190°C (375°F, gas mark 5). Cut the pastry dough into 6 pieces. Roll out each piece thinly on a lightly floured surface and use to line 6 individual, loose-bottomed, non-stick tartlet tins 12.5 cm (5 in) in diameter and 2.5 cm (1 in) deep.

2 Prick the tartlet cases and place on a baking sheet, then 'bake blind' (see page 19) for 12 minutes. Remove the paper and beans, and return to the oven to bake for a further 8–10 minutes or until light golden brown. Remove from the oven. Lower the temperature to 180°C (350°F, gas mark 4).

3 Lightly beat the eggs in a small mixing bowl. Add the yogurt, milk, and salt and pepper to taste, and mix well together.

4 Spread 2 tsp of the cranberry sauce in the bottom of each pastry case, then scatter over the chives and goat's cheese. Pour the egg mixture into the pastry cases, dividing it equally among them. Bake for 25–30 minutes or until the filling is slightly puffed up and golden brown. Serve warm.

Another idea

- For ricotta and watercress tartlets, spread 1½ tsp red pesto sauce in the bottom of each baked pastry case. Divide 100 g (3½ oz) chopped watercress and 6 tbsp chopped sun-dried tomatoes packed in oil, well drained, among the cases. For the custard, beat the eggs with the milk and 115 g (4 oz) ricotta cheese. Pour into the pastry cases, then bake as in the main recipe.

Plus points

- Whether a cheese is made from goat's milk, cow's milk or another milk, it provides protein, calcium and phosphorus as well as several B vitamins.
- Cranberries are not only a rich source of vitamin C, they also contain a natural antibiotic which helps to control some urinary tract infections, mostly notably cystitis.
- Rolled oats are made from the whole oat grain with only the husk removed before they are rolled flat. The nutritional value of the whole grain is therefore retained.

Ham and wild rice pastries

The flavours of smoky, dry-cured Black Forest ham, shiitake and chestnut mushrooms, and courgettes work well with wild rice in the filling for these delicious filo pastries. If you're looking for an interesting lunch dish, this recipe certainly fits the bill and just needs a side salad to serve with it.

Serves 4

5 sheets filo pastry, 30 x 50 cm (12 x 20 in) each, about 150 g (5½ oz) in total
30 g (1 oz) butter, melted
2 tsp poppy seeds

Filling

100 g (3½ oz) mixed basmati and wild rice
300 ml (10 fl oz) chicken stock
1 tbsp extra virgin olive oil
1 red onion, finely chopped
100 g (3½ oz) shiitake mushrooms, sliced
100 g (3½ oz) chestnut mushrooms, sliced
2 small courgettes, diced
140 g (5 oz) Black Forest ham, trimmed of fat and snipped into strips
2 tsp chopped fresh tarragon (optional)
salt and pepper

Preparation time: 40 minutes
Cooking time: 10 minutes

Each serving provides

kcal 352, **protein** 16 g, **fat** 13 g (of which saturated fat 5 g), **carbohydrate** 47 g (of which sugars 2 g), **fibre** 1 g

✓✓	copper
✓	A, B_1, B_2, B_6, C, folate, niacin, potassium, selenium, zinc

1 Preheat the oven to 190°C (375°F, gas mark 5). For the filling, put the rice into a saucepan, pour over the stock and bring to the boil. Reduce the heat to low, then cover and simmer gently for 20 minutes, or according to the packet instructions, until the rice is tender.

2 Meanwhile, heat the oil in a large non-stick frying pan. Add the onion, mushrooms and courgettes, cover and cook for 6–8 minutes, stirring occasionally, until softened. Leave to cool while you prepare the pastry.

3 Lay 4 of the filo pastry sheets out, one on top of the other. (Keep the fifth sheet covered so it doesn't dry out). Trim the stacked filo to make a 30 x 45 cm (12 x 18 in) rectangle. Cut it lengthways in half and then across into 3 to make 15 cm (6 in) squares. You will have 24 squares.

4 Place 4 of the squares on the work surface and brush very lightly with butter. Place another 4 squares on top at a slight angle and butter them. Repeat the layering to make 4 rough piles, each with 6 buttered squares of pastry.

5 Add the rice and ham to the mushroom mixture. Stir in the tarragon, if using, and season with salt and pepper to taste. Divide the mushroom mixture among the filo stacks, spooning it into the centre. Lift up the pastry edges to contain but not completely enclose the filling – the parcels should still be open at the top. Place on a non-stick baking sheet.

6 Cut the remaining sheet of filo pastry in half lengthways and then across into thin strips. Brush the strips with the remaining butter, then scrunch them up and place on top of the parcels to cover the filling.

7 Scatter over the poppy seeds. Bake for 10 minutes or until the pastry is crisp and golden brown. Serve hot.

Plus points

- Over 2,500 varieties of mushrooms are grown throughout the world, though not all are edible. They provide useful amounts of many of the B vitamins and only contain 0.5 g fat and 13 kcal in 100 g (3½ oz).
- Wild rice is cultivated from the seeds of a North American wild aquatic grass. It contains more protein than 'true' varieties of rice.
- Ham is a good source of protein and vitamin B. The fat content can be reduced by trimming off any visible fat.

Some more ideas

- These pastries can be prepared ahead, up to the end of step 7, and kept chilled. Bake just before serving, adding an extra 3–5 minutes to the cooking time.
- To make spicy chorizo, rice and olive pastries, cook 100 g (3½ oz) white long-grain rice in a covered pan with 6 shredded dry-packed, sun-dried tomatoes and 250 ml (8½ fl oz) chicken stock for 10–15 minutes or until the rice is tender and all the stock has been absorbed. Meanwhile, combine 100 g (3½ oz) chopped chorizo sausage, 1 finely chopped red onion and 1 seeded and diced red pepper in a frying pan, cover and cook for 6–8 minutes or until the onion is tender. Add the rice mixture, 45 g (1½ oz) sliced black olives, 1 can sweetcorn, about 200 g, drained, 20 fresh basil leaves, roughly torn up, and seasoning to taste. Use to fill the filo pastries. Scatter over 2 tsp sesame seeds and bake as in the main recipe.

Simple Family Meals

Main dishes to please all ages

The appetising and satisfying dishes here are sure to become firm favourites. Children will love the pizza dough tart filled with ricotta and cherry tomatoes, and the pie made from layers of tortillas and chicken chilli. For a Sunday lunch that all the family will enjoy, why not try a warming beef and chestnut pie with a suetcrust lid, or a lamb hotpot topped with herbed scone triangles? Savoury little rice puddings, rich with Cheddar and asparagus, make a great midweek meal. And who could resist a mash-topped pie with a chicken, apple and cider filling?

Potato tart with tuna, chorizo and black olives

This pizza-style tart uses potato pastry as a base, and is topped with an appetising mélange of tuna, spicy chorizo sausage, peppers and olives. Toppings can easily be varied to include your own favourites. Serve with a salad – watercress and cherry tomato is good – for an easy family meal.

Serves 4

1 quantity Herbed potato pastry, flavoured with 1 tbsp chopped fresh basil (see Some more ideas, page 24), chilled for 30 minutes

Tuna and chorizo filling

8 shallots

100 g (3½ oz) chorizo sausage, thinly sliced

1 red pepper, seeded and thinly sliced

1 yellow pepper, seeded and thinly sliced

140 g (5 oz) tomato passata

1 can tuna in spring water, about 200 g, drained and flaked

30 g (1 oz) stoned black olives, halved

Preparation time: about 1 hour (including making the pastry), plus 30 minutes chilling

Cooking time: 15 minutes

Each serving provides

kcal 408, **protein** 20 g, **fat** 19 g (of which saturated fat 10 g), **carbohydrate** 42 g (of which sugars 8.5 g), **fibre** 4 g

✓✓✓ A, B_{12}, C, selenium

✓✓ B_6, folate, niacin

✓ B_1, E, calcium, copper, iron, potassium, zinc

1 Preheat the oven to 190°C (375°F, gas mark 5). For the filling, place the shallots in a heatproof bowl and pour over enough boiling water to cover. Leave for about 5 minutes, then drain. When the shallots are cool enough to handle, peel and quarter.

2 Place the potato pastry dough on a non-stick baking sheet and roll out to a 28 cm (11 in) round. Bake for 20–25 minutes or until light golden.

3 Meanwhile, gently cook the chorizo in a non-stick frying pan. When the oil starts to run from the sausage, add the shallots and cook for 2–3 minutes or until the shallots are glazed. Add the red and yellow peppers, and cook for a further 1–2 minutes to soften.

4 Spread the passata evenly over the surface of the pastry round, leaving a border clear. Top with the shallot, pepper and chorizo mixture. Scatter over the tuna and olives.

5 Bake the tart for 15 minutes or until the exposed edge is golden brown. Serve hot, cut into wedges.

Another idea

- For a potato tart with sardines and red onion, spread the tomato passata over the surface of the potato pastry base, then top with 1 red onion, thinly sliced, and 1 seeded and thinly sliced red or yellow pepper. Drain 2 cans of sardines in olive oil, about 120 g each, and flake into large pieces. Scatter over the tart together with 6 thinly sliced midget gherkins. Bake as in the main recipe.

Plus points

- Potatoes are a classic source of starchy carbohydrate for everyday meals. Their value as a nutritious and satisfying food was appreciated during the Second World War when the Ministry of Food made sure that they did not become rationed.
- Processed tomatoes in passata contain a high amount of lycopene, a red carotenoid pigment that helps to protect against heart disease and some forms of cancer.
- Chorizo is quite high in fat, but as the paprika-flavoured oil oozes out on cooking, no extra oil need be added to the pan for glazing the shallots.

Yorkshire mince popovers

Yorkshire pudding is a favourite accompaniment to a Sunday roast, but why not enjoy it midweek too, as a main dish? Here it is baked in individual tins, with a savoury pork and vegetable filling. Serve with mashed potatoes mixed with lightly cooked shredded Brussels sprouts for a delicious, well-balanced meal.

Serves 4 (makes 12 popovers)

Batter

125 g (4½ oz) plain flour
2 eggs, lightly beaten
½ tsp sweet paprika
300 ml (10 fl oz) semi-skimmed milk

Pork filling

1 tbsp extra virgin olive oil
300 g (10½ oz) lean minced pork
1 small onion, finely chopped
1 small leek, finely chopped
1 carrot, finely chopped
1 tbsp tomato purée
1 tsp sweet chilli sauce
4 tbsp vegetable stock
1 tbsp chopped parsley
salt and pepper

Preparation time: 45 minutes
Cooking time: 30–35 minutes

Each serving provides

kcal 322, **protein** 26.5 g, **fat** 11 g (of which saturated fat 2 g), **carbohydrate** 32 g (of which sugars 8 g), **fibre** 2 g

✓✓✓	A
✓✓	B_{12}
✓	B_1, B_2, B_6, C, E, folate, niacin, calcium, copper, iron, potassium, zinc

1 First make the batter. Sift the flour into a bowl and add the eggs, paprika, and salt and pepper to taste. Gradually whisk in the milk to make a smooth batter. Leave to stand while making the filling.

2 Heat the oil in a heavy non-stick frying pan. Add the pork and fry over a moderate heat for 5 minutes or until browned, stirring with a wooden spoon to break up the clumps of meat.

3 Remove the pork with a draining spoon and set aside on a plate. Turn down the heat, then add the onion, leek and carrot to the pan. Cook gently for 5 minutes, stirring frequently, until soft and golden. Stir in the tomato purée, chilli sauce and stock. Return the pork to the pan. Cook gently for a further 15 minutes, stirring frequently.

4 Preheat the oven to 220°C (425°F, gas mark 7). Remove the pork mixture from the heat, and stir in the parsley and salt and pepper to taste.

5 Lightly oil 12 non-stick muffin tins that are 7.5 cm (3 in) across and 3 cm (1¼ in) deep. Put them into the oven to heat for 4 minutes.

6 Stir the batter, then transfer it to a jug to make it easier to pour. Divide the batter among the tins so they are half full. Spoon the pork filling into the centre, piling it up.

7 Bake for 30–35 minutes or until the puddings are well risen and golden brown. Carefully turn out the puddings onto 4 plates and serve immediately.

Plus points

- Lean pork is an excellent source of protein, iron and zinc. Combining vegetables with the meat and batter in this dish provides a healthy family meal.
- Though eggs have received a 'bad press' because of their cholesterol content, this is unfair. For most people, eating foods that are high in cholesterol has little effect on blood cholesterol levels.
- Milk is an important source of vitamin B_2 in the diet. As this vitamin is easily destroyed by ultraviolet light, bottles of milk should not be left exposed to sunlight on the doorstep.

Some more ideas

- Instead of sweet paprika, flavour the batter with 2 tsp wholegrain mustard.
- The batter can be made in a food processor. Simply place all the ingredients in the bowl and mix together.
- To make venison toad-in-the-hole, make the batter as in the main recipe but adding 2 tbsp chopped fresh herbs (such as parsley, chives or marjoram) in place of the paprika. Spread out 8 venison sausages, about 300 g (10½ oz) in total, in a lightly greased 22 x 30 cm (8½ x 12 in) roasting tin or baking dish. Bake in a preheated 220°C (425°F, gas mark 7) oven for 10 minutes. Pour over the batter and bake for 10 minutes, then reduce the oven temperature to 200°C (400°F, gas mark 6). Bake for a further 20–25 minutes or until the batter is well risen and golden. Serve straight from the dish, with mashed potatoes and swede plus some seasonal greens.

Smoked haddock and potato pie

Fish pie is usually popular with children, who may not otherwise be keen on fish. In this version, leek and watercress are added to boost the vitamin value, and sliced potato and cheese make an appealing topping. Try it with roasted tomatoes on the vine, cooked for about 15 minutes alongside the pie, and steamed broccoli.

Serves 6

750 ml (1¼ pints) plus 3 tbsp semi-skimmed milk
500 g (1 lb 2 oz) smoked haddock fillets
1 bay leaf
1 large leek, halved lengthways and sliced
550 g (1¼ lb) potatoes, peeled and cut into 5 mm (¼ in) thick slices
3 tbsp cornflour
85 g (3 oz) watercress, thick stalks removed
50 g (1¾ oz) mature Cheddar cheese, coarsely grated
salt and pepper
chopped parsley to garnish

Preparation time: 40 minutes
Cooking time: 25–30 minutes

Each serving provides

kcal 271, **protein** 25 g, **fat** 6 g (of which saturated fat 3 g), **carbohydrate** 32 g (of which sugars 7 g), **fibre** 2 g

✓✓✓	B_{12}, iodine
✓✓	A, B_6, C, niacin, calcium, potassium, selenium
✓	B_1, B_2, folate, copper, zinc

1 Pour the 750 ml (1¼ pints) milk into a wide frying pan. Add the haddock and bay leaf. Bring to a gentle simmer, then cover and cook for about 5 minutes or until the haddock is just cooked.

2 Lift out the fish with a draining spoon and leave to cool slightly, then peel off the skin and break the flesh into large flakes. Set aside. Strain the milk and reserve 600 ml (1 pint), as well as the bay leaf.

3 Put the leek in the frying pan and add the reserved milk and bay leaf. Cover and simmer for 10 minutes or until the leek is tender.

4 Meanwhile, cook the potatoes in a saucepan of boiling water for about 8 minutes or until they are just tender but not breaking up. Drain. Preheat the oven to 190°C (375°F, gas mark 5).

5 Remove the bay leaf from the leeks and discard. Mix the cornflour with the remaining 3 tbsp cold milk to make a smooth paste. Add to the leek mixture and cook gently, stirring, until slightly thickened.

6 Take the pan from the heat and stir in the watercress, which will wilt. Season with salt and pepper to taste. Add the flaked haddock, folding it in gently. Transfer the mixture to a 2 litre (3½ pint) pie dish.

7 Arrange the potato slices on top of the fish mixture, overlapping them slightly. Sprinkle with the cheese, and season with salt and pepper to taste. Bake for 25–30 minutes or until the fish filling is bubbling and the potatoes are turning golden.

8 Sprinkle the top of the pie with parsley and allow to stand for about 5 minutes before serving.

Plus points

- Smoked haddock is an excellent source of iodine and provides useful amounts of vitamin B_6 and potassium. Undyed smoked haddock is now widely available as an alternative to the vibrant yellow-dyed version, which may cause a reaction in susceptible people.
- Potatoes do not contain as much vitamin C as many other vegetables, but they are a valuable source of this vitamin because they are eaten so frequently and in such large amounts.
- Watercress, like other dark green leafy vegetables, is an excellent source of many of the antioxidant nutrients, including beta-carotene, vitamin C and vitamin E.

Some more ideas

- Reduce the amount of smoked haddock to 400 g (14 oz), and add 2 chopped hard-boiled eggs to the fish filling at the end of step 6.
- Use 2 sliced leeks. Omit the watercress and instead, in step 4, add 125 g (4½ oz) baby spinach leaves to the potato slices for the last 1–2 minutes of their cooking time. Drain well. Make a layer of the potatoes and spinach on the bottom of the pie dish. Spoon the hot fish and leek sauce over the top, sprinkle with the cheese and grill under a moderate heat for 5–10 minutes or until bubbling and golden.
- For a smoked haddock, pepper and fennel pie, cook 1 seeded and chopped red pepper, 1 small chopped onion and 2 chopped garlic cloves in 1 tbsp extra virgin olive oil in a large frying pan until the onion is soft. Add 250 g (8½ oz) thinly sliced bulb fennel and cook for a further 5 minutes, stirring occasionally. Stir in 1 can chopped tomatoes, about 400 g, with the juice, and season to taste. Cover and simmer for 25 minutes or until the fennel is tender. Meanwhile, cut the potatoes into chunks instead of slices and cook for 10 minutes or until tender. Pour the pepper and fennel sauce into the pie dish. Lay the skinned smoked haddock fillets on the top (cut to fit if necessary) and scatter over the drained potatoes. Sprinkle with ¼ tsp crushed dried chillies and 30 g (1 oz) freshly grated Parmesan cheese. Bake for about 20 minutes or until golden and bubbling.

Cheddar and broccoli strata

Based on an old-fashioned English recipe, but with an American influence, this satisfying savoury pudding is made up of layers of bread and vegetables with a cheesy egg custard poured over. Served with a quick home-made tomato sauce, it is a tasty and nutritious dish. A leafy salad could be served alongside.

Serves 6

15 g (½ oz) butter
4 shallots, finely chopped
250 g (8½ oz) broccoli, cut into small florets
170 g (6 oz) fine green beans, halved
1 can sweetcorn kernels, about 200 g, drained
9 thick slices of white bread, about 400 g (14 oz) in total, crusts removed and slices cut in half
4 eggs
600 ml (1 pint) semi-skimmed milk
2 tbsp snipped fresh chives
2 tbsp chopped parsley
85 g (3 oz) mature Cheddar cheese, grated
salt and pepper

Tomato sauce

1 tbsp extra virgin olive oil
1 red onion, finely chopped
2 garlic cloves, crushed
2 cans chopped tomatoes with herbs, about 400 g each
2 tbsp tomato purée

Preparation time: 30 minutes, plus 30 minutes standing
Cooking time: 1 hour

1 Melt the butter in a frying pan, add the shallots and cook gently for about 7 minutes or until softened. Meanwhile, cook the broccoli and green beans in a saucepan of boiling water for 4 minutes or until just tender. Drain well, then stir into the shallots together with the sweetcorn. Season to taste.

2 Arrange 6 of the halved bread slices side by side in a lightly greased, deep ovenproof dish. Top with half of the broccoli mixture. Repeat the layers of bread and broccoli mixture, then finish with a layer of bread.

3 Whisk together the eggs, milk, chives and parsley, and season with salt and pepper to taste. Pour over the layered bread and vegetables, and sprinkle the cheese on top. Set aside for 30 minutes, to allow the bread to soak up some of the liquid. Preheat the oven to 180°C (350°F, gas mark 4).

4 Meanwhile, make the tomato sauce. Heat the oil in a saucepan, add the onion and garlic, and cook over a moderate heat for 5 minutes. Stir in the tomatoes, with their juice, and the tomato purée. Bring to the boil, then reduce the heat, cover and simmer for 15 minutes. Uncover the pan, increase the heat slightly and cook for a further 5–10 minutes, stirring occasionally, until the sauce has thickened slightly.

5 Bake the pudding for 1 hour or until set, puffy and golden brown. Just before the cooking time is up, warm the sauce gently. Spoon the strata onto hot serving plates and serve with the tomato sauce.

Plus points

- Cheddar cheese is a good source of protein and an excellent source of calcium. It has a high fat content, but by choosing a mature Cheddar, less can be used while still making a valuable contribution to the flavour and nutritional value of the recipe.
- Sweetcorn provides useful amounts of dietary fibre, which helps to keep the digestive system in good working order.

Each serving provides V

kcal 439, **protein** 23 g, **fat** 17 g (of which saturated fat 7 g), **carbohydrate** 53 g (of which sugars 16 g), **fibre** 5 g

✓✓✓	A, B_{12}, C, calcium
✓✓	B_1, B_2, E, folate, niacin, copper, iron, potassium, selenium, zinc
✓	B_6

Some more ideas

- Replace the shallots with 1–2 sliced leeks.
- Flavour the egg custard with chopped fresh oregano or marjoram instead of chives.
- For a higher fibre dish, use wholemeal bread.
- Use Double Gloucester or Lancashire cheese instead of Cheddar.
- To make a sausage and courgette strata, grill 4 good-quality, high-meat-content herby pork sausages. Meanwhile, cook 1 finely chopped onion and 3 sliced courgettes in the butter for 8–10 minutes or until tender. Slice the grilled sausages and mix with the vegetables. Cut the bread into cubes rather than slices. Layer the bread cubes and sausage mixture in the ovenproof dish. Make the egg custard as in the main recipe, but flavour with 1 tbsp chopped fresh rosemary instead of chives and parsley. Omit the cheese. Leave to soak, then bake. Serve with the tomato sauce, and vegetables such as baby carrots and peas.

Beef and chestnut suetcrust pie

This is a warming dish for the cold weather months, rich with lean beef, celeriac, chestnuts and shallots. The suetcrust pastry lid is flavoured with herbs, and breadcrumbs are added for a light, crumbly texture so the pie is not heavy to eat. For extra vitamins serve with lightly cooked spinach.

Serves 4

1 quantity Herbed suetcrust pastry (see Some more ideas, page 24), made with breadcrumbs replacing 30 g (1 oz) of the flour

Beef and chestnut filling

12 small shallots
1 tbsp extra virgin olive oil
300 g (10½ oz) lean braising steak, trimmed of fat and cut into 2.5 cm (1 in) cubes
400 g (14 oz) celeriac, finely diced
360 ml (12 fl oz) beef or vegetable stock
1 tbsp redcurrant jelly
200 g (7 oz) vacuum-packed, peeled whole chestnuts
1 tbsp plain flour
15 g (½ oz) butter, softened
salt and pepper

Preparation time: 1½ hours (including making the pastry)
Cooking time: 30–35 minutes

Each serving provides

kcal 502, **protein** 23 g, **fat** 24 g (of which saturated fat 11 g), **carbohydrate** 52 g (of which sugars 11 g), **fibre** 7 g

✓✓✓	B_{12}, zinc
✓✓	B_1, B_6, C, niacin, calcium, copper, iron, potassium
✓	B_6, E, folate, selenium

1 To make the filling, place the shallots in a heatproof bowl, pour over boiling water to cover and leave for 5 minutes. Drain and, when cool enough to handle, peel the shallots.

2 Heat the oil in a heavy-based pan or flameproof casserole, add the beef and cook over a moderate heat for 4–5 minutes or until browned all over. Remove from the pan to a plate using a draining spoon.

3 Add the shallots to the pan and cook for 4 minutes or until lightly browned. Add the celeriac and cook, stirring, for 1 minute, then return the beef to the pan. Stir in the stock and redcurrant jelly. Bring to the boil, then reduce the heat and simmer gently for 45 minutes or until the beef is tender, stirring frequently.

4 Using a draining spoon, transfer the beef and vegetables to a 1.2 litre (2 pint) pie dish. Stir in the chestnuts. Set aside.

5 Blend the flour with the butter to make a paste (beurre manié). Stir the paste, a little at a time, into the cooking liquid in the pan and simmer, stirring constantly, until the liquid thickens. Season with salt and pepper to taste, then pour this sauce over the beef mixture in the pie dish. Leave to cool while preparing the suetcrust lid.

6 Preheat the oven to 180°C (350°F, gas mark 4). Roll out the suetcrust dough on a lightly floured work surface to a round or oval to fit the top of the pie dish. Dampen the rim of the dish with water, then lay the dough gently over the top. Press firmly to the rim of the dish to seal. Use a fork to make a decorative edge.

7 Cut 3 small slits in the centre of the pastry lid, to allow steam to escape, then bake for 30–35 minutes or until golden brown. Serve hot.

Plus points

- Beef is an excellent source of protein and iron. Iron from red meat is absorbed by the body much more efficiently than iron from vegetable sources.
- Chestnuts have a higher starchy carbohydrate content and a much lower fat content than other nuts. As a result they are also lower in calories.
- Suet is the fat from around lamb's or beef kidneys, which has been shredded and floured. It contains less saturated fat and more monounsaturated fat than butter.

Another idea

• For a minced beef and lentil suetcrust pie, cook 200 g (7 oz) lean minced beef, without any added fat, over a moderate heat until well browned. Add 1 large onion, 3 carrots and 3 celery sticks, all finely chopped, and cook, stirring frequently, for a further 5 minutes or until softened. Stir in 1 can chopped tomatoes, about 400 g, with the juice, 100 g (3½ oz) split red lentils, 330 ml (12 fl oz) beef or vegetable stock and 1 tbsp Worcestershire sauce. Bring to the boil, then simmer gently for 40 minutes, stirring frequently, until thick. Season with salt and pepper to taste. Cool, then pour into the pie dish. Make the suetcrust pastry dough with breadcrumbs, as for the main recipe, but instead of herbs flavour with 1 tbsp wholegrain mustard added to the water. Use the dough to cover the pie and bake as in the main recipe. This is delicious with steamed spring greens and carrots.

Colcannon chicken and apple pie

Colcannon is a simple, warming Irish potato dish, like bubble and squeak, combining mashed potatoes with shredded cooked cabbage and chopped spring onions. Here it is used as a lovely pie topping for chicken cooked in cider with sliced apples and carrots. The pie is a well-balanced meal in itself, needing no accompaniments.

Serves 4

1 tbsp sunflower oil
1 large onion, sliced
450 g (1 lb) skinless boneless chicken breasts (fillets), cut into chunks
3 carrots, thickly sliced
240 ml (8 fl oz) chicken stock
240 ml (8 fl oz) dry cider
1 tsp wholegrain mustard
1 tbsp chopped fresh tarragon or 1 tsp dried tarragon
2 Cox's apples, thickly sliced
1 tbsp cornflour
salt and pepper

Colcannon topping

700 g (1 lb 9 oz) floury potatoes, peeled and cut into large chunks
200 g (7 oz) Savoy cabbage, shredded
4 tbsp semi-skimmed milk
25 g (scant 1 oz) butter
4 spring onions, finely chopped

Preparation and cooking time: 1¼ hours

Each serving provides

kcal 464, **protein** 34 g, **fat** 10 g (of which saturated fat 4 g), **carbohydrate** 60 g (of which sugars 22 g), **fibre** 8 g

✓✓✓	A, B_6, C, niacin
✓✓	B_1, E, folate, copper, potassium, selenium, zinc
✓	B_2, calcium, iron

1 Heat the oil in a large, deep, non-stick frying pan. Add the onion and cook over a low heat for 5 minutes or until softened.

2 Add the chicken to the pan and cook over a moderate heat, stirring occasionally, for 5 minutes or until it is no longer pink. Stir in the carrots.

3 Combine the stock, cider, mustard and tarragon, and pour into the pan. Bring to the boil, then reduce the heat, cover and cook gently for 10 minutes. Stir in the apples and cook, covered, for a further 10 minutes or until the chicken and carrots are tender, and the apples have softened but are still holding their shape.

4 Meanwhile, cook the potatoes in a saucepan of boiling water for about 15 minutes or until tender. Cook the cabbage in a separate pan of boiling water for 4–5 minutes or until just tender but not soft; drain well.

5 Drain the potatoes and return them to the pan. Add the milk and butter, and mash until smooth. Stir in the cabbage and spring onions, and season with salt and pepper to taste. Cover to keep warm.

6 Using a draining spoon, transfer the chicken, apples and vegetables to a 1.7 litre (3 pint) ovenproof dish. Set aside. Preheat the grill to high.

7 Mix the cornflour with 1 tbsp cold water, stir into the cooking liquid in the frying pan and bring to the boil, stirring until thickened. Season with salt and pepper to taste, then pour over the chicken mixture.

8 Pile the potato and cabbage topping over the chicken mixture, spreading it evenly to cover. Place under the grill and cook for 4–5 minutes or until golden brown. Serve immediately.

Plus points

- Savoy cabbage contains flavonoids that are believed to help suppress cancer-causing cells. It also contains other nutrients with protective properties, such as vitamins C and E.
- Adding a green vegetable such as cabbage to a mashed potato topping is a tasty and clever way of increasing the vegetable content of a meal. It will also be appealing to children who may not always be fond of vegetables like cabbage when they are served separately.

Some more ideas

- Replace the cider with pressed apple juice.
- Instead of cabbage and spring onions, use leeks in the potato topping. Cook 2 sliced leeks in the butter until tender. Mash the potatoes with the milk, then mix in the buttery leeks.
- Make sherried liver topped with minted pea mash. Soften 1 sliced onion in 1 tbsp sunflower oil, then add 400 g (14 oz) lamb's liver, cut into strips and cook for 2–3 minutes. Add 2 sliced courgettes. Combine 250 ml (8½ fl oz) lamb or chicken stock, 2 tbsp medium-dry sherry, the grated zest and juice of 1 orange, and 1 tbsp tomato purée, and pour over the liver mixture. Bring to the boil, then reduce the heat and cook gently for 10 minutes. Transfer the liver and vegetables to the ovenproof dish. Thicken the liquid with 1 tbsp cornflour as in the main recipe, season and pour into the dish. For the topping, cook the potatoes for 10 minutes, then add 200 g (7 oz) mint-flavoured frozen peas. Bring back to the boil and cook for a further 5 minutes or until the potatoes are tender. Drain and crush roughly with a fork, mixing in the milk, butter and 2 tbsp snipped fresh chives. Spread over the top of the liver mixture and grill as in the main recipe.

Herbed lamb cobbler

A hearty hotpot of lean lamb chunks, leeks, carrots, tomatoes and broccoli with a herbed scone topping is sure to satisfy a hungry family. To complete the meal, serve with lightly steamed green beans or another seasonal green vegetable, to boost the vitamin content of the meal.

Serves 4

1 quantity Herbed scone pastry (see Some more ideas, page 23), made with plain low-fat yogurt instead of milk
1 tbsp semi-skimmed milk

Lamb filling

1 tbsp sunflower oil
450 g (1 lb) boneless leg of lamb, trimmed of fat and cut into bite-sized cubes
450 g (1 lb) leeks, thickly sliced
350 g (12½ oz) carrots, thickly sliced
1 can plum tomatoes, about 400 g
200 ml (7 fl oz) lamb stock
2 tbsp chopped fresh thyme
200 g (7 oz) broccoli, broken into florets
salt and pepper

Preparation time: 45 minutes (including making the pastry)
Cooking time: 20 minutes

Each serving provides

kcal 519, **protein** 34 g, **fat** 19 g (of which saturated fat 5 g), **carbohydrate** 55 g (of which sugars 15 g), **fibre** 8 g

✓✓✓	A, C, E
✓✓	B_1, B_6, folate, calcium, iron, potassium
✓	niacin, copper, zinc

1 To make the filling, heat the oil in a non-stick frying pan, add the lamb and cook for 3–4 minutes, stirring occasionally, until lightly browned. Add the leeks and carrots, and cook, stirring, for 1 minute.

2 Add the tomatoes with their juice, the stock, thyme, and salt and pepper to taste. Bring to the boil, then reduce the heat, cover and simmer gently for 30 minutes or until the lamb is tender.

3 Roll out the scone dough on a lightly floured surface to 1 cm (½ in) thickness. Cut into 12 triangles. Preheat the oven to 220°C (425°F, gas mark 7).

4 Add the broccoli to the lamb stew. and stir in. Cover again, increase the heat slightly and cook for a further 5 minutes.

5 Spoon the lamb stew into a 2 litre (3½ pint) ovenproof dish. Arrange the scone dough triangles on top, overlapping them slightly. Brush with the milk to glaze. Bake for 20 minutes or until the scone topping is risen and golden brown. Serve hot.

Another idea

- To make a Hungarian-style turkey cobbler, lightly brown 300 g (10½ oz) skinless boneless turkey breast, cut into bite-sized cubes, in 1 tbsp sunflower oil with 1 thinly sliced onion and 1 crushed garlic clove. Stir in 300 g (10½ oz) peeled, diced potatoes, 200 ml (7 fl oz) chicken stock, 1 can chopped tomatoes, about 400 g, with the juice, and 1 tbsp paprika. Bring to the boil, then cover and simmer gently for 20 minutes. Stir in 300 g (10½ oz) fresh shelled or frozen broad beans. Bring back to the boil, then simmer, covered, for about 5 minutes. For the scone topping, replace the herbs with 1 tbsp caraway seeds, and cut the dough into 12 rounds. Transfer the turkey stew to an ovenproof dish, arrange the scone rounds on top and glaze with milk. Bake as in the main recipe.

Plus points

- Lamb has a reputation for being a fatty meat, but changes in breeding, feeding and butchery techniques have reduced the fat content considerably.
- Carrots are rich in beta-carotene, which helps to protect cells against damage by free radicals. Older, darker carrots contain more beta-carotene than young, pale ones.

Aztec chicken pie

Teenagers especially will love this unusual pie, which layers flour tortillas with diced chicken and red kidney beans in a spicy tomato, sweetcorn and pepper sauce. Serve with a green salad and a side dish of diced avocado sprinkled with lime juice, for a meal with an exciting Mexican flavour.

Serves 6

6 large flour tortillas (wraps)
150 g (5½ oz) plain low-fat yogurt
90 ml (3 fl oz) soured cream
75 g (2½ oz) mature Cheddar cheese, finely grated

Mexican chicken filling

2 tbsp extra virgin olive oil
1 large Spanish onion, chopped
2 garlic cloves, crushed
1 green pepper, seeded and chopped
200 g (7 oz) baby corn, chopped
1 fresh red chilli, seeded and chopped
2 cans chopped tomatoes, about 400 g each
1 tsp ground coriander
1 tsp ground cumin
1 tsp caster sugar
1 good-quality chicken stock cube or 1 tsp chicken bouillon powder
300 g (10½ oz) cooked skinless, boneless chicken breast (fillet), diced
1 can red kidney beans, about 410 g, drained and rinsed
6 tbsp chopped fresh coriander
salt and pepper

Preparation time: 35–40 minutes
Cooking time: 25 minutes

1 First make the filling. Heat the oil in a large pan, add the onion and cook for 10 minutes or until softened. Stir in the garlic, green pepper, corn and chilli, and cook for 5 more minutes.

2 Add the tomatoes with their juice, the ground coriander, cumin, sugar and stock cube or bouillon. Season with salt and pepper to taste, and stir well. Bring to the boil, then reduce the heat and simmer for 10 minutes.

3 Stir in the chicken, beans and half the fresh coriander. Heat through gently for 5 minutes. Preheat the oven to 200°C (400°F, gas mark 6).

4 Lightly oil a large china flan dish, measuring about 28 cm (11 in) in diameter and 5 cm (2 in) deep. Place a tortilla on the bottom and spoon over one-fifth of the filling. Cover with a second tortilla, then spread over another fifth of the filling. Continue layering, finishing with the last tortilla on top. The stack will be slightly higher than the side of the dish.

5 Mix the yogurt with the soured cream, 50 g (1¾ oz) of the cheese and 2 tbsp of the remaining coriander. Spoon over the top of the pie. Sprinkle with the remaining cheese. Bake for 25 minutes or until the top is golden. Sprinkle with the rest of the coriander and serve hot, cut into wedges.

Plus points

- Tortillas, whether made from masa harina, a type of cornmeal, or wheat, are a good source of starchy carbohydrates.
- There is little nutritional difference between canned red kidney beans and cooked dried ones, and canned beans are certainly a lot more convenient.
- Chicken is an excellent source of protein and a good source of many of the B vitamins, particularly B_1 and niacin. Eaten without the skin, it is low in fat and the fat that is present in the meat is mainly the more beneficial unsaturated type.

Each serving provides

kcal 517, **protein** 29 g, **fat** 13 g (of which saturated fat 5.5 g), **carbohydrate** 75 g (of which sugars 17 g), **fibre** 7.5 g

✓✓✓	C, niacin
✓✓	A, B_1, B_6, E, folate, calcium, copper, potassium, zinc
✓	B_2, iron, selenium

Some more ideas

- As an alternative topping, mix 200 g (7 oz) fromage frais with 85 g (3 oz) finely grated Manchego cheese and the 2 tbsp chopped fresh coriander.
- To make a borlotti bean tortilla pie, soften the onion, then add the crushed garlic, 1 seeded and chopped yellow pepper 250 g (8½ oz) chopped courgettes and 500 g (1 lb 2 oz) chopped bulb fennel. Cook for 5 minutes, then stir in the tomatoes, ground coriander, sugar, stock cube or bouillon and seasoning to taste. Simmer for 10 minutes. Add 2 cans borlotti beans, about 410 g each, drained and rinsed, and heat through. Layer the bean mixture with the flour tortillas, top with the yogurt mixture or the fromage frais mixture and bake as in the main recipe.

Chunky vegetable crumble

A tasty mixture of root vegetables and creamy butter beans topped with a savoury cheese crumble makes a nourishing vegetarian dish. Sunflower seeds are added to the crumble for added texture and extra protein.

Serves 4

1 tbsp sunflower oil
1 onion, sliced
2 garlic cloves, crushed
3 carrots, cut into 2 cm (¾ in) chunks
2 parsnips, cut into 2 cm (¾ in) chunks
250 g (8½ oz) baby turnips, quartered
350 g (12½ oz) waxy new potatoes, scrubbed and cut into 2 cm (¾ in) chunks
450 ml (15 fl oz) vegetable stock
generous dash of Worcestershire sauce
1 tbsp tomato purée
2 bay leaves
1 can butter beans, about 410 g, drained and rinsed
3 tbsp chopped parsley
salt and pepper

Sunflower seed crumble topping

85 g (3 oz) wholemeal flour
30 g (1 oz) cool butter, diced
75 g (2½ oz) mature Cheddar cheese, coarsely grated
30 g (1 oz) sunflower seeds

Preparation time: 40 minutes
Cooking time: 20 minutes

1 Heat the oil in a large saucepan, add the onion and cook gently for 10 minutes or until softened. Add the garlic and cook for 1 more minute.

2 Add the carrots, parsnips, turnips and potatoes. Stir in the stock, Worcestershire sauce, tomato purée and bay leaves. Bring to the boil, then reduce the heat, cover and simmer for 20 minutes, stirring occasionally.

3 Meanwhile, make the crumble topping. Put the flour in a bowl and rub in the butter. Sprinkle over 1½ tbsp cold water and mix together with a fork to make large crumbs. Stir in the cheese and sunflower seeds. Set aside.

4 Preheat the oven to 190°C (375°F, gas mark 5). Stir the butter beans into the vegetables and cook for a further 5–7 minutes or until the vegetables are just tender. Remove and discard the bay leaves.

5 Remove a large ladleful of the vegetables and stock, and mash until smooth or purée in a blender or processor. Stir the purée into the vegetable mixture in the pan to thicken it slightly. Stir in the parsley, and season with salt and pepper to taste.

6 Spoon the vegetable mixture into a lightly greased 1.7 litre (3 pint) ovenproof dish. Sprinkle the crumble mixture evenly over the top. Bake for 20 minutes or until golden brown.

Plus points

- Together, parsnips and turnips provide fibre, B vitamins and potassium and are a surprisingly useful source of vitamin C.
- New potatoes, scrubbed but not peeled, have one-third more dietary fibre than peeled potatoes. The nutrients found just under the skin will also be preserved.
- Sunflower seeds are rich in vitamin E. They also offer vitamin B_1, iron and phosphorus.

Each serving provides (V)

kcal 465, **protein** 17 g, **fat** 21 g (of which saturated fat 9 g), **carbohydrate** 55.5 g (of which sugars 16 g), **fibre** 12.5 g

✓✓✓	A, C, E, copper
✓✓	B_1, B_6, folate, niacin, calcium, potassium, selenium, zinc
✓	iron

Some more ideas

- Replace 1 of the carrots with 250 g (8½ oz) quartered kohlrabi.
- For an oaty vegetable crumble, gently cook 1 large sliced onion in 1 tbsp extra virgin olive oil for 10 minutes or until soft. Add 2 crushed garlic cloves, then stir in 1 aubergine, about 200 g (7 oz), 1 acorn squash, about 500 g (1 lb 2 oz) and 300 g (10½ oz) courgettes, all cut into 2 cm (¾ in) chunks. Cook, stirring, for 5 minutes. Add 400 ml (14 fl oz) vegetable stock, 30 g (1 oz) chopped sun-dried tomatoes, 2 tsp chopped fresh thyme and seasoning to taste. Cover and simmer for 15–20 minutes or until all the vegetables are tender. Stir in 1 can of cannellini beans, about 410 g, drained and rinsed. Remove a large ladleful of the mixture, containing mostly squash, tomatoes and beans, and mash or purée, then return to the pan to thicken the mixture. For the crumble, use 30 g (1 oz) freshly grated Parmesan cheese instead of Cheddar, and replace the sunflower seeds with 30 g (1 oz) jumbo oats. Bake as in the main recipe.

Pizza tart with cherry tomatoes

A Parmesan-flavoured pizza dough makes a delicious case for a ricotta cheese and herb filling topped with sweet cherry tomatoes and black olives. Serve with a salad of mixed leaves and poppy, pumpkin and sunflower seeds, toasted to bring out their flavour, for a tempting and nutritious meal.

Serves 4

Parmesan pizza dough

170 g (6 oz) strong white (bread) flour
½ tsp easy-blend dried yeast
30 g (1 oz) Parmesan cheese, freshly grated
120 ml (4 fl oz) tepid water
2 tbsp extra virgin olive oil

Ricotta filling

170 g (6 oz) ricotta cheese
2 tsp chopped fresh oregano
1 tbsp chopped parsley
250 g (8½ oz) cherry tomatoes, halved
50 g (1¾ oz) stoned black olives
2 tbsp balsamic vinegar
1 small sprig of fresh rosemary
1 garlic clove, crushed
salt and pepper

Leafy salad with mixed seeds

50 g (1¾ oz) pumpkin seeds
50 g (1¾ oz) sunflower seeds
2 tsp poppy seeds
1 tsp soy sauce
2 tsp sunflower oil
1 tsp walnut oil
1 tsp cider vinegar
150 g (5½ oz) mixed salad leaves, such as baby spinach, rocket and Oak Leaf lettuce

Preparation time: 35–40 minutes, plus 1 hour rising
Cooking time: 15–20 minutes

1 To make the dough, sift the flour and ½ tsp salt into a bowl, and stir in the yeast and Parmesan cheese. Make a well in the centre. Add the water and 1 tbsp of the oil, and mix to form a dough. Add a bit more water if needed.

2 Turn out onto a lightly floured surface and knead for 10 minutes or until smooth and elastic. Return the dough to the bowl, cover with cling film and leave in a warm place to rise for about 1 hour or until doubled in size.

3 Preheat the oven to 220°C (425°F, gas mark 7) and place a baking sheet inside to heat. Knock back the dough, then turn it out onto the floured surface and knead briefly. Roll out to a 30 cm (12 in) round about 5 mm (¼ in) thick. Use to line a lightly oiled, loose-bottomed, shallow 25 cm (10 in) tart tin, leaving the edges ragged and slightly hanging over the edge of the tin.

4 Mix the ricotta with the oregano and parsley, and season with salt and pepper to taste. Spread evenly in the dough case. Arrange the tomatoes, cut side up, and the olives on top.

5 Gently heat the balsamic vinegar with the remaining 1 tbsp olive oil, the rosemary and garlic in a small pan. Bubble for 1–2 minutes or until it has reduced a little, then drizzle over the tomatoes and olives.

6 Place the tart tin on the preheated baking sheet. Bake for 15–20 minutes or until the case is crisp and golden brown and the tomatoes are slightly caramelised.

7 Meanwhile, make the salad. In a small non-stick frying pan, toast the pumpkin, sunflower and poppy seeds over a moderate heat for 2–3 minutes, turning frequently. Sprinkle over the soy sauce and toss together. The seeds will stick together initially, but will separate as the mixture dries. Remove from the heat.

8 Whisk together the sunflower and walnut oils, vinegar and seasoning to taste in a salad bowl. Add the salad leaves, sprinkle with the toasted seeds and toss together.

9 Remove the tart from the tin and cut it into 4 wedges. Serve hot, with the salad.

Each serving (with salad) provides (V)

kcal 490, **protein** 18 g, **fat** 30 g (of which saturated fat 7.5 g), **carbohydrate** 41 g (of which sugars 4 g), **fibre** 4 g

✓✓✓	A, E, calcium, copper
✓✓	B_1, C, niacin, iron, zinc
✓	B_2, folate, potassium, selenium

Some more ideas

- Use baby plum tomatoes instead of cherry tomatoes.
- Make a prawn and mushroom pizza tart. While the dough is rising, gently cook 300 g (10½ oz) sliced mixed mushrooms in 1 tbsp extra virgin olive oil until just tender. Using a draining spoon, transfer the mushrooms to a bowl and mix with 150 g (5½ oz) peeled raw prawns, 4 skinned, chopped and seeded tomatoes, 1 can of anchovies, about 50 g, drained and chopped, 1 tbsp drained capers, and salt and pepper to taste. Spoon into the pizza dough case and bake as in the main recipe. Serve with a salad of baby plum tomatoes, cucumber and spring onions.

Plus point

- Tomatoes are an excellent source of vitamin C. This important nutrient is found mainly in the jellylike substance surrounding the tomato seeds.

Cheesy rice with asparagus

This is an easy and attractive vegetarian dish. The rice is cooked in stock, then mixed with peas, asparagus and cheese, and baked in individual dishes. Choose a tangy Cheddar cheese for maximum flavour – a little will go a long way. A tomato and herb salad is a perfect accompaniment for these savoury rice puddings.

Serves 4

1 tbsp melted butter
2 tbsp dried breadcrumbs
300 g (10½ oz) long-grain or basmati rice
600 ml (1 pint) vegetable stock
150 g (5½ oz) frozen peas
150 g (5½ oz) asparagus, cut into 5 cm (2 in) pieces
3 eggs
100 g (3½ oz) mature Cheddar cheese, grated
¼ tsp crushed dried chillies
salt and pepper

Preparation time: 25 minutes
Cooking time: 20 minutes

Each serving provides

kcal 508, **protein** 22 g, **fat** 16 g (of which saturated fat 8 g), **carbohydrate** 70 g (of which sugars 2 g), **fibre** 3 g

✓✓✓	B_{12}
✓✓	A, folate, calcium, zinc
✓	B_1, B_2, C, E, niacin, copper, iron, selenium

1 First prepare 4 individual baking dishes that are 360 ml (12 fl oz) capacity. Lightly grease with the melted butter, then dust with the breadcrumbs to coat the bottom and sides. Preheat the oven to 190°C (375°F, gas mark 5).

2 Place the rice in a medium-sized saucepan, pour over the stock and bring to the boil. Reduce the heat, cover tightly and simmer gently for 5 minutes, without stirring.

3 Uncover the pan and stir in the peas and asparagus. Bring back to the boil, then reduce the heat and simmer gently, covered, for a further 5 minutes.

4 Remove the pan from the heat. Stir, then cover again and leave the rice and vegetables to stand undisturbed for 5–7 minutes.

5 Combine the eggs and cheese in a mixing bowl. Add the chilli flakes, and salt and pepper to taste. Mix with a fork until well blended. Add the rice mixture and stir gently until thoroughly combined.

6 Divide the rice mixture evenly among the 4 prepared dishes. Set them on a baking sheet and bake for 20 minutes or until set and the tops are golden and crisp. Serve hot.

Some more ideas

- Instead of peas, use frozen sweetcorn, frozen broad beans or frozen mixed vegetables.
- To make a pepper and tomato rice bake, cook the rice in 600 ml (1 pint) tomato juice with a dash of Tabasco sauce to taste, rather than stock, omitting the peas and asparagus. While the rice is cooking, gently soften 1 red, 1 yellow and 1 green pepper, all seeded and thinly sliced, with 1 crushed garlic clove in 1 tbsp extra virgin olive oil. Divide the peppers among 4 individual baking dishes, or spread over the bottom of a 1.5 litre (2¾ pint) baking dish, greased and dusted with breadcrumbs. Stir the eggs into the cooked rice with 2 tbsp snipped fresh chives and seasoning to taste (omit the Cheddar cheese). Spoon on top of the peppers, then scatter over 2 tbsp freshly grated Parmesan cheese. Bake as in the main recipe.

Plus points

- Rice is the most important cereal grain in the world. It is a source of protein and most B vitamins as well as starchy carbohydrate.
- Asparagus is a rich source of many of the B vitamins, especially folate. Folate not only helps to prevent birth defects such as spina bifida, if sufficient is consumed in the early stages of pregnancy, it may also help to protect against heart disease.

Ham and corn polenta tart

Soft buttery polenta makes a lovely golden tart case, prettily flecked with green herbs. The filling is an appetising combination of diced ham, broccoli florets, baby corn and spring onions in a mustardy egg custard. Serve warm with a salad such as lightly blanched French beans tossed with sliced courgettes.

Serves 4

Herbed polenta

150 g (5½ oz) instant polenta
600 ml (1 pint) chicken stock
25 g (scant 1 oz) butter, softened
2 tbsp chopped fresh chives
2 tbsp chopped parsley
salt and pepper

Ham and corn filling

250 g (8½ oz) broccoli, cut into small florets
85 g (3 oz) baby corn, halved lengthways
200 g (7 oz) lean cooked ham, diced
3 spring onions, thinly sliced
3 eggs, beaten
240 ml (8 fl oz) semi-skimmed milk
1 tsp Dijon mustard
2 tbsp snipped fresh chives to garnish

Preparation time: 25 minutes, plus 10 minutes cooling
Cooking time: 35–40 minutes

Each serving provides

kcal 369, **protein** 25 g, **fat** 14 g (of which saturated fat 6 g), **carbohydrate** 35.5 g (of which sugars 5 g), **fibre** 5 g

✓✓✓	C
✓✓	A, B_{12}, zinc
✓	B_1, B_2, B_6, E, folate, niacin, calcium, iron, potassium, selenium

1 Preheat the oven to 190°C (375°F, gas mark 5). Heat the stock in a large saucepan until boiling, then pour in the polenta in a steady stream, stirring constantly with a wooden spoon to prevent lumps from forming. Cook over a moderate heat, stirring, for about 5 minutes or until thick and smooth, and pulling away from the sides of the pan.

2 Remove from the heat and beat in the butter, chives, parsley, and salt and pepper to taste. Set aside to cool for about 10 minutes.

3 Spoon the polenta into a lightly oiled, straight-sided 25 cm (10 in) loose-bottomed flan tin that is about 4 cm (1½ in) deep. Spread out the polenta with the back of a metal spoon to cover the bottom and sides smoothly and evenly. Set the tin on a baking sheet.

4 To make the filling, cook the broccoli and corn in a saucepan of boiling water for 3 minutes. Drain well and spoon into the polenta case. Scatter over the diced ham and spring onions.

5 Whisk together the eggs, milk, mustard and seasoning to taste. Pour over the ham and vegetables. Bake for 35–40 minutes or until golden brown and just set.

6 To serve, carefully remove the tart from the tin and sprinkle the top with the chives. Serve warm.

Plus points

- Polenta is low in fat and a rich source of starchy carbohydrate. Including it in the diet can help to meet the healthy eating recommendations to increase carbohydrate intake and decrease fat intake.
- Ham is a particularly good source of vitamin B_1, essential for the release of energy from carbohydrate foods such as polenta.
- Broccoli is packed with vitamins, including many of the antioxidants as well as vitamin B_6, folate and niacin. It is also a good source of phytochemicals, particularly indoles which research suggests may be helpful in protecting against breast cancer.

Some more ideas

- Instead of baby corn, use drained canned sweetcorn or frozen sweetcorn.
- For a vegetarian chickpea and corn polenta tart, cook the polenta in vegetable stock, and replace the ham with 1 can of chickpeas, about 410 g, drained and rinsed.
- Make a bresaola and artichoke polenta pie. Flavour the polenta with 4 tbsp chopped fresh basil in place of the parsley and chives. Cool until firm enough to handle, then press two-thirds over the bottom and sides of a lightly greased 23 cm (9 in) metal pie dish. Arrange 100 g (3½ oz) chopped bresaola (air-dried beef), 2 sliced tomatoes and 1 can of artichoke hearts, about 400 g, drained and halved, in the polenta case. Beat 2 eggs with 120 ml (4 fl oz) semi-skimmed milk and seasoning to taste. Pour into the polenta case. Press out the remaining polenta on a lightly floured surface into a round about 5 mm (¼ in) thick, and cut out twelve 4 cm (1½ in) rounds. Arrange over the filling, slightly overlapping. Brush lightly with 1 tsp extra virgin olive oil and sprinkle with 30 g (1 oz) freshly grated Parmesan cheese. Bake in a preheated 180°C (350°F, gas mark 4) oven for 40 minutes or until golden brown.

Savoury Dishes for Entertaining

Special main-dish pies, tarts and puddings

Here are some impressive dishes to disprove the notion that pies and puddings are not dinner party fare. For example, a spinach and goat's cheese pie with a crisp, scrunched-up filo lid looks really grand, as does a filo 'crown' filled with couscous and prawns. An asparagus tart, with an unusual, light-textured yeasted shortcrust case, is very special too. Guinea fowl cooked with mushrooms in Madeira wine is an unexpectedly luxurious filling for a 'pudding in a basin'. This one has a lovely potato pastry crust too, and is baked rather than steamed.

Scrunch-top filo pie

Spinach and tangy goat's cheese make perfect partners in this impressive-looking Greek-style filo pastry pie. Colourful diced tomatoes and toasted pine nuts in the filling add to the appeal. Serve with boiled new potatoes and a dish of mixed vegetables, such as thinly sliced carrots and courgettes tossed with fresh tarragon leaves.

Serves 4

2 sheets filo pastry, 30 x 50 cm (12 x 20 in) each, about 60 g (2¼ oz) in total

1 tbsp sunflower oil

Spinach and goat's cheese filling

30 g (1 oz) pine nuts

675 g (1½ lb) baby spinach leaves, trimmed of any large stalks

200 g (7 oz) soft goat's cheese

2 tsp plain flour

2 eggs, lightly beaten

¼ tsp freshly grated nutmeg

4 tomatoes, about 300 g (10½ oz) in total, diced

salt and pepper

Preparation time: 25 minutes

Cooking time: 25–30 minutes

Each serving provides

kcal 326, **protein** 18 g, **fat** 21 g (of which saturated fat 7 g), **carbohydrate** 17 g (of which sugars 6 g), **fibre** 4.5 g

✓✓✓	A, B_{12}, C, E, folate, calcium
✓✓	B_2, niacin, iron, potassium, zinc
✓	B_1, B_6, copper

1 Preheat the oven to 180°C (350°F, gas mark 4). To make the filling, toast the pine nuts in a large saucepan for 2–3 minutes, stirring frequently, until golden brown. Remove and set aside.

2 Add half the spinach to the saucepan, with just the water used for washing still clinging to the leaves. Cover and cook for 3–4 minutes or until wilted and tender. Tip into a colander to drain while you cook the remaining spinach. Press out excess water, then roughly chop the spinach.

3 Put the cheese in a bowl and sprinkle over the flour, then gradually beat in the eggs. Stir in the spinach, pine nuts and nutmeg, and season with salt and pepper to taste.

4 Spoon half of the spinach mixture into a 1.4 litre (2½ pint) ovenproof dish that is about 5 cm (2 in) deep. Top with the tomatoes, then cover with the remaining spinach mixture.

5 Cut each sheet of filo pastry into eight 12.5 cm (5 in) squares, discarding the excess pastry. Brush the squares with the oil, then crumple them up loosely and place oil side up over the filling. Bake for 25–30 minutes or until the filling is lightly set and the pastry topping is golden brown and crisp. Serve hot.

Some more ideas

• For a lower-fat version, use quark or ricotta cheese instead of goat's cheese.

• To make a squash and cashew nut filo pie, toast 30 g (1 oz) cashew nuts, then coarsely chop. Steam 1 butternut squash, about 600 g (1 lb 5 oz), cut into 1 cm (½ in) cubes, for 6–7 minutes or until just tender. Mix 200 g (7 oz) curd cheese with 2 beaten eggs, then add the squash, cashew nuts, 1 coarsely grated carrot and 25 g (scant 1 oz) pumpkin seeds. Season with salt and pepper to taste and mix well. Spoon into a lightly greased ovenproof dish, top with the scrunched-up filo and bake as in the main recipe.

Plus points

• Spinach is a great source of many of the antioxidants that help to protect against cancer, including vitamins C and E and beta-carotene. The beta-carotene content of spinach is 6 times greater than that of broccoli.

• Pine nuts, also called pine kernels, are a good source of vitamin E and potassium. Though relatively new to many British cooks, husks recovered from Roman camp rubbish tips in the UK suggest that the Romans included pine nuts in their diet.

Mediterranean chickpea pie

Enjoy the taste of the Mediterranean with this vegetarian pie. It's packed with vegetables and chickpeas cooked in red wine with tomatoes and Italian herbs, and is topped with a Parmesan, sun-dried tomato and fresh basil mash. Serve with a seasonal green vegetable, such as Savoy cabbage, for extra vitamins and minerals.

Serves 6

2 tbsp extra virgin olive oil
2 onions, chopped
2 celery sticks, chopped
1 red pepper, seeded and diced
2 garlic cloves, crushed
2 courgettes, sliced
2 cans chickpeas, about 410 g each, drained and rinsed
2 cans chopped tomatoes, about 400 g each
2 tbsp sun-dried tomato paste
150 ml (5 fl oz) red wine
2 tsp dried Italian herb seasoning
salt and pepper

Parmesan and tomato mash

1 kg (2¼ lb) potatoes, peeled and cut into chunks
4 tbsp semi-skimmed milk
1 egg
50 g (1¾ oz) Parmesan cheese, freshly grated
50 g (1¾ oz) sun-dried tomatoes in oil, drained and finely chopped
3 tbsp chopped fresh basil

Preparation time: 55 minutes
Cooking time: 25 minutes

1. Heat 1 tbsp of the oil in a large pan, add the onions, celery, red pepper and garlic, and sauté for 5 minutes. Add the courgettes, chickpeas, tomatoes with their juice, tomato paste, wine and dried herbs. Season with salt and pepper to taste and mix well.
2. Bring to the boil, then reduce the heat. Cover the pan and simmer for 20 minutes, stirring occasionally. Uncover the pan, increase the heat and cook for a further 10–15 minutes, stirring occasionally, until the liquid has thickened slightly.
3. Meanwhile, cook the potatoes in a saucepan of boiling water for 15–20 minutes or until tender. Preheat the oven to 200°C (400°F, gas mark 6).
4. Drain the potatoes well, then return to the pan. Add the milk and the remaining 1 tbsp olive oil, and mash until smooth. Beat in the egg, Parmesan cheese, sun-dried tomatoes, chopped basil, and salt and pepper to taste. Mix well.
5. Spoon the vegetable mixture into an ovenproof dish. Top with the Parmesan mash, covering the vegetables completely. Mark the top of the mash decoratively with a fork.
6. Bake the pie for 25 minutes or until the potato topping is nicely browned. Serve hot.

Plus points

- Chickpeas, like other pulses, are a good source of dietary fibre. This is present mainly as the soluble type of fibre, which is helpful in reducing high blood cholesterol levels.
- Courgettes are a good source of the B vitamins niacin and B_6. It is important to eat the skins as this is where the greatest concentration of these nutrients is to be found.
- Celery provides useful amounts of potassium as well as a compound called phthalide, which is believed to help lower high blood pressure.

Each serving provides (V)

kcal 426, **protein** 18 g, **fat** 15 g (of which saturated fat 3.5 g), **carbohydrate** 54 g (of which sugars 12 g), **fibre** 8 g

✓✓✓	A, B_6, C, E, copper
✓✓	B_1, folate, niacin, calcium, iron, potassium, zinc
✓	B_2, B_{12}

Some more ideas

- Use canned cannellini or flageolet beans instead of chickpeas.
- Replace the celery with 2 chopped carrots.
- Add chopped black olives to the mash rather than sun-dried tomatoes.
- If Italian herb seasoning is unavailable, use any combination of dried basil, oregano, parsley, thyme and sage.
- To make a spiced lamb pie, sauté 2 chopped red onions, 1 red and 1 yellow pepper, both seeded and chopped, 2 crushed garlic cloves, and 1–2 seeded and finely chopped fresh red chillies in 1 tbsp extra virgin olive oil for about 5 minutes or until softened. Stir in 2 tsp each ground cumin and coriander, then add 350 g (12½ oz) lean minced lamb and cook for 3–4 minutes or until browned. Add 1 small diced aubergine, 250 g (8½ oz) halved button mushrooms, 1 can chopped tomatoes, about 400 g, with the juice, 2 tbsp tomato purée and 200 ml (7 fl oz) lamb or beef stock or red wine (or a mixture). Cover and simmer for about 45 minutes. For the topping, cook the potatoes, then mash with 1 tbsp extra virgin olive oil and 100 ml (3½ fl oz) semi-skimmed milk. Mix in 3 tbsp chopped fresh coriander and seasoning to taste. Transfer the lamb mixture to an ovenproof dish, cover with the mash and bake as in the main recipe.

Provençale roasted vegetable and feta slice

This colourful tart combines classic flavours of Provence – peppers, courgettes, tomatoes, garlic and fresh herbs – with piquant feta cheese in a crisp, olive oil pastry case. The tart can be served hot or cold, and would be lovely for a summer picnic or alfresco lunch in the garden.

Serves 4

1 quantity Olive oil shortcrust pastry (see Some more ideas, page 22), rested for 30 minutes

Pepper and feta filling

1 large red pepper, seeded and chopped
1 large yellow pepper, seeded and chopped
2 medium courgettes, thickly sliced
1½ tbsp extra virgin olive oil
2 garlic cloves, sliced
few sprigs of fresh thyme
4 plum tomatoes, quartered
150 g (5½ oz) feta cheese, roughly chopped
2 tsp semi-skimmed milk
1 tsp poppy seeds (optional)
salt and pepper

Preparation and cooking time: 1½ hours (including making the pastry), plus 30 minutes resting

Each serving provides (V)

kcal 446, **protein** 14 g, **fat** 26 g (of which saturated fat 8 g), **carbohydrate** 42 g (of which sugars 9 g), **fibre** 4 g

✓✓✓	A, C
✓✓	B_{12}, E, calcium
✓	B_1, B_6, folate, niacin, copper, iron, potassium, zinc

1 Preheat the oven to 200°C (400°F, gas mark 6). To make filling, put the red and yellow peppers and the courgettes in a roasting tin, drizzle over the oil and turn the vegetables to coat. Sprinkle over the garlic and thyme sprigs, and roast for 15 minutes.

2 Add the tomatoes to the tin and roast for a further 10 minutes. Season the vegetables with salt and pepper to taste, and set aside.

3 Roll out the pastry dough thinly on a lightly floured surface to make a rectangle about 30 x 40 cm (12 x 16 in). Use the pastry to line an 18 x 25 cm (7 x 10 in) non-stick baking tin that is 3 cm (1¼ in) deep. Reserve the pastry trimmings.

4 Prick the bottom of the pastry case. Bake it 'blind' (see page 19) for 10 minutes, then remove the paper and beans, and bake for a further 5 minutes or until golden.

5 Fill the pastry case with the roasted vegetables, spreading them out evenly. Scatter over the feta cheese.

6 Roll out the pastry trimmings and cut into thin strips. Lay the strips in a criss-cross pattern over the filling to make a lattice. Brush the pastry strips with the milk and sprinkle them with the poppy seeds, if using.

7 Bake for 15–20 minutes or until the pastry lattice is golden brown. Serve the tart hot or cold, cut across into thin slices or squares.

Plus points

- Olive oil pastry is lower in saturated fat than shortcrust made with butter. Most of the fatty acids in olive oil are monounsaturated, which are thought to play a part in lowering high blood cholesterol levels.
- Feta cheese has a medium fat content. It is salty, so if you are watching your sodium intake soak the cheese in milk for 15–20 minutes before use (discard the milk).
- Peppers are an excellent source of vitamin C and beta-carotene. Their beta-carotene content depends on the colour of the pepper, with red peppers having the most and green peppers the least.

Some more ideas

• Instead of feta, use Caerphilly or Lancashire cheese.

• Make a Puy lentil and goat's cheese slice. For the filling, soften 1 chopped onion in 1 tbsp extra virgin olive oil with 1 crushed garlic clove and 2 tsp finely chopped, fresh root ginger. Add 200 g (7 oz) Puy lentils, 1 can of chopped tomatoes, about 400 g, with the juice, and 250 ml (8½ fl oz) vegetable stock. Bring to the boil, then reduce the heat and simmer for 10 minutes. Add 250 g (8½ oz) peeled and diced potatoes and cook for 10 minutes, then add 125 g (4½ oz) frozen peas. Bring back to the boil and cook for a further 5–10 minutes or until the potatoes and lentils are tender. Add a little more stock if needed. Stir in 50 g (1¾ oz) chopped watercress and season to taste. Spread evenly in the pastry case and scatter over 100 g (3½ oz) crumbled goat's cheese. Make a lattice top with the pastry trimmings, twisting the strips. Brush with milk and sprinkle with 1–2 tsp fennel seeds, if liked. Bake as in the main recipe.

Chillied potato and leek quiche

If you love quiche but are tired of the usual fillings, here's a new idea to whet your appetite. A vibrant green layer of peppery rocket is sandwiched between sliced potatoes and leeks in a Gruyère-flavoured custard, and the crisp pastry case is speckled with hot chilli and fragrant thyme. Serve warm with a tomato and red onion salad.

Serves 4

Sunflower oil shortcrust pastry

170 g (6 oz) plain flour
2 fresh red chillies, seeded and finely chopped
2 tsp chopped fresh thyme
1 egg
4 tbsp sunflower oil
1 tbsp tepid water

Potato and leek filling

350 g (12½ oz) waxy new potatoes, scrubbed
250 g (8½ oz) leeks, cut into 1 cm (½ in) slices
55 g (2 oz) Gruyère cheese, grated
2 tbsp snipped fresh chives
55 g (2 oz) rocket, roughly chopped
2 eggs
150 ml (5 fl oz) semi-skimmed milk
salt and pepper

Preparation time: 30 minutes, plus 30 minutes resting
Cooking time: 40–45 minutes

Each serving provides

kcal 459, **protein** 17 g, **fat** 22 g (of which saturated fat 6 g), **carbohydrate** 51 g (of which sugars 5 g), **fibre** 4 g

✓✓✓	B_{12}, E
✓✓	A, B_1, B_6, C, folate, calcium
✓	B_2, niacin, iron, copper, potassium, selenium, zinc

1 To make the pastry, sift the flour and a pinch of salt into a bowl. Stir in the chillies and thyme, then make a well in the centre. Whisk together the egg, oil and water, add to the dry ingredients and quickly mix together with a fork to make a dough.

2 Turn out the dough onto a lightly floured surface and knead for a few seconds until smooth. Put into a bowl, cover with a damp tea-towel and leave to rest for about 30 minutes before rolling out.

3 Meanwhile, make the filling. Cook the potatoes in boiling water for 10–12 minutes or until almost tender. Steam the leeks over the potatoes for 6–7 minutes, or cook them in a separate pan of boiling water for 4–5 minutes, until tender. Drain thoroughly and leave until cool enough to handle.

4 Preheat the oven to 200°C (400°F, gas mark 6) and put a baking sheet in to heat. Roll out the pastry dough thinly and use to line a 20 cm (8 in) round, loose-bottomed, fluted flan tin about 3 cm (1¼ in) deep. Scatter half the cheese over the bottom of the case.

5 Thickly slice the warm potatoes and toss with the leeks, the remaining cheese, the chives, and salt and pepper to taste. Arrange half of the potato and leek mixture in a layer in the pastry case. Scatter over the chopped rocket, then spread the rest of the potato and leek mixture on top.

6 Lightly beat the eggs together in a jug. Heat the milk to just below boiling point, then add to the eggs, whisking gently to mix.

7 Place the tin on the hot baking sheet and carefully pour the warm egg custard into the pastry case. Bake for 10 minutes, then reduce the oven temperature to 180°C (350°F, gas mark 4). Bake for a further 30–35 minutes or until the filling is lightly set. Leave in the tin for 5 minutes before removing. Serve warm.

Plus points

- Chillies contain more vitamin C, weight for weight, than citrus fruit. But the quantity of chillies usually eaten means the overall intake of this vitamin is not huge.
- Rocket, like other dark green leafy vegetables, is a good source of folate, a vitamin involved in the production of red blood cells.
- Like many other cheeses, Gruyère is high in saturated fat, which makes it a good source of fat-soluble vitamins such as A and D.

Some more ideas

- For a higher fibre pastry, use half white flour and half wholemeal flour. You'll need an extra 2 tsp water to mix the dough together.
- To make a sweet potato and Swiss chard quiche, cut 350 g (12½ oz) sweet potatoes into cubes slightly larger than 1 cm (½ in) and cook in boiling water for 4 minutes or until almost tender. Shred 170 g (6 oz) Swiss chard (or baby leaf greens) and steam for 4 minutes, or cook in a separate pan of boiling water for about 4 minutes, until tender but still crisp. Drain thoroughly, squeezing out excess moisture. Toss the sweet potatoes with the chard or greens, 25 g (scant 1 oz) coarsely grated Emmenthal cheese, and seasoning to taste. Scatter a further 30 g (1 oz) grated Emmenthal over the bottom of the pastry case. Pack the vegetable mixture into the pastry case, levelling the surface, and pour over the egg custard. Bake as in the main recipe and serve warm.

Pesto rice pie with mozzarella

This open pie, with its richly flavoured 'risotto' crust and Mediterranean vegetable filling topped with melting cubes of soft mozzarella, looks wonderful and tastes sensational! Serve with a chunky green salad of chopped celery and chicory tossed with a little plain low-fat yogurt and chopped fresh mint.

Serves 4

Risotto crust

15 g (½ oz) butter
1 small onion, finely chopped
200 g (7 oz) risotto rice
600 ml (1 pint) hot vegetable stock
1 garlic clove, roughly chopped
25 g (scant 1 oz) fresh basil
25 g (scant 1 oz) Parmesan cheese, freshly grated
15 g (½ oz) pine nuts
1 tbsp extra virgin olive oil
finely grated zest of 1 lemon
1 small egg, beaten
salt and pepper

Mozzarella filling

1 tbsp extra virgin olive oil
1 red onion, sliced
300 g (10½ oz) courgettes, thickly sliced
250 g (8½ oz) tomatoes, cut into chunks
125 g (4½ oz) mozzarella cheese, diced
fresh basil leaves to garnish

Preparation and cooking time: 1¼ hours

Each serving provides (V)

kcal 467, **protein** 19 g, **fat** 23 g (of which saturated fat 9 g), **carbohydrate** 45 g (of which sugars 6 g), **fibre** 2 g

✓✓✓	A
✓✓	B_{12}, C, niacin, calcium, copper, zinc
✓	B_1, B_2, B_6, E, folate, iron, potassium

1 Preheat the oven to 190°C (375°F, gas mark 5). First make the risotto for the crust. Melt the butter in a large, wide pan and cook the onion gently for 4–5 minutes, stirring, until just softened but not browned. Add the rice and stir for 1 minute.

2 Add a ladleful of the hot stock and bubble over a moderate heat, stirring, until it is almost all absorbed, then add another ladleful of stock. Continue adding the stock gradually in this way, stirring frequently. When all the stock has been added and absorbed, the rice should be just tender and the risotto creamy. Remove from the heat.

3 Place the garlic, basil, Parmesan cheese, pine nuts and olive oil in a blender or food processor, and blend together until finely chopped. Stir into the rice with the lemon zest, egg, and salt and pepper to taste.

4 Spoon the risotto mixture into a straight-sided 23 cm (9 in) loose-bottomed flan tin about 3 cm (1¼ in) deep. Spread evenly over the bottom and sides. Set the tin on a baking sheet and bake for 20 minutes or until the crust is lightly browned and just firm.

5 Meanwhile, for the filling, heat the oil in a large pan and cook the onion and courgettes for 3 minutes, stirring, until lightly coloured. Stir in the tomatoes, cover and cook over a moderate heat, shaking the pan occasionally, for 8–10 minutes or until the courgettes are just tender.

6 Spoon the vegetables into the risotto case and level the surface. Scatter the mozzarella over the top. Bake for 8–10 minutes or until the cheese is melted and bubbling. Serve hot, garnished with basil leaves.

Plus points

- Apart from the nutritional benefits of rice, it has been used in natural medicine to treat a variety of digestive problems including indigestion, mild diarrhoea and constipation.
- Pesto, a classic Italian sauce, has a high fat content because of the inclusion of olive oil, pine nuts and Parmesan cheese. However, the majority of fat is present as the more healthy monounsaturated fat rather than saturated fat.
- Mozzarella cheese is lower in fat than many other cheeses and as a result is also lower in calories.

Some more ideas

• To save time, replace the basil, Parmesan cheese, pine nut and olive oil mixture with about 4 tbsp pesto sauce from a jar.

• For an aubergine and halloumi rice pie, make the risotto as in the main recipe up to the end of step 2, adding a pinch of saffron threads to the stock. Instead of the pesto mixture, flavour with 25 g (scant 1 oz) toasted chopped almonds, 2 tbsp chopped fresh mint and the finely grated zest of 1 orange. Stir in the beaten egg and seasoning to taste, then finish the risotto case as in the main recipe. For the filling, fry 3 crushed garlic cloves in 2 tbsp extra virgin olive oil for 30 seconds. Add 375 g (13 oz) diced aubergine and cook on a high heat, stirring, for 10 minutes or until softened and lightly browned. Add 1 can of chopped tomatoes, about 400 g, with the juice, and simmer for 5 minutes or until most of the juice has evaporated. Spoon into the risotto case, top with 125 g (4½ oz) diced halloumi cheese and bake for 8–10 minutes or until golden. Serve hot, garnished with sprigs of fresh mint.

Guinea fowl pudding

Guinea fowl cooked with shallots, 'meaty' chestnut mushrooms, peas and spinach in Madeira wine makes a great pie filling. In this modern version of a traditional favourite, the filling is baked in a pudding basin topped with a lovely, soft-textured potato pastry crust. Serve with Brussels sprouts and baby carrots.

Serves 4

1 quantity Herbed potato pastry (see Some more ideas, page 24) with 1 tbsp chopped fresh tarragon added, chilled for 30 minutes

Guinea fowl filling

2 tbsp extra virgin olive oil

250 g (8½ oz) small shallots, peeled and left whole

400 g (14 oz) skinless boneless guinea fowl breasts (fillets), cubed

250 g (8½ oz) chestnut mushrooms, halved

2 garlic cloves, crushed

90 ml (3 fl oz) Madeira

150 ml (5 fl oz) well-flavoured chicken stock

2 tbsp cornflour

85 g (3 oz) frozen petit pois

100 g (3½ oz) baby spinach leaves

1 tbsp chopped fresh tarragon

salt and pepper

Preparation time: 55 minutes (including making the pastry), plus 30 minutes chilling

Cooking time: 40 minutes

Each serving provides

kcal 536, **protein** 30 g, **fat** 23 g (of which saturated fat 10 g), **carbohydrate** 50 g (of which sugars 6 g), **fibre** 5 g

✓✓✓	A, B_6, niacin, copper
✓✓	B_1, C, folate, potassium, selenium, zinc
✓	B_2, E, calcium, iron

1 Place the potato pastry dough on a large piece of cling film on the work surface. Press out the dough with your hands to make a round that is slightly larger than the top of a 1.4 litre (2½ pint) pudding basin. Lay another sheet of cling film on top and roll up the dough round. Chill while making the filling.

2 Heat the oil in a large saucepan and add the shallots. Cover and cook gently for 8–10 minutes, shaking the pan occasionally, until the shallots are lightly browned all over.

3 Add the guinea fowl to the pan, increase the heat to moderate and cook, uncovered, for 3–4 minutes or until the cubes are no longer pink on the outside, stirring so they cook evenly.

4 Add the mushrooms and garlic. Pour in the Madeira and stock, and bring to the boil. Reduce the heat, cover and cook gently for 10 minutes. Preheat the oven to 190°C (375°F, gas mark 5).

5 Blend the cornflour with 2 tbsp cold water to make a paste. Add to the pan and cook gently, stirring, until the liquid has thickened. Add the petit pois, spinach and tarragon, and season with salt and pepper to taste. Stir for a few more seconds or until the spinach has wilted. Spoon the mixture into the pudding basin.

6 Unwrap the potato pastry round and place it over the top of the pudding basin. Press the edges onto the rim of the basin, pinching them well to seal. Make a hole in the middle so that steam can escape.

7 Set the basin on a baking sheet and bake for 40 minutes or until the pastry is golden brown and the filling is bubbling. Serve immediately.

Plus points

- Originally a game bird, guinea fowl is now classified as poultry. Like chicken it is another low-fat source of protein, especially if the skin is removed, as in this recipe, and it provides B vitamins and iron.
- When potatoes were first introduced into Europe they were believed to have 'weakening' properties. More recently they have been considered fattening. In fact potatoes are very nutritious and low in fat, which makes them a useful food to include in a healthy diet.
- Shallots, a variety of onion, tend to have a much milder and subtler flavour than the onion itself. Like the onion, they contain some vitamin C and B vitamins.

Some more ideas

• Instead of guinea fowl, you can use chicken or turkey breast fillets, as well as skinless boneless pheasant or duck breasts.

• The pastry dough and filling can be prepared ahead of time, then the pie assembled and baked just before serving.

• This is a good way to use up leftover cooked poultry. Skip step 3, and add the diced skinless, boneless poultry with the spinach. Heat through, then spoon into the pudding basin, cover with the pastry lid and bake as in the main recipe.

• For a Chinese chicken and corn pudding, stir-fry 400 g (14 oz) diced skinless, boneless chicken breasts (fillets) in 2 tbsp groundnut oil with 2 crushed garlic cloves for 3–4 minutes. Add 1 seeded and chopped fresh red chilli, 1 tbsp finely chopped, fresh root ginger, 250 g (8½ oz) halved chestnut mushrooms and 150 g (5½ oz) baby corn, sliced at an angle. Stir-fry for 1–2 minutes, then stir in 90 ml (3 fl oz) each dry sherry and water, 2 tbsp light soy sauce, 1 tbsp clear honey and ½ tsp 5-spice powder. Simmer for 10 minutes, covered, then thicken with cornflour as in the main recipe. Add 100 g (3½ oz) shredded spring greens and 4 chopped spring onions. Pile into the pudding basin and top with the potato pastry crust (flavoured with 1 tbsp chopped fresh coriander instead of tarragon). Bake as in the main recipe.

Prawn and couscous filo crown

Here is an impressive filo pastry dish for entertaining. The filling is made with couscous, coloured golden with saffron, prawns, tomatoes, peas, spring onions and coriander. Rocket leaves add a contrasting, fresh green layer through the centre. Serve hot or cold for a special meal for 6, or as the centrepiece of a buffet for 8.

Serves 6

7 sheets filo pastry, 30 x 50 cm (12 x 20 in) each, about 210 g (7¼ oz) in total
2 tbsp extra virgin olive oil
1 tbsp sesame seeds

Couscous filling

300 g (10½ oz) couscous
large pinch of saffron threads
1 tsp harissa or chilli paste
500 ml (17 fl oz) boiling vegetable stock
100 g (3½ oz) frozen peas
250 g (8½ oz) cooked, peeled tiger prawns
200 g (7 oz) tomatoes, skinned, seeded and chopped
3 spring onions, finely chopped
20 g (¾ oz) fresh coriander, chopped
grated zest and juice of 1 lemon
50 g (1¾ oz) rocket leaves
salt and pepper

Preparation time: 40–45 minutes
Cooking time: 20 minutes

Each serving provides

kcal 318, **protein** 18 g, **fat** 7 g (of which saturated fat 1 g), **carbohydrate** 49 g (of which sugars 2 g), **fibre** 2 g

✓✓✓ B_{12}

✓ B_1, C, niacin, calcium, copper, iron, selenium, zinc

1 First make the filling. Put the couscous in a bowl. Add the saffron and harissa to the boiling stock and pour over the couscous. Stir and leave to soak for 10 minutes. All the stock should be absorbed.

2 Meanwhile, cook the peas in a pan of boiling water for 4–5 minutes, or according to the packet instructions. Drain. Preheat the oven to 190°C (375°F, gas mark 5).

3 Rub the couscous between your fingers to separate the grains. Add the peas, prawns, tomatoes, spring onions, coriander, and lemon zest and juice. Mix well and season to taste.

4 Lay a sheet of filo pastry out on the work surface with the short sides to the left and right. (Keep the rest of the filo covered to prevent it from drying out.) Brush very lightly with olive oil. Lay a second sheet of filo above the first so that the long edges overlap by about 10 cm (4 in). Brush this sheet very lightly with olive oil.

5 Lay a third sheet of filo to the right of the first 2 sheets, placing it so a long side overlaps the edges by about 12.5 cm (5 in), to make a rectangle about 67.5 x 50 cm (27 x 20 in). Brush lightly with oil. Repeat with 3 more filo sheets, laying them on top of the first so the rectangle is double thickness.

6 Arrange the rocket leaves in a line near a long side of the pastry rectangle. Pile the couscous mixture evenly on top. Brush the pastry edges with oil, then carefully roll up to make a long sausage shape. Carefully lift onto a non-stick baking sheet and curve round so that the ends meet, to make a circle. Seal the ends together. Brush the pastry ring very lightly all over with oil.

7 Cut the remaining sheet of filo into strips, scrunch them up and arrange on the top of the ring. Brush with the remaining oil and sprinkle with the sesame seeds. Bake for 20 minutes or until golden brown.

Plus points

- Couscous is a staple of many North African countries. Made from semolina, it provides an interesting starchy carbohydrate alternative to rice, pasta or potatoes.
- Filo pastry is lower in fat than many other pastries, especially puff and flaky, and always looks impressive for a special occasion.
- Both prawns and sesame seeds provide good amounts of calcium, essential for keeping bones healthy and strong.

Another idea

• Try a bulghur wheat and smoked trout strudel. Soak 300 g (10½ oz) bulghur wheat in 600 ml (1 pint) boiling vegetable stock, mixed with the harissa, for 30 minutes. Drain off any excess liquid, then stir in the tomatoes and lemon zest and juice (omit the peas, prawns and spring onions). Add 20 g (¾ oz) each chopped parsley and snipped fresh chives, and fold in 200 g (7 oz) flaked smoked trout fillet. Instead of rocket, arrange 85 g (3 oz) roughly chopped watercress on the filo rectangle. Spoon the bulghur wheat filling on top. Fold in the short sides, then roll up to make a sausage shape. Lay diagonally on a baking sheet, without curving into a circle, and top with the scrunched filo. Brush with oil, sprinkle with sesame seeds and bake as in the main recipe.

Deluxe asparagus tart

The filling for this very special tart combines asparagus spears with strips of Parma ham, peas and grated pecorino cheese in a garlic-flavoured egg custard. The pastry case is made from a light yeasted shortcrust that is surprisingly low in fat. Small minted new potatoes would make a perfect accompaniment.

Serves 4

Yeasted pastry
140 g (5 oz) plain flour
45 g (1½ oz) cool butter, diced
1 tsp easy-blend dried yeast
1 egg
2 tbsp tepid water

Garlicky asparagus filling
4 garlic cloves, unpeeled
250 g (8½ oz) slender asparagus spears, cut across in half
30 g (1 oz) pecorino cheese, finely grated
50 g (1¾ oz) Parma ham, trimmed of fat and cut into thin strips
50 g (1¾ oz) frozen peas, thawed
2 eggs
1 egg yolk
250 ml (8½ fl oz) semi-skimmed milk
salt and pepper

Preparation time: 30 minutes, plus 45 minutes resting
Cooking time: 30–35 minutes

Each serving provides

kcal 400, **protein** 21 g, **fat** 21 g (of which saturated fat 11 g), **carbohydrate** 33 g (of which sugars 5 g), **fibre** 3 g

✓✓✓	B_{12}
✓✓	A, folate, calcium, zinc
✓	B_1, B_2, B_6, C, E, niacin, copper, iron, potassium, selenium

1 To make the pastry, sift the flour and a pinch of salt into a bowl, and rub in the butter until the mixture resembles fine breadcrumbs. Stir in the yeast. Lightly beat the egg with the water, and sprinkle over the rubbed-in mixture. Gather together to make a dough.

2 Turn out the pastry dough onto a lightly floured surface and knead briefly until smooth. Put it back into the bowl, cover with cling film and set aside to rest at room temperature for about 45 minutes.

3 Meanwhile, prepare the filling. Put the garlic cloves in the bottom of a steamer with about 5 cm (2 in) of hot water. Place the stalk halves of the asparagus spears in the top of the steamer and steam for 1 minute on a moderate heat. Add the asparagus tips and steam for a further 1–1½ minutes or until just beginning to soften. (Thicker spears may need a few minutes longer.) Remove the asparagus and garlic, and set aside.

4 Preheat the oven to 200°C (400°F, gas mark 6) and put a baking sheet in to heat. Roll out the pastry dough thinly (there's no need to knead it again) on a lightly floured surface and use to line a 25 cm (10 in) loose-bottomed, shallow flan tin.

5 Scatter the pecorino cheese over the bottom of the pastry case, then arrange the asparagus and Parma ham on top, filling the gaps with peas.

6 Squeeze the softened garlic from the skins and mash to a paste. Whisk in the eggs, egg yolk, and salt and pepper to taste. Heat the milk to boiling point, then pour over the egg mixture, whisking to mix.

7 Place the flan tin on the hot baking sheet. Pour the egg custard into the tart. Bake for 5 minutes, then reduce the oven temperature to 180°C (350°F, gas mark 4). Bake for a further 25–30 minutes or until the filling is lightly set and the pastry is golden brown.

8 Leave the tart to stand for about 5 minutes before removing it from the tin. Serve hot or warm, cut into wedges.

Plus points

- Asparagus contains the phytochemical asparagine, which has diuretic properties. Indeed, the ancient Greeks used asparagus in the treatment of kidney problems.
- Parma ham makes a good lean alternative to bacon, especially if any visible fat is trimmed away, as in this recipe.

Some more ideas

• Use freshly grated Parmesan cheese in place of the pecorino.

• For a courgette and blue cheese tart, steam 400 g (14 oz) courgettes, cut into 1 cm (½ in) slices, for 3 minutes, adding the garlic cloves to the water as in the main recipe. Remove the courgettes and pat dry with kitchen paper. Arrange them in the pastry case and scatter over 50 g (1¾ oz) crumbled blue cheese such as Stilton or Roquefort and 30 g (1 oz) roughly chopped walnuts. Make the garlic custard using 3 whole eggs, 200 ml (7 fl oz) semi-skimmed milk, and salt and pepper to taste. Bake as in the main recipe.

Sweet Pies and Tarts

Tempting pastries for all occasions

Pastry and crushed biscuits provide the cases and bases for this delectable assortment of sweet treats. Shortcrust enriched with almonds makes little tartlets filled with luscious berries under a featherlight meringue, while spiced shortcrust wrapped freeform round apples and blueberries is the easiest fruit pie you could wish for. Use filo for a simple strudel filled with fresh cherries, or to make a very pretty lattice topping on a redcurrant tart. Crushed amaretti are the base for a baked cheesecake adorned with fruit – an impressive finale for any meal.

Kiwi-berry cheesecake tart

Impress your family and friends with this tempting baked cheesecake tart, piled high with vitamin C-rich strawberries and kiwi fruit. Unlike many cheesecakes that are high in fat and calories, this recipe uses a lower fat soft cheese for the filling and a crushed amaretti biscuit base made without butter.

Serves 10

115 g (4 oz) amaretti biscuits, crushed
450 g (1 lb) curd cheese
3 eggs, separated
115 g (4 oz) caster sugar
finely grated zest of 1 small orange
150 ml (5 fl oz) whipping cream
30 g (1 oz) plain flour

Fruit topping

300 g (10½ oz) strawberries, halved or sliced
2 kiwi fruit, peeled and sliced
1 tbsp icing sugar, sifted

Preparation time: 30 minutes
Cooking time: 1¼ hours

Each serving provides

kcal 287, **protein** 8 g, **fat** 15 g (of which saturated fat 8 g), **carbohydrate** 31 g (of which sugars 19 g), **fibre** 1 g

✓✓ A, C

✓ B_{12}

1 Preheat the oven to 160°C (325°F, gas mark 3). Grease a 20 cm (8 in) springform tin and line the bottom with greaseproof paper. Sprinkle the amaretti biscuit crumbs evenly over the paper lining on the bottom and set aside.

2 Put the curd cheese, egg yolks, caster sugar, orange zest and cream in a blender or food processor. Blend until smooth and well mixed, then pour the mixture into a bowl. (Alternatively, beat the ingredients together with an electric mixer.) Sift the flour over the surface and fold it in.

3 In a separate clean, grease-free bowl, whisk the egg whites until stiff. Gently fold them into the cheese mixture. Pour into the tin, without disturbing the biscuit crumbs, and level the surface.

4 Bake for 1¼ hours or until slightly risen, lightly set and golden brown. Turn off the oven and leave the tart inside for 15 minutes, then remove and set aside to cool completely. If you like, chill before serving.

5 Remove the cheesecake tart from the tin and place it on a serving plate. Pile the strawberries and kiwi over the top and dust with the icing sugar. Cut into slices to serve.

Some more ideas

- Use the finely grated zest of 1 small pink grapefruit or 1 lime in place of the orange zest.
- Instead of amaretti, sprinkle 140 g (5 oz) crushed digestive or oaty biscuits over the bottom of the tin.
- Top the cheesecake tart with a mixture of sliced peaches or nectarines and blueberries.
- For a raspberry cheesecake tart, sprinkle 140 g (5 oz) crushed ginger biscuits over the bottom of the cake tin. Make the cheesecake mixture as in the main recipe, but using ricotta cheese in place of curd cheese, light soft brown sugar in place of caster sugar and the finely grated zest of 1 lemon in place of the orange zest. After baking, decorate the top with 350 g (12½ oz) fresh raspberries and dust with sifted icing sugar.

Plus points

- Curd cheese contains about half the amount of fat that is found in hard cheeses such as Cheddar.
- Kiwi fruits are an excellent source of vitamin C – a single fruit supplies enough to meet the daily requirement for this vitamin.

Brandied mincemeat purses

Here are some luxurious little 'moneybag' pastries filled with a ginger-spiced mixture of dried fruit, apple and walnuts. The dried fruits are first soaked in brandy, although you can replace the alcohol with fresh orange juice if you prefer. Try these at Christmas-time as a lower-fat alternative to mince pies.

Serves 6 (makes 12 pastries)

6 sheets filo pastry, 30 x 50 cm (12 x 20 in) each, about 180 g (6¼ oz) in total
45 g (1½ oz) unsalted butter, melted
1 tbsp icing sugar, sifted

Mincemeat filling

150 g (5½ oz) mixed dried fruit, such as sultanas, raisins, currants and diced peel
4 tbsp brandy
1 cooking apple, about 250 g (8½ oz)
30 g (1 oz) preserved stem ginger, finely chopped
25 g (scant 1 oz) chopped walnuts
finely grated zest of 1 small lemon

Preparation time: about 25 minutes, plus 1 hour soaking
Cooking time: 12–15 minutes

Each serving provides

kcal 314, **protein** 4.5 g, **fat** 10 g (of which saturated fat 4 g), **carbohydrate** 49 g (of which sugars 30 g), **fibre** 1 g

✓ A, C, copper

1 To make the filling, place the dried fruit in a bowl with the brandy and stir. Cover and leave to soak for 1 hour or until the brandy has been absorbed.

2 Preheat the oven to 200°C (400°F, gas mark 6). Peel, core and coarsely grate the apple. Add to the soaked dried fruit together with the ginger, walnuts and lemon zest. Mix well together.

3 Lay the sheets of filo out, stacking them on top of each other. Cut the stack into six 15 cm (6 in) squares, trimming off the excess pastry. You will have 36 squares. Brush each square very lightly with melted butter and layer them, with the corners offset, to make 12 stacks of 3 squares each.

4 Place about 1 tbsp of the fruit mixture on each stack, then gather up the edges and pinch together at the top to enclose the filling.

5 Place the pastries on a non-stick baking sheet and brush lightly with the remaining butter. Bake for 12–15 minutes or until golden brown. Serve warm, dusted with icing sugar.

Some more ideas

- For an unusual scented flavour, replace the brandy with cold Earl Grey tea, or with a fruit tea such as apple and ginger.
- To make date and apricot parcels, place 115 g (4 oz) ready-to-eat dried apricots and 115 g (4 oz) stoned dates, both finely chopped, in a bowl with 4 tbsp orange juice. Stir, then leave to soak for 1 hour. Add the finely grated zest of ½ orange, 25 g (scant 1 oz) chopped pistachio nuts, ½ tsp ground cinnamon and ¼ tsp orange flower water. Cut 2 stacked sheets of filo pastry into 3 long strips, then cut each strip across in half to measure about 10 x 25 cm (4 x 10 in). Melt 20 g (¾ oz) butter and brush lightly over the 12 pastry strips. Place a rounded tbsp of the filling at one end of each strip. Fold one corner over the filling to make a triangular shape, then keep folding over down the length of the strip to make a triangular pastry. Brush lightly with the remaining butter, place on a baking sheet and bake for 12–15 minutes or until golden brown.

Plus points

- Dried fruit is naturally sweet with fructose, so no sugar is needed in this filling. Dried fruit is also a source of nutrients including dietary fibre, iron, calcium, phosphorus and some B vitamins.
- Herbalists use ginger for its anti-sickness properties and as an aid to digestion. It is also thought to protect against infections of the digestive and respiratory systems.

Meringue-topped berry tartlets

Make these irresistible tartlets at the height of summer when red berries and currants are in season. The luscious fruits fill tartlet cases made with a light almond pastry and are topped with crisp meringue.

Serves 6

1 quantity Sweet almond shortcrust pastry (see Some more ideas, page 22), chilled for 30 minutes

Fruit filling

200 g (7 oz) redcurrants

200 g (7 oz) blackcurrants

2 tbsp caster sugar

125 g (4½ oz) strawberries, chopped

1 tbsp redcurrant jelly

Meringue topping

2 egg whites

55 g (2 oz) caster sugar

Preparation and cooking time: about 1 hour (including making the pastry), plus at least 30 minutes chilling

Each serving provides

kcal 262, **protein** 5 g, **fat** 11 g (of which saturated fat 6 g), **carbohydrate** 38 g (of which sugars 27 g), **fibre** 3 g

✓✓✓	C
✓	A, E, calcium, copper, iron

1 Preheat the oven to 190°C (375°F, gas mark 5). To make the filling, put the red and blackcurrants in a saucepan with the caster sugar and cook very gently for 5 minutes or until the currants are softened but still holding their shape. Remove from the heat and stir in the strawberries and redcurrant jelly. Set aside.

2 Roll out the pastry dough thinly on a lightly floured work surface. Use to line 6 individual, loose-bottomed, non-stick tartlet tins 9 cm (3½ in) in diameter and 2.5 cm (1 in) deep.

3 Prick the tartlet cases and place on a baking sheet. Bake 'blind' (see page 19) for 10 minutes, then remove the paper and beans. Bake for a further 2–3 minutes or until light golden.

4 Remove the tartlet cases from the oven and set aside to cool. Reduce the oven temperature to 160°C (325°F, gas mark 3).

5 Meanwhile, make the meringue topping. Whisk the egg whites in a clean, grease-free bowl until stiff, then gradually whisk in the caster sugar to make a thick, glossy meringue.

6 Carefully remove the pastry cases from the tins and place back on the baking sheet. Fill with the fruit, using a draining spoon (discard any excess juice or use it elsewhere – see Some more ideas, right).

7 Top the tartlets with the meringue, swirling it gently to cover the fruit completely. Bake for 10–15 minutes or until the meringue is set and lightly golden. Serve warm or cold.

Plus points

- Egg whites do not contain any fat, but they are a source of protein and therefore can be a useful addition to a low-fat diet.
- Blackcurrants are an excellent source of vitamin C. On a weight for weight basis they contain 4 times as much vitamin C as oranges.
- Strawberries are not only an excellent source of vitamin C, they also contain the phytochemical ellagic acid, which is thought to help to protect against cancer.

Some more ideas

- When fresh currants and strawberries aren't available, use frozen fruits, thawing them and patting dry with kitchen paper. Or substitute other fruit such as raspberries or blueberries.
- Any juice drained from the fruit filling can be stirred into plain low-fat yogurt, added to a fruit salad or used in a milkshake or smoothie.
- Try gooseberry and apple meringue tartlets. Make the pastry with ground blanched hazelnuts instead of almonds. For the filling, gently cook 350 g (12½ oz) topped and tailed gooseberries and 1 peeled, cored and sliced cooking apple, about 300 g (10½ oz), with 30 g (1 oz) caster sugar for 10 minutes or until softened. Drain off any excess juice, then beat the fruit with a wooden spoon to make a rough purée (it doesn't need to be smooth). Taste and add a little extra sugar if needed. Divide the filling among the tartlet cases, top with meringue and bake as in the main recipe.

Cherry and almond strudel

Austria's famous melt-in-the-mouth pastry, here packed with juicy fresh cherries, looks very impressive, but is surprisingly easy to make. Ground almonds and breadcrumbs are added to the filling to absorb the fruit juices, so the layers of filo pastry bake wonderfully light and crisp.

Serves 6

3 sheets filo pastry, 30 x 50 cm (12 x 20 in) each, about 90 g (3¼ oz) in total
30 g (1 oz) butter, melted
15 g (½ oz) flaked almonds
1 tbsp icing sugar, sifted
Greek-style yogurt to serve (optional)

Cherry filling

30 g (1 oz) fresh white breadcrumbs
55 g (2 oz) ground almonds
45 g (1½ oz) soft light brown sugar
finely grated zest of 1 orange
675 g (1½ lb) fresh cherries, stoned and halved if large

Preparation time: 30–40 minutes
Cooking time: 20 minutes

Each serving provides

kcal 254, **protein** 5.5 g, **fat** 11 g (of which saturated fat 3 g), **carbohydrate** 36 g (of which sugars 24 g), **fibre** 2 g

✓✓	E
✓	C, copper

1 Preheat the oven to 200°C (400°F, gas mark 6). To make the filling, stir the breadcrumbs, almonds, brown sugar and orange zest together in a large bowl. Add the cherries and mix well.

2 Lay a sheet of filo pastry out on a clean tea-towel and brush very lightly with melted butter. Place a second sheet of filo on top and brush very lightly with butter. Place the third sheet of filo on top and brush again with butter.

3 Spoon the filling evenly over the stacked pastry, leaving a 2.5 cm (1 in) margin clear around the edges. Turn in the edges of the short sides.

4 With the help of the tea-towel, roll up from a long side to make a thick sausage shape. Transfer to a lightly greased, non-stick baking tray, curving the strudel slightly to fit, if necessary. The seam should be underneath. Brush with the remaining butter, then scatter over the flaked almonds.

5 Bake for 20 minutes or until the pastry and almonds are golden brown. Dust with the icing sugar and serve hot or warm, with a little Greek-style yogurt, if liked.

Another idea

- For a plum, rum and raisin strudel, soak 50 g (1¾ oz) raisins in 2 tbsp dark rum for 1 hour. Mix with 675 g (1½ lb) sliced ripe plums, 75 g (2½ oz) fresh white breadcrumbs, 30 g (1 oz) chopped walnuts, 45 g (1½ oz) soft light brown sugar and the finely grated zest of 1 small lemon. Spread this filling over the filo pastry, roll up and bake as in the main recipe. Dust the hot strudel with 2 tsp icing sugar sifted with ½ tsp ground cinnamon.

Plus points

- Cherries are used all over the world in many famous dishes as well as being a key ingredient in liqueurs such as Kirsch and Maraschino. Like other fruits they are rich in potassium and they also contain a small amount of iron.
- Almonds are a good source of vitamin E, a powerful antioxidant that helps to protect against heart disease.
- Butter contains useful amounts of the fat-soluble vitamins A and D. Vitamin A is needed for healthy skin and vision. Vitamin D is required for the absorption of calcium and therefore has a vital role in maintaining strong teeth and bones.

Topsy-turvy apple and sultana tart

This delectable tart is rather like the French tarte tatin, being turned out upside-down to serve. The pastry used is shortcrust made with reduced-fat soft cheese and butter, and there is a lot of juicy fruit filling.

Serves 4

Soft cheese shortcrust pastry

115 g (4 oz) plain flour
30 g (1 oz) cool unsalted butter, diced
30 g (1 oz) reduced-fat soft cheese

Apple and sultana filling

5 dessert apples, such as Cox's, about 600 g (1 lb 5 oz) in total
50 g (1¾ oz) light muscovado sugar
1 tbsp lemon juice
30 g (1 oz) sultanas
¼ tsp mixed spice
1 tsp finely grated lemon zest

Lemon and honey yogurt

250 g (8½ oz) plain low-fat yogurt
1 tbsp clear honey
1 tsp finely grated lemon zest

Preparation time: 45 minutes
Cooking time: 20 minutes

Each serving provides

kcal 345, protein 7.5 g, fat 8 g (of which saturated fat 5 g), carbohydrate 65 g (of which sugars 43 g), fibre 4 g

✓✓	calcium
✓	A, B_1, B_2, C, E, potassium

1 First make the pastry. Sift the flour into a large bowl, then rub in the butter and soft cheese until the mixture resembles breadcrumbs. Sprinkle with 1½–2 tbsp of cold water and mix in using a round-bladed knife, to form a soft dough. Gather the dough into a smooth ball, then wrap in cling film and chill for at least 30 minutes while you make the filling.

2 Preheat the oven to 200°C (400°F, gas mark 6). Peel and thickly slice the apples. Put the sugar and lemon juice in a medium-sized saucepan and heat, stirring, to dissolve the sugar. Add the apples, then cover and cook over a low heat for 8–10 minutes, stirring occasionally, until the apples are just starting to soften but not breaking up.

3 With a draining spoon transfer the apples to a 23 cm (9 in) cake tin (not with a loose bottom) or a pie dish. Stir the sultanas, mixed spice and lemon zest into the juice left in the saucepan and simmer for 2–3 minutes. Pour this mixture over the apples. Set aside to cool slightly.

4 Roll out the pastry dough thinly on a lightly floured surface to a round about 25 cm (10 in). Carefully lay the pastry round over the apple filling, tucking the edges down inside the tin. Bake for 20 minutes or until the pastry is golden.

5 Leave the tart to cool in the tin for 5–10 minutes, then carefully turn out upside-down onto a plate with a rim. Stir together the yogurt, honey and lemon zest, and serve with the tart.

Some more ideas

- Make the pastry dough and the filling a day ahead, then assemble the tart and bake just before serving.
- Instead of lemon zest, use grated orange zest in the fruit filling and yogurt.
- For a pear and walnut tart, use Conference or Comice pears instead of apples, and add 30 g (1 oz) chopped pecans or walnuts with the sultanas and lemon zest (omit the mixed spice).

Plus points

- Sultanas are small white seedless grapes that have been dried. As most of the water is removed in the process, sultanas are a much more concentrated source of sugars, vitamins and minerals than the original grapes.
- Yogurt is usually recommended for the contribution it can make to calcium intake, but it is also a useful source of vitamin B_2, which plays a part in releasing energy from food.

Apricot flapjack tart

Make the most of aromatic, golden apricots when they're in season by using them in this attractive tart. It has a sweet orange shortcrust base and is topped with a crumbled flapjack-style mixture of oats, sultanas, hazelnuts and seeds. Serve slightly warm for dessert or with morning coffee or afternoon tea.

Serves 6

1 quantity Orange sweet shortcrust pastry (see Some more ideas, page 22), chilled for 30 minutes

Apricot filling

500 g (1 lb 2 oz) fresh ripe apricots, stoned and quartered
3 tbsp orange juice
½ tsp ground mixed spice
1 tbsp clear honey

Flapjack topping

45 g (1½ oz) porridge oats
15 g (½ oz) sultanas
15 g (½ oz) hazelnuts, chopped
1 tbsp sunflower seeds
1 tsp sesame seeds
1 tbsp clear honey
1 tbsp fresh orange juice

Preparation time: 35–40 minutes (including making the pastry), plus cooling and 30 minutes chilling
Cooking time: 30 minutes

Each serving provides

kcal 278, **protein** 5 g, **fat** 13 g (of which saturated fat 6 g), **carbohydrate** 38 g (of which sugars 18 g), **fibre** 3 g

✓✓ A

✓ B_1, C, E, copper, iron, potassium

1 To make the filling, place the apricots in a heavy-based saucepan with the orange juice and mixed spice. Bring to the boil, then cover tightly and cook on a low heat for 20–25 minutes, stirring occasionally, until the mixture is thick. Allow to cool, then stir in the honey.

2 Preheat the oven to 190°C (375°F, gas mark 5). Roll out the pastry dough thinly on a lightly floured surface and use to line a 23 cm (9 in) loose-bottomed, non-stick flan tin. Prick the bottom of the pastry case.

3 Bake the tart case 'blind' (see page 19) for 10 minutes, then remove the beans and paper. Bake for a further 5 minutes. Remove from the oven and set aside. Reduce the oven temperature to 180°C (350°F, gas mark 4).

4 To make the topping, mix together the oats, sultanas, hazelnuts, sunflower seeds and sesame seeds. Stir the honey with the orange juice, then stir into the oat mixture.

5 Spread the cooled apricot filling evenly in the tart case. Spoon the oat mixture over the top and press it down lightly. Bake for 12–15 minutes or until the flapjack topping is pale golden. Serve warm.

Some more ideas

- If fresh apricots are not in season, replace them with 2 cans of apricots in natural juice, about 410 g each, drained and chopped. Use a little of the drained-off juice to moisten the flapjack topping instead of the orange juice, and sweeten with just 1 tsp honey.
- To make a plum or damson muesli tart, flavour the pastry with lemon zest and juice instead of orange. For the filling, use halved and stoned plums or damsons instead of apricots, and poach with 4 tbsp apple juice and ½ tsp ground star anise. Cool, then stir in the honey. For the topping, mix together 45 g (1½ oz) porridge oats, 1 small dessert apple, peeled and coarsely grated, and 15 g (½ oz) each dried cranberries and flaked almonds. Bake as in the main recipe.

Plus points

- Apricots are a good source of beta-carotene and some of the B vitamins, and also provide some vitamin C.
- Oats are a good source of soluble fibre, which not only helps to reduce high blood cholesterol levels but slows the absorption of glucose in the body, so helping to maintain a steady blood glucose level.

Tropical filo baskets

Here's a very pretty dessert. Filo pastry is baked in individual muffin tins to make crisp, petal-like cases, and these are filled with a creamy mango purée topped with papaya and pineapple cubes and pomegranate seeds. The filo baskets can be made ahead but are best filled no more than 1 hour before serving.

Makes 6

25 g (scant 1 oz) unsalted butter, melted
3 sheets filo pastry, 30 x 50 cm (12 x 20 in) each, about 90 g (3¼ oz) in total

Tropical fruit filling

1 large mango, peeled and stoned
2 tbsp fromage frais
1 papaya, cubed
1 small pineapple, cubed
seeds from 1 pomegranate
finely shredded zest of 1 lime

Preparation and cooking time: 40 minutes

Each serving provides

kcal 189, **protein** 4 g, **fat** 5 g (of which saturated fat 3 g), **carbohydrate** 34 g (of which sugars 25 g), **fibre** 5 g

✓✓✓	A, C
✓	B_6, copper, potassium

1 Preheat the oven to 190°C (375°F, gas mark 5). Lightly grease 6 non-stick muffin tins, 7.5 cm (3 in) across and 3 cm (1¼ in) deep, with a little of the melted butter.

2 Lay the filo sheets out on the work surface, one on top of the other. Cut the stack into 12.5 cm (5 in) squares, trimming off the excess pastry. You will have 24 squares.

3 Line each muffin tin with a filo square and brush very lightly with melted butter. Place another square on top, with the corners offset, and brush with butter. Continue layering the filo squares in this way, using 4 for each tin. Bake the filo baskets for 6 minutes or until golden. Leave to cool.

4 For the filling, purée the mango flesh with the fromage frais in a blender or food processor.

5 Shortly before serving, spoon the mango purée into the filo baskets. Top with the papaya and pineapple, and scatter over the pomegranate seeds and lime zest.

Some more ideas

- Instead of pomegranate, scatter over the pulpy seeds of 2 passion fruit.
- Top the mango purée with other fruits such as strawberries, kiwi fruit, peaches or blueberries – whatever is in season and looks pretty.
- Make an apricot and nectarine filo basket. Cut 5 sheets of filo pastry, about 150 g (5½ oz) in total, in half widthways, then trim to make ten 25 cm (10 in) squares. Use the squares to line a lightly buttered moule à manqué tin (a round cake tin with sloping sides) or an 18 cm (7 in) springform tin, arranging the squares and brushing with melted butter as in the main recipe. Bake this large basket for 8–10 minutes or until golden. For the filling, gently cook 250 g (8½ oz) ready-to-eat dried apricots in 150 ml (5 fl oz) orange juice with 2 tbsp brandy (optional) for 20 minutes or until softened. Purée until smooth. Just before serving, spoon the apricot purée into the basket and top with 4 sliced nectarines. Scatter over 15 g (½ oz) roughly chopped pistachios and dust lightly with sifted icing sugar.

Plus points

- Papaya is a useful source of vitamin A, derived from its beta-carotene content. It also provides good amounts of vitamin C plus calcium, iron and zinc.
- Pomegranate seeds are deliciously sweet-tart and crunchy. They make a contribution of vitamin C and fibre to this pudding.

Lemon banana tart

A crisp, sweet shortcrust pastry case is filled with a layer of strawberry conserve and thickly sliced bananas, then topped with a light but luscious lemon and fromage frais mixture that sets as it bakes. No sugar is needed in the filling as the bananas, fruit conserve and lemon curd provide lots of sweetness.

Serves 8

1 quantity Sweet shortcrust pastry, with the finely grated zest of 1 lemon added (see page 22), chilled for 30 minutes

Filling

4 tbsp strawberry conserve
3 firm bananas
5 tbsp lemon curd
250 g (8½ oz) fromage frais
2 eggs, lightly beaten
strawberries to decorate (optional)

Preparation time: 45–50 minutes (including making the pastry), plus 30 minutes chilling
Cooking time: 30–35 minutes

Each serving provides

kcal 266, **protein** 6 g, **fat** 11 g (of which saturated fat 6 g), **carbohydrate** 37 g (of which sugars 22 g), **fibre** 1 g

✓✓	B_{12}
✓	A, B_2, copper, zinc

1 Preheat the oven to 200°C (400°F, gas mark 6) and put a baking sheet in to heat.

2 Roll out the pastry dough thinly and use to line a 23.5 cm (9½ in) shallow, fluted, loose-bottomed flan tin. Prick the bottom of the tart case. Bake 'blind' (see page 19) for 10 minutes, then remove the paper and beans. Bake for a further 5 minutes. Remove from the oven. Reduce the temperature to 180°C (350°F, gas mark 4).

3 Spread the conserve over the bottom of the warm tart case. Slice the bananas, then arrange evenly over the top. Blend the lemon curd with a little of the fromage frais, then stir in the remainder, together with the beaten eggs. Pour over the bananas and spread out evenly.

4 Bake the tart for 30–35 minutes or until the filling is set and lightly browned. Leave in the tin on a wire rack to cool to room temperature before serving.

Some more ideas

- For a chocolate pastry case, make the pastry substituting 25 g (scant 1 oz) sifted cocoa powder for the same amount of flour, and leave out the lemon zest.
- For a ginger and honey banana tart, flavour the pastry with orange rather than lemon zest. While the tart case is baking 'blind', gently heat 300 ml (10 fl oz) semi-skimmed milk with a 1 cm (½ in) piece of fresh root ginger, roughly chopped, to boiling point. Remove from the heat and infuse for 20 minutes. After baking the tart case, reduce the oven temperature to 160°C (325°F, gas mark 3). Spread 4 tbsp peach or apricot jam over the bottom of the tart case. Arrange 3 sliced bananas over the jam. Blend 1 tsp cornflour with 1 tsp milk in a bowl, then whisk in 2 eggs, 1 egg yolk and 2 tbsp clear honey. Bring the milk back to boiling point and pour onto the egg mixture, whisking constantly. Strain into the pastry case, discarding the pieces of ginger. Bake for 35 minutes or until lightly set. Serve at room temperature.

Plus points

- Bananas have a high potassium content. This mineral is essential for the proper functioning of nerves and muscles in particular, but is also needed by all cells in the body.
- Fromage frais has a wonderfully creamy flavour, but is relatively low in fat. It provides useful amounts of protein, calcium and vitamin B_{12}.

Pear and redcurrant filo lattice

This lovely tart uses sweet and tangy redcurrants with juicy pears for a winning combination. The bright red juice of the currants tints the pears and looks most attractive under the pastry lattice. Although redcurrants only have a short season, they freeze well, so put some in the freezer to make a tart later in the year.

Serves 6

3 sheets filo pastry, 30 x 50 cm (12 x 20 in) each, about 90 g (3¼ oz) in total
20 g (¾ oz) unsalted butter, melted

Filling

2 tbsp redcurrant jelly
1 tsp lemon juice
3 ripe but firm pears, about 170 g (6 oz) each
125 g (4½ oz) redcurrants
45 g (1½ oz) ground almonds

Preparation time: 25 minutes
Cooking time: 15–20 minutes

Each serving provides

kcal 164, **protein** 4 g, **fat** 7 g (of which saturated fat 2 g), **carbohydrate** 22 g (of which sugars 13 g), **fibre** 2 g

✓ C, E, copper

1 Preheat the oven to 200°C (400°F, gas mark 6) and put a baking sheet in to heat. For the filling, place the redcurrant jelly and lemon juice in a small saucepan and heat gently until melted. Remove from the heat.

2 Peel the pears and slice thinly. Add to the jelly glaze and toss gently to coat. Stir in the redcurrants.

3 Lay out 2 sheets of filo on top of each other. (Keep the third sheet covered to prevent it from drying out.) Cut into quarters. Separate the 8 pieces and brush lightly with butter. Use to line a 23 cm (9 in) loose-bottomed, non-stick flan tin, overlapping them slightly, scrunching and tucking in the edges.

4 Sprinkle the ground almonds over the bottom of the tart case. Top with the pear and redcurrant mixture, spreading out the fruit evenly.

5 Cut the remaining sheet of filo crossways in half and brush lightly with butter. Place one half on top of the other, then cut into 10 strips about 2 cm (¾ in) wide, trimming off excess pastry. Twist the doubled strips gently and arrange them in a lattice pattern over the filling, tucking in the ends neatly.

6 Place the tin on the hot baking sheet and bake for 15–20 minutes or until the pastry is crisp and golden brown. Serve warm.

Some more ideas

- Make a pear and raspberry filo lattice by using raspberries instead of redcurrants, and seedless raspberry jam for the glaze rather than redcurrant jelly.
- For a mango and cape gooseberry filo tart, sprinkle the bottom of the tart case with 30 g (1 oz) desiccated coconut. Peel and dice 2 ripe mangoes, about 350 g (12½ oz) each, and mix with 100 g (3½ oz) halved cape gooseberries. Toss the fruit gently with 2 tbsp each of lime juice and light muscovado sugar, then spoon into the pastry case and spread out evenly. Top with the pastry lattice and bake as in the main recipe.

Plus points

- Unlike most fruits, pears contain only a little vitamin C. However in this recipe they are combined with redcurrants, which are a useful source of vitamin C. Pears do offer good amounts of potassium as well as soluble fibre.
- Redcurrants contain more beta-carotene than white currants but less than blackcurrants.

Citrus meringue pie

A modern twist on the well-loved lemon meringue pie, this recipe uses lime and orange as well as lemon in the creamy filling for an exciting citrus flavour. Instead of shortcrust pastry, the case is made with crushed biscuit crumbs held together with egg white, rather than melted butter, to reduce the fat content.

Serves 8

Biscuit crust

150 g (5½ oz) plain biscuits, such as Petit Beurre or Abernethy

1 egg white, whisked lightly to loosen

Citrus filling

grated zest and juice of 1 large lemon

grated zest and juice of 1 large lime

juice of 1 large orange

45 g (1½ oz) cornflour

2 large egg yolks

75 g (2½ oz) caster sugar

Meringue topping

3 large egg whites

85 g (3 oz) caster sugar

Preparation and cooking time: 55 minutes, plus cooling

Each serving provides

kcal 207, **protein** 4 g, **fat** 5 g (of which saturated fat 2 g), **carbohydrate** 40 g (of which sugars 26 g), **fibre** 0.5 g

✓ B_{12}

1 Preheat the oven to 180°C (350°F, gas mark 4). To make the crust, put the biscuits in a polythene bag and crush with a rolling pin. Tip into a mixing bowl, add the egg white and stir until the crumbs are all moistened.

2 Spoon the biscuit mixture into a lightly greased, non-stick 21.5 cm (8½ in) sandwich tin (loose-bottomed if you wish). Using the back of the spoon, press the crumbs evenly over the bottom and sides of the tin in a thin layer. Bake for 7–10 minutes or until firm. Leave to cool while making the filling.

3 Combine the lemon and lime zests and juice with the orange juice in a heatproof bowl. Stir in the cornflour to make a smooth paste. Bring 300 ml (10 fl oz) water to the boil in a heavy-based saucepan. Pour the water onto the juice mixture, stirring constantly, then return to the pan. Stir over a moderate heat until it comes to the boil. Reduce the heat and simmer, stirring frequently, for 1 minute or until thick and smooth.

4 Remove the pan from the heat and cool for a minute. Meanwhile, mix together the egg yolks and sugar in a small bowl. Add a little hot citrus mixture, stirring, then stir this into the remaining citrus mixture until thoroughly combined. Pour into the prepared biscuit case.

5 To make the meringue topping, whisk the egg whites until stiff. Gradually whisk in the sugar to make a thick, glossy meringue.

6 Spoon the meringue on top of the citrus filling to cover evenly, swirling it attractively. Bake in the preheated oven for about 15 minutes or until the meringue is golden brown. Leave the pie to cool before serving.

Plus points

• Eggs are one of the few sources of vitamin D. It is found concentrated in the yolk and is not destroyed on cooking. The vitamin A and vitamin B content of eggs is also concentrated in the yolk rather than the white.

• The iron in eggs is not well absorbed on its own, but the vitamin C in both the lemon and lime juice will aid the absorption of this essential mineral in the body.

Some more ideas

- Use crushed ginger nut or digestive biscuits instead of plain ones.
- For an exotic pineapple meringue pie, make the filling using a can of pineapple in fruit juice, about 430 g. Drain the fruit and reserve the juice. Purée the fruit, then stir in 40 g (1¼ oz) cornflour and the grated zest of 1 lime. Make the drained pineapple juice up to 300 m (10 fl oz) with the juice of the lime and water, then bring to the boil. Pour onto the pineapple purée mixture, stirring well, then return to the pan. Bring back to the boil, then reduce the heat and cook, stirring, until thickened. Cool slightly, then mix with 2 egg yolks and 1 tbsp light muscovado sugar. Pour into the biscuit case. Make the meringue as in the main recipe, but using 45 g (1½ oz) each of caster and light muscovado sugar. Scatter 1 tbsp desiccated coconut over the meringue and bake for 12–15 minutes or until golden brown.

Spiced apple and blueberry pie

Here's the easiest fruit pie you could wish for – a crumbly, half wholemeal shortcrust pastry simply wrapped around a spiced mixture of tangy apples and juicy blueberries, to make a rough parcel with an open top. There's no flan tin to line or pie dish to cover, so it's quick to make and looks sensational too.

Serves 6

Wholemeal shortcrust pastry
75 g (2½ oz) plain white flour
75 g (2½ oz) plain wholemeal flour
1¼ tsp ground mixed spice
75 g (2½ oz) cool unsalted butter, diced
30 g (1 oz) icing sugar, sifted
1 egg yolk

Apple and blueberry filling
550 g (1¼ lb) cooking apples
100 g (3½ oz) blueberries
45 g (1½ oz) light muscovado sugar
1 tsp ground cinnamon
½ tsp freshly grated nutmeg
1 egg white, whisked lightly to loosen

To serve (optional)
vanilla frozen yogurt or Greek-style yogurt

Preparation time: 20 minutes, plus at least 30 minutes chilling
Cooking time: 30–35 minutes

Each serving provides

kcal 261, **protein** 4 g, **fat** 12 g (of which saturated fat 7 g), **carbohydrate** 38 g (of which sugars 20 g), **fibre** 3 g

✓ A, C, copper, selenium

1 First make the pastry. Sift the white and wholemeal flours and the spice into a bowl, tipping in the bran left in the sieve. Rub in the butter until the mixture resembles fine breadcrumbs. Stir in the sugar.

2 Mix the egg yolk with 1 tbsp cold water, add to the flour mixture and mix to form a soft dough, adding a few drops more water if needed. Wrap the dough in cling film and chill for at least 30 minutes.

3 Preheat the oven to 190°C (375°F, gas mark 5). Peel and slice the apples, and mix with the blueberries. Stir together the sugar, cinnamon and nutmeg. Reserve 1 tbsp of the mixture, and stir the rest into the fruit.

4 Roll out the pastry dough thinly on a non-stick baking sheet to make a 30 cm (12 in) round. Brush the dough all over with egg white.

5 Pile the fruit mixture in the middle of the pastry round, then draw up the sides over the fruit, but leaving the centre open. Brush the outside of the case with the remaining egg white and sprinkle with the reserved spiced sugar.

6 Bake for 30–35 minutes or until the pastry is golden brown and the apples are tender. Serve warm, with vanilla frozen yogurt or Greek-style yogurt, if liked.

Some more ideas

- For a pastry with more texture, roll out the dough on a surface lightly sprinkled with fine oatmeal.
- Make a deep dish apple and blackberry pie. Replace the blueberries with blackberries, and sprinkle the fruit with the sugar and 1 tsp ground allspice. Place the fruit in a deep 23 cm (9 in) pie dish. Brush the rim with water. Roll out the pastry dough to a round or oval to cover the dish. Lay the dough over the filling and press the edges to the rim to seal. Crimp the edges. Brush the pastry lid with egg white, and sprinkle with ½ tsp caster sugar and a pinch of allspice. Bake in a preheated 190°C (375°F, gas mark 5) oven for 30–35 minutes or until golden brown.

Plus points

- Blueberries are rich in vitamin C and beta-carotene, both powerful antioxidants that help to mop up free radicals before they can do harm to cells in the body.
- Apples provide good amounts of potassium and of soluble fibre in the form of pectin.
- Combining wholemeal flour with white flour increases the fibre content without making the pie crust too heavy.

Sweet Puddings

Satisfying and good for you too

The sweet dish served at the end of a meal is eagerly anticipated, and when it is a healthier version of a classic no one is disappointed. Try a glamorous bread and butter pudding made with brioche and a rum-spiked custard, or a whisked sponge rolled round fresh raspberries and passion fruit. Or what about an old-fashioned charlotte, its crisp, buttery bread case filled with rhubarb and bananas? For autumn, an upside-down pear and blackberry pudding with an orange-scented sponge is a superb way to use the best fruits in season. And, at the end of the year, you could celebrate with a light, fruity Christmas pudding served with a delicate brandy-laced sauce.

Apricot and rum brioche pudding

This glamorous version of bread and butter pudding is based on brioche, the French bread enriched with eggs and butter, and has an egg custard spiked with rum or brandy for a seductive flavour. Sultanas, dried apricots and apricot conserve provide lots of sweetness, so no sugar is needed.

Serves 4

8 medium-sized slices brioche loaf, about 200 g (7 oz) in total
4 tbsp apricot conserve
50 g (1¾ oz) sultanas
100 g (3½ oz) ready-to-eat dried apricots, chopped
2 eggs
450 ml (15 fl oz) semi-skimmed milk
1 tsp pure vanilla extract
1 tbsp dark rum or brandy

Preparation time: 15 minutes, plus 20 minutes soaking
Cooking time: 30–35 minutes

Each serving provides (V)

kcal 354, **protein** 13 g, **fat** 9.5 g (of which saturated fat 3.5 g), **carbohydrate** 55.5 g (of which sugars 30 g), **fibre** 3 g

✓✓ B_{12}, calcium, copper, selenium

✓ A, B_1, B_2, niacin, iron, potassium, zinc

1 Spread the brioche slices with the conserve. (If the conserve is a little thick, warm it gently so that it can be spread easily.) Cut the slices in half diagonally or into squares.

2 Arrange the pieces of brioche in a lightly greased 1.2 litre (2 pint) ovenproof dish, scattering the sultanas and chopped dried apricots between the layers.

3 Place the eggs in a mixing bowl. Add the milk, vanilla extract and rum or brandy, and whisk together until well combined. Pour the mixture over the brioche, then gently press the brioche down into the liquid. Leave to soak for 20 minutes.

4 Preheat the oven to 180°C (350°F, gas mark 4). If you like, pull up some of the brioche slices to make a peaked effect. Bake the pudding for 30–35 minutes or until it is just firm to the touch. Serve immediately.

Some more ideas

- If preferred, omit the brandy or rum and add another 1 tsp of vanilla extract.
- For a slightly richer pudding, use whole milk instead of semi-skimmed.
- To make a peach and fruited bread pudding, use 8 slices of a fruit bread instead of the brioche, and spread them with 4 tbsp orange marmalade (with or without shreds of peel). Replace the sultanas and dried apricots with 115 g (4 oz) chopped, ready-to-eat dried peaches. Instead of vanilla extract, flavour the custard with the grated zest of 1 orange and use 1 tbsp brandy or orange liqueur. Bake as in the main recipe.

Plus points

- Brioche is made from an enriched yeast dough. Like other varieties of bread, it is an excellent source of starchy carbohydrate and contributes to the intake of several vitamins and minerals.
- Dried apricots are not only a useful source of iron, they also contain good amounts of calcium. Regularly using dried apricots in recipes and enjoying them as a snack will help to boost intake of these essential minerals.
- Many of the essential nutrients in milk are concentrated in the non-fat part. Skimmed and semi-skimmed milk therefore contain more of these nutrients than full-fat milk.

Mocha ricotta tiramisu

This delectable version of the popular Italian dessert includes the traditional sponge biscuits soaked in coffee and liqueur for the base, but rather than a rich topping there is a light and creamy mixture of sweetened ricotta cheese and Greek-style yogurt. A sprinkling of grated dark chocolate is the finishing touch.

Serves 4

8 savoiardi or boudoir biscuits (sponge fingers), about 65 g (2¼ oz) in total
1 tsp Continental roast coffee granules
120 ml (4 fl oz) boiling water
2 tbsp coffee liqueur or brandy
1 tsp caster sugar
200 g (7 oz) ricotta cheese
200 g (7 oz) Greek-style yogurt
25 g (scant 1 oz) icing sugar, sifted
1 tsp pure vanilla extract
25 g (scant 1 oz) good plain chocolate (at least 70% cocoa solids), grated, to decorate

Preparation time: 20 minutes, plus at least 30 minutes chilling

Each serving provides

kcal 253, protein 9 g, fat 12 g (of which saturated fat 7 g), carbohydrate 24 g (of which sugars 20 g), fibre 0.5 g

✓✓ A, calcium
✓ B_2, B_{12}, zinc

1 Break each of the sponge fingers into 3 pieces, then divide evenly among four 240 ml (8 fl oz) glass tumblers or dessert glasses.

2 Place the coffee in a measuring jug and add the boiling water. Add the liqueur or brandy and caster sugar, and stir to dissolve. Pour evenly over the sponge fingers. Leave to soak while you make the topping.

3 Beat the ricotta with the yogurt, icing sugar and vanilla extract until smooth and creamy. Pile on top of the soaked sponge fingers.

4 Sprinkle the top of each dessert with grated chocolate. Cover and chill for at least 30 minutes (but no more than 3–4 hours) before serving.

Some more ideas

- Replace the Greek-style yogurt with fromage frais or vanilla-flavoured low-fat yogurt.
- Instead of grated chocolate, decorate the tops of the desserts by dusting each with ½ tsp of cocoa powder.
- To make an amaretti and raspberry dessert, divide 28 amaretti (or ratafia) biscuits, about 75 g (2½ oz) in total, among 4 glass tumblers or dishes. Add 250 g (8½ oz) raspberries, reserving 12 for decoration. Sprinkle each dessert with 1 tbsp dark rum, brandy or orange liqueur. Make a thick custard using 1½ tbsp custard powder, 2 tbsp caster sugar and 300 ml (10 fl oz) semi-skimmed milk, following the instructions on the label. Flavour with 1 tsp pure vanilla extract. Allow to cool, then blend with 100 g (3½ oz) Greek-style yogurt. Spoon on top of the biscuit and raspberry mixture. Crush 8 more biscuits and scatter the crumbs over the top of the desserts, then decorate with the reserved raspberries. Chill for 30 minutes before serving.

Plus points

- Ricotta is very much lower in fat and calories than the creamy mascarpone that is traditionally used for this pudding. Adding Greek-style yogurt to the ricotta provides creaminess without loading the fat content.
- Dark chocolate is a good source of copper, a mineral that helps the body to absorb iron. As dark chocolate is also a source of iron, there is a double nutritional benefit to including it in this pudding.

Spiced flan

A flan can be both a pastry-based tart and a baked custard, like a crème caramel. The flan here is the latter – a feather-light custard based on butternut squash, eggs and soured cream, fragrantly spiced and flavoured with orange. It cuts beautifully into wedges and is delicious served with more soured cream.

Serves 6

1 butternut squash, about 450 g (1 lb)
grated zest and juice of 1 large orange
2 eggs
100 g (3½ oz) light muscovado sugar
1 tsp ground cinnamon
½ tsp ground ginger
¼ tsp freshly grated nutmeg
¼ tsp salt
1 tbsp brandy (optional)
150 ml (5 fl oz) soured cream

To serve
1 tsp icing sugar, sifted
6 tbsp soured cream

Preparation time: 30 minutes, plus at least 1 hour cooling
Cooking time: 25–30 minutes

Each serving provides (V)

kcal 235, **protein** 5 g, **fat** 13 g (of which saturated fat 7.5 g), **carbohydrate** 27 g (of which sugars 24 g), **fibre** 1 g

✓✓✓	A
✓✓	C
✓	B_{12}, folate, calcium, potassium

1 Peel the squash and cut it into chunks, discarding the seeds. Put into a medium-sized saucepan with the orange juice. Bring to the boil, then lower the heat, cover and cook gently for 20–25 minutes or until tender. Drain, discarding any remaining juice. Purée the squash in a food processor or blender. Preheat the oven to 180°C (350°F, gas mark 4).

2 Lightly beat the eggs in a bowl, then whisk in the orange zest, sugar, cinnamon, ginger, nutmeg, salt, brandy, if using, and soured cream. Add the puréed squash and mix well.

3 Pour the mixture into a 23 cm (9 in) china flan dish or pie dish. Bake for 25–30 minutes or until just set. Loosen the edges with a round-bladed knife, then leave to cool for about 1 hour or, alternatively, until completely cold.

4 Serve slightly warm, or cover and chill before serving. Sprinkle with a light dusting of icing sugar and accompany with extra soured cream.

Another idea

- For a souffléd spiced flan, in step 2, separate the eggs and beat the yolks with the orange zest, sugar, ½ tsp cinnamon, 1 tsp mixed spice, the salt and brandy, if using. Mix with the puréed squash. Whisk the egg whites to soft peaks, then fold into the squash mixture with the soured cream. Pour into a 20–23 cm (8–9 in) ovenproof dish that is 5 cm (2 in) deep. Scatter over 30 g (1 oz) chopped pecan nuts and bake as in the main recipe, until slightly puffy and pale golden. Serve immediately, dusted with icing sugar and with the extra soured cream.

Plus points

- Butternut squash is a good source of the antioxidant beta-carotene as indicated by the bright orange colour of the flesh.
- Soured cream has a lower fat content than double or whipping cream, yet it still adds a rich taste and creamy texture.
- Cinnamon is mentioned frequently in the Old Testament and during the Middle Ages was almost as popular as black pepper. Apart from its culinary use, it appears to have medicinal properties as a nasal decongestant.

Raspberry and passion fruit sponge roll

This light, almost fat-free whisked sponge, rolled up round a crushed fresh raspberry and passion fruit filling, makes a very pretty pudding. It's ideal for late summer, when raspberries are particularly sweet. Children will love it. Serve with home-made custard, if you like.

Serves 8

Fruit filling

350 g (12½ oz) fresh raspberries
25 g (scant 1 oz) icing sugar, sifted
4 passion fruit

Whisked sponge

3 large eggs
115 g (4 oz) golden caster sugar
115 g (4 oz) plain flour
1 tbsp tepid water

To decorate

24 fresh raspberries, about 100 g (3½ oz) in total
sprigs of fresh mint

To serve (optional)

Real egg custard (see page 29)

Preparation time: 15–20 minutes
Cooking time: 10–12 minutes

Each serving provides

kcal 170, **protein** 5.5 g, **fat** 3 g (of which saturated fat 1 g), **carbohydrate** 32.5 g (of which sugars 21.5 g), **fibre** 2 g

✓ A, B_{12}, C, copper

1 Set aside half of the raspberries for the filling. Put the rest into a bowl with the icing sugar, and crush lightly with a fork. Cut the passion fruit in half, scoop out the pulp and stir into the crushed raspberries.

2 Preheat the oven to 200°C (400°F, gas mark 6). Grease a 23 x 33 cm (9 x 13 in) Swiss roll tin and line the bottom with baking parchment.

3 Put the eggs and sugar in a large bowl and beat with an electric mixer until very thick and pale, and the mixture leaves a trail on the surface when the beaters are lifted out. (If using a hand whisk or rotary beater, set the bowl over a pan of almost boiling water, making sure the water is not touching the base of the bowl.)

4 Sift half the flour over the whisked mixture and gently fold it in with a large metal spoon. Sift over the remaining flour and fold in together with the tepid water.

5 Pour the mixture into the prepared tin and shake gently so that it spreads evenly into the corners. Bake for 10–12 minutes or until the sponge is well risen and pale golden, and springs back when pressed gently.

6 Turn out onto a sheet of baking parchment that is slightly larger than the sponge. Peel off the lining paper. Trim the crusty edges of the sponge with a sharp knife and make a score mark 2.5 cm (1 in) from one of the shorter edges (this will make the sponge easier to roll up).

7 Spread the crushed raspberry mixture over the hot sponge, leaving a 1 cm (½ in) border all round. Scatter over the reserved raspberries. Carefully roll up the sponge from one of the short edges and place seam side down on a serving plate.

8 Serve warm or cold, cut into slices. Decorate each serving with a few extra raspberries and a sprig of mint. Serve with custard, if liked.

Plus point

- Raspberries not only provide plenty of vitamin C (32 mg per 100 g/3½ oz), they also contain vitamin E, both of which are powerful antioxidants.

Some more ideas

- For a wholemeal sponge roll, use 55 g (2 oz) plain wholemeal flour and 55 g (2 oz) plain white flour.
- Instead of the raspberry and passion fruit filling, spread the warm sponge with 5 tbsp of your favourite fruit conserve, warmed so that it will spread easily.
- Make an apple, strawberry and hazelnut sponge roll. For the filling, put 225 g (8 oz) cooking apples and 225 g (8 oz) dessert apples, both peeled and finely chopped, in a saucepan with 1 tbsp orange juice. Cover and cook gently for 15 minutes, then remove the lid and cook for a further 5–6 minutes, stirring frequently, until most of the fruit juices have evaporated and the apples are thick and pulpy. Stir in 30 g (1 oz) caster sugar and 170 g (6 oz) sliced small strawberries. For the sponge, replace the flour with a mixture of 55 g (2 oz) each ground hazelnuts and plain flour. Bake, fill and roll up as in the main recipe. When serving, decorate with extra strawberries and sprigs of fresh mint.

Upside-down pear pudding

This comforting pudding is sure to become a family favourite, being perfect for a Sunday lunch on a chilly autumnal day. Pears and blackberries are topped with an orange-scented sponge mixture and baked, then the pudding is turned out upside-down to serve, so the luscious fruit is on top.

Serves 6

55 g (2 oz) golden syrup
3 ripe pears
170 g (6 oz) fresh blackberries
115 g (4 oz) unsalted butter, softened
115 g (4 oz) light muscovado sugar
2 eggs, beaten
170 g (6 oz) self-raising flour
finely grated zest of 1 small orange
2 tbsp semi-skimmed milk, or as needed
To serve (optional)
Greek-style yogurt

Preparation time: 25 minutes
Cooking time: 50–60 minutes

Each serving provides

kcal 401, **protein** 6 g, **fat** 18 g (of which saturated fat 11 g), **carbohydrate** 58 g (of which sugars 37 g), **fibre** 3.5 g

✓✓	A
✓	B_{12}, C, E, calcium, copper, iron

1 Preheat the oven to 180°C (350°F, gas mark 4). Grease a 20 cm (8 in) round, deep cake tin and line the bottom with greaseproof paper.

2 Heat the golden syrup gently in a small pan until it is runny, then pour it over the bottom of the prepared tin. Peel, halve and core the pears. Arrange them, cut side down and in one layer, in the syrup. Scatter over the blackberries.

3 In a mixing bowl, cream together the butter and sugar until pale and fluffy. Gradually add the eggs, beating well after each addition. Fold in the flour, orange zest and milk to give a soft, dropping consistency. Add a little more milk if needed. Spoon the sponge mixture evenly over the fruit in the tin and level the surface.

4 Bake for 50–60 minutes or until risen and golden brown. If the pudding seems to be browning too much towards the end of cooking, cover loosely with foil.

5 Leave to cool in the tin for about 10 minutes, then place an inverted serving plate on top. Turn the tin and plate over, holding them firmly together, so the pudding falls out onto the plate. Serve warm, cut into wedges, with Greek-style yogurt, if liked.

Some more ideas

- For a quick storecupboard pear pudding, use 6 canned pear halves, canned in natural juice, well drained, in place of fresh pears.
- Substitute maple syrup for the golden syrup.
- Try an upside-down pineapple and blueberry pudding, replacing the pears and blackberries with 4 canned pineapple rings, canned in natural juice, well drained, and 170 g (6 oz) fresh blueberries.
- Make an upside-down ginger and plum pudding. Instead of pears and blackberries, arrange 6 halved plums in the syrup. For the sponge mixture use 85 g (3 oz) each of self-raising white flour and self-raising wholemeal flour. Omit the orange zest and add 1½ tsp ground ginger and 3–4 pieces preserved stem ginger in syrup, finely chopped.

Plus points

- Blackberries are high in fibre and vitamin C. They are also one of the richest fruit sources of vitamin E.
- Golden syrup is derived from molasses. It is predominantly made up of the sugars glucose, sucrose and fructose, but because it contains more water and less glucose than table sugar it is not as sweet.

Fragrant gooseberry crumble

Crumbles are always a family favourite and gooseberries are one of the best fruit choices, as their slight tartness partners particularly well with a sweet crumble topping. Here, the flavour of the gooseberries is enhanced with fragrant elderflower cordial and fresh mint, and the crumble topping has oats, hazelnuts and wheatgerm added.

Serves 6

1 kg (2¼ lb) gooseberries, topped and tailed
2 sprigs of fresh mint
2 tbsp elderflower cordial
50 g (1¾ oz) caster sugar, or to taste

Crumble topping

55 g (2 oz) plain white flour
30 g (1 oz) plain wholemeal flour
55 g (2 oz) cool unsalted butter, diced
55 g (2 oz) light soft brown sugar
30 g (1 oz) jumbo oats
30 g (1 oz) hazelnuts, chopped
2 tbsp wheatgerm

To serve (optional)

Real egg custard (see page 29)

Preparation time: 25 minutes
Cooking time: 20–25 minutes

Each serving provides

kcal 275, **protein** 5 g, **fat** 12 g (of which saturated fat 5 g), **carbohydrate** 39 g (of which sugars 25 g), **fibre** 6 g

✓✓	C, E
✓	A, B_1, calcium, copper, iron, potassium, zinc

1 Preheat the oven to 200°C (400°F, gas mark 6). Put the gooseberries in a saucepan with the mint sprigs and elderflower cordial. Cover and cook over a very low heat for 8–10 minutes or until the gooseberries start to soften and release their juices.

2 Stir in the caster sugar until it has dissolved, then transfer to a deep 1.7 litre (3 pint) baking dish, discarding the mint sprigs.

3 Sift the white and wholemeal flours into a mixing bowl, tipping in the bran left in the sieve. Rub the butter into the flour until the mixture resembles breadcrumbs. Stir in the sugar, oats, hazelnuts and wheatgerm. Sprinkle over 1 tbsp cold water and mix in to make a rough crumbly mixture. Spoon the topping evenly over the fruit.

4 Bake for 20–25 minutes or until the topping is golden brown and the fruit filling bubbling. Serve hot or warm, with custard, if liked.

Some more ideas

- For a rhubarb and ginger crumble, cut 1 kg (2¼ lb) rhubarb into 2.5 cm (1 in) lengths and place in a wide, shallow saucepan with 4 tbsp ginger syrup from a jar of stem ginger. Cover and cook gently for 5–6 minutes or until the juices run and the rhubarb is just beginning to soften. Lift out the rhubarb with a draining spoon into the baking dish, leaving the juice in the pan. Sprinkle 45 g (1½ oz) light soft brown sugar over the rhubarb. Simmer the juices for 3–4 minutes or until reduced to about 4 tbsp. Drizzle over the rhubarb. Make the crumble topping with the flours and butter, but add 115 g (4 oz) sweetened muesli instead of the sugar, oats, hazelnuts and wheatgerm. Sprinkle over the fruit and bake as in the main recipe.
- To make a cinnamon plum crumble, quarter and stone 1 kg (2¼ lb) ripe plums and toss with 75 g (2½ oz) demerara sugar and 1 tsp ground cinnamon. Use the crumble topping in the main recipe or the muesli variation above.

Plus points

- This crumble has a lower proportion of fat than the traditional recipe; the crumbly texture is achieved by stirring in a little water. The water evaporates during cooking to give a deliciously crunchy texture.
- Gooseberries are an excellent source of vitamin C. Their high acid content protects the vitamin C, so little is lost during cooking.
- Mint has been used since Biblical times to relieve indigestion. Peppermint tea is still a favourite of many to relieve hiccups and nausea.

Cherry and pistachio rice pots with cherry compote

This is delightful rice pudding, made wonderfully creamy with fromage frais and full of texture and flavour from the addition of dried cherries and pistachio nuts. It's served in individual pots with a fresh cherry compote, which will keep for several days in the fridge. The pudding is equally good served warm or cold.

Serves 4

Rice pudding

45 g (1½ oz) pudding rice
2 tbsp light muscovado sugar
450 ml (15 fl oz) semi-skimmed milk
25 g (scant 1 oz) dried cherries, halved
30 g (1 oz) pistachio nuts, chopped
few drops of pure vanilla extract
250 g (8½ oz) fromage frais

Cherry compote

2 tbsp redcurrant jelly
25 g (scant 1 oz) golden caster sugar
350 g (12½ oz) fresh cherries, stoned
75 ml (2½ fl oz) fruity red wine, such as Beaujolais

Preparation and cooking time: 40 minutes, plus 15 minutes cooling

Each serving provides

kcal 359, **protein** 11 g, **fat** 10.5 g (of which saturated fat 4 g), **carbohydrate** 56 g (of which sugars 46 g), **fibre** 1 g

✓✓ B_{12}, calcium

✓ A, B_1, B_2, C, niacin, copper, potassium, zinc

1 Put the rice in a medium-sized saucepan with the sugar and milk. Stir, then bring to the boil. Reduce the heat and simmer for 20–25 minutes, stirring occasionally, until the rice is cooked and the mixture creamy.

2 Remove the pan from the heat and stir in the cherries, pistachio nuts and vanilla extract. Cool for 15 minutes, then stir in the fromage frais. Spoon into four 170 ml (6 fl oz) little pots or ramekins and set aside.

3 To make the compote, put the redcurrant jelly and caster sugar in a frying pan or wide saucepan and heat over a low heat, stirring, until the sugar has dissolved. Add the cherries and cook gently for 3–4 minutes or until the cherry juices start to run. Pour in the wine, bring just to a simmer and simmer for 1–2 minutes or until the cherries are tender. Serve the compote warm or cold with the rice pots.

Another idea

- For cardamom rice with fresh peach or apricot compote, use flaked rice instead of pudding rice, and add the crushed seeds from 3 cardamom pods with the milk and sugar. Simmer for 15 minutes or until the rice mixture is creamy, stirring occasionally. Cool, then stir in the fromage frais, and pour into pots. For the compote, heat 200 ml (7 fl oz) fruity white wine and 30 g (1 oz) golden caster sugar in a frying pan, stirring, until the sugar has dissolved. Add 4 thickly sliced peaches, or 8 halved apricots. Cover and poach gently for 5–8 minutes or until the fruit is starting to soften. Use a draining spoon to transfer the fruit to a bowl. Boil the liquid in the pan for 6–7 minutes to form a thin syrup. Pour over the fruit, and serve warm or cold with the rice puddings.

Plus points

- Though white rice has less dietary fibre than brown rice, some of the starchy carbohydrate in the white rice is resistant to digestion. This undigested starch seems to aid digestion in a similar way to fibre.
- Fromage frais makes an excellent low-fat alternative to cream for enriching puddings such as this one.

Rhubarb and banana charlotte

This classic English pudding, of fruit baked in a buttery bread case, is often made with apples, but works very well with an unusual combination of rhubarb and bananas instead. The pudding is thought to take its name from Queen Charlotte, the wife of George III, who had a fondness for growing fruits.

Serves 6

500 g (1 lb 2 oz) young pink rhubarb, thickly sliced
2 tbsp caster sugar
½ tsp ground star anise
finely grated zest and juice of 1 orange
2 large, firm bananas
45 g (1½ oz) unsalted butter, melted
11 thin slices white bread, about 330 g (11½ oz) in total
1 tsp demerara sugar

To serve (optional)

Greek-style yogurt or crème fraîche

Preparation time: 25 minutes
Cooking time: 30–35 minutes

1 Preheat the oven to 200°C (400°F, gas mark 6). Put the rhubarb in a saucepan with the caster sugar, star anise, and orange zest and juice. Cover and cook on a low heat, stirring occasionally, for 10–15 minutes or until the rhubarb is tender.

2 Remove the pan from the heat. Peel and slice the bananas, and stir into the rhubarb. Set aside.

3 Brush the inside of a 20 cm (8 in) springform tin with a little of the melted butter. Remove the crusts from the bread and cut into fingers. Brush lightly with a little of the butter.

4 Arrange about two-thirds of the bread fingers, buttered side in, over the bottom and sides of the tin, leaving no gaps. Tip the fruit into the centre, packing it down firmly. Cover with the remaining bread, buttered side down. Press down lightly and brush with the remaining butter.

5 Bake for 30–35 minutes or until golden brown. Cool slightly in the tin, then turn out and sprinkle with the demerara sugar. Serve warm, with Greek-style yogurt or crème fraîche, if you like.

Plus points

- Rhubarb is 94% water and compared with soft fruit and citrus fruit contains very little vitamin C. However, it is a good source of potassium, which functions with sodium to regulate fluid balance in the body.
- Bananas are a carbohydrate-rich food, containing 2–3 times the amount of carbohydrate in fruit such as apples, oranges and pears and about 50% more than grapes. This is why bananas are popular with athletes, who need to maintain muscle stores of glycogen for long-term energy.
- All varieties of breads make a valuable nutritional contribution to the diet – indeed white bread, which is often perceived to be not as 'healthy' as wholemeal, has twice as much calcium as wholemeal bread.

Each serving provides (V)

kcal 254, **protein** 6 g, **fat** 7 g (of which saturated fat 4 g), **carbohydrate** 44 g (of which sugars 17.5 g), **fibre** 2 g

✓✓	selenium
✓	A, B_1, C, calcium, copper, potassium

Some more ideas

- For a change of shape, make the pudding in a 900 g (2 lb) loaf tin instead of a round tin. Bake at the same temperature for the same time as the main recipe.
- To make a plum, pear and blackcurrant charlotte, poach 500 g (1 lb 2 oz) red plums, halved, in 4 tbsp apple juice with 2 tbsp caster sugar and 1 tsp ground cinnamon for about 15 minutes or until just tender. Remove from the heat and add 2 ripe pears, peeled and chopped, and 100 g (3½ oz) blackcurrants. Pour into the bread-lined tin, then finish and bake as in the main recipe. Before serving, sprinkle with 1 tbsp toasted flaked almonds instead of demerara sugar.
- If fresh blackcurrants are not available for the variation above, use canned blackcurrants in natural juice, well drained, and use the blackcurrant juice rather than apple juice for poaching the plums.

Sticky date and walnut pudding

On a chilly winter day, nothing could be more welcoming than a sponge pudding packed with dates and toasted walnuts. This is very easy to make and it has a lovely moist texture achieved by 'steaming' the pudding in a bain-marie in the oven. A tangy pineapple and marmalade sauce makes a perfect accompaniment.

Serves 8

Sponge pudding

170 g (6 oz) dried stoned dates, chopped
3 tbsp semi-skimmed milk
85 g (3 oz) unsalted butter, softened
85 g (3 oz) light muscovado sugar
2 eggs, lightly beaten
115 g (4 oz) self-raising flour
¼ tsp ground cinnamon
½ tsp ground ginger
50 g (1¾ oz) walnuts, toasted and roughly chopped

Pineapple and marmalade sauce

1 can pineapple pieces in natural juice, about 400 g
1 tsp arrowroot
4 tbsp fine-cut orange marmalade

Preparation time: 25 minutes
Cooking time: about 1 hour

1 Preheat the oven to 180°C (350°F, gas mark 4). Lightly grease a 900 ml (1½ pint) ovenproof pudding basin and line the bottom with a small disc of greaseproof paper.

2 Place the chopped dates in a bowl and pour over 2 tbsp of the milk. Stir to coat, then leave to soak while preparing the sponge mixture.

3 Put the butter, sugar, eggs and remaining 1 tbsp milk in a bowl. Sift over the flour, cinnamon and ginger, and beat with an electric mixer for 2 minutes or until smooth. Fold in the soaked dates and the walnuts.

4 Spoon the mixture into the pudding basin. Set the basin in a roasting tin and pour in enough boiling water to come 1 cm (½ in) up the sides of the basin. Cover the tin and basin with a tent of foil.

5 Bake for about 1 hour or until the pudding is lightly risen and springy to the touch, and a skewer inserted into the middle comes out clean. If not, bake for a further 10 minutes or so.

6 Meanwhile, make the sauce. Drain the pineapple, reserving 150 ml (5 fl oz) of the juice. Finely chop the pineapple pieces. Blend the arrowroot with a little of the juice in a small saucepan, then stir in the rest of the juice. Bring to the boil and simmer for 1 minute or until thickened and clear. Stir the pineapple and marmalade into the sauce and simmer for a further 2–3 minutes, stirring occasionally.

7 Lift the basin out of the tin and turn out the pudding onto a warmed serving plate. Spoon a little of the hot sauce over the top and serve with the rest of the sauce.

Each serving provides (V)

kcal 343, **protein** 5 g, **fat** 15 g (of which saturated fat 7 g), **carbohydrate** 51 g (of which sugars 39 g), **fibre** 2 g

✓ A, B_{12}, calcium, copper, iron

Plus points

- Up to 95% of the energy content of dates comes from natural sugars. The fibre content of dates ensures that the glucose obtained from the sugars is released slowly into the blood stream.
- Walnuts have a high unsaturated fat content, particularly as linoleic acid. Some studies have suggested that including a regular, small quantity of walnuts in the diet can help to reduce high blood cholesterol levels and reduce the risk of heart attacks.
- Pineapple canned in natural juice has a total sugar content of 8.5 g per 100 g (3½ oz) compared to 13.2 g for the same weight of pineapple canned in syrup.

Some more ideas

- Use self-raising wholemeal flour rather than white flour. The mixture will need an extra 2 tsp semi-skimmed milk.
- Instead of a pineapple and marmalade sauce, serve the pudding with a pineapple and orange compote. Just mix the pineapple pieces and their juice with 2–3 sliced or segmented oranges.
- To make mini lemon and sultana puddings, soak 85 g (3 oz) sultanas in 1 tbsp lemon juice and 1 tbsp brandy for 1 hour. Lightly grease eight 100 ml (3½ fl oz) deep muffin tins and line the bottoms with greaseproof paper. Make the sponge mixture as in the main recipe, but leave out the dates and walnuts, and instead fold in the soaked sultanas and the finely grated zest of 1 small lemon. Divide the mixture among the tins and bake for 20 minutes. Meanwhile, make a maple, pecan and citrus sauce. Put 120 ml (4 fl oz) maple syrup in a saucepan with 4 tbsp orange juice, 85 g (3 oz) roughly chopped toasted pecan nuts, the segments from 2 oranges and 1 pink grapefruit, and 1 tbsp orange liqueur, if liked. Gently heat until the sauce is just beginning to bubble. Turn out the puddings onto 8 serving plates. Arrange a few extra orange and grapefruit segments around each pudding, then spoon the hot sauce over the tops. Serve straight away.

Peach and vanilla choux ring

An impressive dessert for a special occasion or buffet table, this ring of light choux pastry is filled with fresh peaches and a fluffy mixture of fromage frais and whipping cream. It's ideal for entertaining because the pastry ring can be baked ahead of time. Serve decorated with raspberries and pretty cape gooseberries.

Serves 6

1 quantity Choux pastry (see page 23)
150 ml (5 fl oz) whipping cream
150 g (5½ oz) fromage frais
1 tsp pure vanilla extract
4 fresh ripe peaches, chopped
1 tbsp icing sugar, sifted
To decorate
125 g (4½ oz) fresh raspberries
6 cape gooseberries

Preparation time: 35 minutes (including making the pastry)
Cooking time: 30–35 minutes

Each serving provides

kcal 310, **protein** 7 g, **fat** 21 g (of which saturated fat 13 g), **carbohydrate** 23 g (of which sugars 13 g), **fibre** 2 g

✓✓✓	A
✓✓	B_{12}, C
✓	B_2, calcium, zinc

1 Preheat the oven to 200°C (400°F, gas mark 6). Put the choux pastry into a piping bag fitted with a 1 cm (½ in) plain nozzle. Pipe a ring of choux pastry, 20 cm (8 in) in diameter, onto a non-stick baking sheet. Pipe a second ring inside and touching the first one, then pipe a third ring on top.

2 Bake for 25–30 minutes or until well risen and golden brown. Using a sharp knife, cut the choux ring in half horizontally. Place the top half, cut side up, on another baking sheet. Return both halves to the oven to bake for a further 3 minutes, to dry out the centres. Transfer to a wire rack to cool.

3 In a mixing bowl, whip the cream with the fromage frais and vanilla extract until thick. Fold in the chopped peaches.

4 Just before serving, spoon the peach mixture onto the base of the pastry ring, and replace the top of the ring. Place the filled choux ring on a serving plate. Dust with the icing sugar and decorate with the raspberries and cape gooseberries.

Some more ideas

- Use 500 g (1 lb 2 oz) mixed strawberries and raspberries in place of peaches.
- Instead of vanilla, flavour the cream mixture with the finely grated zest of 1 lemon or 1 small orange, or 1 tsp ground cinnamon or ginger, or a piece of preserved stem ginger, drained of syrup and finely chopped.
- Sprinkle the filling with 30 g (1 oz) toasted flaked almonds before replacing the top of the pastry ring.
- For a lower fat filling, use 250 g (8½ oz) fromage frais and 3–4 tbsp whipping cream.
- Make a coffee and banana choux ring. For the filling, whip the cream with the fromage frais and 1 tbsp coffee-flavoured liqueur, then fold in 4 sliced, firm bananas.

Plus points

- Peaches are an excellent source of vitamin C. A medium-sized peach provides as much as three-quarters of the recommended daily requirement of this vitamin for adults.
- Whipping cream is lower in fat and calories than double cream. When whipped and mixed with fromage frais, it provides a luscious yet healthier alternative to whipped double cream.

Plum cobbler

A cobbler is an old-fashioned pudding made with a light scone topping and plenty of fruit underneath. This version uses plums, but other fruit in season is good too. The scone mixture has some chopped walnuts added for a nice nutty flavour and texture, and is arranged on the fruit in strips to make an attractive lattice top.

Serves 6

800 g (1¾ lb) plums, halved or quartered
grated zest and juice of 1 large orange
1 cinnamon stick
2 tbsp light muscovado sugar

Scone topping
200 g (7 oz) self-raising flour
pinch of salt
1 tsp baking powder
30 g (1 oz) cool unsalted butter, diced
30 g (1 oz) light muscovado sugar
1 tbsp chopped walnuts
100 ml (3½ fl oz) semi-skimmed milk, plus 1 tbsp milk for brushing

Preparation time: 45 minutes
Cooking time: 25–30 minutes

Each serving provides (V)

kcal 269, **protein** 5 g, **fat** 7 g (of which saturated fat 3 g), **carbohydrate** 50 g (of which sugars 25 g), **fibre** 3 g

✓ A, B_1, C, E, niacin, calcium, copper, iron, potassium

1 Preheat the oven to 180°C (350°F, gas mark 4). Place the plums in a 1.2 litre (2 pint) ovenproof dish. Add the orange zest and juice, cinnamon stick and sugar, and mix thoroughly. Gently shake the dish so the fruit settles in an even layer.

2 To make the scone topping, sift the flour, salt and baking powder into a mixing bowl. Rub in the butter until the mixture resembles fine breadcrumbs. Stir in the sugar and chopped walnuts. Make a well in the centre, add the milk and mix to a soft but not sticky dough.

3 Transfer the dough to a lightly floured work surface and knead briefly. Roll out to a rectangle about 1cm (½ in) thick and the length of the ovenproof dish. Using a sharp knife or a pastry wheel, cut into strips about 1.5 cm (¾ in) wide.

4 Dampen the rim of the dish with water, then arrange the strips over the fruit in a lattice pattern, pressing each end of the scone strips onto the rim of the dish and trimming the ends neatly. Brush the lattice with the 1 tbsp extra milk.

5 Bake for 25–30 minutes or until the scone topping is golden and the fruit is tender. Serve hot or warm. Remember to remove the cinnamon stick when serving.

Some more ideas

- Make the cobbler with a mixture of apples and plums or with the traditional blackberry and apples. Other ideas are apples with raspberries, and pears with berries.
- For a strawberry and rhubarb cobbler, replace the plums with 400 g (14 oz) each chopped rhubarb and whole strawberries, and flavour with the orange zest and 2 tbsp redcurrant jelly. Add chopped toasted hazelnuts to the scone topping rather than walnuts. Roll out the dough to an 18 cm (7 in) round that is 1 cm (½ in) thick and cut into rounds using a 3 cm (1¼ in) fluted cutter. Arrange the rounds on top of the fruit, slightly overlapping, brush with milk and bake as in the main recipe.

Plus points

- Plums are a source of both soluble and insoluble dietary fibre. Soluble fibre helps in reducing high levels of blood cholesterol, whereas insoluble fibre has an important role in preventing constipation.
- Using both the zest and juice of oranges boosts the fibre and vitamin C content. Phytochemicals, which have antioxidant properties, are also present in the skin and therefore included when the zest is used.

Prune and apple soufflé

There's no need to be nervous about making a soufflé, as it isn't at all difficult. It just needs to be served hot, straight from the oven, while it is impressively puffed up and is light-as-air to eat. This soufflé is flavoured with prunes cooked in apple juice, both naturally sweet, so the mixture needs no sugar to sweeten it.

Serves 4

125 g (4½ oz) ready-to-eat stoned prunes
120 ml (4 fl oz) apple juice
3 large eggs, separated
2 tbsp double cream
2 tsp icing sugar, sifted

Preparation time: 20 minutes, plus at least 2 hours soaking
Cooking time: 20 minutes

1 Put the prunes in a small saucepan with the apple juice. Cover and leave to soak for at least 2 hours, or overnight if more convenient.

2 Heat the prunes until they start to simmer, then simmer gently for about 5 minutes or until very tender. Purée in the pan with a hand-held blender, or in a blender or food processor.

3 Preheat the oven to 200°C (400°F, gas mark 6), and put a baking sheet in to heat. Lightly grease a 1 litre (1¾ pint) soufflé dish that is 15 cm (6 in) in diameter.

4 In a mixing bowl, lightly whisk together the egg yolks and cream, then stir in the prune purée.

5 In another bowl, clean and grease-free, whisk the egg whites until stiff. Stir 2 tbsp of the egg whites into the prune mixture to loosen it, then carefully fold in the rest with a large metal spoon.

6 Pour the mixture into the soufflé dish. Set on the hot baking sheet and bake for 20 minutes or until the soufflé is risen and just slightly wobbly when very gently shaken. Quickly dust the top with the icing sugar, then serve immediately.

Some more ideas

- For a mango and orange soufflé, replace the prunes with dried mangoes, and simmer in orange juice with 1 tbsp clear honey instead of apple juice.
- To make individual banana and rum soufflés, mash 2 medium-sized ripe bananas until smooth, then stir in 2 tbsp dark rum. Use this instead of the prune purée. Divide the mixture among 6 lightly greased 150 ml (5 fl oz) ramekin dishes. Place on the hot baking sheet and bake for 15 minutes. Dust with icing sugar and serve immediately.

Plus points

- Prunes provide useful amounts of potassium, iron and vitamin B_6. The vitamin C in the apple juice will help the body to absorb the iron in the prunes.
- Although fruit juices like apple have little fibre – unlike the original fruit – they still retain the other nutrients such as good amounts of vitamin C and other antioxidants.
- Eggs are a useful and convenient food, suitable for both sweet and savoury dishes. They are also good for you, boosting the intake of many essential nutrients including protein, vitamins B_{12}, A and D, and zinc.

Each serving provides (V)

kcal 198, **protein** 7 g, **fat** 12 g (of which saturated fat 6 g), **carbohydrate** 17 g (of which sugars 17 g), **fibre** 2 g

✓✓ A, B_{12}

✓ B_2, iron, zinc

Very fruity Christmas pudding

Lighter than the traditional pudding, this is packed with fruit, soaked in sherry and orange juice so it's extra juicy. Served with brandy sauce, this Christmas pudding won't leave you feeling uncomfortably full.

Serves 10

85 g (3 oz) currants
85 g (3 oz) raisins
85 g (3 oz) sultanas
85 g (3 oz) dried stoned dates, chopped
85 g (3 oz) dried apricots, chopped
75 g (2½ oz) dried cranberries
grated zest and juice of 1 large orange
3 tbsp sherry or brandy
115 g (4 oz) unsalted butter, softened
115 g (4 oz) dark muscovado sugar
2 eggs, beaten
1 dessert apple, peeled and diced
1 large carrot, finely grated
30 g (1 oz) flaked almonds, toasted
55 g (2 oz) self-raising flour
2 tsp ground mixed spice
100 g (3½ oz) fresh white breadcrumbs

Brandy sauce

6 tbsp cornflour
900 ml (1½ pints) semi-skimmed milk
3 tbsp caster sugar, or to taste
3 tbsp brandy

Preparation time: 45 minutes
Cooking time: 3 hours, plus 1½ hours

1 Place all the dried fruit in a bowl. Add the orange zest and juice and sherry or brandy, and set aside to soak.

2 Grease a 1.4 litre (2½ pint) pudding basin and place a small disc of greaseproof paper on the bottom.

3 Beat together the butter and sugar until light and fluffy, then gradually beat in the eggs. Add the apple, carrot, almonds and soaked fruits, and mix together. Sift in the flour and mixed spice, and add the breadcrumbs.

4 Spoon the mixture into the pudding basin and smooth the top. Lay a doubled sheet of greaseproof paper and then a doubled sheet of foil on top, and fold together to make a pleat in the centre. Smooth the paper and foil down round the basin and tie securely with string under the edge.

5 Steam for 3 hours, topping up with more boiling water when necessary. Remove the basin from the steamer and take off the foil and greaseproof lid. Cover loosely with a tea-towel and leave to cool.

6 When the pudding is completely cold, cover with doubled sheets of fresh greaseproof paper and foil. Keep in a cool, dark place for up to 3 months.

7 On the day of serving, steam for a further 1½ hours. To make the sauce, blend the cornflour with 6 tbsp of the cold milk. Heat the remaining milk until almost boiling, then pour onto the cornflour mixture, stirring. Return to the pan and stir over a moderate heat until thickened. Simmer for a further 1–2 minutes, still stirring. Add the sugar and brandy, then taste for sweetness, adding a little more sugar if liked.

8 Turn out the pudding onto a serving plate. Pour the hot brandy sauce into a sauceboat or jug and serve with the pudding.

Plus point

- This brandy-laced sauce, made with semi-skimmed milk and thickened with cornflour, provides a much lower fat alternative to cream or brandy butter.

Each serving provides (V)

kcal 432, **protein** 8 g, **fat** 14 g (of which saturated fat 8 g), **carbohydrate** 69 g (of which sugars 53 g), **fibre** 3 g

✓✓✓	A
✓✓	calcium, copper
✓	B_1, B_2, B_{12}, C, E, niacin, iron, potassium, selenium, zinc

Some more ideas

• If preferred, replace the sherry or brandy in the pudding with extra orange juice.

• Make 2 smaller puddings, dividing the mixture between two 750 ml (1¼ pint) pudding basins. They still need 3 hours steaming.

• Rather than steaming, the pudding can be reheated in a microwave. Remove the foil and cook on Medium power for about 8 minutes, or following manufacturer's instructions.

• Make a figgy pudding for Christmas. Use 250 g (8½ oz) chopped dried figs instead of the currants, raisins, sultanas, dates, apricots and cranberries. Soak the figs overnight in 3 tbsp dark rum and the grated zest and juice of 1 lemon. In step 3, use 1 peeled and diced pear in place of the carrot, and add 115 g (4 oz) chopped glacé cherries, rinsed of syrup, and 2 pieces of stem ginger, chopped. Omit the mixed spice. Serve the pudding with a rum and ginger sauce made by flavouring the sweetened white sauce with 3 tbsp ginger syrup (from the jar of stem ginger), 3 tbsp dark rum and the grated zest of 1 lemon in place of the brandy.

A glossary of nutritional terms

Antioxidants These are compounds that help to protect the body's cells against the damaging effects of free radicals. Vitamins C and E, beta-carotene (the plant form of vitamin A) and the mineral selenium, together with many of the phytochemicals found in fruit and vegetables, all act as antioxidants.

Calorie A unit used to measure the energy value of food and the intake and use of energy by the body. The scientific definition of 1 calorie is the amount of heat required to raise the temperature of 1 gram of water by 1 degree Centigrade. This is such a small amount that in this country we tend to use the term kilocalories (abbreviated to *kcal*), which is equivalent to 1000 calories. Energy values can also be measured in kilojoules (kJ): 1 kcal = 4.2 kJ.

A person's energy (calorie) requirement varies depending on his or her age, sex and level of activity. The estimated average daily energy requirements are:

Age (years)	Female (kcal)	Male (kcal)
1–3	1165	1230
4–6	1545	1715
7–10	1740	1970
11–14	1845	2220
15–18	2110	2755
19–49	1940	2550
50–59	1900	2550
60–64	1900	2380
65–74	1900	2330

Carbohydrates These energy-providing substances are present in varying amounts in different foods and are found in three main forms: sugars, starches and non-starch polysaccharides (NSP), usually called fibre.

There are two types of sugars: *intrinsic sugars*, which occur naturally in fruit (fructose) and sweet-tasting vegetables, and *extrinsic sugars*, which include lactose (from milk) and all the non-milk extrinsic sugars (NMEs) – sucrose (table sugar), honey, treacle, molasses and so on. The NMEs, or 'added' sugars, provide only calories, whereas foods containing intrinsic sugars also offer vitamins, minerals and fibre. Added sugars (*simple carbohydrates*) are digested and absorbed rapidly to provide energy very quickly. Starches and fibre (*complex carbohydrates*), on the other hand, break down more slowly to offer a longer-term energy source (see also Glycaemic Index). Starchy carbohydrates are found in bread, pasta, rice, wholegrain and breakfast cereals, and potatoes and other starchy vegetables such as parsnips, sweet potatoes and yams.

Healthy eating guidelines recommend that at least half of our daily energy (calories) should come from carbohydrates, and that most of this should be from complex carbohydrates. No more than 11% of our total calorie intake should come from 'added' sugars. For an average woman aged 19–49 years, this would mean a total carbohydrate intake of 259 g per day, of which 202 g should be from starch and intrinsic sugars and no more than 57 g from added sugars. For a man of the same age, total carbohydrates each day should be about 340 g (265 g from starch and intrinsic sugars and 75 g from added sugars).

See also Fibre and Glycogen.

Cholesterol There are two types of cholesterol – the soft waxy substance called blood cholesterol, which is an integral part of human cell membranes, and dietary cholesterol, which is contained in food. *Blood cholesterol* is important in the formation of some hormones and it aids digestion. High blood cholesterol levels are known to be an important risk factor for coronary heart disease, but most of the cholesterol in our blood is made by the liver – only about 25% comes from cholesterol in food. So while it would seem that the amount of cholesterol-rich foods in the diet would have a direct effect on blood cholesterol levels, in fact the best way to reduce blood cholesterol is to eat less saturated fat and to increase intake of foods containing soluble fibre.

Fat Although a small amount of fat is essential for good health, most people consume far too much. Healthy eating guidelines recommend that no more than 33% of our daily energy intake (calories) should come from fat. Each gram of fat contains 9 kcal, more than twice as many calories as carbohydrate or protein, so for a woman aged 19–49 years this means a daily maximum of 71 g fat, and for a man in the same age range 93.5 g fat.

Fats can be divided into 3 main groups: saturated, monounsaturated and polyunsaturated, depending on the chemical structure of the fatty acids they contain. *Saturated fatty acids* are found mainly in animal fats such as butter and other dairy products and in fatty meat. A high intake of saturated fat is known to be a risk factor for coronary heart disease and certain types of cancer. Current guidelines are that no more than 10% of our daily calories should come from saturated fats, which is about 21.5 g for an adult woman and 28.5 g for a man.

Where saturated fats tend to be solid at room temperature, the *unsaturated fatty acids* – monounsaturated and polyunsaturated – tend to be liquid. *Monounsaturated fats* are found predominantly in olive oil, groundnut (peanut) oil, rapeseed oil and avocados. Foods high in *polyunsaturates* include most vegetable oils – the exceptions are palm oil and coconut oil, both of which are saturated.

Both saturated and monounsaturated fatty acids can be made by the body, but certain polyunsaturated fatty acids – known as *essential fatty acids* – must be supplied by food. There are 2 'families' of these essential fatty acids: *omega-6*, derived from linoleic acid, and *omega-3*, from linolenic acid. The main food sources of the omega-6 family are vegetable oils such as olive and sunflower; omega-3 fatty acids are provided by oily fish, nuts, and vegetable oils such as soya and rapeseed.

When vegetable oils are hydrogenated (hardened) to make margarine and reduced-fat spreads, their unsaturated fatty acids can be changed into trans fatty acids, or '*trans fats*'. These artificially produced trans fats are believed to act in the same way as saturated fats within the body – with the same risks to health. Current healthy eating guidelines suggest that no more than 2% of our daily calories should come from trans fats, which is about 4.3 g for an adult woman and 5.6 g for a man. In thinking about the amount of trans fats you consume, remember that major sources are processed foods such as biscuits, pies, cakes and crisps.

Fibre Technically non-starch polysaccharides (NSP), fibre is the term commonly used to describe several different compounds, such as pectin, hemicellulose, lignin and gums, which are found in the cell walls of all plants. The body cannot digest fibre, nor does it have much nutritional value, but it plays an important role in helping us to stay healthy.

Fibre can be divided into 2 groups – soluble and insoluble. Both types are provided by most plant foods, but some foods are particularly good sources of one type or the other. *Soluble fibre* (in oats, pulses, fruit and vegetables) can help to reduce high blood cholesterol levels and to control blood sugar levels by slowing down the absorption of sugar. *Insoluble fibre* (in wholegrain cereals, pulses, fruit and vegetables) increases stool bulk and speeds the passage of waste material through the body. In this way it helps to prevent constipation, haemorrhoids and diverticular disease, and may protect against bowel cancer.

Our current intake of fibre is around 12 g a day. Healthy eating guidelines suggest that we need to increase this amount to 18 g a day.

Free radicals These highly reactive molecules can cause damage to cell walls and DNA (the genetic material found within cells). They are believed to be involved in the development of heart disease, some cancers and premature ageing. Free radicals are produced naturally by the body in the course of everyday life, but certain factors, such as cigarette smoke, pollution and over-exposure to sunlight, can accelerate their production.

Gluten A protein found in wheat and, to a lesser degree, in rye, barley and oats, but not in corn (maize) or rice. People with *coeliac disease* have a sensitivity to gluten and need to eliminate all gluten-containing foods, such as bread, pasta, cakes and biscuits, from their diet.

Glycaemic Index (GI) This is used to measure the rate at which carbohydrate foods are digested and converted into sugar (glucose) to raise blood sugar levels and provide energy. Foods with a high GI are quickly broken down and offer an immediate energy fix, while those with a lower GI are absorbed more slowly, making you feel full for longer and helping to keep blood sugar levels constant. High-GI foods include table sugar, honey, mashed potatoes and watermelon. Low-GI foods include pulses, wholewheat cereals, apples, cherries, dried apricots, pasta and oats.

Glycogen This is one of the 2 forms in which energy from carbohydrates is made available for use by the body (the other is *glucose*). Whereas glucose is converted quickly from carbohydrates and made available in the blood for a fast energy fix, glycogen is stored in the liver and muscles to fuel longer-term energy needs. When the body has used up its immediate supply of glucose, the stored glycogen is broken down into glucose to continue supplying energy.

Minerals These inorganic substances perform a wide range of vital functions in the body. The *macrominerals* – calcium, chloride, magnesium, potassium, phosphorus and sodium – are needed in relatively large quantities, whereas much smaller amounts are required of the remainder, called *microminerals*. Some microminerals (selenium, magnesium and iodine, for example) are needed in such tiny amounts that they are known as *'trace elements'*.

There are important differences in the body's ability to absorb minerals from different foods, and this can be affected by the presence of other substances. For example, oxalic acid, present in spinach, interferes with the absorption of much of the iron and calcium spinach contains.
• ***Calcium*** is essential for the development of strong bones and teeth. It also plays an important role in blood clotting. Good sources include dairy products, canned fish (eaten with their bones) and dark green, leafy vegetables.
• ***Chloride*** helps to maintain the body's fluid balance. The main source in the diet is table salt.
• ***Chromium*** is important in the regulation of blood sugar levels, as well as levels of fat and cholesterol in the blood. Good dietary sources include red meat, liver, eggs, seafood, cheese and wholegrain cereals.
• ***Copper***, component of many enzymes, is needed for bone growth and the formation of connective tissue. It helps the body to absorb iron from food. Good sources include offal, shellfish, mushrooms, cocoa, nuts and seeds.
• ***Iodine*** is an important component of the thyroid hormones, which govern the rate and efficiency at which food is converted into energy. Good sources include seafood, seaweed and vegetables (depending on the iodine content of the soil in which they are grown).
• ***Iron*** is an essential component of haemoglobin, the pigment in red blood cells that carries oxygen around the body. Good sources are offal, red meat, dried apricots and prunes, and iron-fortified breakfast cereals.
• ***Magnesium*** is important for healthy bones, the release of energy from food, and nerve and muscle function. Good sources include wholegrain cereals, peas and other green vegetables, pulses, dried fruit and nuts.
• ***Manganese*** is a vital component of several enzymes that are involved in energy production and many other functions. Good dietary sources include nuts, cereals, brown rice, pulses and wholemeal bread.
• ***Molybdenum*** is an essential component of several enzymes, including those involved in the production of DNA. Good sources are offal, yeast, pulses, wholegrain cereals and green leafy vegetables.
• ***Phosphorus*** is important for healthy bones and teeth and for the release of energy from foods. It is found in most foods. Particularly good sources include dairy products, red meat, poultry, fish and eggs.
• ***Potassium***, along with sodium, is important in maintaining fluid balance and regulating blood pressure, and is essential for the transmission of nerve impulses. Good sources include fruit, especially bananas and citrus fruits, nuts, seeds, potatoes and pulses.
• ***Selenium*** is a powerful antioxidant that protects cells against damage by free radicals. Good dietary sources are meat, fish, dairy foods, brazil nuts, avocados and lentils.
• ***Sodium*** works with potassium to regulate fluid balance, and is essential for nerve and muscle function. Only a little sodium is needed – we tend to get too much in our diet. The main source in the diet is table salt, as well as salty processed foods and ready-prepared foods.
• ***Sulphur*** is a component of 2 essential amino acids. Protein foods are the main source.
• ***Zinc*** is vital for normal growth, as well as reproduction and immunity. Good dietary sources include oysters, red meat, peanuts and sunflower seeds.

Phytochemicals These biologically active compounds, found in most plant foods, are believed to be beneficial in disease prevention. There are literally thousands of different phytochemicals, amongst which are the following:
• ***Allicin***, a phytochemical found in garlic, onions, leeks, chives and shallots, is believed to help lower high blood cholesterol levels and stimulate the immune system.
• ***Bioflavonoids***, of which there are at least 6000, are found mainly in fruit and sweet-tasting vegetables. Different bioflavonoids have different roles – some are antioxidants, while others act as anti-disease agents. A sub-group of these phytochemicals, called *flavonols*, includes the antioxidant *quercetin*, which is believed to reduce the risk of heart disease and help to protect against cataracts. Quercetin is found in tea, red wine, grapes and broad beans.
• ***Carotenoids***, the best known of which are *beta-carotene* and *lycopene*, are powerful antioxidants thought to help protect us against certain types of cancer. Highly coloured fruits and vegetables, such as blackcurrants, mangoes, tomatoes, carrots, sweet potatoes, pumpkin and dark green, leafy vegetables, are excellent sources of carotenoids.
• ***Coumarins*** are believed to help protect against cancer by inhibiting the formation of tumours. Oranges are a rich source.
• ***Glucosinolates***, found mainly in cruciferous vegetables, particularly broccoli, Brussels sprouts, cabbage, kale and cauliflower, are believed to have strong anti-cancer effects. *Sulphoraphane* is one of the powerful cancer-fighting substances produced by glucosinolates.
• ***Phytoestrogens*** have a chemical structure similar to the female hormone oestrogen, and they are believed to help protect against hormone-related cancers such as breast and prostate cancer. One of the types of these phytochemicals, called *isoflavones*, may also help to relieve symptoms associated with the menopause. Soya beans and chickpeas are a particularly rich source of isoflavones.

Protein This nutrient, necessary for growth and development, for maintenance and repair of cells, and for the production of enzymes, antibodies and hormones, is essential to keep the body working efficiently. Protein is made up of *amino acids*, which are compounds containing the 4 elements that are necessary for life: carbon, hydrogen, oxygen and nitrogen. We need all of the 20 amino acids commonly found in plant and animal proteins. The human body can make 12 of these, but the remaining 8 – called *essential amino acids* – must be obtained from the food we eat.

Protein comes in a wide variety of foods. Meat, fish, dairy products, eggs and soya beans contain all of the essential amino acids, and are therefore called first-class protein foods. Pulses, nuts, seeds and cereals are also good sources of protein, but do not contain the full range of essential amino acids. In practical terms, this really doesn't matter – as long as you include a variety of different protein foods in your diet, your body will get all the amino acids it needs. It is important, though, to eat protein foods every day because the essential amino acids cannot be stored in the body for later use.

The RNI of protein for women aged 19–49 years is 45 g per day and for men of the same age 55 g. In the UK most people eat more protein than they need, although this isn't normally a problem.

Reference Nutrient Intake (RNI) This denotes the average daily amount of vitamins and minerals thought to be sufficient to meet the nutritional needs of almost all individuals within the population. The figures, published by the Department of Health, vary depending on age, sex and specific nutritional needs such as pregnancy. RNIs are equivalent to what used to be called Recommended Daily Amounts or Allowances (RDA).

RNIs for adults (19–49 years)

Nutrient	RNI
Vitamin A	600–700 mcg
Vitamin B_1	0.8 mg for women, 1 mg for men
Vitamin B_2	1.1 mg for women, 1.3 mg for men
Niacin	13 mg for women, 17 mg for men
Vitamin B_6	1.2 mg for women, 1.4 mg for men
Vitamin B_{12}	1.5 mg
Folate	200 mcg (400 mcg for first trimester of pregnancy)
Vitamin C	40 mg
Vitamin E	no recommendation in the UK; the EC RDA is 10 mg, which has been used in all recipe analyses in this book
Calcium	700 mg
Chloride	2500 mg
Copper	1.2 mg
Iodine	140 mcg
Iron	14.8 mg for women, 8.7 mg for men
Magnesium	270–300 mg
Phosphorus	550 mg
Potassium	3500 mg
Selenium	60 mcg for women, 75 mcg for men
Sodium	1600 mg
Zinc	7 mg for women, 9.5 mg for men

Vitamins These are organic compounds that are essential for good health. Although they are required in only small amounts, each one has specific vital functions to perform. Most vitamins cannot be made by the human body, and therefore must be obtained from the diet. The body is capable of storing some vitamins (A, D, E, K and B_{12}), but the rest need to be provided by the diet on a regular basis. A well-balanced diet, containing a wide variety of different foods, is the best way to ensure that you get all the vitamins you need.

Vitamins can be divided into 2 groups: *water-soluble* (B complex and C) and *fat-soluble* (A, D, E and K). Water-soluble vitamins are easily destroyed during processing, storage, and the preparation and cooking of food. The fat-soluble vitamins are less vulnerable to losses during cooking and processing.

• ***Vitamin A*** (retinol) is essential for healthy vision, eyes, skin and growth. Good sources include dairy products, offal (especially liver), eggs and oily fish. Vitamin A can also be obtained from *beta-carotene*, the pigment found in highly coloured fruit and vegetables. In addition to acting as a source of vitamin A, beta-carotene has an important role to play as an antioxidant in its own right.

• ***The B Complex vitamins*** have very similar roles to play in nutrition, and many of them occur together in the same foods.

Vitamin B_1 (thiamin) is essential in the release of energy from carbohydrates. Good sources include milk, offal, meat (especially pork), wholegrain and fortified breakfast cereals, nuts and pulses, yeast extract and wheat germ. White flour and bread are fortified with B_1 in the UK.

Vitamin B_2 (riboflavin) is vital for growth, healthy skin and eyes, and the release of energy from food. Good sources include milk, meat, offal, eggs, cheese, fortified breakfast cereals, yeast extract and green leafy vegetables.

Niacin (nicotinic acid), sometimes called vitamin B_3, plays an important role in the release of energy within the cells. Unlike the other B vitamins it can be made by the body from the essential amino acid tryptophan. Good sources include meat, offal, fish, fortified breakfast cereals and pulses. White flour and bread are fortified with niacin in the UK.

Pantothenic acid, sometimes called vitamin B_5, is involved in a number of metabolic reactions, including energy production. This vitamin is present in most foods; notable exceptions are fat, oil and sugar. Good sources include liver, kidneys, yeast, egg yolks, fish roe, wheat germ, nuts, pulses and fresh vegetables.

Vitamin B_6 (pyridoxine) helps the body to utilise protein and contributes to the formation of haemoglobin for red blood cells. B_6 is found in a wide range of foods including meat, liver, fish, eggs, wholegrain cereals, some vegetables, pulses, brown rice, nuts and yeast extract.

Vitamin B_{12} (cyanocobalamin) is vital for growth, the formation of red blood cells and maintenance of a healthy nervous system. B_{12} is unique in that it is principally found in foods of animal origin. Vegetarians who eat dairy products will get enough, but vegans need to ensure they include food fortified with B_{12} in their diet. Good sources of B_{12} include liver, kidneys, oily fish, meat, cheese, eggs and milk.

Folate (folic acid) is involved in the manufacture of amino acids and in the production of red blood cells. Recent research suggests that folate may also help to protect against heart disease. Good sources of folate are green leafy vegetables, liver, pulses, eggs, wholegrain cereal products and fortified breakfast cereals, brewers' yeast, wheatgerm, nuts and fruit, especially grapefruit and oranges.

Biotin is needed for various metabolic reactions and the release of energy from foods. Good sources include liver, oily fish, brewers' yeast, kidneys, egg yolks and brown rice.

• ***Vitamin C*** (ascorbic acid) is essential for growth and vital for the formation of collagen (a protein needed for healthy bones, teeth, gums, blood capillaries and all connective tissue). It plays an important role in the healing of wounds and fractures, and acts as a powerful antioxidant. Vitamin C is found mainly in fruit and vegetables.

• ***Vitamin D*** (cholecalciferol) is essential for growth and the absorption of calcium, and thus for the formation of healthy bones. It is also involved in maintaining a healthy nervous system. The amount of vitamin D occurring naturally in foods is small, and it is found in very few foods – good sources are oily fish (and fish liver oil supplements), eggs and liver, as well as breakfast cereals, margarine and full-fat milk that are fortified with vitamin D. Most vitamin D, however, does not come from the diet but is made by the body when the skin is exposed to sunlight.

• ***Vitamin E*** is not one vitamin, but a number of related compounds called tocopherols that function as antioxidants. Good sources of vitamin E are vegetable oils, polyunsaturated margarines, wheatgerm, sunflower seeds, nuts, oily fish, eggs, wholegrain cereals, avocados and spinach.

• ***Vitamin K*** is essential for the production of several proteins, including prothombin which is involved in the clotting of blood. It has been found to exist in 3 forms, one of which is obtained from food while the other 2 are made by the bacteria in the intestine. Vitamin K_1, which is the form found in food, is present in broccoli, cabbage, spinach, milk, margarine, vegetable oils, particularly soya oil, cereals, liver, alfalfa and kelp.

Nutritional analyses

The nutritional analysis of each recipe has been carried out using data from *The Composition of Foods* with additional data from food manufacturers where appropriate. Because the level and availability of different nutrients can vary, depending on factors like growing conditions and breed of animal, the figures are intended as an approximate guide only.

The analyses include vitamins A, B_1, B_2, B_6, B_{12}, niacin, folate, C, D and E, and the minerals calcium, copper, iron, potassium, selenium and zinc. Other vitamins and minerals are not included, as deficiencies are rare. Optional ingredients and optional serving suggestions have not been included in the calculations.

Index

Titles in italics are for recipes in 'Some more ideas'.

Printing and binding: Tien Wah Press Limited, Singapore
Separations: Colour Systems Ltd, London
Paper: StoraEnso

Book code: 400-196-01
ISBN: 0 276 42802 1
Oracle Code: 250008438S

Family History comes to LIFE

Foreword

Just as societies which lack knowledge of their past are disadvantaged in the pursuit of understandings of their present, so too do human beings who are unaware of their origins have a diminished consciousness of who they are in the world they inhabit.

The quest for our origins in distant times and places has a perennial fascination. Without knowledge of these, we may not know whence we came. Nor may we properly understand history which, reduced to its most essential element, is the study of process — of change through time. I have the most vivid memory of how, thirty years ago and travelling in Europe for the first time, I climbed the dusty hill to the Acropolis in Athens, and among its ruins knew that I was at the wellspring of Western culture and the Western imagination, without either of which I should not be as I am, no matter how much time out of mind, how many generations, how vast a geographical distance and how much technological change lay between me, a young person from an emergent society on the edge of the Pacific Ocean, and the ancient Greeks.

Family history is an important component of this quest for roots in other times, other places. I have an equally vivid memory of how, a few weeks earlier on that trip, I had wandered the grounds of Nurney House, County Kildare, Ireland, and seen where my maternal forebears had lived in the 18th and 19th centuries, until declining circumstances compelled one to make the long voyage out to the Australian colonies, where in the second half of the 19th century he eked out a precarious living as a prospector, storekeeper and 'remittance man' in the wilds of tropical North Queensland.

In some large part, the person I was had emerged from conjunctions of these geographical and historical spaces: I sensed this essential truth then, and have pursued the conjunctions ever since, tracing the history of my mother's

family in greater detail, seeing the attendant family sites in Northumberland, travelling more about the world, informing myself of the pasts of Australia and Europe. At one point, I wrote the life of Admiral Arthur Phillip, the founding governor of the British colony in New South Wales. Some of the research for this biography gave me a very good understanding of the problems in tracing family relationships when many of the details are either missing, or tenuous at best, or the consequence of rumour.

Those pursuing family history usually encounter many twists and turns, sometimes blind alleys and, frequently, misinformation. It is important to be alert to difficult terrains and pitfalls. Otherwise, the results are false; and false results are not worth the having. Peter Cuffley has written a most valuable handbook for those wishing to know their family's history truly.

In a series of logically arranged chapters, he advises about the necessary computer capabilities and software programs. He indicates the major sources of information, many of which are now available on CD-ROM and, increasingly, at web sites on the Internet. He describes, first, the beginning steps and then, the more advanced ones in the intricate processes of accessing, recording, writing up and publishing this data. And he discusses the preservation and use of visual materials such as maps, miniatures and photographs. Much of the work is concerned with sources relevant to Australians of Anglo-Celtic backgrounds, but there is also a most valuable summary of those relevant to other major ethnic groups.

Peter Cuffley writes clearly and well. The basic content of the chapters is always informative and up-to-date. He enlivens this basic content with neat, sometimes intriguing, examples from his own quests; and he has illustrated this work extensively and appropriately.

Altogether, this is a most valuable handbook for those who wish to trace, record and publicise the history of their family. Beginners at this fascinating quest will find it most useful, but it also has good pointers for more advanced students.

I should have benefited much for having this work when I was researching the life of Governor Phillip. Hopefully, it will show you how to proceed, and how to avoid errors in your own quests.

I commend it enthusiastically to you.

Professor Alan Frost
Department of History
La Trobe University, Victoria

The church and churchyard at Lutterworth, Leicestershire, a late 19th-century engraving. Researching the homeplaces of your ancestors, and collecting relevant images, is one of the most pleasurable aspects of working on a family history.
Source: Collection, Peter Cuffley

Contents

Introduction

We live in an exciting era when it comes to exploring family history. Resources are improving year by year and there is now a serendipitous alliance between the world of computers and the ancient art of record-keeping. Technology is also providing new and often inexpensive ways to restore old images such as precious family photographs.

Genealogy and family history rank with popular pastimes such as gardening and household crafts. The purpose of this book is to show you how family history can become more accessible for people of all ages. Instead of being tucked away in a drawer or cupboard, rarely seen and mostly forgotten, there is a positive way of creating more immediate reminders of where we have come from. Well presented pictures in attractive frames, whole galleries of family faces, visions of old homeplaces and treasured heirlooms, these help bring our heritage to life. Books, albums, videos and compact discs can all be produced to a high standard and shared with family and friends or with the wider community.

Searching out ancestors or relatives, as well as ancestral places, can be a wonderful voyage of discovery. It involves not only the use of standard resources and methods but also, at times, real detective work and more than a modicum of lateral thinking. Your explorations will unearth the full range of human experiences. Transcendental moments, simple joys, heart-wrenching sadness, stories of triumph and loss, prosperity and hardship. The best moments are when the past reaches out to touch you in a very special way. A powerful feeling of connection can be suddenly manifested. When a letter or a diary turns up, the words breathe life into any gathering of plain facts. Another dimension is to find relatives, family friends or others who can offer their own insights and a different perspective. Travelling to places which have

This photograph from a family album shows two brothers, Walter Story Young (1892–1944) and Frederick Albert Young (1890–1970), dressed up in their best sailor suits. They were the sons of John and Mary Young (née Story) of Sedgwick, Victoria.
Source: Courtesy Gwen Shaw

significance in the family story can bring both rewards and disappointments. Ideally it will engender a sense of place and a deep-felt spiritual belonging.

A desire to reach back into history and pride in one's forebears has been a primary motivation for generations of family historians. In the 19th and early 20th centuries there was also a widespread belief that somewhere a lost family fortune was waiting to be found. Before large-scale lotteries, it was the one great hope of instant wealth and therefore security. An industry grew up with agents, lawyers and professional searchers often growing fat on claims which would never realise a penny for the folk who paid out their hard-earned money. Charles Dickens had offered a warning of chasing money held in chancery in Bleak House, first published in serial form in 18534, but many ignored the moral of the tale. Apart from the few who were able to make a successful claim, the most positive outcome was the spotlight focussed on family trees and collections of records. Surviving correspondence and papers relating to family connections often owe their existence to family fortune hunting. If the facts are accurate, they can be of great value or there might at least be some useful clues. The danger for us is that details were sometimes altered if there was a need to make spurious connections.

Understanding that human nature has not changed dramatically over time allows the modern family historian a more realistic view of people in earlier times. Add to that a knowledge of the social and economic conditions and lives can be seen in a meaningful context. A perfect example of this is the publication of well-researched studies of the thousands of convicts who were transported to the Australian colonies. Convict ancestry, once something to

hide, is now happily proclaimed. While every story is different, we now know that a large percentage of those convicted made good when offered new opportunities. Copies of old documents such as a Ticket of Leave or a Conditional Pardon are now proudly displayed and make interesting conversation pieces. New settlers in Australia since the First Fleet in 1788, have come for myriad reasons under all sorts of conditions. These journeys become part of history and have great significance to those who undertake them and to all succeeding generations.

Bringing family history to life is not only about celebrating old stories and images as well as treasuring heirlooms; it is also about creating such things for future generations. Some would say that an object only becomes an heirloom when it has been passed from generation to generation and, strictly, that is true. However, we can consciously set out to fashion things which we hope will be cherished for a long, long time. Needlework is a notable field where pieces can immediately take on heirloom status. A typical example is the making of beautiful quilts which record events. Remember, history is about our yesterdays and today will very soon be history.

An oval shape was chosen for many portrait photographs in the second half of the 19th century and early decades of the 20th century. Here we have Jane Alice 'Allie' Semmens who lived from 14 September 1896 to 13 June 1995. In 1920 she married Walter Story Young of Sedgwick, Victoria.

Source: Courtesy Gwen Shaw

Chapter One
FAMILY HISTORY ADVENTURES

FACT AND FICTION

Family lore can be an important resource for historians. Tales handed down, a few key words, a useful date, even the subtle nuances of beliefs and attitudes; these are all worthy of our attention. Alongside them we need to place the ability to sort out the elaborations, distortions and fanciful creations which, in time, can become part of family traditions.

Word of mouth is the ancient means of passing on facts and folklore; later came the picture and the written or printed word. In the 19th century, the invention of photography allowed us to capture images. Family photographs were soon a familiar part of household life. In the 20th century, moving pictures were increasingly available as a means of recording people and places. Video cameras continue to evolve and are now so accessible and easy to use that family events are as likely to be captured with sound and movement as they are in still photographs.

It is fascinating to learn about the occupations of our ancestors. This is a bird-catcher in London in the 19th century.
Source: Collection, Peter Cuffley

Generally speaking, recent history is well recorded. Reliable records become scarcer as we move back through the centuries. In some places, relatively modern records have, for various reasons, been poorly kept or have been lost. Flood, fire, war and social unrest are just a few of the causes, and let's not forget neglect or over-zealous housekeeping. People may have long resented the intrusions of bureaucracy, but family historians are ever grateful to those who carefully compiled official records such as census returns or really informative entries for births, deaths and marriages.

My grandmother came to live with us at the end of her life. Thankfully I was inspired to ask her questions about the family and also to identify some of the people in old photographs. I was a teenager then and over the decades

British migrants line the decks of the SS Borda *as it leaves Tilbury docks for Australia on 14 January 1921. The face in the circle is Henry Standen who was accompanied by his wife Florence (née Steadman), twin sons Fred and Harry, daughter Freda and his sister Amy. Henry had initially wanted to migrate to Rhodesia but settled on Australia after being offered a job in Sydney.*
Source: Courtesy Tim Freer, great grandson

since her death I have thoroughly researched the stories. She spoke of three Cuffley brothers who were said to have had a brewery in Surrey, England. Later I found that the brewery had been in the Melbourne suburb of Fitzroy and that only two brothers were involved. The third had died of yellow fever in Rio de Janeiro long before the enterprise was established. Surrey turned out to be an important county in the family story and, over time, some fascinating records have turned up. This illustrates the importance of collecting all the family tales, even if you later find that the facts have been somewhat distorted or rearranged.

Family history is a captivating pursuit for many people, while for others it can be an area of painful memories or even a complete lack of information. Taking an interest in a family or families which are not part of your own story can also be very rewarding. To choose a person or family of particular interest, but not yet researched, offers the possibility of an intriguing journey. Local history groups are always seeking to add new material to their collections.

Celebrating Convict Ancestry

Through learning about people's lives, particularly in past eras, we can begin to learn about ourselves and even what the future may hold. Generally the fear of finding family 'skeletons' has been modified by a greater understanding of human nature and the forces acting upon each individual. For

many Australians there is the challenge of coming to terms with convict ancestry. In the late 19th century, it was a subject for novels and a degree of popular curiosity, but older family members preferred it be forgotten and younger ones were told stories carefully refashioned to avoid the truth. Many former convicts were still alive in the early 20th century and it is interesting to read the obituaries of this period which were sometimes a blend of fact and fiction. It is perfectly understandable that the new existence grown out of fresh opportunities would be the story to celebrate.

A frigate of the type seen in the convict era. They were armed ships of war but not as large as a ship of the line.
Source: Collection, Peter Cuffley

Researching the life of my maternal great great grandfather, Thomas Sweeney, in the 1960s, I found a wall of resistance suddenly erected when I proposed to older cousins that he was very likely a convict. Thomas and Margaret Sweeney were respected pioneer settlers of Eltham, Victoria, having purchased 110 acres in 1842. Three and a half decades of research have revealed a remarkable story and I now feel I know Thomas Sweeney very well.

Margaret remains a shadowy figure because she wasn't a convict or active in business or community affairs. As a traditional wife and mother she was the homemaker who would have toiled alongside her husband to create a secure family place.

They had married in Sydney in March 1838 and by September were living in Melbourne, a very new village of huts, tents and an increasing number of more substantial buildings. It was a place of endless, oozing mud in the winter and choking dust in the summer. Family tradition says that Patrick, the first child of Thomas and Margaret Sweeney, was born in Flinders Street. We do know from the registers of St Francis Church that he was born on 6 December 1838 and baptised on Sunday, 26 May 1839. Father Geoghegan, the first Catholic priest in the settlement, caught up on the backlog of unbaptised children on that second Sunday after his arrival.[1]

To draw a clearer picture of the unfolding life of Thomas Sweeney I have constructed a timeline listing all the records found up to the present date. It begins in Tipperary in 1803, the year of his birth, and follows through to his death at Culla Hill, Eltham, in September 1867. A linear or sequential record of all the known facts is an ideal ready-reference and also shows up any major gaps or conflicting dates. A livelier narrative can then be created by interweaving further details, background information and notable events into the framework.

When Thomas was captured at Cullahill in the Parish of Bourney, County Tipperary on Sunday, 2 March 1823 'about midnight', he was with a band of 'Whiteboys' or 'Rockites'. These rural guerrilla groups were engaged in a struggle against the payment of tithes by poor farmers and also struck at certain landlords or their agents. Michael Connors who styled himself 'Captain Rock' and was the leader, was captured with Thomas Sweeney, and within a month they had been tried at Clonmel and were on their way to the prison hulk *Surprise* in Cork Harbour. They were transported to Sydney on the convict ship *Isabella* (3) and survived an outbreak of fever as well as the plottings of a group of desperadoes who were looking to stage a mutiny.

Thomas was well behaved and was fortunate in being assigned to a good master. Between 1823 and 1831 he learned all he could about survival in the

ABSOLUTE PARDON.

No. 44/9

HIS Excellency Sir George Gipps Knight *Captain General, Governor and Commander-in-Chief in and over Her Majesty's Territory of New South Wales and its Dependencies, and Vice-Admiral of the same, &c. &c. &c.*

To all Her Majesty's Officers aud Ministers of Justice within the Territory of New South Wales and its Dependencies for the time-being, and to all other Her Majesty's Subjects whom these Presents may Concern;

GREETING:—

WHEREAS Michael Connor late of Tipperary (a description of whose Person is on the back hereof for the greater certainty written,) was Tried and Convicted of at the Assizes holden at Tipperary on the Day of in the Year of Our Lord One thousand eight hundred and twenty three and he the said Michael Connor for his said Offence was adjudged or ordered to be Transported to the said Territory of New South Wales for the Time or Term of his Natural Life: AND WHEREAS the said Michael Connor was for said Offence duly Conveyed and Transported from Tipperary to, and arrived in the said Territory of New South Wales by the Ship Isabella [illegible] Master, in the Year of Our Lord One thousand eight hundred and twenty three AND WHEREAS in consideration of the good Conduct of the said Michael Connor since his arrival in the said Territory of New South Wales, I, the said Sir George Gipps have thought fit to extend the Royal Mercy to him the said Michael Connor and to REMIT the whole of the Remainder of the Time or Term for which he the said Michael Connor hath been so Transported as aforesaid; NOW THEREFORE KNOW YE, That I, the said Sir George Gipps in virtue and exercise of the power and authority in me, the GOVERNOR of the said Territory of New South Wales as aforesaid, vested by the Commission of his late Majesty King GEORGE THE THIRD, duly made and granted under the Great Seal of Great Britain, in pursuance of the Act of Parliament in such case made and provided, and bearing date at Westminster in the Thirty-first Year of the Reign of His said late Majesty, do hereby ABOLUTELY REMIT the whole of the Time or Term yet to come and unexpired of the Time or Term for which he the said Michael Connor was adjudged, or ordered to be, and hath been Conveyed and Transported to the said Territory of New South Wales as aforesaid; PROVIDED ALWAYS, however, and this Instrument of Remission is made and granted upon the following Condition, that is to say, That the said Michael Connor do and shall Quit the Colony of New South Wales and its Dependencies at any Time when he shall be required by the GOVERNOR so to do: And if the said Michael Connor shall fail well and truly to keep and perform the said Condition, then this Instrument shall be void and of no effect, and the said Michael Connor shall be exposed to all the Penalties of the Original Sentence.

GIVEN under my Hand and the Seal of the Government of the said Territory of New South Wales, Sydney, this first *Day of* May *in the* Sixth *Year of the Reign of Her Majesty* ~~King~~ Queen Victoria *and in the Year of Our Lord One thousand eight hundred and* ~~thirty~~ forty three

(signed) Geo Gipps

colonies and on gaining his Ticket of Leave, he set about becoming a coastal trader. He was soon dealing with the great Sydney merchants and some of the best-known settlers in the Illawarra region. By 1833 he owned a half share in a small vessel called *Sarah*, he had purchased one hundred acres of land, and fifty head of cattle, and he was building a craft of some forty tons. He had also married his first wife Bridget Coleman, a young free settler, and stated in a petition for an early pardon to Governor Bourke that he had no desire to return to his native land. In fact, he had been sentenced to transportation for life so even if he wanted to he couldn't have returned to Ireland.[2]

If the documents I found helped capture the scenes and progress of Thomas' life, it was the maps and illustrations which added real depth to the story. Finding sketches and paintings of Illawarra and Sydney in the 1820s and 1830s and plotting the significant places on maps gave his life story a new dimension. Having absorbed these images, my next move was to experience the settings as they are today. Much has changed, but standing on the sand at Brighton Beach, Wollongong, still a modest harbour filled with small boats, evening shadows and the soft swish of the waves, there really was a sense of times past. A visit to Marshall Mount, the historic property built by Henry Osborne, brought scenes of rolling pastures, towering cabbage palms, remnant rainforest and the great escarpment which dominates the Illawarra

FAR LEFT: *On Sunday, 2 March 1823 'about midnight', Michael Connors alias 'Captain Rock' led an attack on a house at Cullahill in the Parish of Bourney in County Tipperary. The police had been alerted and so Connors was captured along with a younger protégé Thomas Sweeney. At the Clonmel Spring Assizes, both were sentenced to hang under the Whiteboy Act. This was commuted to transportation for life, though for some reason Michael Connors was given an Absolute Pardon in 1843.*
Source: State Records of New South Wales

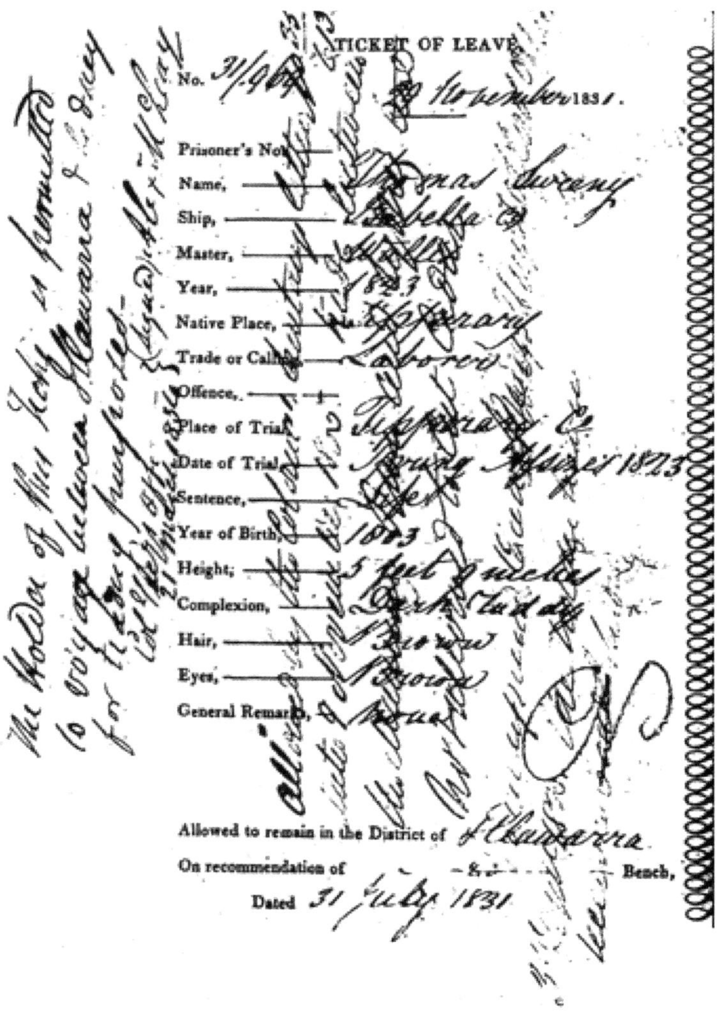
TICKET OF LEAVE.
No. 31/964 November 1831.
Prisoner's No.
Name, Thomas Sweeny
Ship, Isabella
Master,
Year, 1823
Native Place, Tipperary
Trade or Calling, Laborer
Offence,
Place of Trial, Tipperary Co.
Date of Trial, Spring Assizes 1823
Sentence, Life
Year of Birth, 1803
Height, 5 feet 9 inches
Complexion, Dark Ruddy
Hair, Brown
Eyes, Brown
General Remarks, None
Allowed to remain in the District of Illawarra.
On recommendation of — & — Bench,
Dated 31 July 1831.

LEFT: *This Ticket of Leave butt is filled with information relating to Irish convict Thomas Sweeny (Sweeney). In July 1831, it permitted him the freedom of the Illawarra district south of Sydney. By March 1834 he was allowed to voyage as a coastal trader between Illawarra and Sydney.*
Source: State Records of New South Wales

Ten to twenty-ton cutters of this type were used as coastal trading vessels throughout the Australian colonies.
Source: Collection, Peter Cuffley

landscape. Thomas Sweeney carried goods to and from Sydney for Osborne, a man of great enterprise who was exceedingly rich when he died in 1859. In a reference to the petition for early pardon, he writes of Sweeney's most excellent character and notes that he is 'an Industrious and Honest Fellow.'[3]

On entering Sydney Harbour, Thomas would sail into Darling Harbour and tie up at the Market Wharf. He leased a property in Kent Street to use as a warehouse and in June 1834 raised £50 by assigning it to Isaac Simmonds, a well-known merchant.[4] While Darling Harbour (previously called Cockle Bay) has totally changed, some of the feeling of early Sydney and its maritime history survives in The Rocks and the flash of sails on the glittering water. Sweeney descendants are now scattered throughout Australia and New Zealand with Culla Hill at Eltham, Victoria, the main place of pilgrimage. Thomas and Margaret's old house sits snug on its hillside above the Yarra River and, with its wonderful barn of stone and brick, has gained enough significance to be on the Register of the National Estate. The road is as yet unmade and lined with old gums; paddocks sweep down to the river flats which once grew potatoes to be carried to the goldfields. A new subdivision will increase the reliance on memories and old photographs, but thankfully much of the essence remains.

Finding Long-lost Relatives

Family history journeys can involve all sorts of people and places from the very recent past to times now centuries removed. They can also have a spiritual dimension or be part of a healing process. My wife's paternal grandmother died of tuberculosis in 1926 at the age of 27. We knew little of her except that she played the piano and had long, delicate hands and a beautiful complexion.

Early in our search we found she had borne seven children with only two surviving beyond infancy. Her eldest son, Barbara's father, had died at 48 leaving only those few memories of his mother which he had shared with his family. He was a quiet man who seemed to carry a deep sadness. We knew why when the records began to reveal a tragic tale. When his mother died he was handed over to relatives and his baby brother went to a different family and was given a new surname.

Gradually some parts of the story were reconstructed, yet there was obviously so much more that was missing. How to find Lily Carlisle Williamson's childhood home became an important question. She and her siblings had their births registered at Colac in Victoria's Western District, so we looked up a 1911 Post Office Directory and suddenly all was revealed. There was an entry for Charles Williamson, selector, Carlisle River. The country towns section of the Post Office Directory informed us that Carlisle River was in the Colac area and as we knew Lily's father was Charles it fitted perfectly. As soon as a chance came up we headed for Colac and then with the aid of a map wended our way to the relatively isolated settlement called Carlisle River.

Surrounded by forest on all sides, we found it to be a small farming

community situated at the confluence of two rivers and nestled into the Otway Ranges. At the second door we knocked on we found some very kind people who could tell us much of the history of the area. After ringing ahead, they sent us off to visit another family in Colac who would be able to help us with more information. Welcoming cups of tea, a beautiful cottage garden and a generous sharing of stories were the order of the day. Many photographs were produced, but best of all, a copy of the souvenir booklet, 'Back-to-Carlisle River 1967' was presented to us by the author herself. Inside the booklet a school photograph, taken about 1909, showed us the face of Lily Carlisle Williamson for the first time.

Our next breakthrough came in a conversation with someone called Williamson on a Puffing Billy trip in the Dandenong Ranges. He was from Colac and while there was no connection with the Carlisle River Williamsons, he did promise to make enquiries for us. In a short while he contacted us with the news that Lach and Fran Gardiner of Colac, who were retired Carlisle River farmers, actually had a photograph of Barbara's grandmother standing on the bridge at Carlisle River (see below). After a number of telephone

Lily Carlisle Williamson is the taller of the two sisters on the bridge at Carlisle River in Victoria's Otway Ranges. The photograph was taken by Charles Silk, a local farmer and keen amateur photographer.
Source: Courtesy Lach and Fran Gardiner

conversations with the Gardiners it was arranged that we should visit them. What a trip that was! Both of them have a lifetime of stories about Carlisle River and the Otways generally. Lach in his younger days worked on the roads as well as on the family farm. He also recalls taking supplies to the Cape Otway lighthouse with a bullock team, collecting them from the narrow gauge railway at Lavers Hill and heading down the steep gradients to the coast then through swampy ground where no motor truck could go.

Lach Gardiner's sister turned up a newspaper cutting about the 1967 Back

What did your forebears do?
Source: Collection, Peter Cuffley

to Carlisle River gathering which included a picture of one of the Williamson girls. Importantly it had her married name, so we were able to follow a trail which led to death notices in the paper in 1984. We knew the youngest sister born in 1915 was named Lenora Albertina Williamson; the great hope was that she would still be alive. The death notices implied that she was the only surviving sister and once again finding her married name in the notice was a vital piece of information. Our search through the newspapers that day at the State Library continued with the current electoral rolls.

Happily, Lenora was still listed when we searched in 1994, ten years after her sister's death. The unusual given names offered certainty that we had the right person and the address was an outer suburb we knew quite well. By this time we were very excited and decided to head for the nearest telephone. Many would hold that a letter is the only acceptable means of first contact. While genealogical etiquette usually favours this approach, the telephone is considered a reasonable option by many people in this age of multiple forms of communication. Perhaps the choice should be based on common sense and instinct.

We decided to telephone after finding a listed number. Barbara's great aunt answered, her surprise turning to absolute joy that 'Lily's family' had finally found her. 'We have tried so hard to find you over the years,' she said, and Barbara by this time could not speak for crying. I took over the phone and it was quickly resolved that she would be more than delighted to have us come for afternoon tea that very day. Within two hours Barbara and her great aunt were at last together and the healing of sixty-seven missing years had begun. The story of the Williamson family really did come to life from that first meeting.

Since then we have absorbed and recorded the first-hand memories, studied and copied the photographs and shared all the information found in our continuing researches. Friends, relations and serendipity have all played a part in finding four more photographs of Lily Carlisle Williamson. One is a postcard with a note on the back written by Lily's mother, Mabel, who was just coming to terms with the death of her own mother. 'I often fancy I see and hear her — she is best off. No doubt you [also] heard how ill poor Lillie [sic] is. She is way up in Mooroopna Hospital. We were called to bid her goodbye a fortnight ago but God was good and spared her. She is improving now — the climate is lovely.'[5]

SOCIAL HISTORY

Placing lives in the broader context of recorded history makes both the lives and the history more interesting. To make sense of the movements of families and individuals or notable changes in their circumstances, we need to be familiar with the forces and events bearing upon them at a local, regional, national or even international level. An ancestor tramping the roads in search of work may be a small story in itself, while the crash on Wall Street in 1929 is of world significance. The fact that the first is related to the second is the essential connection to make.

A humble weatherboard cottage at Toongabbie in Gippsland, Victoria, was home to the Veitch family. The adults from left to right are: David Veitch and his wife Eliza Ann, Eliza's mother Mrs Dyer, Edwin Veitch, Lizzy Boddy, Agnes Veitch (née Pentridge), second wife of Edwin Veitch, Lillian Veitch (née Finn) and husband Robert Veitch. Edwin Veitch and his first wife, Ellen, were at Cochrane's Creek near Moliagul, Victoria, in the early 1860s. Edwin's niece, Violet Veitch, was the mother of famous English entertainer, Noel Coward (1899-1973).

Source: Courtesy Gwen Shaw

Similarly, if your family arrived in Australia as immigrants, there must be a social context. It could have been a simple desire to begin a new life in a time of peace and relative prosperity, or a desperate need to escape famine, social unrest, persecution and war. Some people came with no intention of staying and through various circumstances became part of the ongoing story. This was a common occurrence in the era of the great gold rushes. We must also remember that a significant percentage of the earliest arrivals were convicts, who by and large were unwilling immigrants, although it was not unheard of for people to commit crimes so they would be transported at government expense to a land of opportunity.

If your family story includes a more recent arrival in Australia there is a greater chance that the events which led to the migration will be a strong memory, or at least someone will be found to give a first-hand account. Moving back to the beginning of the 20th century and beyond, the story changes and we increasingly rely on the printed word and the work of photographers and illustrators. Great social upheavals such as the potato famine in Ireland, the highland clearances in Scotland or the pogroms in Russia could be the pivotal elements in a family history and therefore need to be well understood.

It may be known that someone in the family witnessed an important event in history such as the opening of the Liverpool and Manchester Railway in 1830, or the Russian Revolution in 1917. There are Australian families who proudly claim an ancestor who fought at the Eureka Stockade in 1853 and many more who had someone at Gallipoli in 1915. My great grandfather passed on memories of being at Royal Park in Melbourne for the departure of the Burke and Wills Expedition on 20 August 1860. Thousands of people

Published illustrations are a valuable resource in finding an early view of a parish church with family associations. This example is from a series of prints published in the 1820s by Charles Thomas Cracklow. The series title is: Views of all the Churches and Chapelries in the County of Surrey. *Here we see* All Saints, Banstead *before the rebuilding of the south chapel in 1837 and overall restoration in the 1860s.*
Source: Guildhall Library, London

were there and he joined with a straggling group of well-wishers who walked the first few miles with the great cavalcade.

Along with the indigenous population, and an ever-increasing diversity of immigrants since 1788, the Australian nation has an extraordinary mixture of origins. Even within the dominant groups from the British Isles and Europe, there has been much intermarriage so that old tribal, regional, social and religious divisions have been blurred or refashioned. The suspicion and outright hostility of sectarian views has been undone by couples from different backgrounds who fall in love and can't see the sense in keeping up the old barriers in a new country. Settlers taking up land in Australia have sometimes remained in relatively homogenous groups, but most of the new communities were made up of people from a wide range of backgrounds. The need to work together and to help each other in times of difficulty or disaster overcame a lot of the old prejudices.

Family historians in the Old World may find interesting origins in their ancestry such as noble or even royal blood, or dramatic shifts from riches to poverty or vice versa. We may all share in these possibilities as well as the story of migration to a distant land. Sometimes we are described as a new nation and said to have little history compared to the Old World. In fact, we live in an ancient land with a fascinating history. Our heritage from other lands is a rich and complex story which grows with every new arrival. Understanding our past and the people who made us is a great challenge. Hopefully it will also lead to a greater understanding of humanity in general and a better appreciation of multiculturalism.

Local Networks

Family historians are an interesting study in themselves. Genealogy and family history groups or societies are found throughout the country and around the world, and any view of us as being generally old and conservative misses most of the story. Many people do take up this interest in their later years when retirement offers the time, but you only need to look at the Internet to see that every adult age group is represented. Family historians are usually more familiar with new technology than their peers in the general community. Conversations between active researchers may include references to microfiche, microfilms, CD-ROMs, new web sites and the growing range of computer programs for family historians. Many are well travelled and by various means keep a close watch on everything that is happening in the field. Virtually every society or group has people working on research projects or

This graveyard at Cowfold, West Sussex, is interesting for the number of gravestones with Celtic crosses. These are comparatively modern works based on ancient designs. The use of gravestones as we know them dates back to the 17th century and, at first, only affluent families were likely to have them. In the 19th century, churchyards were extended and cemeteries developed to cope with a widening demand for permanent grave sites with memorials or headstones.
Source: Collection, Peter Cuffley [Photograph by Toni Lumsden]

specialised indexing. These may cover local or regional subjects or be part of a wider span of interest. One of the very important activities is the conservation of cemeteries, burial grounds and lonely graves. Transcribing and indexing memorials or gravestones is a vital task as weather, neglect and vandalism all take their toll. Similarly, burial records are conserved, copied and indexed as important records.

State, regional and local libraries throughout Australia have sections devoted to family history and many are continually extending the resources offered. Our nearby Bendigo Library is the headquarters of the North Central Goldfields Regional Library Corporation. We have two very active family history groups who have their own collections in the reference area and the library itself has a growing collection of resources for genealogists, family historians, students and researchers in general. The library has also become a repository for original local records making it an important regional archive. Volunteers from the two family history groups offer help to the general public

No.

KINGDOM OF SCOTLAND,

COUNTY OF DUMFRIES.

PARISH OF GRETNA.

These are to Certify To all whom these presents shall come, that George . Story from the Parish of Aspatree in the County of Cumberland and Ann Briggs . from the Parish of Belforde in the County of Northumberland being now here present, and having declared themselves single persons, were this day Married after the Manner of the Laws of the Church of England, and agreeably to the Laws of Scotland ; as Witness our hands, Allison's Bank Toll-House, this 5th day of May -- 1850

By John Murray { George Story

Witnesses, } Ann Briggs

Thomas Donely

Jane Murray

The Scottish border town of Gretna became a place noted for irregular or clandestine marriages. After 1856, English couples needed to be resident in Scotland for at least three weeks. John Murray was one of the notable 'marriage merchants' and ran a profitable business at Allison's Bank or Starkbridge Toll Bar. Here we see one of his impressive certificates made out for George Story of Aspatree, Cumberland (1821–1868) and Ann Briggs of Belforde, Northumberland (1828–1900). George went to Australia in search of gold and Ann followed in 1857 with their children Mary (1851) and Robert (1853). They eventually took up land at Emu Creek near Bendigo, Victoria.
Source: Courtesy Gwen Shaw

on three days of each week and the library staff are always keen to help. Anyone setting out to explore their family history should seek out the libraries and the organisations which offer the guidance and resources to make a very positive start. Joining one of these societies or groups can bring a whole range of benefits including publications, research services, courses and seminars, guest speakers, and best of all, friendly interaction with family history buffs.

Australia's premier family history organisation is the Society of Australian Genealogists, founded in Sydney in 1932. It now has some 8000 members and the largest non-governmental genealogical reference library in Australia.[6] The society's Australasian collection is at Richmond Villa, 120 Kent Street, Sydney and its overseas collection at Rumsey Hall, 24 Kent Street, Sydney. Between the two libraries there are more than 20000 volumes as well as records in microform and on computer, an extensive card index and some 20 000 manuscripts including family papers, pedigrees, photographs and other documents.

The Genealogical Society of Victoria was founded in 1941 and offers a range of services to its members including a research consultancy. Its comprehensive library holds a large collection of books, journals, microfiche, microfilm,

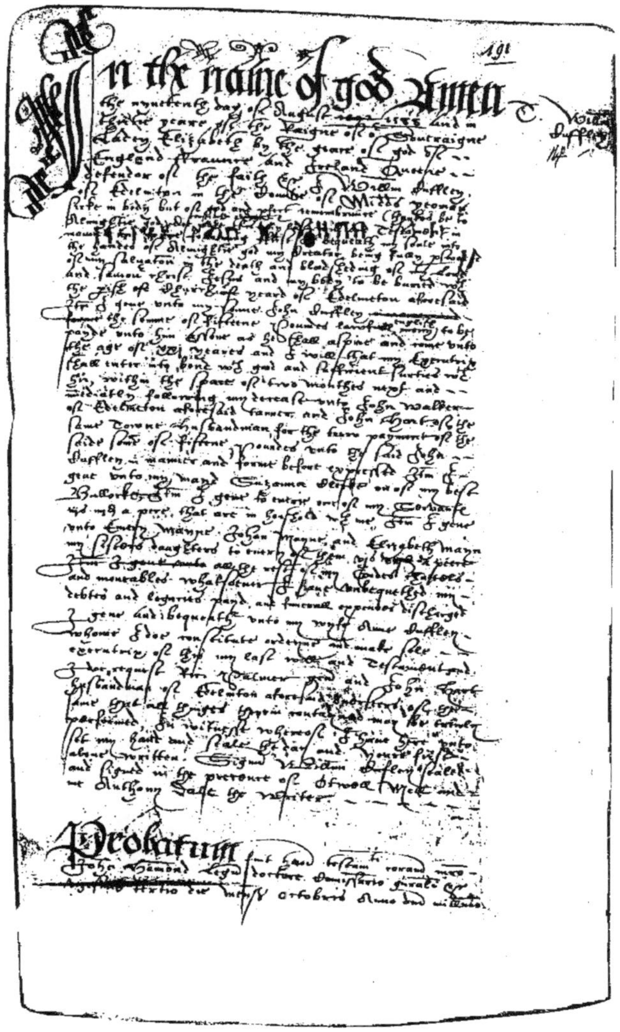
In the name of god Amen

Probatum

This fine example of ornamented penwork dates from 1588 and is the will of William Cufley of Edmonton, Middlesex. Queen Elizabeth was in the thirtieth year of her reign when it was written. Thankfully it is in English and not Latin, and is relatively easy to decipher. The spellings 'Cufley' and 'Cuffley' have both been used over many centuries. At the time this will was made, a single 'f' could well look like a double 'f'.

Source: Guildhall Library, London

CD-ROMs, indexes, convict records, cemetery records and published family histories. A new society called the Australian Institute of Genealogical Studies was founded in Melbourne in 1973. Its stated aim is 'to promote and encourage the study of genealogy, heraldry, family history and allied subjects throughout Australia and to assist members in their research.' Commonly known as the AIGS, this organisation has its headquarters and library in the Melbourne suburb of Blackburn with a number of groups in the metropolitan area and country Victoria. The library has a wide range of research material including an extensive collection of films of the British census and parish registers.

All of the larger societies offer valuable services such as the purchase of sterling cheques and a form of courier service for overseas certificates of birth, death and marriage as well as copies or transcriptions of British wills.

Medical Records

One of the special areas of interest in genealogy and family history is the recording of medical information. Human genetics has become an extremely important area of research in modern times with many controversial aspects.

Cottages, cabbages and the Crofts family, a delightful photograph taken at Wandiligong, Victoria around 1900. At the back from the left we have Frederick James Crofts, Mary Ann Hingston Crofts (née Tickell), William Frederick Crofts and Josephine (Nin) Crofts. In front from the left are Mary Winifred (Win) Crofts, Florence (Florrie) Crofts, Susanna (Susan) Crofts and Mabel Crofts. Sadly, Frederick Crofts died in 1904 at 55 years of age. William Frederick, who is looking so solemn in his top hat, died in 1913 at a mere 28.
Source: Courtesy Lauren Thomson

Inherited genes are the building blocks from which we are constructed and there are many good reasons for keeping track of inherited characteristics and conditions. Now that we have increasing evidence for the genetic component in many common medical conditions, it seems perfectly logical to search back through the generations so that we are at least aware of any predisposition to certain problems.

This is not meant to create yet another source of anxiety in this world of many pressures, but rather to build a positive awareness. After all, prevention is a primary goal of clinical genetics. Medical science has benefited from the mass of work which has already gone into genealogy or family history. If we are fortunate enough to have good civil and other records covering the life and death of our parents, grandparents and great grand-parents, there is a strong possibility that some medical notes, even if only a cause of death, can be recorded for everyone in each generation.

At various times in our life we are more acutely aware of inherited characteristics. Often it is first pressed upon us at school when our stature, colour of hair, eyes and perhaps skin can be remarked upon, become the source of a nickname, or even lead to some form of persecution. We see familiar elements in the faces and general characteristics of brothers and sisters, cousins, aunts and uncles, grandparents and in generations beyond. I have a number of very old portraits as yet not confidently identified, which bear such a likeness to the typical 'family face' of one part of the family that it is almost eerie looking at them.

A charming photograph of a curly-headed, fair- skinned great grandmother always comes to mind when I see so many curly heads and similar complexions at family gatherings. One of the benefits of having an ancestor who is described in official records is the word picture it offers when writing a family history. Best of all are the detailed descriptions given in many convict records. Even scars and tattoos are included in the most informative examples. An interesting argument has arisen out of the various studies of convicts shipped to Australia. Some accounts have taken height statistics and contemporary observations to label the mass of convicts as 'runts'. Recent research based on broad analysis and logical comparisons concludes that, in fact, the convicts were of the same stature as recruits into the British Army and the Marine Society in the early 19th century.[7] We are reminded that average heights were less than they are now with diet and general standards of health much improved.

The Golden Rule

Careful analysis of as much evidence as can be found is a golden rule of family history research as it is for other fields of enquiry. It is good to remember that because something is in print it is not necessarily reliable. Many old histories include speculation, fanciful ideas and absolute fabrications. Generally the newer works given the approval of respected authorities are the ones to rely on, though there are older reference books which have stood the test of time.

We still see highly romanticised accounts of past ages on our television screens and in the theatre so that a study of the real facts usually has a balancing effect. For example, the *Oxford Companion to Local and Family History* points out that the so-called traditional costumes of the highlands of Scotland and Wales, were 'the joint invention of romantics and commercial interests in the early 19th century'.[8] Poor highlanders had worn belted plaids in earlier centuries, but it seems that distinctive tartans related to clans were not worn before the rebellion of 1745. The tartans evolved from the ones developed for highland regiments which were formed from the mid-18th century. King George IV was portrayed wearing a kilt as part of his visit to Edinburgh in 1822 and this encouraged local businesses to invent distinctive tartans for many clans which had not previously possessed them.[9]

A tragic reality in the story of Scotland is that the highlanders were cleared out in great numbers and forced to migrate. In contrast, Scots from the lowlands often emigrated freely and came from a highly urbanised and industrialised society. They mostly had lived ordinary working lives in towns and cities. Migrants in general often come to a softer or more romantic view of the land they left behind. While there is natural beauty and the romance of the old in so many homeplaces, the life led by peasants and poor workers in past times was often just a battle to survive. When we seek to add a lively dimension to our family history it is important to make sure it is well tempered with reality.

Scottish military costume in the 18th century is clearly illustrated in this engraving entitled A Piper from a Highland Regiment. *The original was included in Grose's* Military Antiquities *(1786) and later used in* Irish Minstrels and Musicians *(1913) as part of a chapter on bagpipes.*

Source: Courtesy Saul Roche

Chapter Two

Finding the Essential Facts

Most people researching family history set out to trace one or two lines of particular interest. Some stay on these selected trails; others are soon captivated by the thought of finding origins in all of the possible directions. There are limits to such a broad range of enquiry, for mathematically we have hundreds of ancestors within seven generations. If we count back for twenty generations, the numbers of ancestors would be over two million. This raises the question given that populations were much smaller, say, a thousand years ago — where do we find all those people? The logical conclusion is that we are all more closely related than we realise, even from country to country. In any case, a well-documented family line back to the 17th or 18th centuries should keep most family historians happy, so the exponential increase in ancestors will not present a problem. At seven generations we have 254 ancestors

Taken at Warrnambool, Victoria, in 1926, these are the Pattison children. From left to right, it's Grant, Byron, Dorothy, Jinny and Noel. Five people of this generation would typically have 100–150 descendants by the year 2000.
Source: Collection, Peter Cuffley

counting our parents, grandparents and so on. If we add to that all of the other relatives, it can be quite a figure. Looking at the more recent past and making sense of just how we and our families got to where we are, is a fascinating challenge.

Two factors are important in present day genealogy and family history. First, we now have computers which can store, collate and readily retrieve information, so that researching a number of family lines is not so difficult. Second, for most of us, the limitation of available records will bring us to a halt before too long and so having an interest in a wider range of ancestral lines is more rewarding. It also means that if the search in one direction comes to a standstill while you wait on information or a miraculous breakthrough, you can still be undertaking productive and enjoyable searches in another direction.

Following a family name back through the generations is a time-honoured approach. Because women in Western societies have traditionally taken on their husband's name, this is usually a patriarchal line. If a name on the female side is seen as interesting, then this often becomes the starting point. My daughter asked if I could research her matriarchal line and I was happy to take up the challenge. We had good fortune in records and the use of family names as given names and soon were back seven generations from mother to mother. I was able to find actual dates of birth for all but one generation and the trail led to a very picturesque Scottish village in what was Perthshire and is now Tayside.

The curled forelock was fashionable in the 1860s, but how did William 'Bill' Cuffley achieve that wave in his beard?
Source: Collection, Peter Cuffley

Who Do We Believe?

A well-known genealogist, Janet Reakes, has her audiences chuckling when she reminds them that you can really only rely on the certainty of the maternal line. To feel confident of the reliability of the information given in old documents you need to have additional evidence or at least feel that the parts of the jigsaw fit perfectly. A clear continuity of dates, such as a sequence of births, is reasonable evidence if no conflicting material turns up. Ideally two or more pieces of documentary information will agree, thus establishing a fact beyond reasonable doubt.

One of the real dangers in genealogy and family history research, is taking as gospel those earlier works which have a solid air of authority, but are in reality as fictional as any romantic novel. A notable English genealogist, Horace Round (1854–1928), took on the great books of printed pedigrees in the 1890s, attacking their lack of consistent scholarship and supporting evidence. An earlier historian, Edward Augustus Freeman (1823–92) had attacked those hallowed publications *Burke's Peerage* and *Burke's Landed Gentry* for containing in some parts, 'monstrous fictions'. We all need to be wary of accepting family traditions and stated fact without critical appraisal. There is a great deal of reliable information to be had from the efforts of previous generations who set a high standard in research. All of us owe so much to the keepers of the records, the conservers of documents, the hardworking pioneers who transcribed, indexed and very often published the surviving material.

Construction of Queen Victoria Street in London in the late 1860s provided an unusual panorama. This is the city captured forever in the works of Charles Dickens. In fact, this street construction saw the demolition of Doctors Commons where he had lived for a while in the 1830s. The church of St Andrew by the Wardrobe in the centre of the picture survived a bomb through its roof in World War II. In the mid-19th century, William and Joan Cuffley lived at number 32 St Andrews Hill just three doors up from the building immediately behind the crane.
Source: Guildhall Library, London

Considering the many dangers official and unofficial documents have faced, it is a miracle that so many have survived. Think of the entries in an old parish register written two or three or even four hundred years ago. Apart from natural deterioration through age, they have also survived mishandling, hungry vermin, leaking roofs and creeping damp, not to mention wars and civil disturbances. Government registers of births, deaths and marriages, dating from the present day back to their beginnings in the 19th century, have in some cases, been lucky to survive.

Family history research has progressed in great leaps and bounds for those of us who remember the frustrations of the era before indexes on microfiche and CD-ROM. I can recall in the mid-1960s, thinking how extremely useful it would be to have access to the indexes at the Registrar's office. Now there are microfiche for most needs, and even better, computer indexes which can be searched using the frailest of clues to find lost records. With only the names of parents, family trees can rapidly be assembled, before the work of checking and further documenting each group.

Old Methods and New Technology

If you are at the very beginning of your great adventure, or at any stage along the way, things can only get better from here on as far as the availability of information is concerned. Computers have given us the information explosion, but thankfully they have also given us the means to handle large quantities of research and family records. Not that people who work without a computer should feel left out. Computers are already helping you even if you are not aware of it, and you can get along quite nicely with good old pen

and paper if that is the choice or the only option. While I have thousands of names entered into a family history program on a computer, I still enjoy keeping two kinds of notebook. I have a well-bound, old-fashioned ledger-style volume with good quality paper which I purchased from a stationers decades ago. This contains all sorts of family records in an indexed format. I write in waterproof, fade-proof ink with a hope that it will survive for generations. I am also building a collection of modern binders with plastic pockets where I can keep notes, letters, printouts and copies of documents. It really seems important to have such readily accessible records which are safe from any failures in the power grid or the upsets computers can suffer (see chapter 3 for details on electronic storage).

Technology has given us compact and very portable notebook computers, with the promise of all sorts of advances still to come. Beyond that, a pen and a notebook or folder is the low cost combination for all. If you are using a traditional notebook which you may want to keep for a long time, buy one that is well made and has acid-free paper. The other useful items for the researcher are a tape recorder and camera. A very compact battery-operated tape recorder is ideal for using in interviews or for other records collected verbally. Having a portable photocopier is a boon when the chance arises to copy material which you cannot borrow.

Most people's working lives were far removed from the formality we see in studio portraits.

Source: Courtesy Lach and Fran Gardiner [Photograph: Charles Silk]

Where to Begin

Step-by-step guides to family history research have appeared in many forms over the years. This is still the most useful format for readers who have no previous knowledge of the subject. Hopefully, this chapter also provides many useful ideas for researchers who are already experienced.

Two things should happen at the beginning. First, build up your documentation and then survey all possible sources which might soon be lost. As an example, my great aunt had failing health and was keen to tell us her stories. With her permission a tape recording was made, a wonderful gathering of memories and essential details. That interview was in 1967 and now the transcript is a marvellous insight into a time beyond memory. With additional notes made at various family gatherings, plus all of the newly available facts from the records, there is a rich resource to build a detailed family history. The time to do such things is as soon as possible. How many people express regret about missing an opportunity to talk about the past with someone who would have known so much. Also, people sometimes fail to copy documents and photographs before they are lost in a clean-up or just disappear. Remember, sharing every aspect with other members of the family is not only the right thing to do, it acts as an insurance against future loss.

You may begin with a simple notebook, a set of blank family group sheets or a sophisticated computer program. Standard pro-forma record sheets are an essential item for gathering and compiling genealogical information. You can purchase a book of standard designs to suit the various sorts of records you'll accumulate and all you need to do is to make photocopies as you use them.

Step 1: the very first thing to do

Write down all of the details you have about your immediate family including the significant dates in your own life.

Step 2: assess what is needed and find all available documents

Locate any available documents or photographs and begin the process of assessing their relevance.

Step 3: check to see if anyone else has been working on your family's history

Once you have decided to follow a specific family line with associated connections and branches, you can then establish names and details of parents, grandparents, aunts, uncles, cousins, and so on. Having talked to various family members you may also find that someone else has gathered or is still gathering the same information.

At various stages in your quest you need to check for the existence of family research. The further away from the family circle, the more likelihood of there being a family researcher you were not aware of, who may well be able to save you doubling up on a lot of effort and expense. Magazines and publications such as the *Genealogical Research Directory* will alert you to anyone interested in the same family or perhaps distant connections.

Step 4: gather the essential records needed to start the family search

Apart from any certificates or other documentation you may have in your family, you can now begin the process of locating and acquiring the records which are the building blocks of the family story. If you have ancestors who lived in states and countries with good documentation, you are most fortunate. Others could strike difficulties fairly early in their research.

Certificates of birth, death and marriage from government authorities vary in the amount of information they offer. The process of civil registration, where the government issues official documents for births, deaths and marriages, was introduced in Victoria on 1 July 1853 using a system devised by William Henry Archer who was Victoria's first Registrar-General.[1] He included a broad range of questions which, if fully and correctly answered, are a boon to the genealogist and family historian.

The Archer System was introduced to Scotland where it was used from 1 January 1855, and was also the model for New South Wales registrations which began on 1 March 1856. Other states varied in the content of their certificates. Tasmania had introduced registration on 1 December 1838, a mere seventeen months after it began in England (1 July 1837). Western Australian civil registration began on 9 September 1841, South Australia on 1 July 1842, and Queensland dates from the same time as New South Wales because it was still part of that colony until 1859.

There are a number of important items of information you can hope to find in official records of births, deaths or marriages. In the case of a birth you may want the exact date and place of birth and the names of the parents. The most informative birth certificates will give you details such as the age and place of birth of each parent, the date and place of marriage and, if applicable, the names of previous children. The rank or profession of the father, the signature and address of the person giving the details (the informant) will also be included. If a doctor was present the name will be given along with a nurse or midwife and the name or names of witnesses.

A death certificate will have date and place of death, name and surname, sex, age, occupation and, generally, cause of death. The signature, description and residence of the informant can be a useful detail as it is usually a member of the family. Really informative certificates will give details of a marriage or marriages, the children in order of birth, the length of time in the colony or state, along with the date and place of burial plus the name of the minister and any witnesses.

Certificates of marriage will, at least, give the date and place of the event, the names of the parties, their ages, condition (i.e. bachelor and spinster) their rank or profession, place of residence, name of celebrant and official witnesses. Additional details could include the names and occupations of the respective fathers and, in the best certificates, both parents will be given for each party. One of the frustrations of research is to have questions such as names of parents and place of birth left blank. We can only guess that one or both of the parties were uneasy about their origins or simply were not in possession of the facts. I have two marriage certificates which have been left blank in the spaces allotted for the place of birth of the parties and for the parents' names. In both cases I suspect it was the grooms who were rejecting

Many letters have survived which give a first-hand account of arriving in Australia after a long sea voyage. Here we see Emigrants Landing at the Queen's Wharf, Melbourne, *an engraving from a sketch by Nicholas Chevalier. It was published on page one of the* Illustrated Australian News *of 25 August 1863 and accurately captured a scene which many readers would have found familiar.*

Source: La Trobe Picture Collection, State Library of Victoria

their backgrounds, one because his father was a philanderer and the other to cover a convict record.

Sometimes people gave false information and often they would adjust their age to suit the situation. One of my great grandmothers was thirty-four when she married in 1880. Great grandfather was twenty-four, so he put his age as twenty-six and she opted for twenty-five. Ministers and priests must have had their suspicions at times. I heard another tale about a wedding held at Eltham, Victoria, in 1884. The priest asked the couple their ages. Bridget answered honestly that she was thirty-four. When Mick was asked he said with a twinkle in his Irish eyes, 'Thurrty two.' Guessing that he was somewhat older, the priest said, 'You're all that Mick!' Civil registration was generally treated as a serious matter, for there were warnings of prosecution for those giving false information.

For the genealogist and family historian, acquiring a sought-after certificate can be an exciting time or at least give you a sense of satisfaction in having important questions answered. New horizons are suddenly revealed and the next possible step is at hand. You may for the first time be able to pinpoint the birthplace of a grandparent or great grandparent. The names of their parents will also allow you to search for siblings. Sometimes a piece of information will be quite unexpected and open up an entirely new direction in your research. It is always wise to begin with a belief that we cannot stand in judgement over past lives. Coming to an understanding of the times and situations faced in other eras is an essential ingredient in family history research.

STEP 5: PREPARE SOME CHARTS AND MEANS OF RECORD-KEEPING

One of the most important requirements for keeping track of how you are progressing and the directions to be taken is the setting out of some form of pedigree chart which will readily explain how people are related. Basic information such as dates of births, deaths and marriages, along with relevant locations will give a ready reference. If you are entering information into a computer program, there will be a facility to create various types of print-outs. The alternative is to use a pro-forma chart from a book and fill in the spaces; or draw up your own design. I find an A3 sheet a good size to hold a few generations and with a straight edge and pen you can create a descending chart (see page 23). This type of sheet can be photocopied and with a single fold fits into a plastic pocket to be carried around as a handy reference when you are working on research. A dropline chart from a family history computer program is also useful (see page 45), but for a number of generations you need a few pages. Your research folder should also carry more detailed sheets in the form of family group charts (see example page 47).

Setting out possible relationships in the form of a pedigree chart can be a useful tool, but it is important to mark it as 'speculative chart' or with the warning 'relationships not yet proven'. If it goes wandering or is found in your papers in future times, you don't want it taken as proven fact. You may also be sending it to someone for comment and so you need to make its status clear.

OPPOSITE: *A large number of Australians have ancestors who came in search of gold and stayed on to become part of the community. After growing up in London, William Cuffley (1824–1903) spent seven or eight years on the Victorian goldfields before going into business as a brewer and publican in Melbourne. The letter addressed to him at 'Bleak House, Argyle Gully, McIvor' is a 32-verse poem on the 1856 rush to Spring Creek (Graytown). Source: Collections — Gwen Shaw and Cuffley family [Photograph: Dennis Russell and Peter Cuffley]*

SHIPPING INTELLIGENCE.
HOBSON'S BAY.
CERTIFICATE OF MARRIAGE.
In the Colony of Victoria.
[Original Certificate.]
In Memory of
MRS. JANE CUFFLEY,
Who died 3rd October, 1872,
AGED 79 YEARS.
COLONY OF VICTORIA.
No 55
£1
ADVANCE AUSTRALIA
Miner's Right.
Issued to
under the provisions of the Act of the Governor and Council, 21 Victoria, No. 32, to be in force until
NOT TRANSFERABLE.
Letters of Administration
William Cuffley Esqr
McIvor
RUCTION, CONNECTING THE WORKINGS WITH
RTON TRAMWAY CO.'S LINE.

BROWN & OSBORNE, CASH DRAPERS, 318 & 320 BOURKE S
EIGHTEENTH
SUCCESSFUL CONCERT SEASON.
ON HIS MAJESTY'S SERVICE
Mrs M. G. Smale
Devon Park
Seymour
NEW NUMBERS, 318 & 320
Gloster's Paddock.
Grand Building Allotments
Land to sell colored thus
FORM AND CONDITIONS OF LICENSE UNDER SECTION 19
OF "THE LAND ACT 1869."
Know all Men
Probate
BAND OF HOPE
WALKER'S
LINCOLNSHIRE
Wednesday, 30th May, '88.
AT TWO O'CLOCK, ON THE GROUND.
Great Sale of Choice
BUILDING ALLOTMENTS
Gloster's Paddock, Seymour.
WALLDER, HARTE & WALLD
Section of the Land Act, 1869
Survey Fees.
Mileage.
Total.
GOVERNMENT CONTRACT SURVEYOR.

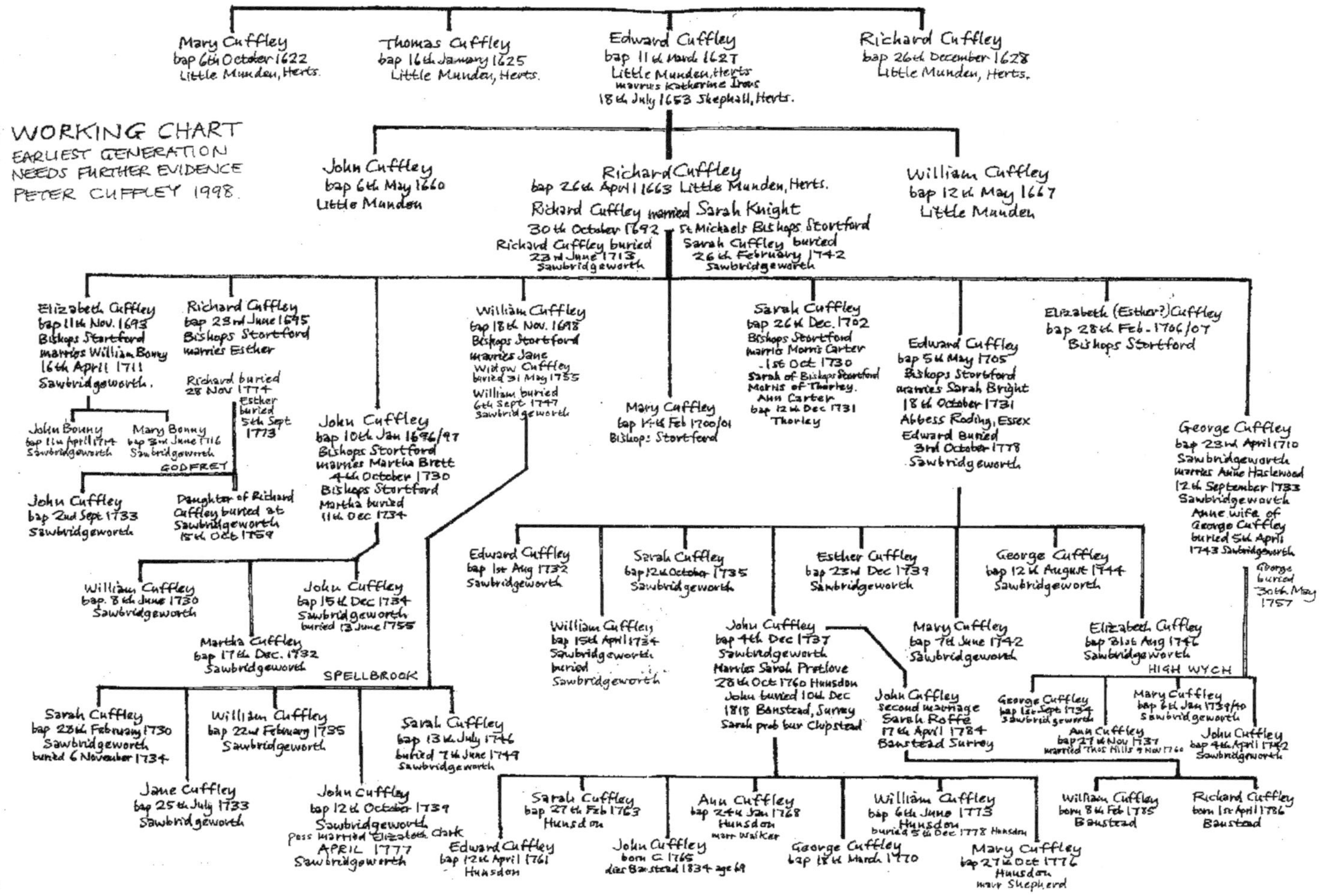

When your research goes back a few generations then you may discover that various family groups or individuals are linked. Building a framework is a good start to your research. You then set to work to find the documentation which either supports the speculative chart or demands it be reworked or scrapped altogether.

For this chart-building stage you need to have familiarised yourself with the standard terms and abbreviations used in genealogy and family history research. The *Family History Research Manager* (see Bibliography) is an ideal resource for pro-formas, glossary and Chapman County Codes for the British Isles. The latter are three-letter standard abbreviations devised by Colin Chapman to denote the counties of Great Britain and the Republic of Ireland. There are many other standard abbreviations for countries, states and cities which help in condensing information. You will find a guide to these in an excellent resource, the *Genealogical Research Directory* (see Bibliography). Because you will write some things many times over while researching, it is more efficient to use standard abbreviations. The core examples are:

D — death
B — birth
bapt — baptised
M — marriage
W — will
c — circa (around this date).

Creating a working chart of the kind seen here offers a clear overview of relationships within five generations of a family. This example was produced on an A3 sheet, but is still readable when reduced to A4.

Source: Peter Cuffley

OPPOSITE: *One of the core areas of documentation in the history of families relates to the acquisition, holding and distribution of land or property. This includes Crown grants, selections, freehold titles, leases, land tax, land sales, subdivisions, conveyances and wills. If documents do not survive in the family's hands, solicitors offices, historical societies, government titles offices and official archives may well be holding interesting material.*

Source: Collection, Peter Cuffley [Photograph: Dennis Russell and Peter Cuffley]

ABOVE AND OPPOSITE: *Carte-de-visite from the 1860s and 1870s. These women look like they are dressed in their finest for a photograph which would have been taken using a glass-plate camera.*
Source: Collection, Peter Cuffley

Marriage is also shown by an equals sign (=) placed between the partners' names. It is also helpful to be able to abbreviate months of the year. Some well-accepted abbreviations are: jan; feb; mar; apr; may; jun; jly; aug; sep; oct; nov; dec.

There are many lists of abbreviations in books and other publications devoted to genealogy and family history. Here are a few of the abbreviations that you're more likely to encounter:

A.B. — able seaman
BDM — Births, deaths and marriage
Co. — County
dau — daughter
d.i.i. — died in infancy
Dist. — District
Div. — division
div. — divorce(d)
d.s.p. — died without issue (*decessits sino prole*)
Govt. — government
inf. — infant
Jnr. — junior
P.P. — parish priest
pr. — proved
PRO — Public Record Office
Prob. — probate
Regt. — regiment
Rev. — Reverend

Beyond the logical methods of recording your findings, it is also essential that you carefully note all of the sources from which you have drawn information. Writing notes on scraps of paper will suffice if circumstances dictate this, but remember such records can soon become confusing or even meaningless if you have not marked them with the relevant source and some identification relating to your own files. If you want to produce a worthwhile family history, it is important to include your sources, preferably in a manner which accords with the standard practice for citation. There is a book published on this subject especially for family historians (see Bibliography).

Step 6: locate the sources to search for relevant records

Census Returns

To begin with, civil registration is the central source, at least back to the mid-19th century. There are also other records of great importance to the family historian. Census returns, where they survive, will help you check the details such as the make-up of the household. The best returns offer the address of the household, full names, marital condition, age, occupation, place of birth and relationship with the head of the household. Unfortunately for those whose ancestors were here in Australia in the 19th and early 20th centuries, very few censuses have survived.

If, however, you trace your family back to England, Wales or Scotland, there are surviving census records from 1841 to the present time. In some cases, a few of the earlier censuses have survived. The years now available to the public are: 1841, 1851, 1861, 1871, 1881, 1891. The British census for 1901 becomes public in 2002. The 1841 census for England and Wales is somewhat limited in the information given but can still be important in what it does record. In this census, the age of

anyone over fifteen had to be rounded down to the nearest five or zero so that thirty-eight became thirty-five and forty-two became forty. The column for occupation is useful but the place of birth column required only a yes/no answer about whether the person was born in the county, and there was a separate column for place of birth in 'Scotland, Ireland or Foreign Parts'.

For many people in Australia, the civil records here lead to a record in England, Wales or Scotland which gives an exact address or at least the name of a town or village. If the date of your record is close to a census date or in the broad period 1840–95, there is a strong chance that you will find a return. The place of birth is recorded in the census from 1851 onwards so the all-important step back to earlier parish records can be made. Sometimes a marriage or death certificate in Australia will give enough information to take the search directly back to a village, town or city in the Old World. That does not mean that you ignore the census records for they offer an insight into families and households not available from any other source except perhaps from a detailed will.

Where the family trail goes back to early colonial times in Australia, the surviving censuses can be of great value. The most comprehensive and best known is the 1828 census of New South Wales. It can be found, along with other published census material, in the libraries of the various genealogical and family history societies as well as most larger public libraries. Best of all, the 1881 census of England, Wales and Scotland is now available on CD-ROM and microfiche. There are also various indexes for the 1851 census, and the counties of Devon, Norfolk and Warwick are on CD-ROM.[2] This puts a large proportion of census information into a readily searchable form.

Many people in the 1851 census records were born before Captain Cook charted the east coast of Australia and a few were more than one hundred years of age. This serves to remind us that a census entry of the mid-19th century can take us back to an earlier family location in the 18th century. My great great grandfather, William Cuffley, was living in St Andrews Hill, London, in 1851. However, the census shows that he was born in Banstead, Surrey, around 1785. In the 1960s, Miss Flowers, a professional searcher in England, looked up the registers of the All Saints Church, Banstead and, sure enough, there was William's baptism dated 6 March 1785. Happily his date of birth was also given (8 February 1785) and, armed with the parents' names and their marriage in 1784, the search continued.

Census records for Ireland before 1901 are something of a patchwork of fascinating pieces. You may be lucky and find a surviving census for a parish which includes your ancestors or relatives. The Irish records have been described as 'diverse and widely scattered', and you'll need to consult a publication such as *Irish Genealogy, A Record Finder* (see Bibliography) for a list of material for each county. In the 19th century when the whole of Ireland was still under British rule, there was a census taken every ten years from 1821. In that oft-mentioned tragedy, the fire at the Four Courts in Dublin in 1922, all but a few volumes for the years 1821, 1831, 1841 and 1851 were destroyed. The returns for 1861 and 1871 had been officially destroyed after the extraction of general information. After that there is a gap until 1901 and this census has survived to become a highly valued resource.

As a partial substitute for the loss of the mid-19th century censuses, you can refer to the Primary Valuation of Ireland, generally known as Griffith's Valuation. It records only each householder and the owners and occupiers of land — there are no personal particulars. Nevertheless, it does offer names, townland addresses, acreages held, whether a garden and outbuildings were included and the estimated net annual value of the holding. Until recently the only way to search this valuable resource was to use the index provided as part of the microfiche of the original records. The quest has been made much easier with the release of the *Index to Griffith's Valuation* on CD-ROM.

Baptismal font at St Andrew's Church, Colebrooke, Devon.
Source: Imperial Dictionary *(1861)*

The Church of Jesus Christ of Latter-Day Saints has some European censuses on microfilm. To find out what is currently available, you need to check their Family History Library Catalogue which is available on microfiche, CD-ROM and on the Internet.

If you're searching for Tasmanian records, you are fortunate because there are musters and census returns dating from 1803–51. Surviving returns, such as those for 1848, usually only have the name of the head of the household, the address, number of occupants along with occupation, status, religion and age. The musters for New South Wales usually included Norfolk Island and 1811 includes Van Diemen's Land. Those for 1800–2, 1805–6, 1811, 1822 and 1837 are all available in book form. To determine the availability of census returns for each state there are a number of useful publications. *Tracing your Family History in Australia* has a complete listing of the records that exist.

Parish Registers

While governments are the major keepers of the essential records, there was a transition from church to state which took place at different rates in different countries. There is also a tendency to forget that church registers continued after civil registration was introduced. Such registers can be an important resource, often giving details such as date of birth which would normally be obtained only by applying for a civil certificate. When it comes to the era before civil registration, it is the church records which cover most aspects of life.

One very useful collection of Scottish registers is often called the Old Parochial Registers. It contains parish records from 1553 to 1855, and you'll find it invaluable if you are searching for baptisms and marriages or, to a lesser extent, deaths.

For indexes of births, deaths and marriages in Australia, the church records provide the early years from the registers of baptisms, burials and marriages. They may not be as informative as civil registrations but they are the essential stepping stones for the journey back through time. Entries from Australian church registers obtained from the Registrar's office in each state may give a date of birth as well as the date of the event in the case of a baptism. In marriage entries, the names of the witnesses can be a useful clue.

Marriage Documentation

Marriage certificates and associated documents can contain fascinating details. If the person was a convict, the words 'with the consent of the

68 *WIMBLEDON PARISH REGISTER.*

1780	Feb.	20	Charlotte d. of Jacob & Sarah Hubbard
	Jan.	23	Robert Godfrey s. of Godfrey & Anne Hattemley
	Feb.	13	William s. of Robert & Elizabeth Wright
	Mar.	5	Mary d. of James & Anne Coote
		12	Nicholas Thomas s. of William & Mary Everatt
		5	William & Edward twin children of Edward & Sarah Cuffley
		19	Thomas s. of Robert & Mary Moseley
		24	Joseph s. of A. & B. Wrey, Strollers & left by them in the workhouse
	April	22	Robert s. of John & Mary Phipps
		6	Eleanor Martha d. of John & Barbara Watney, r. c. 23 April
		23	William s. of Thomas & Mary Berkshire
		12	James s. of James & Anne Yenneck of the Parish of St. Peter's, Cornhill, r. c. June 4
	May	7	Margaret d. of Abraham & Mary Kill

Many English parish registers have been transcribed and published. This sample is from the registers of Wimbledon, Surrey, published in 1924 for the John Evelyn Club for Wimbledon.
Source: Collection, Peter Cuffley

Governor' may appear on the marriage record. A Ticket of Leave holder (a form of probation) may have T.L. after their name. Convicts who applied to marry in New South Wales in the period 1826–51 have been indexed (see Bibliography) enabling researchers to readily find the record on microfilm.

Surviving documentation such as affidavits made by individuals wishing to marry by licence can include important historical details. Many interesting people have an affidavit and certificate relating to a marriage by licence. For instance, Edward Hammond Hargraves applied for one on 26 December 1836, some fourteen years before he would be credited with the discovery of gold near Bathurst, New South Wales. At this time he was under twenty-one years of age and he needed the consent of his father John Edward Hargraves. The affidavit tells us that his wife-to-be was Eliza Mackie, daughter of John Mackie, the master and owner of a number of small trading vessels. Both Edward and Eliza lived in Sydney at this stage but would later become settlers at Wollongong in the Illawarra region.[3]

Family historians have benefited greatly from the Act for the Better Preventing of Clandestine Marriages which came into force on 25 March 1754. Popularly called Lord Hardwicke's Marriage Act it confirmed ecclesiastical law by requiring that all marriages be either preceded by banns or authorised by licence. Only Quakers and Jews were exempted. All other ceremonies had to be performed in Church of England chapels or churches even if the parties belonged to another denomination (see Non-conformists and Others, page 30).

Marriages under the Marriage Act, in contrast to earlier records, had to be registered in a prescribed form. Many earlier marriage entries in parish registers give only the names and the date. From 1754 onwards, witnesses are named and important details, such as the parish each party belonged to, are recorded. You can ascertain whether they were both single (a 'Bachelor' or 'Spinster') or if one or both had previously been married ('Widow' or 'Widower'). A note was also made about whether the marriage was by banns or licence. These details may be found in marriage records before 1754, but after this time they became mandatory responses.

Marriage by banns involved the registration of the intention to marry and the reading of the banns in the parish church on three successive Sundays. In

AFFIDAVIT

To be made separately by both Parties wishing to be married by licence.

This day came before me, one of His Majesty's Justices of the Peace for the Colony of New South Wales Edward Hammond Hargraves of Sydney in the said Colony: Bachelor and voluntarily made Oath, that he is at this present time under twenty-one Years of Age, free, and unmarried; also, that there is no lawful impediment of consanguinity, affinity, dissent of Parents or Guardians concerned, or any other cause whatsoever, to hinder a Marriage between the said Edward Hammond Hargraves, and Eliza Mackie of Sydney in the said Colony: Spinster with whom he is now desirous of proceeding to the solemnization of true and lawful Matrimony, according to the Rites and Ceremonies of the Church of Scotland, one of the Parties being a Presbyterian.

Sworn before me, at Sydney in New South Wales, this 26th day of Decr 1836

H. Semhill J.P. (Signature of Magistrate.)

E H Hargraves (Signature of Party.)

CERTIFICATE

To be added to the above, by the Parent or Guardian, when the Applicant is under twenty-one Years of Age.

I John Edward Hargraves of Sydney in the Colony of New South Wales, Householder do hereby certify that my Son the above-named Edward Hammond Hargraves is under twenty-one Years of Age; that I have given my consent to his Marriage with the above-named Eliza Mackie of Sydney and that to the best of my knowledge and belief, there is at this present time no lawful impediment thereto, by reason of any pre-contract or Marriage, (or suit or controversy touching the same), or of consanguinity, affinity, or any other cause whatsoever.

In testimony whereof, I have hereunto set my hand at Sydney in the said Colony, this 31st day of December in the year of our Lord 1836, in the presence of the two witnesses whose names are likewise hereunto subscribed.

Signed in the presence of us John McGarvie, Jno Mackie Witnesses.

John Edward Hargraves (Signature of Guardian.)

Edward Hammond Hargraves was to become the person credited with the discovery of gold in New South Wales. In 1836, he needed the permission of his father, John Edward Hargraves, before he could marry Eliza Mackie, daughter of coastal trader, John Mackie.
Source: State Records of New South Wales

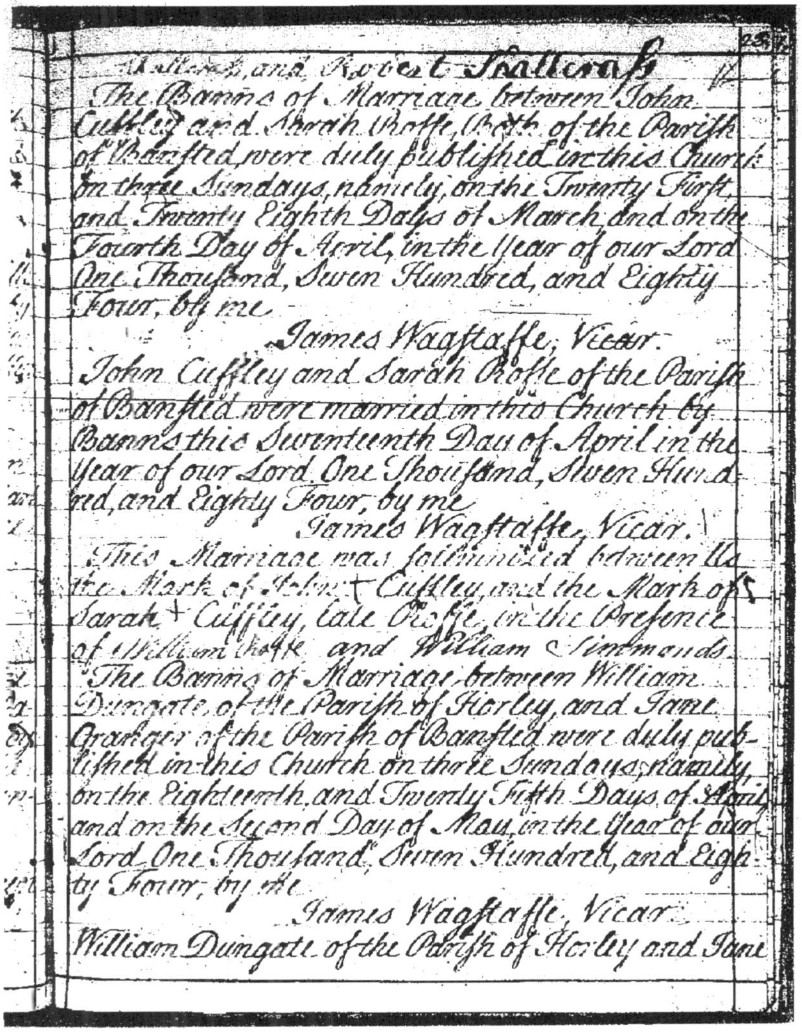
[illegible] and Robert Shallcross

The Banns of Marriage between John Cuffley and Sarah Roffe, Both of the Parish of Bansted, were duly published in this Church on three Sundays, namely, on the Twenty First and Twenty Eighth Days of March and on the Fourth Day of April, in the Year of our Lord One Thousand, Seven Hundred, and Eighty Four, by me

James Wagstaffe, Vicar.

John Cuffley and Sarah Roffe of the Parish of Bansted were married in this Church by Banns this Seventeenth Day of April in the Year of our Lord One Thousand, Seven Hundred, and Eighty Four, by me

James Wagstaffe, Vicar.

This Marriage was solemnized between Us the Mark of John + Cuffley, and the Mark of Sarah + Cuffley, late Roffe, in the Presence of William Roffe and William Simmonds.

The Banns of Marriage between William Dungate, of the Parish of Horley, and Jane [illegible] of the Parish of Bansted were duly published in this Church on three Sundays, namely, on the Eighteenth, and Twenty Fifth Days of April and on the Second Day of May, in the Year of our Lord One Thousand, Seven Hundred, and Eighty Four, by me

James Wagstaffe, Vicar.

William Dungate of the Parish of Horley and Jane

English parish register entries varied greatly, but after 1754 marriage entries should include witnesses, parish of residence for each party and their status such as bachelor and spinster. The register of All Saints Church, Banstead, Surrey, records the marriage of John Cuffley and Sarah Roffe on 17 April 1784, as well as the dates on which the banns were read.
Source: Courtesy Surrey History Centre and All Saints Parish, Banstead

some cases a Banns Register entry survives as well as the one in the Marriage Register. Other examples are found of the banns being included with the record of the marriage. For example, the details of the banns and the marriage of John Cuffley and Sarah Roffe on 17 April 1784 at Banstead, Surrey, take up almost two-thirds of a page in the register.

Marriage by licence was a more expensive option and was therefore generally only available to the more affluent levels of society. Licences were favoured by people who wanted more choice in the time and place of marriage. Some were avoiding the publicity of the reading of the banns; others were in a hurry. While few licences survive, there are registers of allegations, which are the sworn statements made when one of the couple applied at an official registry. There may also be a bond or sworn statement from relatives or friends that the couple were free to marry, that this would take place in a specific church and they were prepared to forfeit a stated sum of money if the partners did not comply with the licence.

Since late in the 19th century indexes to marriages in the British Isles have been a resource of growing importance. Perhaps the best known by an individual is the one compiled by Percival Boyd which contains between six

and seven million names. *Boyd's Marriage Index* includes entries from some 4300 English parishes and is estimated to cover twelve to fifteen per cent of marriages between 1538 and 1837.[4] Many county record offices have created indexes of marriages as have a number of family history societies.

The International Genealogical Index (IGI)

The International Genealogical Index, usually referred to as the 'IGI', is by far the largest index of baptisms and marriages. It covers an ever-increasing number of British records, but that is only part of the story for it also includes Europe, North America, Central and South America, the southwest Pacific (including Australia and New Zealand) and a limited representation from Africa and Asia. This index, compiled by the Genealogical Society of Utah, is available on microfiche, CD-ROM and on the Internet at: [`http://www.familysearch.com`].

At the present time, it is said to contain entries for more than 240 million people. The Genealogical Society of Utah was established by the Church of Jesus Christ of Latter-Day Saints to facilitate genealogical research. Church members seek to identify their relatives back through the generations so that they can be baptised into the Mormon faith. In undertaking this work they have accumulated a vast collection of genealogical records which are available to members and the general public through the church-sponsored libraries called Family History Centres.

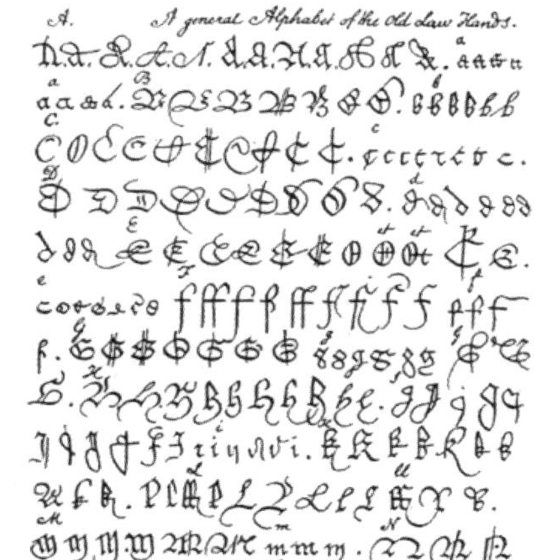

Letter forms typical of the 16th and 17th centuries. You'll eventually become familiar with this old-style writing.
Source: Collection, Peter Cuffley

An important point about the IGI is that it must be seen as a finding aid or research tool. While you can construct speculative charts using the IGI, it is essential to check the source material as well as searching for supporting evidence not necessarily included in records covered by the index. If you have ancestors in the sections of the IGI that contain a large percentage of available church records, then you are indeed fortunate. For example, London is very well covered as is Yorkshire, Warwickshire and Cornwall. Scottish records of births, baptisms and marriages can be found on both the IGI and the indexes to the Parochial Registers of 1553 to 1855 in both CD-ROM and microfiche forms at the Latter-Day Saints (LDS) Family History Centres. Unfortunately Ireland is not well covered. The majority of entries are for surviving records of the Church of Ireland. For Roman Catholic baptisms and marriages you will need to locate the relevant Heritage Centre in Ireland or deal directly with the parish or diocese.

If you or your family have arrived in Australia in the decades since World War II, it is likely that you may still have family connections or at least friends back in your place of origin. This is also possible if you left your homeland early in the 20th century and even beyond that time; however, the links generally become frailer with each decade that passes. The survival of civil, church and other records is going to vary from place to place. Record-keeping in countries such as Germany, Italy and Greece is discussed in chapter 5.

Ancestral File

The Church of the Latter-Day Saints also holds an enormous database called Ancestral File. It contains information on families and pedigrees which have

mostly been submitted by church members. Apart from over 35 million names, the database also tells you the name and address of the person who submitted the details.

Records of Deaths and Burials

Dates of death and burial are considered important by most genealogists and family historians to round off the story of each individual. It can be frustrating when dates of birth and death before the introduction of civil records prove difficult, if not impossible, to find. In fact, death dates rarely appear in church records and the only hope is that they may be found on a gravestone or memorial, in a family bible, in a published obituary or in family papers including wills and associated documents. That wonderful resource, the IGI, does not include deaths or burials, but the microfilms of parish registers made by the Genealogy Department of the Church of Jesus Christ of Latter-Day Saints generally include burials. To find these you need to consult the Family History Library Catalogue on microfiche, CD-ROM or the Internet.

Having located the register of burials covering the period you want to search, you order the relevant film at your nearest LDS Family History Centre. To do this you will need to give basic details of the section of the film, for instance: 'Parish of Little Munden, burials 1680–1812, item 2–4, film number 1040815 (British Film Area).' If the film is not already in Australia, it will travel from Salt Lake City to the library and you will be notified of its arrival so that a booking can be made to use a microfilm reader. The current cost for this useful service is $A6 per film. In most cases you will be looking at a filmed copy of the original record, and the feeling of being closer to the world of your ancestors will suddenly become very strong. Parish registers containing baptisms, marriages and burials sometimes have other notes such as details of repairs to the church, even recipes for herbal remedies! Much more about the everyday life of the parish is revealed on the films containing the accounts of the Overseers of the Poor, and the Vestry Minutes.

There is room for a number of small-time villains in these village stocks.
Source: Imperial Dictionary *(1861)*

Non-conformists and Others

The terms non-conformists, non-parochials, and dissenters, appear in descriptions of records which deal with people who did not belong to the Church of England. England was Catholic until 1559 when the final separation from Rome was completed.[5] Acceptance of both the people who remained Catholic and the increasing number of Protestant dissenters improved over the centuries with the passing of a number of Acts.

The Toleration Act of 1689 allowed Protestant dissenters to secure licences to conduct worship in stated places. Quakers and Jews were exempted from Lord Hardwicke's Marriage Act of 1753. All others were required to be married in the Church of England, even if they were Baptists, Methodists, Roman Catholics or any of the other separate groups. Such people were labelled as dissenters from the established church. Most of the remaining prohibitions on Catholics were removed by the Catholic Emancipation Act of 1829. It came as a result of the political campaign to liberate the Catholic majority in Ireland and its effects were felt not only in the British Isles but also in the colonies.

Wills and Administrations

When people made highly detailed wills, they wouldn't have realised that future family and social historians would be giving thanks for these splendidly informative documents. Wills do vary and some are limited in value with very little in the way of useful details. The best kind of will gives information on a whole family both immediate and extended. It will also identify properties, mortgages, debts, shares, interests, businesses and professions, as well as listing possessions such as clothing, jewellery, pictures, books, furniture, horses, carriages, wagons, cars, boats, basic household items and tools of trade. When my ancestor, John Cuffley, made his will in 1807, he asked his executors to sell by public or private sale, the growing crops, stock and utensils in trade of his farm at Perrotts in the Parish of Banstead, County of Surrey.

When ancestors owned property or at least were of some substance, we can hope to discover a will. It is disappointing though to find that there is often not a will and that people must have passed on their worldly goods by other means, or simply did not have anything to leave. If there was no will, there was often an administration, which means an offical division and distribution of assets took place. For probates and administrations in Australia, each state has indexes which are an important research tool because they pinpoint the date of death and from that many other records can be found, apart from the will or administration and associated papers.

In England, the Probate Act of 1857, which came into force on 12 January 1858, moved the responsibility for wills and administrations away from

John Cuffley (1737–1818) made his will on 29 May 1807. Apart from instructions to sell the growing crops, stock, 'utensils in trade' and household furniture of his farm at Banstead, Surrey, it also mentions his sons John, George, William and Richard, along with his daughters Ann Walker and Mary Shepherd.
Source: Public Record Office, London

I John Cuffley of the Parish of Banstead in the County of Surry Farmer being in good health and sound disposing Mind and Memory blessed be God for the same do hereby publish and declare this to be my last Will and Testament in manner and form following that is to say first I desire all my just Debts funeral expences with the proving of this my will may be fully paid and satisfied also I desire as soon as convenient after my decease my Executors do sell or cause to be sold by public or private sale the growing Crops Stock Utensils in Trade household furniture &c of my Farm at Perrotts in the Parish of Banstead in the County of Surry the produce of which outstanding Debts or any other property due to me or whatsoever it may be or of whatsoever the same may consist I give & bequeath to my Children John Cuffley Ann Walker George Cuffley Mary Shepherd William Cuffley and Richard Cuffley to be divided between them share and share alike or in case of the death of either of my aforesaid Children to their Child or Children the same share their Parent would have been intitled to if living but in case either of my aforesaid Children should die without issue then their proportionate share to be divided between the survivors of my said Children and I do hereby nominate and appoint Thomas Langham of Wimbledon in the County of Surry Callico Printer and William Potter of the Parish of Wimbledon Cutler my Executors of this my Will and I do hereby publish and declare this to be my last Will and Testament making void all other Wills by me heretofore made In witness whereof I have hereunto set my hand and Seal this 29th Day of May 1807. John Cuffley, his mark In the presence of. Samuel Gibling, James Pursell

Proved at London 12 January 1819 before the Worshipful Samuel Rush Meyrick D. of Laws and Surr by the Oaths of Thomas Langham and William Potter the Executors to whom Admon was granted being first sworn duly to adm:

ecclesiastical courts and the Courts of Chancery to a newly established civil Court of Probate.[6] Searching for post-1858 wills and administrations is usually more straightforward than for the period before that date. The choice is either to read up on the subject or have a professional searcher do the work for you.

In Scotland wills are called testaments and, until 1868, the law provided that the eldest son should receive all real property which meant land and buildings. If there was no son, any daughters would share equally and if there weren't any children, the inheritance would go to the surviving spouse. Only moveable property, such as money, jewellery, furniture and livestock, was subject to a testamentary disposition. After 1868, all property could be devised or bequeathed in the manner familiar to us today.

The administration of Irish wills is covered by various jurisdictions, and there are detailed works on the subject. While there is much that can be found, the disastrous 1922 fire in Dublin was a huge loss for family historians. A fair amount of work has been done to replace the lost records so if you think your ancestors in Ireland may have left wills it is always worth investigating.

Directories and Electoral Rolls

For tracing addresses and occupations, some of the most useful resources are the various types of directories and the electoral rolls. Since Australian federation in 1901 we have had comprehensive electoral rolls covering both state and federal divisions. Joint rolls covering the two spheres were introduced in Tasmania in 1908, South Australia in 1920, Victoria in 1924 and New South Wales in 1927. Queensland and Western Australia still maintain separate rolls.[7] A listing of electoral rolls for the colonial period is included in *Tracing your Family History in Australia* along with a guide to surviving directories and almanacs for each state.

Before the need for telephone directories, there were so-called post office directories compiled by private companies. These directories were weighty tomes filled not only with people's names, addresses and occupations, but also information on cities, suburbs, towns and settlements as well as trades and businesses. They are valuable tools for tracing the whereabouts and the overall movements of individuals and families. An increasing number have been made available on microfiche and are usually to be found in libraries with a section devoted to history and genealogy. Directories covering the British Isles from the 18th century onwards are also widely available, both as microfiche and facsimile reprints.

Trade and business journals are an excellent source of information about occupations. This ironmongers' works is located in Birmingham.
Source: Collection, Peter Cuffley

Occupational Records

One of the most important ways to learn about the lives of our ancestors is to gather information on their occupations. If you are keen to go further, you can try to acquire some of the knowledge they would have needed, and perhaps even some of the skills, or touch upon the experiences which we know confronted them. This can mean anything from prospecting for gold, working with hand tools, sewing and weaving, traditional food preparation, sailing on a square rigger or walking a long distance under difficult conditions.

We often gain an insight into old trades and industries through works of art. In 1747 William Hogarth (1697-1764) the English painter and engraver, created his Industry and Idleness *series. This is* The Fellow 'prentices at their Looms, *a typical 'moral narrative' which maintained its appeal in the 19th century when this engraving 'from the original design' was published.*
Source: Collection, Peter Cuffley

Many books have been published on specific occupations but if you find there is little available, it represents an opportunity for some real research. One of our family was a calico printer in the 18th century which raised the question, what did such an occupation involve? Through reading and correspondence I was able to learn something of the growth of this industry in the Industrial Revolution. Directories, histories, maps, land tax assessments, settlement papers and wills all helped build up a picture.

There are many occupations that are well recorded, including lists of apprentices, certified tradespeople and qualified professionals. Employees in both government and private occupations can be found in a range of records. For instance, employment records of railway workers, service personnel, postal officers, teachers and merchant seamen have been located and published, or may be available at the headquarters of the relevant body or in a general archive. Registers of professionals in areas such as medicine, architecture and the law are an important resource, as are the records of associations, companies, guilds and trade unions. Once again we can be thankful to the institutions, organisations and individuals who have worked to index a wide range of sources which relate to occupations. An overall guide is *Specialist Indexes in Australia* (see Bibliography). *Tracing your Family History in Australia*, which I mentioned earlier, has an extensive coverage of occupational records. Some indexes are particularly helpful to us because they are very detailed. *An Index to Victorian Railway Employees of the 19th Century* (see Bibliography) has in most of its entries, the date of birth as well as period of employment.

The history of occupations in Britain is particularly well served by publications which are both affordable and accessible. *Occupational Sources for Genealogists: A Bibliography* is an overall index to information on a great diversity of occupations (see Bibliography). The records of people in the

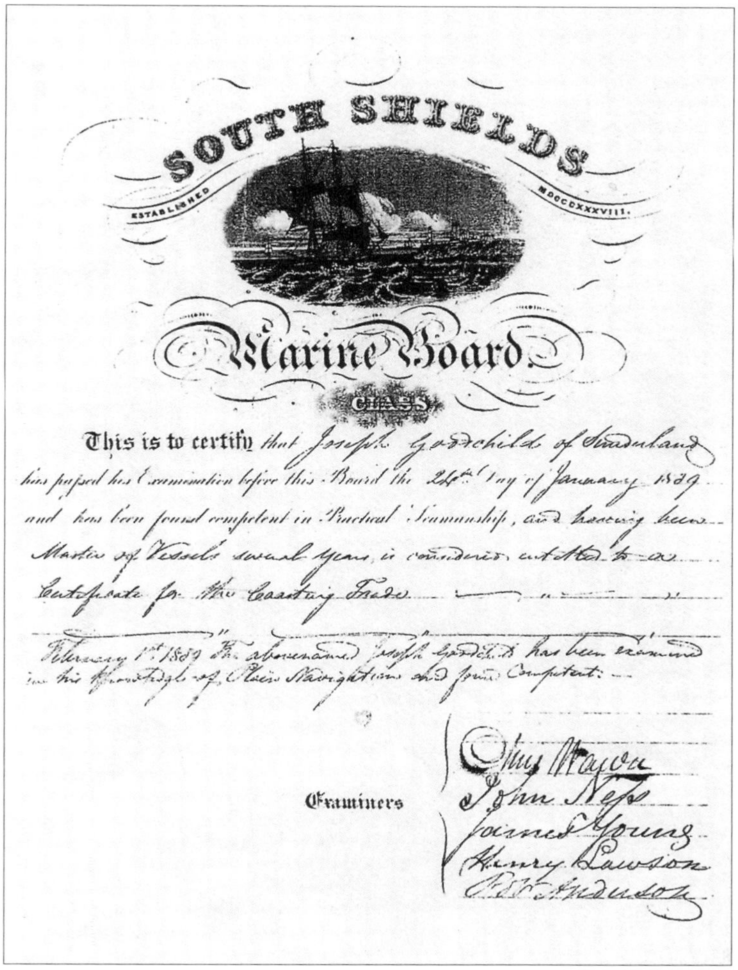
SOUTH SHIELDS

ESTABLISHED MDCCCXXVIII.

Marine Board.

CLASS

This is to certify that Joseph Goodchild of Sunderland has passed his Examination before this Board the 26th Day of January 1829 and has been found competent in Practical Seamanship, and having been Master of Vessels several years, is considered entitled to a Certificate for the Coasting Trade.

February 1st 1829 The abovenamed Joseph Goodchild has been examined in his Knowledge of Plain Navigation and found Competent.

Examiners

John Ness

James Young

Henry Lawson

[illegible]

This superbly engraved document of 1829 notes that Joseph Goodchild has been the master of vessels for several years and is considered entitled to a certificate for the coastal trade. Born in Sunderland, Durham, in 1809, Captain Goodchild gave up the sea in the early 1850s.

Source: Collection, Goodchild family

services have become a great resource and most countries have accessible archives. The Australian War Memorial in Canberra and the National Archives of Australia are important starting points when searching for those who served in the defence forces (see Useful Addresses).

There are many other resources which will help build a comprehensive account of the lives of earlier generations. You may seek out school and university records, land and property records, registers of shipping and seamen, convict records, immigration registers as well as naturalisation and citizenship records. The subject of immigration, including naturalisation, is covered in chapter 5. This chapter is intended to help you make a start, if you haven't already! Consult the Bibliography (pages 182–5), the guides provided at libraries and research centres, and the catalogues of booksellers who specialise in genealogy and family history along with local and world history.

Chapter Three
Computers and your Family History

People who haven't been closely involved with computers sometimes tend to feel that it is a big area which would be difficult to learn for anyone beyond a certain age. Their speedy nature, alien language, and the obvious connection with the 'now' generation, all raise unnecessary barriers to a fascinating world of useful technology. Family history is one of the areas of high activity for home computers and, in the wider sphere, computers have become a powerful tool for the creation of indexes, storage of records and above all, in disseminating information. They have come a long way since the early 1980s, and software designers are making them ever more simple to operate. We all need time to learn at our own pace and, thankfully, home computers offer room to move at every level of expertise. In the current jargon they are user-friendly.

As an author I still find excuses to write my manuscripts in double-spaced longhand, though there are many good reasons for using the word processor. With two-finger typing I have entered some 3500 individuals into 'Reunion', a genealogy database program. I've become adept at getting the best out of indexes on CD-ROM and can travel the Internet with confidence. My wife Barbara has worked with computers since the days when they were lumbering giants. She has a breadth of knowledge in the field which becomes clearer with every small step I take. Together we make a good team, though at both levels we are the first to admit that computers can always throw up new challenges or moments of sheer frustration.

The good news is that computers are becoming more and more affordable as well as being easier to operate for basic tasks such as entering family history

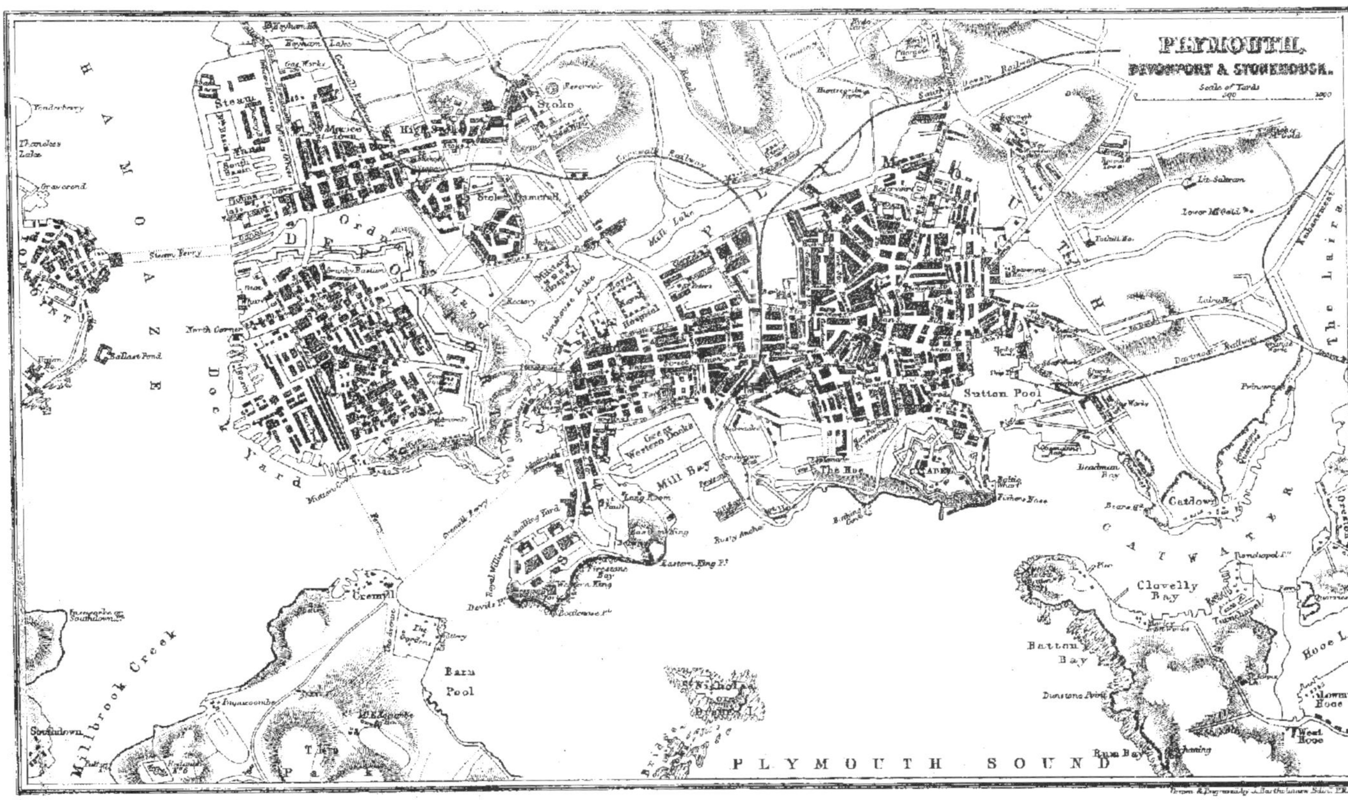
PLYMOUTH,
DEVONPORT & STONEHOUSE.
Stoke
Dock Yard
Mill Bay
Sutton Pool
The Hoe
Cremyll
Millbrook Creek
Barn Pool
Clovelly Bay
Batten Bay
PLYMOUTH SOUND
The Laira
Cattedown

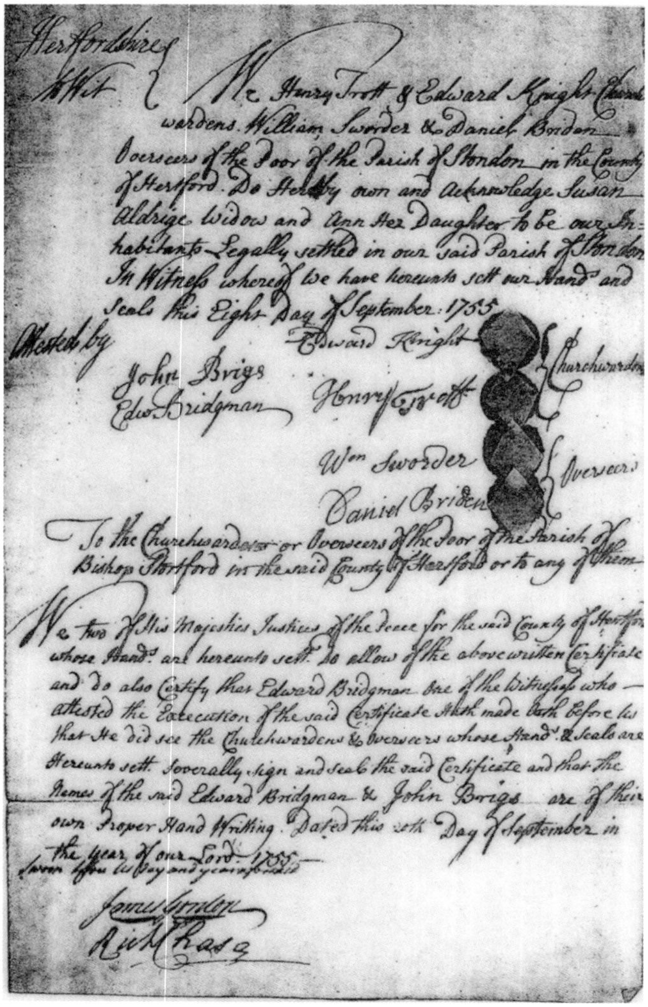
Hertfordshire to Wit

We Henry Trott & Edward Knight Church wardens William Sworder & Daniel Briden Overseers of the Poor of the Parish of Standon in the County of Hertford Do Hereby own and Acknowledge Susan Aldrige Widow and Ann Her Daughter to be our Inhabitants Legally settled in our said Parish of Standon In Witness whereof We have hereunto sett our Hand and Seals this Eight Day of September 1755

Attested by
John Brigs
Edw. Bridgman

Edward Knight
Henry Trott
Churchwardens

Wm Sworder
Daniel Briden
Overseers

To the Churchwardens or Overseers of the Poor of the Parish of Bishop Stortford in the said County of Hertford or to any of them.

We two of His Majesties Justices of the Peace for the said County of Hertford whose Hands are hereunto sett do allow of the above written Certificate and do also Certify that Edward Bridgman One of the Witnesses who attested the Execution of the said Certificate Hath made Oath before us that He did see the Churchwardens & Overseers whose Hands & Seals are Hereunto sett Severally sign and seal the said Certificate and that the Names of the said Edward Bridgman & John Brigs are of their own Proper Hand Writing. Dated this 20th Day of September in the year of our Lord 1755

Sworn before us the day and year above said

James Gordon
Richd Hase

LEFT: *This settlement certificate of 1755 allows Susan Aldrige (widow) and her daughter Ann to reside in the parish of Bishops Stortford, Hertfordshire, while still being legally settled in the parish of Standon. The churchwardens and overseers of the poor in Bishops Stortford could send them back to Standon if they became paupers and were likely to require relief from the parish funds. Documents such as this can be scanned and then incorporated into a print-out from a family history database. Some record repositories are creating digital images from original documents and these will be available through the Internet.*

Source: Hertfordshire Archives and Local Studies

data, printing out charts and reports, or writing text. Prices range from \$300 to \$3000 and upward. A second-hand or rebuilt home computer can be purchased at the lower end of the price scale and an average model with enough power to play CD-ROMs and link up to the Internet can be between \$1000–\$2000. Whether you are just beginning to work on your family history or are reasonably well advanced, you should seriously consider the advantages of having a computerised data program to keep your records efficiently. These programs are able to produce lists, charts and even integrate images such as photos, drawings or copies of documents to share with other family contacts. The added advantage of being 'on-line' and accessing the Internet is very appealing and, again, user-friendly.

People who have been researching their family for many years will naturally have found very efficient ways of recording, storing, and retrieving information. We belong to a local family history group and it is interesting to note that each year more and more members are getting computers. Those taking the plunge to computerise are being encouraged by their friends and family insisting that they 'can do it' and with a little help have taken the step. The computer is a great organising tool for those of us who tend to be somewhat haphazard in our filing or record-keeping.

FAR LEFT (TOP): *A hardworking Stewart truck and three generations of the Just family of Haden near Crows Nest in south-east Queensland photographed about 1934. Grandfather Theodore Christian Just, here seen leaning on the front mudguard, emigrated to Australia from Germany in 1884. A civil engineer, he worked as a gold-miner, drover and carpenter and in 1887 was granted a 160-acre selection at Goombungee. His son, Maxmillian Edward William Just, better known as 'Bill' used the truck for his carrying business. He married English-born Freda Garrett in 1917 and they had fifteen children. You could scan any of your family photographs and send them by e-mail to relatives.*

Source: Courtesy Doris Walker

FAR LEFT (BOTTOM): *Plymouth was one of the important departure points for emigrants leaving the British Isles. Also, voyages which began in London would often take on passengers here. This map is from the fifth edition of* Black's Guide to the Counties of Dorset, Devon and Cornwall *published 1871. Old maps are increasingly available on CD-ROM.* *For information on computer-generated maps, turn to page 130.*

Source: Collection, Peter Cuffley

We know from the words on the back of this postcard of January 1918, that the young sailor was stationed at the depot in Williamstown, Victoria and expected to be sailing to England on 2 February. It is addressed to Mrs Collins from Edie and Perce of 11 College Street, Hawthorn. Indexes of births, deaths and marriages on CD-ROM *can help identify people when the initial information is limited. In this case, the electoral roll is a logical first step.*
Source: Collection, Peter Cuffley

Genealogy database programs provide standardised places to record your findings and to keep records of your research, which is highly desirable if you don't want to waste time doing research only to find that you have already searched that particular list or record. These programs allow you to produce lists in various ways that may reveal where you have missing data, and this could lead you to the next step in your research. You can also print out your family trees in formats such as box charts, descendant charts, and family history reports.

OPPOSITE (TOP): *This painting of St Pauls, London, from the south bank of the Thames, was done by Thomas H. Shepherd (1792–1864) in the 1820s. It shows us a slice of a great city which would have been familiar to many of those who came to Australia as convicts, sailors, gold-diggers or settlers. An engraving of this view appeared in Thomas Shepherd's* London and its Environs in the Nineteenth Century, *published in 1829.*
(Oil painting on copper panel, 216 mm x 317 mm)
Source: Collection, Clive L. Lloyd, Shere, Surrey

OPPOSITE: *Scottish painter, Thomas Faed, is known for his anecdotal pictures of humble folk. There is a wealth of authentic detail in this work, including the threadbare carpet and the boy's boots with the soles worn away. Faed painted* Reading the Bible *in 1845, capturing the kind of family who may have emigrated if that was at all possible.*
(Oil on canvas, 1125 mm x 1528 mm)
Source: Geelong Art Gallery, gift of Miss L.J. McPhillimy, 1935

Equipment to Get You Started

The computer itself is called the 'hardware' in computer terminology and the programs that run inside it are referred to as 'software'. The hardware you buy is determined by the type of software you want to run. The two main types of computers are Macintosh and IBM (or IBM compatible). Frequently IBM or IBM-compatible computers are referred to as personal computers (PCs). A greater variety of general purpose software and family genealogy programs exists for the IBM-compatible computers. You will also need a printer for your computer.

If you just wish to record your family in the simplest form, you will get by with a lower priced, second-hand computer. An IBM-compatible computer should have at least a 486 processor chip, 100 Mb (megabytes) of storage memory on the hard disk, and at least 16 Mb of RAM (Random Access Memory), which runs the software.

Every program you load onto your computer will use some of the 16 Mb of RAM while the program is open and running. Some programs require 2 Mb, others 4 Mb or more. Bear in mind, this is a minimum requirement. Processing time tends to slow down if your 16 Mb RAM is substantially utilised. You may need a computer which can be upgraded to run a CD-ROM and a modem for on-line access, should you decide later to do this. The computer should come with a VGA colour screen and also have an external floppy disk drive to take 3½ inch disks (1.4 Mb storage).

DRAPER &C
R POYNTER
88
ESTD 1860
88
MILLINERY
AD 1872
FLYING SQUADRON HOTEL
84
82
W. CUFFLEY'S
FLYING SQUADRON
BAR
SAMPSON TARTAKOVER
PAWNBROKER & MONEYLENDER

F.M. RYAN
GENERAL STORE
COOL
DRINKS
GENERAL
STORE

If you wish to you can purchase the latest computer with all the bells and whistles. This is a very exciting thing to do but be assured it will be superseded fairly soon. The main advantage of newer model computers is the accelerated processing speed. They also support the state-of-the-art accessories such as fast CD-ROM players, external back-up or storage systems, high speed modems for faster on-line access to the Internet, as well as supporting hi-tech scanners and printers. With the right equipment you can store hundreds of scanned images of your ancestors. You'll need a large hard disk as scanned images take up a significant amount of computer memory considering they output proportionately small images. Or you could purchase an external drive (e.g. a Zip drive) which will copy your large files on to disks that each store up to 100 Mb.

To assist you in basic computing you should make sure your computer comes with an operating system such as Windows, and it should have documentation and installation disks as well. Legally you must own the copy of the operating system you use. You may also need to re-install the system at some later date and the technician will ask for your installation disk(s).

It is desirable to purchase your computer with a word processing program installed, and these may vary from the small but useful inbuilt Windows Notepad to a commercial application like WordPerfect or Microsoft Word. Some genealogy programs use your word processing program to generate reports. For instance, Reunion for Windows requires you to nominate a word processing program and if you want to generate a family history report it does so in that program, not in Reunion. This is an advantage because you are not limited by the rigid output of a certain format. Before printing, you can rearrange the format of the document, enlarge the type size, repaginate it, add extra information such as your address, or extra details not required or able to be stored by your genealogy program.

Programs to Run on Your Computer

Basically, computers can assist us to organise our family history research. There are a number of types of programs which can be very useful.

Genealogy Specific Database Programs

These are programs designed for entering the names of our ancestors and relatives along with details of important events, and notes or anecdotes to make their story more interesting.

To help you choose a program suitable for your needs, you may be able to speak to someone who uses a certain program, or you could join one of the genealogy computer groups such as a Dead Persons Society in your state, or one of the larger societies, which usually have a computer group. In Victoria, there is an excellent organisation called Genealogists Using Microcomputers (GUM), which publishes regular reviews of the computer programs in their monthly newsletter.

There are a number of essential basic requirements for the program you ultimately decide on.

OPPOSITE (TOP): *After the failure of Parker Brothers Fitzroy Brewery in 1873, William Cuffley became the publican of hotels both large and small. The Flying Squadron in Smith Street, Collingwood, was hardly more than a bar and is seen here as it was in 1884.*
(Acrylic on hardboard, 1968)
Source: Peter Cuffley, original work

OPPOSITE: *Small general stores or mixed businesses have been part of the lives of many Australians. Frank and May Ryan purchased their business at Tynong, Victoria in 1926. Unpaid debts in the worst years of the Great Depression forced them to drive away in an old Ford truck with only the happier memories for comfort.*
(Acrylic on hardboard, 1997)
Source: Peter Cuffley, original work

ABOVE AND OPPOSITE: *Carte-de-visite from the period 1860–1890s. Why aren't these gentlemen smiling? Perhaps to avoid blurring the shot (because of the relatively long exposure time), or maybe the photographer has a concealed head brace to avoid the possibility of movement altogether!*
Source: Collection, Peter Cuffley

Ease of Entering your Data

Does the program enable you to link details of father and mother as well as record events about their lives? Does the program allow you to enter marriage details? It is also important to be able to record notes and anecdotes, sources for the records, research progress, and many different but nevertheless important facts such as baptismal and death dates and places, burial details, and so on.

Can you Transfer your Data or Receive Incoming Data from Other Family Members?

Before you start entering your data, make sure your chosen program has the ability to transfer data to and from other programs. Quite often, you would like to run two programs, or you find another program that would suit your needs better, and so you need to be able to transfer all the entered records to and from each program safely. With this in mind, make sure your program has import/export facilities. The standard format for this is called GEDCOM (GEnealogical Data COMmunications).

Can you Generate Charts and Reports?

It is important to be able to print out basic charts and lists that will aid you in identifying and recording your family. Ancestor charts (also known as pedigree charts), descendant charts, family group sheets and individual details sheets are all fundamental. Check to see if there are variations available on these charts and sheets such as displaying other details that you consider important. Some of the charting and listing abilities are very limited indeed. I feel that the place of marriage or birth is an essential item but not many programs include this and only the dates are allowed.

Some Genealogy Database Programs to Consider

Programs vary in complexity and cost and so your research goals or what you most want out of your records will influence your choice. There are many programs on the market as well as a few which can be downloaded from the Internet as free 'shareware'. Typically, the popular commercial programs include a comprehensive manual with either CD-ROMs or disks from which the program is installed. Some include more than one CD-ROM and have additional indexes and guides.

You can usually obtain demonstration copies of the commercial programs and shareware programs and try them out. This enables you to enter some names and details then print out a sample chart to see if the program's capabilities and character suit your requirements.

The Master Genealogist

Described as a family history project manager, The Master Genealogist (TMG) operates on IBM-compatible computers which have Windows 3.1, Windows 95, or Windows 98 as the operating system. It comes in a budget priced Silver Edition or the premier Gold Edition. Both need the minimum of a 486 computer with 16 Mb of RAM. This is one of the programs at the high

end of the scale in its range of capabilities and special features. It has all of the tools an experienced genealogist would require, as well as being readily accessible for the beginner.

There is unlimited capacity to include individuals, families, any number of events per person, relationships, free-form text, images per person, sources and citations. When you type in a person's name, you are allowed one hundred characters each for the title, given name, surname and suffix. Place names can have up to one hundred characters on each of six separate lines (fields). The program has the capacity to handle conflicting data, adoptions, unwed parents, uncertain dates, 'old style' dates, disproved data, spelling changes, contradictory sources, multiple lines of descent, missing data and sensitive data. An example of handling of sensitive data is that the program will, if instructed, suppress specific citations or the details of living people from generated reports. There may be details of the parentage of a family member which are to be withheld for a specified time or until they or their children have passed on. Some people sending out charts or other reports may want to suppress details such as specific dates of birth for living people.

As previously mentioned, it is important to be able to transfer data from other programs and this is usually done through GEDCOM. The Master Genealogist has a feature called GenBridge which enables the direct transfer of genealogical data from a long list of programs. This is supposed to be an improvement on GEDCOM transfers and overcomes the errors and omissions which can occur.

Another feature is the Custom Report Writer which widens the options for the presentation of narrative reports and enables you to write in your own style. The publication of a family journal or book is made easier with the publication tools in the program, and there are many handy functions such as text editor, research log, relationship calculator, spell checker, regnal date converter (gives the reigning English monarch(s) from dates supplied), date calculator and address book. The creation of timelines is also of great value and TMG includes a number of historical timelines to give a wider context to the family story.

One of the important attributes of family history programs is the amount of information on the screen at a given time, such as how many individuals are shown when you select a section of the family tree. Most programs display three generations. The Master Genealogist will display up to twenty-six offspring covering three generations with birth and death dates as well as spouses. In the Gold Edition, it also produces most reports in HTML format (see page 59) for displaying on the World Wide Web. Both versions have important multimedia features which support graphics formats, digital sound and scanning directly into the program. There are many more features which, though ancillary, are very helpful and you can discover them as you go along.

Generations (Deluxe Edition, Version 4.2)

Generations (deluxe edition, version 4.2) is the successor of a highly acclaimed genealogy program called Reunion for Windows. Having used Reunion to record my family I can vouch for its user-friendly character.

Register Report

First Generation

---

1. ROBERT PURTON. Born Circa 1760. Occupation TRAVELLER. Religion CHURCH OF ENGLAND. He married MARY PRITCHETT, 25 Oct 1784 in CAPEL SURREY ENGLAND. They had the following children:

	i.	JAMES PURTON; Died in NEW BRUNSWICK CANADA?. Religion CHURCH OF ENGLAND.
	ii.	JOHN PURTON;
	iii.	GEORGE PURTON
2	iv.	WILLIAM PURTON
3	v.	SHADRACK PURTON

Second Generation

---

2. WILLIAM PURTON. Born 1787. Christen 2 Dec 1787 in EAST GRINSTEAD SUSSEX ENGLAND. Died 14 Feb 1869 in SKENE ST NEWTOWN GEELONG VIC. Buried 14 Feb 1869 in WESTERN CEMETERY GEELONG. Occupation CARTER. Religion CHURCH OF ENGLAND.

He married MARY ANN MOORE, 25 Oct 1819 in AYLESFORD, KENT, ENGLAND. Born Circa 1787 in KENT ENGLAND. Died 24 Nov 1872 in SKENE ST NEWTOWN GEELONG VIC. Buried 26 Nov 1872 in WESTERN CEMETERY GEELONG. Occupation SHOPKEEPER.
They had the following children:

4	i.	MANSELL PURTON
	ii.	GEORGE PURTON; Born 1823 in WORMSHILL NR MAIDSTONE KENT. Christen 7 Sep 1823 in WORMSHILL NR MAIDSTONE KENT.
	iii.	SOLOMON PURTON; Born 1826 in WORMSHILL NR MAIDSTONE KENT. Christen 21 May 1826 in WORMSHILL NR MAIDSTONE KENT.
	iv.	JOHN PURTON; Born 1828 in WORMSHILL NR MAIDSTONE KENT. Christen 29 Jun 1828 in WORMSHILL NR MAIDSTONE KENT.
5	v.	ELEANOR [ELLEN] PURTON
	vi	MARIA JANE PURTON; Born 1834 in WORMSHILL NR MAIDSTONE KENT. Christen 23 Mar 1834 in WORMSHILL NR MAIDSTONE KENT. Died 1837 in DIED AT SEA.
6	vii.	MARY ANN PURTON
	viii.	ELIZA JEAN PURTON; Born Circa 1839 in TASMANIA. Died 1918 in BALLARAT EAST VICTORIA.

3. SHADRACK PURTON. Born 1795 in GREAT PECKHAM KENT ENGLAND. Died 7 Jul 1871 in WESTBURY TASMANIA. Buried in WESTBURY CEMETERY. Occupation SOLDIER--OVERSEER--FARMER. Religion CHURCH OF ENGLAND.

He married SARAH SMITH, Jun 1822 in ST JOHNS NEW BRUNSWICK CANADA. Born Circa 1800 in MAIDSTONE KENT ENGLAND. Died 29 Apr 1886 in WESTBURY TASMANIA. Buried in WESTBURY CEMETERY. Religion CHURCH OF ENGLAND.
They had the following children:

7	i.	GEORGE SMITH PURTON
8	ii.	JAMES PURTON
9	iii.	SHADRACK PURTON
10	iv.	JOHN PURTON
11	v.	ROBERT PURTON
12	vi.	WILLIAM PURTON
	vii.	AMY [EMMA] PURTON; Born 31 Oct 1837 in WESTBURY TASMANIA. Christen 23 Jan 1839 in WESLEYAN CHURCH LAUNCESTON TAS. Died 14 Sep 1903 in LAUNCESTON TASMANIA. Religion WESLEYAN. She married GEORGE BEST, 13 Apr 1872 in HAGLEY NR WESTBURY TASMANIA.
	viii.	MARIA PURTON; Born Circa 1841 in WESTBURY TASMANIA. She married JOSEPH BELL SIMPSON, 14 Feb 1862 in FRANKLIN,TAS..

An example of a register report generated by Reunion for Windows in rich text file (RTF) format. A print-out such as this provides a clear overview and yet contains a reasonable amount of detail.
Source: Peter Cuffley

Generations requires a minimum 486 computer with 2 Mb of RAM and it operates in Windows 3.1, 95 or 98. Entering family information including names, dates, facts, personal notes and mailing addresses is easy, and details already entered such as place names, can be re-used to save typing them again. While its capacity for individuals or families is not unlimited, in both cases it will handle up to 30 000 entries. Apparently, Generations is built using a fast genealogy database engine so that it is not slowed down by the increasing amount of information being entered.

Personal data for family members is stored in a section called Easy Tree. Various kinds of charts, including a five-generation overview chart are created in Easy Chart. You can have access to some fifty-seven million records from the United States in Easy Viewer, an inclusion which may or may not be useful to researchers in Australia. A set of tools called Internet Detective facilitates on-line searches of over 26 000 genealogy web sites. The program comes with a printed reference manual and a web site [www.sierra.com] which offers further support along with e-mail or telephone contact. Generations will import data from GEDCOM or from someone else's Generations program. Export of data is limited to GEDCOM for Ancestral File, or All Data to ASCII text or Tab Delimited.

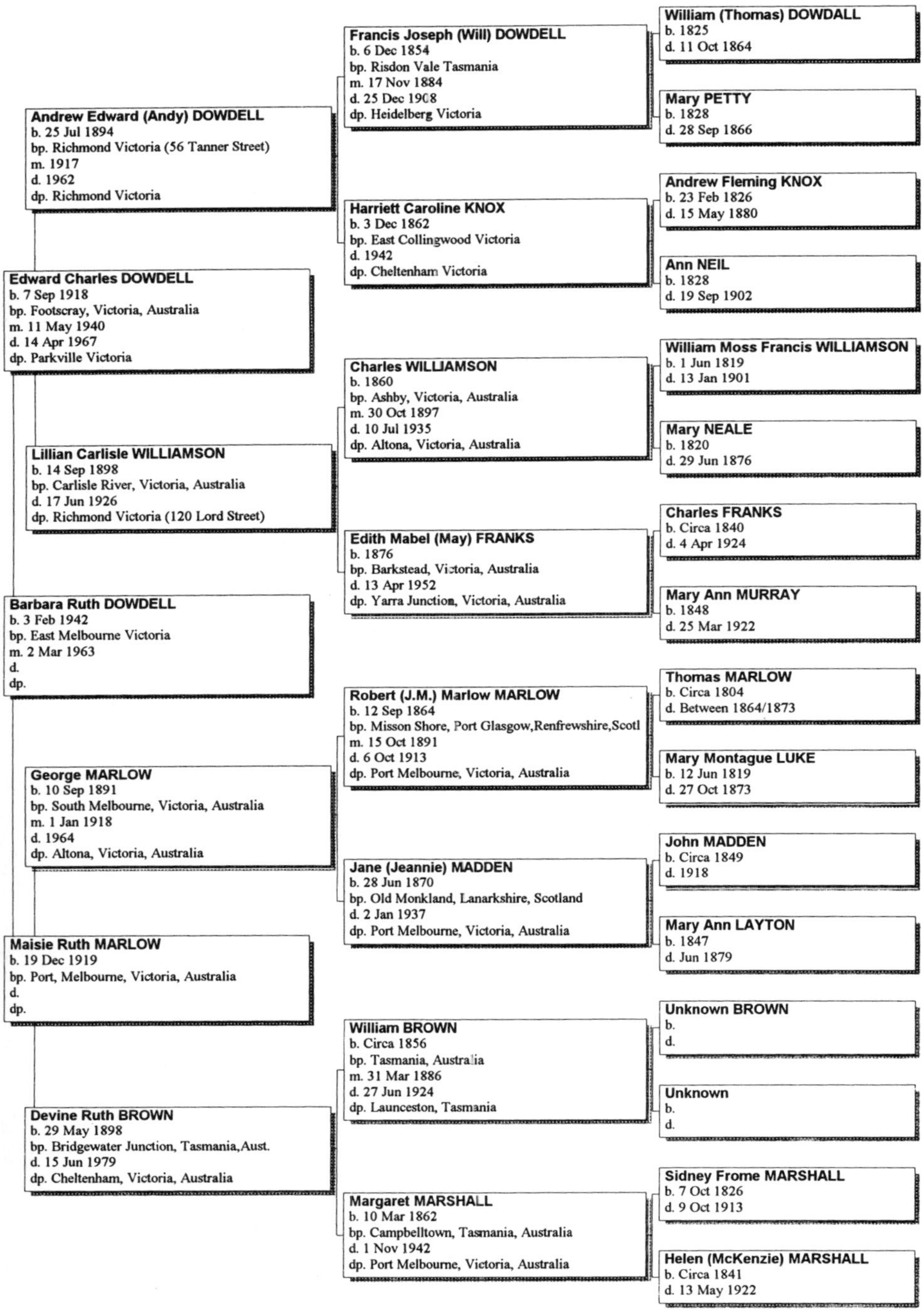

A five-generation chart offers a very accessible one-page pedigree and emphasises any gaps.
Source: Peter Cuffley

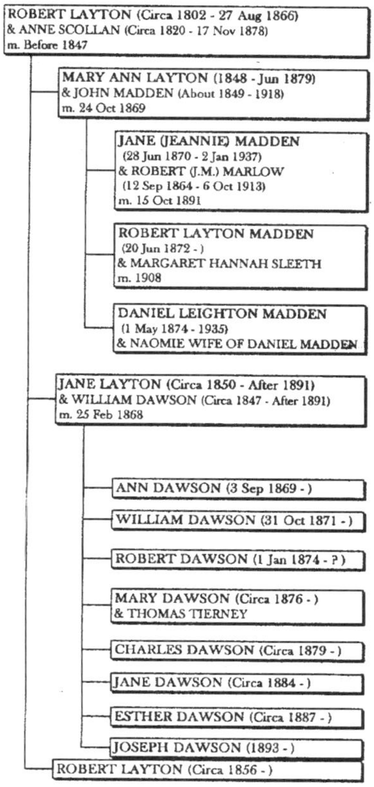

ABOVE AND OPPOSITE: *These drop-line box charts were generated in Reunion. The example on the right has been truncated to show just one generation. Charts of this type are unlimited in the number of generations they can show.*
Source: Courtesy Barbara Cuffley

Family Tree Maker (Edition III, Version 5.0)

Three versions of Family Tree Maker (basic edition, standard edition III, deluxe edition III) offer you a wide variety and price range. A 486 computer is the minimum requirement with Windows 3.1, 95 or 98 as an operating system and 16 Mb of RAM.

This program organises names, dates, facts and photographs, and will print a broad range of family trees and reports. All the editions can create multimedia family albums, though many of the special features such as the step-by-step 'how-to' guide are not on the basic edition, which is purchased as a single CD. Edition III of Family Tree Maker comes in a four-CD set. The deluxe edition III has five additional cds of existing family trees. These family trees were created by people in other countries, although most are American families. It is possible that some may be relevant to you.

You can enter an unlimited number of families per database and events per person. The space for sources and source citations for each name and each event is also unlimited. Version 5 provides a specially designed hourglass family tree which shows both descendants and ancestors for a given individual. Also included are historical timelines, colour coded family trees, requests for information in other languages (form letters), a research journal, and married or maiden name control for female entries. Data can be imported through gedcom, or directly from PAF or someone else's Family Tree Maker. It lets you make use of the Internet through InterneTree which produces a family tree style especially for the World Wide Web.

Ultimate Family Tree

The genealogy software called Ultimate Family Tree comes in a standard edition and a British edition. The latter will suit those who have ancestry in the United Kingdom because it includes an historical timeline along with tutorial articles including guides to civil registration in England and the British census records. It also has an extensive collection of genealogy links for the Internet which are related to United Kingdom web sites. Ultimate Family Tree requires the minimum of a 486 computer with Windows 3.1, 95 or 98, and 8 Mb of RAM although 16 Mb is recommended. It requires 35 Mb of hard disk space, an SVGA monitor with 256 colours and a CD-ROM drive.

Once you have entered the available information on your family, a range of charts and reports can be generated easily. Some of the features include basic and advanced editing modes, inclusion of family photographs in reports, and the ability to create a family journal with title page, endnotes and index. You can also print out birthday and anniversary calendars, historical timelines, family group sheets and relationship lists. The chart designs include fan charts, box charts, family trees and pedigree charts. People or families per database and the number of events per person are all unlimited. Six names per person can be entered, which helps if there are aliases, religious names or nicknames as well as the primary name.

Data import is from GEDCOM, or directly from the program Roots III, or Ultimate Family Tree and its predecessors. Data export is to GEDCOM (version 4.0– 5.5), or GEDCOM for Ancestral File. It will also export reports to ASCII

text or directly to Delimited Tab and many other formats. Most reports can also be produced in HTML format for pages on the World Wide Web.

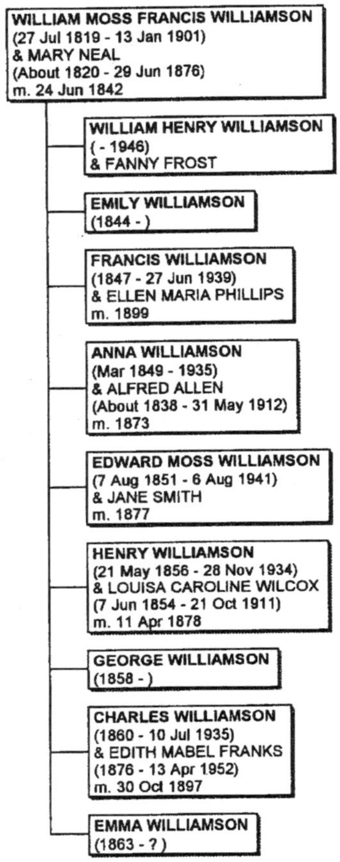

Family Origins for Windows

Considered to be the best budget program available, Family Origins (version 6.0) has many desirable features. The minimum system requirements are 486 computer with Windows 3.1, 4 Mb of RAM and 4 Mb of hard disk space. Installation floppy disks are included in the package for those without a CD-ROM drive.

This is another user-friendly program with unlimited space for entering family details. It automatically links entries and has a built-in relationship and date calculator to automatically calculate ages, years married and so on. A Find feature allows you to quickly locate anyone in your database.

The Source List Report prints a complete list of your sources. Reports can be exported in the Rich Text Format (RTF) to suit most word processors, so you can reformat the information if you wish. There is also a guide to creating your own web page and the program supports the production of reports in HTML format. A Scrapbook Report allows you to print pictures in a photograph album format, or you can generate a family tree with integrated images.

Family Heritage

Offered in standard or deluxe packages, this is a substantially upgraded version of the program formerly known as Corel Family Tree Suite. Minimum requirements are a 486 computer with Windows 95 as the operating system, 8 Mb of RAM (12 Mb recommended), 40 Mb of hard disk space, CD-ROM drive and a VGA monitor with 256 colours.

Family Heritage has easy-to-use tools for building a range of attractive charts or trees. You can create multiple photograph albums for each person or event as well as report layouts with various graphics. Ancestor, descendant and register reports can be assembled for print-out or publication with the Auto Format Wizard. You can publish on the World Wide Web using your free home page at the Family Heritage web site, or distribute family trees to family and friends using a floppy disk. Included in the package are 200 000 surname histories and coats of arms. The deluxe version contains Corel Photohouse for restoring or modifying family photographs.

Brother's Keeper

This program is available as shareware you can download from the Internet, or there is a fully registered version which you buy that offers additional features. There is a Windows version which needs the minimum of a 386 computer with Windows 3.1 or 95, 3 Mb of hard disk space and 4 Mb of ram. The old DOS version requires 2 Mb of hard disk space and 640 Kb of RAM.

When you key in a person's details, it can be found or accessed again either by name, partial name or record number, and each database can hold up to a million names. Pedigree charts with four to six generations per page can be created as well as multi-page pedigree charts. Descendant box charts have boxes connected by lines. Import and export facilities use GEDCOM and you

can import scanned pictures into the program. An instruction manual for both Windows and DOS versions is supplied.

Relatively Yours II for Windows

This is an Australian program which includes all of the features typically found in the imported programs as well as extra features such as a timeline of historical events with an Australian emphasis. Designed for Windows 95 or 98, it requires a minimum of 16 Mb of RAM. The Relatively Yours web site [`http://www.relativelyyours.com`] is a source of useful advice, and registered users can download program updates.

The method for entering data is simple. You point and click on an icon to add new entries or further details to an existing person. Relatively Yours has a unique mapping facility which relates recorded events to places. The user clicks on 'hyperlinked' names, dates and places to bring up a screen of personal information, details of events that occurred on the date selected, or a map showing where the place is situated.

Charts produced directly from the program are in the standard indented descendant format.Other types of chart need to be created by using gedcom to a separate charting program. Scanned photographs, sound recordings and home videos can all be integrated into the system. The program is purchased on CD-ROM.

Reunion for Macintosh

This program is considered the ideal one for Macintosh or Power Macintosh. As previously mentioned, Reunion is known for its user-friendly character and wide range of capabilities. A variety of descendant and pedigree charts can be created with full on-screen editing of box colour, font and font size, shadows, borders, connecting lines and captions. It will create book style reports including Ahnentafel and register reports, and family history reports. All of these are automatically opened in your word processor and are fully formatted with page numbers, page breaks, headings, and so on. Import and export is by GEDCOM.

Relational Database Programs

For the more adventurous, owning a relational database program provides sophisticated avenues to access the data that you accumulate. It allows you to search through information using selected criteria, say, any surname 'Thomas' with a date of birth occurring in the 1880s. So if, for instance, you visit an LDS Family History Centre or a general library which has the International Genealogical Index (IGI) on CD-ROM, you can save selected records to a floppy disk to bring home with you, and you can either open the results into your word processing program as a text file or you can import them into a relational database such as Microsoft Access or dBASE IV. My wife Barbara uses Microsoft Access and can manipulate imported data from the Pioneer Indexes and the IGI into further searchable lists which can be sorted by date, place, occurrence of name, and so on. She saves the raw information onto a 3½ inch disk and brings it home to import into her

HUNSDON PARISH REGISTERS
1546-1837

THIS BOOKE or Registrye of Christninge Mariage and burialls had, done and solemnized w[th]in the church and parishe of Hunsdon of the dioces of London within the Countie of Hertford taketh begiñinge in the yere of oure lorde god one thowsand fyve hundred fortie and syxe, and in the first yere of the raigne of owre most gracious Soveraigne lorde Edwarde the syxte by the grace of god kynge of england Fraunce and Irelande, defendo[r] of the faithe &c. & in yearth next under god of the church of England and Irelande supreme governo[r] and began his Raigne the xxxj[st] of Januarye

BURIALLS.

John Foster	7 September	1546.
John Kynge	23 "	
John Greene	17 July	1547
John Obson	" "	
Agnes Addam	3 December	
Marian Horsly	6 February	
John Tylbury	19 March	1548
Stephen Berman	6 September	
Peter Addington	11 September	
Robert Addams	27 October	
Thomas Addams sonne	29 "	
Mother Jones	31 "	
Margaret Dawes, widdowe	31 December	
Prudens Ferris	1 January	
Johan Addams wyfe to Thomas Addams	13 "	
Gilbert Shelly	24 "	
Robert Dyer	17 February	
Jhone Docket	23 April	1549
Robert Harrison	26 "	
Agnes Homes	1 May	
Elizabeth Fleming	3 November	
Father Homes servant to S[r] John Carye	2 December	
Jane Pynchback	23 January	
Thomas Boshell	20 March	
Lawrence Byrchet	12 May	1550
Thoms Pavy	20 "	

This transcript of a parish register represents an early form of data collection. It was the published at the beginning of the 20th century.
Source: Collection, David Cufley

database program at her leisure. There are free programs available on the Internet (freeware or shareware) that convert information from the IGI so that it can go straight into your own genealogy program.

Genealogical Data on Cd-Rom

The list of CD-ROMs specifically for family history researchers grows longer with every week that passes. People all around the world are busy indexing, and this material along with earlier indexes in books or on microfilm (especially microfiche) is gradually being transferred to CD-ROM in a searchable database format.

This has revolutionised research from a number of points of view. For example, you may be searching for a birth record, and have the first name or names, and the year, but not the surname. The computer will rapidly sort though the whole database to see if any entries match the information you have entered. To help matters along, you may type in the given name for the mother or father or both, if you have it. A single result could soon be confirmed as the one you have been searching for, or perhaps a few possibilities will need to be given further attention. The latest CD-ROMs of births, deaths and marriages in Australia are now being released with software (Digger) which has a given-name thesaurus to solve the problems with common given name abbreviations. For instance, the revised Victorian Pioneers Index 1836–88 contains a given-name thesaurus as well as a gazetteer of Victorian place names. In the original index many of the place names were abbreviated and were sometimes very difficult to identify.

One of the important attributes of a searchable database is that you can easily find a name in a list which isn't alphabetical, such as the microfiche

Family Group Sheet Page 1 of 1

Husband	**Andrew Edward (Andy) DOWDELL**		
Born	25 Jul 1894	Richmond Victoria	
Died	1962	Richmond Victoria	
Occupation	Soldier		
Father	Francis Joseph (Will) DOWDELL (185	Mother	Harriett Caroline KNOX (1862-1942)
Married	1917	Victoria	
Wife	**Lillian Carlisle WILLIAMSON**		
Born	14 Sep 1898	Carlisle River, Victoria, Australia	
Died	17 Jun 1926	Richmond Victoria (120 Lord Street)	
Occupation	Home Duties		
Father	Charles WILLIAMSON (1860-1935)	Mother	Edith Mabel (May) FRANKS (1876-1952
Children			
1 F	**Mavis Carlisle DOWDELL**		
Born	1917	Victoria	
Died	1917	Newport Victoria	
2 M	**Edward Charles DOWDELL**		
Born	7 Sep 1918	Footscray, Victoria, Australia	
Died	14 Apr 1967	Parkville Victoria	
Occupation	Labourer/Welder		
Spouse	Maisie Ruth MARLOW		
Married	11 May 1940	Port Melbourne Victoria	
3 M	**Malcolm Lindsay DOWDELL**		
Born	1920	Newport Victoria	
Died	1921	Newport Victoria	
4 F	**Edith Jean (Twin) DOWDELL**		
Born	1922	Victoria	
Died	1922	Newport Victoria	
5 M	**Norman Keith (Twin) DOWDELL**		
Born	1922	Victoria	
Died	1922	Newport Victoria	
6 M	**Raymond Jeffrey DOWDELL**		
Born	1924	Victoria	
Died	1924	Newport Victoria	
7 M	**Desmond Lyle DOWDELL**		
Born	1926	Victoria	

Family group sheets are readily created by computer programs such as Reunion for Windows. These print-outs are a ready-reference to carry in a research folder and also can be included in a family history publication.
Source: Courtesy Barbara Cuffley

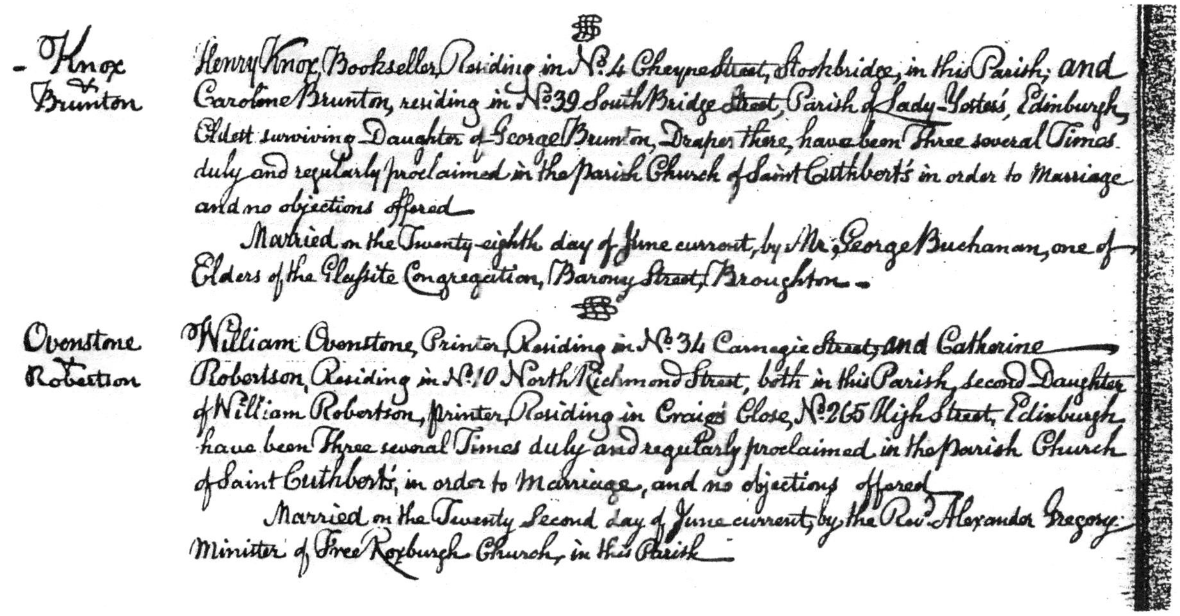

Knox & Brunton — Henry Knox, Bookseller, Residing in No 4 Cheyne Street, Stockbridge, in this Parish; and Caroline Brunton, residing in No 39 South Bridge Street, Parish of Lady Yester's, Edinburgh, Eldest surviving Daughter of George Brunton, Draper there, have been Three several Times duly and regularly proclaimed in the Parish Church of Saint Cuthbert's in order to Marriage and no objections offered.
Married on the Twenty eighth day of June current, by Mr George Buchanan, one of Elders of the Glassite Congregation, Barony Street, Broughton.

Ovenstone & Robertson — William Ovenstone, Printer, Residing in No 34 Carnegie Street, and Catherine Robertson, Residing in No 10 North Richmond Street, both in this Parish, second Daughter of William Robertson, printer, Residing in Craig's Close, No 265 High Street, Edinburgh, have been Three several Times duly and regularly proclaimed in the parish Church of Saint Cuthbert's, in order to Marriage, and no objections offered.
Married on the Twenty Second day of June current, by the Revd Alexander Gregory, Minister of Free Roxburgh Church, in this Parish.

Marriage entries for the parish of St Cuthbert's, Edinburgh, dating from 1849 offer, apart from the essential information, some very useful details such as name, occupation and address of the bride's father as well as her place in the family. All of this information helps build a family tree and can readily be entered in a genealogy program on your computer.
Source: National Archives for Scotland

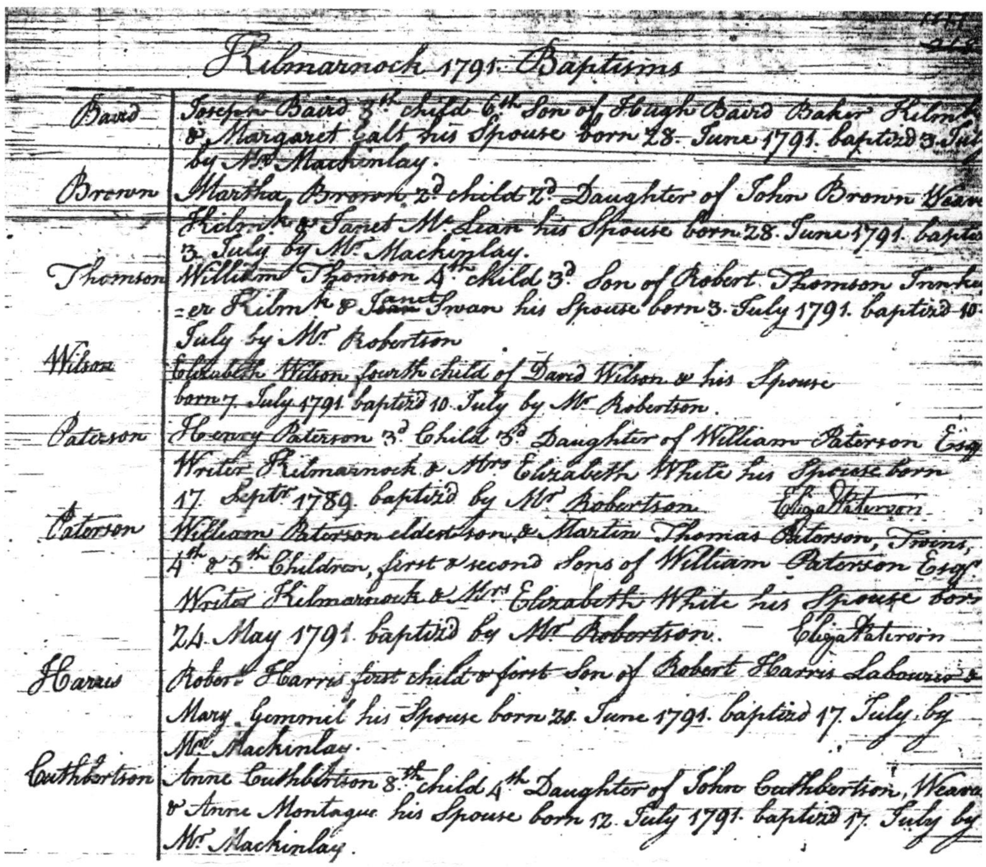

Kilmarnock 1791 Baptisms

Baird — Joseph Baird 8th child 6th Son of Hugh Baird Baker Kilmk & Margaret Galt his Spouse born 28 June 1791 baptized 3 July by Mr Mackinlay.

Brown — Martha Brown 2d child 2d Daughter of John Brown Weaver Kilmk & Janet McLean his Spouse born 28 June 1791 baptized 3 July by Mr Mackinlay.

Thomson — William Thomson 5th child 3d Son of Robert Thomson Innkeeper Kilmk & Janet Swan his Spouse born 3 July 1791 baptized 10 July by Mr Robertson

Wilson — Elizabeth Wilson fourth child of David Wilson & his Spouse born 7 July 1791 baptized 10 July by Mr Robertson.

Paterson — Henry Paterson 3d Child 3d Daughter of William Paterson Esq Writer Kilmarnock & Mrs Elizabeth White his Spouse born 17 Septr 1789 baptized by Mr Robertson Eliza Paterson

Paterson — William Paterson elder son & Martin Thomas Paterson, Twins, 4th & 5th Children, first & second Sons of William Paterson Esqr Writer Kilmarnock & Mrs Elizabeth White his Spouse born 24 May 1791 baptized by Mr Robertson. Eliza Paterson

Harris — Robert Harris first child & first Son of Robert Harris Labourer & Mary Gemmil his Spouse born 20 June 1791 baptized 17 July by Mr Mackinlay.

Cuthbertson — Anne Cuthbertson 8th child 4th Daughter of John Cuthbertson, Weaver & Anne Montague his Spouse born 12 July 1791 baptized 17 July by Mr Mackinlay.

Family historians are ever grateful for detailed entries in parish registers. This example from the register of baptisms for the Parish Church of Kilmarnock, Ayrshire, Scotland, gives not only date of birth and baptism, but also the child's place in the family. For example, Anne Cuthbertson is the '8th Child 4th daughter of John Cuthbertson, weaver and Anne Montague his spouse.' In earlier times, a mass of names, dates and facts could be difficult to keep track of. Computers have made the storage of information much more efficient.
Source: National Archives for Scotland

versions of the indexes of births, deaths and marriages. It is possible to search for mothers' maiden surnames in both births and deaths indexes, or maiden surnames for women whose deaths are recorded under their married name.

Ordinary indexes are usually by surname at a given time. When researching a married woman, her parents' names only appear if you have a database which is able to search for them. You will need to look for marriage

records (may give you her father's name, if the woman is not a widow or previously married); a birth record (maiden name usually given); a death record (usually parents' names are given, if known). The database program can also look for a mother's name for a male death given that we know his surname is the same as his father's surname.

Another option is to instruct the program to produce a list of entries based on parents' names. Say, a request for all of the children born to Edward Taylor with a mother Mary Brown, or even just a mother Mary, will quickly produce a list of entries. Whether you can be sure that they all belong to one set of parents will depend on the rarity of the names and other identifying factors such as place of birth.

Misspellings are one of the difficulties you may face at various stages of your research. In earlier centuries, before general literacy, there was little standardisation and people relied on phonetics. Family and given names might even be spelt in a number of different ways within a single document or a short period in a register. The spelling of names can vary right up to the present time for a number of reasons. Less common names, being unfamiliar, are often misread or misheard, and all names are subject to spelling mistakes or typographical errors.

We get letters with Chuffley, Cussley or Cuttley, all of which might be missed in searching an index. Some of my wife's relatives were recorded in Melbourne in 1842 as Mansfield (correct), Mansel and Maunsell. They were Irish immigrants, so perhaps we can imagine that the official writing down the name was having trouble with their accents. At that time, of course, not so many people were literate, though many illiterate people did learn how to make a crude signature, rather than have to make a mark (usually a cross).

The indexes of births, deaths and marriages on CD-ROM help catch spelling errors or variations by enabling you to use a surname prompt. For example you can enter Swe*y to catch Sweeney, Sweeny or Sweney. Or you can enter the first few letters followed by an asterisk to produce a larger range of names and possible variations. In this case you might enter Gri* to get Grieg, Grigg or even Grig. In the CD-ROMs published by Royal Melbourne Institute of Technology (INFORMIT) in association with the various Australian State registries, you enter a name, or a few letters, and can call up a list of variants. The ones you want to include in the search are then tagged by pressing F9 on your keyboard.

Apart from spelling mistakes made at the time of registration of a birth, death or marriage, there is always the chance of a later mistake in the indexing. In my own family research I was at a dead-end looking for a birth for Morrish until I chanced to find it under Monish. An entry for the death of Edward Smale in 1857, turned up under Smele. When the certificate was posted to me I could see how the original handwriting could be easily misread by the person doing the indexing. Recently I was searching for a Timothy Keary in a ship's passenger index and found him entered as Timy Carey. Obviously it helps when you apply lateral thinking to the puzzle so that even the oddest possibilities are tested. Sometimes the answer is so obvious it's embarrassing to admit that it has been missed. A search for Robert Layton or possibly

Libraries with substantial sections devoted to family history usually offer a good range of material on CD-ROM. This is a display board at Bendigo Library, a busy centre for genealogists and historians, including two family history groups.

Source: Courtesy Bendigo Library and Sally Routledge

Leighton was getting us nowhere and causing a bit of frustration for ourselves and a professional researcher in London. When the penny finally dropped that he was entered under Leyton we all felt a bit silly! Computers and searchable indexes will not solve every problem, but they certainly provide answers to a lot of conundrums in the area of given names and surnames.

When we know that our forebears or members of the family would have been giving information using an accent not well-understood by an official, we can expect some strange variations in the records for given names and surnames and places of origin. Sometimes it helps to find someone with an identical, or similar, accent and ask them to pronounce the surname or words, then write them down as they might have been interpreted.

Other Genealogical Programs

New products are appearing constantly and I expect that exciting new genealogical computer software will continue to be released. Information is always available on the Internet and downloadable demonstrations are helpful in making a choice to suit your needs.

Genealogy and family history are benefiting from the ever-increasing list of computer software. CD-ROMs covering subjects such as 19th century Australian history, Cornish origins, New South Wales land grants and regional or world history are all of great value. The information resource *Family History On Disk* is a single CD which combines a selection of family history databases such as the Australian Historic Records Registry and the Australasian Military History Database. And someone was thinking big when they began the task of putting the 1881 British census and National Index on to CD-ROM. Over thirty million individuals are listed on twenty-four CD-ROMs covering England, Scotland, Wales, Channel Islands, Isle of Man, and the Royal Navy. The *Index to Griffith's Valuation of Ireland 1848–64* is available on CD-ROM too, which makes access to these records so much easier. There are other useful CD-ROMs including interactive atlases, biographical indexes and telephone directories for Australia and other countries.

Genealogy and multimedia resources are one of the exciting facets of the use of computers for family history and we are really only beginning to explore a field with extraordinary potential.

Chapter Four
Treasures from the Internet

For family history researchers of the pre-computer era, the marvels of the present age are either just another confusing aspect of a changing world, or a dream come true. The first sign of change was the arrival, in genealogical libraries, of microfiche and microfilm. Anyone who knew the library of the Genealogical Society of Victoria (GSV) in the 1960s or before that time, will recall that it had a charming old-world air, in part due to its situation in the historic Block Arcade building at 282 Collins Street, Melbourne. My work took me away from the city for some years, and when I next found an opportunity to do some research at the library, the International Genealogical Index (IGI) had arrived on microfiche and I was soon eagerly scanning columns of names on the screen of a fiche-reader. The release of this

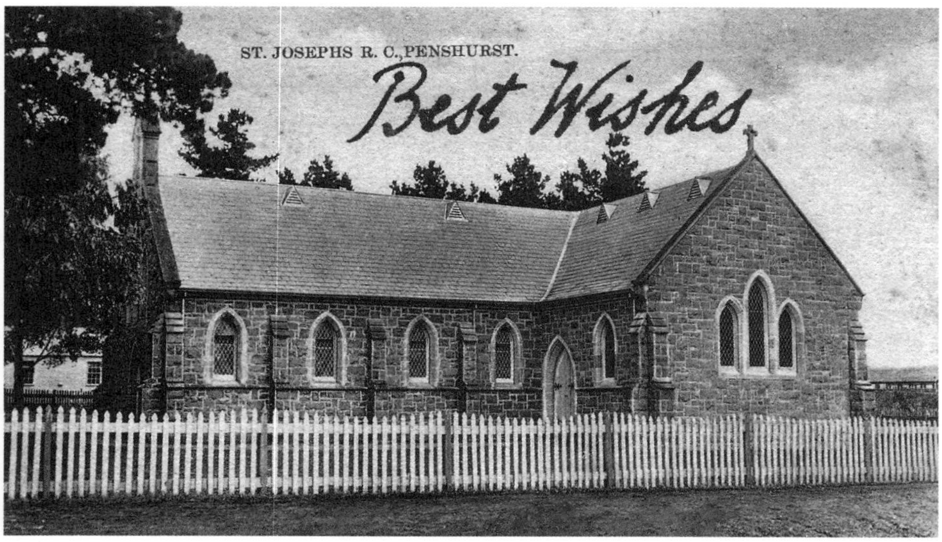

Penshurst is in Victoria's Western District. There is always a chance that a church with family associations might have appeared on a postcard. Nowadays, the Internet is an important resource in the search for old postcards. There are web sites created in Australia, and others overseas, where you can view or purchase postcards.
Source: Collection, Peter Cuffley

Michael Blake was born near Templemore, Tipperary, in 1816 and died there on 8 February 1913. His granddaughter, Ann Agnes Brennan, migrated to Victoria and in 1911 married Martin Dwyer. Something of the story of Ireland in the 19th century is conveyed in this wonderful portrait. Web sites about individuals, families, social history and places of interest are all on the Internet, and there is always an interest in Irish ancestry wherever Irish people have settled.
Source: Courtesy Denis Dwyer, great grandson

computer-produced first edition of the IGI resource in 1970 was a precursor to the many exciting developments of the following decades. Home computers equipped with genealogical databases proliferated in the 1980s, and the Internet began to boom in popularity in the early 1990s.

The Internet is not easily defined and certainly cannot be quantified. It offers access to a vast amount of information and in a year's time, or a month, it will have much more. Only a portion is of use in researching, disseminating or celebrating your family history, but even that encompasses an enormous and growing range of possibilities.

What is the Internet?

For those who have no clear picture of how the Internet works there are ways to visualise its structure. The words 'net' or 'web' are essential clues. Try to imagine the pattern of a fishing net with a computer at every knot, or a road network with a computer at every intersection. The definition 'a network of computer networks' describes the linking up of computers by telephone cable, optical fibre, or satellite transmission so that information can travel from one to the other in all directions. The networks are globally linked so we have the term Internet.

The Internet began with the Defence Department in the United States. They wanted a method of sending data from one computer to another that didn't rely on a single pathway which could well be rendered inoperable by a

system's breakdown, natural disaster, sabotage or enemy attack. In this network, a computer would receive data and then check to see whether it was addressed to itself, or was to be passed on through the network. What started as a system of regional networks, grew larger with the inclusion of government agencies, as well as colleges and universities. In time the wider links were made and it became accessible to everyone through Internet service providers. Electronic mail in the form which has become familiar to us as e-mail began in 1972.[1] The World Wide Web, a term coined to describe the information network which you have access to through the Internet, became operational in March 1989.[2]

Information, commentary, services, directories, person-to-person communication, message posting and broadcasting are just some of the ways in which the Internet is used. A large percentage of information on the Internet is free, but there are also many different kinds of services and products which require a monetary transaction. Family historians can be thankful that the ideal of sharing ensures that a large body of records, indexes and useful information is available cost-free. When charges are made they are very often based on the need to cover the expense of gathering, conserving and presenting material, though commercial enterprise is sometimes an important component.

Service Providers

Once you have purchased a computer, including a modem to facilitate your connection to the Internet, you'll need to subscribe to a commercial Internet Service Provider. These organisations are like junction boxes — they will put you in touch with the World Wide Web via your modem for a fee, which is often based on the time you spend connected ('on-line'). In some areas there is little or no choice because only one or two providers can offer a link. In built-up areas and the larger cities, there is competition which translates into a range of services at various prices.

Using the Internet

To get the maximum benefit from the Internet, you need to understand how to make the right connections. This means learning something of the different facets of this extraordinary resource and how you can link to specific individuals, groups, institutions or sites. A 'site' is an electronic address which has been created by either an individual or group. It is often referred to as a web page or a home page.

Genealogy or family history sites are always interesting but you can also contact individuals working on a particular surname, family group or specific place or region. In fact, there are family or surname associations and surname lists. Libraries, archives or record offices might have information you need; towns and cities which are important to your story can be represented in their own right or as part of a regional site. Information about restoration and conservation is there under a variety of titles or headings. Directories,

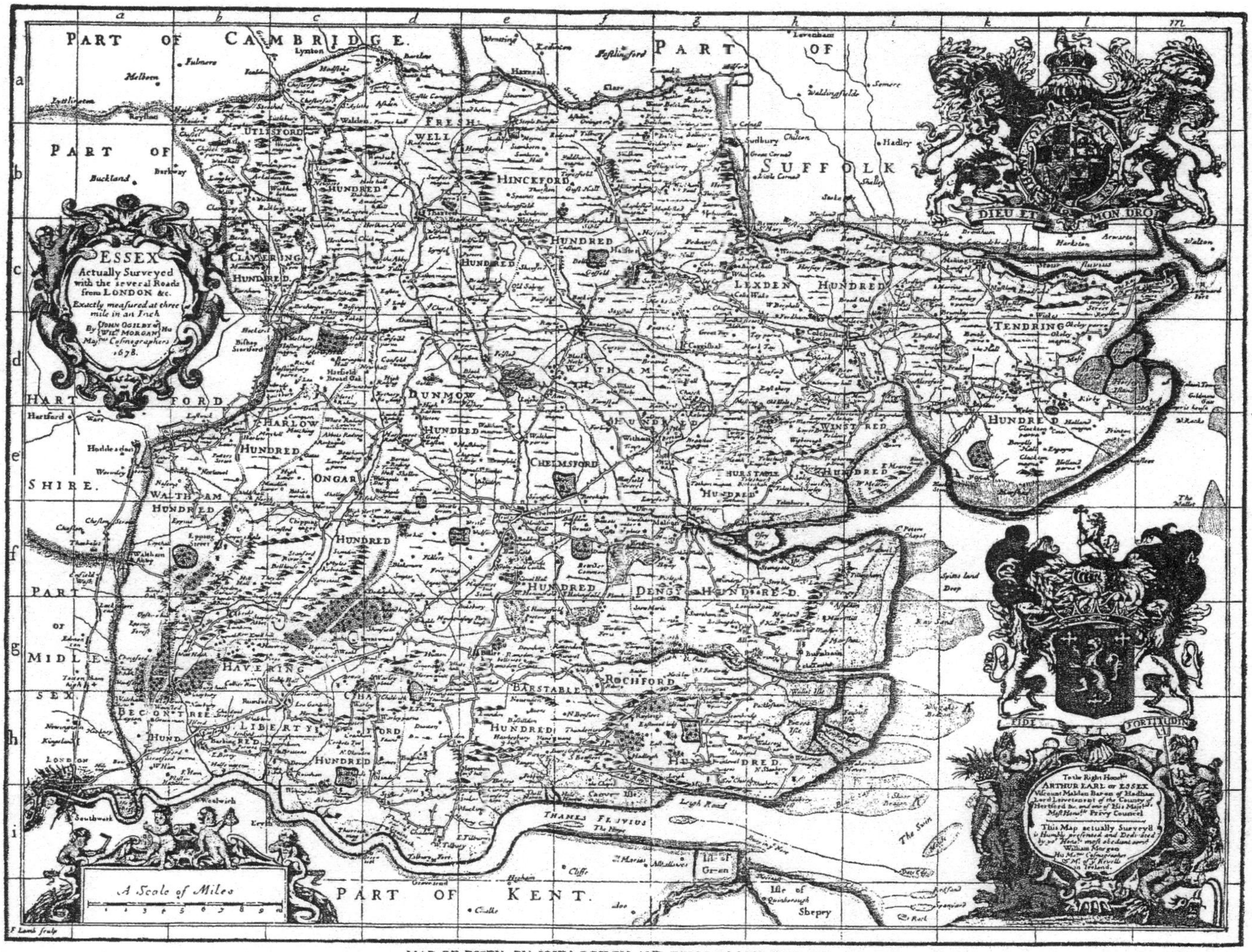

MAP OF ESSEX, BY JOHN OGILBY AND WILLIAM MORGAN, 1678 — Essex Record Office

Old maps can be both informative and decorative. This example is the county of Essex by John Ogilby and William Morgan and dates from 1678. Catalogues of maps and details of collections in archives can all be found on the Internet.

Source: Reproduced by courtesy of the Essex Record Office

gazetteers and maps, both historic and contemporary, are there for the finding.

Your research may lead you to specific books or other publications and these can be found in on-line catalogues. Antiquarian and specialist book dealers can be contacted and if a particular title is not in stock, they will keep your request on file and send you an e-mail if it turns up (see Internet bookshops, page 64).

In summary, there are two basic ways to use the Internet. There is electronic mail which allows you to communicate directly with anyone else on the Internet. Then there is the World Wide Web which is like an enormous encyclopaedia and shopping mall combined.

Electronic Mail (e-mail)

Old-fashioned letters continue to be part of my world, though I must admit, for rapid communication faxes or e-mails are ideal. For the efficient exchange of questions, requests, information and general messages, the electronic mail on the Internet is the way to keep your family history investigation moving

along at a reasonable pace. Person-to-person communication can be almost like a conversation, especially if you are both receiving and sending within the same time span.

Being able to give an e-mail address on ordinary letters, cards, or in directories and journals, ensures that people can contact you immediately, and once the e-mail addresses are in the system at both ends, messages and replies are automatically addressed so that all you need to do is click on 'send'. In order to have your own e-mail address, you need to be connected to a service provider first, then you follow some simple instructions from the provider to assign yourself an address. Usually your address is your own name, the service provider, and the location on the Internet. For example: bsmith@snakeville.com.au. Short messages can be composed and sent while you are on-line but generally it is best to type your message off-line, then next time you are on-line make sure it is sent, so very little on-line time is used.

Mailing Lists

Apart from direct communication, you can also use e-mail to subscribe to a mailing list. My wife is a member of Genealogists Using Microcomputers (GUM) and subscribes to that group's mailing list. The word 'subscribe' in this context means indicating your desire to be part of a group. Subscribing to

There are many sites on the Internet devoted to Scotland and Scottish history. The tartan sites are particularly interesting. Robert Oliver, a central Victorian grazier, is clearly very proud of his Scottish heritage. The photograph was taken by Verey of Castlemaine in the 1920s.
Source: Collection, Ashley Tracey

All Saints Church, Morston, is on the north Norfolk coast. The villages of Stiffkey, Morston and Blakeney look out over salt marshes and there are flat sand and shingle beaches. Giles Daniel (c. 1825–1910), a pioneer of Oakleigh, Victoria, migrated from this area in the 1840s. His son Giles Felix Daniel, visited Morston in 1887 and came home with this treasured photograph of the church. Images of parish churches including Morston, can be found on the Internet.
Source: Courtesy Fran Townsing (née Daniel)

a mailing list means that every e-mail that each member sends to the mailing list address of the group is received by all subscribed members of the mailing list. You need to be careful as some mailing lists consist of lots of members, and the resultant incoming mail from these lists can add up to some hundreds each day.

Fortunately, you can choose how you receive these messages, either as individual e-mails or in a digest form. The digest groups a certain number of the e-mails in one e-mail transmission and lists the subjects at the beginning of the e-mail, then you can scroll through it in its entirety depending on your interests. This reduces the incoming e-mails considerably. If your e-mail program allows, you can also filter incoming and outgoing e-mails into their own specific mail boxes and this helps keep track of a selected area of interest. A common way of subscribing to a mailing list is to go to the group's home page on the World Wide Web and click on a box to indicate your wish to subscribe. Then you fill in your own e-mail address and become a member of the list. It's fun!

The Victorian group, GUM, serves all states and can be found on the Internet at: [http://www.vicgum.asn.au]. For a very modest annual fee, members receive a monthly newsletter which offers all kinds of useful information. Importantly there is a 'Dial Help' service where volunteers assist members free of charge. Both telephone numbers and e-mail addresses are given, so that advice on genealogy software, the Internet and many other related subjects is readily available. One of the important aspects of this organisation is its Australian perspective which ensures that it reflects local experience, including evaluations of imported software.

When you join a mailing list, you become part of a group with shared interests. In genealogy and family history research, give and take should be the central philosophy. You help others and they help you; the more we share the more there is to go around. Information, helpful hints, interesting

experiences, even warnings of traps for the unwary, these can all be sent out as messages to the whole group. On the other hand, you may be able to help one particular member and therefore you would respond directly to them using the e-mail address given when they posted a query or comment.

For those of you who are keen to see more mailing lists, there is a web site which is home to the largest collection of genealogy mailing lists on the World Wide Web at: [http://www.rootsweb.com/roots-l/]. If you think you would like to subscribe to one of the mailing lists you just have to click on your choice, then an e-mail form comes up and you type in 'subscribe' in the body of the e-mail (not the subject line, leave that empty).

Newsgroups

Newsgroups also use e-mail addresses and function in a similar way to mailing lists. In this case, you e-mail a message to a 'news server' and it is posted on a public message board. Before you can access a newsgroup, your service provider must have access to the group via a 'news feed'. Alternatively, if your provider doesn't have this connection, you can view and 'post' messages to newsgroups quite simply on the Internet at various sites such as [http://www.dejanews.com].

There are thousands of message boards on the Internet and the genealogy messages boards have multiplied to such an extent that the popular ones have been subdivided into specific interest newsgroups. Groups are categorised in hierarchies. For a genealogical example, the most relevant newsgroup is called soc.genealogy ('soc' is the first level, 'genealogy' is the second level). At the time of writing, there are twenty-six newsgroups at the next level under soc.genealogy. One newsgroup [soc.genealogy.surnames], was reorganised into seven groups. Five of them cover specific regional areas. The seven newsgroups are:

- [soc.genealogy.surnames.britain] — Great Britain, Channel Isles, Isle of Man;
- [soc.genealogy.surnames.canada] — Canada;
- [soc.genealogy.surnames.german] — German-speaking areas of Europe;
- [soc.genealogy.surnames.ireland] — Republic of Ireland and Northern Ireland;
- [soc.genealogy.surnames.usa] — United States of America and territories;
- [soc.genealogy.surnames.misc] — other countries;
- [soc.genealogy.surnames.global] — worldwide.

All the information you need on the soc.genealogy.surnames family of newsgroups and associated surnames mailing lists can be found on the Internet at: [http://www.rootsweb.com/~surnames/#posting].

Other soc.genealogy newsgroups include: [soc.genealogy.australia+nz], [soc.genealogy.britain] and [soc.genealogy.ireland]. If you want to search an index of surnames which have already been posted by newsgroup contributors, try the Rootsweb Surname List at: [http://rsl.rootsweb.com/cgi-bin/rslsql.cgi].

Scottish Towns

Muthill

Three miles south of Crieff on the A822 in lush agricultural land is the picturesque conservation village of Muthill with a total of 96 "listed" buildings which include some of the finest examples of 18th century Scottish vernacular architecture.

Whilst the correct pronunciation is "Mewthill," strangers understandably say "Mutt-hill" which gave rise to the dubious explanation of the ancestry of the name Moot Hill ("hill of meeting"). This Anglo-Saxon lineage is hotly disputed by Gaelic speakers who insist that the name was originally "Meaothail" - ("soft place"). "Meeting place" or "soft place," this settlement on a major route north has seen and suffered countless military incursions; from the Romans in the 1st century to the Jacobites in the 18th.

Town Map | Local History | Museum | Drummond Castle | Highlandman's Green | Parish Church | Accommodation | Visitor Attractions

Crieff & Strathearn

An ever-increasing number of towns and villages can be found on the Internet. Most of these homepages are illustrated and often there is a short history. Muthill is at [`http://www.scottish-towns.co.uk/perthshire/muthill/index.htm`*].*
Source: Courtesy The Perfect Solution. Drawing from Aiton Fine Arts, Crieff, Scotland

Before posting a message with a newsgroup I suggest that you spend some time checking that any questions you might ask haven't been answered previously. You can also get a sense of the working of the group and the kind of queries, comments or information that would be appropriate by watching the postings for a while. This is called 'lurking' and helps you absorb the formal and informal rules which enable the newsgroup to work efficiently.

So, if you want to subscribe to a newsgroup via your e-mail, remember there are subscription addresses and posting addresses, and that you need to have access, via your service provider, to the newsgroup. The subscription address is a link to the administrator of the newsgroup, and the posting address is for posting an actual message. For example, if you are interested in Polish genealogy and want to subscribe to the newsgroup 'genpol', you send a

'subscribe genpol' command to the subscription address: [listserv@ plearn.edu.pl]. The address for postings is: [genpol@plearn.edu.pl].

WORLD WIDE WEB

Since its inception in 1989, the World Wide Web (WWW) has become the primary means of accessing the vast quantities of information being placed on the Internet. It is described as a system for viewing and using multimedia documents and we do this by means of Web browsing software. Netscape Navigator and Microsoft Internet Explorer are two of the best-known browser programs. HyperText Markup Language (HTML) is used to create web documents with each web site being made up of one or more pages. A hypertext reference (HREF) is a highlighted word or phrase which is a link that you can click on with your cursor. This takes you to another part of the document you are in or to another site entirely that has some reference to the current site.

Search Engines

Having obtained a connection to the World Wide Web by means of your Internet service provider (ISP), you can then go on-line. If you already have the address of a site you wish to go to, you type it into the location box at the top of the screen and press the return key. The connection will be made if the site is available. A web site addresses is known as a URL (Uniform Resource Locator) and consists of a long group of letters and symbols, for example: [http://home.netscape.com/au/].

If you are not sure of the URL or have no idea of it, you can elect to search for its address by using a 'search engine'. Your browser has a 'search' button built in, or your home page, provided by your ISP, often has a group of search engines you can use. Choose a search engine such as Alta Vista and in the box provided enter some key words that reflect your search requirements. Press return and the engine goes away and searches the web for the occurrence of

The clipper ship Blue Jacket *was launched at East Boston, Massachusetts on 27 August 1854. Her first Australian voyage was to Melbourne, having departed Liverpool on 6 March 1855 under Captain E. Underwood. Taking the great circle route, it made the journey in 68 days, and a painting by Thomas Baines shows her passing an iceberg in latitude 49 degrees south. A detailed description of the ship can be obtained from the Internet by entering 'clipper ship blue jacket' on a browser.*

Source: Collection, Peter Cuffley

ABOVE AND OPPOSITE: *Mid-19th century illustrations of sailing vessels. Source: Collection, Peter Cuffley*

these key words. When the search engine has finished the search you will be presented with a number of sites that have your key words in them. It is a matter of finding the one most relevant to your needs. Remember that each search engine has its own protocol for searching so it is a good idea to look at the tips or helpful hints on the search engine you have chosen.

Being a lateral thinker I thoroughly enjoy the challenge of turning up useful information from all kinds of sites by using a selection of key words. Often such searches are very straightforward in that one, two or three words will immediately bring up the results you want. Unexpectedly detailed returns are always welcome. For example, I wanted to find out about a clipper ship *Red Jacket* which made a voyage to Melbourne in 1855. I typed the words 'ship Red Jacket' and clicked on the search button and up came a good selection of sites. One turned out to be a description and chronology which confirmed the dates I had for the voyage and also the captain's name (Milward). The site included newspaper accounts of some of the Boston-built clippers which were on the England to Australia run. There was also a clipper ship called *Blue Jacket*. Turn back to page 59 to see an engraving of it in full sail.

But even if your query seems obscure, you should always be optimistic, for the Internet is a place you can find the most unlikely information. No library on the planet could have as broad a range of material, however, in many cases the information offered is only a summary or extract and lacks the depth of a hard-copy publication. The time and space required to download information encourages brevity. An important function of the Internet is to make available material which signposts the directions you might take with archives, books, documents and papers. It may also inspire journeys in real time, having whetted your appetite with words and images.

Selection Criteria

Search engines comb through vast indexes of information to find the sites and resources which may fit the search request you have entered. The indexes are generated by programs called Robots, which in turn, have gathered the material from the Internet. While there is some variation in the way search engines operate, at a basic level, a search request is entered in more or less the same way. If you type in a single word, the only question is whether to begin with a capital letter. Given names are sometimes more easily identified when they begin with capitals, but most search engines will find what you want if the request is all lower case.

The next option is to use two or more words and decide how they can be linked. If you type in the following two words — Italian surnames — you will get a long listing of sites which include the word 'Italian' and lots which have the word 'surnames'. To ensure both words appear in the same document, you normally place a plus sign (+) between them — Italian+surnames. In some search engines the plus sign is placed in front of each word. If you want to find words appearing together — history of Italian surnames — you enter the words within quotation marks — 'history of Italian surnames'.

You need to be logical and sometimes imaginative in the key words or phrases you submit though you should also take care not to make requests

which will return a huge number of results (hits). Each search engine provides 'search tips' and any other help you might require.

When you are searching for information about a village, town or city, it is best to add the county, state or country in case there are a number of places with the same name. My wife has ancestors who lived in Halifax, Yorkshire (West Riding). If you just enter Halifax, places including Halifax, Nova Scotia will turn up. Unusual names are naturally easier to locate, but even then it is surprising how many additional hits you can get with people's surnames, the name of a business or organisation, or even a street name.

Special Interest Sites

Beyond all of this, there is a wealth of information to be had from all kinds of sites. Sometimes individuals have put extracts from old gazetteers or histories on their sites, or have created a contemporary picture of a place simply because they live there. Libraries, museums and archives also offer information on places or place names, while local authorities, organisations and companies promoting tourism are very keen to tell their story.

Remember that the Internet is universal and multi-lingual, so you can search for places anywhere on the planet and if you find them, the site may well be in a language other than English. Sites relating to genealogy or family history in a non-English speaking country are often created in English in regions such as North America or Australasia, by descendants of migrants. My son and daughter have Norwegian ancestry and there are very informative sites on Norway which originate in parts of the United States with a strong Scandinavian heritage. The 1801 census of Norway is available on the World Wide Web at: [http://rsl.rootsweb.com/cgi-bin/rslsql.cgi]. This is part of a site called 'How to Trace Your Ancestors in Norway' created by an individual enthusiast.

One of the sites of special interest to Australians with Irish ancestry is 'Views of the Famine' compiled by Steve Taylor at: [http://vassun.vassar.edu/~sttaylor/FAMINE/]. The first page of this web site has a dramatic painting of famine victims, and then there is a long list of black and white images taken from illustrated newspapers and journals. You'll also find a heart-wrenching six-page account of a journey through Ireland in the year 1847, called 'Narrative of a Journey from Oxford to Skibbereen During the Year of the Irish Famine' by Lord Dufferin and the Honorable G.G. Boyle. Many family historians researching Irish convicts have had positive results from an on-line search of the Transportation Records at the National Archives of Ireland home page at: [http://www.nationalarchives.ie/search01.html].

On-line Searches

There are many searchable indexes which are linked to web sites. For instance, the Scots Origins site is a pay-per-view database of the genealogical records of the General Register Office for Scotland. Inaugurated in April 1998, this on-line service can be a great help to researchers who cannot visit New Register House in Edinburgh or one of the centres which hold records on film.

On-line access for twenty-four hours currently costs £6 sterling, so you can search the database for a birth, christening or marriage on the Old Parochial Records, or a birth, marriage or death on the Statutory Indexes (after 1855), or the 1891 Census of Scotland.

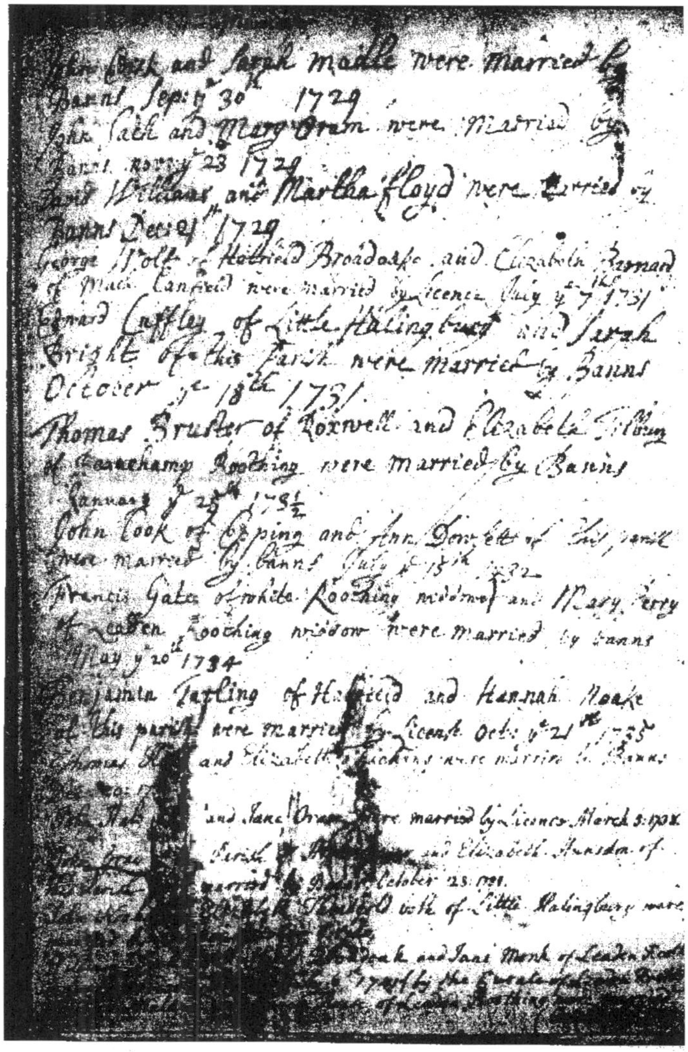

A page from the marriage register of Abbess Roding (Abbess Roothing), Essex, showing the marriage of the author's ancestors Edward Cuffley and Sarah Bright in 1731. This copy was obtained from the Essex Record Office which has an informative web site at: [http://www.essexcc.gov.uk/heritage].
Source: Reproduced by courtesy of the Essex Record Office

When a list of possible records is displayed you can decide whether you need to narrow the search or use one of your ten page credits to display and print-out the selected group of detailed entries. If one or more of these is a record you would like to purchase as a full certificate, you can follow the Extract Ordering procedure and pay the fee required by credit card. This is done by means of a secure payment site which you will have already used to pay the initial fee. At present a certificate costs £10 sterling and will be mailed to the address you supply. One point to make is that once you have paid a fee for twenty-four hours of access, you are given a user ID and password so you can log off or on at any time within that period.

To maximise the value of the service, you need to be well prepared with all of your possibilities on a list, so you are not scrambling through bundles of

papers while on-line. We thoroughly enjoyed our first search session and found it was something like a challenging computer game. Being at home you can really get excited when you realise you have found a vital record, whereas in the more subdued atmosphere of a library, you have to contain that desire to yell 'Bingo!'. Having cups of tea or coffee close to hand is another benefit of being at home. My wife obtained a couple of key certificates from that first session with Scots Origins and these opened up new areas of research which have proved very rewarding. If you want to learn more about this on-line database, you can download general information and sample extracts from: [http://www.origins.net/GRO/about.html While assurance is given that use of your credit card for on-line services is within secure systems, you may want to use a card based on an account with limited funds for any such transactions.

Another on-line resource, 'Immigration to Victoria 1852–69', is useful for tracing people who arrived in Victoria in the 1850s. This searchable database from the Public Records Office of Victoria can be found at: [http://shipping.cohsoft.com.au/cgi-bin/db/ship.pl]. The information at the site includes surname, given names, age, month and year of voyage, name of ship and a cross-reference to the fiche records. These records comprise photographs of the actual pages of ships registers of passengers, and can be consulted in many libraries. Most states have these records but only Victoria has a searchable site as yet.

A number of states in Australia offer pay-per-view searchable databases which give you access to records of births, deaths and marriages. Eventually, these sites will have scanned images of the actual records which you'll be able to download for a fee.

A quantum leap in on-line research came with the release on the World Wide Web of the FamilySearch Internet Genealogy Service in early 1999. Apart from the International Genealogical Index, this remarkable site offers access to Ancestral File, the Family History Library Catalogue, the Source Guide, the location of Family History Centres, collaboration mailing lists, and links to thousands of web sites. The Church of Jesus Christ of Latter-Day Saints has once again shared its vast resources with the whole community. The address of this site is: [http://www.familysearch.com].

Most record offices and archives now have home pages on the Internet with details of their collections and services. Often these are listed in sites which offer direct links. One example is UK Archival Repositories on the Internet which can be found at: [http://web.ukonline.co.uk/ddlg.uk/uksites.htm]. It covers many county record offices and records held at university libraries.

One of the sites I was pleased to find lists the date of Easter Sunday in any year complete with a full calendar for that year. As my very handy universal calendar only goes back to 1749, it is useful to be able to match a date to a day of the week, for any year before that time. This resource comes from the Anglican Diocese of Ely in England and can be found at: [http://www.ely.anglican.org/cgi-bin/easter]. I'm also interested in sites devoted to bell ringing because the names of English parish churches,

Carte-de-visite from the period 1860–1870. Two boys solemnly posing for posterity.

Source: Collection, Janet Goodchild-Cuffley

Carte-de-visite from the period 1860–1880. Peeping pantalets and triple frills, for a special occasion.
Source: Collection, Janet Goodchild-Cuffley and Peter Cuffley

which are not included in many entries found in the International Genealogical Index, can often be found there. The Hertford County Association of Change-Ringers established in 1884, has a Bishops Stortford District home page at: [http://www.crsshll.demon.co.uk/hcacr/main.htm]. By clicking on Thorley, for example, you find the parish church is St James the Great.

Cyndi's List

On a different scale altogether, you can access resources such as the famous Cyndi's list of genealogical sites on the Internet at: [http://www.cyndislist.com]. At the time of writing, this web site had over 40 000 cross-referenced links in over ninety categories. Some general categories to explore are: Australia and New Zealand; heraldry; LDS and Family History Centres; maps, gazetteers and geographical information; United Kingdom and Ireland General Index; societies and groups; citing sources; libraries, archives and museums.

This site also has a Genealogical Home Page Construction Kit and a list of personal home pages which will lead you to a vast network of genealogists and family historians. Links to this site are continuously being added or updated. To keep up with updates of Cyndi's list you can register your e-mail address and details will be sent to you.

The first home page to list and link genealogy sites was Genealogy Home Page at: [http://www.genhomepage.com] It was created and is still maintained by Stephen Wood. Australasian Genealogy Web (AGWeb) provides a comprehensive range of links of special interest to family historians in this region. It is found at: [http://home.vicnet.net.au/~AGWeb/].

If there is a chance that a surname you are researching is registered with the Guild of One-Name Studies, you should visit their home page at: [http://www.one-name.org/]. Members of this international organisation can offer help and information and are always pleased to receive research and documentation which could be added to their studies.

Transferring Data

The direct transfer of files, databases, indexes and images is an important function of the Internet. File Transfer Protocol (FTP) enables transfers to take place between computers if the appropriate software has been loaded. While you need authorisation to download files in many instances, there are also many sites which allow 'anonymous' as a login or user-name with your full e-mail address as the password.

Text files, shareware and freeware can all be downloaded including updates of commercial software. Family history material can also be transferred as an 'attachment' on an e-mail. Both text and images can be sent this way; the text will be a .TXT file and images are best sent in the smallest file size possible such as a .JPG or a .TIF file.

Internet Bookshops

Books and journals are still an essential resource, even in this age of electronic wonders, and the Internet is another means of locating and acquiring books,

alongside the traditional bookshop and mail-order catalogue. Many sites contain information about books and some have lengthy reading lists which are useful in studying the social or geographic aspects of family history. For example, information on British and Irish rural history is contained in works listed in the Rural History Database, an on-line bibliography of over 40 000 records available to subscribers. Details of the bibliography and a subscriber contact can be found on the Rural History Homepage at: [http://www.reading.ac.uk/Instits/im/rural/bib.html].

The Weald and Downland Open Air Museum at Singleton, Chichester, West Sussex, can be a great source of information on English rural life in earlier centuries. Their web site at [http://www.wealddown.co.uk/] includes information on exhibits and a long list of publications on traditional architecture, agriculture, trades, crafts, household life and building conservation.
Source: Photograph by Toni Lumsden

Another source of genealogical books and supplies which are British Isles in focus, is the Institute of Heraldic and Genealogical Studies Family History Bookshop at http://www.cs.ncl.ac.uk/genuki/IHGS/Catalogue.html]. This bookshop is physically located in England.

Two notable sources in Australia with home pages on the Internet are Gould Books based at Gumeracha, South Australia, and Macbeth Genealogical Services based in Melbourne. Some 7500 titles are listed in the Gould Books on-line catalogue and the web site is at: [http://www.gould.com.au]. Macbeth Genealogical Services offer a series of catalogues, including a 'must have' book list for Australasian genealogy. Their web site address is: [http://www.macbeth.com.au].

Every year that passes from the writing of this chapter will expand the horizons of the Internet. In the meantime, family historians have a plethora of on-line resources to enjoy right now.

Chapter Five
Cultural Diversity

Among the thousands of people who arrived in the period 1788 to 1900, there were Chinese, Italians, French, Swedes, Danes, Norwegians, Greeks, Indians, West Indians, Lebanese, Melanesians, Polynesians, Portuguese, Spanish, Afghans, Hungarians, Maltese, Finns and citizens of the United States who, in turn, were of various origins. As a group, Jewish people were represented on the First Fleet and grew steadily in number throughout the 19th century.

If statistics show that Australian immigration since 1788 has been predominantly from the British Isles and Western Europe, it is important to remember that among these groups there is an abundance of cultural and ethnic diversity. The three main groups of early immigrants were the English, the Celts and the Germans. Within these broad categories, the people from England generally identified with county or regional origins, while the Irish, Scots, Welsh and Cornish were all proud of their differences.

Cologne is situated on the west bank of the Rhine and was part of Prussia after 1814. The river trade was important until the arrival of the railways. This view is mid-19th century.
Source: Collection, Don and Zara Latimer

German-speaking Settlers

German-speaking settlers came from various states, kingdoms and principalities. The province of Silesia in Prussia was a major source of migrants for Australia. In fact, Germany did not become a single state until 1870, long after the 1838 settlement scheme in South Australia under the auspices of entrepreneur George Fife Angus.[1] As well as the main group from Silesia, there were also Poles and Slavic Wends to add to South Australia's cultural mix.

Queensland was the other colony which received a large share of German migrants. First in 1838, a small group settled on the coast north of Brisbane and then from the early 1860s sizeable numbers began to arrive. Victoria received its early German population by direct migration and from the drift of settlers across the border from South Australia. By 1857 there were nearly 8000 Germans living in Victoria and a number of notable settlements were established.[2]

Making a New Life

The population of involuntary migrants over the period 1788–1868 was around 160 000. The number of convicts of non-British origin has been estimated as high as 3000, including a few West Indians of African descent.[3] My convict ancestor, Thomas Sweeney, was assigned in December 1823 to James Chandler of 'Bexley' south-west of Sydney, and he would have known another convict also assigned to Chandler, William Cornwallis, who was listed as a 'St Domingo black'.[4]

Apart from John 'Black' Caesar, often described as Australia's first bushranger, the best known of the West Indians was Billy Blue, a Jamaican convict who was transported in 1796. He became a legendary ferryman on Sydney Harbour and gave his name to Blue's Point.[5]

This happy picture is of a Greek family picnic at Seaford, Victoria, around 1929. From 1952 Melbourne's Greek population grew dramatically.
Source: La Trobe Picture Collection, State Library of Victoria

Overall, the convict system was seen as a source of low-cost labour and for many free settlers it was an essential component in the creation of businesses and landed estates. When transportation to New South Wales came to an end in 1840, the availability of cheap labour became an important question. In 1847 Benjamin Boyd, an entrepreneur and landowner, brought workers from the New Hebrides to Boydtown on the south coast of New South Wales. In the following year, contract labourers from China arrived, some five years before the gold rushes began to attract Chinese in large numbers. Although gold had been found in New South Wales and Victoria before 1851, it was the discoveries of that year which unleashed a social phenomenon of far-reaching effect.

Jumping Ship

A great flood of immigration began with people from all over the world arriving at the various ports. To add to the tide, ships' crews deserted in droves and many a sailor stayed on to become a permanent resident.

My son and daughter have a maternal ancestor who was Norwegian. He sailed into Melbourne in 1857, and later told his family that by sunset on the day of arrival the whole crew had deserted. As the ship's cook he had stayed behind with the captain who was also a family friend.

After several days there seemed no hope of finding a new crew, so William Schmidt asked for permission to leave the ship to head for the goldfields. The captain said, 'Schmidt, you cannot leave me!' But during the night he rolled up his bundle of belongings and went over the side. Because jumping ship was a serious matter, he became William Smith and was known by that name for the rest of his life. When official statistics are quoted, I often wonder how many people in earlier times had simply arrived without ever being recorded and just melted into the landscape.

Records of Arrivals

From the beginning of organised migration to Australia right up to the present day, there has always been some form of documentation. Mostly it has survived and is kept in various archives. The amount of information on each individual varies from the barest details such as name, age and origin, to highly informative papers of great value to family historians.

Before 1947 government immigration schemes were directed towards people from the British Isles. The only exception was the recruitment and assistance given by the Queensland government to people from Germany and Scandinavia. However, due to World War I, German immigration was banned from 1914 to 1925.[6] A great change in official policy took place immediately after World War II, when the assisted migration schemes were widened to include refugees and displaced persons from Europe. Agreements between the Commonwealth government and individual countries also resulted in a broadening range of migrants not necessarily affected by the war, but who were seeking new lives and greater opportunities.

If members of your family came to Australia as assisted or unassisted migrants or as refugees, at any time since the founding of the Commonwealth

A dramatic background of ringbarked trees is testimony to the need for settlers to establish themselves quickly in the early years of taking up a selection. This family of pioneers, thought to be of German origin, was photographed in the 1890s in the Murra Murra (Haden) area of south-east Queensland.
Source: Collection, Carbethon Folk Museum and Pioneer Village, Crows Nest, Queensland

of Australia in 1901, there will be a number of resources which offer vital records for your family history. Apart from the story surrounding the migration, there could well be facts revealed of great value in your research relating to earlier generations and places of origin. Commonwealth government immigration records are listed in detail in *Finding Families*, published by the National Archives of Australia in 1998.

Passenger records are an important aspect of your search even from the earliest decades of settlement. Various kinds of indexes are available for arrivals in the 19th century and these are being added to as work progresses. There are no consolidated indexes for 20th century arrivals and this means the name of the ship, approximate date of arrival and place of embarkation, are facts you will hopefully have before approaching the archives. The same applies to arrivals by air. For ships and aeroplanes, there are passenger lists and passenger cards, the former from 1852 to 1973, and the latter from 1948. Passenger cards substitute for passenger lists after these were discontinued in 1973.[7] State archives also hold rolls of migrants in certain cases and *Finding Families* has a guide to both national and state holdings. The Australian National Archives is an important resource for this type of search. Their web site is at: [http://www.naa.gov.au].

Records for immigrants and refugees can include case files, selection documents, accommodation records and naturalisation and citizenship records. The National Archives has published a series of fact sheets which you may want to refer to. Two examples are: No. 66 Migrant Selection Documents in Canberra, and No. 68 Naturalisation Records Held in Canberra. In February 1904, the Commonwealth of Australia issued its first certificate of naturalisation. Before that time the colonies and states were

responsible for naturalisation. Some indexes of these records have been published such as the index for naturalisations in South Australia. It should be noted that until 1948, people became a 'British subject'; the concept of Australian citizenship came after that time.[8]

When it comes to researching family history outside the British Isles, the quantity of resource material varies to a great degree. Australian families of German origin are well served with many published histories and an accumulation of records and resources. Other groups of settlers such as the Italians, Swiss–Italians, Greeks, Chinese and Maltese have all been well represented in publications and research projects. The existence of books, guides, indexes and accessible records, depends on the interest and commitment of individuals, groups and institutions.

In some cases, material relating to immigrants from a particular country may be scarce or even impossible to find. However, people from the same country may have gone to Canada or the United States in larger numbers, so that resources exist there which could prove very helpful. One such umbrella group with a long list of web sites is the Federation of Eastern European Family History Societies, which is based in Salt Lake City, Utah, but has links to fourteen countries. The Internet address is: [http://www.feefhs.org]. An affiliated group, the Slovenian Genealogical Society, has chapters in twelve states of the USA, two in Canada and one in Australia. Their address is: [http://www.feefhs.org/slovenia/si/frg-sigs.html].

In Search of Your European Roots: A Complete Guide to Tracing Your Ancestors in Every Country in Europe is an excellent guide for anyone setting out to research ancestry in Europe (see Bibliography). This book offers a wealth of information on the availability and whereabouts of records and how you can access them in person or by correspondence.

Atlases and maps are an essential tool wherever you are searching. It is especially important that you are able to take account of changes in borders, town or village names, and political history which may lead to a change of name for a country, state or region. The next section lists places of origin outside the British Isles with some directions for your family history research.

OPPOSITE (TOP): *From its opening in 1869, the Suez Canal became a part of the experience for many people who travelled to Australia by sea. This coloured postcard captures Port Said as it was in the first half of the 20th century.*
Source: Collection, Peter Cuffley

OPPOSITE: *Celebrated for his goldfields' pictures, Samuel Thomas Gill painted some fine views of Adelaide in the 1840s. This delightful work is entitled* Port Adelaide looking across Gawler Reach. *This was the gateway for thousands of immigrants who settled in South Australia in the 19th century.*
Source: S. T. Gill, born England 1818, arrived Australia 1839, died Melbourne 1880 Port Adelaide looking across Gawler Reach *1848, watercolour, body colour on paper 28.2 x 46.1 cm*
Art Gallery of South Australia, Adelaide Gift of the South Australian Company 1890 0.646

Western Europe

Germany

How you go about tracing your German ancestors depends on when they arrived in Australia and the amount of information already in hand. If you know your forebears came here in the 19th century, you could well find a published history which will give you a flying start. The State Library of Victoria has a marvellous site on the World Wide Web which includes a searchable index of surnames found in German–Australian family histories of the 19th and 20th centuries. This can be found at: [http://www.slv.vic.gov.au/slv/genealogy/german/g_ger_b.htm]. Many entries include summaries of the stories of individuals and families.

A number of social histories and detailed studies can be found in libraries and some of these are listed in the Bibliography. The South Australian

PORT SAID VUE GÉNÉRALE DU CANAL

This Indenture
GOODCHILD
&
STEPHENSON
THE NEW AUSTRALIAN CLIPPER
NOTICE
AUSTRALIAN PACKET OFFICE.
TOWER CHAMBERS,
LIVERPOOL.
NAUTICAL WAREHOUSE.
JOHN & S.A. CAIL
Mathematical & Optical Instrument
Makers &c.
45, Quayside
NEWCASTLE on TYNE.

Settlers with a German wagon in the Barossa Ranges, South Australia. This view by John Skinner Prout (1805–1876) was published as an engraving in Australia Illustrated *in 1873.*
Source: Collection, Peter Cuffley

Genealogy and Heraldry Society has an index of settlers of Germanic or Polish stock which is continually updated. It gives name, ship and date of arrival, and often the place of embarkation (see Useful Addresses). There is also an Internet site called 'German Genealogy: Tips for Researchers' at: [http://www2.genealogy.net/gene/www/ghlp/tips.num]. This site has various links to other sites and a list of resources.

Netherlands

The Dutch settled in Australia in large numbers after World War II, but remember also that Australia was visited by early Dutch mariners and was called New Holland. Most researchers will be making that step back to the Netherlands within a generation or two and so a good resource is the Nederlandse Genealogische Vereniging (see Useful Addresses).

Basic information is available on its home page at [http://www.ngv.nl/ngv-en.htm]. Many families of Dutch origin have come to Australia from the former Dutch East Indies and other colonial outposts.

France

People from France and French colonies or territories have been coming to Australia since the early decades of European immigration. Many came during the great gold rushes and we are indebted to gold-miner, writer and photographer Antoine Fauchery for some wonderful records of those times.

The Internet has many useful paths you can follow. An important article entitled 'French Genealogy and the Internet' by Dr Jean-Marie Thiebaud,

OPPOSITE: *If papers and relics from seafaring ancestors have not been passed down through the family, there are records in archives and a wide range of sources for maritime collectibles. Joseph Goodchild, 1809–1879, was apprenticed to ship-owner Caleb Wilson in 1823 at age 14, and by 28 was a ship's captain. On 26 May 1838 he married Hannah Clark Stephenson, daughter of Captain John Stephenson at Jarrow near Newcastle on Tyne. The ticket is for Joseph's trip to Australia in 1852 when he was most likely off to the goldfields.*
Source: Collection, Goodchild family [Photograph: Dennis Russell and Peter Cuffley]

President of the French Federation of Genealogy, is found at: [http://www.karolus.org/actual/ac-inter/jmt-k-ot.htm]. A vast amount of information and actual records has been made accessible on the Internet through Karolus, a special service managed by the Institute for Documentation on Family History. The address is: [http://www.easynet.fr/karolus/].

The Family History Department of the Church of Jesus Christ of Latter-Day Saints offers a wide range of records for people researching French origins, including a microfilmed manuscript collection. The Family History Library Catalogue can be consulted at your local LDS library. There is also the well-known Internet site, Cyndi's List, which will lead you to many sources for researching French origins. The address is: [http://www.cyndislist.com].

Switzerland

It is a simple matter to find the canton and village your surname relates to in a book *Familienna menbuch der Schweiz,* which gives the place and earliest registration of some 48500 surnames. A microfiche version is at LDS Family History Centres (#6053507). *Swiss Genealogical Research*, an inexpensive handbook, is also useful.

Swiss Genealogy on the Internet is found at: [http://www.eye.ch/swissgen/schweiz-en.htm]. Swiss immigrants were an important part of the development of the wine industry in Victoria in the 19th century. *The Settlement of Swiss Ticino Immigrants in Australia* by Joseph Gentilli is filled with detailed information on individuals and families of Swiss–Italian origin in the Daylesford–Bendigo region of Central Victoria.

Belgium

A good starting point for Belgian family history research is the web site found at: [http://www.ping.be/picavet/]. And, once again, the LDS Family

Thomas Guiliani and his wife Louisa (née Trewel) with their son Antonio Harry (1910) and daughter Thelma Margaret (1914) on the steps of their home in Tuff Street, Eaglehawk, Victoria in 1924. There was a sizeable community of people from Italian-speaking Switzerland in the Daylesford–Bendigo region from the 1850s.
Source: Collection, Peter Cuffley

History Centre is an essential resource. Apart from direct migration, many families fled to England during times of crisis, and their descendents have often come to Australia.

Among the Protestant refugees who crossed the English Channel in earlier centuries were French-speaking Walloons from the Low Countries. In fact, the word 'refugee' passed into the English language from the French. There is a Hugenot Society in Britain and many publications on families which originated in Holland, Belgium and France.

People brought their memories of traditional customs from the Old World to Australia. This illustration entitled Outside the Stadhaus, Hanover, *portrays a market scene complete with outdoor umbrella.*
Source: Collection, Peter Cuffley

Austria

Most church records in Austria, a predominantly Roman Catholic country, are still in their original parishes. Very little has been microfilmed which makes research difficult. General information on genealogy in Austria can be found at: [http://www.rootsweb.com/~autwgw/] or [http://w3g.med.uni-giessen.de/gene/reg/AUT/#soc]. The address for the Heraldic Genealogical Society Der Adler is in Useful Addresses.

Southern Europe

Italy

People from Italy came to Australia in ever-increasing numbers from the mid-19th century. They mined for gold or worked as labourers, canecutters, fishermen, gardeners and so on, and others were professional people. The statistics show there were 4000 Italians here by 1891, mainly in New South Wales and Queensland.[9] Some 200 applied for citizenship in Victoria before 1870.[10] The book *Tracing Your Italian Ancestors for Victorians* has general information which can be applied universally.

Mass migration from Italy took place in the 1950s and 1960s, so the step from searching local records to searching Italian records is, for many, close at hand. On the Internet the Italian Genealogy home page is found at: [http://www.italgen.com]. It offers all kinds of useful information, including 'Straight Talk About Genealogical Research Conditions in Italy' by Louis Mendola of the Italian Genealogical Heraldic Institute. The mailing address of the Institute is in Useful Addresses.

Greece

The beginning of Greek migration to Australia has been traced back to 1827.[13] While Hellenic people settled in many parts of the country, the great migration after World War II was mostly to Victoria, and Melbourne became a city with a notable Greek presence. For some insight into public records in Greece, look up the web site called Hellenes-Diaspora found at: [http://www.geocities.com/southbeach/cove/4537/research.htm]. It has a link to a site which offers a sample letter in Greek for sending to government offices in search of vital records. Civil registration began in Greece in 1925 and before that civil copies of church records are the official source for births, deaths and marriages. There are surviving census returns back to the 1820s.

The Reverend Serafim Phocas was fifty when he arrived in Sydney in 1899 with his wife and five daughters. His eldest daughter, Anna, married John Comino in 1901 at the new Greek Orthodox church in Surry Hills. Another daughter, Eftehia, married Harry (Haralambos) Corones in 1914. Harry Corones became a noted hotelier and businessman at Charleville in Queensland, was an original shareholder in Qantas and in 1965 was appointed MBE.
Source: Collection, Corones family

Portugal

Clear proof that Portuguese mariners discovered Australia before the British set about their explorations is yet to be found. They certainly came in the 19th century, in search of gold or a new life. Again, many seafarers jumped ship and may have changed their name to avoid detection. Interestingly, I have met families whose Portuguese ancestors wanted to assimilate. In each case, the husband assumed the wife's name, which was more Anglo-sounding, and they quickly became part of the larger community.

The LDS Family History Centres have many Portugese church records on microfiche and the Internet is quite helpful. Portugese Resources on the Web can be found at: [http://www.maui.net/~makule/port.htm]. There is also Fernando Candido's Portugese genealogy home page at [http://fu2.freenet.edmonton.ab.ca/~fcandido], which has all the basic information on records available in Portugal.

Malta

Maltese migrants were the first group from the Mediterranean region in the great period of migration following World War II. This came as a result of an agreement made in 1949 between the authorities in Malta and the Australian government. The subject of earlier Maltese immigrants is covered in

the book *Empire and Race, the Maltese in Australia 1881–1949*. The first Maltese immigrant to come to Australia was Antonio Azzopardi who arrived in 1838.[12] Information on Maltese genealogy can be found on the Internet at: [http://www.searchmalta.com/genealogy/index.shtml].

Spain

People of Spanish origin have been migrating to Australia since early in the colonial period. Much later on, an immigration agreement between Spain and Australia was signed in 1958.[13]

Civil registration began in Spain in 1870. For baptisms, marriages and deaths before that date it is necessary to search parish or Bishopric archives. There is an Internet site for Spanish genealogy [http://genforum.familytreemaker.com/spain/] where you can post your surname or request information about your family.

Eastern Europe

Since the opening up of Eastern Europe with the retreat of communism, a great deal of work has been done in gathering church and other records. Much has been lost through wars and political unrest and the identity of countries and people has often changed.

The Federation of Eastern European Family History Societies (FEEFHS) is an important organisation which offers links to a diverse range of family history sources (see Useful Addresses). Cyndi's List of genealogy sites for Eastern Europe on the Internet [http://www.cyndislist.com/easteuro.htm] is a valuable resource. Some of the following sites may be of interest as well:

- Albanian Research List at: [http://www.feefhs.org/al/arl.htm].
- Armenian Genealogical Society at: [http://www.feefhs.org/am/frg-amgs.htm].
- The Carpatho–Rusyn Society at: [http://www.feefhs.org/rusyn/frg-crs.htm].
- Croatian Genealogical and Heraldic Society at: [http://www.feefhs.org/cro/frg-cghs.htm].
- Czechoslovak Genealogical Society International Inc. at: [http://www.feefhs.org/czs/cgsi/frg-cgsi.htm].
- Moravian Heritage Society at: [http://www.feefhs.org/czs/frg-mohs.htm].
- Polish Genealogy and Heraldry Society at: [http://www.feefhs.org/pol/frg-pghs.htm].
- Russian Heritage Society at: [http://www.feefhs.org/frg-rhs.htm].
- Genealogy Helplist Russia at: [http://www.perso.club-internet.fr/montardi/berdnikov/Genealogy-Helplist-Russia].
- Slovak Genealogical Research Center at: [http://www.feefhs.org/slovak/frg-sgrc.html].
- Slovenian Genealogical Society (Australian Chapter) at: [http://www.feefhs.org/slovenia/frgsgau.htm].

Middle East

Lebanon

Immigrants from Lebanon were represented in Australia in the latter part of the 19th century. More than 1500 are listed as being Lebanese or Syrian in the records for 1901.[14]

Unassisted migrants continued to arrive after World War II and in the 1960s and 1970s the numbers increased. The Lebanon Genealogical Forum can be found on the Internet at: [http://genforum.familytreemaker.com/lebanon/].

Turkey

In October 1967, the Australian government signed an immigration agreement with Turkey. Small numbers of Turkish people had arrived before that time. Information about Turkish history is available on the Internet at Turkish Odyssey: [http://www.turkishodyssey.com/turkey/history]. The Turkey Genealogy Forum is at: [http://genforum.familytreemaker.com/turkey/.

Asia

Tracing family history in many of the countries which come under the broad description of Asia, can vary greatly and as usual depends on the existence and availability of records. The AsiaGen Web Project is being established to help with research and can be found at: [http://www.rootsweb.com/~asiagw].

China

The history of Chinese immigration to Australia is both long and fascinating. Some 40 000 arrived during the gold rushes of the second half of the 19th century, but around two-thirds of these single men returned to China. Those who stayed often married non-Chinese women and established families that can be traced through the various civil records.

A number of books have been written on the Chinese in Australia and there are groups and individuals dedicated to researching Chinese–Australian family history. *Sources for Chinese Local History and Heritage in New South Wales* is particularly useful for anyone researching the Sydney area. The National Archives of Australia has also published a guide, *Chinese Immigrants and Chinese-Australians in NSW,* which is on the Internet at: [http://www.naa.gov.au/publicat/guides/chinese/guide.htm].

If you're in Victoria, there is a wonderful Chinese museum in Bendigo called the Golden Dragon Museum which has an extensive archive.

This Christmas greetings card winged its way from Hong Kong to Australia, from an older brother to a younger brother, in the 1950s.

Source: Courtesy Marty Kemp

Philippines

Filipinos have two kinds of surnames — original surnames in use before an 1849 edict of the Spanish Governor General, and the 'approved' names assigned to families from that date. The purpose of this edict was to give surnames to people who did not possess them, as well as overcoming the

Alfred Lam Sun married Mary Josephine 'Josie' Schultz in 1917. This family portrait by Verey of Castlemaine was taken in the late 1920s. Alfred, who was the son of Lam Woon Toom and Si Wang, died in Bendigo in 1951 aged 70. His wife Josie, the daughter of George Schultz and Ann Keiser, died in 1971 aged 78.
Source: Collection, Ashley Tracey

arbitrary adoption of saints' names which caused much repetition and therefore administrative confusion.[15] At the time, a catalogue of family names was compiled, including indigenous names collected by religious orders, the Spanish surnames that were acquired, and surnames furnished by the vegetable and mineral kingdoms, geography, the arts and so on.

Philippines sites on the Internet can be found at: [www.geocities.com/heartland/Ranch/9121/gensites.htm] and [http://www.filipinolinks.com/home/genealogy.html].

Scandinavia

Close connections with the sea ensured that many sailors from Scandinavia found themselves in Australian ports. Quite a few went searching for gold in the second half of the 19th century and there was a wave of Danish emigration to Queensland which began in the 1860s.[16] In fact, there is a Danish Association in Queensland which is on the Internet at: [http://www.gil.au/va/heimdal/].

Sites with information for those of you tracing Scandinavian origins are well represented on the Internet. The Danish Emigration Archives at Aalborg, Denmark, is found at: [http://www.feefhs.org/dk/frg-deaa.htm]. The Finnish Genealogy Group is found at: [http://www.feefhs.org/misc./frgfin.mn.htm]. For an extensive list of links to sites relating to ancestors and records in Norway you can look up Norwegian Research

Sources at: [http://www.rootsweb.com/~wgnorway/Norlinks.htm]. The Federation of Swedish Genealogical Societies even has an 'E-zine' called *Rötter*, details of which can be found at: [http:// www.genealogi.se/index.htm#sok].

The LDS Family History Library is also an important source for Scandinavian family history research and many of the church records are in the International Genealogical Index.

Jewish Genealogy

Because Jewish people live in so many places, there are records scattered throughout the world. In Australia, there has been a notable Jewish presence since the early decades of European immigration. The Australian Jewish Genealogical Society has branches in Sydney, Melbourne and Adelaide with members throughout Australia.

A newsletter, *Kosher Koala*, is published quarterly. Information on the Society can be found on the Internet at: [http://www.zeta.org.au/~feraltek/genealogy/ajgs/ajgstxt.htm]. There is a site called Routes to Roots for Jewish Record Searchers at: [http://feefhs.org/jg/frg-rtr.htm]. The web pages of the Federation of Eastern European Family History Societies are linked to many Jewish history specific sites. The Links Database JewishGen is at: [http://www.Jewishgen.org/links/].

Australia's First People

People of Aboriginal descent may face difficulties in researching their family history. Much work is being done to gather together all the available records and there are now some helpful publications. In 1990, the Aboriginal Studies Press published *Looking for Your Mob: A Guide to Tracing Aboriginal Family Trees*. The publication *My Heart is Breaking: A Joint Guide to Records about Aboriginal People in the Public Record Office of Victoria and the Australian Archives* was published in 1993.

There are many other useful and up-to-date publications including: *Aboriginal and Torres Strait Islander People in Commonwealth Records: A Guide to Records in the Australian Archives ACT*, *Finding Families* (chapter 3) and *The Guide to the National Archives of Australia for Genealogists* (see Bibliography). *My Place* by Sally Morgan tells of the joys and disappointments of searching for family.

A broad sweep of people now call Australia home, and part of that sense of belonging begins with a pride in our origins whatever they may be. Family trails link us to all kinds of communities and hopefully as we make the journey we will be touched by our shared humanity.

Chapter Six
Homeplaces and Hallowed Ground

Some years ago my wife and I went to a family picnic at Devon Park near Seymour. It was held at Uncle Bert's place on about sixteen hectares of what was once a 240-hectare property, intersected by Stoney Creek and edging the Goulburn River. This piece of land is, for us, hallowed ground. Gnarled red-gums, some of which would have been old in 1856 when the homestead block was first purchased, give an air of timelessness; a single pepper tree marks a family grave. This place is filled with stories, and the three generations at the picnic walked its undulations with a warm reverence.

Great great grandmother was widowed in 1857, a thirty-one-year-old mother of three children. Born in the Devonshire village of Abbots Bickington on 22 June 1825, she was baptised on 10 July in St James parish church, a humble edifice dating from the early 14th century. It was a community of farmers, farm labourers and cottage workers. People were generally made of the stuff to survive adversity and we can see from Mary's portrait (see page 98), that she was a determined soul. My great aunt who knew her well said she could be a stern grandmother and yet also had a light-hearted side. Her religion, originally Church of England and then Methodist, gave her a belief that life's hardships would end in a glorious heaven.

Her brother-in-law, Richard Smale, arrived from England to help her with the farm in 1859. Tragically he drowned in the Goulburn River in April 1863 while making a crossing with a dray and two horses. Constable Robert Strahan, who was also drowned, had commandeered Richard and his vehicle because he needed to get back to the township side, after losing track of an escaped prisoner.[1]

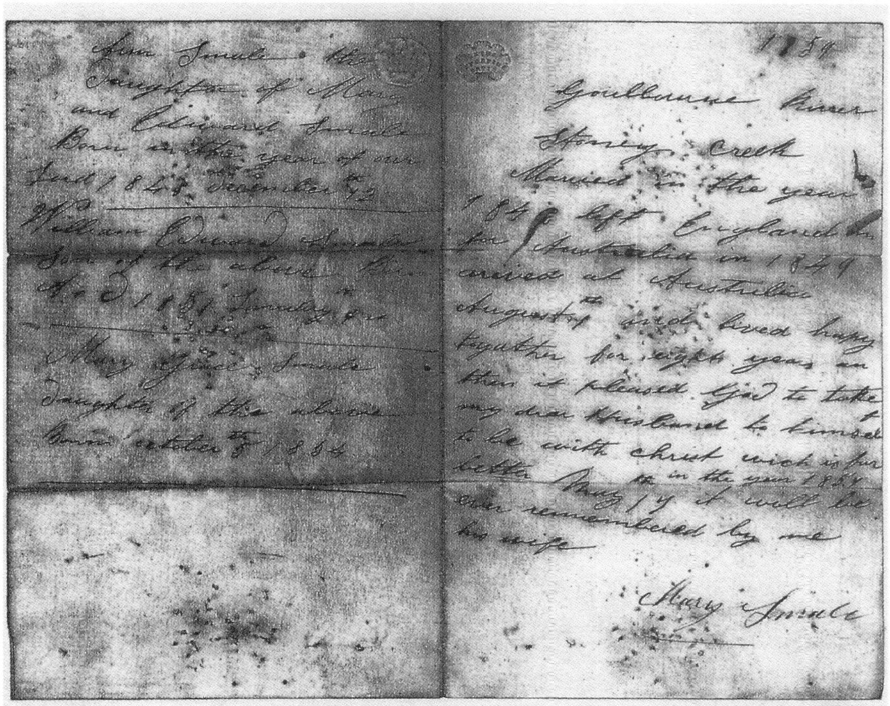

'1859

Goulbourne River

Stoney Creek

Married in the year
1848 left England an
for Australia in 1849
arrived at Australia
August 1st and lived happy
togather for eight years an
then it pleased God to take
my dear Husband to himself
to be with christ wich is for
better May 17th in the year 1857 it will be
ever remembered by me
his wife

Mary Smale.'

A statement and family record written by Mary Smale in 1859. When Edward Smale died in May 1857, she was left to pioneer her farm on the Goulburn River near Seymour, Victoria. She would later name it Devon Park after the county of her birth.
Source: Collection, Peter Cuffley

In 1860, Mary gave birth to a fourth child who was registered as Albert Morrish, son of Mary Morrish [Mary Smale's maiden name], widow. An entry in *Victoria and its Metropolis* (1888) moves the date of her husband's death to 1859, and it was long believed that Albert was born in that year. In fact, he was born exactly three years after the death of Edward Smale. We'll never know who fathered Albert. It could have been Richard Smale, a sober lay preacher and farm labourer.

Mary lived on in relative isolation and managed to create a prosperous farm which in memory of her birthplace she called Devon Park. In 1888 it was noted that, 'Mrs Smale has at present 520 acres, which she uses for cultivation and dairy purposes and also for raising cattle.'[2] It was generally good land although the creek and the river were a haven for tiger snakes and floods would refashion the eastern boundary at irregular intervals.

Albert Morrish Smale was my great grandfather and from all we know of him he was a fascinating character. He had an absolute passion for the bush and all of its elements. As a youngster he would set off for Northwood School on his horse, but often get only as far as the top of the drive where he would turn left instead of right. A day wandering the bush was far more attractive than a country schoolroom. Much of his time was spent with young people from the local Aboriginal tribe. In later life, he passed on a deep respect for the original inhabitants of the land to his children and grandchildren and was highly protective of any ground he knew was sacred to them. It is remembered that he was heartbroken at the loss of his childhood friends when few Koories survived in the district. Ironically, his own freedom and prosperity had come from the land appropriated by the government and settlers.

My grandmother, Mary Ann (May) Smale, was the third of six daughters of Albert Smale and Catherine Smale (née Keogh). She seemed to have a

natural affinity with her father's side of the family and spent a lot of time in her earlier years wandering the bush and countryside with him. He was happy to share all that he knew about the natural world and the original inhabitants of the area.

They closely studied birds and insects and took a particular interest in the rocks and stones they found in the river. Even when she had her own family and lived in Melbourne, and further away in Gippsland, she would make an annual pilgrimage for her father's birthday and would once again be walking the beloved homeplaces. As May Ryan, she became a well-known amateur in the fields of geology, palaeontology and astronomy. Her fossil discoveries in the cliffs on the eastern side of Port Phillip Bay attracted the attention of notable scholars of the day. We also bless her for being interested, in the 1920s, in family history, heirlooms, early photographs and old documents.

Researching Homeplaces

Veteran family historians know the rich memories and the important material that can be gathered on journeys to places which have a special significance. Such activities can vary from forays to nearby cemeteries, churches, schools, houses, and sites, to grand expeditions reaching distant parts of the world.

AT BLACK ROCK

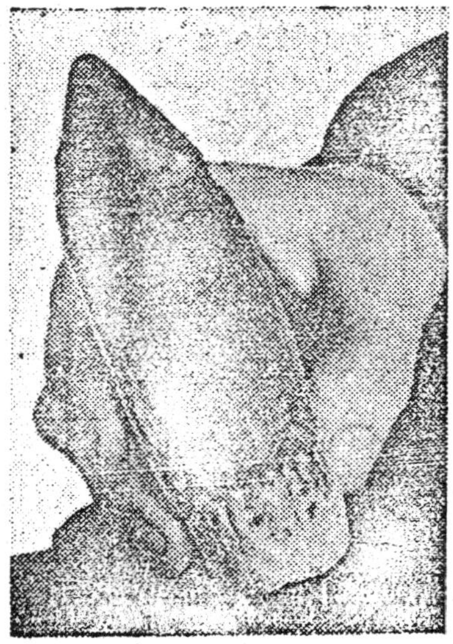

Age-Old Whale Tooth

By Charles Barrett

Recent storm damage to the cliffs at Black Rock revealed a relic more than 500,000 years old—a tooth of an extinct species of whale.

It was found by Mrs M. A. Ryan, of Fifth Street, Black Rock, who is a keen collector of fossils.

Similar relics of the toothed whales have been collected at Beaumaris, from the Kalimnan beds.

Mr F. Chapman, former Commonwealth palaeontologist, described a well-preserved tooth belonging to a new form of scaldicetus. Another species with slender teeth, was discovered in the same geological series, near Hamilton.

"In only one other locality besides Australia does the genus occur," Mr Chapman says, "namely, at Antwerp, Belgium, in crag deposits of Lower Pliocene Age."

Mrs Ryan has made many interesting finds along the cliffs at Black Rock, Beaumaris and Mornington.

She began fossil hunting at the seaside nearly 20 years ago. She now has about 2000 specimens, including some 200 teeth of extinct sharks. One tooth measures three inches across at the top.

Item published in The Herald *(Melbourne) 21 July 1936.*
Source: Collection, Peter Cuffley

Mary Ann 'May' Ryan (1889–1937) and son John Francis Ryan (1924–1945). With an interest in astronomy, palaeontology, geology and natural history, May Ryan was a remarkable woman in her time.
Source: Collection, Catherine Cuffley (née Ryan)

You can also go on a voyage of discovery without ever leaving home by researching a chosen place in times before the present day. This is a reasonable quest for all who cannot travel.

There are many places which were part of our ancestors' lives which simply do not exist in any recognisable form today. Many of the great medieval cities and towns of Europe were completely devastated by the two world wars. Other places have been swept aside by development and bear little resemblance to any earlier form. Having said this, it must be admitted that actually being in a place which has long family associations or has been very important for a short while, is the ideal way to absorb that indefinable and yet very powerful resonance. A feeling of connection may come not only from the subtle elements in the physical nature of the place, but there may also be a spiritual energy, a deep-felt belonging which offers no rational explanation. This has also been described by people who have visited ancient ruins, very old dwellings or landscapes and sites which have been the settings for dramatic events or mystical experiences. We can learn a great deal from Aboriginal people about the energy in certain places.

Friends have spoken of being overcome by emotion in places which only later were found to have been important in the lives of their ancestors. One friend told me about arriving in a coastal village in the south of England for the first time. His father had grown up there but left to go to sea and later settled in Australia. Not only was my friend recognised by many of the villagers, some even called him by his father's name. He felt completely at home, far more than he ever imagined he would. In that place there was a very close connection, and layers of human experience going backwards in time, which were part of the family story.

Some would argue that our genetic inheritance gives us a kind of cosmic memory. That great Australian artist Lloyd Rees once related in an interview that he was overwhelmed by certain places in Wales on his first trip to Britain.

The homeplaces and landscapes familiar to past generations in our family have remained relatively unchanged. This beautiful lane is between Cadbury and Thorverton in Devon.
Source: Collection, Peter Cuffley
[Photograph: Toni Lumsden]

He explained that as a child in Brisbane he created pictures which seemed to come from deep within, mysterious ancient places with forms and colours quite alien to his childhood in the sun-drenched antipodes. When he saw Wales he was struck by the familiarity of it all and came to think in terms of some form of race memory or Celtic dreaming.

Homeplaces and hallowed ground can be captured to various degrees through words, sounds and images. These can be newly created, gathered from the recent past or drawn from very old sources. Music we know is a very powerful means of unlocking memories or bringing times beyond memory to life. The spoken, written and printed word can each offer their distinctive forms of storytelling. I use the term 'written word' in the sense of handwriting, that great art which has become something of a rarity. Thankfully, the revival of calligraphy has given recent generations some idea of the possibilities in the use of the pen or brush. Letters, diaries and journals have long been valued for the information and emotions they can convey.

The family treasures of this kind are sometimes only for the immediate circle; in other instances they have a much wider significance. Historians, and readers in general, have found published works such as *The Letters of Rachel Henning* and *The Diary of a Welsh Swagman* invaluable insights into life in Australia in earlier times (see Bibliography). A brief but important record of the life of a farm-worker in the Illawarra region of New South Wales in the 1830s, *The Paulsgrove Diary*, was published by the Illawarra Historical Society in 1988. Imagine how happy I was to find that the diarist mentioned my great great grandfather seven times and gave details of his activities. We rarely have any hope of such a finding.

Places of relevance to family history are found in published works from various eras ranging from the letters, diaries and journals mentioned above, to accounts of travels and explorations, memoirs, directories and gazetteers, historical works and surveys. For instance, if Scotland has a place in your family history, you'll find the *Statistical Account of Scotland 1790–1799* compiled by Sir John Sinclair, a Scottish politician and improver of agriculture, to be a marvellous resource. He asked ministers in each parish to gather information in a suggested format, and the returns made up twenty-one volumes.

Details for each parish include the location and extent, the state of agriculture, population, occupations, manufacturers, schooling, state of the poor, roads and antiquities. There are also observations on manners and morals which, in many cases, provide a rare and valuable picture of the character of the people. You will be pleased to know that these records have been published on microfiche by the State Library of Victoria and can be consulted in libraries which have a comprehensive genealogy and family history section.

Gazetteers and Directories

A gazetteer is a geographical dictionary with descriptive entries for cities, towns and villages as well as large regional divisions. Some are single books; others run to many volumes. They were published by governments and

Old postcards are ideal for views of places which have significance in a family story. This example shows The High Street, Stockbridge, Hampshire, around 1900. At the beginning of the 20th century, many towns and villages were much as they had been in the previous centuries.
Source: Collection, Peter Cuffley

private interests. Many of the earlier gazetteers have also been released on microfiche as have Post Office directories. The *Gazetteer of England and Wales 1841* (26 fiche) and *Lewis' Topographical Dictionary of Ireland* (14 fiche) are two excellent resources in sets of affordable microfiche. Both of these works provide detailed locations of villages and towns and a useful description which varies according to the size or importance of the place.

Searching for an Irish Homeplace

In Ireland, the 'townland' is an identification of a unit of land in rural areas. On average it is around 140 hectares (350 acres) and can be entirely agricultural or may contain small groups of houses and perhaps a village or town. It is very useful to be able to locate the townland because while Ireland does have parishes, there are three kinds, so you need to know which one you are dealing with. There are the civil parishes which are referred to in census returns and valuations, the ecclesiastical parishes of the Church of Ireland which are usually made up of a number of civil parishes, and finally the Roman Catholic parishes which sometimes share boundaries but can also cover a different area.

Overall, Ireland is made up of four provinces: Ulster, Connaught, Leinster and Munster. These in turn are subdivided into counties of which there are thirty-two. Next come the baronies which number 325, and then approximately 64 000 townland divisions. In 1838 poor law unions were created out of multiples of townlands and equate to the unions we find in English records from 1834.[3] They were an attempt to rationalise the management and distribution of poor relief. Each union had a workhouse managed by an elected board of guardians.

One of the difficulties of searching for a homeplace in Ireland is that even

Visiting an old family home on the other side of the world is a powerful experience for those fortunate enough to have such a place and the opportunity to travel. This house at Ardmone, County Cavan, Ireland, was occupied by generations of Gibsons. John Gibson decided to emigrate and arrived in Victoria on the Conway *on 15 September 1858.*
Source: Courtesy Shirley Stone

if you have a village or townland name, there are sometimes two or more called by the same name. For example, my convict ancestor Thomas Sweeney was associated with a place called Cullahill, Tipperary; it took years for the evidence to turn up which confirmed that it was Cullahill townland in the Parish of Bourney and not the other one in the same general area, which was in the Parish of Glenkeen. Both of these townlands are near the town of Templemore and to add to the confusion there is a town called Cullahill just across the border in County Laois or Leix (formerly Queens County). Thomas Sweeney indicated the importance of Cullahill in his life by naming his farm in Victoria, Culla Hill. The name actually comes from Collchoill and means hazelwood, so the 'hill' in Cullahill is misleading. As with most other countries, the spelling of place names in Ireland varies over time. Nevertheless, having a parish, town or townland name is a wonderful help compared to only knowing that your ancestor came from Tipperary.

With the difficulty of the repetition of names and the lack of records, many Australians of Irish descent have to be satisfied with a county of origin or perhaps a parish. To give life to the family story then means building a picture of how people might have lived in the general area at that time. There are useful accounts and studies from the 19th century, and modern

opposite (top): *Simple vernacular buildings were a familiar aspect of life for all of our forebears who lived and worked in areas not greatly affected by the demands of fashion. This group is in Bibury, Gloucestershire, one of the much-loved Cotswold villages.*
Source: Collection, Peter Cuffley [Photograph: Robert Hadden]

opposite: *The beautiful coastal town of Dunmore East, in County Waterford, is a tourist destination for a lot of people. For others it is a homeplace with a powerful resonance and never more so than after much of a lifetime on the other side of the world.*
Source: Courtesy Saul Roche [Photograph: Gordon Jones]

overleaf (top left): *Cape Schanck lighthouse has been looking out over Bass Strait since 1859. With Cape Otway and Point Lonsdale it guided ships to Port Phillip Heads. Nicholas Chevalier painted the scene in 1865 and called it Castle Rock, Cape Schanck. This version was painted by James Flintoff.*
(oil on board, 395 × 560 mm)
Source: Collection, Peter Cuffley

overleaf (bottom left): *One of the legendary 19th century ships, the SS* Great Britain, *is seen here about to depart from Liverpool. Built in Bristol and employing both steam and sail, it was launched in July 1843. It carried migrants to Australia for over twenty years, the forebears of a quarter of a million present-day Australians. SS* Great Britain *has now been restored, see [http://www.ss-great-britain.com/3.htm].*
(oil on canvas, 760 × 1060 mm)
Source: Mitchell Library, State Library of New South Wales

overleaf (right): *Mellow, golden stone is the hallmark of England's Cotswold region. Here we see the doorway of the church of St Peter at Farmington in Gloucestershire. The Bishops transcripts of its registers from 1617–1812 have been published, and baptisms and marriages are also in the International Genealogical Index.*
Source: Collection, Peter Cuffley [Photograph: Robert Hadden]

scholarship is producing detailed works. Many of these can be found in Australian libraries, while specialist booksellers both here and overseas offer extensive lists and can also search for other titles.

We found the Tipperary Historical Society on the Internet and from their excellent site were able to study the contents of each edition of the *Tipperary Historical Journal*. In the 1990 edition, we found an article by Maria Luddy called 'The Lives of the Poor in Fethard in 1821'. Such works provide valuable insight into the realities of life in Ireland including the types of dwellings most families occupied.

Old Family Dwellings

Small cottages reflecting the vernacular architecture of the British Isles were once built in many parts of Australia. Of these, very few offer a picture of the one- or two-roomed cabins which made up a large percentage of housing in Ireland and were familiar to poor migrants who settled in Australia. A proper chimney was something to be proud of, as was a small window which actually had glass in it. Many cabins simply had a hole in the thatch to let the smoke out and there was often no lining to the roof.

It is also important to realise that a large proportion of the population in Ireland slept on the floor on piles of straw, rushes, bracken, heather or even old rags .[4] One or two stools by the fire were typical items of furniture. Next may come a table, a mantle shelf, a chest, a dresser and perhaps some proper chairs. The simplest wooden bed raised up from the damp or cold of an earth or stone floor was highly desirable. The bed may have been constructed to give protection from draughts, and a canopy would have saved the occupants from falling particles or dust from the thatch. The character of Irish cabins or basic houses is very well covered in an excellent reference work entitled *Irish Country Furniture 1700–1950* (see Bibliography).

When you try to picture the kinds of dwellings your forebears may have lived in, you need to begin by finding their relative position in the society in question. If they were at the lower end of the scale in terms of income or land occupation, it is fairly certain they they would have lived in a very humble dwelling. Single room or 'one-bay' thatched cottages were the typical rural worker's accommodation in the English countryside. Most of these have disappeared and it is the more substantial or extended cottages which have survived to become idealised visions of rural life. Ancestors who were owners or occupiers of larger dwellings tend to leave behind more records such as detailed wills, property deeds and land tax assessments. Notable figures may well find their way into local histories and if you are really fortunate, their house will have survived.

Old family dwelling places are one of the focal points in comprehensive family histories. Broadly, they can be divided into two categories — those which still exist and those which do not. Images, memories and written descriptions keep many houses alive even if they have vanished without trace. A much happier state is the survival of a family home as well as documentation and relics from earlier stages of its existence. Rarest of all is the

IRELAND.
County Seats:
Battlefields:
Elevations in English Feet:
Depths in English Feet:
Railroads:
Principal Steamship Routes:
Canals:
Submarine Telegraph:
Light Houses:
Importance of places is indicated by style of type, approximately, as follows:
NOTE:
TO NEW YORK
TO GLASGOW 490 MILES
DUBLIN
CORK
Killarney
Dundalk
Coleraine
Lough Foyle
Lough Neagh
LOUTH
MEATH
Dingle Bay
Dungarvan Harbor
Waterford Harbor
Youghal
Tralee

place which has survived more or less completely intact from an earlier time. Buda, a historic home and garden in Castlemaine, Victoria, is a remarkable entity now open to the public. Here is a family's life between 1861 and 1981, carefully conserved and maintained so that we could well believe that the last of the Levinys is out visiting friends and may return at any moment. Meroogal at Nowra in New South Wales is similarly endowed, as is Calthorpes' House in Canberra. These houses are open to the public as are other examples of equal importance in various parts of Australia.

Tracing a family home, or indeed any other building or property which has a part in your story will require varying degrees of effort. A house or homestead which is well known to local people may be found readily. On the other hand, a residence which was one of many in a street or road where numbers have changed or are simply not recorded means careful research is required.

Old directories are a first step and sometimes the only way to locate your family on a particular site. If they were ratepayers then the rate books are your best resource. The difficulty with ratebooks is their survival and accessibility. Their importance as historical records is now widely recognised and through microfilming they can be easier to access. If they survive, rate books should also enable a date of construction to be fixed as well as any substantial enlargement of the building. Various libraries, archives and local historical societies may be able to help with records and with some luck could even have

By far the most common housing in rural Ireland was of the type seen here. They are often called cabins, but rarely cottages, which is a term the English might use. This example, photographed in Donegal in the 1890s, illustrates various means of survival such as keeping pigs, spinning yarn and small-acre farming.
Source: Courtesy Rachel Tonkin

OPPOSITE (TOP): *This simple white church is at Killeter, near Strabane, in County Tyrone, Ireland. Family history trails lead many travellers to chruches such as this one.*
Source: Courtesy Gwen Shaw

OPPOSITE: *Set in picturesque countryside with the Western Tiers in the distance, this is the Union Church at Cleveland in Tasmania's midlands.*
Source: Collection, Peter Cuffley [Photograph: Barbara Cuffley]

A large proportion of old postcards were actually real photographs and can be easily copied and enlarged. There is always a chance that you will find a picture of an ancestor's homeplace. or at least a scene which portrays the character of the times.
Source: Collection, Peter Cuffley

a picture of the house. If that is too much to hope for, there is always a chance that it may appear in a wider view.

When an old family place still exists but has gone out of family ownership, you may be able to engage in a beneficial exchange of information with the current or other owners. We live in an 1864 cottage built by Henry Gough and later owned by his father-in-law, William Froomes senior. Descendants of both the Froomes and the Gough family have contacted us and passed on information and we, in turn, have given them all we can find including details from the rate books. The title deeds gave us the succession of owners, and noting that Mr Froomes sold out in September 1888, it was possible to find a sale notice in the local paper which gave a detailed description of the property. Sometimes current owners are less than friendly, but generally they will be welcoming if you are clearly genuine in your interest.

I heard a funny story about a woman who went to an old family location and asked if she could show some friends her mother's birthplace. The present owner was a little puzzled. The matter became clearer when the woman discovered that 'grandma's house' had been moved out to their family farm years ago and the present house on the site had nothing to do with their family!

Misleading information is something to be wary of in printed or verbal form. For example, in 1940, the *Australian Home Beautiful* published a five-page article on Culla Hill, the old Sweeney farm at Eltham, Victoria. When I first began researching the family in the 1960s the article was a great

inspiration. As I began to delve into original records, inconsistencies became apparent. I still give thanks for the photographs and the general information in the story, but even now have to warn relatives that some of the 'facts' given in the magazine are simply not correct.

Useful Collections

Our larger and longer-established libraries have important collections of books relating to the social history of the British Isles. Antiquarian or local histories were favoured acquisitions in the 19th and early 20th centuries when librarians were either born in Britain or looked to the Old World as their cultural mecca. We have also benefited immensely from the efforts of those who collected Australiana long before it had captured the interest of a wider public.

The Mitchell and Dixson collections in the State Library of New South Wales constitute an outstanding repository relating to the history and development of Australia. We owe a great debt to David Scott Mitchell and Sir William Dixson who were pioneer collectors in the field. The Mitchell collection began in the latter half of the 19th century and the Dixson from around 1900. They include a mass of material of direct interest to the family historian such as family papers, diaries, letters, notes, portraits, photographs and artworks, which help capture the scenes our ancestors knew so well.

Publications from the late 19th or early 20th centuries often have delightful illustrations of churches, villages and the countryside. Dealers in old books and prints can be very helpful in your search for views of a particular place. This beautifully composed photograph is of St Mary's Church, Wendover, Buckinghamshire, and dates from the early 20th century.
Source: Collection, Peter Cuffley

I noted that a drawing listed in an exhibition catalogue was entitled '*Boat Harbour Wollongong, July 8/35* by Conrad Martens, collection Mitchell Library'.[5] On applying to the library I was able to purchase a photograph of the drawing to aid in my research. This 1835 view perfectly captures the harbour and its environs, right at the time my ancestor Thomas Sweeney was sailing in and out in his trading boats. I've read that at this stage no major harbour works had been undertaken so small vessels anchored off Brighton Beach. Passengers were carried to the shore or out to the boats in small rowboats. Livestock, which included pigs and calves, were either taken out by the same means or were made to swim.[6]

The Mitchell and Dixson libraries and Dixson galleries began with two outstanding collections and have continued to grow. Each state has its important libraries and each of these have collections to enrich the field of social and family history. In Canberra, the National Library of Australia has become yet another treasure-house of words, images and artefacts. Then there are the various government archives or record offices which are a notable resource for historians of every sort.

English local history is very well documented in a remarkable enterprise called the *Victoria History of the Counties of England.* At the present time over 200 volumes have been published and there are more to come. The original plan when it all began in 1899 was to have a series of 160 volumes in six years. It was also hoped that the project would return a handsome profit for its founders, however, from 1910 it began to falter and in 1933 production was transferred to the Institute of Historical Research of the University of London.[7]

Earlier volumes placed emphasis on churches, country houses and the nobility or gentry and generally included coats of arms. More recent volumes have paid greater attention to vernacular architecture and general social history, and photographs are used in place of line drawings. The work is considered complete and comprehensive for only a few counties. Beyond this, Westmorland, Northumberland and the West Riding of Yorkshire have not yet been included in the project.

I was pleased to find many volumes of this history in the State Library of Victoria. It can similarly be found in the State Library of New South Wales and the library of the Society of Australian Genealogists in Sydney. The plans of All Saints Church at Banstead, Surrey, were of particular interest to me as were the footnotes which suggested further lines of enquiry. They also helped me sort out the ownership of some estates in the parish of Chipstead, one of which was leased by Edward Cuffley from 1782–88.

An advertisement from the 1870s.
Source: Collection, Peter Cuffley

Through books, documents, plans, maps, photographs and works of art, homeplaces and other sites of significance can be traced, evaluated, illustrated and conserved.

BURIAL PLACES

Trips to our homeplaces at Culla Hill and Laurel Hill have long been important to our family, though the cemetery is the most regular place of pilgrimage. Our ancestors intended it to be the hallowed ground, the last

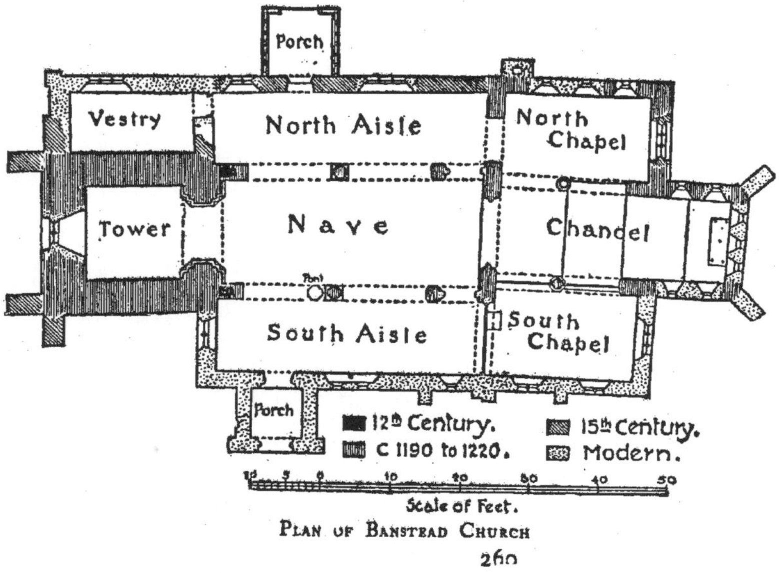

All Saints Church at Banstead, Surrey, as with many others, is made up of elements which reach from modern times back to the Middle Ages. This plan is from the Victoria County History of Surrey *which was published in 1911.*
Source: State Library of Victoria

resting place, a dignified setting for family memorials. Thomas Sweeney was a foundation member of cemetery trusts in the Parish of Nillumbik and now rests in one of the earliest marked graves in Eltham cemetery. Recently the wife of a cousin was buried there on one of those suitably sombre days. Softly falling rain, a flock of umbrellas, dark cypresses and a few Celtic crosses gave life to the Irish origins of the mourners. With no family houses available close by, the gathering moved on to the Eltham pub and among many other stories, recalled that an early Sweeney once rode his horse into the bar.

Cemeteries and graveyards make some people uneasy, but most of us find them fascinating. Our ancestors expected that family and future generations would come to pay their respects and if enough money was available, some sort of marker, headstone or memorial would usually be erected. Burial places vary enormously in their scale and condition. Some are superbly rustic with old trees, shrubs and naturalised flowers; others are sparse, even bleak, with none of the traditional character we might hope for.

Graveyards associated with historic churches can be very picturesque. Visions of English parish churches come to mind along with remembered words from Thomas Gray's *Elegy Written in a Country Churchyard,* first published in 1750. The churchyard which inspired those immortal lines is that of St Giles, Stoke Poges, Buckinghamshire. A professor of history and a poet, Gray spent his later years wandering the field paths and green lanes of Stoke Poges, as well as contemplating the meaning of life in this typical English churchyard. We can see such a figure in the illustration on page 92.

Something of the character of these hallowed places can be found in a number of Australia's older settled areas. I recall an unforgettable frosty sunrise in Carrick, Tasmania, with its old stone church and picturesque graveyard. Bright sunlight cut through gaps in the hawthorn hedge and lit up sheets of bluebells which had naturalised themselves under the oak trees. Where I live in Central Victoria, the country cemeteries are varied in their trees and overall character, though beautiful white gums are often part of the

The church and churchyard at Stoke Poges, Buckinghamshire, the inspiration for 'Gray's Elegy'.
Source: Collection, Peter Cuffley

scene, along with the traditional cypresses. They are also places where heritage roses have survived, along with old varieties of daffodils and jonquils.

Many groups and individuals take an interest in the welfare of our cemeteries and graveyards, though there is still both official and arbitrary vandalism. When I say official vandalism I mean the wholesale destruction of gravestones to create low maintenance public space, the over-zealous clean-ups which see heritage plants eliminated and the intrusion into older sites of modern elements which destroy the historic character.

Our forebears may have approved of a reasonable degree of rustic character in an old cemetery. Mind you, they also would have hoped that the graves remained dignified and received some care and attention. The growing interest in family history brings more visitors to burial grounds and now graves are often restored or new memorials set in place on family plots which were previously unmarked. Homeplaces and hallowed ground are essential elements in any family story.

Chapter Seven
A Heritage of Photographs

Looking at old photographs and seeing a 'family face' is one of the intriguing aspects of searching out the past. We can count ourselves fortunate if such pictures have survived and that our ancestors and relatives had the means and the opportunity to have portraits taken, or in later times were able to take their own snapshots.

It was in 1839 when news of the 'daguerreotype' process began to spread through Europe. Most people were delighted at the thought of capturing images directly from life, though others saw it as the work of the devil and were sure it would never be accepted.[1] Louis Jacques Mandé Daguérré pioneered this early photographic method along with Joseph Nicéphore Niepce.

Before the general introduction of the use of negatives and multiple prints on sensitised paper, portraits were one-off images usually kept in protective cases. A family portrait taken by the daguerreotype process in the 1840s or 1850s is a precious object indeed. Ambrotypes were a less expensive and therefore more common method of recording very early portraits but nonetheless they can hold a special place in family collections. Portrait photography from the 1850s grew to be an enormous industry and few households were without their elaborate albums and framed pictures.

Drawings and paintings of individuals and groups was an important element in family life for the more affluent levels of society. Then photography made the portrayal of the family into an almost universal expectation. While it was comparatively expensive, the daguerreotype was dubbed, 'the poor man's portrait'. There had been some use of relatively cheap and often itinerant portrait artists by less affluent families, including the production of silhouettes or 'shades' made from skilfully-cut black paper.

Travelling photographer J. H. Nixon was in the vicinity of Reedy Creek in south-east South Australia when he photographed the family of John and Mary Payne. Using a portable backdrop and a square of carpet he could set up anywhere. The children, from left to right, are George (1854), Henry (1858), William (1861), Annie (1863), Thomas (c. 1865) and Walter (1866).
Source: Collection, Peter Cuffley

Better quality silhouettes and finely-painted miniatures were displayed in good quality frames in the best rooms of genteel households.

One of the exciting aspects of early photographs is the fact that we can actually look at people who knew a world which now seems a great distance from our own era. The portrait of Grace Morrish on page 100 is an interesting example in that she was born on 19 March 1788, less than two months after the arrival of the First Fleet at Sydney Cove. Her picture is an ambrotype, taken on glass, probably in the late 1850s and in turn this was re-photographed in the following decades. Born at Sutcombe, Devon, she travelled to Australia in 1861 and lived with her daughter near Seymour, Victoria. When she died in 1884 it was proudly stated on her death certificate that she had lived '96 years, 6 months and 5 days'.

A desire to capture images of places reaches back to the very beginning of photography. Early pictures of cities, towns, villages, seascapes and landscapes can all have relevance to family stories. Photographs of family residences in the mid-19th century are uncommon and highly valued. Even views taken in a later era can be rare in many circumstances. When a professional photographer was engaged to record a family home, it suggests both domestic pride and money for the fees. By contrast, an itinerant photographer would probably offer reasonable rates, ensuring that humbler houses might also be recorded.

Both amateurs and professionals photographed places of interest including dwellings on every scale. The picturesque cottage or bush hut was a favourite subject. If we are lucky, a particular house or property will appear in a general view, offering a chance to enlarge and enhance the relevant section. For example, a town may have been photographed from a vantage point, hopefully using a large format camera, and there in the distance, or even close by, is a house or property of importance to the family you are researching.

Photographs of holiday trips and family picnics proliferated in the early 20th century and at the same time the motor car opened up new horizons for those prosperous enough to own them. Included in this group are Horace and Betsy Coombs, an English couple from Moonee Ponds, Victoria, and the Cuffley family from Essendon.
Source: Collection, Cuffley family

Our cottage of 1864 appears in a view of the town which was once displayed in a railway carriage.

At their best, these old black and white images are unsurpassed in a number of ways. First, they were usually taken on a large format camera with a good lens and so the quality of the image is very high. Second, they were well lit and well composed and the best of them have a dramatic presence. Thirdly, they are not only finely detailed, but have been skilfully processed using materials which are very stable and can, under the right conditions, last for many generations.

Photographs of Every Kind

Daguerreotypes

For you to identify the types of photographs you may have inherited it is helpful to understand something of how photography evolved. The daguerreotype arrived in Australia in 1841 and by December 1842 the first studio had opened on the roof of Sydney's Royal Hotel.[2] The cost of the picture, frame and case was said to be 'less than the cost of a new hat, or a box at the theatre.'[3] That still put them beyond the reach of ordinary folk, so it was mostly the upper levels of colonial society whose likenesses were captured in the first decade of photography in Australia.

A daguerreotype has a mirror-like quality and needs to be held at a certain angle for the image to be seen. It was created using a highly polished silver-plated copper sheet which was made light sensitive by exposure to the fumes of iodine. Then the picture was taken and the image developed by exposing the surface again, but this time to the fumes of heated mercury. Wherever light had hit the surface the mercury condensed and remained to form the lighter tones. The darker areas were formed by dissolving the silver-iodide layer, leaving the surface to reflect like a mirror. The image taken directly from the subject was a reverse portrait just as we see ourselves in a mirror. Various improvements were made after 1840, including the speeding up of exposure times to less than a minute, and by the 1850s it was down to around thirty seconds under average conditions.

In 1854, Batchelder's Daguerrean Rooms in Collins Street, Melbourne, offered likenesses, 'taken in all weathers, beautifully coloured, and inserted in Frames, Cases, Lockets, Pins, Rings, Bracelets, &c.'[4] They also noted that the pictures were warranted not to fade, 'each likeness being subject to a gilding process, by which a transparent coating is formed over the entire picture, preserving all of its original beauty, unaffected by light, air or age'. This was a gold-chloride treatment which not only helped stabilise the fragile film of mercury, but also enhanced the contrast and warmed the colour of the image. A more stable surface was also better suited to the application of colour with a brush.[5]

Most commonly, daguerreotypes were produced on a 'one-sixth plate' (84 mm x 70 mm) and were carefully enclosed in glass to preserve their delicate image. The glass was held away from the picture surface by a paper or metal spacer which usually formed a decorative frame, or mat. The edges of this sandwich were sealed to make it airtight.

This elaborate and patriotic photograph album celebrates Australian federation. Source: Collection, Don and Zara Latimer

Typically this ensemble was then given a protective case of morocco leather, tortoiseshell or perhaps wood covered with a thin skin of leather or velvet. The 'union case' was popular too. It was an American invention made of thermoplastic, which consisted of compressed shellac, gum, sawdust fibre and black pigment. Heated and pressed into moulds, there were all sorts of decorative patterns available.

As previously mentioned, lockets, brooches, bracelets and even rings were designed to hold tiny daguerreotype portraits. Surviving examples vary greatly in quality and some are tarnished to the point that the image is hardly visible. Even work that was good quality originally can deteriorate when the edge seal is broken or removed. Cheaper, poor quality images are also likely to become blackened with age. It requires expert restoration to recover a tarnished daguerreotype, so it is not advisable to tinker with them.

Ambrotypes

It is easy to confuse ambrotypes and daguerreotypes because they are both kept in the same kinds of mounts and cases. Ambrotypes are actually a very thin, under-exposed negative on glass, with a black backing of paint, paper or cloth. This image looks like a normal positive image because light is reflected by areas of silver and those with no silver appear black. Ambrotypes are

This illustration entitled Photographic Saloon, East End of London *is from Henry Mayhew's* London Labour and the London Poor, *published between 1851 and 1862. It shows us the most basic of establishments which would have produced portraits at six pence or a shilling.*
Source: Collection, Peter Cuffley

correctly described as collodion positives and are sometimes called collodiotypes. Their period of popularity was 1855 to 1865, having first appeared in Australia in 1854.[6] Being a less delicate process than that used for daguerreotypes, all sorts of operators moved into the business and portraits for sixpence or a shilling (five or ten cents) were turned out in huge quantities.

In Henry Mayhew's articles 'London Labour and the London Poor', published between 1851 and 1862, we meet a busker turned photographer who offers a rare insight into all the tricks of the trade in cheap portraits. After describing the dodge of selling bits of varnished paper as 'air-preservers' to be placed in ambrotype cases, he comments, 'Another dodge is, I always take the portrait on a shilling size; and after they are done I show them what they can have for a shilling, — the full size, with the knees; and table and a vase on it, — and let them understand that for sixpence they have all the background and legs cut off; so as many take the shilling portraits as sixpenny ones.'[7]

It seems that Sunday was the best day for shilling portraits because people had their wages and were probably dressed up for church or a stroll through the neighbourhood. We can see a photographer of this era at work in the illustration above. His 'photographic saloon' is a rough and ready affair in London's East End.

When ambrotypes have lost the protection of their cases or frames and have suffered various sorts of destructive forces, it may still be possible to recapture much of the character of the original image. On page 98 you can see a battered ambrotype and two types of restoration of that image which illustrate that all is not lost, even when it might seem hopeless. In this case we found the original in an old envelope without a protective cover glass, backing, frame or case. The dark varnish on the back was scratched and crazed and the image on the face of the glass is scratched and pitted. We placed the image on to a black background and it suddenly looked much better. It was photographed at this stage, then new enlarged prints were used for the restoration.

A

B

C

D

Example C shows the image restored using the traditional technique of removing all the scratches by painstakingly painting them out. A fine paintbrush or an airbrush in the hands of a skilled restorer can achieve remarkable results. Example D is the same image restored using the latest digital technology.

Computer programs such as Photoshop can be used to alter the tonal range, sharpen edges and details, remove scratches, lines, stains or blotches, and fill in tears and gaps. If you have a scanner and a suitable program on the computer, there is no reason why you should not try some photo restoration.

Calotype

William Henry Fox Talbot, an Englishman, developed the negative–positive process from which multiple prints could be made. He experimented with photo-sensitised paper and patented the Calotype process in 1841.[8] This was a salted paper print made from a paper negative. It was also called a Talbotype. These images are rarely found in ordinary family collections. Examples seen in books are usually in museums.

Collodion Negative

While modified and improved systems based on Talbot's principle were central to the development of modern photography, his paper negative system fell out of usage when the wet-plate collodion process was successfully introduced. Wet-plate negatives were used to produce positive prints on albumen paper. It was a process done on a one-to-one basis, so larger prints required larger negatives. Carte-de-visite photographs were made by this method, as were the large format pictures, until gelatin dry-plate negatives were introduced in the 1870s.

Most family photographs taken in the mid to late 1800s are on albumen paper, which is coated with a solution containing egg white. The paper had an exceptionally fine emulsion surface with a natural sheen, although prints made after 1875 were sometimes given a high-gloss enamelled finish. It was also thin paper and needed to be pasted on to a card backing. On the reverse of the card or mount you will usually find the name and address of the photographer, often in a very decorative design which may include coats of arms, monograms or exhibition medallions.

That rich purple-brown colour seen in old photographs was achieved by toning them with cold chloride, a treatment which also aided their long-term preservation. The practice of double-toning photographs, first with gold and then with platinum produced a warm, neutral-toned image. Double-toned images have generally survived in very good condition.

Carte-de-visite

Parisian photographer Andre Adolphe Disderi patented a system of taking eight small pictures on a 204 mm x 254 mm plate (8 inch x 10 inch) in 1854. His camera had four lenses and every time the full plate negative was printed, it made eight small prints.[9] The idea didn't become popular until 1859, and then millions upon millions of carte-de-visite or 'cartes' were made in the period 1860–90. They were relatively inexpensive, and could easily be sent through the mail. The size was an international standard so carte albums became a part of the worldwide craze.

Early examples are usually on fairly thin card with square corners. Often

FAR LEFT: *The restoration of photographs is a complex subject. Sometimes an image needs a minimum of work; in other examples, a great degree of knowledge and skill is required. This portrait of Mary Smale (1825–1901) is an ambrotype taken in the late 1850s. Image A is the original photographed on a white background to show how much wear and tear it has suffered. When placed on a black background, as seen in image B, the legibility improves dramatically. This photograph was then used as the basis for the hand restoration C and the digital restoration D. Both types of restoration required considerable expertise and many hours of work. As with anything old and interesting, there is an argument for leaving much of the character which reflects the passing of the years. Real damage which dominates the image is worthwhile repairing.*

A Ambrotype on white background
B Ambrotype on black background
C Hand restoration on an enlarged print
D Digital restoration by Geoff Sayer of Bendigo
Source: Collection, Peter Cuffley

RIGHT: *Early photographs were often copied at a later date, even in the 19th century. This example is an 1870s or 1880s print, the size of a carte-de-visite, taken from an ambrotype of the late 1850s. The original, now much deteriorated, can be seen above. The subject is Grace Morrish (née Glover) who was born at Sutcombe, Devon, on 10 March 1788 and died at Seymour, Victoria, on 16 December 1884.*
Source: Collection, Ellie Goss

you'll notice that they have been hand-cut with scissors. If there is printing on the back of the carte-de-visite it is usually just a few words, perhaps with a coat of arms or monogram. Through the 1860s the larger establishments went for more impressive designs often taking up the entire back of the card.

Better quality card with more elaborate printing is typical of the 1870s and 1880s. I've seen gold-leaf, gold edging, coloured inks and elaborate lettering used on cream, yellow, pink, brown or even red cards. Carte-de-visite taken by itinerant photographers sometimes have a crude stamp, a small label or perhaps even just a handwritten name.

Tintype or Ferrotype

The tintype is a positive image created directly on to a prepared metal plate, a variation on the system used for ambrotypes. It was patented by Hamilton Smith in 1856. Incidentally, the word 'tin' is misleading because they really used a thin sheet of iron coated with black or brown varnish (japanned).[10]

Tintypes found in Australia mostly date from the period 1880 to 1890, though in America they were made in huge quantities from the early 1860s. Prices could be as low as a shilling per dozen for 'gems', the little postage stamp-size tintypes which were made thirty-six to a plate.[11] Because they were often crudely processed, and because they are very easily bent, the protective coat of varnish can crack, allowing air and moisture to form rust.

Charles A. Woolley was a notable photographer in Hobart, Tasmania.
Source: Collection, Peter Cuffley

Sennotype

This system was an interesting attempt to achieve a three-dimensional effect by placing an albumen print, which was waxed to make it transparent, over the top of an identical unwaxed print. One or both could be hand-coloured and then it was protected by a sheet of glass. Sennotypes were made by well-known photographers in sizes from a quarter plate upwards.

Cabinet Photographs

Demand for a format larger than the carte-de-visite saw the introduction of cabinet photographs. They were more than twice the size of a carte-de-visite, measuring 115 mm x 165 mm (4½ inches x 6½ inches). Though they were seen in Australia as early as 1866, the main period of production was 1880 to 1900.[12]

Panel Photographs

The 'Paris Panel' was an entire plate of prints trimmed and mounted on a card measuring 174 mm x 248 mm (6⅞ inches x 9¾ inches). This popular form of mount apparently reached Australia about 1881 and was part of a trend towards larger prints for framing. The grand panel was 350 mm x 580 mm (13¾ inches x 19 inches) and there was an intermediate size.

Opalotypes

An opalotypes was created printing a photographic image on to white glass. It was available in Australia in the early 1880s and was most popular in the decade 1890 to 1900. Opalotypes are often so heavily retouched or coloured that people think they are 'paintings on glass'.

Amateurs and Snapshots

For people who could afford the equipment, photography offered the amateur a fascinating hobby, even in the decades up to 1880 when processes were complicated, cameras were bulky, and a travelling darkroom was required for work out of doors. In 1880, the dry-plate negative was first used in Australia, a great step forward for both indoor and outdoor photography.[13] George Eastman patented paper-backed film in 1884 and in 1888 placed the Kodak camera on the market.

Modern roll-film cameras began with the 'Kodak' of 1898. The legendary 'Brownie' which first appeared in 1900 was an easy-to-operate box camera at a price ordinary people could afford. Snapshots became part of family life,

bringing a new informality to the family album. One of the ways of dating photographs is by the costume worn. *Dating Family Photos 1850–1920* is a very useful book for family historians (see Bibliography).

Restoring Old Photographs

This is a complex and engrossing subject. There are dozens of methods used to copy, restore, duplicate and store images. But don't feel bamboozled; remember that the primary aim of saving old photographs by using the best technology, both old and new, is to ensure their survival for a long time to come. Most of us can think of a precious photograph which we would be greatly pained to lose. Then consider how many have been lost and how many have survived more by luck than careful conservation.

Before You Do Anything Else

First, have a copy made of any photograph you believe is the only one surviving, then make sure a print or the negative is stored in a safe place. Distribute a number of copies around the family, with details of the person or place pictured, and you will have insured against future loss.

If you cannot arrange for professional copying and restoration, at least try to make your own copies. Often this can be done with ordinary colour film in a basic camera, though for small pictures you will need a lens capable of taking close-ups. If you get reasonably proficient at taking shots of old photographs, you would then be able to copy pictures which cannot be borrowed. Most people will let you take a photo of a photo because it can be done on-site. Having heard so many tales of borrowed photographs never being returned, it is easy to understand why people are nervous. The other option is to let them arrange for copies to be made and you pay the cost.

Black, White and Grey

Old 'black and white' photographs are usually a mass of different tones of 'grey' with 'white' at one end of the scale and 'black' at the other. When a picture is mostly light and dark tones with little in between, we describe it as having too much contrast. These are usually difficult to restore because of the lack of a good tonal range; in other words they are missing the softer details. By comparison, a photograph can be very faded but still have a well balanced tonal range. Many people look at these and give up hope, when in fact this condition lends itself to restoration either by photographic means or through a computer program.

Photographic Restoration

The photographic approach involves making a new negative and controlling the quality of print. A particular kind of film may be chosen and a filter placed on the camera lens if that will help correct some of the problems in the old image. In the case of 'silvering' or oxidation which sometimes spoils old photographs, a polaroid filter can be used in conjunction with polarised

OPPOSITE (TOP): *An example of the system for copying and restoring old photographs called dye sublimation computer imaging. Typically these are done at a local photographic shop and involve an electronic scan which is used to produce a print-out on photographic-type paper. Restoration of the digitised portrait has been done on a computer screen.*
Source: Collection, Peter Cuffley

OPPOSITE: *A rare Australian double portrait of Andrew and Rebecca Watt, Bendigo, Victoria, c. 1863. Married at Dunbar, Lothian, Scotland c. 1839, they migrated to Australia c. 1857 (see page 117). An interesting detail in the painting is the small gold kangaroo on Andrew's watch chain.*
Source: Courtesy Kevin and Willi Carney

This Indenture
Austral
Omnia Veritas
GOODCHILD
&
STEPHENSON
NAUTICAL WAREHOUSE
JOHN & S.A. CAIL,
Mathematical & Optical Instrument
Makers &c.
45, Quayside
NEWCASTLE ON TYNE.
Mr Richard Small
Five Lanes
Alternun
Cornwall
With Speed
Wm. H. ALLEN & Co., 7, LEADENHALL STREET.
LIVERPOOL:—J. AND A. WALKER, SOUTH CASTLE STREET.
EDINBURGH:—OLIVER AND BOYD.
1850.
Joseph Goodchild

lights. With careful adjustment the reflective effect will be neutralised in the new negative and the dark areas returned to their original tones.

When it comes to printing with a new negative, the picture can be manipulated in a number of ways. The whole image can be darkened or the contrast increased. In some cases certain sections can be masked to allow the darkening of a selected area. Photographic papers have various qualities or characteristics and one can be chosen which spreads the range of tones so that all the subtlety remains in the scale of greys, but the lightest areas will be brighter and the darkest areas more intense.

Computer Restoration

To begin the process of restoring a photograph using a computer program, the photograph needs to be scanned with a simple hand scanner or on a flat-bed scanner. This converts the picture into a digital image which can be copied on to a computer disk or CD-ROM. The larger processing firms will now supply your photographs as images on disk even if they have been taken on film.

Most home computers and printers lack the capacity to tackle high-resolution work but you can do a lot with a graphics program and a reasonable printer. Professional restoration of family photographs using a powerful computer and high resolution printer will give results comparable with, or

OPPOSITE (TOP): *This tinted ambrotype with gilt mount dates from the early 1860s. It is thought that the subject could be Mrs Charles E. Glass (Jemima Alexa Harvey Curle) and her daughter Frances Curle Glass, who was born in Castlemaine, Victoria, in 1862.*
Source: Collection, Castlemaine Art Gallery and Historical Museum

OPPOSITE (LEFT): *A 'picture wall' is an ideal way to present family photographs. It could vary from a compact group to a scattering of pictures over a wider area.*
Source: Courtesy Alison and Les Waddell [Photograph: Dennis Russell]

OPPOSITE (RIGHT): *The Cooper family at Mt George, New South Wales.*
Source: Collection, Manning Valley Historical Society Inc.

A remarkable digital restoration has rescued this portrait of Emily Maud Arthur (née Gray) (1860–1930).
Source: Restoration by Geoff Sayer of Bendigo, great grandson of the subject

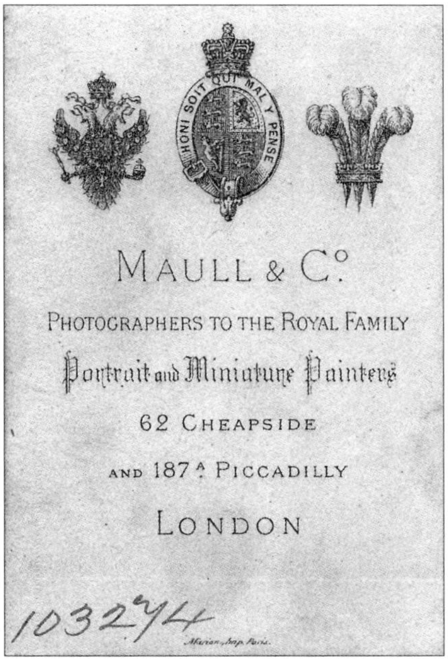

This reverse side of a carte-de-visite is an opportunity to impress clients and potential clients with the studio's talents, awards and general ambience.
Source: Collection, Peter Cuffley

even superior to, traditional restoration techniques. While restoration using a computer program still involves a skilled operator, it is generally less labour intensive than handwork with a paintbrush or airbrush. Lower cost should be the result, and that can be an important consideration for most family historians. Remember to establish a clear understanding of what can be expected from the process and what exactly you will be getting for your money.

Computer programs used to restore photographs usually have a graph which shows the range of grey tones with black at one extreme and white at the other. For a 'washed out' image, the graph will appear with a hump in the middle, and it won't extend to the 'black' or 'white' at each end of the range. Some programs have pointers representing these extremes and by moving them you can alter the graph and therefore the image. This is called improving the 'tone mapping'. These adjustments are not final so that you can return to the earlier condition if you are not happy with the result.

When photographic images are stored on disk or scanned directly into a computer, they are recorded digitally in an image file which is measured in 'pixels' or picture elements. When you enlarge a computer image the pixels appear like a mass of building blocks. The more pixels in a picture on the screen, the more it seems to have a continuous tonal gradation.

While we can have a high resolution on the screen, it is the print-out that gives the final result and here the quality of the image is dependent on how fine the printing is or, in other words, the number of dots per inch (dpi). Ordinary home computers are likely to have a laser-jet or ink-jet printer with 300 dpi resolution. These printers tend to produce a picture that looks slightly grainy, which is acceptable for reference or inserts in your family history computer programs. If it is for book production or framed display, the best move is to have the image printed elsewhere on a machine which produces 1200 or 1800 dpi.

At whatever level the work is done, computer restoration involves working on the photograph as a graphic image file. Well-known programs such as Paint Shop and Corel Photo House can then be used to modify and repair the photograph. A range of 'tools' covers all possible needs from adjusting the brightness or contrast, to 'painting' out spots, scratches and tears. Edges can be sharpened, selected areas diffused, and missing sections can be filled with texture, shading or detail which is copied or 'cloned' from elsewhere in the photograph.

A whole section of background may be missing or badly stained. This can be corrected by blending in a range of tones from another part of the background. The task is often made easier by the softly impressionistic painted backgrounds used in many photographic studios in earlier eras. On the other hand, if architectural elements or curtaining is present or represented in *trompe l'oeil* paintwork, surviving sections may be used as the basis for the replacement of missing or damaged sections.

Figures can be separated from a group, or even brought together to make a combination portrait. Some computer programs allow you to give a vignette quality to the picture by having the centre in focus with gradual softening

towards the edges. Traditionally, portraits in an oval or circular form would be given this soft-focus effect with a mask or template.

When photographs are converted to a digital format, some companies will offer you a number of grades of resolution for each image on the one disk. For instance, a small thumbnail image is useful for selecting and previewing photographs and it can be at a very low resolution (128 x 192 pixels). A snapshot (256 x 384 pixels) can be used for image manipulation at low resolution and will help you with the placement of photographs if you are compiling your family history in book form. The standard image can be supplied at a moderate resolution (512 x 768 pixels), which matches the resolution of a 300 dpi colour printer, that is, each printer dot corresponds to a pixel. Being TV-compatible, this moderate resolution image is good for viewing on a computer monitor or television. Higher resolution (1024 x 1536 pixels) is ideal for image manipulation and printing out on colour printers of 600 dpi or higher. For the finest photographic quality image with full detail, there is a very high resolution (2048 x 3072 pixels) which can be used with one of the professional computer graphics programs.

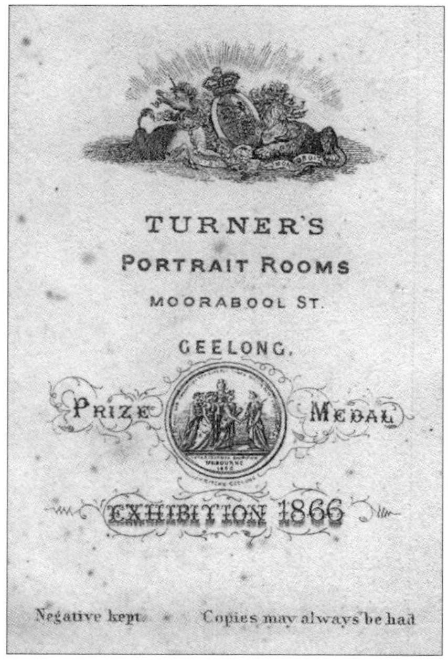

Dye Sublimation Computer Imaging

A popular method of copying old photographs is to have them scanned and reproduced using a process called digital thermal dye transfer or dye sublimation computer imaging. These are usually done at your local photographic shop and involve an electronic scan which is used to produce a print-out on photographic-type paper.

While a photo-quality copy is the immediate result, it is important to know that the print is achieved using dyes. Even with the protection of ultraviolet filtering on the surface, these images will begin to fade over time if displayed under ordinary household conditions. They are not silver-based photographs like old black and white prints and so cannot be expected to last for generations.

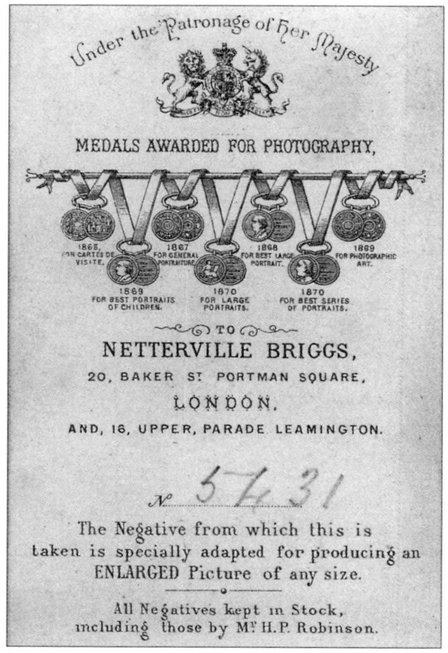

Storing your Collection

If your images have been restored photographically, with or without hand-retouching and repair work, you'll usually be given a copy negative of the completed work to produce prints for your own purposes. Most restoration specialists will give you both the negative and a good quality print, though some prefer to hold the negative and offer multiple prints at a set price.

Photographs restored by means of a computer program can be stored on the hard disk of your computer as well as presented as a print-out on archivally stable paper. Pictures restored by the pre-electronic method can also be stored on disk and this raises the question of which technology will best serve the long-term interest. Storage of pictures in digital form seems to offer marvellous possibilities for the family historian. For example, the Photo CD by Eastman Kodak will hold up to one hundred images and these can be accessed by a computer equipped with CD-ROM.

Mind you, your computer with CD-ROM drive could eventually become

Frederick Peppin (1828–1911) and Sarah Ellen 'Ellen' Peppin (née Morgan, 1835–1910) taken at 'Fernbrook', Loch, Gippsland, Victoria. Frederick was the son of George Hall Peppin and with his father, and brother George, had developed the famous Peppin Merino on their properties in the Riverina. The family left their farm at Dulverton in Somerset and arrived in Melbourne on the Anna Maria *on 11 December 1850. At first they leased a station in Victoria, then in 1858 purchased South Wanganella Station on Billabong Creek near Deniliquin, NSW. In 1861 they bought Morago Station, 35 miles west of South Wanganella. Frederick married Sarah Ellen 'Ellen' Morgan in 1862 and they lived at Morago with his father and mother. In 1872, George Hall Peppin died and Morago was sold. In 1873, Frederick and brother George purchased Boonoke which adjoined South Wanganella. Here Frederick and Ellen lived until the properties were sold following the death of George junior in 1876. They settled in Melbourne in 1877, purchasing six acres in St Kilda and properties at Epping and Loch.*
Source: Courtesy Margaret Winmill, great granddaughter

a curiosity from a bygone age. Though we anticipate that CD-ROMs will have a long life, the operating systems that run them may be difficult to find in fifty years. New technology should bring greater security in the storage and retrieval of words, sounds and images from earlier times. For the present though, it seems wise to keep 'hard copies' of everything we value, while still taking advantage of new systems.

It is difficult to establish an ideal storage environment in an ordinary household, but if long-term preservation is a priority for you, certain standards need to be achieved. Australian Archives suggest that as a minimum general standard you would need to store photographs in a clean, dark environment at 8–12°C and 45–55 per cent relative humidity.[14] The ideal

environment to store black and white material is at 8–12°C and 30–40 per cent relative humidity, and colour prints or negatives at less than 5°C and 30–40 per cent relative humidity.

Long-term survival of contemporary photographs depends on the quality of both the processing and the materials used. It is important to know that you are getting a high standard of work when you have copies made of old black and white family photographs. Sepia-toning or selenium-toning usually ensures a longer life for photographs. This is because they are additional processes applied to a standard black and white print and you can expect that this work would be done with due care.

Black and white photography remains a most reliable form of archival technology. Metallic silver in a gelatine emulsion on a stable base of polyester film or archival quality paper should last, under reasonable storage conditions, for hundreds of years.

Colour photographs are not as durable as black and white. Colour negatives and prints contain dyes which cannot hope to match the stability of silver-based photography. However, a system called UltraStable offers the best possibility for long-lasting colour prints (see Useful Addresses). Considered a world standard for fine art colour photographs, the prints should last for 500 years before noticeable fading or staining occurs. Unfortunately they are probably beyond the pocket of most family historians, but worth considering if you have a highly valued colour image which might become an heirloom piece.

The sad news is that most ordinary colour prints will show a marked degree of fading after fifteen to twenty years.[15] Colour laser printer copies may last up to forty years before real deterioration becomes evident, though the choice of paper may also make a difference.

I have a set of photographs taken in the late 1970s which are badly faded and have changed their colour balance. However, the negatives are in a good condition and a new set of prints made in recent years is as good as the originals were when first printed; perhaps even better. The next question is how will these fare over the coming decades and what kind of image will survive in fifty or a hundred years? There is no easy answer to this question because of the many variables.

As you have probably gathered, there is a difference between photographs kept in the dark and those subject to everyday light sources. Sunlight is particularly detrimental to all kinds of colour prints, including colour photographs. Direct sunlight is one thousand times stronger than normal household lighting so always ensure that displayed photographs are in areas away from direct sunlight and from strong daylight. Those kept in albums or some form of dark storage will fare better if the temperature is low and the relative humidity is less than 40 per cent.

It is preferable also to have archival quality albums. This means that the materials of which they are made will not have a detrimental effect on the photographs. Those albums with 'magnetic' or self-adhesive pages should be avoided. The best paper-based albums use archival quality board, the photographs are held by photo corners and each page is interleaved with a protective sheet. If you choose to use an album with plastic pockets, at least make sure the materials are acid free.

Australian Archives suggest that lint-free cotton gloves be used when handling photographic material. We tend to forget that moisture or oils from the skin can cause deterioration over time. They also advise us never to write on the photographs or attach labels to them. It is best to identify the picture on the storage envelope or album page. I think in the case of family photographs there is an argument for writing on the back to ensure that some details go with the picture. My choice is to write carefully along an edge on the reverse so as not to affect the image. A number or code may suffice if it relates to a corresponding list of details. The only question then is, can you be sure the list will not go astray?

This photograph of a street scene in Sydney was taken by W. McGuire & Co. Along the border of the picture we found the name 'James King' and a very faint arrow pointing to the upright, bearded gentleman in the centre.
Source: Collection, Peter Cuffley

Once you have successfully restored your photographs, then you can present them as part of a lively family heritage (see chapter 12). We should always remember that the survival of old photographs is a blessing from the past. Photographic images reaching back through the generations help history to come alive!

Chapter Eight
Images of Every Kind

In the 19th century, the invention of photography and printing machines brought a new dimension to the lives of ordinary people. By the end of that century, even the poorest household had pictures on the walls. The movement towards universal education had created a growing readership for books, and technology allowed the mass printing of them.

The pictures in cottages and average houses were generally popular reproductions of notable paintings and were in either black and white or richly coloured. Between 1860 and 1900, photographs became more accessible to the general population, and the size of the photographs grew. Large framed portraits were displayed in various rooms of the house especially the parlour or sitting room but also the hallway and even bedrooms were considered suitable places. Affluent families may still have favoured portraits by well-known artists though photographs in good quality frames found a place even in luxurious interiors.

Narrative or storytelling paintings were the accepted genre and prints of these had a ready market. Most had a moral to them or at least celebrated a universal sentiment. When many settlers were still clearing and developing their land in the late 19th or early 20th century, prints of pioneering scenes by Australian artists were both a comfort and an inspiration.[1] Images of royalty, the heroes of the British Empire or nostalgic visions of distant homelands were also considered highly acceptable.

People kept illustrated books, journals, magazines and souvenir issues of newspapers just as we do today. The imagery in advertisements was popular. Many households gave the famed Pears soap print 'Bubbles' pride of place.

There are two basic types of pictorial matter which help bring family history to life. First, you can draw on images directly related to your own

This charming portrait has been painted in a somewhat naive or formulated style often associated with colonial painters. In fact, the photograph at right is of an original English painting probably done in the Manchester area in the 1830s. It is thought to be of Elizabeth Prince (née Wood) who was born in Manchester in 1811, married William Prince there in 1830 and died in 1849. Her son, John, may have been the person who brought the photograph to Australia in 1864.
Source: Courtesy Sandra Geddes

family and then, as your next option, you can locate general illustrations which add an important dimension to the family history. All kinds of factors have an effect on whether family pictures have survived up to the present day. Some families, or individuals in families, are great hoarders. Luckily for me, all four of my grandparents kept a great deal from their own and earlier generations.

Most of us have a story of the loss of family photographs, heirlooms and documents or have certainly heard them from others. Things survive by default or by being carefully handed down, and yet much just gets lost or is deliberately destroyed when a major change takes place. The leaving of a long-time family home is a typical event and apart from the clean-up there can be battles over who gets what, with important family records becoming prizes for whichever faction is victorious. There is a great need for generosity if family history is to be saved for everyone. Modern technology ensures that everything can be copied and duplication makes good sense in a number of ways.

The Importance of Copies

Years ago we could only dream of the wonders of the colour copier and now they are everywhere! Bear in mind though that old images need to be protected and constantly exposing them to the bright light of the electronic copier is not advisable. However, in most cases, a few exposures will do no more harm than the item being subject to daylight for a given length of time.

Photocopiers are ideal for drawings, engravings, documents and some decorative pieces, such as needlework samplers.

The size, condition and importance of an item can mean that photography is the best method of copying it. Having a negative or negatives (or a digital record) allows for multiple images without the need to access the original more than once. Light is the essential element for the appreciation of one-dimensional objects and yet it is also destructive over time. This again is an argument for making good copies of originals if they cannot be displayed in ideal or at least reasonable conditions.

I think of poorly conserved museum collections seen in country towns in years gone by. We must be thankful that people were at least history conscious, but what pain it was seeing original photographs, works of art and printed matter, all fading in the light as well as being attacked by silverfish. One curator in a nearby town simply refused to apply conservation principles to a highly valuable local history collection. The words 'copying', 'conserving' or worse still 'reproducing in a book' were likely to cause him apoplexy. Unsuitable conditions still exist, though generally there has been a great awakening to the need for protection of our fragile heritage.

Sources of primary and secondary images

Mention of local museums reminds us that they are often the only source of family photographs or other images of importance. Such places are usually under the care of the local or regional historical society or perhaps the National Trust. These organisations can also have an archive or some form of storage where material not permanently displayed is kept. Other important repositories are private museums, local libraries, family history libraries, state or regional libraries, the larger museums, art galleries, official archives and educational institutions. If you do have a collection of images relating to family history these resources may well provide further material.

Where there are no surviving family pictures, there is always hope that something of primary interest will turn up in a collection. You could find your

A street of very simple cabins in Rathnew, County Wicklow, Ireland photographed early in the 20th century. This picture by W.A. Green was included in as magazine series entitled Hutchinson's Beautiful Britain *published in the mid-1920s.*
Source: Collection, Peter Cuffley

St Mary's Wynd; View from the Pleasance *is an Edinburgh scene of the 1820s by Thomas H. Shepherd. The book,* Edinburgh in the Nineteenth Century, *was published in 1829 and contains 86 views of the 'Modern Athens'.*

Source: Collection, Peter Cuffley

ancestor in a framed collection of portraits such as was typically assembled to honour a group of pioneers, a committee or a shire council.

Pictures of secondary interest, but important to your family story, may be of a school, business, building, town or an important event your ancestor was involved in. For example, I was sent a copy of a delightful oil painting of St Paul's London, from a private collection in England (see opposite page 38). This work is of general interest, but is also specifically important to my family story because the tower of the parish church of St Andrew by the Wardrobe is visible, as are the wharves on the Thames where great great grandfather was a warehouse foreman and corn chandler. The fact that Thomas Shepherd (1792–1864) painted this scene in the 1820s when the Cuffley family had just settled in the area between St Paul's and the Thames, makes it an important image for descendants who are interested in the family story.

Print Galleries and Published Works

Aside from the many different collections which may hold primary or secondary images for your family history, there are a number of ways you can independently search for images. Art galleries, and more specifically print galleries, that deal in works of historical interest often have views of towns, ports, notable beauty spots, businesses and properties, important landmarks and historic places. They can also have pictures of traditional occupations, various types of transport or people at their leisure. Most print dealers will

have works relating to Australia and to many other parts of the world. They can usually be purchased properly mounted ready for framing so you can have a copy made for your history files or a family publication and then put the framed original on the wall. Australian scenes are not so easy to find in old books, but you can be lucky. These can be copied without causing any damage so you have both the book and a looseleaf copy.

Modern photocopiers handle all sorts of tasks and, in the hands of a skilled operator, will make excellent copies to whatever size you require. Remember that we are considering old material not covered by copyright. Anything in more recent books is a different story and you cannot reproduce pictures for a family history unless you have the written permission of the owners of the work or the copyright holder if that is relevant.

This postcard photograph is of Vivienne Camille Moss, born near Maldon, Victoria, 27 July 1909. Affectionately known as 'Babs', she was the daughter of farmer and engineer, Frederick Moss, and his wife, Elizabeth (née Ewing).
Source: Collection, Peter Cuffley

Picture Postcards

Picture postcards became popular from the end of the 19th century. They provided an easy means of communication, and their value today lies in both the pictorial content and the message on the reverse. For family historians they offer a chance to find views of a selected village, town or city, or possibly a building such as a church, school, community hall, post office, general store or hotel.

Postcard fairs are probably the ideal place to find a wide selection but they can also be found at outdoor markets, antique centres, antiquarian bookshops or specialist outlets. The best stalls have their cards sorted into subjects such as 'Transport' or 'World War I' with views of places divided by country, state or region. While many of the views are of notable sites and tourist attractions, there are thousands which show ordinary towns and villages. Prices can range from a few dollars to five or ten times that price if the card is considered rare. A number of businesses in Britain offer original postcards of churches while others supply old postcard reproductions (see Useful Addresses).

There are also sites on the Internet which list postcards for sale and some will search for requested items. Museums and the various state libraries have postcards of Australian views, pioneer life and notable events in their pictorial collections. Some of these collections are on fully searchable sites on the Internet.

Postcards were sometimes designed with a decorative border. This picture of a family on a day out was taken in Tasmania.
Source: Collection, Peter Cuffley

A district picnic day at Carlisle River, Victoria, around 1910. This unmistakeably Australian scene was captured by Charles Silk, a farmer and keen amateur photographer.
Source: Courtesy Lach and Fran Gardiner

Postcard photographs were also made by amateur photographers and these were generally limited to a few prints for friends and family although sometimes a local amateur would produce enough to meet the needs of the district. We have reason to be grateful to people who used their hobby to record family, friends, community gatherings and local views. Importantly, they often photographed ordinary houses and buildings which may not have attracted the eye of the photographer from the postcard company.

If you are really lucky, you may be able to find local amateur postcards which have your own family in them. Charles Silk of Carlisle River in Victoria was both a farmer and an amateur photographer early in the 20th century. My wife was able to identify her Williamson family in a delightfully informal scene taken during a district picnic and sports day. Mr Silk was a very keen photographer who sent prints to the *Weekly Times* newspaper and entered competitions.

Illustrated Newspapers

This dynamic illustration of swagmen in search of work was included in Australian Sketches, *which appeared in* The Leisure Hour 1897–8. *Pictorial publications from the 19th and early 20th centuries can be an important source of images relating to the lives of people in past eras.*
Source: Collection, Peter Cuffley

Pictorial newspapers and journals are another important possibility for pictures to enhance a family history. Victoria's *Weekly Times* has been a favourite publication for country people since 1869. Such papers contain general pictorial matter including advertisements with all sorts of items and occupations that could relate to your story. More specifically, the pages of photographs showing local events such as country shows, field days, school or town reunions, balls and dances could well include ancestors or family members. Each state has had this type of newspaper, and there have also been publications with a wider circulation such as the *Illustrated Australasian*. In Western Australia there was the *Western Mail*, Queensland had *The Queenslander*, Tasmania had the *Illustrated Tasmanian Mail*, and New South Wales was home to the *Southern Cross*. City and suburban newspapers also had pictures of social gatherings, civic events, race meetings and community picnics.

The quality of the photography varies greatly, though most history-minded people are happy enough to find an image which has some significance to their research. Occasionally a proper photographic print turns up in a collection or in a family album. It was probably purchased at the time from the newspaper or magazine by an interested party. Sometimes these photographs were also sold as postcards.

Mining was of great importance to Australia, and was illustrated in many mediums.
Source: Collection, Peter Cuffley

Reconstructing a View

My grandfather's school appears on a carte-de-visite photograph which was taken around 1880. This shot is important to us, though I would describe it as of secondary interest. Another photograph in the same format is definitely a primary image. It shows my grandparents outside their small hotel in the Melbourne suburb of Collingwood. In recent years with the help of cousins in Sydney we have been able to identify a third figure in the picture as my great grandfather's niece, Emma Rosina Cuffley. With the family name on the building and the family identified, it is a centrepiece in our collection.

In the early sixties I hadn't yet discovered that old street directories are kept in most libraries, so the location was still unknown. As soon as I was able to place it in Smith Street, Collingwood, I went to see if the building still existed. Eighty years had passed, but I was delighted to find that, apart from the removal of the pillar-supported verandahs, it was much the same, as were the adjoining buildings. I took a series of photographs including one from the same angle as the original picture then had the idea of painting a streetscape based on both old and new images. The 1884 street directory gave the names of the businesses on each side and a search through a Collingwood newspaper of the period yielded an illustration of Poynters drapery and millinery establishment at number 88. It all required quite an effort but in the end the painting was an accurate full colour recreation of a slice of old Collingwood (see opposite page 39). Now over thirty years on, I can see a few things I could correct, though I suppose the work itself is history and reflects the era in which it was done.

New Portraits From Old

Any reputable artist can be commissioned to paint a family history portrait. For instance, you may decide to have an oil painting done from an old photograph of an ancestor or a family home which has now been changed completely or demolished. Such an approach may upset some of the purists, but why not have work created which you can hang on the wall for your own and your family's enjoyment. Illustrations are commissioned for all sorts of published works and if you can find an artist who is within your budget, there is no reason why the family history should not have some lively images.

Local real estate agents use artists to produce drawings for selling houses; perhaps you could commission one to produce an attractive picture of an old family property. This approach allows you to remove some of the undesirable modern elements which can make it hard to obtain a satisfactory photograph. The same artist may also be prepared to create some interesting illustrations from

A

A photograph from the mid-1880s (C), a sketch from an old newspaper illustration (D) and a photograph taken in the 1960s (A) were used by the author to create the painting of the Flying Squadron Hotel in Smith Street, Collingwood, Victoria (B). The name refers to a British naval squadron. Executed in 1968 using poster paint mixed with woodworking glue, the work is inspired by colonial painters.
Source: Collection and original work, Peter Cuffley

B

C

D

old photographs which may not, in themselves, do justice to a house or property.

Remember that it is always wise to be clear on a number of matters. First, be sure the artist can produce the kind of work you want. Second, make sure they know exactly what you expect in the result. Third, have an agreed price or at least an upper limit set before they begin.

Back in the 1890s, one of the Sweeney girls paid a visiting artist, Charles Bertie, to paint a picture of our old family home, Culla Hill. In the 1960s she died and the picture passed to her son. Fortunately the owners of Culla Hill, by now called 'Sweeneys', had a really good photographic copy made of the original because it has now disappeared. Such things happen under various circumstances and once again we are reminded of the need to duplicate documents, photographs and images in case of loss. Family history magazines sometimes have photographs of old portraits with accompanying requests for help to find the originals. The chances are probably not very strong of such a work being found, though pictures do go on strange journeys and can reappear in odd places.

IDENTIFYING A PORTRAIT WITH A FEW CLUES

Friends once owned a splendid mid-19th century portrait of 'Mr A.W. Watt & Mrs Watt' (see opposite page 102). It was inscribed on the back, so we knew the identity of the couple, and some additional words read, 'presented to Mrs Griffiths by her father A.W. Watt'. Having admired this painting over many years, I had never thought to use the clues given to find out more about the subjects and their daughter, Mrs Griffiths. The ever-valuable *Victorian Pioneers Index 1837–1888*, an index to birth, death and marriage records on CD-ROM, makes a search such as this a whole lot easier. I also knew the painting had been found in Central Victoria. An interesting clue confirmed the portrait as being an Australian work. We spotted a tiny gold kangaroo hanging from Mr Watt's watch chain.

In searching the pioneers index, the combination of Griffiths with a maiden name Watt instantly turned up the marriage of Rebecca Watt to James Griffiths in 1869. After finding the children of this union, I searched for Rebecca's death and found it registered at Kangaroo Flat near Bendigo in 1912. Her age is given as 72 and her parents as Andrew Watt and Jane Gibson. I also noted that her sister had died in Victoria in 1871. The next step was to search for Andrew and Jane Watt. The death of Jane Watt, daughter of Charles Gibson and Rebecca Ford, was registered in 1887, again at Kangaroo Flat. Once the certificate arrived I saw that she was born in Edinburgh and married Andrew Watt at Dunbar, Scotland, circa 1839.

From these few very important details on the back of a painting, a whole story can be developed. With no inscription and no other clues, Andrew and Jane would have been yet another anonymous couple staring out at us from an earlier age. Not many of us can claim that we have diligently written on the back of every photograph in our keeping, so we really cannot be annoyed with our forebears for leaving behind so many unidentified pictures.

Illustrations of Migrant Ships

Few of us can hope to own a first class painting of a migrant ship, but we can generally find some sort of illustration of a particular vessel. In the light of Australia's strong maritime heritage, it is not surprising that many of our museums and libraries have collections of paintings, drawings, prints and photographs of ships and related subjects. From the First Fleet to well after World War II, immigrants arrived by ship. At first the ships were sailing vessels, then a combination of steam engines and sail, then entirely steam, and finally modern passenger liners with internal combustion engines. Boat people arriving in northern Australia have added a further chapter to maritime immigration.

Pictures of ships can be wonderfully evocative. Many of the surviving works are superbly crafted and often given a picturesque or dramatic setting. The romance of it all would quickly fall away if we were asked to take a voyage under the same conditions many of our ancestors endured. Nevertheless, there were better times with good ships in capable hands praised by those who enjoyed a relatively fast and comfortable voyage.

Marine paintings vary in quality as much as any other form of art. Mostly we would like to have an accurate rendition of the ship. There are also drawings, engravings, lithographs and the ordinary line blocks used in old newspapers and other publications. From late in the 19th century, photographs were reproduced in publications. Old prints of ships at sea or in identified ports are readily available and can generally be purchased for a reasonable price.

Finding a painting for sale which depicts a ship you have linked to the family would be a very rare piece of good fortune. A copy or reproduction of a work in a collection is the most likely option. There is more hope of finding an original print or photograph, but again there would be some luck involved as well as persistence. Newspapers, magazines and books are all possible sources for a picture of a certain ship, but usually the best move is to approach the museums or libraries.

Various kinds of sailing vessels might be seen on the open ocean in the 19th century, and all were used to carry immigrants at one time or another. The Dutch Galleot (above) was rigged like a schooner (top) but was broader, with an almost flat bottom. These illustrations are from Every Boy's Book *(1855).*
Source: Collection, Peter Cuffley

Searching for ship illustrations has become much easier with aids such as Nick Vine Hall's *Ships' Pictures Index 1490–1991*. Available as a set of three microfiche, it includes many of the ships which carried migrants to Australia in the 19th and early 20th centuries. The list includes details of where you may locate a relevant illustration.

Maritime museums are a logical place to find information and pictorial matter. The Australian National Maritime Museum in Sydney is an important resource and offers a series of information sheets. They hold a maritime illustration index for the *Illustrated Sydney News 1853–1889*, the *Illustrated London News 1842–1891*, and *Australian Sketcher 1873–1889*. You can also use the Internet and search sites such as the State Library of Victoria's pictorial collection. For example, the famous clipper ship *Red Jacket* is illustration number 838573. A copy of the image you can see on the screen can be ordered from the library, which holds the reproduction rights.

Libraries may possess a diverse range of books on maritime subjects

Leith Harbour was Edinburgh's access to the Firth of Forth which in turn led to the open ocean. Apart from being a busy shipping port, it was also a manufacturing area. This engraving was made by Thomas Shepherd in the 1820s and appeared in his book Edinburgh in the Nineteenth Century. *Print galleries and antiquarian booksellers are an important resource in the search for relevant images.*

Source: Collection, Peter Cuffley

including many on ships. *Emigrant Ships: the Vessels which carried Migrants Across the World, 1946–1972* is an important work for families who migrated to Australia by sea after World War II, and *Emigrant Ships to Luxury Liners* is another comprehensive reference. For any kind of written records which are known to exist of ships relevant to Australia, there is a three-volume work, *The Log of Logs*, by maritime historian Ian Nicholson. In this publication you can find details of each vessel along with the voyages and any logs, diaries, journals or other accounts in libraries, museums or private collections.

For anyone with convict ancestry, the standard reference is *The Convict Ships* and it gives an alphabetical list of all the convict ships with the number of people on board, place of arrival and the source and call number of the indent or assignment list (see Bibliography). There were 1040 voyages that brought convicts to Australia. For a graphic insight into life on board the 19th-century immigrant ships, I recommend Michael Cannon's *Perilous Voyages to the New Land* (see Bibliography).

Searching for a picture of the ship your ancestors arrived on means that you need to have the details of the vessel and the dates of the voyage. If you have yet to locate this information, the good news is that more and more records are now indexed and readily accessible.

Migration in the 20th century is discussed in chapter 5, but it is worth mentioning again that excellent guide to the National Archives of Australia called *Finding Families*. This publication details the kind of information and pictorial material which might be found for your family history (see

Bibliography). If a photograph of your family or one of its members is too much to hope for, there is a chance that a government or news photograph may have recorded the arrival of the ship or plane. Perhaps more likely is a series of photographs of migrant accommodation which could include a place your family experienced as a first taste of life in a new land.

Photographs in Government Archives

Government archives have collections of photographs covering a wide range of subjects from workers in national or state-run services to the registration of 'aliens'. This outmoded term referred to people born in another country who had not gained citizenship by naturalisation. During the first and second world wars, many so-called 'enemy' aliens were detained by the Australian government and placed in internment camps. Both official and unofficial photographs have survived of these places and of the people detained. Others who arrived as prisoners of war were also held in camps. Both internees and prisoners of war worked on government projects or were assigned as farm labour.

Defence Service Records

Many Australian family histories record stories of service in the defence forces. This is an area of rich documentation and, in many cases, relates to experiences still within living memory. Our greatest resource, aside from all of the memories and relics retained by individuals or their families, is the Australian War Memorial in Canberra, a monument, museum and archive of incredible depth and distinction.

No. 10

No. 26

Service in the regular army, or involvement during wartime, may lead you to a range of interesting documentation. These photographs were issued as cigarette cards.
No. 10 Wounded Australians on the Menin Road.
No. 26 Australians cooking dinner in support trenches at Bullecort, May 1917.
No. 25 Australian transport returning from the line at the gallop, Bullecort, April 1917.
Source: Collection, Peter Cuffley

No. 25

While it is not our only repository of records relating to the armed services and all who were associated with them in the Australian experience of war, it does hold a vast quantity of records including works of art, photographs, film and sound recordings and written or printed documents. A visit to the Australian War Memorial is an ideal but not essential step in your research, for much can be obtained at a distance, including publications. There is also a site on the Internet which offers information and possible leads for further research (see Useful Addresses). The Returned Services League will also help people who are searching for individuals or groups, and they may be able to help with enquiries relating to family members who served in a particular division, battalion, unit or squadron.

People at Work in Past Eras

Occupations are another central theme in the history of a family. This is such a huge field that readers are best advised to seek out the many reference books which cover this fascinating subject. These will usually contain pictorial material or suggest resources. Family history magazines also regularly feature trades or occupations and old trade or professional journals have biographical and general information as well as useful illustrations.

My researches into horse-drawn vehicles and the coach-building trade alerted me to the value of journals such as the *Australasian Coachbuilder and*

The tents and huts seen in this view at Silverton near Broken Hill in the late 19th century illustrate the conditions many of our forebears endured. Developments such as the building of railways, dams, water channels and roads, often saw whole families living under canvas or makeshift shelters.
Source: Collection, Peter Cuffley

Working by candlelight was never easy on the eyes. Taking in sewing was a common means of survival for many poor households. This illustration is Meg Veck's Garret *and dates from 1845.*
Source: Collection, Peter Cuffley

Saddler, which began publication in 1890.[2] This particular journal contains stories of companies and individuals and often has portraits along with pictures of the factories and the vehicles being manufactured. Similar material appears in the 'cyclopaedias' which were popular in the late 19th and early 20th centuries. Publications such as the *Cyclopaedia of Tasmania* and the two-volume *Cyclopaedia of Victoria* are rich in biographical information, the history of trades, businesses and other pursuits as well as offering photographs of towns, businesses, farms, houses and individuals.

Specialist publications usually provide a long list of job titles relating to occupations. There is also the *Dictionary of Old Trades & Occupations* to help sort out some of those less familiar terms such as a kitter (a maker of wooden tubs and buckets), or a slubber (a person who dresses fibres prior to spinning yarn).[3] Old encyclopaedias and dictionaries will often yield illustrations of people working at various trades and occupations. Newspaper advertisements and wholesale or retail catalogues are sources for machinery, tools of trade or people working at specific tasks.

In many ways the search for pictures to include in your family history can be as interesting a challenge as the documentation and the words.

Chapter Nine
Maps, Plans and Papers

Being able to pinpoint on a very old map the roads and tracks, towns and villages that were familiar to your forebears helps you develop an understanding of their world. To see and, perhaps, hold documents related to the ownership of land, the building of a house, or a dramatic change in an ancestor's life, engenders a great sense of connection. Reading a will or series of probate papers, may alert you to names, places and properties which were previously unknown to you.

Maps offer endless possibilities for bringing family history to life. They are more likely to be found than documents directly related to the family story and yet in themselves can be presented in such a way that makes them essential and enjoyable elements in the saga.

Four kinds of map can be used to tell the tale. First, there are hand-drawn originals which can be old, new or even something you have created yourself. Alternatively, you may discover old printed maps from various eras. Then there are commercial reprints of old maps or reproductions in books, and last but not least are the copies of maps you make yourself and have modified especially for the family history.

These maps may show anything from a street or property layout to an entire hemisphere. Family journeys can cover at least half a world while other important trails might be across a city or from village to village. In Australia, the map may be of a farm or station property which can be equal in area to an entire parish or even a county in the Old World. Importantly, you can set the scale you want to best illustrate your narrative or make the strongest impression. Modern photocopiers are a wonderful aid, not only in making very good copies, but also in changing the scale of a map or selecting one portion of it and enlarging that to whatever dimensions offer the right

interpretation. Maps can be simple, no nonsense works which accurately portray the chosen subject, or at the other end of the spectrum they can be highly decorative and at times imaginative, with beautiful lettering, pictorial elements and subtle colouration.

Maps are created for all sorts of reasons. This one showing the town of Enfield in Middlesex was drawn up for an 1850 report to the General Board of Health on a preliminary enquiry into the sewerage, drainage, supply of water and the sanitary condition of the parish. Foul-smelling privies, cesspools, open drains and ditches were all noted in some parts of Enfield town.
Source: Local History Unit, London Borough of Enfield

Sourcing Old Maps

Because interest in family and general or social history is burgeoning it has become much easier to find the maps we want. There is now an extensive catalogue of reprinted maps for the British Isles, while those for other regions and specific countries, states, counties or cities vary in relation to demand. With a large percentage of Australians claiming some ancestry in Great Britain or Ireland there is reason to celebrate the efforts to make available

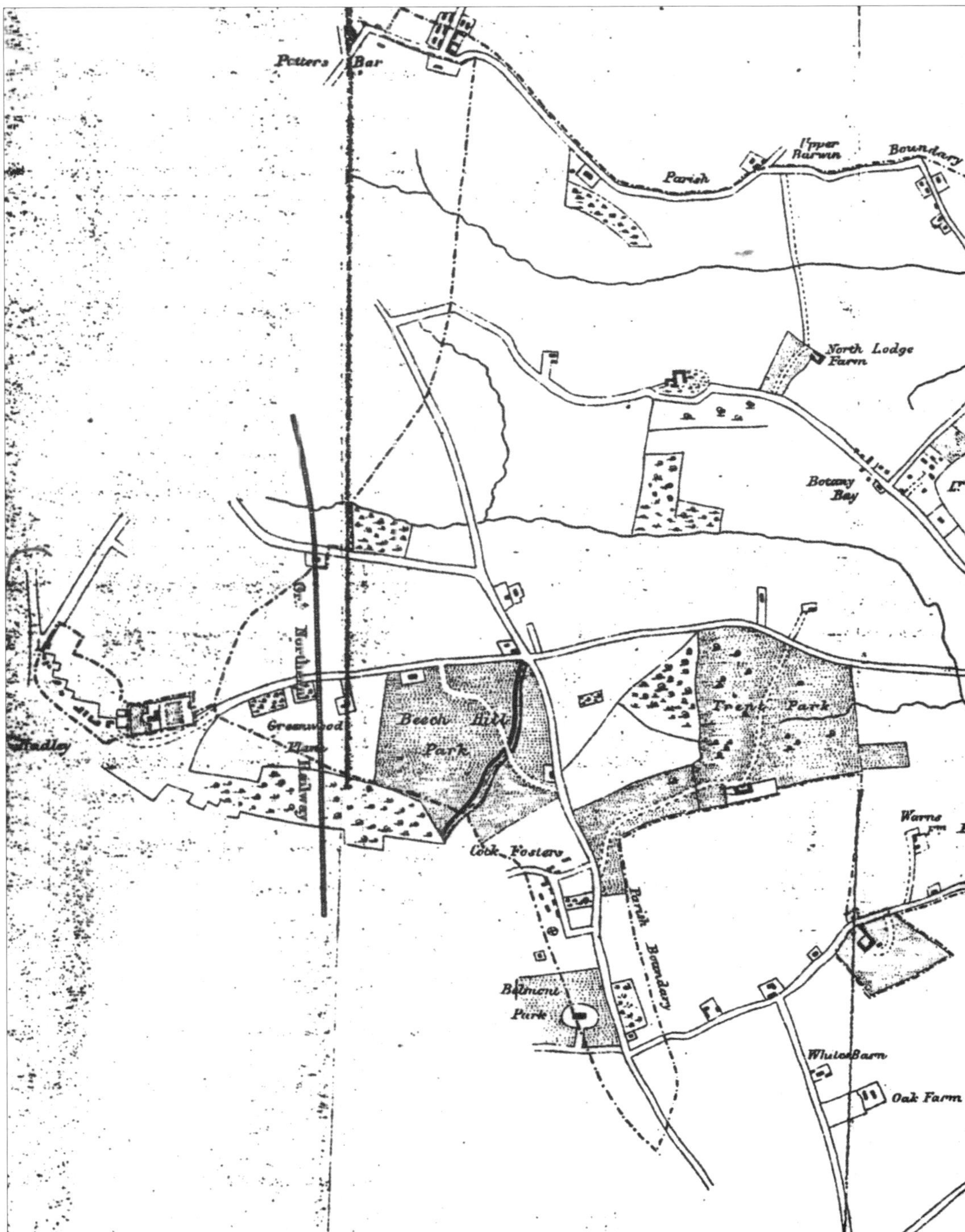

reprints of the old Ordnance Survey maps, including Town Plans for England, Wales, Scotland and Ireland. While the latter naturally only cover the cities and the larger towns, they are of great value if they do include a place of interest, because the amount of detail is marvellous. Individual buildings including private dwellings are all there, along with footpaths, tram tracks, railway lines, canals and sundry other elements.

On a larger scale, the standard 'one inch to the mile' Ordnance Survey maps made in the 19th century are ideal for their coverage of whole regions on a scale which offers the important smaller details as well as the relative placement of each town, village, notable house or farm. For research purposes you can then enlarge sections to study a given area. The reprints are available through specialist map dealers and family history bookshops at a very reasonable price. They fold down to an easily carried size, although for a

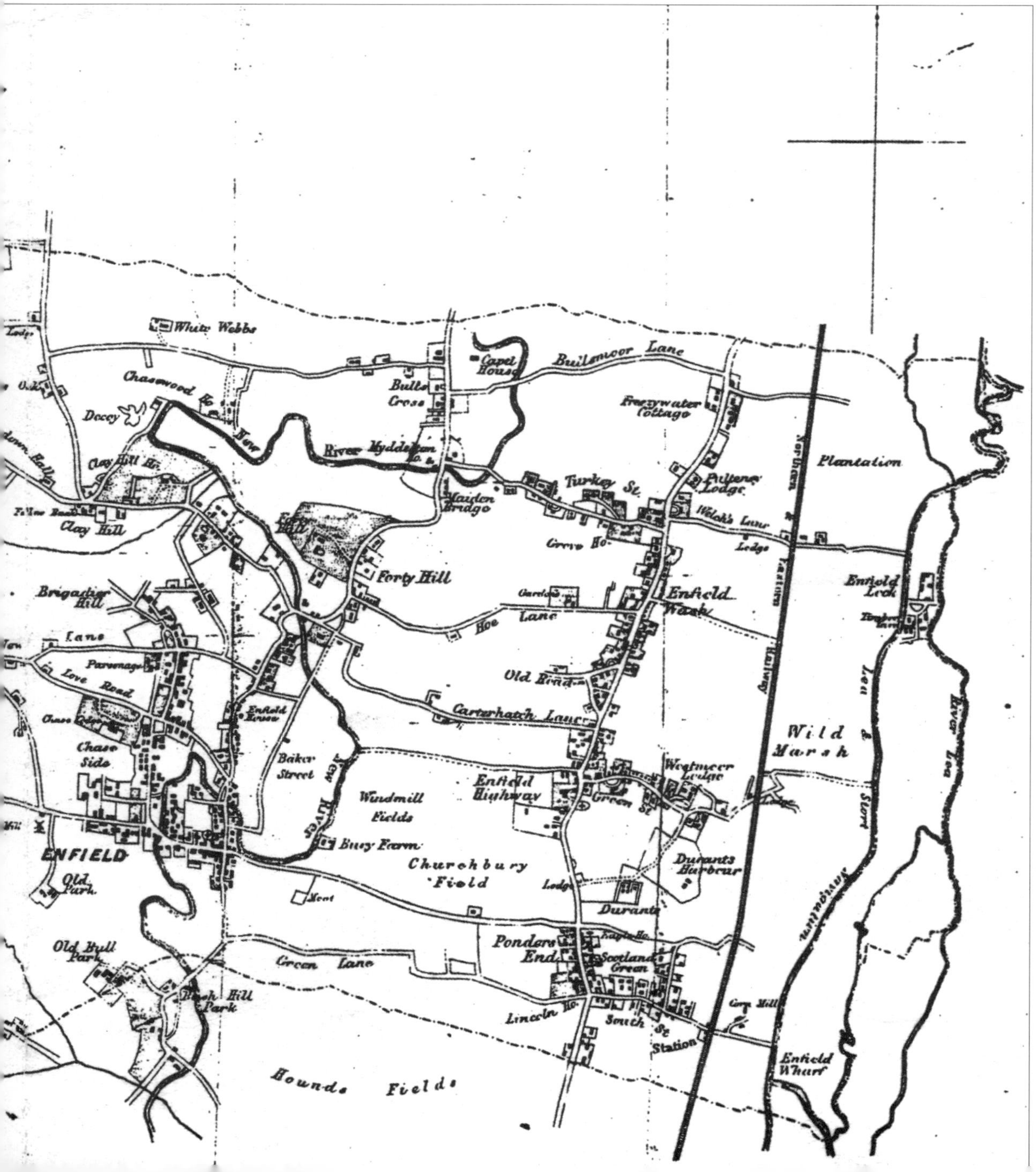

The rise of the printing industry created a vast number of printed works which are now a resource for family historians.
Source: Collection, Peter Cuffley

handy reference a portion can be copied to A4 size and placed in a plastic pocket or laminated. When it comes to copying maps for your own published family history you need to be sure you have the appropriate permission if the work is still under copyright or ownership is claimed by a present day publisher. Very old maps in your own possession should be free of any such restraints. However, if you obtain copies of an old map from a library or museum collection, you will need permission to reproduce it in a book.

Dealers in old prints usually include maps in their stock. You may not be able to locate a detailed map of a specific area such as a parish, but there could be examples covering English counties, the countries of Europe or individual Australian states. Atlases from the beginning of the 20th century and back into the 19th certainly do turn up in secondhand and antiquarian bookshops and these may yield some useful maps. Local museums and historical societies will have maps relevant to the area, but could also have some covering other places. Old gazetteers can have beautifully engraved maps, usually finely detailed and often with a pictorial element.

To pinpoint the area map you hope to find, you may need to start with a gazetteer or directory so you can establish the exact locality of the town, village, settlement or property which is relevant to your research. Some topographical dictionaries give the latitude and longitude for each entry and this can be a great help in finding the right map.

Zooming in from the state or county map to the subdivisions such as townlands, parishes, shires or boundaries of suburbs is the next step. Some areas are well-mapped, others not. Fortunately there are all kinds of local maps now on microfiche and these are often in the family history sections of libraries. For example, in Victoria there are old parish maps on microfiche showing crown allotments — an invaluable resource. Parish and county maps may be available at the sales section of your state lands and natural resources office or at a retail outlet selling a range of maps (see Useful Addresses).

Families in Australia whose forebears came from Prussia or Poland and, in particular, from Silesia, will be interested in reprints of maps surveyed in the 1890s obtainable from Gould Books (see Useful Addresses). On a scale of one to one hundred, they are shaded relief maps with a great amount of detail.

Reprints of old maps as single sheets, or produced in book form, may cover countries and regions for various periods in history. I've seen beautifully produced facsimiles of 17th century maps of the English counties drawn by Johan Blaeu (*Atlas Novus*, 1648) reprinted by John Bartholomew & Son Ltd of Edinburgh. These are in full colour on good quality paper. Many of the English counties are rendered in black and white on maps made in 1761 by John Rocque, and there are other reprints of 18th century maps which are important references for people who have traced family lines to the British Isles in that period.

Aerial Photographs

Local and overseas government departments involved in surveying and mapping may also hold early aerial photographs of a place of interest. Sections can be enlarged to bring up a particular town, settlement or farm. Many of

these aerial photographs were taken more than fifty years ago and so record places before the dramatic changes which took place in certain areas after World War II. In the Old World, the destructive forces of war altered cities and towns and led to large scale reconstruction and development.

Place Names

Obtaining copies of maps for selected periods in history is essential if you are going to make sense of the relative importance of towns, villages or settlements. There is also the question of the spelling of place names at a given time, the position of any boundaries and the way the road network or physical barriers affected people's lives. If you know where people went to church or to market, the main access to a larger town or a city, the location of the manor or country estate, then you have a good framework on which to build your story.

The variation in the spelling of names for both people and places is one of the very interesting aspects of ancestor hunting. Many place names on maps and in records have changed over time. Sometimes you'll see a variation in the spelling, but often a name will have altered in its form or even lost its original

Enlargements of old maps which focus on a particular area are useful tools in family history research, and also make interesting illustrations. This is a section of a map of Bedfordshire in volume one of the Parliamentary Gazetteer of England and Wales, *published in 1854.*
Source: Collection, Peter Cuffley

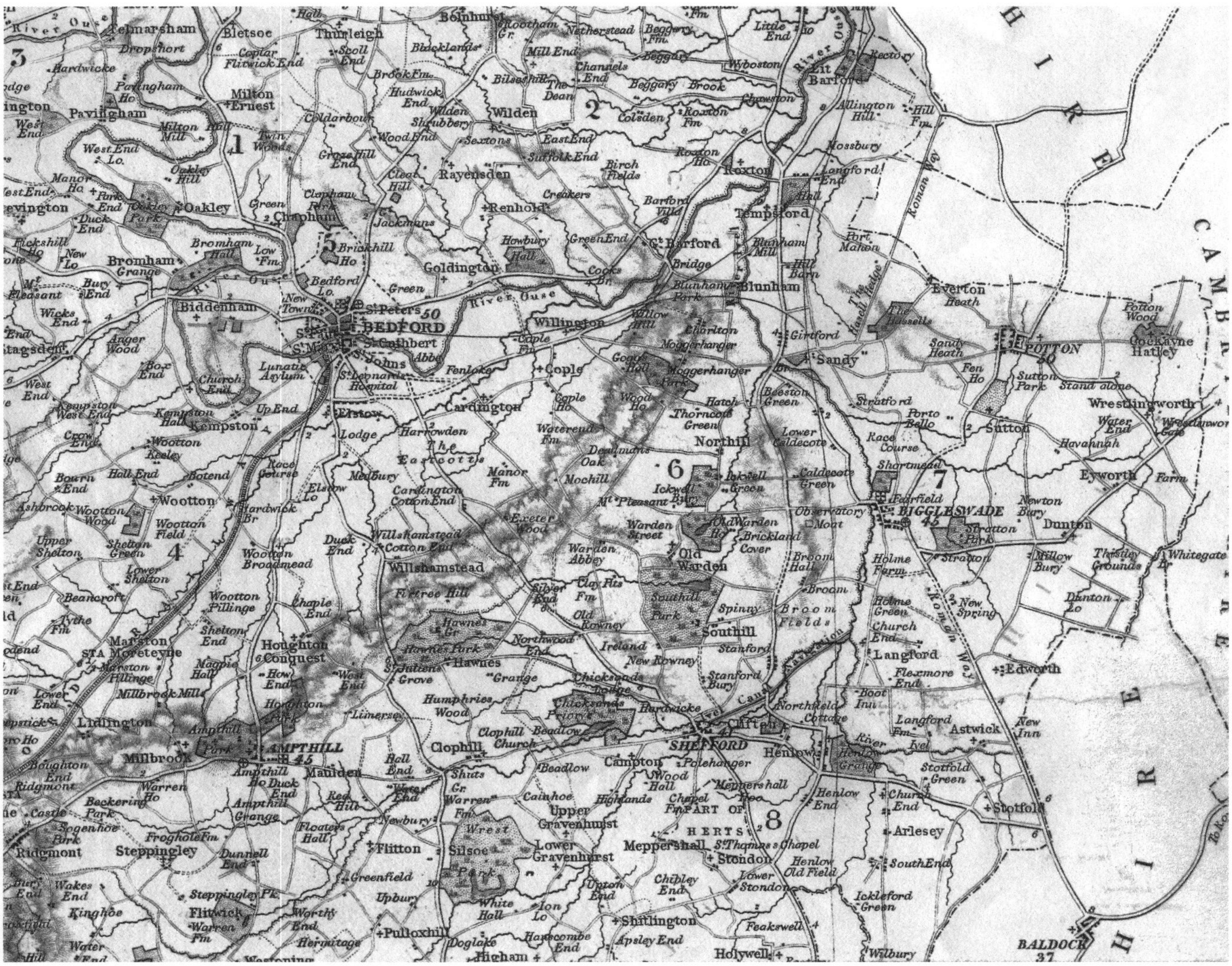

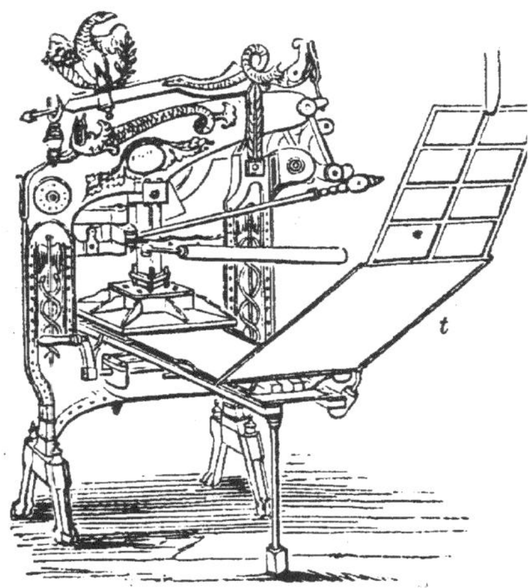

ABOVE AND OPPOSITE: *Nineteenth-century printing presses.*
Source: Collection, Peter Cuffley

meaning. The spelling of both place names and surnames depended on the small proportion of the population who were literate, and even then there were no rules or demand to be consistent.

In the Assize Rolls of 1255, the place now called Cuffley in Hertfordshire was written as Kuffele, and in 1275 as Caffeleye.[1] By the 16th century it may have been Coffley or Cuffley, and it was the latter which finally became the standard in the late 19th century.

Boundaries

County maps showing the names and boundaries of the parishes in both Britain and Ireland have been published in a number of books. The best known source for England, Wales and Scotland is the *Phillimore Atlas and Index of Parish Registers* (see Bibliography). The English and Welsh maps included were produced by the Institute of Heraldic and Genealogical Studies, and they are available as single sheets in a larger format. These maps show the counties of England and Wales as they were before 1974 and give the commencement dates of the parish registers which have survived. For Ireland, *A New Genealogical Atlas of Ireland*, contains maps of counties, dioceses, baronies and civil parishes.[2] This book also shows the areas of jurisdiction of civil probate registries and the poor law unions.

If your ancestors came from rural areas in England or Ireland, there may be detailed maps showing the layout of fields and the location of dwellings and other buildings. Between 1838 and 1854 in England, tithe apportionment maps were prepared for areas where tithes had survived.[3] Each parish or township was shown with each field, house or garden numbered. The apportionment schedule gives a description of each parcel of land, the names of the owners and occupiers, and specifies the rent payable.

For Ireland, there are 'six inch to the mile' maps dating from between 1835 and 1846. These were the work of Ordnance Survey and show details such as buildings, field boundaries, bogland and groups of trees, but not the kind of topographical shading we find on the 'one inch to the mile' (1:63 360) Ordnance Survey maps. The 'six inch to the mile' maps also lack descriptive writing. This extra information went into notebooks which survive for only nineteen of the thirty-two counties.[4] The maps themselves are on microfiche as 'The Townland Survey of the Counties of Ireland' and a set of these is held by most state libraries.

I find it best to work with a series of maps for a given area because one may contain information not found on the other. It is often worthwhile to use a photocopier to bring the maps to a common scale if you are studying a small area. Photocopies on transparent film can be used as overlays which enable you to combine two surveys. Of course, they will need to match in scale and be accurately surveyed in the first place. When this is possible using an old map and a modern one, you'll be able to pinpoint old sites, early roads and sometimes survey lines or boundaries.

If your research has led you to a manor or an estate in the British Isles, it may be that maps survive in the records. Your forebears could have owned the manor or estate but more likely they were tenants or landless workers. The

difficulty in locating relevant records comes from them being in various collections, both public and private. If you know the name of a manor or estate and perhaps something of the families long associated with it, you can approach a county record office or local archive for information on surviving records.

Another major source is the Historical Manuscripts Commission in London (see Useful Addresses) which has the Manorial Documents Register and the National Register of Archives (NRA). It is important to remember that a village or a number of villages may appear on a map of a manor or estate complete with the names of the tenants.

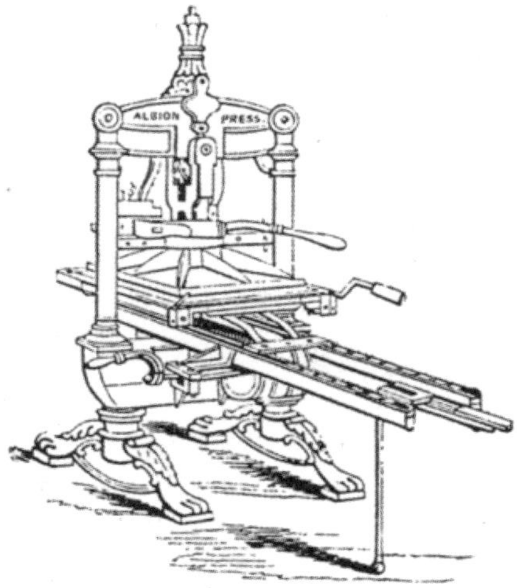

Australian Maps

With more than two centuries of European settlement in Australia, there are maps to complement and illustrate every family story. Again we benefit from the widespread interest in history which has seen so many fine old maps reprinted. There is a 1789 map of Sydney Cove showing the first buildings and a plan of Sydney by James Meehan dated 1807. My favourite maps show Sydney in the 1820s and 1830s because I can visualise the movements of my great great grandfather Thomas Sweeney, both as a convict and as a coastal trader. The site of Melbourne in 1837 is depicted in an interesting map by Robert Russell and I'm also keen on a coloured map of Van Diemen's Land in 1831 published by Henry Teesdale & Co.

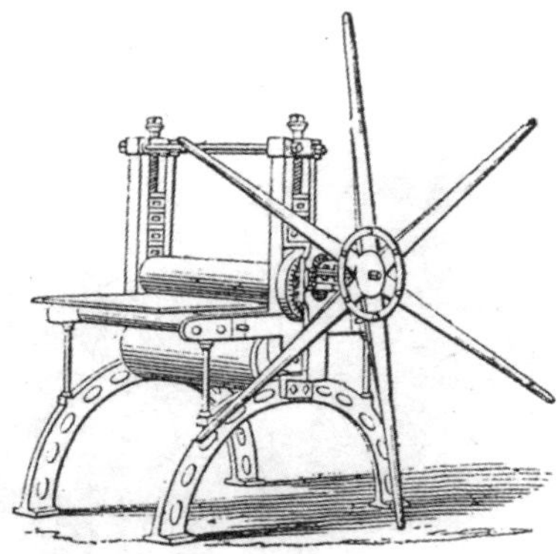

To appreciate how far Australia had developed by the middle of the 19th century, take a look at some of the maps produced by John Tallis and Company, which are both informative and superbly decorative. Published in the early 1850s as steel engravings, they have been reproduced in colour and are ideal for mounting or framing. The collection includes an overall map of Australia along with one each for New South Wales, Tasmania, Victoria, South Australia and Western Australia (Swan River). Two sources for map reprints are MapWorks in Victoria and Gould Books in South Australia (see Useful Addresses).

Government Issue Maps

Government surveys exist for each colony or state in Australia and can be a valuable resource for the family historian. For example, in Tasmania there are 1:100 000 scale topographic maps, in various editions up to the present time, which show the names of properties and the position of the main residence on each one. Many of the larger estates employed and housed both families and individuals in a way of life which reflected the Old World.

Until recent times, county charts were the key to the original crown allotments in Tasmania. The information they contain has been applied in an updated form to a 1:25 000 scale Crown Land Series of maps.[5] Both the earlier and the current publications will help you find the boundaries of crown allotments, the relevant numbers, the grantee, the area of grant and in some instances correspondence file numbers. Tasmap supplies maps in print, and for earlier material there is the Land Titles Office or the Archives Office of Tasmania (see Useful Addresses).

OTHER MAPS AND PLANS

As well as the comprehensive government maps, there are countless privately published works which show the layouts of towns and villages, land subdivisions, canal or railway schemes, housing estates and properties for sale. Such maps and plans can be found in old newspapers and journals, or as brochures, folders, posters or leaflets, distributed by promotors of schemes, land developments and property sales. Many of these are now in libraries, archives and local historical museums.

In the 19th century, the 'bird's eye view' became very popular and combined the qualities of a relief map and a three-dimensional view. One of the best known is *A Balloon View of London* (1851) showing the central city and the Thames from Greenwich to Chelsea. Australian cities and larger towns have been presented in a similar fashion. Coloured aerial views frequently had a border of illustrations showing notable buildings, businesses, street scenes, landmarks or beauty spots. Advertising for land subdivisions often combined maps, aerial views and attractive scenes to entice prospective buyers. A land sale map may provide an interesting illustration for your history and these can be found in libraries and museums or you may be able to acquire an original document from a dealer in ephemera.

Maps on Computer

Your family history research can be presented geographically using a computer program such as GenMap. This particular program displays and prints maps of historical or genealogical data related to the British Isles. It can be used to plot the distribution and movement of a surname through space and time, and combines a full coastline map and historical county boundaries.

You are given a choice of dot distribution or county-floodfill. The latter shows the degree of concentration of a family in each county by means of a colour fill. Information from your computer records is imported into the program and linked to counties or specific places on the map.

Plans

An assortment of plans may be linked to the story of a family or individual including plans for dwellings, private or public gardens, buildings such as churches, schools or prisons, ships, steam engines, bridges — in fact, anything of relevance. An illustration and floor plan of a family home is likely to survive if the house was built through a housing scheme or development company. Most of the so-called 'bank houses' built between 1900–1950 are sure to be in catalogues or bank archives.

KEY DOCUMENTS

Documentation in the form of wills, probate inventories, land applications, titles and transfers, indentures, mortgages, memorials, petitions, convict pardons, naturalisation certificates and educational qualifications are all

FAR RIGHT: *Under English church law, marriages by licence required a bond to be taken out on the validity of the union. They were compulsory from 1579 until 1823. The example shown is a standard printed form, contrasting with the poor handwriting of whoever filled it in. It states that Thomas Langham of the parish of St Andrews, Holborn, was applying for a licence to marry 'Sa Cuppley'. By other evidence this is Sarah Cuffley born in 1735 at Sawbridgeworth, Hertfordshire. The marriage took place on 1 September 1754 at Hunsdon and daughter Sarah was baptised on 20 November, which explains the rush.*

Source: Reproduced by courtesy of the Essex Record Office

Langham

A Half Penny Pr Sheet

Know all Men by these Presents that We Thos. [Langham] of ye Parish of St Andrews Holborn London & William Sewell of ye Parish of Hunsdon in ye County of Hertford

are held and firmly bound to the Rt. Revd. Father in God Thomas Lord Bishop of London in two hundred

Pounds of lawfull Money of Great Britain to be paid to the said Bishop or his certain Attorney Executors Administrators or Assigns for the true Payment whereof We bind ourselves and each of us by himself for the whole and every part thereof and the Heirs Executors and Administrators of us and each of us firmly by these Presents. Sealed with our Seals Dated the [blank] Day of [blank] in the 28th Year of the Reign of our Sovereign Lord George by the Grace of God of Great Britain France and Ireland King Defender of the Faith And in the Year of our Lord one Thousand Seven Hundred and 54

The Condition of this Obligation is such: That if there shall not hereafter appear any lawful Lett or Impediment, by reason of any Pre-contract, Consanguinity, Affinity, or any other just Cause whatsoever; but that the above bounden Tho: Langham & Sa: Cuppley

may lawfully Marry together: and that there is not any Suit depending before any Judge Ecclesiastical or Civil, for or concerning any such Pre-contract: and that the Consent of the Parents, or others the Governors of the said Parties be thereunto first had and obtained: and that they cause their said Marriage to be openly solemnized in the Face of the Parish Church of Hunsdon in ye County of Hertford between the Hours of Eight and Twelve of the Clock in the Forenoon: And do and shall save harmless and keep indemnified the abovenamed Bishop his Surrogates and all other his Officers and Successors in Office, for and concerning the Premises; That then this Obligation to be void and of none Effect, or else to remain in full Force and Virtue

Sealed and delivered in the Presence of

Daniel Linsell

Elizabeth Glascock

Thomas Langham

William sewell

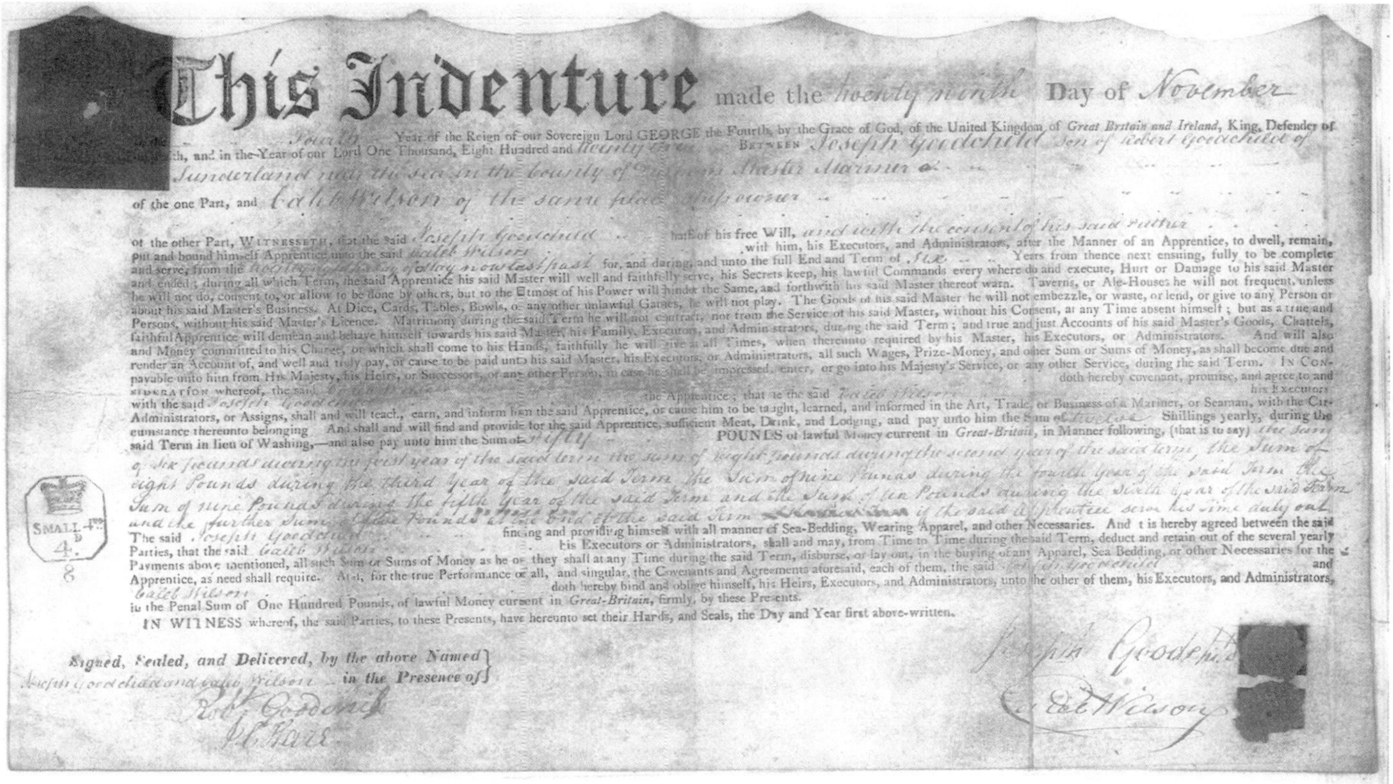

This Indenture made the *twenty ninth* Day of *November* in the *Fourth* Year of the Reign of our Sovereign Lord GEORGE the Fourth, by the Grace of God, of the United Kingdom of *Great Britain and Ireland*, King, Defender of the Faith, and in the Year of our Lord One Thousand, Eight Hundred and *twenty three* BETWEEN *Joseph Goodchild Son of Robert Goodchild of Sunderland near the sea in the County of Durham Master Mariner* of the one Part, and *Caleb Wilson of the same place Shipowner* of the other Part, WITNESSETH, that the said *Joseph Goodchild* hath of his free Will, *and with the consent of his said Father* put and bound himself Apprentice unto the said *Caleb Wilson* with him, his Executors, and Administrators, after the Manner of an Apprentice, to dwell, remain, and serve, from the *twenty eighth day of May now last past* for, and during, and unto the full End and Term of *Six* Years from thence next ensuing, fully to be complete and ended; during all which Term, the said Apprentice his said Master will well and faithfully serve, his Secrets keep, his lawful Commands every where do and execute, Hurt or Damage to his said Master he will not do, consent to, or allow to be done by others, but to the Utmost of his Power will hinder the Same, and forthwith his said Master thereof warn. Taverns, or Ale-Houses he will not frequent, unless about his said Master's Business. At Dice, Cards, Tables, Bowls, or any other unlawful Games, he will not play. The Goods of his said Master he will not embezzle, or waste, or lend, or give to any Person or Persons, without his said Master's Licence. Matrimony during the said Term he will not contract, nor from the Service of his said Master, without his Consent, at any Time absent himself; but as a true and faithful Apprentice will demean and behave himself towards his said Master, his Family, Executors, and Administrators, during the said Term; and true and just Accounts of his said Master's Goods, Chattels, and Money committed to his Charge, or which shall come to his Hands, faithfully he will give at all Times, when thereunto required by his Master, his Executors, or Administrators. And will also render an Account of, and well and truly pay, or cause to be paid unto his said Master, his Executors, or Administrators, all such Wages, Prize-Money, and other Sum or Sums of Money, as shall become due and payable unto him from His Majesty, his Heirs, or Successors, or any other Person, in case he shall be impressed, enter, or go into his Majesty's Service, or any other Service, during the said Term. IN CONSIDERATION whereof, the said *Caleb Wilson* doth hereby covenant, promise, and agree to and with the said *Joseph Goodchild* the Apprentice; that he the said *Caleb Wilson* his Executors Administrators, or Assigns, shall and will teach, learn, and inform him the said Apprentice, or cause him to be taught, learned, and informed in the Art, Trade, or Business of a Mariner, or Seaman, with the Circumstance thereunto belonging. And shall and will find and provide for the said Apprentice, sufficient Meat, Drink, and Lodging, and pay unto him the Sum of *twelve* Shillings yearly, during the said Term in lieu of Washing,—and also pay unto him the Sum of *fifty* POUNDS of lawful Money current in *Great-Britain*, in Manner following, (that is to say) *the Sum of six pounds during the first year of the said term the sum of eight pounds during the second year of the said term, the Sum of eight Pounds during the third year of the said Term the Sum of nine Pounds during the fourth year of the said Term the Sum of nine Pounds during the fifth year of the said Term and the Sum of ten Pounds during the sixth year of the said Term and the further Sum of* [illegible] *Pounds at the End of the said Term* [illegible] *if the said Apprentice serve his time duly out.* The said *Joseph Goodchild* finding and providing himself with all manner of Sea-Bedding, Wearing Apparel, and other Necessaries. And it is hereby agreed between the said Parties, that the said *Caleb Wilson* his Executors or Administrators, shall and may, from Time to Time during the said Term, deduct and retain out of the several yearly Payments above mentioned, all such Sum or Sums of Money as he or they shall at any Time during the said Term, disburse, or lay out, in the buying of any Apparel, Sea Bedding, or other Necessaries for the Apprentice, as need shall require. And, for the true Performance of all, and singular, the Covenants and Agreements aforesaid, each of them, the said *Joseph Goodchild* and *Caleb Wilson* doth hereby bind and oblige himself, his Heirs, Executors, and Administrators, unto the other of them, his Executors, and Administrators, in the Penal Sum of One Hundred Pounds, of lawful Money current in *Great-Britain*, firmly, by these Presents.

SMALL 4th D 4. 8

IN WITNESS whereof, the said Parties, to these Presents, have hereunto set their Hands, and Seals, the Day and Year first above-written.

Signed, Sealed, and Delivered, by the above Named *Joseph Goodchild and Caleb Wilson* *in the Presence of*
Robt. Goodchild
J. C. Hare

Joseph Goodchild
Caleb Wilson

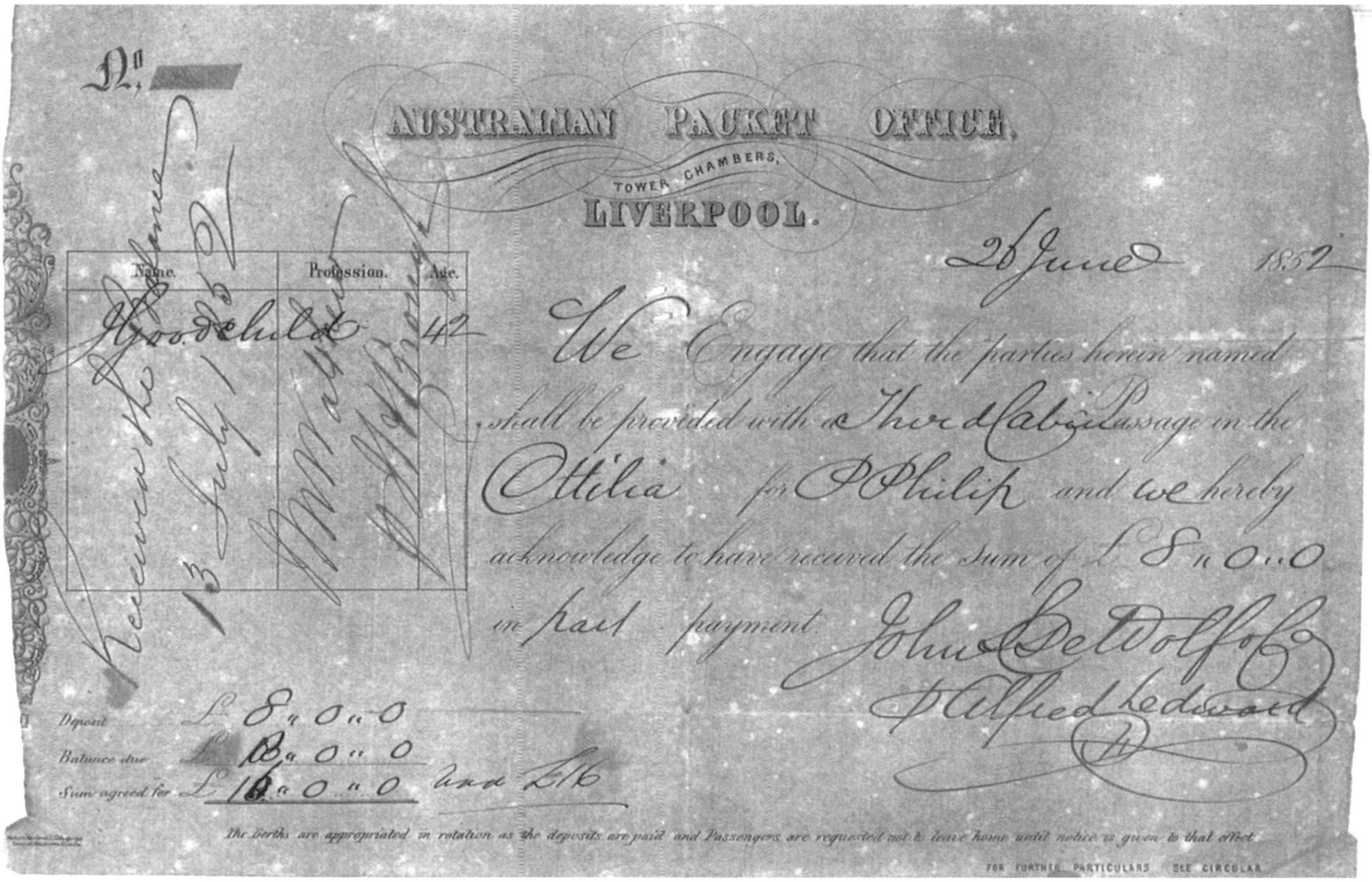

No.

AUSTRALIAN PACKET OFFICE.
TOWER CHAMBERS,
LIVERPOOL.

26 June 1852

Name.	Profession.	Age.
J. Goodchild		*42*

We Engage that the parties herein named shall be provided with a Third Cabin Passage in the Ottilia for P. Philip and we hereby acknowledge to have received the sum of £ 8 " 0 " 0 in part payment. *John [illegible] Wolfe*
P. Alfred Edwards

Received the balance 13 July 1852 [illegible]

Deposit £ 8 " 0 " 0
Balance due £ 13 " 0 " 0
Sum agreed for £ 16 " 0 " 0 *and £16*

The Berths are appropriated in rotation as the deposits are paid and Passengers are requested not to leave home until notice is given to that effect.

FOR FURTHER PARTICULARS SEE CIRCULAR

items of family interest. Their importance as historical records depends on their age, rarity and content, while their pictorial value will come from inherent or acquired character. A fine piece of calligraphy accompanied by stamps, seals and ribbons makes a legal document more visually effective than a plain set of words. Sometimes a selected portion of calligraphy, perhaps with robust scroll decoration will make an effective illustration.

Printed certificates may also have finely worked lettering, delicate scrolls and borders, and, in some examples, one or more illustrations. Among our family papers we have a South Shields Marine Board certificate (see page 34) which was awarded to Captain Joseph Goodchild (1809-1879), a Sunderland-born master mariner who paid his own fare to Victoria in 1852, probably to seek his fortune on the goldfields. His wife and children arrived as assisted immigrants on the *Hotspur* in June 1855. Goodchild's 1852 ticket for a passage from Liverpool to Melbourne on the *Ottilia* has survived and is an interesting combination of decorative elements and simple copperplate script (see opposite).

One of the key documents relating to the life of Joseph Goodchild is his apprenticeship indenture of 1823 (see opposite). Along with the seals and a stamp, it has Joseph's signature, his father's, Captain Robert Goodchild, the ship owner's, Caleb Wilson, and witness, J.C. Hare. The terms of the apprenticeship are intriguing, including the agreement that young Joseph would not play at 'Dice, Cards, Tables, Bowls, or any other unlawful Games'. He would earn fifty pounds ($100) over six years, plus twelve shillings ($1.20) per year 'in lieu of Washing'. While he was given 'sufficient Meat, Drink and Lodging', he was to provide himself with 'all manner of Sea-Bedding, Wearing Apparel, and other Necessaries'.

Family papers which have survived for generations are naturally to be treasured. The problem is that the survival rate is not very high, so that only a small percentage of people researching their family history have access to such items, or can expect they will turn up. The exceptions to this are wills, title deeds, lease indentures, mortgages, property transfers, and the various official records such as papers relating to military service. All of these can be located and copied if they are not already in the possession of the family (see chapter 2, pages 31–4).

Some wills and related papers are one or two pages long and well suited to display in your home as illustrations in a family history or as framed documents. In many wills the opening section has character and strong visual appeal. Other lengthier documents are best used as an addendum, if they are included.

Property Titles

Title deeds, memorials, indentures and other papers relating to land or property are all eminently collectable. In Britain, Ireland and Australia, there are two basic forms of records: the collections of title deeds and other documents which were used to prove ownership or right of occupation, and the registers of deeds of title which have been created by government

FAR LEFT (TOP): *This well-preserved apprenticeship indenture provides a detailed record of the conditions under which a young man might begin a seafaring life. Joseph Goodchild, born in 1809 at Sunderland, in the county of Durham, was apprenticed to shipowner Caleb Wilson in 1823. The document is signed by his father, Robert Goodchild, master mariner. In January 1839, Joseph's mother, Mary Goodchild (née Dove) applied for a pension. Captain Robert Goodchild's ship, the* Alexander, *had gone down in the North Sea with the loss of all hands.*
Source: Courtesy Goodchild family

FAR LEFT: *A 19th-century ticket to Australia is a relatively rare item. Joseph Goodchild paid his own way, leaving his wife and children behind. No doubt he was looking to make his fortune on the goldfields.*
Source: Courtesy Goodchild family

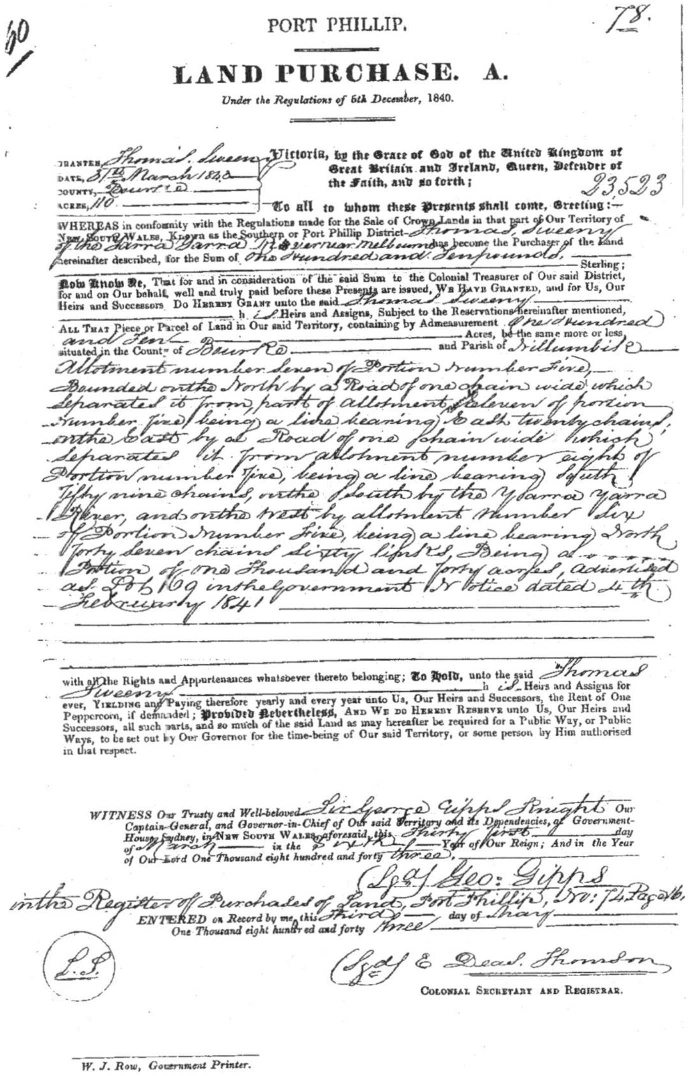

PORT PHILLIP.

78.

LAND PURCHASE. A.

Under the Regulations of 6th December, 1840.

GRANTEE, Thomas Sweeny
DATE, 31st March 1843
COUNTY, Bourke
ACRES, 110

Victoria, by the Grace of God of the United Kingdom of Great Britain and Ireland, Queen, Defender of the Faith, and so forth;

23523

To all to whom these Presents shall come, Greeting:—

WHEREAS in conformity with the Regulations made for the Sale of Crown Lands in that part of Our Territory of New South Wales, Known as the Southern or Port Phillip District— Thomas Sweeny of the Yarra Yarra River near Melbourne has become the Purchaser of the Land hereinafter described, for the Sum of One hundred and Ten pounds, Sterling;

Now Know Ye, That for and in consideration of the said Sum to the Colonial Treasurer of Our said District, for and on Our behalf, well and truly paid before these Presents are issued, We Have Granted, and for Us, Our Heirs and Successors Do Hereby Grant unto the said Thomas Sweeny his Heirs and Assigns, Subject to the Reservations hereinafter mentioned, All That Piece or Parcel of Land in Our said Territory, containing by Admeasurement One hundred and Ten Acres, be the same more or less, situated in the County of Bourke and Parish of Nillumbik

Allotment number Seven of Portion number Five, Bounded on the North by a Road of one chain wide which separated it from part of allotment Eleven of portion number five being a line bearing East twenty chains; on the East by a Road of one chain wide which separates it from allotment number eight of Portion number five, being a line bearing South fifty nine chains, on the South by the Yarra Yarra River, and on the West by allotment number Six of Portion number Five, being a line bearing North forty seven chains sixty links, Being a Portion of one Thousand and forty acres, advertised as Lot 169 in the government Notice dated 4th February 1841

with all the Rights and Appurtenances whatsoever thereto belonging; To Hold, unto the said Thomas Sweeny his Heirs and Assigns for ever, Yielding and Paying therefore yearly and every year unto Us, Our Heirs and Successors, the Rent of One Peppercorn, if demanded; Provided Nevertheless, And We do Hereby Reserve unto Us, Our Heirs and Successors, all such parts, and so much of the said Land as may hereafter be required for a Public Way, or Public Ways, to be set out by Our Governor for the time-being of Our said Territory, or some person by Him authorised in that respect.

WITNESS Our Trusty and Well-beloved Sir George Gipps Knight *Our Captain-General, and Governor-in-Chief of Our said Territory and its Dependencies, at Government-House, Sydney, in* New South Wales *aforesaid, this* Thirty first *day of* March *in the* Sixth *Year of Our Reign; And in the Year of Our Lord One Thousand eight hundred and forty* three.

(Sgd) Geo: Gipps

in the Register of Purchases of Land, Port Phillip, No: 74 Page 16.

ENTERED on Record by me, this Third *day of* May *One Thousand eight hundred and forty* three

L.S.

(Sgd) E. Deas. Thomson

Colonial Secretary and Registrar.

W. J. Row, Government Printer.

A land document may have many levels of significance beyond the details given. For many settlers, land ownership was a new experience which contrasted greatly with the lack of opportunity in the Old World. The purchase of 110 acres in the Port Phillip District in 1842 was a triumphant step for former convict Thomas Sweeney and his wife Margaret.

Source: Registrar-General's Office, Victoria

OPPOSITE (TOP): *Wireless Operator/Air Gunner Sergeant Fred James Deem, 202 Squadron (Sunderlands) was killed on 20 November 1944 when the plane crashed in Wales returning from patrol duties in bad weather. His daughter Shirley, born in May 1945, emigrated to Australia in 1966.*

Source: Courtesy Shirley Smith

OPPOSITE (BELOW LEFT): *Australian flowers add a distinctive touch to this certificate of thanks for service in World War I.*

Source: Collection, Manning Valley Historical Society Inc.

OPPOSITE (BELOW RIGHT): *Illuminated addresses and ornamented certificates can tell a story and be wonderfully decorative. This address to John Andrews is a superb example of a one-off piece. It also has a list of fellow citizens who benefited from his diligent service as postmaster at Woodside, NSW. The building shown was the Andrews home and the post office. Built about 1842, it is now the oldest surviving residence in the Manning Valley.*

Source: Collection, Manning Valley Historical Society Inc.

departments. Many of the earlier deeds remained in the possession of families or were lodged with their solicitors. As registration has taken over, many of the old papers have become redundant, having been replaced by certificates of title.

The rules in Britain from 1925 said that a seller was only required to prove ownership of the property in question during the previous thirty years, and the requirement is now half that time. This meant a great number of old documents were considered worthless. I still read of firms destroying old documents when they are replaced by modern records, but hopefully there is growing awareness of their value. Fortunately record offices, archives and libraries have gathered together collections. Nonetheless it is strange to see very old deeds or indentures for sale in antique markets, though at least they have not been dumped or burnt.

The land purchase document (pictured above) records Thomas and Margaret Sweeney's purchase of 110 acres (44.5 hectares) at Port Phillip dated 31 March 1843. In April 1842, Thomas had written to C. J. LaTrobe, wanting

IN PROUD AND GRATEFUL REMEMBRANCE OF
FRED DEEM,
OF
ROCKWELL GREEN
WHO GAVE HIS LIFE FOR HIS COUNTRY DURING THE WORLD WAR 1939-1945.
"GREATER LOVE HATH NO MAN THAN THIS, THAT HE LAY DOWN HIS LIFE FOR HIS FRIENDS."
P H Scott

FOR LIBERTY & JUSTICE
MUNICIPALITY OF TAREE
NEW SOUTH WALES
The Mayor, Aldermen and Citizens of the Municipality of Taree
Hereby place on record their Thanks for and Appreciation of the conduct of
Nº 1387 Tpr Jas Gore. 1st Light Horse.
who served his King and Country in the Great War of 1914–1919.
In Witness Whereof the Corporate Seal of the Municipality is hereto attached in the presence of
Mayor
Town Clerk
Dated

TO
John Andrews, Esq
J.P.,
WOODSIDE,
MANNING RIVER.
Dear Sir,
ON this, the eve of your retirement from the position of POSTMASTER at Woodside, which you have held since the 1st July, 1890, we feel we cannot let the occasion pass without expressing our regret that the exigencies of the Postal Service have caused the closing of the Woodside Post Office in which you have rendered such good service.
In your official capacity you have at all times carried out your duties efficiently and well, and exhibited remarkable tact in the execution of any unpleasant instructions or duties entrusted to you.
The firmness, judgment, and impartiality with which at all times you conducted yourself, have earned for you the respect and esteem of all respectable and law-abiding citizens with whom you have come in contact, and on their behalf we wish you good health and prosperity, feeling sure you will by your actions, in whatever sphere you may occupy, earn the same regard and esteem as you have done as Postmaster here.
We are, Yours sincerely,
WOODSIDE, APRIL, 1916.

THOMAS

to purchase land with the £100 he had deposited in the Sub Treasury. Acquiring freehold land in the parish of Nillumbik, in present-day Eltham, is pivotal to their story. They were among the first people to be able to purchase a smaller allotment (rather than a large acreage) outside of Melbourne or Geelong.[6] This means they were in the first group of people to become small freeholders in what would become rural Victoria, but was then New South Wales. Thomas Sweeney, having been an Irish convict who fought against tithes on small landholders or leaseholders in Ireland had, in a sense, triumphed over the odds.

It had taken Thomas Sweeney more than eleven years to be able to gain freehold title to a parcel of land. As a convict holding a Ticket of Leave from 1831 to 1838, he could not legally own property and relied on the goodwill of friends and business associates.[7] In 1833 he claimed to own 100 acres, but there is no record of this so he must have come to a special arrangement.

Convict Documentation

Thomas Sweeney's Ticket of Leave, dated 29 November 1831, allowed him to remain in the district of Illawarra. The butt of a Ticket of Leave (see page 5) is one of the interesting documents you can hope to find if you had a convict ancestor in New South Wales. These exist for the period 1827 to 1875 and are held by State Records of New South Wales. Many libraries hold copies on microfiche as part of the Genealogical Research Kit.

The information given on the Ticket of Leave butt is invaluable, though even more interesting are the various notations which can often be referred back to correspondence. In the case of Thomas Sweeney the first note states, 'The Holder of this Ticket is permitted to voyage between Illawarra and Sydney for trading purposes (signed) Alex McLeay, Colonial Secretary's Office 21 March 1834.' A later notation reads: 'Allowed by the Colonial Secretary's letter no. 35/613 dated 9 November 1835 to trade between the Manning River and Sydney but not allowed to cut Cedar.'[8]

Conditional and Absolute Pardons have also survived and are held by State Records of New South Wales (formerly the Archives Office of New South Wales). These too are available on microfiche. A framed photocopy makes an interesting conversation piece. Remember that you will need official permission to reproduce such documents in a published work. For those who claim convict forebears in Tasmania there are some remarkably detailed records. For example, the Conduct Registers covering the period 1803–53 give name, place and date of trial, the nature of the offence, date of arrival, religion, ability to read or write, trade, age, physical description, native place, assignments to service, any illness or hospitalisation, an application to marry, bad behaviour or offences and the nature and date of a pardon. In the column detailing service history, you'll often find names, places and dates which can become the basis for a timeline and further research.

A page from the Conduct Register usually takes up an A3 sheet when photocopied and is sure to be a significant document in any family history.

OPPOSITE (TOP): *Needlework has long held a central place in the creation of heirloom pieces. The patchwork quilt on the left dates from the 19th century; that on the right has the names of members of the Presbyterian Church, Chatsworth, [NSW?] and is dated 1929. Mary Lofthouse of Clitheroe, Lancashire, worked the sampler on the left in 1820. The scrapbook was a present to Helen Jane Baird of Horsham, Victoria, on her 14th birthday in 1881. Also seen are a World War I d'oyley, a 'crazy patchwork' tea cosy, a pair of booties and a Christening bonnet.*

Source: Collections — Valmai and Clark Massie, Di and Spenser Tunks, Phyllis and John Murphy

OPPOSITE: *Needlework designs such as this family tree are readily available and are an ideal way to tell a family story.*

Source: Courtesy Mary Thomas

These records are held at the Archives Office of Tasmania (CON 31,33,40,41) and you will need to supply the name of the convict, date of arrival and name of the ship. There are indexes on microfiche which contain this information and these can be consulted in libraries with comprehensive family history sections.

The indents of convicts sent to Tasmania directly from Britain form an important set of records in the Archives Office of Tasmania (CON 14,15,16,17). They answer questions about whether the convict was married or single, children (if any), religion, ability to read or write, relatives, apprenticeships, last place of residence, character on board ship and offences. The column for relatives and the last place of residence is often valuable because it may give the first names of one or both parents and any brothers or sisters. Sometimes there is an additional clue such as the regiment of a brother in the army. The entry for my wife's ancestor Mary Petty (1828–66) states that she arrived with seven-month-old Sarah in her arms; also that she had lived for four years with James Romford (Rumfit) who was tried with her at York Assizes in July 1851.

Family history research would be quite straightforward if all our ancestors were as well recorded as a large percentage of the 160000 convicts who came to Australia. By reading the surgeon's report for the voyage of the *Sir Robert Seppings* which began on 17 of March 1852, we discovered that Mary Petty made the sick list from 30 June to 4 July, while suffering from catarrh.[9] The Transportation Registers covering a large proportion of the convict ships which came to Australia are kept at the Public Record Office in England. Under the Australian Joint Copying Project (AJCP) these records and the surgeon's reports are available on microfilm at reference centres including state libraries and the National Library in Canberra. The AJCP covers a vast number of records relating to all aspects of Australia's colonial development.[10]

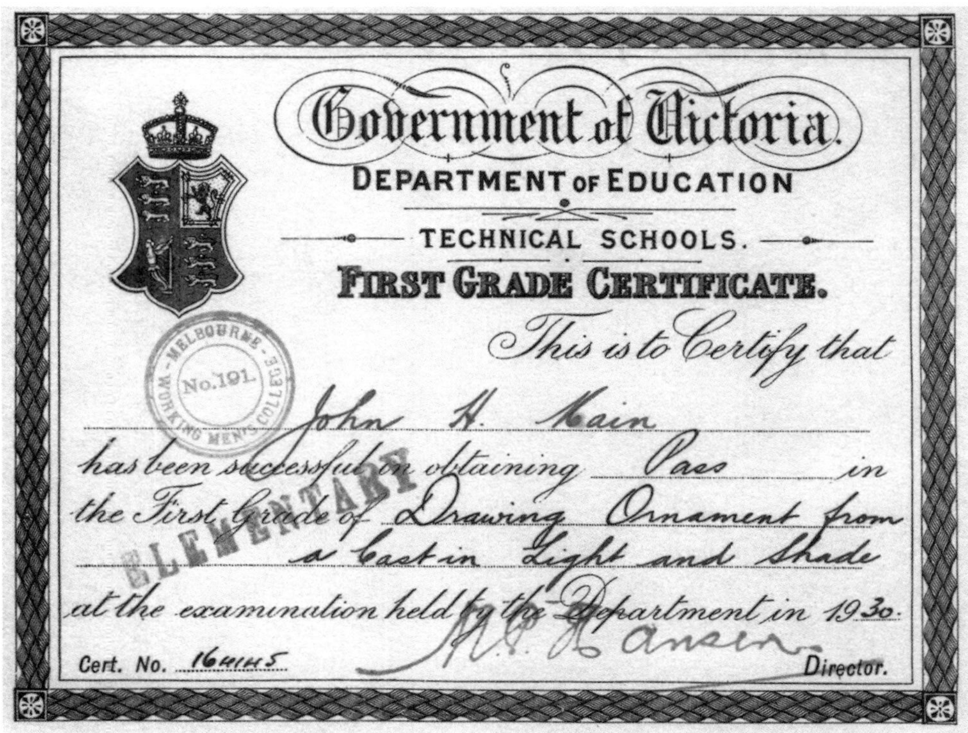

Government of Victoria
DEPARTMENT OF EDUCATION
TECHNICAL SCHOOLS.
FIRST GRADE CERTIFICATE.
This is to Certify that
John H. Main
has been successful in obtaining Pass in
the First Grade of Drawing Ornament from
a Cast in Light and Shade
at the examination held by the Department in 1930.
ELEMENTARY
MELBOURNE WORKING MEN'S COLLEGE No. 191.
Cert. No. 164145
Director.

Certificates have been issued for all manner of qualifications over hundreds of years. It is interesting to note the traditional character of this example.
Source: Collection, Peter Cuffley

Ellener Meredeth (Eleanor Meredith), who died in Gippsland, Victoria, in 1904, was memorialised in a highly decorative document which displays a number of symbols including the cross, sheaf, anchor, bluebirds, a weeping willow, a crown and a church spire. Born c. 1832, she was the daughter of Stephen Russell and Margaret Davis.
Source: Collection, Peter Cuffley

Licences and Certificates

Many kinds of documents are connected with the lives of previous generations. There are the licences issued for occupations and activities from selling alcoholic beverages to fishing for pleasure or profit. Cab owners have almost always needed licences, although private motorists early in the 20th century were able to simply purchase a car and take to the road. Membership of organisations has generated a bewildering array of certificates including those for lodges, trade unions, temperance societies, friendly societies, boy scouts and girl guides, cubs and brownies, lifesaving clubs, birdwatchers' leagues, and the many sporting clubs. Certificates of service can be both decorative and an important record. All of these and many more can find a place in bringing each era to life.

There are many ways in which death was memorialised. The framed poem on page 138 is very touching. It was written in 1886 and begins: 'Farewell dear Alf, a long farewell, On earth we'll meet no more, But we shall meet on that Great Day; On Zion's happy shore'. Alfred Page lived and died at Port Sorell on Tasmania's northern coast. More typical are the small cards, often pierced and embossed which were distributed to the family and friends of the departed. The card commemorating the death of my great great grandmother Jane (Joan) Cuffley (see page 138) records important details such as her age and the date of death. It also states that her burial took place at Nunhead

This touching farewell poem to Alfred Page by William Archer was found in Deloraine, Tasmania. It seems that Alfred lived all of his nineteen years at Port Sorell on Tasmania's northern coast.
Source: Collection, Peter Cuffley

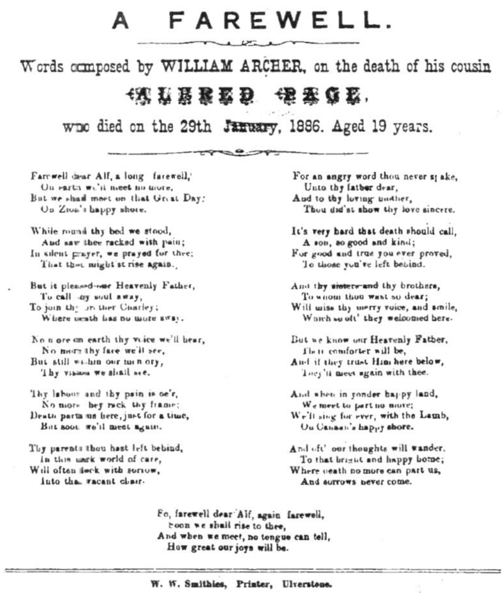

A FAREWELL.

Words composed by WILLIAM ARCHER, on the death of his cousin

ALFRED PAGE,

who died on the 29th January, 1886. Aged 19 years.

Farewell dear Alf, a long farewell,
On earth we'll meet no more,
But we shall meet on that Great Day:
On Zion's happy shore.

While round thy bed we stood,
And saw thee racked with pain;
In silent prayer, we prayed for thee;
That thou might'st rise again.

But it pleased our Heavenly Father,
To call thy soul away,
To join thy brother Charley;
Where death has no more sway.

No more on earth thy voice we'll hear,
No more thy face we'll see,
But still within our memory,
Thy vision we shall see.

Thy labour and thy pain is o'er,
No more they rack thy frame;
Death parts us here, just for a time,
But soon we'll meet again.

Thy parents thou hast left behind,
In this dark world of care,
Will often look with sorrow,
Into that vacant chair.

For an angry word thou never spake,
Unto thy father dear,
And to thy loving mother,
Thou did'st show thy love sincere.

It's very hard that death should call,
A son, so good and kind;
For good and true you ever proved,
To those you've left behind.

And thy sisters and thy brothers,
To whom thou wast so dear;
Will miss thy merry voice, and smile,
Which so oft' they welcomed here.

But we know our Heavenly Father,
Their comforter will be,
And if they trust Him here below,
They'll meet again with thee.

And when in yonder happy land,
We meet to part no more;
We'll sing for ever, with the Lamb,
On Canaan's happy shore.

And oft' our thoughts will wander,
To that bright and happy home;
Where death no more can part us,
And sorrows never come.

So, farewell dear Alf, again farewell,
Soon we shall rise to thee,
And when we meet, no tongue can tell,
How great our joys will be.

W. W. Smithies, Printer, Ulverstone.

BELOW: *Cards were often made to commemorate the death of a loved one. This is Jane (Joan) Cuffley (c. 1795–1872), great great grandmother of the author.*
Source: Collection, Peter Cuffley

BELOW RIGHT: *An extract from a register of baptisms, dated 1887, and a vaccination certificate.*
Source: Collection, Peter Cuffley

Cemetery which was established in 1840. London's first public cemetery was Kensal Green, a 79-acre site opened in 1827.[11] Urban churchyards had simply run out of space.

As much as we grumble about bureaucracy in the modern world, credit should be given to the record-keeping habits of earlier generations. Paperwork can be overwhelming at times, and yet when it comes to ancestor hunting and family history, we are always delighted to find some form of reliable documentation. Maps can show the way and even prove a fact; plans can tell us how things were or at least were meant to be; documents of every kind are the stepping stones and the building blocks.

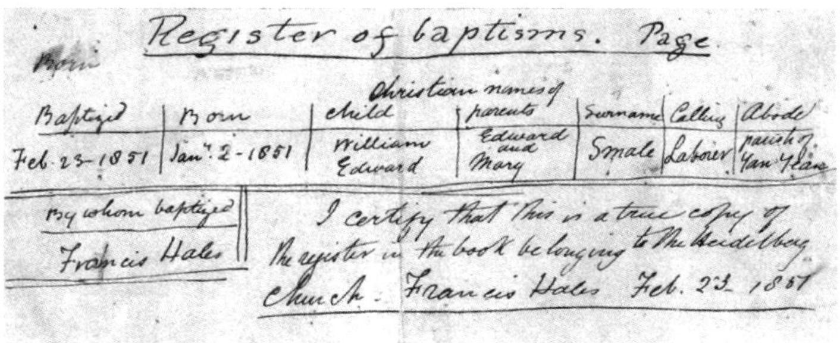

Register of baptisms. Page

Baptized	Born	Christian names of child	Christian names of parents	Surname	Calling	Abode
Feb. 23-1851	Jan. 2-1851	William Edward	Edward and Mary	Smale	Laborer	parish of Yan Yean

By whom baptized: Francis Hales

I certify that this is a true copy of the register in the book belonging to the Heidelberg Church. Francis Hales Feb. 23. 1851

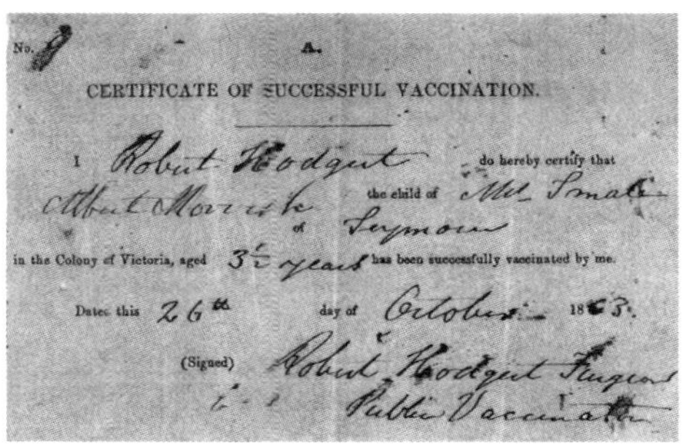

No. 9 A.

CERTIFICATE OF SUCCESSFUL VACCINATION.

I Robert Hodgert do hereby certify that Albert Morris the child of Mr Smale of Seymour in the Colony of Victoria, aged 3½ years has been successfully vaccinated by me.

Dated this 26th day of October 1863.

(Signed) Robert Hodgert Surgeon Public Vaccinator

Chapter Ten

LETTERS, DIARIES, WORDS IN PRINT

In 1860 my great grandfather and his brother Benjamin were establishing their brewery and hotel business in the Melbourne suburb of Fitzroy. Late in that year they each sent letters home on pictorial 'letter sheets'. William or 'Bill' Cuffley had some eight years on the goldfields behind him and was answering the concerns of his mother and sister in London that he had not written in ages, that at thirty-five he should have been married and settled at home as a man of property:

> 'Melbourne, Australia,
> October 14 1860
>
> Dear Mother and Sister,
>
> I was glad to receive your welcome letter barring the jacketting although it was no more than I might expect not having written to you so long. To the charge you bring against me I feel I must plead guilty, in fact I have been courting all my life and to speak my sentiments I think in many circumstances it is the pleasanter part, yet I must admit the possibility of being over head and ears some day and then matrimony will be inevitable. The bricks and mortar you place very prominently in your letter and seem to forget that the same material exists on this side of the globe where I could accept them with better grace — but more of this another time or I may say more than I intend.
>
> Ben has told you in his letter a full account of our movements and therefore has left little for me to say on this point. Our speculation is a little more promising lately and I hope dear Mother we may have the

> pleasure soon to give you a proof of our success. There is not a stone we have left unturned in the endeavour to attain it. The struggle in this colony seems to meet fresh difficulties every year, although at the present time the general opinion is that we will be more prosperous.'[1]

At the end he writes: 'Dear Mother and Sister, I must now conclude with my kind love hoping this will meet you in good health. I remain, Yours Affectionately, William Cuffley. My kind love to all my cousins.'

The finding of this letter, and others, in England was possibly the most important breakthrough I have had in over three decades of family history research. The husband of a descendant of Rosina Jane Cuffley, the sister addressed in the letter, had been clearing out the house of his recently deceased mother-in-law, when he came upon some very interesting items. There were three letters written on illustrated sheets called 'The News Letter of Australasia' (see opposite), a school writing book dated 1800 belonging to my great great grandfather William Cuffley (1785-1854), an embossed memorial card and a needlework sampler by Rosina dated 1846.

Rosina Cuffley's descendant contacted David Cufley, the keeper of the Cuf(f)ley one name study, which is registered with the Guild of One Name Studies [http://www.one-name.org] and is a logical contact point. When David received a call about the find he was elated and he immediately drove to Otford, not far from his own home at Dartford (Kent). Within a very short while we had an e-mail from David telling us all about the letters, book, card and sampler. He knew I would be over the moon, because they were clearly connected to my family.

Pictorial lettersheets were very popular in the gold-rush era of the mid-19th century and featured the work of some of the well-known artists of the day including S.T. Gill, Ludwig Becker, Nicholas Chevalier and Eugene von Guerard. The lyrebird 'news letter' is folded to make three pages to write on. It weighs less than half an ounce (15 g) and the paper is very thin. The writing has bled through to the reverse making it somewhat difficult to decipher the words where there is writing on both sides.

FAR RIGHT (TOP): *This lightweight letter sheet was published in March 1858 and sent to London from Melbourne in October 1860.*
Source: Collection, Peter Cuffley

FAR RIGHT (BOTTOM): *Timothy Keary (1835–1876) was from Galway, Ireland, and arrived in Melbourne on the* Commodore Perry *on 14 August 1860. His sister, Eliza, had married Laurence Bourke in 1855 and was living at Little Eltham in a comfortable hut on an acre of land. In the page illustrated from a letter home written a week after his arrival, Timothy tells of his walk out to Eltham and life for the Bourke family.*
Source: Collection, Keary family, Woodford, Galway, and Jim Considine

Reading Between the Lines

Old letters offer a candid view of the lives and day-to-day preoccupations of our forebears. They are as varied in character and style as the people who wrote them. It is can be rather overwhelming to read about the hardships many faced in what would have been an accepted way of life, and yet the universal concerns and general optimism are timeless elements.

My maternal grandfather Frank Ryan wrote to congratulate his Uncle Joe and Aunt Bridget on their golden wedding anniversary in September 1935. He included a question on family history, which is still unanswered today, in his typically dry manner: 'I often think I would like to hear from you Uncle a little about our relations in Ireland. I know they hopped off from Clonmel, but that is all I know about them. When my children read in the papers about a Ryan in America who is a millionaire and ask me if he is related, I can only

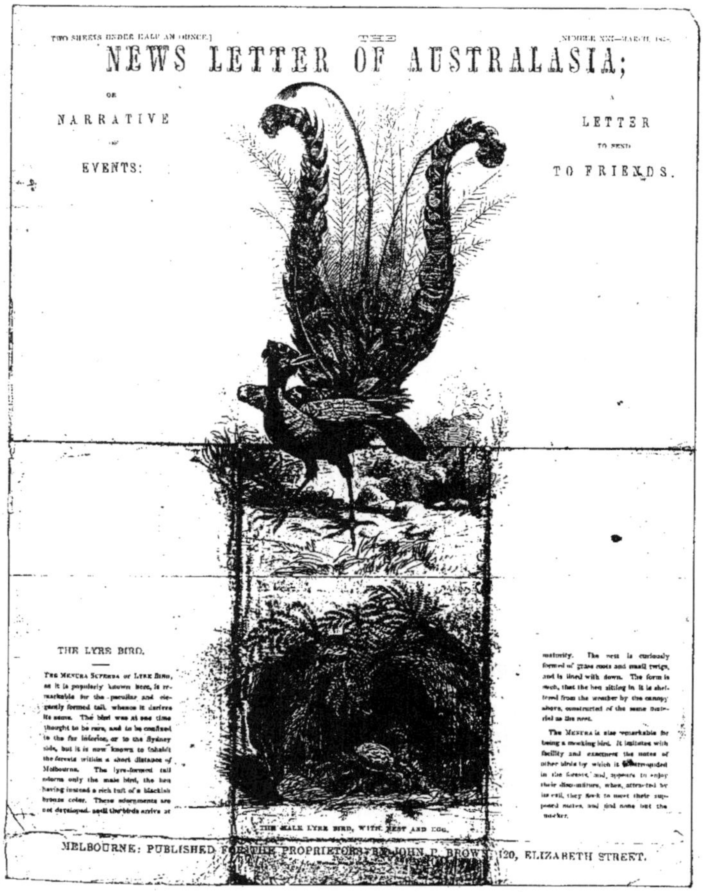

TWO SHEETS UNDER HALF AN OUNCE.] THE [NUMBER XXI—MARCH, 18..

NEWS LETTER OF AUSTRALASIA;

OR NARRATIVE OF EVENTS:

A LETTER TO SEND TO FRIENDS.

THE LYRE BIRD.

THE MENURA SUPERBA or LYRE BIRD, as it is popularly known here, is remarkable for the peculiar and elegantly formed tail, whence it derives its name. The bird was at one time thought to be rare, and to be confined to the far interior, or to the Sydney side, but it is now known to inhabit the forests within a short distance of Melbourne. The lyre-formed tail adorns only the male bird, the hen having instead a rich tuft of a blackish bronze color. These adornments are not developed until the birds arrive at maturity. The nest is curiously formed of grass roots and small twigs, and is lined with down. The form is such, that the hen sitting in it is sheltered from the weather by the canopy above, constructed of the same material as the nest.

The MENURA is also remarkable for being a mocking bird. It imitates with facility and exactness the notes of other birds by which it is surrounded in the forests, and appears to enjoy their discomfiture, when, attracted by its call, they seek to meet their supposed mates, and find none but the mocker.

THE MALE LYRE BIRD, WITH NEST AND EGG.

MELBOURNE: PUBLISHED FOR THE PROPRIETORS BY JOHN P. BROWN, 120, ELIZABETH STREET.

is beautiful all a forest of large trees it is called the Bush all the province is this way, there is some nice villages on the way Government townships, Eltham is a township and a large one too the first man I met on entering Eltham was Laurence, poor Eliza was very Glad to see me she feared the Ship went down, she has two fine little boys as ever I seen she lost the Eldest as you know already Laurence is a quite decent fellow he has £2 5s a week he goes in to Melbourne twice a week with Leather to his masters Store and spends the rest of the week at tanning I never seen such real happiness in my life as there is in this little family Eliza looks very well an excellent housekeeper they have a hut of their own and an acre of land cleared off Which they paid £53 for and £5 for title deeds so they pay neither rents or taxes there is a tanner lodged in house with them paying them £1.0.0 for board he is nice fellow he stopped from work these 2 days to show me the diggings and life in the Bush so we went Kangarooing through the Bush until we came to the diggings on Stony creek there was only a few men working there scarcely able to earn their supper We had Bernard out with us Saturday & Sunday we went to Mass 6 miles from Eltham, Bernard went to town by the Mail car on Sunday evening to Watch the Advertisements I go in early in the morning with Laurence to see if anything turns up if not we will go out the Bush or to some other town we cannot live idle, I wrote to the Lallys the other

There is always a chance that old letters relating to your family will turn up, so it is good planning to make your interests widely known.
Source: Collection, Peter Cuffley

say he is, but can't prove it. You will quite understand my anxiety in that direction.'[2]

If the chance of old family letters turning up seems remote, I can only say that wonderful things happen when you combine lateral thinking with positive energy. If there are letters out there somewhere, just who might have them and how can the connections be made? By good fortune a letter may survive, though it may pass to people unknown to you and possibly half a world away. Research directories, notices in magazines, list of members' interests from family history societies all increase your chances, as do the registers of family history searchers on the Internet.

Tracking down lost branches of the family can yield all sorts of interesting items connected to earlier generations. A cousin in Canada saw one of my entries in the Australian annual, *Genealogical Research Directory*, and wrote to me about her branch of the family. I was able to send copies of old letters and early photographs, all of which would have been an unexpected windfall for her.

There is always a chance that an ancestor or relative will be mentioned in a letter or diary held in a public or private collection. For example, many shipboard diaries mention passengers by name and sometimes, if they were relatives or friends of the diarist, there can be more than just a word or two. Moreover, if an accident, a birth or death, or some notable merriment occurred as they crossed the equator (a King Neptune ceremony), names and details may well be given. The *Log of Logs*, now in three volumes, lists any diaries or accounts known to exist of a particular voyage.[3]

Diaries

My great great grandfather's brother, John Cuffley, was a sailor on the migrant ship *Bombay* which sailed from Plymouth on 29 August 1852. The *Log of Logs* noted two surviving diaries of the voyage, one by Richard Moffat held at the Australian National Maritime Museum in Sydney and the other by Archibald Gilchrist in the collection of the State Library of Victoria.

So I sent to Sydney for a copy of the diary of Richard Moffat from Roxburgh, Scotland. On 10 December, after more than three months at sea, he wrote about the first glimpses he had of the Victorian coastline.

> 'This morning a good many of the Emigrants rose by break of day in hopes of seeing the Land, but they were disappointed, but about Midday Land was descried from the mast-head, so a great many of us went aloft to see it. There were 6 vessels in sight today. We passed one, the *Isle of Sky* from London bound for Port Phillip — she left 3 weeks before us. We came up alongside of Land in the afternoon. A little to the left about sunset the Light-House came in sight; it is a revolving Light, very pretty, 80 miles from Melbourne.'[4]

After the excitement of entering Port Phillip Bay, there was the frustration and worry of being held in quarantine and having to fly the yellow flag. The scourge of typhoid had killed over 200 of the 800 passengers on the *Ticondaroga* which was at the quarantine station when they arrived. They anchored about a mile out from the station and the doctor came on board to inspect the passengers and crew. It took up to two weeks for the migrants to finally get their feet on land.

You may be fortunate in finding a business card, advertisement, bookplate, trademark or letterhead which has family significance. Often these are decorative and finely executed, lending themselves to use as items in a family history or display in a frame.
Source: Collection, Janet Goodchild-Cuffley

Richard and Catherine Moffat with a child, Robert, and a baby, Jessie, marvelled at the hearty meals served at the immigration depot and saw it as their Christmas cheer, it being 24 December. Little did they know they would only have the coming year together — Jessie died on 30 January 1854 and her father three weeks later. Catherine married again in 1855 and lived until 1914 when she died at the age of 86.[5]

Letters and diaries relating the experience of travelling halfway around the world can vary from matter-of-fact accounts to lively and often very moving insights into the experiences of the travellers who braved conditions most of us can scarcely imagine. Twenty-five-year-old Timothy Keary from Woodford in County Galway, Ireland, wrote home to his family in August 1860 about a nightmare voyage to Melbourne in the emigrant ship *Commodore Perry*, as it attempted to take the 'Great Circle' route and sailed south as far as 45 degrees latitude. A great circle route is the shortest distance between two

Exploring Voyage.

KING WILLIAM STEAMER.

With the view of enabling the Public to ascertain the extent and capabilities of the Big River, and its tributary Streams,

THE Undersigned proposes sending this Vessel, early in the month of May, from Sydney, direct, laden with fuel, provided a sufficient number of Passengers offer to defray the expenses. The light water draught, and great power of this Vessel, it is expected will enable her to reach the fall, estimated at one hundred and sixty miles from the sea, also, up its navigable branches. It is believed the M'Leay River will afford advantages of soil and water conveyance to the Agriculturist and Grazier, unknown in any other part of New Holland.

The Terms for the Trip out and home will be £.0 each Person, £5 for each Horse, and 5s. per day to the Steward for Provisions. Such Gentlemen as wish to promote the object, are requested to communicate how many Tickets they will require, between this and the 20th of April, that timely notice may be given of starting.

J. H. GROSE.

March 28, 1839.

For Passengers Only.

THE BARQUE ABEL GOWER, Henderson, Commander, will call here from Newcastle, to fill up, and remain one week; has excellent accommodation for Passengers. Apply to

R. DACRE,

Jamison-street,
5th April, 1839.

For Hobart Town,

THE Packet Brigantine, MARIAN WATSON, Will positively sail on Saturday next, 23rd instant. For Freight or Passage, having superior accommodations, apply to the Master, on board; or, to

DANIEL EGAN,
Lower George-street.

March 18th, 1839.

APPRENTICES.

WANTED, One or Two Lads, as Apprentices to the Printing Business. Apply at the *Australian* Office.

Clerk Wanted.

WANTED, by the Undersigned, a Young Man well acquainted with Accounts. None need apply whose character for Sobriety, &c., will not bear the strictest investigation.

W. HEBBLEWHITE,
Auctioneer.

Lower George-street,
April 10, 1839.

WANTED,

A YOUTH, as an Apprentice in a Surveyor's Office; he may live with the family if necessary—One who has been instructed in the rudiments of Geometrical Drawing would be taken without a premium; otherwise, a small premium will be required.

JOHN BIBB.

Elizabeth-street, South,
April 1, 1839.

WANTED,

A SITUATION as Superintendent of an Agricltural and Stock Establishment, by a gentleman many years accustomed to the management of Stock and Agricultural pursuits —Salary not so much an object as a respectable situation. Address, post paid, to J. R, at *The Australian* Office.

1*st January*, 1839.

WANTED to Purchase, an Order to select a Section of Land. Apply to Mr Campbell, Accountant, Hunter-street.
Sydney, April 2, 1839.

TWO, OR FIVE POUNDS REWARD.

LOST, from Bora Creek, in February last, a Dark Brown Mare, branded C on near shoulder, and F under saddle. Any person giving such information as will lead to recovery of the Mare shall receive Two Pound, and if stolen, Five Pounds on conviction of the parties.

Apply to Mr J. Coumd, Mettagong, near Bong Bong.

Thirty Pounds Reward.

STOLEN.

A LIGHT BAY MARE, with black points, long mane and tail, branded on the

Shipping notices and general advertisements can yield specific information and general background for family stories. In the convict era there were lists of absconders, Tickets of Leave and pardons both conditional and absolute. This cutting is from The Australian *(Sydney) 13 April 1839.*
Source: Collection, Peter Cuffley

points on the earth. In this case, the journey between Liverpool and Melbourne involved going close to the Antarctic region and forgoing the usual call at Cape Town.

On this voyage they were battered by storms:

> '. . . the water coming in so strong, it broke the deck skylights and hatchhouses, and got down to between decks, smashing bunks and trunks, posts and tables, washing over beds, provisions, clothes and everything that was in the berths. This was a frightful scene. While the ship did roll and roll fearfully during the gale, the screams of the women

and children were worse than all. The men had right good courage and fell to work quickly to clear out the water with buckets. It took us six hours.'[6]

No sooner had they finished than they were being pounded once again. Twelve people were severely injured, some suffered broken legs and others had broken arms. Timothy noted that they had travelled 20 000 miles on account of headwinds and going so far south. 'We had 20 deaths on board — 16 children died from measles and whooping cough, and two men and two women. One of the men, it is supposed, threw himself overboard in a fit of despondency. It was night. He couldn't be saved.'

Timothy states that there were three births, 615 passengers and a crew of seventy. I looked up the register of passengers in the Public Record Office and found 458 adults and seventeen children listed, though the number varied with births and deaths. A count of the total entries came to 512 passengers on board.[7]

Timothy may have erred in his passenger estimate, but clearly had reason to be concerned. 'I think you will see something about it in the newspapers at home as a great many passengers are determined to expose the company, the captain and the commodore, and the whole system of emigration from Liverpool. It is but right.'[8] The *Commodore Perry*, a 1964-ton clipper, was built by Donald McKay at East Boston, Massachusetts in 1854. She was to be the pioneer in McKay's line of European packet-boats, but was sold before completion to James Baines of Liverpool, for his Black Ball line of Australian clippers.[9]

The postage stamps from letters written by distant ancestors are a great inclusion in your family history.
Source: Collection, Peter Cuffley

It is important to remember that people emigrating to Australia travelled on all kinds of sailing vessels from less than 100 tons to around 2000 tons. The conditions on ships carrying assisted migrants were supposed to be supervised. However, the ships carrying unassisted passengers during the gold-rush years of the 1850s were either obsolete vessels pressed into service, or fast clippers pushed to the limit to reduce the sailing time to record levels. The clipper *James Baines* set a Liverpool-to-Melbourne record of sixty-five days in 1854.[10]

Two months at sea may sound like a long time in this age of jet travel, but it was a lot better than four months, even with the added risks of sailing at latitudes below 45 degrees south, which often meant frozen rigging, mountain-ous seas and the danger of icebergs. In November 1869, the Suez Canal was opened and in 1875 the British Government acquired a 40 per cent interest.[11] Migrants from the British Isles and Europe now had a more direct route to Australia and with ancillary steam power they were not entirely subject to the vagaries of the wind.

Letters

Before the advent of long distance and international telephone services, people managed to keep in touch by post even if the letter was delivered many months after it was sent. The arrival of mail was an emotional time, stirring up thoughts of home and family. On the other side of the world it meant news of loved ones' efforts to make a new life.

During the gold rush there were thousands upon thousands of letters

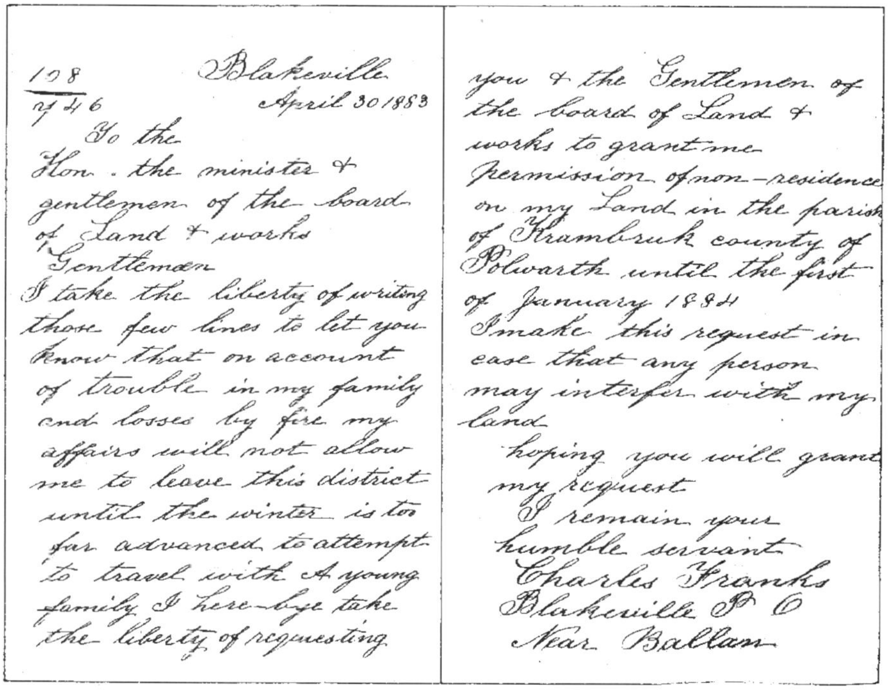

128
7/46
Blakeville
April 30/1883
To the
Hon. the minister &
gentlemen of the board
of Land & works
Gentlemen
I take the liberty of writing
those few lines to let you
know that on account
of trouble in my family
and losses by fire my
affairs will not allow
me to leave this district
until the winter is too
far advanced to attempt
to travel with A young
family I here-bye take
the liberty of requesting
you & the Gentlemen of
the board of Land &
works to grant me
Permission of non-residence
on my Land in the parish
of Krambruk county of
Polwarth until the first
of January 1884
I make this request in
case that any person
may interfer with my
land
hoping you will grant
my request
I remain your
humble servant
Charles Franks
Blakeville P O
Near Ballan

Archival collections of documents connected with the settlement of land can include complete files relating to a single holding. Often there are letters which can be an interesting addition to the family history. Charles Franks (c. 1840–1924) selected land at Krambruk (Apollo Bay) Victoria, in 1883 but was having difficulties in occupying it. Under the terms of the Act of 1869, a selector could take up land under licence from the Crown for three years. The annual rent was two shillings per acre, which came off the total purchase price of one pound per acre. The selector was required to live on the land and to make improvements which equalled in value the overall cost of the land. These were inspected by government officers and usually consisted of buildings, boundary fences, a proportion of land cleared for grazing or crops, and other improvements such as dams. After three years, the payment of rent could continue to reach the total purchase price, or the balance owing could be paid in a lump sum to give immediate freehold title. In many areas, the odds were against success.

Source: Reproduced with the permission of the Keeper of Public Records, Public Record Office of Victoria (VPRS 626, Unit 947, Land Selection Files)

addressed care of post offices, and people relied on notices in the papers or the government gazette which listed unclaimed letters. If your ancestors were here at that time, it is sometimes possible to trace their movements through these lists. At least we can note that someone thought they were in a particular place even if they had long since moved on.

I found a typical entry in the *Victorian Government Gazette* of January 1858: 'William Cuffley, Heathcote, letter 4d at G.P.O.' Before the opening of the Suez Canal, mail travelled via the Gulf of Suez, having been overlanded by camel train from Cairo.[12] When steamships were withdrawn for use in the Crimean War, in the mid-1850s, the mail came on clipper ships travelling the Great Circle route.[13]

If your forebears had cause to write to government departments there is always a chance that the letter survives. In files about the selection and purchase of land it is possible to come across a case where a bundle of documents has been kept. There may be original letters which raise issues, answer questions or give details of circumstances such as a crop failure or the effect of bush fires. When selectors were finding it difficult to meet official requirements for clearing, fencing and other developments, they would often write a pleading letter or get someone to write it for them.

Handwriting Samples

It is probably a good idea to collect signatures and samples of handwriting that you know belong to earlier generations of the family. Comparisons can then be made if letters turn up. My ancestor, Thomas Sweeney, could sign his name and probably could read enough to survive in business, but he always had a friend or a professional scribe write the letters he sent to government departments. Usually they would also sign on his behalf, though I do have

one letter with his distinctive signature. It is the same one he made when sworn as a witness at the Illawarra Magistrates Bench in July 1834, on his marriage certificate of 1838, and his will of 1867.

In the Bottom of a Box, Trunk or Drawer

Various factors can play a part in the survival of letters, cards, diaries and any other handwritten items. Many have been kept for sentimental reasons and then by later generations because they were becoming old and interesting. A good number survived simply by being safe in the bottom of a box, trunk or drawer of a cabinet. In the case of postcards they may have been in an album, or simply be kept because they were attractive.

When postcards first became popular in the 1870s, they were not as sumptuous as later on. Publishers and printers used every means at their disposal to capture a share of the booming postcard market in the decades between 1890 and 1930. Richly decorated greetings were immensely popular as were portraits of notable people or picturesque views. A commercial picture may be relevant to your family history, or a personalised card depicting your own relatives or homeplaces is a real find. The best postcards have a family picture on the front and more than a few words on the reverse. I have a number of examples which really amount to short letters and so have considerable significance for my family story. Even those with a few lines can capture a mood or the feeling of an era.

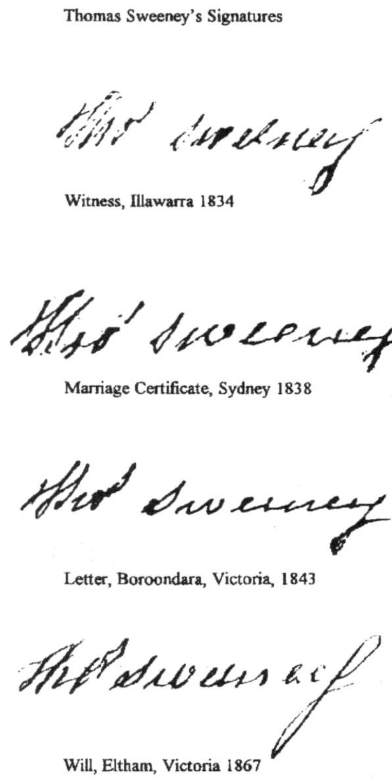

If your ancestors could sign their name, it is interesting to collect reference copies. The 1834 Illawarra signature was essential in proving that Thomas Sweeney of Eltham, Victoria, had been a convict in New South Wales.
Source: Collection, Peter Cuffley

MEMOIRS

Publication of letters, diaries, journals and memoirs is a grand old tradition. One of the best-known works over many years is the diary kept by an Englishman, Samuel Pepys, between January 1660 and May 1669. First

Weddings were important news in country communities and were usually given detailed coverage in local newspapers. This farewell to the bride and groom is at Glenmaggie in Victoria's Gippsland region.
Source: Photograph by Cornelius Gleeson, courtesy the Hill family, Maffra

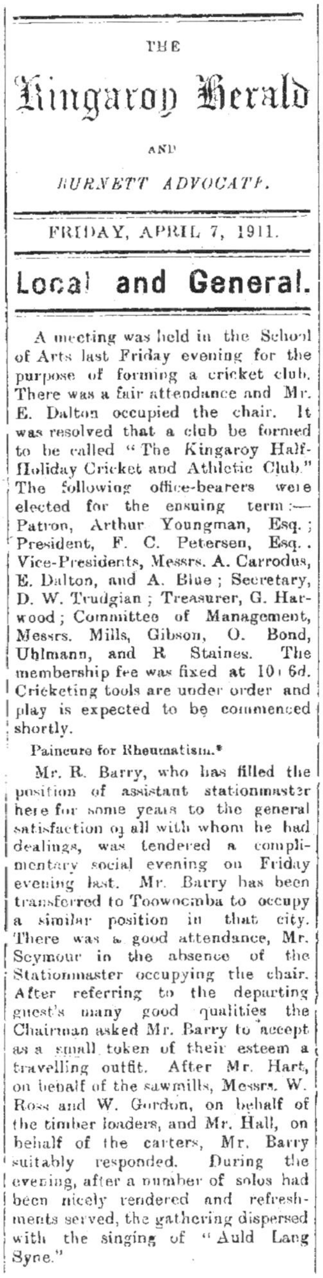

THE

Kingaroy Herald

AND

BURNETT ADVOCATE.

FRIDAY, APRIL 7, 1911.

Local and General.

A meeting was held in the School of Arts last Friday evening for the purpose of forming a cricket club. There was a fair attendance and Mr. E. Dalton occupied the chair. It was resolved that a club be formed to be called "The Kingaroy Half-Holiday Cricket and Athletic Club." The following office-bearers were elected for the ensuing term:—Patron, Arthur Youngman, Esq.; President, F. C. Petersen, Esq.. Vice-Presidents, Messrs. A. Carrodus, E. Dalton, and A. Blue; Secretary, D. W. Trudgian; Treasurer, G. Harwood; Committee of Management, Messrs. Mills, Gibson, O. Bond, Uhlmann, and R Staines. The membership fee was fixed at 10/6d. Cricketing tools are under order and play is expected to be commenced shortly.

Paincure for Rheumatism.*

Mr. R. Barry, who has filled the position of assistant stationmaster here for some years to the general satisfaction of all with whom he had dealings, was tendered a complimentary social evening on Friday evening last. Mr. Barry has been transferred to Toowoomba to occupy a similar position in that city. There was a good attendance, Mr. Seymour in the absence of the Stationmaster occupying the chair. After referring to the departing guest's many good qualities the Chairman asked Mr. Barry to accept as a small token of their esteem a travelling outfit. After Mr. Hart, on behalf of the sawmills, Messrs. W. Ross and W. Gordon, on behalf of the timber loaders, and Mr. Hall, on behalf of the carters, Mr. Barry suitably responded. During the evening, after a number of solos had been nicely rendered and refreshments served, the gathering dispersed with the singing of "Auld Lang Syne."

Committee lists, sporting teams and reports of community gatherings can all be useful in tracing the lives of our forebears. The details given for a farewell social could provide very useful clues in tracing an individual's life.
Source: Collection, Peter Cuffley

transcribed in 1822, it is regarded as a wonderful insight into the life and times of a scholarly man. He was a keen observer of all that went on around him and has been described as 'a journalist of genius'.[14] Pepys had intended that his journal should be private so he kept it in complete secrecy and wrote in shorthand. Other writers have created memoirs with publication in mind and these have become invaluable in explaining the lives of our ancestors.

Here in Australia we are well served by a growing list of memoirs and published letters or diaries. *The Letters of Rachel Henning* captured a wide audience when they were first published in the *Bulletin* in 1951 and early 1952. They were soon offered in book form with drawings by Norman Lindsay.[15] Rachel Henning's letters were written between 1853 and 1882 in both England and Australia. Born in 1826, she came to Australia in 1854 then was drawn back to England in 1856 but returned in 1861. After marriage in 1866, she settled here permanently. We owe Rachel Henning a great debt for her detailed descriptions of life in the town and the bush; for clear visions of simple interiors and gardens both large and small; and for giving us insightful, if sometimes class conscious, observations.

My other favourite memoirs reflect my regional bias but readers will no doubt bring to mind similar works which have national, regional or local significance. For enjoyable reading, I recommend: Mary E. Fullerton's *Bark House Days* (1921) which recalls a pioneer childhood at Glenmaggie in Victoria's Gippsland; *The Diaries of Sarah Midgley and Richard Skilbeck* (1967), centred around Koroit in Western Victoria; and *Diary of a Welsh Swagman* (1975) which talks about the countryside between Ballarat and Bendigo in the period 1869–94. Most importantly, all such records, both published and unpublished, are a great resource for family and social historians.

Newspapers and Magazines

Newspapers and magazines are another essential resource and none more so than the local or regional newspapers. These have traditionally published detailed accounts of community gatherings, notable events, weddings and sometimes funerals, as well as recollections of earlier times by local old-timers who have taken up the pen.

Obituaries are very helpful in establishing relationships, connections and an overall picture of a life. It is always wise of course to check the 'facts' given and look for other documentation. We need to remember a writer's natural tendency to give an obituary a positive glow. The same goes for first-hand accounts of local history found in newspapers. They can be of great importance to the family historian in capturing the broad sweep of an important period from the local or regional point of view and they may well mention family figures and even give a fulsome account of their activities.

A noteworthy piece of historical writing, 'Reminiscences of Illawarra by Old Pioneer' appeared in the *Illawarra Mercury* between 1923 and 1925. Historians are still not sure of the identity of 'Old Pioneer', but it is generally believed that he was Frank Young, a well-known local resident and journalist on the newspaper.[16] The reminiscences are a patchwork of memories from

The Avoca Mail.

TUESDAY EVENING JULY 8 1947

The Borough of Maryborough has informed Lexton Shire Council that the services of the borough engineer (Mr Hill) will be made available for the purpose of preparing a report on the proposed water scheme for Lexton. Mr Hill will carry out an inspection, with local residents, of the proposed site and other likely sites. The Lexton Shire secretary (Mr C. F. Loxley) will make arrangements for local residents to meet the engineer when he is available.

OBITUARY

MR BENJAMIN PELLETT

It is with regret that we announce the death of Mr Benjamin Pellett, an old resident of the district, which took place at his home on Monday after an illness of some considerable time. Deceased was well known and highly respected. In his early life he carried on farming pursuits at Mt. Lonarch, later coming to Avoca, where he has been resident up till the time of his passing. A wife and family of two are left to mourn. Members of the family are Frank and Kathleen.

The funeral took place this afternoon, leaving his late residence for the Avoca cemetery at 2.30 p.m.

SOCIAL GOSSIP

Mr Stan Trickey, of Kennedys Creek, accompanied by his wife and four daughters, spent the week-end with relatives.

The many friends of Mr Colin Evans, who has been an inmate of the Maryborough Hospital for some considerable time, will be pleased to learn that he is progressing favourably and hopes to leave the Hospital by the end of the present month.

Week-end visitors to Mr and Mrs M. C. Sanderson, of High st., were the latters parents, Mr and Mrs Peekin and daughter Ruth, and Mr Alan Krepp, all of Mortlake.

Friends of Mr Archie Wolfe of High st., will regret to learn that he is at present indisposed, and an inmate of the Maryborough Hospital.

Helen Shiell, daughter of Mr and Mrs L. Shiell, Homebush, underwent an operation for appendicitis in the Maryborough District Hospital on Thursday last.

Move To Improve Avoca Fire Alarm

Following a discussion on the effectiveness or otherwise of the Avoca Urban Fire Brigade's electric siren, it was agreed at the brigade's monthly meeting on Thursday night to leave

LEFT: *Local newspapers are an important resource for family historians. The obituary for Benjamin Pellet is comparatively short; some can be very detailed. He was born at Amphitheatre, Victoria, not far from Avoca, and married Jane Auld in 1897.*
Source: Collection, Peter Cuffley

FUNERAL NOTICE.

THE Friends of Mrs. STROHFELDT are respectfully invited to attend the Funeral of her deceased Husband (Charles), which will move from her residence, Spring street, Middle Ridge, THIS DAY, at 2 p.m.

BOSENSTENGEL and KLEIMEYER, Undertakers and Embalmers.

Advertisement from the Darling Downs Gazette *(Queensland), 20 November 1902.*
Source: Collection, Peter Cuffley

various people including some who wrote to the paper in response to the earlier articles. They are rich in detail and often include delightful vignettes which would be treasured by descendants of the family concerned, but also have significance in the social history of Australia as a whole. The following is a small taste of the Old Pioneer's column:

> 'Just past where the railway line goes under the road is the residence where Tom Tiffels lived. The house has now gone. Tom, with his wife and daughter, was a maker of cabbage-tree hats. Tom and his family were artists at the work and he did a big trade in hats from the cabbage-tree. This class of hat was much used by the early residents, and a fair number were sent from the district to Sydney.'[17]

Cabbage-tree palms still grow in the Illawarra region, even in open farmland. The finely woven hats were highly valued by all who owned them and are celebrated in colonial literature.

Weddings, balls, concerts, fêtes and sports days are just some of the occasions which warrant detailed accounts in local or district newspapers. At

PRAHRAN PIONEERS

Four Generations

Members of the Prahran Pioneers' Association celebrated their anniversary yesterday, when they gathered on the Prahran bowling green and reminisced.

Stirring stories of the early days were recounted by those who minded the time when busy Chapel-street was merely a paddock, in which blackfellows held corroborees.

One family was represented by four generations, Mr. H. Ryall, aged 95, a 70 years' resident of Prahran; his son, Mr. W. Ryall, aged 65, his married daughter, and her child.

Other Prahran veterans included Mr. T. Stewart, aged 79; Mr. F. Fowler (80), Mr. W. Stewart (81), Mr. G. H. Greenwood (71), who was born in Chapel-street, where his father erected the second house; Mr. W. Ilsley (66), Mr. J. H. Furneaux (66), who is secretary of the association; and Mr. W. Davies (70).

The secretary's mother, Mrs. R. Furneaux, who is 85 years of age, was the oldest woman pioneer present, while Mrs. W. Head claimed to be the oldest Prahran-born woman. These and others claiming distinction by virtue of age or residence were subsequently the recipients of gifts.

Gatherings of old pioneers were often reported in local or city papers. This example is from the Sun News Pictorial *(Melbourne), 9 March 1923.*
Source: Collection, Peter Cuffley

OPPOSITE (TOP): *Simple black frames with gilt slips or applied gold were favoured in the 19th century for small- to medium-sized pictures. The silver-plated oval frame is early 20th century, as is the souvenir plaque showing St Paul's Cathedral, London. See page 137–8 for details of the farewell to Alfred Page.*

Source: Collection, Peter Cuffley [Photograph: Dennis Russell and Peter Cuffley]

OPPOSITE (BOTTOM) : *The beautiful photograph album (at back) was presented to Mr E. Hague by the Congregational Church and Sabbath School in Truro, Cornwall, on 30 October 1884. There is an invitation to a ball at the Exhibition Building, Melbourne, in 1860 in honour of Queen Victoria's birthday; also invitations to the weddings of Emilie Robinson and John W. Miller (1884) and Annie Teresa Villiers and William Henry O'Grady (1881), both in Melbourne. The letter dated 'March 3 1849', was written by Edward Smale to his brother Richard while Edward, Mary and baby Ann waited on board the ship* Hope *in Plymouth Harbour before it sailed for Australia. It is believed that the teapot was a wedding present in 1848 and came with them on the voyage. Next to the teapot is an ornamented clay pipe, a very popular item in the 19th century. There is also a programme of the visit by the American fleet to Australia in 1908.*

Source: Collections — Don and Zara Latimer, Peter Cuffley

the turn of the century most weddings had a few lines in the paper, and some reports took up one or two columns. If one or both of the parties were well known there may also be reports of functions leading up to the great event.

When my paternal grandparents were married in 1906, the local paper carried a report of the wedding as well as a separate account of the 'Farewell Social' for my grandfather, who for many years had been choirmaster at his parish church. Some wedding reports give descriptions of the church decorations, the clothes worn by the bridal party and the immediate family, the wedding ceremony, the wedding breakfast and the farewell to the honeymooners. If a dance or concert followed, it was usually reported and, most importantly, a list of wedding presents, complete with names of those who gave them was also likely to be appended.

Concerts and bazaars or fêtes are generally well covered in local newspapers, with lists of participants and all the highlights. In many instances, the entire concert programme is published with songs, instrumental solos, duets, recitations and comic monologues. For bazaars and fêtes, names are often given of organisers and the people running each stall or attraction. Sunday school anniversaries are covered and, again, many names mentioned. Reports of school presentation nights can be equally informative. Articles on local and district sports days, along with general reports and prize lists from the agricultural show may mention your ancestors or relatives and add another dimension to the story of their lives.

While old newspapers contain all sorts of notices, lists and articles which will add to your family saga, they can be hard work if you have no specific dates to search and they have not been indexed. Fortunately, more and more newspapers are being indexed. Also, the number of newspapers held on microfilm is always increasing, not only because of the need to conserve the originals, but also to make them more widely available. State libraries generally have the largest collections, though regional and local papers may

Pioneers in isolated places looked forward to letters and newspapers to ease that feeling of being cut off from the wider world. Described as 'Mrs Coles old home', this cottage with its humble garden is in Western Australia.

Source: Collection, J.S. Battye Library of West Australian History, No. 10664B

A FAREWELL.
Words composed by WILLIAM ARCHER, on the death of his cousin
ALFRED PAGE.
who died on the 29th January, 1886. Aged 19 years.

American Fleet
Programme
DUNOLLY DETACHMENT 5 COMPANY
ANNUAL MILITARY BALL
In Memory of

THE
NATIONAL
GALLERY
OF
VICTORIA.

still be found in their place of origin, in both public and private collections. One of the intriguing aspects of old newspapers is that they tended to borrow stories from each other so that many items considered to be of wider interest will turn up in papers far removed from the locality to which they relate.

Before the latter half of the 19th century, newspapers rarely concerned themselves with the details of the lives of ordinary people. If they were involved in a newsworthy event they might rate a mention. Of course, there were reports of court appearances for those who fell foul of the law. Sometimes the writer gives a detailed account of the alleged crime, though many have just a few words and tend to devote more space to general homilies and the status of those sitting in judgement. Reports of trials are usually found in the main newspapers of the city or town where the trial was held, but again, these reports may also have been taken up by other publications. If you have a date and place of trial for a convict ancestor, it is best to begin with the record office or central library nearest to the place of the trial. If the required newspaper is not held there, they may direct you to another library which holds a broader collection.

Published Histories

Finally, don't overlook the possibility of finding important material for your family story in general, local or family histories. Besides the broad social context for the lives of earlier generations, you may find parallel stories which offer new insights and suggest directions for research. With luck there could be references to families or individuals which are of relevance to your work, and best of all, they could be given more than just a mention. If you can track down comprehensive local histories, the chances of inclusion increase considerably. Sadly, there are times when an author has not been able to find much on a particular family or individual. Your work may well ensure that they are represented in any future publications.

Published family histories are constantly being added to the shelves of public libraries, and to the collections of genealogical and historical societies. It is always a good idea to peruse the index in case a familiar name pops out. Well-researched books will have notes and a good bibliography which could be very helpful with your own lines of enquiry. Apart from library and book-sellers' catalogues, there are lists of published family histories on the Internet, for example at: [http://www.gould.com.au]. Consulting local historians or members of a local society is worthwhile, too, as they may well alert you to a little-known work which could offer the breakthrough you were looking for.

OPPOSITE (TOP): *Names, initials, momograms and detailed inscriptions make heirlooms and collected items especially interesting. In the centre is a silver locket and chain by Fisher of Geelong with the monogram ABR. The cufflinks were presented to Frederick Goodchild (1888–1957) and the beaded purse bears the name R.B. Anderson, 1871. The small locket ringed with pearls once contained a lock of hair from William Swaine who dide 24 October 1802, aged 14.*
Source: Collections — Don and Zara Latimer, Janet Goodchild-Cuffley

OPPOSITE: *Hester Anne Welton (née Biggs), seen in the portrait (at left), was given the bible by her husband Henry Welton in 1853. Both the silver jug and the silver ladle have her monogram on them. 'Family Worship' is the title of the Pears print of 1911, an evocation of cottage life and the joy of a new generation. The so-called 'bible box' would have held anything of special value. An example of creating a future heirloom is seen in the decoupage box recently made for the author by Anne Hadden.*
Source: Collections — Phyllis and John Murphy, Di and Spenser Tunks, Janet Goodchild-Cuffley [Photograph: Dennis Russell and Peter Cuffley]

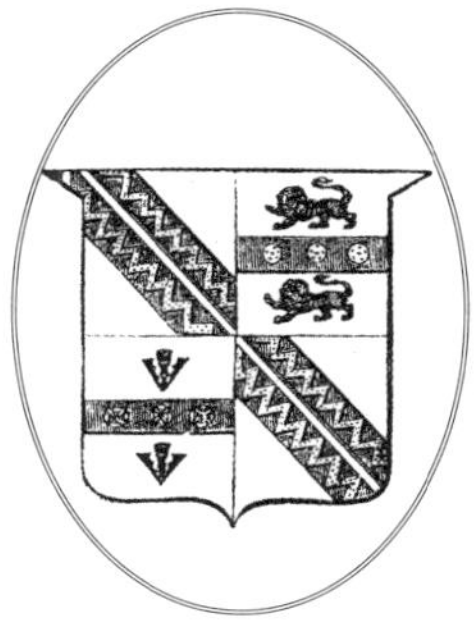

Chapter Eleven

Heirlooms and Coats of Arms

Nowadays any object handed down through a family is described as an heirloom, although the original definition refers to a special custom where a piece of furniture or personal property is passed on to a designated 'heir-at-law'. These days we are generally more concerned about handing things on to whoever will take care of them. Most people would agree that it is a good feeling to know that an object in their possession has been part of the lives of their ancestors.

Heirlooms can be valuable in their own right or of little worth to anyone except members of the family. My maternal grandmother treasured a copper lustre teapot which was said to have been brought to Australia by her grandparents in 1849. In the early 1930s it was carefully carried home to a safe place among the other family pieces she had gathered. Importantly, she placed a note inside which would remind the coming generations of its origins.

Silverware, Samplers and Special Objects

When I think of things people have treated as heirlooms, a great variety of objects come to mind — a Windsor chair which has been in a family for generations, an inscribed powder flask from the days of muzzle-loader guns, needlework samplers with names and dates. Wooden trunks or chests very often have a story and the best still have the name of the original owner painted on the lid or front panel. Some have those intriguing words 'wanted on voyage' to indicate they were not to be stowed in an inaccessible part of the ship's hold.

Silverware and ceramics often become heirlooms, especially if they carry particular initials, monograms, crests or coats of arms. Silver spoons are

Photographs of interiors were difficult to achieve in earlier times. If we look beyond everyone being carefully posed, there is a host of detail to observe. Apart from family photographs and other framed pictures, there are many other items which were, or would become, heirlooms. Clocks and vases are likely to be handed down as are cherished pieces of furniture. This was taken at 'Lynditha', the Semmens family home at Sedgwick, Victoria, around 1919.
Source: Courtesy Gwen Shaw

great survivors and many of them have engraved handles. Other engraved presentation pieces such as cups, trophies, trays, bowls, writing cases, snuff boxes, christening mugs, or plaques applied to marble-cased clocks or wooden-cased barometers are all part of the long tradition of family history. Gold or silver watches, lockets and bracelets are frequently engraved with names, dates, or an expression of endearment. How tantalising it can be to read about an engraved silver hot-water kettle in an old newspaper reporting on a farewell presentation to an ancestor, then later, to hear that someone had found it in an antique shop.

Family bibles are one of the more common heirlooms, and they are especially valued if they contain family records. Bibles were often kept in a compact 'table desk' or simple box along with other books and papers. These bible boxes often had initials and dates carved on them as well as decorative work (see opposite page 151). Europeans also brought larger decorated boxes, usually with names and dates as part of the design. Often described as blanket boxes, many have survived in families descended from German immigrants or have been placed in museums.

Creating an Heirloom

If you are not fortunate in having family pieces such as these you can always begin a tradition by creating a future heirloom or having one specially made. While names and dates from the family history can be applied to such items,

Cottage life has been the subject of many writers and poets. We owe a debt to people like Thomas Hardy for celebrating relatively humble household items as heirlooms.
Source: Collection, Peter Cuffley

it is wise to add the present date so that future generations will know its origins. Remember also that names of the current era will become history so these too have a place.

The revival of old crafts is important because it enriches the community with skills that would otherwise be forgotten. Many currently fashionable arts and crafts lend themselves to the creation of heirloom pieces. Boxes or containers are ideal candidates for decoupage and folk art painting. Here is a way to celebrate selected aspects of the family story. For a detailed pictorial effect, decoupage is the best medium because you can combine printed elements, coloured photocopies and hand painting.

Imagine a decoupage box with historic scenes, portraits in shaped panels, names and dates, and even a few lines of text or portion of a document. Colour photocopies are relatively colour-fast and can be fixed or sealed before the finishing coats of clear polyurethane. Boxes have a wide appeal and can be used for all sorts of purposes including the holding of family records and memorabilia. Other items which can be similarly made into future heirlooms are small cupboards, occasional tables, mirror frames, picture frames, spoon racks, trays and clock cases.

Keepsakes

In times past, wooden items have been carved, incised, pierced and burnt with hot irons. The making of wooden spoons is a fine old tradition from Wales and also from Scandinavia. Welsh 'love spoons' were made by ardent

Welshmen for their sweethearts. Decorative character, ingenuity and the sheer amount of labour involved were all messages of love. Hearts, rings, keyholes, wheels, carved chains and spheres inside cages to show the man's heart was held captive were all popular symbols.[1] Another form of love token was the stay busk, a flat or flattish insert used to make the bodice of a dress perfectly straight from waist to bust. Being close to the heart they were often inscribed with symbols of devotion and many were given initials and dates. They were made from wood, bone or ivory and mostly date from the late 17th century through to the end of the 18th century.

Sailors made these keepsakes on long sea voyages along with other kinds of scrimshaw such as incised whales' teeth and pastry-cutting jagging wheels made from whale bone. Families who churned their own butter usually had carved wooden moulds which would transfer a name, initials or symbol to the final product. Cream and milk cans sometimes had a small brass plaque with the name of the family and the address or district. Stencils for wool bales, bags and boxes, and brands used for livestock often had initials and names of significance.

A peddlecar from the 1940s or 1950s is likely to stir up nostalgia for aging baby-boomers. Each era has its significance in the family story.
Source: Collection, Lach and Fran Gardiner

Tools and Toys

Even tools carefully handed down and treated with reverence can be described as heirlooms. An old and much used spinning wheel or perhaps a wool winder are also in this category. Home-made toys such as vintage dolls' houses which have been used and loved by generations of children are real treasures. Doll-house furniture and, of course, the dolls themselves can have important family associations. My grandmother's doll-size teaset is still in existence, as is the nursery lamp she had for her own children.

The subject of heirloom dolls, or new dolls carefully fashioned to become heirlooms is a book all of its own. Do consider, however, that dolls can tell a family story in a most appealing way. Dolls in national costume are an ongoing celebration of family origins; others can be dressed to represent

Even old tools can be passed down as heirlooms. This photograph was taken in the 1920s on the Taylor farm at Glassnamullen, County Wicklow, Ireland. In the middle is George Taylor (b. 1879) and on the left his nephew, Robert William Taylor (1896–1971). The boy has not been identified.
Source: Courtesy Leslie Taylor and Shirley Stone

figures from various eras in history. If you have some good pictures of your ancestors it could be an interesting challenge to translate the images into heirloom dolls. Dolls representing convicts, pioneer farmers and people in pursuit of gold may fit your narrative, as could a host of different subjects from various eras.

Embroidery and Needlework

In the community generally there is an ongoing tradition of commemorative needlework which displays individual creativity, as well as pieces made with commercial kits. The sheer number of needlework samplers done over the past few centuries has ensured that many survive. A revival of interest in the old ones has also had the positive effect of encouraging the working of new examples. My family was delighted when the 1846 sampler by Rosina Jane Cuffley was found in England.

Apart from conserving a frail original, the piece can be copied by the needleworkers in the family as replicas for display. The old one might be framed and placed on a wall but only under conditions which would protect it from further deterioration.

Kits are readily available for new samplers, although there is nothing wrong with creating your own design, choosing traditional elements, then adding the current date, your name and any other details which seem appropriate. A sampler style or, indeed, any suitable technique can be used to create an heirloom piece giving the date and other details of an important event. Births, christenings, weddings, graduations, family reunions and the passing of loved ones can all be recorded in a way which perfectly expresses the shared sentiments.

Handmade lace has long been passed on from generation to generation as has the art of lace-making. Here we see lace-makers at Olney, Buckinghamshire in the mid-19th century.
Source: Collection, Peter Cuffley

A family tree can be worked from a contemporary design (see opposite page 135) to display at least three generations. Many interesting works of this type have been done and again, the possibilities for individual pieces on every scale are only limited by the necessary skill and patience. Most forms of needlework, tapestry, weaving or knitting can be used to create family keepsakes which, in time, become heirlooms. Tablecloths and coverlets for beds are two old favourites for displaying needlework skills.

Needlework potentially can be used to create pictures which have a clear family connection. There are embroidery kits which offer designs that can be personalised and some firms offer chart sets or kits specifically designed from your reference for working in cross-stitch or tapestry (see Useful Addresses). Portrait photographs can be translated into a counted cross-stitch pattern in warm sepia tones. When worked in coloured threads, the result is a piece of needlework which perfectly captures a family face. I've seen a design for a silkwork replica of a decorated page from a Victorian photograph album. Many needleworkers design their own pictures based on photographs, paintings, coats of arms, family crests or combinations of decorative elements and words or text. Those 'illuminated' certificates and testimonials from past eras could provide inspiration for the use of floral elements, borders and various symbols.

Family homes can be interesting subjects for embroidery, appliqué or tapestry. Commercial kits and books of designs will help with the drafting of a suitable layout to best capture the house and garden. If you have a picture of a ship which is part of the family story, that too could become a needlework picture. You may be able to modify an existing design if you are daunted by the idea of planning the whole picture. Then you can simply change the ship to fit your reference.

Apart from having a company translate your chosen picture into a cross-stitch design you can purchase a computer program that will do it for you. The result is a counted cross-stitch chart in either colour or black and white. Information and sample programs are available on the Internet (see Useful Addresses).

Monograms were used for needlework, penwork (cards, bookplates), engravings and any other application where it was appropriate to place someone's initials. These examples are from the 1870s.
Source: Collection, Peter Cuffley

Presentation frames

There has always been an art to framing and happily we are well served in the present era by the availability of skilled and imaginative framers. If you choose to do your own framing there are lots of ready-made frames. Some beautiful period style examples are available covering a wide range of effects from richly ornate to simple country style.

Australia's German immigrants have been notable for heirlooms such as wedding veils and other accessories kept in decorative presentation frames. Protected under glass, the items were carefully arranged to be a constant reminder of sacred vows and that happy day. A special place in the best room was the right setting for this memorabilia. I've also seen needlework anniversary pieces, usually with names and dates. Apparently these were mostly made up from kits imported from Germany in the period 1880 to 1940.[2]

Veils, gloves, shoes, garlands, good-luck horseshoes, garters and artificial flowers have all been kept as memories of a wedding day. When carefully framed or kept under a glass dome they have become treasured heirlooms. From the back of this delightful photograph we know that the bride is Harriet Burton and the groom Alf Webster.
The wedding took place on 10 April 1910; the question is, where?
Source: Collection, Janet Goodchild-Cuffley

Patchwork Styles

The patchwork quilt is a classic which has been with us for centuries. Australia's patchworking tradition came at first from the British Isles and has been with us since the earliest years of European immigration. There are two basic types: pieced patchwork where pieces are joined at the edges; and appliqué quilts where the patch of fabric is sewn on to a larger piece of material. American-style 'crazy patchwork' became popular from the mid-1880s and in the 20th century the influence of the wider American tradition came to dominate the craft of quilt making.

In 1816 that great reformer, Elizabeth Fry (1780–1845), introduced patchwork as an occupation for women in London's Newgate Prison. From 1818, the female prisoners on convict ships were given materials for sewing and knitting, including patchwork pieces. At the end of the voyage the patchwork could be sold, as could other needlework.[3] Many quilts, ranging from the plain and practical to finely detailed works, which were veritable showpieces, came to Australia with pioneer settlers. Together with the quilts made in Australia, they represent a marvellous heritage of needlecraft.

Historic patchwork along with other types of bedcovers or counterpanes are treasured heirlooms in families fortunate enough to own them. Many have found their way into local, regional or state collections and can be seen in galleries, museums, or historic houses. While the provenance of many quilts is well recorded, some actually have names and dates sewn on making them especially valuable. If you would like to be inspired by quilts which are part of the story of this country, I recommend you study Margaret Rolfe's fascinating book, *Patchwork Quilts in Australia*.

MARITIME HEIRLOOMS

There are many objects associated with the sea which can become heirlooms. A dear friend, now dead, had a wonderful brass clock which belonged to his sea captain father. It struck the watches, rather than every hour, giving their house a nautical flavour. My great aunt presented me with an ivory marline-spike when I was still quite young and it stirred up visions of Moby Dick and other sea stories.

Many families have passed down models of ships, some made by seafaring ancestors, others just acquired as picturesque conversation pieces. A framed ship model is a variation which combines a half model on a painted background. Sometimes these were created by shipbuilders to illustrate the design of a hull, but mostly they are simply examples of marine art made by sailors or ship lovers. In many picture models the sea has been given a three-dimensional character by the use of a moulded material such as putty.[4] Ships in bottles are a well-known tradition with the best being masterly creations made with great ingenuity. Navigation instruments and associated books have passed down the generations, as have sea chests and brass bound chests of drawers.

Schooners were favoured trading and passenger vessels on short to medium runs. They were an important link between the various colonies or settlements before overland routes were established.
Source: Collection, Peter Cuffley

RELICS FROM THE PAST

Relics from the lives of your ancestors serve as a reminder of many different times and places. Some are clearly associated with the broad sweep of history or, conversely, with a relatively obscure aspect of an ordinary life. Wartime service may be memorialised with medals, ribbons, colour patches, badges, items of uniform, weapons, flags, and various accoutrements. For others there are civilian mementos, some sentimental, some grim reminders of a terrible time. Souvenirs may recall great journeys and presentation pieces highlight great achievements. Medals and keepsakes have been made to record every kind of human endeavour. Collecting souvenirs relating to places and events is an interesting way to bring to life the progress of the family or its individual members.

Companies producing souvenirs and keepsakes can turn out limited runs of selected items for family reunions or other significant events. You'll need to supply suitable words and pictures and the company will consult you about the design. Drinking glasses or mugs are popular, as are wine glasses and china plates (see Useful Addresses).

For very special occasions, one-off ceramic pieces can be made by skilled china painters. Cups, mugs, plates, bowls, sugar basins and tea or coffee pots all lend themselves to commemorating an historic occasion or memorialising our forebears. If you look to the past for inspiration there are some delightful examples of text, illustrations and decorative details.

Mugs or jugs with illustrations of rural scenes and lines such as 'Speed the Plow' were great favourites in earlier times. Sunderland and Staffordshire in England both produced light-coloured earthenware with a printed transfer or hand-worked decoration. An amusing Sunderland plate in speckled lustreware has illustrations of a ship in full sail, a plough and a lamb, with the words 'Success to the Fleece, to the Plough and the Sail, May our Taxes Grow Less and our Commerce Never Fail.'[25]

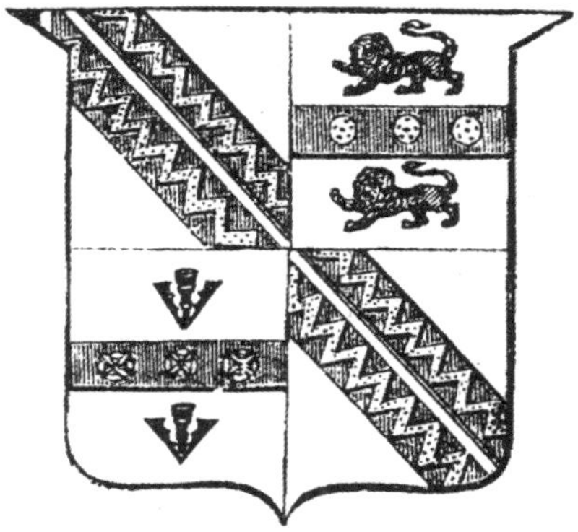

Here we see an example of quartering in heraldry. The word quartering is used if three or more than three other arms are included with those of the family.
Source: Imperial Dictionary *(1861)*

Collectable pieces may have pictures of houses, churches, bridges, inns or scenes from daily life. Notable people were likely to be depicted and various coats of arms or flags were also used. In many designs there is a single panel for the words or text with a decorative surround. Some have an illustration with text below, or all within the border; others have separate pictorial panels. A skilled craftsperson will suggest the best ways to achieve desirable results.

Coats of Arms

Coats of arms and crests have been liberally applied to all manner of items, from public buildings to personal bookplates. Companies offer family coats of arms painted on vellum, parchment, cast metal shields, glassware and ceramics, or woven into fabrics.

However, heraldry is a very complex field to investigate — finding a family crest is rarely as simple as leafing through a book of names and designs. It all depends on what sort of heraldry you are considering and especially its country of origin. I have a 1904 book of Irish history and heraldry which lists 735 family names and illustrates the relevant shield, crest and motto. Unfortunately the notion of there being 'family' coats of arms in Ireland belonging to anyone with a given surname was wrong then and is wrong now.

Heraldry

Heraldry as we know it today was introduced into Ireland by the Anglo-Normans. The system which continues to exist in Great Britain and in the Republic of Ireland is based on the grant of arms to individuals. Direct descendants of these persons have a right to bear those arms. The heraldic authority in the Republic of Ireland is the Chief Herald of Ireland, who is at the Genealogical Office, 2 Kildare Street, Dublin.

In England, the College of Arms in Queen Victoria Street, London is the heraldic authority, under the control of the Earl Marshal who acts on behalf of the Queen. In Scotland, the Lord Lyon King of Arms and the heralds at New Register House, Charlotte Square, Edinburgh control the granting and use of arms. Whereas in England a grant of arms allows all male descendants, and sometimes females, to establish a claim, in Scotland, the grant can only

FAR RIGHT: *A beautifully engraved page of arms from* A Genealogical and Heraldic History of the Colonial Gentry *by Sir Bernard Burke, C.B., LL.D., Ulster King of Arms (vol. 1, 1891; vol. 2, 1895). Wyndham, Skene, Moore, Stuart and A'Beckett were all resident in Australia while Acland, Arkwright, Johnson and Woollcombe were in New Zealand.*
Source: Collection, Bendigo Library

Wyndham
of Leconfield

Skene
of Marnoo

Moore
of Springwood

Acland
of Holnicote

Arkwright
of Overton

Johnson
of Wellington

Stuart
of Sydney

Woollcombe
of Ashbury

À Beckett
of Melbourne

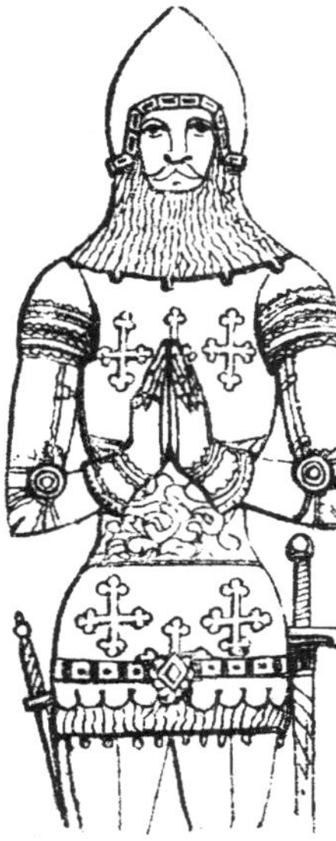

descend from eldest son to eldest son. Younger sons of the original grantee, or of his heirs, can only apply for a variation of the original arms.

Distinctive Designs

Use of the word 'arms' and 'armory' usually refers to the device placed upon a shield. These have been traced to the 12th century when signs or symbols were adopted to suggest some military status.[6] In medieval tournaments, a blend of sport and warfare, groups of knights fought on open battlefields. The pageantry and heroism of these events encouraged the decoration of shields, helmets and lance flags with colourful devices, in a sense to make a statement rather like a modern trademark or advertising logo.

It must be said that this was before the time of full suits of armour, so it is not true to say that heraldry was created to allow knights in closed helmets to be identified. The coat of arms was a textile 'surcoat' worn over various kinds of armour. Eventually this became identified as a person's armorial bearings. Individual designs were associated with courage and great deeds and sons would naturally desire to inherit the swords, shields and other accoutrements of their noble fathers.

During the Crusades, men from throughout Christian Europe went to capture the Holy Land from the Muslims. The rivalry between countries and between individuals to achieve great honour in what was seen as a 'holy war', strengthened the role of distinctive devices or marks, including the use of colours. An intermingling of fighting men from many different countries, in a single cause, helped spread the principles and practice of armory throughout Europe.

The Granting of Arms

Most of the rules and terms of heraldry became more or less universal, even if over the centuries the adopting or granting of arms differed from country to country. While official regulation of the right to bear arms has long been in place in the British Isles, in other European countries the story is somewhat different. Grants of arms have been made by sovereigns and emperors, and these were naturally given high status. Conversely self-assumption has also been a common way to acquire arms. While the story might begin at the upper levels of the social order, in the end all sorts of people acquired arms which would then be passed on through the generations. The passage of time gave them respect and legitimacy if they were not at some stage given official recognition.

Rich landowners, powerful merchants and burghers sometimes adopted arms on their own authority as did craftsmen, tradesmen and even peasants. If your family background is in Europe, there is a possibility you may find a family coat of arms. With less regulation, and in many instances a wider spectrum of people bearing arms, your chances could be reasonable.

There are numerous books on the subject and many listed on the ever-increasing number of sites on the Internet. An interesting site to look at, called 'Frequently Asked Questions on Italian Heraldry', is found at:

[http://caltrap.bbsnet.com/frequent.htm]. Here we read that 'a person descended in the legitimate male line from an armigerous ancestor is entitled to display a coat of arms as his own.' However, the article also makes it clear that the adoption of arms in Italy was limited to the noble families and in a few cases extended to minor nobility, so be cautious about firms that offer a coat of arms based on your surname with no proper genealogical research.

The Office of Honours and Heraldry in Rome does not claim authority to grant arms to individuals or to protect those which have existed from earlier times. Their concern is mainly with armorial bearings for towns and other corporate entities. The Collegio Araldico is a private organisation which publishes a peerage directory and this includes the titles of nobility and coats of arms of living Italians.

It seems there are traps for the unwary in many countries. Remember, if you are serious about family history, a coat of arms or crest will be relevant only if the connection is properly documented.

Achievements

A combination of the shield, helmet and crest, with a motto on a scroll and, in some examples, supporters on each side of the shield is called an achievement. The term coat of arms more properly refers to the shield and whatever it contains. Very elaborate achievements have supporters as well as a complicated arrangement called a mantle or lambrequin coming from beneath the wreath or coronet. This mantling has evolved as a highly decorative and stylised representation of the textile covering worn on the helmet. Some historians suggest that the ragged or slashed character of the mantle design is supposed to indicate heroism in that the wearer has been 'in the forefront of a fight'. Many designs have an unmutilated cloth tied at the upper corners and displayed behind the armorial bearings, which some authorities consider derives from the robe of state.

Crests

The term 'crest' refers to the symbolic element which is on top of the helmet, or simply sits on a wreath or torse placed centrally above the shield. Crests evolved from fan-shaped ornaments placed on the top of helmets. These were both decorative and practical in that they could break the force of a downward blow. Elaborate crests were mainly used to make an impression at tournaments or ceremonial occasions.

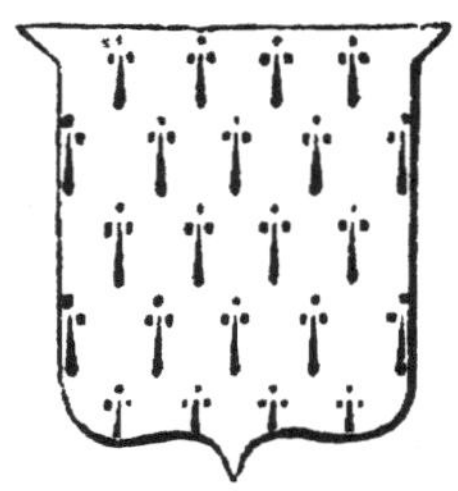

The use of crests in arms was at first reserved for the nobility but, in time, they were more liberally applied and eventually all coats of arms issued in Britain were granted with a crest. It has been pointed out that in English heraldry a coat of arms can legally exist without a crest, but a crest cannot exist without a coat of arms.[7] If you see a crest on a piece of silverware or other objects, it means you should be able to trace it back to a coat of arms. This presumes, of course, that the crest is genuine and not simply a creation to impress the world at large. It may also be a borrowed crest which really only relates to another family.

The Right to Bear Arms

For the family historian, the confirmation of a right to bear arms can open up the possibility of a rich vein of genealogical information. During the 16th and 17th centuries, the heralds in England visited each county about every twenty or thirty years to record all of the coats of arms then in use. Part of their work was to record the pedigrees of families who were required to show that by grant or long use they were entitled to bear arms. These are called visitations and the records of them, along with a vast amount of other material, is kept at the College of Arms in London. In the 19th century, publications such as *The General Armory of England, Scotland, Ireland and Wales* became standard references.

One of the outcomes of the Industrial Revolution in the 18th and 19th centuries was that as certain families became more affluent they wanted symbols of their status. A coat of arms was an essential acquisition and if no legal right to bear arms could be found or bought, they would often simply borrow those of another family. The advent of businesses promising a family coat of arms for the payment of a fee began at this time. Such services continue to be offered, along with mail order 'family history' books which again are not based on research and have no standing in the world of the serious historian.

Heraldry can have an important place in some family stories, while in others it has no relevance, except perhaps for the arms of towns, authorities or important landowners which touched upon the lives of ordinary people. Thankfully, we have left behind much of the elitism of earlier times and value individuals and families as we find them, rather than on inherited status.

Edinburgh Castle was an important military headquarters over many centuries. This dramatic view is from Edinburgh in the Nineteenth Century *by Thomas H. Shepherd, published in 1829.*
Source: Collection, Peter Cuffley

Chapter Twelve
Conservation and Presentation

Many of our ancestors had posterity in mind and were intent on leaving some sort of legacy; others were too busy surviving to give a thought to anything beyond their own immediate world. Some deliberately covered their tracks, or managed to ensure future confusion by telling untruths or altering facts. A great danger for the researcher is to be so immersed in the past that present and future generations may not receive the benefit of all the work that has been done. It is extremely important to pass on accumulated knowledge in an accessible form.

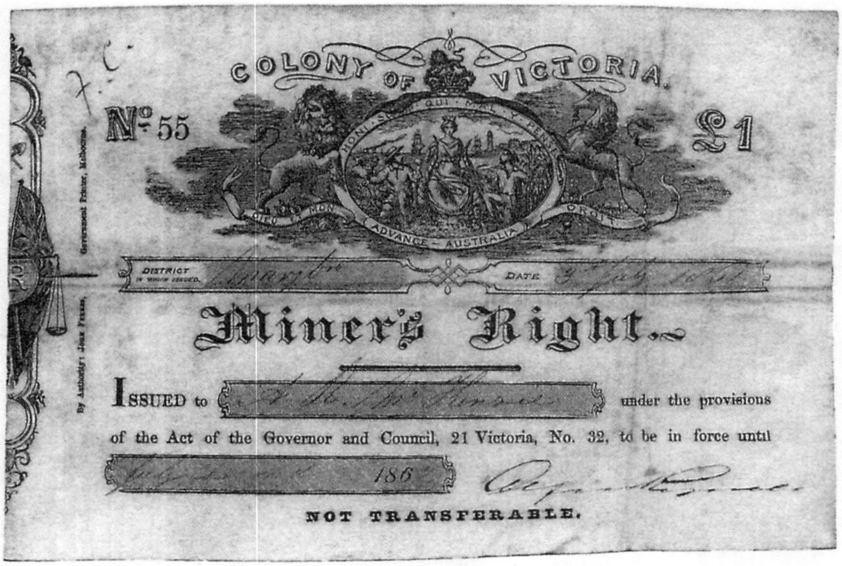

COLONY OF VICTORIA.

No 55 £1

ADVANCE AUSTRALIA

DISTRICT IN WHICH ISSUED. DATE

Miner's Right.

ISSUED to under the provisions of the Act of the Governor and Council, 21 Victoria, No. 32, to be in force until 186

NOT TRANSFERABLE.

Considering that most miners would have carried their Miner's Right on their persons, it is surprising that quite a few have survived in good condition. The paper is a type of waxed parchment so that would have helped. Such items need to be kept in acid-free pockets or framed with long-term preservation in mind.
Source: Courtesy Gwen Shaw

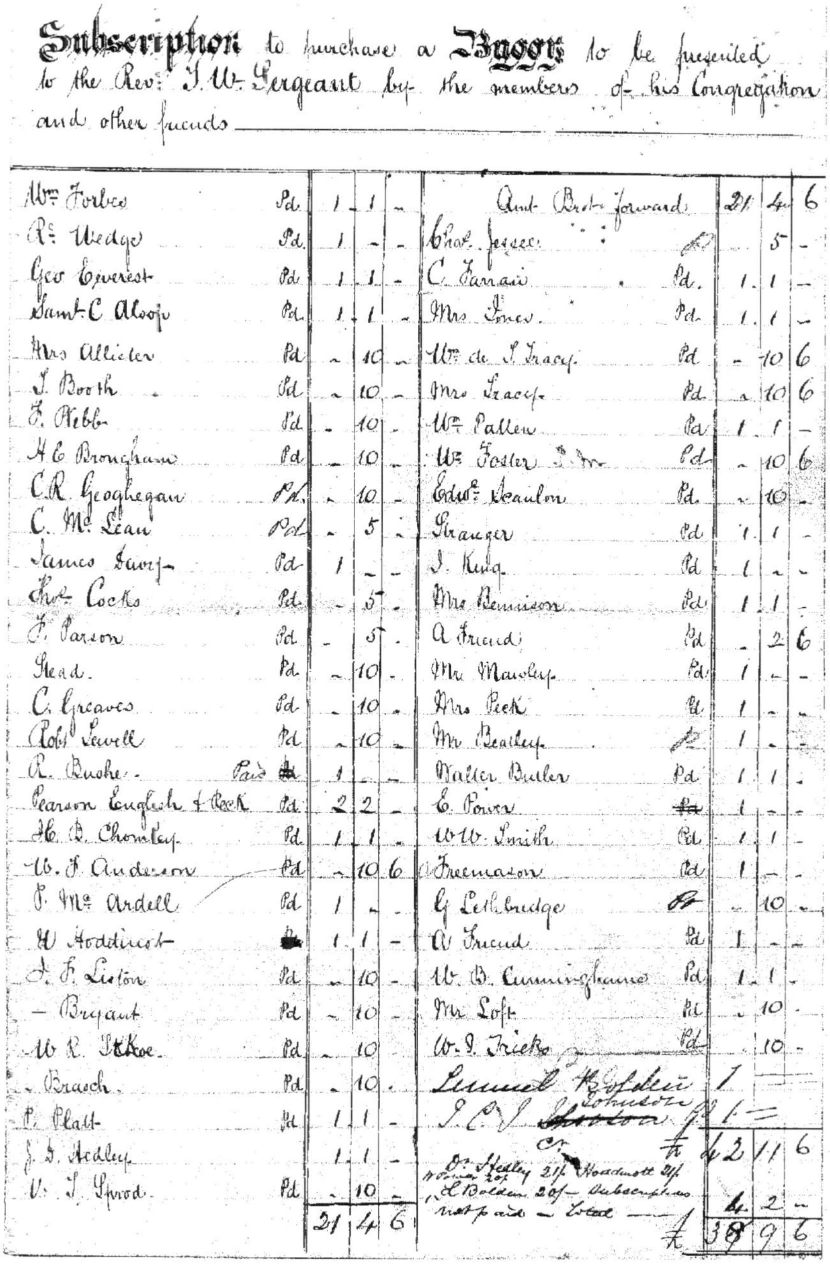

Subscription to purchase a Buggy to be presented to the Revd T. W. Sergeant by the members of his Congregation and other friends

Name		£	s	d	Name		£	s	d
Wm Forbes	Pd	1	1	–	Amt Brot forward		21	4	6
Rd Wedge	Pd	1	–	–	Chas Jessee	Pd		5	–
Geo Everest	Pd	1	1	–	C. Farrar	Pd	1	1	–
Saml C Aloof	Pd	1	1	–	Mrs Jones	Pd	1	1	–
Mrs Allister	Pd	–	10	–	Wm de S Tracy	Pd	–	10	6
J. Booth	Pd	–	10	–	Mrs Tracy	Pd	–	10	6
F. Nebb	Pd	–	10	–	Wm Pallen	Pd	1	1	–
H C Brougham	Pd	–	10	–	Wm Foster J.m.	Pd	–	10	6
C.R. Geoghegan	Pd	–	10	–	Edwd Scanlon	Pd	–	10	–
C. Mc Lean	Pd	–	5	–	Stranger	Pd	1	1	–
James Savey	Pd	1	–	–	J. King	Pd	1	–	–
Thos Cocks	Pd	–	5	–	Mrs Bennison	Pd	1	1	–
F. Parson	Pd	–	5	–	A Friend	Pd	–	2	6
Head.	Pd	–	10	–	Mr Mawley	Pd	1	–	–
C. Greaves	Pd	–	10	–	Mrs Peck	Pd	1	–	–
Robt Sewell	Pd	–	10	–	Mr Beasley	Pd	1	–	–
R. Bushe	Paid	1	–	–	Walter Butler	Pd	1	1	–
Pearson English & Beck	Pd	2	2	–	E. Power	Pd	1	–	–
H. D. Chomley	Pd	1	1	–	W W. Smith	Pd	1	1	–
W. F. Anderson	Pd	–	10	6	Freemason	Pd	1	–	–
P. Mc Ardell	Pd	1	–	–	G Lethbridge	Pd	–	10	–
H Hoddinott	Pd	1	1	–	A Friend	Pd	1	–	–
J. F. Liston	Pd	–	10	–	W. B. Cunningham	Pd	1	1	–
– Bryant	Pd	–	10	–	Mr Loft	Pd	–	10	–
W R. McKee	Pd	–	10		W. J. Fricke	Pd	–	10	–
Brasch	Pd	–	10	–	Samuel H Golden		1		
P. Platt	Pd	1	1	–	J. C. J Johnson		1	1	–
J. S. Hedley		1	1	–	Cr	£	42	11	6
V. J. Sprod	Pd	–	10	–	Dr Hedley 21/ Hoddinott 21/ L Bolden 20/- Subscriptions not paid — total		4	2	–
		21	4	6		£	38	9	6

A buggy was a very practical presentation to give to the Reverend Thomas Woolcock Serjeant (correct spelling). He was at Sale in Gippsland, Victoria, in the 1860s and members of his congregation there make up most of the list, though friends from elsewhere are also included. Having gained a B.A. at Exeter College, Oxford, in 1846, he married Harriette Charles in 1850 and they migrated to Australia in 1860.
Source: Collection, Margaret Winmill, great granddaughter

Ideally, you could produce a printed family history which is both a narrative and a well-documented collection of facts. The recent trend has also been to place the family story in a broader context so that it relates to social and economic history.[1] Albums or framed pictures and documents, with integrated or attached information, are another important means of enjoying and sharing family history.

If publishing the family history seems an impossible task, at least consider producing a set of notes or a summary of the information you have gathered. This can be given to family, local libraries, historical societies and the various genealogical or family history groups. Even a modest booklet ensures that family members or other interested parties who go searching will be aware of the work done and can either track you down or, in the future, have a clear direction to take.

No 7/557

SESSION CLERKS OFFICE.
1 CLYDE TERRACE.
GORBALS.

PROCLAMATIONS ENTERED FOR
GORBALS, HUTCHESONTOWN, TRADESTON,
POLMADIE & LITTLE GOVAN.

That William Crozier, Weaver Glassford Parish of [illegible]
have been Proclaimed in the Church here, in order for
Marriage, three several times, and no objection made,
is attested at Gorbals, the Thirteenth day of December
One thousand, Eight hundred, and Sixty Nine years by
Thomas Smith Session Clerk.

N.B.—Upon production of this Certificate, the parties will obtain from the Registrar of the Parish or District within which the Marriage is intended to be Solemnised, a Copy of Schedule C, which the Registrar will fill up, and the Schedule must be returned to him within Three Days after the Marriage, under a Penalty not exceeding £10 Sterling.

Although damaged, this certificate is both historically and visually interesting. It records that the banns have been read and we know from the records that William Crozier married Martha Campbell Pettigrew on 17 December 1869 at Hutchesontown, Lanark, Scotland.
Source: Courtesy Robyn Brett (née Crozier)

By now you may be using a computer program to store a growing number of records. These can be printed out to create folders of information; or duplicate files can be made for distribution. It is important to note, however, that computer disks are vulnerable in two ways. Physically, they have a limited life, and then you must also consider that the software and hardware needed to read them may not be widely available in coming years. CD-ROMs seem to have better prospects of survival, though new storage systems are still being developed and even CD-ROMs may be superseded.

After putting a lot of work into researching the past and rescuing photographs, documents, heirlooms and memorabilia, the matter of long-term conservation is your final step. Experts tell us that records and artefacts are all degrading in one way or another; the question is how can we slow the process down? You also need to protect against dramatic changes, such as a leaking roof, which can cause immediate damage or rapid decline. Presentation and conservation are two vital components in the great family history adventure.

Writing and Publishing

Published family histories are as diverse as people who create them. They can be brief accounts or great sagas, humble booklets or weighty volumes. Most are interesting, but some stand out as fine examples of a lively synthesis of all

How did your ancestors travel before the age of the motor car?
Source: Collection, Peter Cuffley

available data. A good family history is based on solid research and is written in a manner which offers accessible information and a sense of the times and places in which real people lived.

Family anecdotes, insights into character and beliefs, all help elevate the story above being a collection of names and dates. If you can include pictorial material, there is even greater certainty of engaging people's interest. Members of the judging panel for the prestigious Alexander Henderson Award for published family histories in Australia have stated that the essential components in such a work are:

1 a comprehensive index;
2 a clearly defined title page with publication (imprint) details on the reverse;
3 an introduction stating the purpose of the book;
4 acknowledgement of all those who have provided information or pictorial matter;
5 clear illustrations;
6 a bibliography or list of reference sources;
7 properly documented footnotes or endnotes;
8 a foreword or author's preface;
9 a list of contents;
10 a list of illustrations;
11 genealogical tables and charts;
12 appendices.[2]

The need for an index is mentioned first because so many publications lack this vital component.

Financial considerations will generally determine the physical character of a published family history. The best quality available within a specified budget is what most people aim for. Costs depend on many factors, including the extent of the text and the complexity of both text and layout, how much material is supplied print-ready (such as charts and whole pages), the quality of the paper, printing and binding, and the size of the print run. When my first book was being prepared in 1972, we still had long strips of paper called galley-proofs, taken from metal type, to paste up the final pages. All this has changed with electronic typesetting. Pages of text can now be created on a home computer. This process is called 'desktop publishing'.

There are various methods of printing a book to achieve different quality end-products. A commercial printer can produce a high-quality publication by creating film directly from your disk. Or they can print from laser proofs and achieve a very good result. Many family historians have computers, but not the expertise or quality of equipment needed to handle a large-scale production.

Companies who are specialists in the field of family history, or small-run publications, offer a range of services and most can handle book production at whatever quality or size of print run that is required (see Useful Addresses). There are a number of books on writing and publishing a family history and

these are listed in the Bibliography. It is important to establish the likely demand for your published work before committing yourself to the desired quality and print run. Taking firm orders or pre-selling the book is the safest way to proceed because a realistic budget can then be set.

Well-produced family histories generally involve much hard work but the final result always makes your effort seem worthwhile. By applying for an ISBN number from the National Library of Australia in Canberra, and sending them a copy of the published book, you will have established a claim to the words and any other elements which are your original creation.

The reverse side of the title page (imprint page) should have the date of publication, the name and address of the publisher, a copyright symbol (©) with your name and the date, a full title and ISBN number. Be generous in your acknowledgements and make sure credit is given where credit is due. It is important for the acceptance of your work that it is inclusive and balanced, so that other members of the family do not feel alienated or sense an unnecessary bias. Statements of fact should be well supported by all of the available evidence.

Pedigree Charts

In the past, drawing family trees or other kinds of charts was usually sheer hard work. These days genealogy computer programs will generate clear, easily understood charts which are readily fitted into a specified page design. A number of standard print-outs can be created to suit a vertical page. Charts which work downwards from a selected ancestor are called drop-line pedigrees. These have been around since the 16th century and are also described as rectilinear charts. Programs will produce variations such as the drop-line 'waterfall' design or a descending box chart that can continue over many pages (see page 44–5). Another popular form has each generation indented from the previous one.

A very useful five-generation pedigree chart in a horizontal form works in reverse by having yourself or a family member on the left-hand side of the page, then parents, then grandparents and so on until you have sixteen great great grandparents on the right-hand side. This chart is generated in most up-to-date family history programs for home computers. One thing it clearly illustrates is just how far back in each line the research has gone.

The traditional family tree is another type of pedigree chart. It shows early ancestors at the base and the generations spreading upwards and outwards. Family trees can be completely drawn by hand with hand-lettering, or typeset names can be applied.

Wall charts are available with blank spaces for the names and details to be filled in. Colourful wall charts can be purchased from the British magazine *Family Tree*. These begin with an individual at the base of the tree and go to six or seven generations (see Useful Addresses). There are also circular charts which begin with two ancestors and radiate in all directions. On the Internet I found a supplier offering wall-size charts (90 cm x 150 cm) which cover nine generations. To find sites dealing in these products simply type in 'pedigree charts' or 'family tree charts'.

A framed display of Sergeant Joseph Charles Sloper's war record with medals. He was in the 12th Field Company, Engineers, AIF, in World War I, and was awarded the Distinguished Conduct Medal for gallantry in the field. This is the highest honour next to the Victoria Cross.
Source: Courtesy Pauline Humphreys

Videos and CD-Roms

A video is an exciting way to record the story of your family. It could begin by showing a sequence of family photographs with titles and background music, though more elaborate examples can be created which incorporate old home movies or videos, as well as some form of narrative.

Family history videos or photography albums stored on CD-ROM can also feature personal items, service medals, keepsakes, memorabilia, awards, heirlooms; the list is endless. Look up a professional service on the Internet or in the Yellow Pages under Video Productions, or do it yourself! Some firms offer editing, choreography (planning the sequence and effects), background music, voice overs and character-generated titles.

Framing and Presentation

For immediacy and value-for-money it is hard to beat a well-framed picture or collage of documents. Presenting images, text, and all sorts of items, in a tasteful frame provides a constant reminder of times past and our various connections. For hundreds of years, people have presented and displayed precious objects in frames. Authenticity and impact are two key words to bear in mind as you decide on a design. Valued family pictures deserve to be framed in a way which is in keeping with their age, character, style and potential impact.

A pre-printed frame or border is a simple and effective way of presenting photographs. This subject here is Ann Cuffley (née Dowling) c. 1836–1924. Born is Kilkenny, Ireland, she came to Australia as an assisted migrant in 1854.
Source: Collection, Peter Cuffley

Sometimes the logical choice will be an original fame or at least a reproduction of a period style. For other pieces, the framing might perhaps allude to a particular era, while remaining clearly contemporary.

Before you decide on a frame, you should be aware that it is important never to trim original documents or pictures to fit them into a frame. It is always better to leave them as they are. Untrimmed photographs and other such items are easier to mount and the trimming of documents and maps can greatly decrease their value.

Nineteenth-century photograph albums were often sumptuous creations, though unfortunately they rarely meet modern conservation standards.
Source: Collection, Peter Cuffley

Historical Styles and Fashions

Typically the date range of family pictures and other frameable pieces extends from the latter half of the 19th century up to the present time. This span covers an extraordinary diversity of framing styles and techniques as well as the changing notions of how pieces might be displayed. The drift of fashion in framing and presentation is naturally closely allied to the changing tastes and ideals in furniture design and interior decoration. For instance, very plain frames using timbers such as oak reflected the mood of the Arts and Crafts movement. No varnish or polish was used and the only relief was the gilt trim in some examples. By contrast, in the Victorian era, many frames were given ornate decoration, often in combination with richly-coloured plush fabrics.

Frames are available in countless styles. Oil paintings were traditionally displayed in heavy frames with a predominance of gilded finishes. When a work was protected by glass and was less robust, the frame would be lighter and at times quite slim. Prints, watercolours and photographs from the 1850s onwards were often seen in frames that had a veneer of birds-eye maple with a gilt inner trim called a slip. In the early 20th century, prints and photographs were typically in the slimmest of frames. Black was a popular colour with a contrasting white mat surrounding the print. Often the mat was quite large, with a bigger proportion of mat below the work to give an aesthetic or Japanese look.

Catalogues over the period 1800 to 1920 depict a wide range of frames for photographs with particular emphasis on the 'cabinet' and 'Paris Panel' sizes. Solid glass frames with gilt borders, velvet-covered frames with embroidered silk flowers and nickel mounts, and even ormolu frames with imitation precious stones were the height of fashion. Moulded frames with a gilt finish were popular as were the different woods, oak, maple, rosewood and imitation olive wood.

Apart from the standard rectangular, square, or oval frames, a universal favourite was the Oxford 'cross-corner' design which appeared during the Aesthetic movement that first took hold in the 1870s (see page 172). They were meant to be exotic and were made in imitation olive wood, black with gilt, or in assorted woods. Many other materials were used to create frames including papier maché, ivory, leather, brass, painted metal and early forms of plastic such as celluloid.

Composition cases made of compressed plastic material were used to display daguerreotypes and ambrotypes. A similar technique was employed to make composition frames in a variety of sizes. There are examples from the

FANCY WOODEN FRAME

No. C 719.
Double Cabinet Sheet Glass Photo Frames, with Gilt Corners, and assorted Hand-painted Floral Decorations.

No. C 691.
Sheet Glass Cabinet Photo Frames, with Cut Edges and Assorted Floral Decorations.

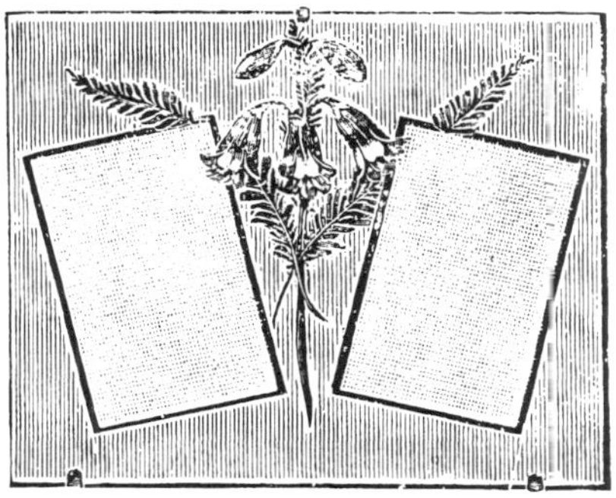

No. C 720.
Double Cabinet Sheet Glass Photo Frames, with assorted Hand-painted Floral Decorations.

OXFORD FRAME

Glass Panel Photo Frames, with Silvered Borders, Inlaid with Pearl.

The 'cross-corner' or 'Oxford' frame was a great favourite in the late 19th and early 20th century. The 'fancy wooden frame' was made from steam-pressed timber and was a popular choice for photographs and prints. Glass photo frames were made for standing on a cabinet or mantelpiece.
Source: Collection, Peter Cuffley

mid-19th century which have been given an ivory finish. Some were grained to look like wood and others were gilded.

Apart from plain moulded wooden frames there were frames made from sheets of plywood with applied decoration. The influence of Art Nouveau was evident in both the shape of the cut-out plywood and in the moulded decoration. Homemade 'craft' pieces made from wooden panels cut into shapes, such as the map of Australia, would probably be regarded as kitsch today. Some frames were decorated by using a type of carving known as chip carving. Soldiers of the World War I era are typically seen in wooden frames.

Decorative elements were applied to wooden picture frames with a form of plaster called gesso. In affluent households you could also find carved wooden frames finished with gold-leaf.

The mats used for artworks, prints and photographs varied from plain or gilded card to velvet, brass or ormolu. In the early 20th century, thin oak ply or a thin sheet of oak on card would complement an oak frame to give a 'woodsy' or 'craftsman' effect. A few decades earlier high fashion demanded rich colours and so red, blue, green or gold plush fabric would surround a picture. One of the most popular shapes of mat was the style given a curved upper inside edge.

When we study the methods and styles of framing in past eras a number of key elements emerge. In fact, there is a hierarchy of quality and style depending on the work framed and the social level to which it belonged. This is something to keep in mind if you are framing works of art or family photographs and you want to capture the authentic character of the period of the work.

Framing and Displaying Photographs

Many works of art in the 19th century were given ornate frames, but photographic portraits were generally presented more simply. Black frames with gold slips or a gold inner trim were seen as tasteful and dignified for small- to medium-sized pictures. Arranging photographs as a group on the wall was a favoured device in Victorian and Edwardian best rooms. Later on the Aesthetic movement and eclecticism had an influence and pictures of various sizes in all manner of frames were displayed in a broad band around the walls of fashionable rooms. Some were placed in an 'artistic' asymmetrical arrangement; others were symmetrically hung for a balanced effect. Groups of small pictures were sometimes placed on either side of a large picture or a number of small works arranged one above the other and between two larger pieces.

When photographic enlarging became possible at the end of the 19th century, many small-format portraits taken some thirty to fifty years earlier were re-photographed, blown up to large scale and framed in one of the fashionable styles of the day.

Happily an older style of presentation, where a number of photographs are displayed in the one frame, has returned to favour. In the past there were some wonderful composites created of family members, teams, lodges, service personnel, civic leaders and old pioneers. Names and other details were usually finely inscribed, with additional decorative elements drawn or painted.

My wife and I were recently invited to see a collection of family photographs and found them beautifully and imaginatively framed, with names, dates, places and other essential or interesting details annotated in fine calligraphy. One particularly impressive piece had a photograph and a copy of a newspaper cutting in the one frame with additional penwork. The two items in juxtaposition each gained from the other. Sections of maps, drawings of properties, certificates and letters can all be framed with a relevant photograph or a whole set of pictures.

Archival Standards

All flat items including prints, photographs and documents can be mounted and framed attractively, as well as meeting basic archival standards. The board used to back and mount an item should be archivally stable. Australian Archives suggest that materials used with photographs need to have passed the 'Photographic Activity Test' (PAT). This technical information is available from suppliers and relates to whether the material is acid-free.[3]

Scottish heritage is celebrated in the costume of this little boy. The photograph dates from around 1900 and unfortunately has developed spots of fungus or mould. This condition, described as 'foxing', results from the interaction of moisture or humidity and impurities in the card used for the mount. The photograph could be restored by creating a new image and retouching by hand or digitally (see chapter 7). Old and new photographs should be stored in acid-free tissue paper in an area that has dry circulating air.
Source: Collection, Peter Cuffley

If possible it is best to suspend the item you are framing using an archival quality tape along the top edge or at the top corners, rather than glueing it to the backing board. This leaves it free to expand and contract as conditions change. Use a mounting mat or some form of spacer to keep the protective sheet of glass away from the surface of your photograph or document. It is even better if the glass is filtered against the ultraviolet (UV) in the light spectrum, as this is the most damaging portion of both natural and artificial light.

Visible light can also damage photographs and documents. Coloured inks or dyes are highly susceptible to light damage. Original photographs, documents, general ephemera and artworks such as watercolours, if displayed at all, should be kept away from bright light sources. Fluorescent lights emit a high amount of ultraviolet rays compared to ordinary incandescent light globes. Specially filtered fluorescent tubes are recommended for storage areas and for lighting items on display. If it is possible to create good quality copies

Old photographs of sporting teams are always interesting if players can be identified. Family connections make them ideal as items for a history or for display. Darley is a rural area near Bacchus Marsh, west of Melbourne. This premiership photograph dates from 1923.

Source: Collection, Peter Cuffley

of documents, artworks or paper ephemera it is always preferable to have these on display and the originals stored under archival conditions. With photographs it should be standard practice to display copy prints which can be replaced, rather than the originals. And even copies need to be given adequate care if you want to enjoy them for a reasonable length of time.

Archival framing works in a number of ways to protect original items or copies. Dust, dirt and various air-borne impurities are kept from the surface of the piece. If archival quality backing boards and mats are used they will not contribute to degradation of the framed item. Uncoloured boards are used because the dyes in coloured boards can cause problems. The use of 'hinges' made from archival quality paper (such as strips of Japanese mulberry paper) to attach the item to the backing board not only allows for expansion and contraction, but avoids damaging glues. The glue used for the paper hinges is often a wheat starch paste with a fungicide added. Commercially prepared archival tape can be purchased from specialist suppliers.

Heat and fumes or smoke from fireplaces and heaters can be a problem, so keep valuable pieces away from these. Damp is also a factor; be sure to choose a dry position. The internal surface of an outside wall may transmit

moisture, therefore internal partition walls are preferable as display areas in many households.

When you want to create long-lasting copies of letters, newspaper articles or notices, or other documents, the best move is to photocopy them on to an archival quality paper. Acid-free 'buffered' paper is ideal and can be purchased from specialist outlets or ordered through a local stationery supplier. Buffered or alkaline paper has a pH value over 7.0, whereas standard acid-free paper has a pH of 7.0 and can become acidic over time. Buffering neutralises acids and prevents their migration from other sources.

It is also good practice to use a UV filter on photocopiers when copying photographs, documents or other original items. Polyester film for filtering UV is available and can be placed between the light source and the material being copied.

Papers made with wood pulp or liquin become acidic with age and have a tendency to go yellow or brown. That's what happens to your newspaper cuttings. Original single or folded sheet items should be stored in acid-free buffered folders. When more than one item is placed in a folder or box, a piece of acid-free tissue should be placed between each item.

A good way to keep documents which might occasionally be viewed by yourself or others is to use archivally stable plastic pockets made from polypropylene, polyethylene or polyester (Mylar).[4] Small- to medium-sized documents can be viewed from both sides without removing them from the pocket. Larger items such as maps, plans or newspaper pages require large plastic sleeves, though some may be stored rolled up in cylinders if interleaved with archival tissue. Storing paper items in plastic pockets and sleeves can be a problem in climates with a high humidity because it can lead to mould growth or adhesion between items.

Three-dimensional pieces, including heirlooms made from various materials, should be stored in boxes with archivally stable plastics or paper to act as a shock absorber. Don't use crumpled-up newspaper, brown paper or coloured paper because they can cause long-term problems.

Both two- and three-dimensional items in a family collection may potentially be affected by pollution and pests. Wood, leather, rubber and certain plastic materials can produce acid vapours as they age. Silverfish, book lice, carpet beetles, mice and even termites can be a threat to items on display or in storage. Good housekeeping is the primary method of deterrence, which means regular inspections of stored collections.[5]

Displays Under Glass

There is a long tradition of displaying family keepsakes, memorabilia and heirlooms in frames, under glass domes or in small glass boxes or display cases. Heritage framers can create collages using both flat and three-dimensional items. For example, a framed display may include a wedding photograph, a satin goodluck horseshoe, a garter, the wedding invitation and artificial flowers. Another might have baby pictures, woollen booties, a birth notice and other keepsakes. A more general family collage can include documents,

photographs, cards, small heirloom pieces, war service medals or other medals and ribbons. In fact, any object can be grouped to fit a chosen theme and the available space.

A framed display to be hung on a wall cannot be too deep, whereas a dome or case can be whatever size is deemed suitable. Again, it is advisable to choose materials which are not going to damage the items being celebrated. Except for the frame itself and the base of a dome or case, it is best to avoid using wood. Non-corrosive metal is a good choice, as are archival quality boards, including those which have a foam core. A polystyrene box, cut down from one used to pack vegetables, can be combined with a suitable frame to make a collage, or you can buy an archival box from a supplier.

To protect pieces from vermin, try to make your case airtight and keep the display area clear by good housekeeping and the judicious use of insecticide. Remember, never allow sprays to come in contact with photographs, documents, fabrics or other materials being preserved. Camphor products such as mothballs should also be avoided as they can have a deleterious effect on photographs and documents.

Needlework with Pictures

Patchwork quilts in earlier times were linked to the family story through the use of names and other words, dates and appliqué pictures. Nowadays heritage or heirloom quilters can use patches which have transferred reproductions of family photographs. When combined with traditional patchwork elements they look very striking — it's yet another way of preserving portraits or other images.

There are a number of systems for transferring photographs on to fabric. Silk-screening of photographs on T-shirts is popular, and there are several methods for copying photographs on to quilt panels for family history quilts,

The stereograph below pictures children engaged in adult activity. This was considered humorous at the time. Nowadays we can use these images to garner details of domestic life.
Source: Collection, Peter Cuffley

anniversary quilts, pillows, wall hangings and so on. One method uses a colour scanner to transfer the image to a computer program. At this stage, the image is reversed and then laser printed on a transfer sheet, which in turn is heat-pressed on to the selected fabric. White, off-white or ivory-coloured one hundred per cent cotton is considered an ideal base for the reproduction of family photographs. Another method uses a colour laser copier to produce a transfer sheet. This is then heat-pressed on to the chosen fabric. Both colour and black-and-white photographs can be transferred, as can any other suitable images. Signatures, invitations, old greeting cards and engravings of sailing ships are just some of the possibilities. The heat-pressing is supposed to be permanent and able to withstand machine-washing in cold to warm water, low-heat tumble drying and ironing on a low to medium setting.[6]

If you've started a family history research project, you'll undoubtedly have discovered that travelling back through time can be exciting, frustrating, and sometimes painful. Making sense of what you find, sharing the outcomes, creating an accessible record for future generations, are all vitally linked, and come together in the final product. And as we pore over books, leaf through magazines and explore the Internet, remember we are making family history come to life!

Notes and Sources

1 Family History Adventures

1 Fr D. F. Bourke, *A History of the Catholic Church in Victoria,* Catholic Bishops of Victoria, Melbourne, 1988, p. 8.
2 Memorial for an early pardon, dated 15 August 1833, to His Excellency Major-General Richard Bourke, Governor of New South Wales: The Humble Memorial of Thomas Sweeny, a prisoner for life holding the indulgence of a Ticket of Leave. 33/397, State Records of New South Wales.
3 Memorial for an early pardon, dated 15 August 1833, 33/397, State Records of New South Wales.
4 Memorial, June 1834, Registry of Land Titles and Deeds, no. 95, Book G, Sydney, NSW.
5 Postcard addressed to Mrs Gardiner from Mabel Williamson, n.d., private collection.
6 John Titford, 'The Society of Australian Genealogists', *Family Tree Magazine*, December 1997, p. 17.
7 Stephen Nicholas (ed.), *Convict Workers: Reinterpreting Australia's Past*, Cambridge University Press, Sydney, 1988, p. 82.
8 David Hey (ed.), *The Oxford Companion to Local and Family History*, Oxford University Press, Oxford, 1996, p. 138.
9 ibid., p. 97.

2 Finding the Essential Facts

1 N. J. Vine Hall, *Tracing Your Family History in Australia,* Rigby, Sydney, 1985, p. 131.
2 1851 British Census (Devon, Norfolk, and Warwick only). 1997 Edition, Family History Resource Files of the Church of Jesus Christ of Latter-Day Saints.
3 *New South Wales and Port Phillip General Post Office Directory for 1839*, James Maclehose, Sydney.
4 Mark D. Herber, *Ancestral Trails: The Complete Guide to British Genealogy and Family History,* Sutton Publishing/ Society of Genealogists, Stroud, Gloucestershire, 1997, p. 116.
5 ibid., p. 202.
6 ibid., p. 178.
7 *Finding Families: The Guide to the National Archives of Australia for Genealogists*, National Archives of Australia, in association with Hale & Iremonger, Alexandria, NSW, 1998, p. 221.

4 Treasures from the Internet

1 Clark Cerf Leine, et al., *A Brief History of the Internet,* February 1997, on-line: [http://www.isoc.org/internet-history/brief.html].January 1999, p. 3.
2 Lenny Zeltser, *The World-Wide Web: Origins and Beyond,* February 1997, on-line: [http://www.seas.upenn.edu/~lzeltser/WWW/] January 1999. p. 3.

5 Cultural Diversity

1 Geoffrey Sherington, *Australia's Immigrants 1788–1978*, George Allen & Unwin, Sydney, 1980, pp. 43,44
2 Noris Ioannou, *The Barossa Folk: Germanic Furniture and Craft Tradition in Australia*, Craftsman House, Roseville East, NSW, 1995, p. 21.
3 James Jupp, *Australian Retrospectives: Immigration*, Oxford University Press, Melbourne, 1991, p. 42.
4 Philip Geeves & James Jervis, *Rockdale: Its Beginning and Developments*, Council of the Municipality of Rockdale, 1986, p. 18.
5 Suzanne Mourot, *This Was Sydney: A Pictorial History from 1788 to the Present Time,* Ure Smith, Sydney, 1969, pp. 134–5.

6 James Jupp, *Australian Retrospectives: Immigration,* Oxford University Press, Melbourne, 1991, p. 38.
7 Margaret Chambers (comp.), *Finding Families: The Guide to the National Archives for Genealogists*, National Archives of Australia, in association with Hale & Iremonger, Alexandria, NSW, 1998, p. 5.
8 ibid., p. 42.
9 W. D. Borrie, *Italians and Germans in Australia,* Cheshire, Melbourne, 1954, p. 35.
10 Bette Leone Maiuto, *Tracing Your Italian Ancestors for Victorians,* Co.As.It., Carlton, Vic., 1993, p. 1.
11 Demetra Egan, *Greek Australians: An Introduction,* [http://www.glavx.org/Australi/into.htm.] 27 August 1998.
12 Barry York, *How Many Maltese in Australia,* Wir-, Malta, April 1995, vol. 1, no. 10, Toronto, Ontario.
13 James Jupp, op cit., Oxford University Press, Melbourne, 1991, p. 77.
14 ibid., p. 50.
15 Claveria's Decree on Filipino Surnames, 21 November 1849, from the 'Introduction' of Dr Domingo Abella in *Catalogo Alfabetico Apellidos* (1849); reprinted, National Archives, Manila, 1973.
16 Eileen Johnson, *Tracing Danish Ancestors,* Australian Family Tree Connections, September 1998. p. 24.

6 Homeplaces and Hallowed Ground

1 Police Report, Seymour, 4 April 1863, Public Record Office of Victoria, VPRS:937.
2 Alexander Sutherland, *Victoria and its Metropolis*, Melbourne, 1888, vol. II, p. 331.
3 Marilyn Yurdan, *Irish Family History*, Batsford, London, 1990, p. 7.
4 Claudia Kinmonth, *Irish Country Furniture 1700–1950,* Yale University Press, London, 1993, p. 151.
5 Pencil sketch, *Boat Harbour Wollongong July 8/35,* Mitchell Library (MLC295 f.42), Sydney.
6 Mr Albert Organ recalling his father's descriptions of life in Wollongong in the 1830s from *Old Pioneer's Reminiscences of Illawarra (1830s–1920s),* Illawarra Historical Publications, 1989, p. 63.
7 David Hey, *The Oxford Companion to Local and Family History,* Oxford University Press, Oxford, 1996, p. 473.

7 A Heritage of Photographs

1 Russell Miller, *Click,* Marshall Cavendish, London, 1974, p. 26.
2 Alan Davies & Peter Stanbury, *The Mechanical Eye in Australia, Photography 1841–1900,* Oxford University Press, Melbourne, 1985, p. 8.
3 *Sydney Morning Herald*, 13 December 1842.
4 *Age*, 17 October 1854, p. 7.
5 *Conservation of Photographs: Early Photographic Processes,* Eastman Kodak Co., New York, 1985, p. 26.
6 Davies & Stanbury, ibid., p. 112.
7 Peter Quennell (comp.), *Mayhew's Characters*, Spring Books, London, n.d., p. 291.
8 *Conservation of Photographs*, p. 27.
9 William B. Becker, *A Brief History of the Carte-de-Visite,* [http://www.Photoarts.com/gallery/becker/histsw.html7≥] 30 November 1998.
10 *Conservation of Photographs*, p. 31.
11 Davies & Stanbury, op cit., Oxford University Press, Melbourne, 1985, p. 113.
12 ibid., p. 114.
13 ibid.
14 Australian Archives, *Protecting and Handling Photographs,* Paper no. 7, August 1997, p. 4.
15 David Yeske, 'When the Only Colour Is the Blues', *Ancestor,* vol. 22, no. 5, Autumn 1995, p. 44.

8 Images of Every Kind

1 From the recollections of J. K. Andrews, 1873–1973, copy of an unpublished manuscript in the possession of descendants.
2 Peter Cuffley, *Buggies & Horse-drawn Vehicles in Australia,* Pioneer Design Studio, Lilydale, Victoria, 1981.
3 Andrew & Sandra Twining, *Dictionary of Old Trades & Occupations*, 2nd edn, published by the authors, Woodcroft, SA, 1995.

9 Maps, Plans and Papers

1 Gerald Millington & John Higgs, *Cuffley and Northaw Past,* Jack Edwards, Waltham Cross, Hertfordshire, 1985, p. 4.
2 Mark D. Herber, *Ancestral Trails: The Complete Guide to British Genealogy and Family History,* Sutton Publishing/ Society of Genealogists, Stroud, Gloucestershire, 1997, p. 246.
3 B. Mitchell, *A New Genealogical Atlas of Ireland,* Genealogical Publishing Co. Inc., Baltimore, Md, 1986.
4 Marilyn Yurdan, *Irish Family History*, Batsford, London, 1990, p. 121.
5 Anne M. Bartlett (comp. & ed.), *Local & Family History Sources in Tasmania,* Genealogical Society of Tasmania, Inc., Launceston, 1994.
6 Letter to the Colonial Secretary from C. J. LaTrobe dated 27 December 1842, 43/122, Archives Office of New South Wales; explains reason for sale of portion of larger allotment.
7 An Act of Parliament, dated 11 July 1832, stated that 'no such person shall be capable of acquiring or holding any property' until they had gained a pardon', *Sydney Gazette,* 13 December 1832.
8 Ticket of Leave Butt, No. 31/969, 29 November 1831, Archives Office of New South Wales.
9 Report of Surgeon Superintendant S. J. Cunningham, ship *Sir Robert Seppings*, March–July 1852, AJCP Reel 3210.
10 Frances Brown, *The Australian Joint Copying Project: What's In It for Me?*, Family History Conference Papers, Melbourne, 1995, pp. 28–39.
11 David Hey, *The Oxford Companion to Local and Family History,* Oxford University Press, Oxford, 1996, p. 71.

10 Letters, Diaries and Words in Print

1 Original letter in the possession of the author.
2 Letter from F. M. Ryan of Black Rock, Victoria, to Joseph and Bridget Ryan of Wardell, New South Wales, collection of the author.

3 Ian Nicholson, *Log of Logs,* vol. 2, Roebuck Book, published by the author, Yaroomba, Qld, 1993.
4 *Aboard the Bombay: The Diary of Richard Moffat*, published by George W. Flowers, Melbourne , (undated); Australian National Maritime Museum, Sydney, 910.450 92 MOF.
5 Great War Index, Victoria 1914–1920, Registry of Births, Deaths and Marriages, Victoria (Vic. Heritage), Melbourne, 1997.
6 Extracts from the letters of Timothy Keary published in *From Praties to Puha,* compiled by Fr Jim Consedine for the family reunion of Keary Descendants, Coromandel, New Zealand, January 1997.
7 Passenger List, Commodore Perry, Inward Passenger Lists, British Ports, 1860, Public Record Office of Victoria.
8 Timothy Keary's letter, 21 August 1860, Keary family collection.
9 Lars Bruzelius, *'Commodore Perry' (1854)*, Maritime History Virtual Archives.
10 Michael Cannon, *Melbourne After the Gold Rush*, Loch Haven Books, Main Ridge, Vic., 1993, p. 24
11 Richard A. Smith (comp.), *The Oxford Companion to British History*, Oxford University Press, Oxford, 1997, p. 897.
12 Cannon, op cit., p. 243.
13 ibid.
14 Prof. J. A. Cannon, 'Samuel Pepys (1633–1703)', *The Oxford Companion to British History*, Oxford University Press, Oxford, 1997, p. 742.
15 David Adams (ed.), *The Letters of Rachel Henning,* Penguin, Ringwood, Vic., 1969.
16 M. Organ & A. P. Doyle (comps), *Old Pioneers' Reminiscences of Illawarra (1830's–1920's),* Illawarra Source Books, Illawarra Historical Publications, Woonona, NSW, 1989.
17 ibid., p. 107.

11 Heirlooms and Coats of Arms

1 Hugh Johnson, *The International Book of Wood,* Michael Beazley, London, 1976, pp. 206–7.
2 Noris Ioannou, *The Barossa Folk: Germanic Furniture and Craft Traditions in Australia,* Craftsman House, Roseville East, NSW, 1995, p. 278.
3 Margaret Rolfe, *Patchwork Quilts in Australia*, Greenhouse, Richmond, Vic., 1987, p. 20.
4 Vaughan Evans, 'Sea and Sail', in *First Fleet to Federation: Australian Antiques,* National Trust of Australia (NSW) 1977, p. 116.
5 Bernard Hughes, *The Collectors' Encyclopaedia of English Ceramics,* Abbey Library, London, 1968, p. 144.
6 David Hey, *The Oxford Companion to Local and Family History,* Oxford University Press, Oxford, 1996. p. 216
7 Arthur Charles Fox-Davies, *A Complete Guide to Heraldry*, Thomas Nelson & Sons Ltd, London, 1925. p. 383.

12 Conservation and Presentation

1 Anthony Camp, 'Family History', *The Oxford Companion to Local and Family History,* Oxford University Press, Oxford, 1996, p. 171.
2 Donald. W. M. Grant, 'Alexander Henderson Award' 1996, *The Genealogist*, vol. VIII, no.11, September 1997, p. 494.
3 Australian Archives, *Caring for Your Family Archive,* Archives Advice 10, July 1997.
4 ibid.
5 Henry Ford Museum, *The Care and Preservation of Archival Materials, 24* May 1994: [http://www.hfmgv.org/histories/cis/archival.htm] 12 December 1998.
6 *Graphics on Fabric: Frequently Asked Questions*, Perfect Impressions on Fabric, Colorado Springs, Colorado, [http://shell.rmi.net/~mcurry/piof.html] 30 December 1998, p. 4.

Bibliography

Key references

Barrett, John & Iredale, David. *Discovering Old Handwriting.* Shire Publications Ltd, Princes Risborough, Buckinghamshire, 1995.

Begley, Donal F. *Irish Genealogy: A Record Finder.* Heraldic Artists Ltd, Dublin, 1981.

Black, George F. *The Surnames of Scotland.* New York Public Library, New York, 1946.

Bromell, A. *Tracing Your Family History in New Zealand.* GP Publications, NZ, 1991.

Camp, Anthony J. *Wills and Their Whereabouts.* 4th edn. Published by the author, London, 1974.

Chambers, Margaret. *Finding Families: The Guide to the National Archives of Australia for Genealogists.* National Archives of Australia, in association with Hale & Iremonger, Alexandria, NSW, 1998.

Herber, Mark D. *Ancestral Trails: The Complete Guide to British Genealogy and Family History.* Sutton Publishing/ Society of Genealogists, Stroud, Gloucestershire, 1997.

Hey, David. *The Oxford Companion to Local and Family History.* Oxford University Press, Oxford, 1996.

Holton, Graham S. & Winch, Jack. *My Ain Folk: An Easy Guide to Scottish Family History.* Tuckwell Press, East Linton, East Lothian, 1998.

Humphery-Smith, Cecil (ed.). *The Phillimore Atlas and Index of Parish Registers.* Phillimore & Co. Ltd. Chichester, Sussex, 2nd ed., 1995.

Johnson, K. A. & Sainty, M. R. (comps). *Genealogical Research Directory.* Library of Australian History, North Sydney, 1999 (published annually).

Rogers, Colin D. *The Family Tree Detective: Tracing Your Ancestors in England and Wales.* 3rd edn. Manchester University Press, Manchester, 1996.

Vine Hall, Nick. *Tracing Your Family History in Australia: A Guide to Sources.* Scriptorium Family History Centre, Albert Park, Vic., 1994.

Family History in the British Isles

Alcock, N. W. *Old Title Deeds: A Guide for Local and Family Historians.* Phillimore, Chichester, Sussex, 1986.

Cairns-Smith-Barth, John Lawrence. *Scottish Family History: A Research and Source Guide,* vol. 1. Melbourne, 1986.

Cole, J. & Titford, J. *Tracing Your Family Tree.* Countryside Books, Berkshire, 1997.

Cole, Jean & Church, Rosemary (comps). *In and Around Record Repositories in Great Britain and Ireland.* 4th edn. Armstrong, Boon, Marriott Publishing, Huntingdon, Cambridgeshire, 1998.

Cory, K. B. *Tracing Your Scottish Ancestry.* Polygon, Edinburgh, 1991.

Cracklow, Charles Thomas. *Views of all the Churches and Chapelries in the County of Surrey (1823–c.1827).* Phillimore & Co. Ltd, Chichester, Sussex, 1979.

Fox-Davies, Arthur Charles. *A Complete Guide to Heraldry.* Thomas Nelson & Sons Ltd, London, 1925; reprinted by Wordsworth Editions Ltd, Ware, Hertfordshire, 1996.

Gibson, J. S. W. (comp.). *Wills and Where to Find Them.* Phillimore, Chichester, Sussex, 1974.

Gibson, Jeremy (comp.). *Probate Jurisdictions: Where to Look for Wills.* 4th edn. Federation of Family History Societies, Birmingham, 1980, 1994.

Lewis, Samuel. *A Topographical Dictionary of Ireland (in two volumes)*. 1837; Genealogical Publishing Company Inc., Baltimore, Md, 1984, 1995.

Lewis, Samuel. *A Topographical Dictionary of Scotland (in two volumes)*. 2nd edn, 1851; Genealogical Publishing Company Inc., Baltimore, Md, 1989.

Mitchell, B. *A New Genealogical Atlas of Ireland.* Genealogical Publishing Co. Inc., Baltimore, Md, 1986.

Moule, Thomas. *The County Maps of Old England.* Studio Editions, London, 1990.

Pelling, George. *Beginning Your Family History.* 6th edn. Federation of Family History Societies, Birmingham, 1995.

Rowlands, S. *Welsh Family History: A Guide to Research.* Federation of Family History Societies, Birmingham, 1993.

Shepherd, Thomas H. *London and its Environs in the Nineteenth Century.* Jones & Co., London, 1829; new edition, Bracken Books, London, 1983.

Wood, Tom. *An Introduction to Civil Registration.* Federation of Family History Societies Birmingham, 1994.

Yurdan, Marilyn. *Irish Family History.* Batsford, London, 1990.

Family History in Europe

Baxter, Angus. *In Search of your European Roots: A Complete Guide to Tracing Your Ancestors in Every Country in Europe.* 2nd edn. Genealogical Publishing Company Inc., Baltimore, Md, 1995.

Hennekam, Eric. 'Research in the Netherlands'. *The Genealogist,* vol. viii, no. 7, September 1996, p. 291.

Nedredo, Yngve. How to Trace Your Ancestors in Norway. [http://rsl.rootsweb.com/cgi- bin/relsql.cgi].

Family History in Australia

Deverall, M. & MacFarlane, I. (comps). *My Heart Is Breaking: A Joint Guide to Records about Aboriginal People in the Public Record Office of Victoria and the Australian Archives.* Victorian Regional Office; AGPS, Canberra, 1993.

Frost, Lenore. *Searching for Mary Ann: Researching Women Ancestors in Australia.* Published by the author, Essendon, Vic., 1994.

Genealogical Research Kit. Principal Superintendant of Convicts, Register of Applications to Marry 1826–51. Microfiche, Archives Office of New South Wales, 3rd edn, 1988.

Gentilli, J. 'The Settlement of Swiss Ticino Immigrants in Australia'. *Geowest,* no. 23, University of Western Australia, Nedlands, WA, 1988.

Killion, Martyn C. H. & Garnsey H. E. (eds). *Cemeteries in Australia: A Register of Transcripts.* Australasian Federation of Family History Organisations, Sydney, 1994.

Kopittke, Eric. 'German Emigration to Australia in the 19th Century'. *Australian Family Tree Connections.* vol. 6, no. 5, 1998, pp. 19–21.

Leone Maiuto, Bette. *Tracing Your Italian Ancestors for Victorians.* Co.As.It., Carlton, Vic., 1993.

Lucas, R. 'Genealogies and Registers: A Resource for Aboriginal History'. *Australian Aboriginal Studies,* no. 1. 1986.

MacFarlane, Ian. 'Koori and Chinese Genealogy, an Initial Exploration', *The Genealogist,* vol. vii , no. 3, September 1992, p. 120.

McClaughlin, Trevor. *From Shamrock to Wattle: Digging up Your Irish Ancestors.* Genealogical Society of Victoria, Melbourne, 1990.

McClaughlin, Trevor. *Irish Women in Colonial History.* Allen & Unwin, St Leonards, NSW, 1998.

Morgan, Sally. *My Place.* Fremantle Arts Centre Press, Fremantle, WA, 1987.

Pascoe, R. *Buongiorno Australia: Our Italian Heritage.* Greenhouse Press, Melbourne, 1987.

Prentis, Malcolm D. *The Scots in Australia: A Study of New South Wales, Victoria and Queensland, 1788–1900.* Sydney University Press, Sydney, 1983.

Reakes, J. *How to Trace your Convict Ancestors: Their Lives, Times and Records.* Hale & Iremonger, Sydney, 1992.

Shearer, J. D. *Bound for Botany Bay: Impressions of Transportation and Convict Life.* Summit Books, Sydney, 1976.

Smith, D. & Halstead, B. *Looking for Your Mob: A Guide to Tracing Aboriginal Family Trees.* Aboriginal Studies Press, Canberra, 1990.

Stacker, J. & Stewart, P. *Chinese Immigrants and Chinese-Australians in NSW.* Guide no.1, Australian Archives, 1996.

Struve, Walter. 'Germans in Victoria in the Second Half of the Nineteenth Century''. *The Genealogist,* vol. viii, no. 3, September 1995, pp. 100–4.

Tampke, J. & Doxford, C. *Australia, Willkommen: A History of the Germans in Australia.* New South Wales University Press, Sydney, 1990.

Thornton, Bob. *An Index of Victorian Railway Employees of the 19th Century.* Library Council of Victoria, Melbourne, 1988.

Vondra, J. *German Speaking Settlers in Australia.* Cavalier Press, Melbourne, 1981.

Webster, J. *Specialist Indexes in Australia: A Genealogist's Guide.* Published by the author, Brisbane, 1998.

York, Barry. *Empire and Race: The Maltese in Australia 1881–1949.* University of New South Wales Press, Kensington, NSW, 1990.

Young, F. & Harris, D. *Birth, Death and Marriage Certificates in Australia.* AIGS, Blackburn, Vic., 1992.

Young, Faye & van Barneveld, Nicole. *Sources for Chinese Local History and Heritage in New South Wales.* Published by the authors, Kareela and Alexandria, NSW, 1997.

Arrival by Sea

Bateson, Charles. *The Convict Ships 1787–1868.* Brown Son & Ferguson, Glasgow, 1959.

Cannon, Michael. *Perilous Voyages to the New Land: Experiences of Australian Pioneer Families on the High Seas.* Today's Australia Publishing Co., Mornington, Vic., 1997.

Chuk, Florence. *The Somerset Years.* Pennard Hill Publications, Ballarat, Vic., 1987.

Cooke, Anthony. *Emigrant Ships: The Vessels Which Carried Emigrants Across the World, 1946–1972.* Carmania Press, London, 1992.

Hawkings, David. *Bound for Australia.* Library of Australian History, North Sydney, 1988.

Nicholson, Ian (comp.). *Log of Logs: A Catalogue of Logs, Journals, Shipboard Diaries, Letters and All Forms of Voyage Narratives 1788 to 1988.* Ian Nicholson, Yaroomba, Qld, vol. 1, 1990; vol. 2, 1993; vol. 3, 1999.

Num, Cora. *How to Find Shipping and Immigration Records in Australia.* C. Num, Canberra, 1996.

Parsons, Ronald. *Trying to Find a Seafaring Ancestor.* Gould Books, Gumeracha, SA, 1988.

Plowman, Peter. *Emigrant Ships to Luxury Liners.* University of New South Wales, Sydney, 1994.

Public Record Office of Victoria. *Coming South: Victorian Archives of Immigration 1839–1923, A Guide.* Public Record Office of Victoria, Melbourne, 1995.

Snelson, Adrian John. 'Liverpool Packets and Clippers to Australia'. *The Genealogist,* vol. viii, no. 1, March 1995, pp. 6–9.

Vine Hall, Nick. *Ships Pictures Index 1491–1991, An Index to Ships Pictures in Print.* On three microfiche. Published by the author.

Photography

Bradley, Alan. 'Improving Old Photographs with Your PC'. *Family Tree Magazine,* vol. 12, no. 1, November 1995, pp. 25, 26.

Davies, Alan & Stanbury, Peter. *The Mechanical Eye in Australia: Photography 1841–1900,* Oxford University Press, Melbourne, 1985.

Eastman Kodak Company. *Conservation of Photographs.* Eastman Kodak Co., Rochester, NY, 1985.

Frost, Lenore. *Dating Family Photos 1850–1920.* Published by the author, Essendon, Vic., 1992.

Pols, Robert. *Dating Old Family Photographs.* Federation of Family History Societies, Birmingham, 1992.

Social Histories

Adams, David (ed.). *The Letters of Rachel Henning.* Bulletin Newspaper Co. Pty Ltd, Sydney, 1952; new edn, Penguin, Ringwood, Vic., 1969.

Broome, Richard. *The Victorians: Arriving.* Fairfax Syme & Weldon Associates, McMahons Point, NSW, 1984.

Cannon, Michael. *Old Melbourne Town Before the Gold Rush.* Loch Haven Books, Main Ridge, Vic., 1991.

Cole, G. D. H. & Postgate, Raymond. *The Common People 1746–1946.* Methuen, London, 1938; new edition, 1946.

Cox, Jane. *London's East End: Life and Traditions.* Weidenfeld & Nicolson, London, 1995.

Dingle, Tony. *The Victorians: Settling.* Fairfax, Syme & Weldon Associates, McMahons Point, NSW, 1984.

Evans, Marcia. *The Place of the Rural Blacksmith in Parish Life 1500–1900 (With particular reference to Somerset and Dorset).* Published by Michelle Merrick on behalf of the Somerset and Dorset Family History Society, Weymouth, Dorset, 1998.

Evans, William (ed.). *Diary of a Welsh Swagman 1869–1894.* Macmillan, Melbourne, 1975.

Fauchery, Antoine. *Letters from a Miner in Australia.* Georgian House, Melbourne, 1969.

Fullerton, Mary. *Bark House Days.* S. J. Endacott, Melbourne, 1921; paperback edn, Melbourne University Press, Melbourne, 1964.

Harris, Alexander. *Settlers and Convicts, or Recollections of Sixteen Years' Labour in the Australian Backwoods.* London, 1847; reprinted Melbourne University Press, 1953; reprinted with new foreword, 1964.

Hasbach, W. *A History of the English Agricultural Labourer.* Frank Cass, London, 1966.

Hughes, Robert. *The Fatal Shore: A History of the Transportation of Convicts to Australia 1787–1868.* Collins Harvill, London, 1987.

Isaacs, Jennifer. *Pioneer Women of the Bush and Outback.* Lansdowne Press, Sydney, 1990.

Jurgensen, Manfred & Corkhill, Alan (eds). *The German Presence in Queensland Over the Last 150 Years.* Department of German, University of Queensland, Brisbane, 1988.

Kunz, Egon F. *Displaced Persons: Calwell's New Australians.* Australian National University Press, Sydney, 1988.

Marshall, Dorothy. *English people in the Eighteenth Century.* Longmans, Green & Co., London, 1956.

Mayhew, Henry. *London Labour and the London Poor.* Selections published as *Mayhew's London*, Spring Books, London, n.d.

Mourot, Suzanne. *This Was Sydney: A Pictorial History from 1788 to the Present Time.* Ure Smith, Sydney, 1969.

Nicholas, Stephen (ed.). *Convict Workers, Reinterpreting Australia's Past.* Cambridge University Press, Sydney, 1988.

O'Farrell, P. *The Irish in Australia.* New South Wales University Press, Kensington, NSW, 1987.

Organ, M. & Doyle, A. P. (comps) *Old Pioneers' Reminiscences of Illawarra (1830's–1920's).* Illawarra Historical Publications, Woonona, NSW, 1989.

Priestley, Susan. *The Victorians: Making Their Mark.* Fairfax, Syme & Weldon Associates, McMahons Point, NSW, 1984.

Quennell, Peter (ed.). *Mayhew's Characters.* Selected from Henry Mayhew, *London Labour and the London Poor*, Spring Books, London, n.d.

Sherington, G. *Australia's Immigrants 1788–1988.* George Allen & Unwin, Sydney, 1990.

Sutherland, Alexander. *Victoria and Its Metropolis,* vols 1 and 2. McCarron Bird, Melbourne, 1888.

Thompson, Flora. *Lark Rise to Candleford.* Oxford University Press, London, 1945.

Twining, Andrew & Sandra. *Dictionary of Old Trades and Occupations.* 2nd edn. Twining's Secretarial, Woodcroft, SA, 1995.

Watts, Christopher J. *My Ancestor Was a Merchant Seaman.* Society of Genealogists, London, 1986.

Heirloom Arts and Crafts

Ioannou, Noris. *The Barossa Folk: Germanic Furniture and Craft Traditions in Australia.* Craftsman House, Roseville East, NSW, 1995.

Isaacs, Jennifer. *The Gentle Arts: 200 years of Australian Women's Domestic and Decorative Arts.* Lansdowne Press, Willoughby NSW, 1987.

IELTS Speaking Success:

Skills Strategies and Model Answers

About the author

I have been teaching English as a second language for over fifteen years in Taiwan and Australia, in language centers and universities. My area of specialization is teaching students how to pass the IELTS exam. I particularly enjoy teaching IELTS because I find it challenging to teach students the necessary skills and strategies that they need to pass, and I also find that my students are highly motivated – this is a joy for a teacher!

Other books in this series available at:

http://www.ieltsanswers.com/IELTS-Books.html

IELTS Task 2 Essay Writing

IELTS Task 1 Writing Academic Test

IELTS Task 1 Writing General Test

Ways to follow me!

http://www.ieltsanswers.com/

http://www.youtube.com/user/IELTSanswers

https://www.facebook.com/IELTSanswers

Copyright

Contents

1. INTRODUCTION

The IELTS speaking test lasts 11-14 minutes. The test is divided into three parts. The IELTS examiner will ask you different types of questions in each part as follows below.

Part 1: Short question and answers about familiar topics.

This part of the test lasts from 4 to 5 minutes and consists of questions about you and the country you are from. There is a maximum of three different sets of topics and each topic has a maximum of four questions. The first topic will be about whether you work or study, the place you are living in, or the place you are from. The other two topics are usually fairly straightforward topics such as hobbies, holidays, sports, and entertainment.

Part 2: Long Turn

You are given a card with a topic and then given 1 minute to prepare a 1 to 2 minute answer to this topic. You should try to talk for 2 minutes if you are able. Topics include describing or commenting on a person, place, object, activity, or experience. The topic also has sub-topics, which are provided to assist you to plan your response. The examiner may ask one or two rounding-off questions at the end of this part of the test. These should be answered briefly.

Part 3: Discussion

This part of the test lasts from 4 to 5 minutes and consists of questions roughly based on the topic area of the Part 2: Long Turn. Questions typically ask you to compare, analyze, speculate, or give your opinion on the given topic. In this part the examiner may push you hard to see the limits of your ability.

Overview of the three parts of the test

PART	REQUIREMENT
Part One General questions 4-5 Minutes	Answer up to four questions for three topics . Try to speak for about 2-4 sentences for each question.
Part Two Long Turn 3-4 Minutes	1. The examiner will hand you a card with a topic on it. 2. You have one minute to prepare for the topic. 3. Speak for one to two minutes. [Longer answers are need for higher scores!]
Part Three 4-5 Minutes	A discussion based on Part Two. This normally takes the form of the examiner asking a series of questions related to your topic in Part Two.

1.1 GRADING

Your speaking test is graded and marked from 1-9 in accordance with the four key criteria shown below:

The four criteria are explained in more detail in the sections following the tables. You can also refer to my YouTube videos for further explanation of the grading: https://www.youtube.com/watch?v=p3uSntDcKTU

Fluency and coherence:

6	7	8
Speaks at length, but some effort is required	Speaks at length without noticeable effort	speaks fluently; hesitation is usually to think of ideas and rarely to search for language
some loss of coherence due to repetition, self-correction, or hesitation	no loss of coherence due to repetition, self-correction, or hesitation	develops topics coherently and appropriately
some inappropriate linking words	wide range of linking words used	wide range of linking words used that assist to make information highly coherent

[Note that the criteria described in this section are based on the Public Version of the speaking band descriptors at: https://www.ielts.org/PDF/UOBDs_SpeakingFinal.pdf]

Pronunciation:

6	7	8
uses a range of intonation, stress, rhythm; but with mixed control and it is not maintained	Good usage of intonation, stress, rhythm; sustains flexible use of these features, with only occasional lapses	uses a wide range of pronunciation features flexibly and appropriately
can generally be understood throughout, though mispronunciation of individual words or sounds reduces clarity at times	easy to understand throughout; accent has minimal effect on intelligibility	easy to understand throughout; accent has no effect on intelligibility

Vocabulary: [lexical resource]

6	7	8
Vocabulary is sufficient to discuss topics at length and make the meaning clear in spite of some errors	vocabulary used flexibly to discuss a variety of topics	uses a wide range of vocabulary readily and flexibly to convey precise meaning
generally paraphrases successfully	uses paraphrases effectively	uses paraphrases effectively as required
insufficient advanced language is used to award 7	uses some less common and idiomatic vocabulary and shows some awareness of style and collocation, with some inappropriate choices	uses less common and idiomatic vocabulary skillfully, with rare inaccuracies

Grammar: [grammatical range and accuracy]

6	7	8
uses a mix of simple and complex structures, but with limited flexibility	flexibly uses a range of complex structures	uses a wide range of structures
may make frequent mistakes with complex structures, though these rarely cause comprehension problems	frequently produces error-free sentences	most sentences are error-free with only very occasional errors that are not repeated

Level 9 Grading Criteria

Fluency and coherence	speaks fluently like a native speaker and any repetition or self-correction is extremely rare; and any hesitation is to think of ideas and not to think of vocabulary or grammar speaks coherently using a wide range of appropriate cohesive features responses to question are relevant and developed fully
Pronunciation	uses a full range of pronunciation features with precision and subtlety sustains flexible use of pronunciation features throughout can be understood effortlessly
Lexical resource	uses vocabulary with full flexibility and precision for all topics uses idiomatic language naturally and accurately
Grammatical range and accuracy	uses a full range of structures naturally and appropriately produces consistently accurate structures apart from 'slips' characteristic of native speaker speech

FLUENCY AND COHERENCE:

Fluency is about your ability to speak at a normal speed without excessive hesitation and restarting of words or phrases. **Coherence** refers to your speaking being easy to understand. In order to score highly you need to show willingness to talk at length and develop your topic, use **connectives** and **linking words**, avoid pauses and restarts.

Speaking speed

In order to score well, you need to speak at a good speed. This can be challenging when speaking in a foreign language. In order to improve this become familiar with the way the test is conducted, and the types of questions that get asked, so that you are able to respond in a quicker way. In addition, you do not have to speak quickly throughout the whole test you just need to show that you are able to speak at a good speed in parts of the test. Therefore, in areas where you are more comfortable try to speak at a quicker speed to show this ability to the examiner, and in parts that are a bit more challenging you might have to slow down a little.

Hesitations [pauses]

Try to avoid having hesitations in the middle of sentences. These types of hesitations suggest to the examiner that you are trying to think of the necessary words or grammar to complete the sentence. Hesitations at the start of sentences are not as serious as they may be a result of trying to think of ideas for your response to the question. For this reason it is better to hesitate at the start of a sentence rather than in the middle of it.

Transitions and Linking phrases

Transitions are words or phrases that suggest a change in direction to the listener. These include phrases like: *in addition, however, consequently*. These words increase coherence because the examiner is able to clearly know that you have changed topic or the direction of the topic you are talking about. To increase your score use a wide range of these and don't repeat any phrases excessively.

PRONUNCIATION:

Your grade is influenced by the level to which your accent makes it difficult to understand what you are saying, and also the degree to which you use language features of a native speaker such as **chunking, stress, and intonation**.

Specific sounds

Many candidates have errors with specific sounds such as: *th, w, v, r, l, long vowel sounds [name].*

If you think you have these kinds of errors then ask a teacher or at least a native speaker their opinion. And if you do have these errors they are definitely going to have an impact on your score for pronunciation. You must get rid of them! You must practice saying them correctly... and practice doing it every day. This is because our pronunciation is based on habits. We speak without thinking about our actual pronunciation. Therefore if you have a bad habit of mispronouncing a sound you need lots and lots of repetition of saying that sound correctly in order to create a new habit. Bad habits are hard to change!

Chunking

Chunking is how words are characteristically grouped together in spoken segments. You can think of these as being like clauses or sentences when we write. Between these 'chunks' you should have pauses at the appropriate places. Think of a comma when speaking as a short pause, and a full-stop is a longer pause including a breath. Each chunk is an idea and the pauses help the listener to know when you are moving onto a new idea. One of the best ways to improve your chunking is to notice the way native speakers naturally do this. Watching movies is a good way to achieve this!

Stress of syllables and words and sentences

Stress has to do with where speakers put the emphasis on particular syllables or words. In English every word has one of the syllables emphasized more than the others [PHOtograph, phoTOgrapher and photoGRAPHIC.] If you incorrectly stress syllables of words, then it can make it difficult for the listener to understand what you're saying. A lack of stress at the sentence level can make your speech sound flat and make it difficult for the examiner to catch the key point of the sentence. As with chunking, one of the best ways to improve this is to notice the way native speakers naturally do this. You also need to understand how altering the stress of words in sentences changes the meaning of the sentence:

I didn't say <u>HE</u> stole the money = I think someone else stole the money

I didn't say he <u>STOLE</u> the money = I think he didn't steal the money...maybe he borrowed it.

Intonation

As with stress above, if you speak without any intonation your speech will sound flat and boring to the examiner. Intonation is about how the tone of the voice rises and falls during speech. This intonation needs to be done naturally or it can have the influence of lowering your score. Essentially, if the intonation occurs in the wrong place or in the wrong way it will lower your score for pronunciation. For instance, we usually end a statement with a falling tone. A rising tone is often used when asking a question that is expected to result in a yes or no answer. This is probably one of the hardest aspects of learning English, and as a result it can be one of the factors that can prevent a score of eight. As with other elements of pronunciation the only real way to make progress here is by observing the way that native speakers naturally use intonation. Actively watching movies and actively noticing the intonation of native speakers is very important.

VOCABULARY: [lexical resource]

To score highly you must use higher level words, pay attention to **collocation** (which are words that go together). In addition, control your **word endings** (use the correct form of a word such as noun, verb, or adjective). As well is this, you should try to show ability to **paraphrase** (rephrase words) and use **colloquial language** (conversational style language). Show precision with vocabulary by modifying your verbs with adverbs [*extremely* busy] and nouns with adjectives [*magnificent* city]

Errors with word choices

Errors with word choices lower your score according to how frequently they occur, whether they are repeated errors or just isolated errors, and also depending on how seriously they interfere with communication. Try to avoid words you are unsure of. However, you do need to show talent to the examiner, so use more advanced language where possible. Remember it is a language test!

Errors with word forms

This is an error where you use the correct word, but not the correct form of the word. For example, a noun where a verb is needed ("You need to ~~management~~ manage your business"). These errors are less serious than the errors with word choices, but still lower your score. If you know you have frequent errors with any aspects such as confusing adverbs and adjectives then try to work on reducing these errors by doing quizzes and reviewing the rules.

Lack of talent

In order to get beyond six requires that you show the examiner some advanced language such as idiomatic language or topic-based language. If you have lots of time before your exam, then learn language related to a wide range of topics. I'm also a big fan of learning idiomatic language because it can be applied to a wide range of topics. My main suggestion here is that rather than trying to learn lots of new words and phrases you focus on learning a few well so that you are able to use them effectively in the exam. This is covered in detail in Chapter 6 and 7.

GRAMMAR: [Grammatical Range and Accuracy]

To score highly you need to avoid grammatical errors, such as with articles and prepositions and sentence order especially when they make your speaking difficult to understand and also use a variety of sentence types (simple, compound, complex, passive). Using lots of complex sentences is particularly important. These are sentences that have a dependant and independent clause. Grammar is covered in detail in Chapter 8.

Use complex sentences

To score well for grammar requires you to use a wide range of sentence types. Especially, complex sentences which are sentences with a dependent and independent clause. As with my advice regarding vocabulary, I suggest you don't try to learn too many types of sentences. Instead focus on learning a few and learning them really well. My two top suggestions are learning how to use conditional phrases; [if phrases] and relative pronouns [who, which, that, when], which enable you to add extra information about the subject of the sentence. This is covered in more detail in Chapter 8.

Tenses

For the most part you can limit the number of errors with tenses by just sticking to the tense of the question. If the examiner is asking you a question about your childhood then it is likely that your answer is going to be in the past tense. When you read the Part Two question card you should think about what tenses you need to use in your answer.

Word order

This type of error is very serious and easily noticed by the examiner. A common cause is due to differences in the sentence structure between your native language and the English language. It is a good idea to become aware of what the main differences are. You may need to frequently review these differences.

Prepositions and Articles

Errors with prepositions [in on at]; and articles [a, an, the] are minor and are likely to be not noticed or forgiven by examiners. However, if you frequently make mistakes with these then it will start to limit your score for grammar. Repeated errors make it difficult to get to 7 and almost impossible to get to 8. As with other aspects of grammar you need to review the rules and perhaps do some quizzes to become more familiar with them.

1.2 PREPARING FOR YOUR TEST

To improve your score in the IELTS speaking section, you should focus on the following areas:

1. Understanding how the speaking test is graded
2. Preparing for and practicing common questions that are asked
3. Learning ways of structuring your answers to extend your answers and to improve your coherence
4. Learning to paraphrase, which is when you use a phrase to explain a word you can't think of
5. Improving your pronunciation, and ensuring you can make all sounds correctly (th, l, r, long vowel sounds) and also getting natural sounding stress, intonation, and connected speech.
6. Improving spoken grammar by correcting any frequent errors, and learning to use a couple of complex sentence structures such as conditional phrases or relative pronouns.
7. Broadening your vocabulary especially by building common phrases that can be used for a variety of responses, such as connectives and linking words and idiomatic language.

2. GENERAL STRATEGIES

This section introduces strategies that can be used in all three parts of the test. The strategies will be briefly introduced in this section, and then the way to use these strategies will be explained under each part of the test.

BAD EXAMPLE OF A SPEAKING TEST:

Do you like to watch movies: **yes**

What sort? **Drama**

Do you have a particular favorite? **no**

Do you have a favorite actor? **no**

It is really important to produce language in the test to get a good score for all four grading criteria. The example above fails to do this. It is very short so the examiner is not able to see any fluency. Very few words have been spoken so it is difficult to assess pronunciation, vocabulary, and grammar.

The strategies outlined below can be used in all three parts of the test to extend your answer. You may also like to see my YouTube video on this topic. It is my most popular video with hundreds of thousands of viewers!
https://www.youtube.com/watch?v=j4VYB-hXNkw

Extend your answers

The strategies below are used to answer the question:

"What kind of food do you like?"

1. DIVIDE INTO 2 OR 3 PARTS:

This strategy involves giving 2 or 3 reasons for your answer, as follows:

Well, there are three kinds of food that I'm really keen on.

The one I like best is *Italian food* because...

I also really like to eat *Korean food* as it's very...

I'm also kind of partial to *Mexican food* because it is...

Well, there are three kinds of** food that I'm really keen on.* ***The one I like best *is Italian food* because I am a big fan of pasta. ***I also really like*** *to eat Korean food as it's* very healthy and flavorsome. ***I'm also kind of partial*** *to Mexican food because* it is so hot and spicy.

2. GENERAL TO SPECIFIC

This strategy involves giving a general reason for your answer, and then explaining it more specifically, and even giving an example as follows:

> **Well, I'd have to say that I'm a big fan of** seafood. **In particular**, I really like to eat Japanese seafood because it's always so fresh. **For instance**, sashimi is delicious because the raw fish is so flavorsome.

general = seafood

specific = Japanese seafood

example = sashimi

3. DEPENDS: describing different situations

This strategy involves giving different reasons for different situations for your answer, as follows:

> *I think it **depends** really.*
>
> ***If** I'm working **I prefer** to get something like fast food such as McDonalds because I only have a short break.*
>
> ***But, if** I'm out with friends **I would rather have** something more exotic such as Thai food or Indian food.*

4. CONCESSION:

This strategy involves making a main point and then giving a counterargument to it, as follows:

> *Well, recently I'd have to say that I have been enjoying eating steak and each time I feel like a steak I go to Outback Steak House because the steaks there are huge.* ***However,*** *I think that it may not be all that healthy to eat so much red meat, as I've heard it can lead to high levels of cholesterol.*

5. AVOIDANCE:

This strategy involves not directly answering the question at first, and then answering it, as follows:

> ***Well, to be honest, I don't really have*** *a favorite food;* ***but I guess that if I had to choose one,*** *then I'd go for something like pizza– you know, I just love all that cheese and tomato sauce.*

Avoiding phrase = *Well, to be honest, I don't really have...*

Answering phrase = *but I guess that if I had to choose one...*

Speak at a variable speed rate

Your grade for fluency requires that you speak at a good speed. You must demonstrate this to the examiner, but you do NOT need to speak quickly throughout the entire exam. Vary your speed as follows:

Slow down when you...

1. reach a difficult area or are unsure of what you will say
2. want to emphasize something
3. are using high level language to make the examiner notice it

Speed-up when you...

1. are comfortable with the topic and what you are saying
2. are giving less important information

Use redundant language

Redundant language is words that don't have any real meaning such as: **oh, well, actually**. Research shows that native speakers use lots of redundant language, but non-native speakers rarely use it. So use it to be more native-like!

Use punctuation

When we speak we use punctuation. Spoken punctuation takes the form of pauses and these pauses act like punctuation in writing. They guide the listener. A short pause signals a new clause. A longer pause with a breath of air signals a new idea. And, an even longer pause signals a change of topic.

comma = short pause

full-stop = longer pause with a breath of air

paragraph= even longer pause

Use lots of adjectives and adverbs

Adjectives make things more interesting. There is a difference between eating a nice dessert, and eating a bowl of the freshest, sweetest fruit, topped with a delicious chocolate sauce! Adverbs allow you to explain an activity more precisely. Again, there is a difference between running and running swiftly.

Adjectives and adverbs increase the precision of your language and this increases your score for vocabulary.

We can also use adverbs with adjectives to add even more precision and show even more talent with vocabulary to the examiner. The following adverbs are organized from providing weak modification to strong modification of an adjective:

slightly tiring

fairly tiring

particularly tiring

really tiring

extremely tiring

Listen carefully for key words in the questions

In English the key words of questions usually come at the very start of the sentence. If you miss this word, you may struggle to know what the examiner is asking. Some common question words are listed below:

Question	Function	Example
what	asking for information about something	What types of shops do you like?
when	asking about time	When do you usually go shopping?
where	asking about a place	Where do you like to go shopping?
which	asking about a choice	Which is more important to you the quality or the price of a product?
who	asking about other people	Who do you usually go shopping with?

Entering the test room

When the time comes for your speaking test you will enter a room with a table and two chairs and usually sit opposite the examiner. In theory, your test does not begin until after the examiner has checked your identification (passport). In reality though, as soon as you enter the door the examiner is forming an opinion about you!

You may feel nervous. It's pointless to tell the examiner you feel nervous as they hear this often. The best thing is to try to hide the nervousness. Try to show confidence and calmness. Try to show the examiner that you are confident to speak English. It can be helpful to smile at the examiner to establish warmth between you. Overall, you don't really need to worry about doing anything because the examiner is experienced and will guide you through the process of the exam.

Before your test starts the examiner needs to record some details such as the date and time. You should stay silent during this. However, you can use this as an opportunity to get accustomed to the examiner's accent and pronunciation. Essentially, you can be tuning your listening to make it easier to catch the questions when the examiner starts asking them.

The examiner also needs to check your identification and will ask you a few questions such as: *What is your full name? Where are you from? Can I see your identification please?* The test has started at this point, but just give simple answers to these questions. This is not the time to be giving extended answers. You will frustrate the examiner if you do this!

After the examiner has finishing checking your identification the examiner will say something like *"Now, I would like to ask you a few questions about yourself"* and the examiner will introduce a topic and start asking you questions about it.

3. PART ONE: QUESTIONS ON FAMILIAR TOPICS

Part One	Requirement	Suggestions
4-5 Minutes	Answer up to 4 questions about 3 different topics. The examiner can repeat the question one time. You can ask the meaning of a word but the examiner cannot rephrase the whole question.	1. Full response – not just yes/no 2. Try to speak for about 2 or 4 sentences for each question. 3. Focus on language not ideas or real opinions.

Requirement

This part of the test lasts from 4 to 5 minutes and consists of questions about you and the country you are from. In this part of the test the examiners read questions directly from their examiner's book. There is a maximum of three different sets of topics and each topic has a maximum of four questions. The first topic will be about whether you work or study, the place you are living in, or the place you are from. The other two topics are usually fairly straightforward topics such as hobbies, holidays, sports, or entertainment.

Procedure

1. After checking your ID the examiner will start Part One of the test.

2. The examiner will say: "*Now, I am going to ask you a few general questions*"

3. The examiner will ask three or four questions according to different topics. The examiner will then introduce the topic by saying something like:
"Now, let's talk about where you live"

Make sure you pay attention to the keywords the examiner uses to introduce the topic. This is because you will have three or four questions based on this topic and you want to be clear what the topic is about.

4. The examiner will ask you three or four questions based on the topic, such as:

Do you live in a house or an apartment?
Which room do you like the most in your home?
In the future, what sort of home would you like to live in?

5. When the examiner has finished asking you 3 or 4 questions based on the topic, the examiner will move onto the next topic, by saying something like:

"Now let's talk about your hobbies and interests"

6. After three sets of topics [each with three or four questions] the examiner will finish Part One and move onto Part Two of the test. Note that Part One of the test lasts 4 to 5 minutes. If you give longer answers, it is possible that you may only get two topics. This could be an advantage because there is less chance of getting an unfamiliar topic!

3.1 STRATEGIES

1: Expansion

Expansion is making something bigger. In IELTS it is good to give expanded answers to questions. This shows that you understand the question, and gives you more chance to show your language ability and get a higher score. This is illustrated below:

QUESTION: Do you like riding bicycles?

BAD RESPONSE: "*Yes*"

BETTER RESPONSE: *"Yes, because it's fun, good for health, and doesn't cost a lot."*

GREAT RESPONSE:

> Well, I like to ride bikes for a few reasons. **The main reason** I like to cycle is that I think it is really fun and it is a good way to go sightseeing. **I'd also like to point-out** that riding a bike is very good for my health because it can help me to lose weight. **I would also like to add** that recently I haven't been riding my bike much, as I am quite busy at work.

You should refer back to Chapter 2 about the different ways to expand your answers which include:

1. Dividing your response into two or three parts:

2. Explaining something from general terms to specific and maybe giving an example

3. Depends: describing different situations

4. Concession: making a main argument and then giving a concession to it

5. Avoidance: not directly answering the question at first and then answering it

2: Show language

QUESTION: What colors do you like?

BAD RESPONSE: *"I like green and blue."*
[This answer has no advanced vocabulary.]

BETTER RESPONSE: *"My favorite colors are **light green** and **navy blue**."*
[This answer is more precise and precision increases your score for vocabulary.]

EVEN BETTER RESPONSE:

Well, My favorite color is **magenta**, I guess that's because I'm really into bright and bold colors. I also like **turquoise**, I find that a very relaxing peaceful color that reminds me of the ocean.

This answer uses some less common colors, and can impress the examiner with your vocabulary about colors. It also includes the idiomatic expression *"I'm really into."* This means to like something.

3. Buy time to think

There are a few ways to buy some time to think of your answer. Note that you shouldn't use any particular method too often! Use a range of these methods below:

Repeat the question: One way to do this is to rephrase the words of the question *"Oh, so you're asking about my favorite color."*

Ask the examiner to repeat the question: In Part One of the test the examiner is permitted to repeat the question one time. Note that the question cannot be repeated a second time and the examiner is not supposed to rephrase the question. You could ask the question to be repeated just so that you can have time to think of how to

respond to it. Essentially, while the examiner is repeating the question you are thinking of what you can say. Doing this once won't lower your score, but obviously if you do it often it will lower it!

You can use language like: *"I'm sorry I didn't quite catch that...could you please repeat the question."*

Use some memorized phrases to start your answer: if you memorize a few phrases, while you are saying these phrases you can be thinking of how you will actually respond to the question. Some phrases could be:

"Well, that's a really interesting question"

"Oh I'm not too sure about that... Let me think for a minute...Oh yes it is...."

"With regards to your question, I guess I would have to say that....."

4. If you don't understand the question

If you do not hear or understand the question, the examiner can repeat each question one time. If you do not understand the meaning of a word you can ask the examiner to explain that word. However, the examiner is not able to rephrase the whole question if you are not able to understand it, except in Part Three. If you didn't answer the question it doesn't mean you've failed your exam, but you wouldn't want to do this more than once or twice. If you can't understand the question then tell the examiner. The worst situation is that you stay silent and make the examiner unsure about whether you will give an answer or not. This makes both you and the examiner uncomfortable. Another choice is to listen out carefully for key words in the question and then try to give some sort of response to the question. This is a bit of a gamble! Do you feel lucky?

3.2 TYPES OF QUESTIONS

Note that this section will use the general strategies outlined in Chapter 2. More than one of the strategies could be used for any particular question. The purpose of this section is to show you how to actually use these strategies to answer questions.

The following types of questions are outlined below:

Question Type	Strategy
description	divide into 2 or 3 parts
types of	divide into 2 or 3 parts
liking	general to specific
disliking	general to specific
habits	depends
yes/no	depends
"Wh" questions	concession
when you were a child	concession
in the future	avoidance
comparing	avoidance

1. DESCRIPTION QUESTIONS

STRATEGY: divide your response into two or three parts

STRUCTURE: point 1 + point 2 + point 3

SAMPLE QUESTION: "*Tell me something about your hometown?*"

> **Well,** I come from Taipei and I have lived here all my life. **I'd like to begin by saying that** it's the capital of Taiwan and also the cultural center. **On top of that I can also add that** It's very crowded, maybe even one of most congested cities in Asia I guess. The roads are so jammed that even the locals have problems finding their way around! **Finally, I'd also like to mention** that it offers splendid examples of contemporary architecture. Actually some of the most renowned landmarks are in the middle of Taipei, such as Taipei 101, the second tallest building in the world.

USEFUL LANGUAGE

Starting-off (redundant language)

ok, then; actually; alright; well, you know;

Point 1

I'd like to begin by saying ...

The first thing I'd like to mention is ...

The main thing you need to know is ...

Point 2

On top of that I can also add that ...

Another interesting point ...

Not only that, but ________is also exceedingly .....

Point 3

Finally, I'd also like to mention ....

And, I shouldn't forget to mention that...

I guess I could also say that (it's) sort-of ....

Practice Questions:

1. What sort of work do you do?
2. What does your house look like?
3. What does your neighborhood look like?
4. What does your city/town look like?
5. What sort of clothes do you like to wear?
6. Describe a city you would like to visit?
7. Describe a country you would like to visit?
8. Describe a park you have visited?

2. "TYPES OF" QUESTIONS

STRATEGY: divide into 2 or 3 parts

STRUCTURE: general statement + type 1 + type 2

SAMPLE QUESTION:

"Tell me about the different types of public transportation in your city."

> **Well, you know there's quite a mixed variety of** public transportation in my city. **I think the most common one** is buses because they seem to go everywhere. **In addition**, the trains **are also extremely popular** for those people who are lucky enough to live near a train station.

USEFUL LANGUAGE

Rephrasing types: kinds, sorts, variety, range of, array

Useful phrases to start [General statement]

There's quite a mixed variety of ...

There's a fairly wide range of ...

There's quite a diverse mixture of ...

Type 1

I think the most common one is...

The main one is....

The first one that comes to mind is...

Type 2

In addition, X ...is also extremely popular

Another kind is ...

Not only that, but X ...is also exceedingly.....

Type 3 [if needed]

And I shouldn't forget to mention that...

I guess I could also say that...

Finally, I'd also like to mention...

Practice

1. What kinds of restaurants are popular in your country?
2. What types of shops can be found in your local area?
3. What types of things do people collect in your country?
4. How do you spend your free time?
5. How do people spend their free time in your country?
6. What sorts of TV programs do you watch?
7. What sorts of TV programs are popular in your country?
8. What sort of things do people collect in your country?

3. LIKING

STRATEGY: general to specific

STRUCTURE: general statement + more precise statement + reason

SAMPLE ANSWER

"What kind of animals do you like?"

> **Well, in general I would say <u>I'm pretty fond of</u>** small animals. **In particular, <u>I'm really keen on</u>** cats and dogs; **and, I guess this is because** we often kept them when I was growing up, and they were good companions for me.

Rephrasing "liking"

I'm pretty fond of...

I'm really keen on...

I'm a big fan of...

I'm extremely passionate about...

General statement

Well, in general I would say ...

Generally speaking...

Overall, I think that...

More precise statement

In particular,

Specifically,....

To be more precise...

Reason

And I guess this is probably because...

I think this is due to the fact that...

The reason for this is because...

Practice:

1. What do you like about your hometown?
2. What do you like about your job/studies?
3. What sort of music do you like?
4. What sorts of books do you like reading?
5. What type of movies do you like?
6. Where do you like to shop?
7. What types of food do you like?
8. What types of free time activities do you like?

4. DISLIKING

STRATEGY: general to specific

STRUCTURE: General dislike + more precise statement + reason

SAMPLE ANSWER

"Is there anything you don't like about your hometown?"

> **Generally speaking...I'd have to say** that I'm not really fond of the weather. **To be more specific**, I really can't stand the summer months. **I think this is due to fact that** it is always humid, so it makes me feel quite hot and sweaty!

Rephrasing "Disliking"

I really can't stand...

I'm not really fond of...

I'm not much of a fan of...

... simply gets on my nerves.

General statement

Generally speaking...

Well, in general I would say ...

Overall, I think that...

More precise statement

To be more specific...

To be more precise...

Specifically,....

Reason

I think this is due to the fact that...

And I guess this is probably because...

The reason for this is because...

Practice

1. Is there anything you don't like about your hometown?
2. Is there anything you don't like about job/studies?
3. Is there any food you don't like?
4. Are there any clothes that you don't like?
5. Are there any colors that you don't like?
6. What type of weather do you dislike?
7. What type of noises do you dislike?
8. What type of movies do you dislike?

5. Habits

STRATEGY: Depends

STRUCTURE: Depends + if preference 1 + if preference 2
[note that the structure uses conditional clauses which can increase your score for grammar]

SAMPLE QUESTION

What do you usually do at the weekend?

> **Well, it is contingent upon** how I feel.
>
> **If I'm** exhausted after working all week **I prefer to** do something relaxing like chilling out on the sofa with a good book.
>
> **But, if** I feel energetic **I would rather** do something more exciting like go hiking or camping.

LANGUAGE

Depends

Well, it is contingent upon...

I think it depends really.

Well, to be honest, I would have to say that it really depends.

Preference 1

If I'm... I prefer to...

Usually, I prefer...

Sometimes, I prefer to...

Preference 2

But, if I... I would rather...

Although, sometimes I would rather...

However, if I have...

Note: To describe past habits we can also use "used to' or 'would", with an appropriate adverb of frequency:

When I was a child, my brother often ***used to*** *take me fishing.*

My mother ***would always*** *tell me a story to get me to fall asleep*

Practice

1. What do you usually do on the Internet?
2. Where do you usually study?
3. What do you like to do for holidays?
4. When do you go shopping?
5. What do you do to relax?
6. How much sleep do you usually get?
7. How do you celebrate festivals in your country?
8. How much TV do you watch?

6. Yes/no questions

STRATEGY: Depends

STRUCTURE: Depends + preference 1 + preference 2

SAMPLE QUESTION

Do you eat healthy food?

Well, to be honest, I would have to say that it really depends. Usually I prefer to eat something quick and convenient such as instant noodles because I am very busy with my studies. **Although, sometimes I would rather** spend a little more time and cook something healthier such as a rice and veggies *.

[*veggies = vegetables].

LANGUAGE

Depends

Well, to be honest, I would have to say that it really depends.

Well, it is contingent upon...

I think it depends really.

Preference 1

Usually I prefer...

If I'm... I prefer to...

Sometimes I prefer to...

Preference 2

Although, sometimes I would rather...

But, if I... I would rather...

However, if I have...

Practice Questions

1. Do you like the weather in your country?

2. Do you enjoy eating food from other countries?

3. Do you enjoy your work/studies?

4. Are there enough festivals in your country?

5. Do you enjoy going shopping?

6. Do you like to get up early?

7. Do you play or watch any sports?

8. Are you planning any vacations?

7. "WH" Questions

[these are questions that start with the words: **who, where, why, what,** and **how**]

STRATEGY: CONCESSION (making a main point and then giving a concession to it)

STRUCTURE: main point + concession

SAMPLE QUESTION

"What sort of restaurants do you usually eat at?"

> Well, recently I'd have to say that I have been enjoying eating steak and each time I feel like a steak I go to Outback Steak House, because the steaks there are huge. **Although, I suppose it could be argued that** it may not be all that healthy to eat so much red meat, as I've heard it can lead to high levels of cholesterol.

LANGUAGE

Concession

Although, I suppose it could be argued that...

However, I'm quite aware that...

Nevertheless, it is worth remembering that...

DIFFERENT TYPES OF "WH" QUESTIONS

QUESTION	FUNCTION	EXAMPLE
what	asking for information about something	What types of shops do you like?
when	asking about a time	When do you usually go shopping?
where	asking about a place	Where do you like to go shopping?
which	asking about a choice	Which is more important, the quality or the price of a product?
who	asking about other people	Who do you usually go shopping with?
why	asking for a reason	Why do you go with that person?

PRACTICE QUESTIONS

1. What do you do at the weekend?
2. When do you usually read?
3. Where do you usually go for holidays?
4. Which do you prefer, reading a book or watching T.V?
5. Who do you spend your evenings with?
6. When do you usually sleep?
7. Why do you work/study there?

8. How often do you play or watch sports?

8. When you were a child

STRATEGY: Concession

STRUCTURE: main point + concession

SAMPLE QUESTION

What games did you enjoy playing when you were a child?

> Well, I was always very keen on playing video games. I spent almost all my free time playing them. **However, I'm quite aware that...** It wasn't the healthiest way to spend my childhood and perhaps it's contributed to my myopia*.
>
> [* myopia is an eye problem of short-sightedness]

Concession

However, I'm quite aware that...

Nevertheless, it is worth remembering that...

Although, I suppose it could be argued that...

Practice Questions

1. What colors did you like when you were a child?
2. Did you like to wear bright clothing when you were a child?
3. Did you like any sports when you were a child?
4. What type of food did you like when you were a child?
5. Did you have a lot of friends when you were a child?
6. What types of indoor activities did you do when you were a child?

9. In the future

STRATEGY: avoidance [not directly answering the question]

STRUCTURE: avoiding phrase + answer to the question

SAMPLE ANSWER

"Where would you like to go for your next vacation?"

> **Well, to be honest, I don't really have** a clear plan **but I guess that I will probably** go overseas to some exotic location like Nepal because I'm really into hiking and exploring new areas.

Avoiding phrase

Well, to be honest, I don't really have...

Actually, I'm not really sure about that.

Oh, I've never really thought about that.

answer to the question

... but I guess that I will probably...

... but I guess that if I had to choose one, then I'd...

... perhaps the end result will be that

Practice Questions

1. Would you like to learn a new language in the future?
2. In the future, what sort of home would you like to live in?
3. In the future, do you think people will use mobile phones more than now?
4. In the future, do you think people will be healthier or less healthy than now?
5. Do you think your hometown will change much in the future?
6. Do you think you will have more free time in the future?

10. Comparing

STRATEGY: avoidance [not directly answering the question]

STRUCTURE: avoiding phrase + answer to the question

SAMPLE ANSWER

"Do you prefer to read a book or watch TV?"

> **Oh, I like them both so it's hard to choose only one. But I guess that if I had to choose one, then I would** rather read a novel **and the main reason for this is because I slightly prefer** the storylines of novels to TV.
>
> [Note: the comparative words are underlined]

Avoiding phrase

Oh, I like them both, so it's hard to choose only one.

Well, to be honest, I don't really have...

Actually, I'm not really sure about that.

Oh, I've never really thought about that.

Answer to the question

... but I guess that I will probably...

... but I guess that if I had to choose one, then I'd...

... perhaps the end result will be that

Comparatives

I slightly prefer..

I'd much rather

I enjoy X much more than Y

Practice Questions

1. Do you prefer studying in the morning or in the evening?
2. Do you prefer taking photos with your phone or with a camera?
3. Would you rather live in a place with hot weather or cold weather?
4. Do you like to take lots of short holidays or one long holiday?
5. Do you prefer to write by hand or using a computer?
6. Do you prefer to send text messages or to call someone

3.3 COMMON TOPICS

There are a wide range of topics that can be asked at any particular time. As well as this the questions used in the test change frequently, so it's difficult to predict exactly what topics you will receive.

Note that the first topic you receive is likely to be about your work or study, your home, where you are from, or where you are living now. In this case it makes sense to be really well prepared to answer these questions. I am amazed when I have students that don't know how to describe their job or pronounce their job title correctly! Or, have no ideas about their hometown. Prepare well for these sets of questions, so that you can get your test off to a good start. This will make a favorable impression with the examiner and also help you to relax.

Important note: Do you work or are you a student?

If the examiner asks whether you work or study, it makes things difficult for the examiner if you don't specify one clearly. I suggest that if you are working and studying you talk about the one that is the easiest for you to talk about and use higher-level language. And, if you're not doing anything, I suggest you talk about what you were doing most recently. If you want to avoid having to talk in the past tense, then just pretend that you're still doing it! It's okay to pretend in the exam. According to one of my Buddhist students, even though it is not okay to lie...it's okay to tell stories!

Sample questions and answers

...Let's talk about your job...

What kind of work do you do?

Well now, I'm an athletic trainer in a small gym, and I also have to help out at the reception desk and also in the retail shop we run. I guess you can say that I have to wear many hats. [The underlined phrases are explained in the section below regarding idiomatic language]

Why did you choose that kind of work?

Ok, that's quite an easy question. It's because I've always been keen on sports, so when I was trying to find a job, I decided to look for something I'm familiar with. Luckily I found a golden opportunity at the gym just down the road from my house.

Did you have to do any training or study for this job?

Well, for this type of job there is no formal training. I mostly learnt from the other staff and through hands-on experience.

Is there anything you don't like about your job?

Well there are some things I don't like, but it's not related to the job itself. I mean this job is great, I love to guide people about how to exercise, it's meaningful. However, the one thing I don't like is that there is not much team spirit amongst my co-workers. I guess you could say that my gym has low workplace morale. I think this is the only thing bothering me.

Nouns	Meaning
deadline	to finish a project by a specific time
occupation	type of job
overtime	needing to work beyond your normal working hours
perks	extra benefits you get from a job
shift work	working at different times of the day
social skills	the ability to communicate and interact well with others
morale	team spirit

Verbs	Meaning
be involved in	to be doing
concentrate	to focus attention towards an activity or problem
help out	help [phrasal verb]
persevere	to not give up. To keep doing something.
procrastinate	to delay or put off doing something

Adjectives	Meaning
casual	relaxed and not following strict rules
exhausting	tiring
formal	observation of conventional forms and rules
hectic	busy
inspirational	motivating
monotonous	boring
passionate	intense or strong emotional feeling about something [positive]

Idioms	Meaning
golden opportunity	an excellent opportunity *An internship at Google would be a <u>golden opportunity</u>.*
hands-on	to learn by actually doing. *We can get <u>hands-on</u> experience by actually doing things.*

on the go	busy *I've been <u>on the go</u> all week so I haven't had a chance to play golf.*
wear many hats	someone who has to do many different types of tasks or roles. *My job description is very broad, so I have to <u>wear many hats</u>.*
work flat out	work very hard *Sometimes I have to <u>work flat out</u> to finish my work on time.*

Practice questions about your job

1. What kind of job do you do?
2. Was it easy to get this job?
3. Did you like your first day at work?
4. Why did you choose this kind of work?
5. Have you always wanted to do this type of work?
6. How long have you been doing this job?
7. How long will you continue to do this type of work?
8. Would you like to do a different job in the future?

Studies

Sample questions and answers

...let's talk about your studies...

Where are you studying?

I'm studying at Sydney University. It's a very prestigious university, and the lecturers are really demanding and give lots of assignments, so I often have to study <u>until the wee hours</u>. [Underlined words are explained below in the idioms section.]

Why did you choose to study there?

Actually I chose the school for a few reasons. Most importantly, I chose to study there because it has the most <u>up-to-date</u> knowledge in my area. As well as this, the University has a student centered approach, so I feel my learning needs are really taken care of.

Did you enjoy your first day there?

Yes, it was really great because I got to meet lots of fantastic new people. That first day was quite relaxing, but after that the course got really intense and I found that I had to <u>hit the books</u> every day just to keep up.

What would you like to do after you finish your studies?

Well I think it depends. I think that my course will help me to <u>set the stage for my future career</u>. I'd like to join one of the top five accounting companies, but if my grades aren't high enough I will go to work at my uncle's accounting firm.

Nouns	Meaning
nurture	to help grow or develop
pedagogy	the way of teaching including the instructional methods that are used
qualification	what someone gets when they graduate from school. For instance, a diploma is a qualification.
student centered education	a philosophy of education where the student is the central focus
the curriculum	the entire school program including course materials and testing of students. Everything that a school aims to teach.
tuition	the fees for studying a course

Verbs	Meaning
enroll	to join a class
graduate	to pass a course or level of study
interpret	to understand in a particular way. For example, we need to interpret the meaning of a painting.
revise	to review materials that have already been taught

Adjectives	Meaning
academic	relating to education especially universities.
multi-disciplinary	involving several different subjects or areas of study.
pedagogical	relating to teaching methods and principles.
prestigious	of high reputation
tertiary education	university or vocation school
vocational	concerns teaching the skills necessary for a particular job. This concept is often applied to trade schools. So if you are studying cooking or plumbing you are going to a vocational school.

Idioms	Meaning
hit the books:	to study hard *I have to hit the books because I have a 5,000 word essay due tomorrow.*
set the stage for	create conditions to allow something to happen in the future. *I think that my course will help set the stage for my future career.*
the wee hours	very early in the morning *I often have to study until the wee hours because my course has a really heavy work load.*
up-to-date	the most recent *I chose to study there because it has the most up-to-date knowledge in my area.*

Practice questions about your studies

1. What are you studying?
2. Why did you choose to study this?
3. Is it easy to study this?
4. Have you always wanted to study this?
5. Is there anything about your subject that you don't like?
6. How long will you continue to study this?
7. What do you hope to do in the future when you have finished your studies?
8. Who are more important to you, your teachers or your classmates?

Sample questions and answers

Let's talk about where you live...

Do you live in a house, or an apartment?

Oh, I live in a high-rise apartment complex in an up-market neighborhood on the east side of the city. [Underlined words are explained below in the idioms section.]

Do you like living there?

Yes I really do. Even though it's my uncle's house he really makes me feel at home. And it's a fantastic apartment complex because it includes a lot of facilities such as a swimming pool and a gymnasium. As well as that I have become friends with some of the neighbors and we often hang out together.

Which is your favorite room?

Oh, it's definitely the living room. I live on the 25th floor and it has lots of windows that give me a bird's eye view of the city. I love to sit on the sofa and drink my coffee in the morning and enjoy the fantastic view.

Is there anything you don't like about your home?

There are a couple of things. I guess the main thing is that it is quite an old apartment and it has become a bit run down. My uncle really needs to renovate his apartment. As well is this, it has really lofty ceilings and so it's difficult to keep the rooms warm in the cooler months.

Nouns	Meaning
apartment complex	an apartment building. Especially when there are multiple buildings.
architecture	the style of the design of a building
ceilings	the inside of the roof
detached house	a house that is separated from other houses by land
neighbors	the people who live next to or near someone
neighborhood	area that someone lives in

Verbs	Meaning
commute	regular travel. For instance, commuting to work every day
having access	being able to easily get somewhere or use something
reside	live. I reside in a five-storey building

Adjectives	**Meaning**
built-up	an area with many buildings, especially tall ones
cozy	comfortable
classic	old or traditional style
contemporary	modern
fantastic	wonderful, really good
lofty	tall; e.g. lofty ceilings
modest	not large or expensive
rooftop	something that is built on a roof [it has a rooftop garden]
spacious	lot of space inside [a spacious room]
well-appointed	attractive or expensive decoration and furniture

Idioms	Meaning
bird's eye view	a view from a high point *I live on the 25th floor, which gives me a <u>bird's eye view</u> of the city*
feel at home	To feel comfortable in a place *Even though it's my uncle's house he really makes me <u>feel at home</u>.*
run down	in bad condition *My neighborhood is not so good because many of the houses are owned by poor families and their houses are <u>run down</u> and need to be repaired.*
up-market	expensive *I live in an <u>up-market</u> neighborhood on the east side of the city*

Practice questions:

1. What sort of furniture does your home have?
2. How do you think your home could be improved?
3. How long have you been living there?
4. Do you think you will live there for a long time?
5. In the future what kind of home would you like to live in?
6. What do you like about the area where you live?
7. Is your neighborhood a good place for families with children?
8. What do you like about the rooms in your home?
9. Is there anything you don't like about your home?
10. What sort of home would you like to live in, in the future?

Sample questions and answers

...Let's talk about your hometown...

Tell me about the hometown you come from?

Well as you can probably guess I come from Taipei and I have lived here all my life. The first thing that most people notice about Taipei is that it's very crowded, and you know it's one of the biggest cities in Asia. It's so congested that there can be traffic jams at any time of the day! Another significant characteristic is that it offers splendid examples of contemporary architecture. Actually some of the world's most renowned landmarks are in the middle of Taipei, such as Taipei 101, the second tallest building in the world. [Underlined words are explained below in the idioms section.]

Is it a good place for young people?

It's a great place for a few reasons. One of the main ones is that it is a fun place to hang out with friends because we have access to lots of different types of entertainment. There are lots of different places to go to such as night markets and up-market cafes. As well as this it's a really convenient place to live because the public transportation is excellent and there are even free bicycles to ride around the city.

What would you like to change about your hometown?

Well if it's possible, it would be good to have more parks and green spaces. You know sometimes it feels a bit like a concrete jungle here because you just feel surrounded by tall buildings. Another thing would be to try to make the city a little bit less crowded. Sometimes the hustle and bustle of the city really gets to me.

Do you think your hometown will be better in the future?

Well I think that depends. If the local government can continue its plan to develop the subway system and reduce the traffic congestion I think it will be better. However, if the public transportation can't be increased quickly enough I think the traffic is going to get much worse... And this is going to make our daily commute much worse.

Nouns	**Meaning**
architecture	the character or style of buildings
downtown	the city centre
green spaces	parks, gardens and areas with trees, plants, or grass
landmarks	a highly noticeable building or place
subway system	an underground train system in a city
suburbs	the residential areas outside of the city centre
traffic congestion	traffic jams

Verbs	Meaning
commute	regular travel. For instance, commuting to work every day
have access	being able to easily get somewhere or use something
reside	live in
surrounded by	encircled [the house is surrounded by trees= the house has trees all around it]

Adjectives	Meaning
built-up	an area with many tall buildings
contemporary	modern
distinctive	clear and easy to notice [Taipei 101 is a distinctive landmark]
industrial	relating to industry. An industrial area has lots of factories.
residential	relating to living. A residential area has lots of homes.
splendid	wonderful, amazing
sprawling	built over a wide area in a spread out way
unique	only one in existence. [Taipei 101 is a unique building]

Idioms	Meaning
concrete jungle	an environment dominated by large tall buildings
hustle and bustle	busy and noisy *The city is really crowded, so there is a lot of hustle and bustle.*
traffic jams	streets crowded with slow-moving traffic
up-market	fashionable and expensive

Practice questions:

1 Do you live in a city or a town?

2 What is the best thing about where you live?

3 Do you know many people who live near you?

4 How do you think your city/town could be improved?

5 Do you think your city/town will be better in the future?

6 Will you live in this city/town in the future?

Other topics

There are lots of other potential topics that you may get asked in Part One. You can read the sample questions below to help prepare for these. In addition, you can find more Part One questions and vocabulary for different topics in Chapter 7 of this book.

Now let's talk about birthdays

How do you usually spend your birthday?

Who do you prefer to spend your birthday with?

Are birthdays important in your country?

What is the most important age or birthday in your country?

Let's talk about children

Do you like children?

Do you know many children?

When do you usually meet children?

What kind of child were you like when you were young?

Now let's discuss games

What kind of games did you like to play when you were a child?

Did you prefer outdoor or indoor games?

Nowadays, do you like to play computer games?

Do people in your country enjoy playing computer games?

Now let's talk about cars

Do you have a car?

Do you have a driver's license?

Do you prefer to be the driver or the passenger in a car?

Do you often go on long car journeys?

Now let's talk about swimming

Have you learnt how to swim?

Do you think all children should learn how to swim?

Are there a lot of places for swimming in your country?

Do people prefer to swim in swimming pools or the ocean in your country?

Let's discuss weekends

What do you usually do at the weekend?

What did you do last weekend?

What are you going to do next weekend?

Do you like your weekends now more than when you were a child?

Now let's talk about dancing

Do you like to dance?

Have you ever taken any dancing lessons?

Do you like to watch other people dance?

When do people dance in your country?

Let's move onto the topic of giving gifts

When do people give gifts or presents in your country?

Do you ever take a gift when you visit someone in their home?

When did you last receive a gift?

Do you enjoy looking for gifts for other people?

Now let's talk about telephones

How often do you make telephone calls?

Who do you talk to the most on the telephone?

Do you prefer to call people or send text messages?

Do you think sending e-mail is more convenient than calling people?

Let's move onto the topic of history

Do you like to learn about history?

Do you think learning about history is important?

Do you think history should be a compulsory school subject?

What do you think is the best way to learn about history?

Let's discuss the ocean

Do you enjoy visiting the ocean?

Do you like to do any activities at the ocean?

Would you like to live by the ocean?

Do many people in your country live by the ocean?

Now let's talk about toys

What sorts of toys did you like when you were a child?

Did you have a favorite toy?

Was playing with toys very important to you?

Do you still have any toys?

Let's talk about Days of the week

Which is your favorite day of the week?

Which is your busiest day of the week?

How many days off do you have every week?

What do you like doing on your days off?

Let's discuss clothes and clothing

What sort of clothes do you usually wear?

Do you wear the same sort of clothes as your friends?

Do you spend a lot of money on clothes?

When did you last shop for clothes?

4. PART TWO: SPEAK FOR 2 MINUTES

<table>
<tr><th>Part Two</th><th>Requirement</th><th>Suggestions</th></tr>
<tr><td>1-2 minutes
Long Talk</td><td>Prepare a topic for 1 minute and then speak about it for up to 2 minutes.</td><td rowspan="2">PREPARATION
1. identify key words in the question
2. choose a response for the topic that is familiar to you
3. choose a response that you have language to describe
2. think about the tenses required
3. write down some key points

SPEAKING
1. answer the topic directly at the beginning of your talk
2. expand your key points to make your talk longer
3. make it clear when you move onto a new key point
4. use high level language</td></tr>
<tr><td>Possibly 1 or 2 follow-up questions</td><td>Briefly answer any follow-up questions.</td></tr>
</table>

Requirement

In this part you are given a card with a topic and then given 1 minute to prepare an answer of up to 2 minutes on this topic. Topics usually include describing or commenting on a person, place, object, activity, or experience. The topic card also has sub-topics, shown as bullet points. These are only provided to assist you to plan your response and you do NOT have to respond to all of these. The examiner may ask a brief rounding-off question at the end of this part of the test.

Procedure

1. The examiner will introduce Part Two by saying:
Now I am going to give you a topic and I would like you to talk about it for 1 to 2 minutes. I will give you a pencil and paper to make notes. Do you understand?

2. The examiner will pass you the topic card and say:

Here is your pencil and paper for making notes....and here is your topic, I would like you to talk about... [first sentence on topic card]

3. The examiner will now stay silent and give you 1 minute to prepare your answer. You should use this time to prepare your topic and write down some notes to help you.

4. After 1 minute the examiner will ask you to start speaking by saying:

Remember you have 1 to 2 minutes for this, so don't worry if I stop you. Can you start speaking now please.

5. If you stop talking before 2 minutes is up the examiner will pause a few seconds and then tell you: *"You still have time if you want to add anything."*

[This is to give you the opportunity to say more]

6. The examiner will be timing this part of the test and once two minutes is reached the examiner will ask you to stop talking. You MUST stop talking. The examiner will say something like *"Thank you"* and then ask a follow up question if it is appropriate Answer a follow up question in one sentence. DO NOT talk at length here as the examiner needs to start Part Three of the test. You will frustrate the examiner if you start talking at length here, and the examiner may cut you off in the middle of your sentence.

4.1 PREPARING YOUR ANSWER

You only have 1 minute to prepare your answer so you should use it wisely. Focus on the following things:

1. Identify key words in the question

2. Think about the tense required

3. Choose to talk about something familiar to you and that you have language to describe. This is really important!

4. Write down some key points

5. Write down some key vocabulary [if you have time for this]

Important note: You do not need to stick to the sub-questions on the topic card; as long as you are talking about the topic you can say anything about it. You also do not need to cover ALL of the sub-questions.

Sample question

Describe a place that you have visited that you particularly liked.

You should say:

a. When you visited there?

b. Who you went with?

c. What was most memorable?

And explain what you liked most about this place.

Procedure to answer the topic

1. Read the question and then underline the key words. It should look something like below.

Describe a place that you have visited that you particularly liked.

You should say:

a. When you visited there?

b. Who you went with?

c. What was most memorable?

And explain what you liked most about this place.

2. Decide the place you will describe then write down some notes. You are given paper for this and you can keep your notes during your talk.

Place: San Francisco, USA

Sub-questions	**A few key points**
a. When you went there?	• For 4 months in 2013 • summer
b. Who you went with?	• friend who is from Viet Nam • vegetarian guy • brother was an artist
c. What was memorable?	• lots of cool places to visit such as Fisherman's Wharf and Alcatraz Island
d. What you liked most	• Multi-cultural people • great restaurants and cafes • relaxed lifestyle

Your handwritten brainstorm might look a bit like this:

	When	*4 months* *2013* *Summer*
	Who	*Thomas from Viet Nam* *Vegetarian* *Brother artist*
San Francisco	*Memorable*	*Fisherman's Wharf* *Alcatraz Island*
	Like most	*Multi-cultural* *restaurants and cafes* *lifestyle*

3. Introduce your answer, rephrasing the question and directly answering it, to show you clearly understand the question.

Well, a fantastic place I went to is San Francisco in California.

4. Use phrases to signal when you change to a new subtopic:

I went there in ...

I went there with ...

The thing I remember most is ...

Some of the things I enjoyed were ...

MODEL ANSWER

Well, a fantastic place I went to is San Francisco in California. It's definitely the best holiday I ever went on, so it's a place I will never forget.

I went there in 2013 for about four months during summer. I remember the climate is weird at this time of year as it got really foggy at about four o'clock every day and also it was surprisingly chilly during the night.

I went there with a chum of mine who is from Viet Nam, and we shared an apartment together. He is a vegetarian, so I also became a vegetarian during that time. You know I had to give up eating some of my favorite food like sirloin steak and lamb chops. We only ate veggies and I remember eating a loss of pasta with shiitake mushrooms. I also remember his brother who was a very talented artist.

The thing I remember most about San Francisco is that there were many cool places to visit such as Fisherman's Wharf, which is famous for its delicious seafood and sour dough bread. Oh, and Alcatraz Island, which used to be a prison for murderers and other serious criminals.

Some of the things I enjoyed most about San Francisco were the different types of people and the easy-going relaxed lifestyle they seem to be leading. As well as that, there were many trendy places to hang out and also some great restaurants and cafes.

4.2 STRUCTURAL LANGUAGE

Opening: Introductory phrases to use when you start your talk:

I'm going to talk about...

OK, I'm going to describe...

Well, I'd like to talk about...

The first point:

The first thing I'd like to mention is ...

I'd like to begin by highlighting that...

The most important point about [rephrase question] is...

In terms of [rephrase question], I would like to mention...

The second point:

Going on to [rephrase question], and what I'd like to highlight here is that ...

Now concerning the matter of [rephrase question], what I would like to mention here is that ...

The third point:

Progressing to the subject of [rephrase question]. I would like to explain that...

Moving onto the question regarding [rephrase question], what I would like to make clear is that...

The last point:

Finally, I'd like to discuss [rephrase question]

Finally then, if there is still enough time, I would also like to mention that...

Phrases for adding details:

At that time...

It happened...

It took place...

It's been going on since...

It's near...

Phrases to describe something that had an effect on you

... influenced me

... had an effect on me

... impressed me

... motivated me

... touched me deeply

4.3 STRATEGIES

Prepare some high-level language

Most of the questions are about people, places, things, activities, experiences. It is a good idea for you to brainstorm higher level words that you know that can be used to respond to these types of questions. For instance, for any topic about a person you could describe them as an INTROVERT [shy] or an EXTROVERT [outgoing]. For places you could talk about the AMBIENCE [the atmosphere of the place]. To describe an object like a smart-phone you could have language to describe its size as TINY [small], shape as RECTANGULAR and the color of its case as MAGENTA [purplish-red]. Try to start by thinking about the words you already know. To assist you with this process you can also refer to Chapter 7.

Prepare some model answers

In addition to preparing language about the common topic areas of people, places, things, activities, experiences; a good way to prepare for Part Two is to prepare a model answer for each of these common topic areas for a couple of reasons:

1. If you prepare for a question about a person, let's say your best friend, you could apply this answer to other questions about people. For instance, if you are asked to describe an adventurous person you could talk about your best friend and explain why he or she is adventurous in some way. And, let's say you get asked to describe a good teacher; if you are good at telling stories, you could even pretend your best friend was your teacher!

2. No matter what the topic, you should be able to say something about people, places, and things. By preparing some vocabulary and ideas about these topic areas you will essentially be preparing for any question.

NOTE A COUPLE OF THINGS:

1. You should not prepare too many model answers. The idea is to just prepare a few for each of the common categories [people, places, things, activities, experiences].

2. Before you take your test you should practice using your model answers to respond to different questions. Look at different Part Two questions and think which of your model answers could best fit it. And, if none of them perfectly fit it you might have to start off your answer by directly answering the specific topic, and then moving onto one of your prepared topics, or even use parts of different prepared answers.

3. You may need to customize the answer to fit the specific question. For instance, if you have prepared the topic about your best friend and the question is about your neighbor then at the start of your talk you either need to say that your best friend is your neighbor, or else just pretend that your best friend is your neighbor without actually saying it.

4. With practice you should be able to answer almost any question with just a few model answers that you can customize to answer specific questions. Note that this is an excellent way to increase your score because you will be familiar with the topic which will enable you to speak fluently and if you prepare the topic well it will have high-level vocabulary and grammar in it.

How many words are needed for a model answer?

You should ideally speak for 2 minutes. A native speaker speaks at about 145-160 words per minute and then there are pauses between ideas. A non-native high-level speaker may speak a bit slower perhaps 110 words per minute. A lower level speaker may speak at fewer than 100 words. You might want to work out your speaking speed, to get an idea of how many words you will need to speak. If you plan your model answer to be 250 words, that will be more than enough.

Tell a Story

Stories are useful to extend a talk in Part Two of the speaking exam. They often come out very fluently, are interesting, and result in the expression of a wide range of vocabulary and grammatical structures. The following explains these benefits in more detail:

1. It is often easy to speak fluently as ideas can often come out more quickly. This is because stories are often clear in our mind and we have told people certain stories many times and so they come out fluently in the exam.

2. Stories can also be helpful to speak for 2 minutes because there are often different parts to them such as a beginning, middle, and end; or a cause, effect, and solution.

3. Stories can be really interesting and can help the examiner to be interested in what you are saying.

4. Stories can also allow you to make things up which can help you to extend your talk and also use higher-level language. For instance, in the real story there might have been a white dress... but in the IELTS story you might change it to a magenta dress with a dark blue ribbon.

5. The story may not take up the whole of your response. You may start by focusing more on the topic card and then later move onto the story. Because of this aspect stories can be particularly useful with topics that you find difficult to talk about. Essentially, start by talking about the topic and then shift to a story that is somewhat related to the topic. Imagine you have been asked to talk about *"your favorite wild animal"*. Maybe, after half a minute, you have said all you know about pandas! Now you can tell a story about going to the zoo and seeing a panda!

Time sequencing words

To make clear the sequence of events in a story use time words such as:

In the beginning

After that...

Subsequently...

In the end...

Tenses for stories

Stories occurred in the past so when we are describing what happened in the story we need to use the past tense.

"I went to my best friend's birthday"

However, we need to use the present tense if we are describing facts and opinions about these past events.

"She is a kind woman"

[Note that if we use the past tense then it suggests that she is no longer kind!]

4.4 ANSWERING ROUNDING-OFF QUESTIONS.

You may be asked a follow-up question at the end of your 2 minute speech. You just want to give a short single sentence answer to this, unless you didn't speak for very long [under 2 minutes]. This is because the examiner needs to move onto Part Three of the test quickly. You can use this technique to answer a follow-up question:

1. Brief answer, repeating the auxiliary verb [have and do in the examples below]

2. Use the same tense

EXAMINER: *"Have you done this type of work before?"*

CANDIDATE: *"No, I haven't."*

EXAMINER: *"Do you know anyone who has"*

CANDIDATE: *"Yes, I do, my cousin does this job."*

4.5 TYPES OF QUESTIONS

The purpose of this section is to help you prepare for the common categories of topics that get asked in this part of the test. Most of the questions in Part Two of the test are about: PEOPLE, PLACES, THINGS, ACTIVITIES, and EXPERIENCES.

This section includes the following information:

1. sample questions for each category

2. model answers for each category

3. aspects you can consider when dealing with each category

4. structures that can be used to answer questions in each category

5. language related to these common topics

4.6 PEOPLE

Many of the questions in this part of the test are about people. As well as this you can often discuss a person when you are answering other types of questions. For instance, if you are describing a place you might describe the person you go there with.

GRAMMAR

Tenses

If the question asks you to describe someone you know now. e.g. *Describe a person who is interesting,* you should describe the person using the present tense. If you are asked to describe someone you know from the past you should still describe the person using the present tense, unless the person is now dead. In this case you will use the past tense. Illustrative examples:

My neighbor Brian ***is*** *a senior citizen.* [present tense is used because he is still alive]

Audrey Hepburn ***was*** *a petite woman.* [past tense is used because she is dead]

For all types of people, describe any actions they have already done using the past tense. For example, *"He* ***learnt*** *how to fly a plane last year."*

Use relative pronouns [who, whose]

Use who to add information about the subject.

My neighbor, <u>who</u> is really old, seldom goes outside.

Use whose as a possessive relative pronoun.

He is a rich man <u>whose</u> house is very large.

VOCABULARY

To make your answer more interesting use lots of descriptive vocabulary, e.g. extrovert, slender, and so on. You could talk about the following aspects:

1. appearance
2. personality
3. relationship to you
4. their lifestyle

1. APPEARANCE:

Height: petite [short], lofty [tall]

Build: slender [thin], overweight [fat], well-built [muscular]

Age: toddler [young child], adolescent [young adult], senior citizen

Facial features: clean shaven, full beard, goatee beard, moustache

Hair: short cropped hair, long thick hair, ponytail, bald

Audrey Hepburn was a petite woman with short cropped hair. Hepburn was boyish, and yet feminine simultaneously. She was famous for wearing little black dresses that had a way of making her look glamorous. [past tense is used because she is dead]

Brian is a senior citizen, with a goatee beard, a moustache, and a short grey ponytail. He always wears sunglasses because he has eyes that are sensitive to sunlight. [Present tense is used because he is still alive].

Sarah, who is in her early forties, is quite tall and has a medium build. She has thick black hair that is plaited into a waist length ponytail. She usually wears jeans and a red sweater.

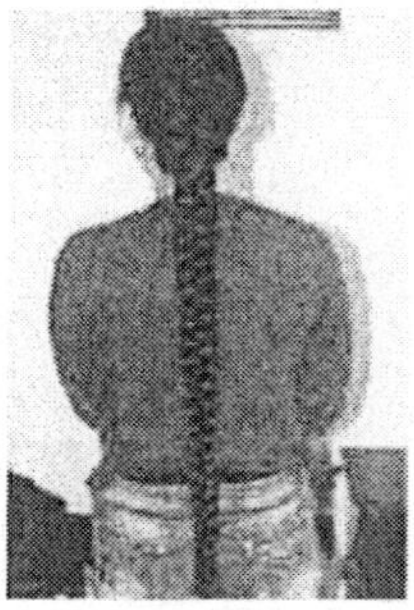

2: PERSONALITY

You can talk about positive and negative features of a person's personality.

Positive: warm, fun loving, intelligent, charming, kind-hearted, extrovert [outgoing]

Emma is quite an extrovert. She is always the life of the party because of her warm-hearted and fun loving nature.

Negative: mean, selfish, cruel, arrogant, introverted, a pain in the neck [annoying]

Steven is rather introverted, he usually sits quietly in the corner at parties. He is also a pain in the neck because he always bothers me when he needs help with his computer.

3. RELATIONSHIP: pal, soul-mate, classmate, colleague, family member, mentor

I have been pals with Peter since high school. I guess you can say that now he is my soul-mate. As well as this his father has always been somewhat of a mentor to me, as he is my soccer coach.

4. LIFESTYLE: hobbies, interests, work

My sister is a college student and a part-time assistant in an office, so she has little time to socialize at the weekend or play badminton.

Some advice about vocabulary:

1. Have short lists; you only need 2 or 3 words for each category

2. Focus on high-level language = language to impress the examiner and increase your score

3. The truth doesn't matter, use language to describe a person even if that is not true. For instance you might say your uncle is an extrovert even though he isn't! This is to increase your score for vocabulary.

Model answer

Describe a famous celebrity from your country who you admire

You should say:

who the person is

what kind of celebrity this person is

describe why this person has become successful

and explain why you admire this person.

Alright then, I'm going to talk about Faye Wang, who's the most famous female singer in China.

I'd like to begin by highlighting that Faye is considered as the all-time diva among the young generation. She was born in Beijing, but became famous in Hong Kong as a pop singer. Her fame is due to her career as a highly successful and influential singer, songwriter and actress; and she's also known as an icon of fashion due to her amazing and impressive makeup and clothing styles.

Now let's move on to the point of why I hold Faye in high regards. What I have to mention here is that the admiration I have for her dedication to help others. Her daughter was born with a cleft lip, and she took her to California for surgery. Once she realized how much money is required for cleft lip surgeries, she decided to establish a foundation to help people receive proper treatment.

Apart from this, what I'd like to mention is that Faye is a highly family-oriented person. She is a traditional Chinese woman and in the mid-1990s she left Hong Kong at the peak of her career and moved to Beijing to live with her husband, who was a successful rock star. Although her marriage failed, everyone took pity on her and respected the career sacrifice she made for her family.

Practice questions

Describe one of your neighbors.

You should say:

what sort of person your neighbor is

do you like this neighbor

when do you usually meet this neighbor

and explain if this person is a good neighbor.

Describe an old person you admire.

You should say:

who this person is

how long you have known him/her

what qualities they have

and explain why you admire him/her.

Describe someone you know who is a good teacher.

You should say:

who this person is

how you know him/her

what kinds of subjects they teach

and explain why this person is good at teaching.

Describe an interesting person who you know.

You should say:

what sort of person this is

where you first met him/her

why you met him/her

and explain why you think this person is interesting.

Describe a friend you remember from your childhood.

You should talk about:

who the person is

how you knew this person

what you used to do together

and explain what you remember most about this person.

4.7 PLACES

Many of the questions are about places. As well is this you can often discuss a place when you are answering other types of questions. For instance, if you are describing an activity you might describe the place you do it.

CITIES/COUNTRIES:

Location: on the coast, in the mountains, in the heart of the country,

People: kind-hearted, hospitable, polite, rude, arrogant, cosmopolitan [mix of cultures]

Cityscape: picturesque, contemporary architecture, skyscrapers, classical architecture, polluted and contaminated

Entertainment: bustling and lively, a wide variety of entertainment facilities, dull and boring, touristy

San Diego is located on the west coast of America, near the border of Mexico. The thing which makes tourists enjoy visiting this city is the kind-hearted and hospitable nature of the people. It's a picturesque setting due to its location on the coast. The downtown has lots of skyscrapers which can make it seem a bit like a concrete jungle. However, within an easy drive there are a wide variety of entertainment facilities such as SeaWorld, the zoo, and for nature lovers Torrey Pines State Reserve, which is an excellent place to go hiking and see a wide range of fauna and flora*.

*fauna = animals; flora = plants

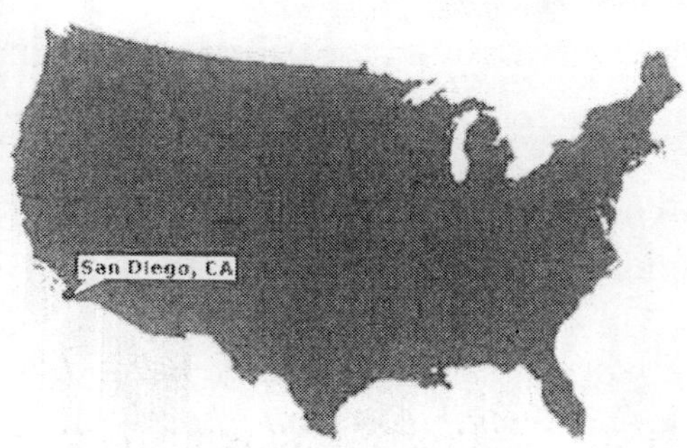

BUILDINGS

Location: downtown, at the corner of a hectic street, quiet cul-de-sac

Exterior: elegant, plain, contemporary designed, classical architecture

Interior: well lit, dark and dingy, lofty ceilings, compact, spacious

Atmosphere: cozy, comfortable, tranquil ambience, lively and upbeat

St Martin's church is located at the end of a quiet cul-de-sac. It was built using contemporary architecture; the back wall is plain brick, facing a private garden, which gives it a very tranquil ambience. The main entrance is well lit and when you step inside the main building it has giant windows all the way up to the lofty ceilings. During the day the building is well lit without the need for artificial lighting.

Positive expressions:
awe-inspiring, breathtaking, delightful, eye-catching, majestic, picturesque, tranquil,

The castle, standing at the top of the mountain has majestic views over the city that are quite eye-catching and picturesque.

Negative expressions:
bleak, dilapidated, inhospitable, squalid

The bleak concrete building was in a dilapidated state, inside it was squalid, and it was located in an inhospitable neighborhood.

PLACES OF NATURAL BEAUTY:

Location: remote, just outside the city, along the coast, in a mountainous area,

Visitors: visitors flocked to, seldom visited, deserted

Activities: go sightseeing, hiking, doing extreme sports like bungee jumping and abseiling, experiencing indigenous species

Contents: fauna [animals], flora [plants], lake, waterfall

Opinions: amazing, breathtaking, spectacular

Golden Gate park is located in the west of San Francisco city and due to its spectacular scenery many local residents and tourists flock to it. Many residents of San Francisco feel this spacious public park is similar to Central Park, in New York City. Undoubtedly, the feature that will disappoint many tourists is the lack of opportunities to see native fauna and flora there. Really this is an inner-city park, it doesn't have a lot of wide open spaces, but there are lots of activities to do here. One of the interesting activities that you can do in the park is horse-shoe throwing.

Model answer

Describe an attractive outdoor place you visited as a child

You should say:

where this place is

when and how you went there

what the place looked like

and say what you found attractive about this place.

I'm going to describe a really beautiful park I used to visit when I was a child. It is a national park about 100km away from my hometown of Ho Chi Minh City.

With regards to the question of when I used to go there, my parents and I often went there whenever we had a long weekend. Since, it's not far away we used to drive our car. We would set off in the wee hours to avoid the hellish rush hour traffic of my city. I am not an early bird so I usually slept during the journey... and woke up in paradise!

Now concerning what this place looks like, I really felt over the moon every time I went there. It is a wonderful place with fascinating and marvelous natural beauty. There is a large salt lake in the centre of this park with extremely clean water, in which I could see the reflection of the blue sky, white clouds and green hills.

Another thing that really attracted me was that there are many kinds of fish in this lake, such as carp and trout. We often went boating and fishing in the lake. Once I even caught an angelfish, which is a beautiful fish with long fins. I wanted to bring it home as my pet, but I was afraid that I couldn't take care of it, so I just set it free.

Finally I'd like to mention that the most attractive feature is that the lake there is surrounded by a variety of tropical fruit trees, including lichi trees, durian trees and mango trees. Usually, after fishing we would have a BBQ for our lunch under those fruit trees. In the afternoon, we would rent a tandem bicycle and ride together on a small path around the lake, enjoying the tranquility and fresh air.

Practice questions

Describe a house you have visited which you particularly liked.

You should say:

what kind of house it is

why you visited the house

how it is different to other houses you have visited

and why you particularly liked it.

Describe a cafe you know that about you would recommend to others.

You should say:

where this cafe is

what type of food and drinks the cafe serves

how often you go to this cafe

and explain why you would recommend this cafe.

Describe a city that you would like to travel to.

You should say:

where this city is?

how you would travel there?

who you would go there with?

and explain what you like about this city.

Describe a place you have visited where you learned something.

You should say:

where this place is

when you went there

why you went there

and explain what you learned there.

Describe a room you like that you spend a lot of time in.

You should say:

where this room is

what this room looks like

what you do in this room

and explain why you like to spend so much time in this room.

4.8 OBJECTS

Many questions ask you to describe an object. As well is this, when you answer other types of questions it may be useful to describe an object. For instance, if you are describing a sport you might describe some of the objects that are required to play this sport. Some of the aspects you can think of when discussing an object are as follows:

1. size
2. color
3. texture
4. weight
5. material
6. age
7. shape
8. reason for being special

1. size

Small: tiny, miniscule, microscopic

Big: enormous, huge, gigantic

2. color

Magenta = a bright pinkish purple

Turquoise = bluish-green

3. texture

Coarse = rough

Smooth = flat

4. weight

Heavy: weighs a ton [idiomatic expression]

Light: lightweight, feather light

5. material

Wooden

Metallic

6. age

Contemporary = modern

Classical = old and following tradition

7. shape

oval 	diamond 	cube 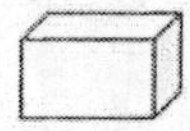
crescent 	rectangle 	hexagon 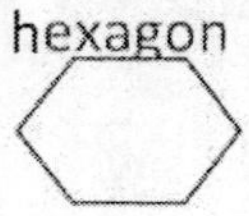
arc 	heart 	donut 

8. Reason for being special:

family heirloom, birthday present, Christmas gift, from a soul mate

<table>
<tr>
<td>

Describe something expensive that you bought recently [<u>not</u> a computer].

You should say:

what it was

what it looks like

how much it cost

and explain why you bought it.

</td>
<td>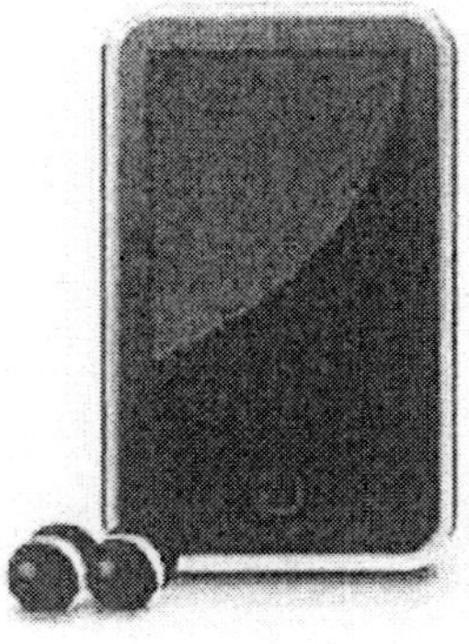</td>
</tr>
<tr>
<td colspan="2">

Well, the expensive item that I would like to talk about is my smart phone. It is made by Apple and it's a sixth generation iPhone.

The first thing I'd like to mention is that the color of the phone is magenta, which is extremely rare for an iPhone. I believe that Apple only released about 1,000 of these in my country. Other than that, there's nothing too special about my iPhone. Like other iPhones, it has a tiny camera just above the screen, on the front of the phone for taking selfies. On the back of the phone, there is a slightly larger camera, for taking high resolution photos of things like scenery.

Going on to the price of the phone, what I'd like to highlight here is that I got an excellent deal. I was able to buy the phone at a 20% discount, and that included a free pair of lightweight ear-bud headphones.

Finally I'd like to mention the reason why I bought the phone. I'm going abroad to study in Australia and I want to be able to keep in touch with friends and family and also show photos of some of the spectacular scenery.

</td>
</tr>
</table>

Practice questions

Describe a purchase you were dissatisfied with.

You should say:

what you bought

when you bought it

where you bought it

and explain why you were dissatisfied with it.

Describe something old you have kept for a long time.

You should say:

what the object is

explain why you have kept it

discuss how long you have kept it

and explain what you like about it the most.

Describe an important letter or email that you received.

You should say:

who wrote it

what the letter or email was about

how you felt about it

and explain why it was important.

Describe a book you have read that you think is interesting

You should say:

how you know about this book

where you got this book from

what it is about

and explain what you find most interesting about this book.

Describe a toy that was special to you when you were a child.

You should say:

what it looked like

where you played with it

who gave it to you

and explain what was most special about the toy.

4.9 ACTIVITIES

I recommend students to focus on people, places, and objects first. This is because these aspects can also be used when you discuss activities. Activities often occur with other people, in particular places, and involve objects such as equipment. Therefore, there are lots of ideas and language from the three previous sections that can be used here:

Who: get ideas from the previous section on people

Where: get ideas from the previous section on places

What you need: get ideas from the previous section on objects

ADDITIONAL ASPECTS

When: on weekends, in the winter, at dawn [daybreak], at dusk [sundown]

Why: unwind, relax, have a lot of fun

Preparations: planning and equipment needed

What happens: before the activity, during the activity, after the activity

Your feeling: excited, bored, scared

STRUCTURE

A good way to structure an activity is like a story. Talk about what happened before the activity, during the activity, and after the activity.

Before the activity: give the activity name, time/date, place, and reason for celebrating the event, describe the preparations for the event, explain any of the equipment that was needed.

During the activity: describe the event itself; what happened at the start, middle and end of the event; discuss the people involved, describe the location

After the activity: describe your feelings about the event, say something that happened after the event

Model answer

Describe an outdoor activity you would like to try for the first time.

You should say:

what the activity is

where you would do it

what preparations and equipment you would need

and explain why you would like to do this activity.

Well, the outdoor activity I'd like to talk about is bungee jumping because I have seen that on TV and it really looks like a lot of fun.

In terms of where I would most like to do it, the answer is definitely New Zealand. This is because the sport was invented by a New Zealander and I also heard that New Zealand has some of the best bungee jumps in the world. You know ...you can jump off a bridge and fall about 100m before you start your ascent up again. Another choice is off the Auckland Sky Tower, but I think it would be more dangerous... I'm not sure if I'm brave enough for that!

Now concerning the question of the equipment that I would need to do this, I think that most of the equipment would be provided by the bungee jumping company. I think it goes without saying that I would need to wear extremely comfortable clothes. I can imagine that it would be uncomfortable wearing a tight pair of jeans, so I would probably wear something like a tracksuit and sneakers.

Finally if there is still enough time I would like to tell you why I would really like to do this. **I guess the main reason is because** it's a kind of challenge to overcome. I think it is a physically and mentally demanding activity, so I want to try it. You know... It's a kind of a once-in-a-lifetime experience... something to brag about with friends!

Practice questions

Describe an activity you enjoy doing in your free time.

You should say:

What this activity is

who you do this with

where you do it

and explain why you like to spend your free time this way.

Describe a practical skill you have.

You should say:

what the skill is

how often you use it

who taught it to you

and explain why the skill is practical.

Describe a sport you have enjoyed playing or watching.

You should say:

what this sport is

where this sport is played

how the sport is played

and explain what you like most about this sport.

Describe a foreign language you would like to learn (not English).

You should say:

what the language is

how you would learn it

what difficulties you might have when learning this language

and explain why you would like to learn this language.

Describe an activity that you do to stay healthy.

You should say:

what activity you do

when you started doing this

how much time you spend doing this

and explain what benefits you get from this activity.

4.10 EXPERIENCES

I recommend students to focus on people, places, and objects first. This is because these aspects can be used when you discuss experiences. Experiences often occur with other people, in particular places, and involve objects such as equipment. Therefore, there are lots of ideas and language from the three previous sections on people, places, and objects that can be used here:

Who: get ideas from the previous section on people

Where: get ideas from the previous section on places

What you need: get ideas from the previous section on objects

ADDITIONAL ASPECTS

When: during my childhood, when I was an adolescent, in my twenties

Why: chill-out, necessary in order to..., unavoidable

What happened: before the experience, during the experience, after the experience

Your feeling: nervous, bored to death, terrified

Model answer

Describe a challenge that you faced at high school

You should say:

what the problem was

how it happened

how you felt about this problem

and explain how you felt when you solved the problem

I'm going to talk about the challenge I faced to pass the exams I had to take for university entrance. In my country every student has to take exams in order to get into a university.

I'd like to begin by highlighting the fact that whilst my grades were always high, I had always been terrible at mathematics and always struggled to get passing grades. Unfortunately for me, this was one of the most critical subjects that I needed to pass in order to get into a tertiary institution.

Going on to how I overcame this problem, I knew that in order to pass this subject I would have to work flat out, and I even hired a tutor to assist me. Although I'm not an early bird, I got up at 6 AM every morning to start studying.

Moving on to the question of my feelings regarding this challenge, I was really stressed-out and felt down in the dumps every day. You know... I really felt depressed. To be honest, I never would have made it through this difficult time without the words of encouragement from my soul mate.

And if there is still time, I'd also like to mention that after I passed this test I really felt over the moon, so I invited all my friends over for a party to celebrate my success!

Practice questions

Describe a class you remember taking at high school.

You should talk about:

what the class was

what the class was about

who taught the class

and explain what you remember most about attending this class.

Describe an important challenge that you had to overcome in the past.

You should say:

what the challenge was

why you had this challenge

who helped you face this challenge

and explain how you overcame this challenge.

Describe an important decision you might have to make in the future.

You should say:

what the decision is

how you will make your decision

what the results of the decision are likely to be

and explain why this decision is so important.

Describe an educational trip that you went on when you were in school.

You should say:

where you went

what you did there

who went with you

and explain what you learned on this trip.

Describe an interesting talk or speech you heard recently.

You should say:

who the speaker was

where and when you heard it

what it was about

and explain why you found it interesting.

5. PART THREE: THE DISCUSSION

Part Three	Requirement	Suggestions
4-5 minutes Discussion	Respond to the examiner's questions related to your topic in Part Two for 4-5 Minutes. You are allowed to ask the examiner to repeat or rephrase the question. You can ask a checking question: *"Are you asking me about..."*	1. Give extended responses. Ideally your responses should be twice as long as in Part One of the test. So you want answers that are about 4 to 6 sentences. 2. Try to support your main points, by adding details, giving explanations, or giving examples 3. If you are really stuck about how to answer a question, do not sit there in silence! Say it: *"Gosh that's a tricky question I've never thought about that before."* Then try to give some sort of answer. If you can't then just tell the examiner. Of course this is not ideal, but the worst thing is to sit there in silence.

Requirement

This part of the test lasts from 4 to 5 minutes and consists of questions roughly based on the topic area of the Part Two: Long Turn. Usually you will be asked two to three questions on two different topics. The major difference with this part of the exam is that you are asked questions about people in general rather than about yourself. This can be more challenging. Essentially, it's more difficult to talk about other people than it is about ourselves. Another key difference is that the examiners are able to ask their own questions, and they are not limited to the questions written in their book like in other parts of the exam. In this part the examiner may push you hard to see the boundaries of your ability. You may feel this part is the most difficult! It is called the discussion section because the examiner follows some of your answers with a follow-up question that is based on the answer you just gave.

Procedure

1. The examiner will introduce Part Three saying:
"We've been talking about [topic from Part Two], now I'd like to ask you a few general questions about that."

2. The examiner will introduce the topic more specifically.

"Let's talk about [specific topic]". For example: *"Let's talk about shopping in your country."*

3. The examiner will then ask you two or three questions related to this specific topic:

What are some of the different types of places where people can go shopping in your country?

Do you think people spend more time shopping these days than they did in the past?

Do you think this is a positive trend or negative trend?

4. The examiner will move onto the second specific topic and ask two or three questions about this.

Let's move on and talk about ....[introduce topic]

5. After 4 to 5 minutes the examiner will end the exam saying:

Thank you, this is the end of the speaking exam.

6. You should thank the examiner and leave the exam room. You could say something like:

Thank you, I appreciate your time.

7. Try to smile at the examiner and then leave the room.

8. Do not do any of the following:

Have any further conversation with the examiner unless the examiner initiates it.
Apologize for your poor English!
Ask the examiner what your score is.
Try to explain any mistakes that you made.

9. After you leave the exam room, don't forget to collect any of your belongings if you have left items outside the exam room.

5.1 STRATEGIES

Buy time to think

One of the biggest problems in this part of the test is that the questions can be quite challenging. You may struggle to think of what you want to say, let alone how you are going to say it. There are some strategies you can use to deal with this situation.

Start with a memorized set phrase

Use some memorized set phrases to buy time to think about what you are going to say:

1. Off the top of my head I would say...

2. Well, it's difficult to say, but ...

3. That's an interesting question and I think I would have to say that...

4. Mmm ... I'm not really sure, but...

5. Actually, that's not something I've really thought about, but...

6. I don't really know much about that, but...

[Lots of set phrases for different types of questions are explained in the next section.]

Ask for the question to be rephrased

Another way to buy time is to pretend you didn't understand the question and ask the examiner to rephrase it. While the examiner is doing this you can think about what you want to say. This won't lower your grade, unless you do it repeatedly in which case it's going to start to lower your score for vocabulary. You could say something like:

"I'm sorry I didn't quite catch that, could you please rephrase it"

Focus on language and not ideas

In this section it is very important that you don't waste time trying to think of your real opinion, that doesn't matter; what is important is that you give an opinion and then support it. In addition, it is a language test so it's more important that you use higher-level language than have clever ideas.

Speak at length

This part of the test is designed for you to give responses that are twice as long as Part One. If you are looking for a higher score you should try to show the examiner you have the ability to talk at length. Also, this part of the test is limited to 4 to 5 minutes and the questions are designed to increase in difficulty. Therefore, if you give longer answers you are going to get fewer questions and then there is less chance of you getting a question that you are unable to respond to or lack the language to give a strong reply. Ideally you want answers that are about 4 to 6 sentences, and if you really feel comfortable with a question you could even speak longer!

You should use the strategies outlined in Chapter 2 to enable yourself to produce longer answers. To summarize these are:

1. Divide your response into two or three parts

2. Describe from general to specific (maybe give an example)

3. Depends: describe different situations

4. Concession: make a main argument and then give a concession for it

5. Avoidance: do not directly answer the question at first, and then answer it.

Produce language

You need to say something. If you are unable to say anything at all in response to a question this will have a severely negative impact on your score. Especially your score for fluency and coherence! Say something even if it doesn't have any real meaning. You can think of politicians here and the way they answer questions that they don't like. Let's say you're asked your opinion about something, and you really don't know what to say...you could say something like:

"Well I think that's a really interesting question, but I never thought about it before. I guess I'd have to say that I agree"

Think about past writing tasks you have completed

Some Part Three questions are very similar to, or even exactly the same as some Task Two Writing test questions. The Writing test questions are asking questions that are related to many of the same functions as Part Three of the speaking test such as your opinion, the advantages and disadvantages of something, and problems and solutions. If you are lucky you may get a question that you have already written an essay about. You should be able to use some of the language you used in that essay!

Likewise, if you have prepared for the academic test report writing then you should have language related to comparing things, describing trends, and making predictions. This language could be used in Part Three of the speaking test for functions such as comparing and making predictions.

Getting out of trouble

Sometimes you will find yourself in an uncomfortable situation in this part of the exam. It is important to stay calm and manage this as best as you can. The following advice relates to some of the typical situations that might occur.

YOU JUST GAVE AN UNCLEAR POINT

Due to the difficulty of this section, sometimes you may finish a sentence and realize that you haven't really made the point clearly. I suggest you can rephrase the point you just made more clearly beginning with one of the following phrases:

In other words...

Well let me clarify that by pointing out that...

How can I put this better ... Oh yes, what I mean to say is that...

Another way to put it is...

YOU DON'T KNOW HOW TO FINISH A SENTENCE

Another common problem is you may end up starting a sentence and not quite knowing how to finish it. I suggest the following solutions:

Restart your sentence

What I mean to say is...

Sorry I have lost my train of thought what I'm trying to say is...

Oh, I seem to have lost my train of thought a bit, let me see, oh yes, that's right, what I mean to say is...

Move onto your next point

A long period of silence is the worst situation, especially for your score for Fluency and Coherence. If you can't finish an idea fairly quickly, it is sometimes best to just move onto the next point. If you're lucky the examiner might not even notice! Say something quickly like:

Oh and I would also like to mention...

Which reminds me that...

Pretend you forgot the question!

This strategy can really only be used once! Just pretend you forgot what the original question was and say something like:

Oh... Gosh... Sorry what was the question again?

[My feeling is that this doesn't really have a negative effect on your score if you do it only one time. It is definitely much better than a long silence. With the examiner unsure whether you are going to speak any more or whether they should move onto the next question].

5.2 TYPES OF QUESTIONS

It's difficult to predict exactly what questions you will get asked in the third part of the exam, but usually they will have a close connection to the topic that was discussed in Part Two of the exam. The questions are based on the following functions, which will be discussed further in this section:

1. **Different kinds of**
2. **Comparing (time/objects/concepts)**
3. **Predicting**
4. **Advantages**
5. **Disadvantages**
6. **Problems**
7. **Solutions**
8. **Opinion (why)**

1. Different kinds of

This is a very common first question in this part of the test. It is a question like:

What are some of the different kinds of shops in your country?

Note carefully:

Avoid just repeating the information or language that you used in Part Two. This is because it will not show the examiner anything new and not give them any new rateable language. In addition, another common mistake that people make is to just give one kind of shop, but the question clearly asks for more than one kind of shop. I suggest the following approach:

MODEL ANSWER:

What are some of the different kinds of shops in your country?

Well, there are a wide range of places to go shopping.

One of the most popular types is department stores. **I think this is because** they stock high-quality products and always offer a money back warrantee if you are unsatisfied with your purchase.

Another, trendy place that people in my country enjoy shopping at is night markets. **I guess this might be because** it's a lot of fun and the prices are usually cheaper than in the stores.

Steps to answer the question:

1. Paraphrase the question:

Well, there are a wide range of places to go shopping.

2. Introduce the first type and perhaps a reason:

One of the most popular types is....[type of shop]. *I think this is because...*[reason]

3. Introduce the second type and perhaps a reason:

Another, popular place that people in my country enjoy shopping at is [type of shop]. *I guess this might be because...* [reason].

USEFUL LANGUAGE

Introduction

Well, there are a wide range of...

Actually, there is quite an array of...

There are many options to choose from.

First type

One of the most popular types is...

Probably the most common is...

Second type

Another, trendy option is

Many people are also keen on...

Giving reasons

I think this is because

I guess this might be because

OTHER STRUCTURES

We can also use different strategies here to structure our answer. For instance you could use the **depends strategy** that was introduced earlier. In this case your answer will be something like:

MODEL ANSWER: based on depends strategy

What are some of the different kinds of shops in your country?

> **Well, I think it depends on** the age of the person.
>
> **One of the most popular types** for young people is night markets. I guess this might be because it's a lot of fun and the prices are usually cheaper than in the stores.
>
> **However**, older people seem to enjoy shopping in department stores. I guess this might be because they are looking for famous brands and high-quality products.

Steps to answer the question:

1. State that it depends:

Well, I think it depends on the age of the person.

2. Introduce the first type and perhaps a reason:

One of the most popular types for young people is....[type of shop]. I think this is because...[reason]

3. Introduce the second type and perhaps a reason:.

However, older people seem to enjoy shopping at [type of shop]. I guess this might be because... [reason].

language used in the depends model

Well, I think it depends... [first situation] However, [second situation]

Practice Questions

1. What are the different types of leisure activities that are popular in your country?

2. What types of sports do young people like to play?

3. What types of people are famous in your country?

4. What are some of the different types of restaurants in your country?

5. What types of products are more popular these days?

2. Comparing

Another common type of question in this part of the exam is for you to compare two different things. This type of question can be asked in different ways, but usually you are asked to compare different **time periods** [now and the past]; **things** [such as houses and apartments]; or different types of **people** [older/younger, and different genders]. For all these types of questions you could use language of comparison (cheap<u>er</u>, <u>more</u> expensive, X is more/less than Y) .

Comparing time periods

What are the differences in the topics that people talk about these days and the topics they talked about in the past?

> **Well, I think they are like chalk and cheese. I feel the most fundamental would be that** people these days prefer to talk about technology and the economy, **whereas** people in the past used to talk about politics more. **Moreover, a further distinction might be that** these days people like to talk a lot about their interactions on social network sites. **While on the other hand**, people in the past talked more about their face-to-face interactions with their friends.

Comparing things

What are some of the differences in the types of homes that people live in these days compared to the past?

> **Well, obviously there are a number of clear differences. Perhaps the most significant difference is that** most people used to live in houses; whereas these days it is becoming increasingly common to live in high-rise condominiums. **In addition,** a subsequent contrast could be that in the past many houses used to be made out of wood. **Conversely, these days** most houses are made out of concrete.

Comparing people

What differences are there in the topics that men and women discuss?

> **Well obviously there are a number of clear differences. Perhaps the most significant one would be** that men tend to <u>talk more about</u> sports such as baseball or basketball. **Whereas,** women <u>have a preference</u> to chat about things like going shopping or what sort of clothes they like to wear. **In addition, a subsequent contrast could be that** women like to gossip a lot. **Conversely**, men <u>prefer</u> to talk more about politics and business.

[language of comparison is underlined]

Step-By-Step Approach [based on the answer above for comparing people]

1. opening phrase:

Well obviously there are a number of clear differences.

2. introduce and describe the first difference:

Perhaps the most significant one would be that men tend to talk more about sports

4. develop this first difference with a linking word:

<u>*such as*</u> *baseball or basketball.*

5. use a comparative linking structure and add a contrasting idea:

whereas, women prefer to chat about things like going shopping or what sort of clothes they like to wear.

6. introduce and describe the second difference.

In addition, a subsequent contrast could be that women like to gossip a lot

7. Signal a contrast and state the difference

Conversely, men prefer to talk more about politics and business.

Complete model answer [repeated from above about comparing people]

Well obviously there are a number of clear differences. Perhaps the most significant one would be that men tend to talk more about sports such as baseball or basketball. **Whereas, women prefer** to chat about things like going shopping or what sort of clothes they like to wear. **In addition, a subsequent contrast could be that** women like to gossip a lot. **Conversely, men would rather** talk more about politics and business.

USEFUL LANGUAGE

Opening:

Well, I think they are like chalk and cheese. [An idiom for really big differences]

Well obviously there are a number of clear differences.

The first difference:

Perhaps the most significant difference is ...; whereas...

I feel the most fundamental would be that ... On the contrary, ...

The second difference:

In addition, a subsequent contrast could be that ... Conversely,...

Moreover, a further distinction might be that ... While on the other hand,...

To show similarity: [essentially you are giving a concession to the question]

However, one thing that seems the same is....

On the other hand, I think they are both similar with regards to...

Practice Questions

1. Do men and women prefer to buy different types of products?
2. Do young people prefer to do different activities than older people?
3. What differences are there in the activities people do these days compared to the past?
4. How are shops today different to the shops when you were younger?
5. What changes have occurred in the buildings in your country?
6. Nowadays do families spend more time together or less?

3. Predicting

Another common type of question in this part of the exam is about the future. This type of question often occurs after a question that asks you to compare the past to the present. Essentially, you are now being asked to compare the current situation to a future one. In many cases you will need to use the future tense:

will + verb

The buildings will be much taller

going to + verb

People are going to live much longer

USEFUL LANGUAGE

Opening:

I am sure that in years to come we will see some major developments.

It is difficult to predict the future, but I think there are going to be some major changes with regard to...

The first prediction:

It's hard to predict the future, but I suppose...

I'm not sure exactly what will happen, but one possibility is...

The second prediction:

As well as this, we will probably start to see...

Furthermore, this might sound a bit crazy, but I think one day...

Future idioms

on the cards = probably will

Yes, doing some study is <u>on the cards</u> tomorrow

bank on = almost certainly will happen

You can <u>bank on</u> the Internet being more popular in the future.

SAMPLE QUESTION:

How do you think housing will change in the future?

It is difficult to predict the future, but I think there are going to be some major changes with regard to residential buildings.

I'm not sure exactly what will happen, but one possibility is the rising demand for housing and the scarcity of land may lead to people only living in apartment buildings and so I think the disappearance of detached houses is **on the cards.**

Furthermore, this might sound a bit crazy, but I think one day, we may even have to start building houses on the ocean. There just doesn't seem to be enough land left in many metropolitan areas like Shanghai to build anywhere else.

Step-By-Step Approach

1. opening phrase:

It is difficult to predict the future, but I think there are going to be some major changes with regard to residential buildings.

2. introduce and describe the first prediction:

I'm not sure exactly what might happen, but one possibility is the rising demand for housing and the scarcity of land may lead to people only living in apartment buildings and *the disappearance of detached houses.*

3. Use a linking phrase and introduce and describe the second difference:

Furthermore, this might sound a bit crazy, but I think one day, we may even have to start building houses on the ocean. There just doesn't seem to be enough land left in many metropolitan areas like Shanghai to build anywhere else.

Practice Questions

1. What will schools be like in the future?
2. What will cars be like in the future?
3. Do you think people will have more free time in the future?
4. Do you think we will get the news in different ways in the future?
5. What will your country be like in 20 years?
6. Do you think the climate will be hotter in the future?

4. Advantages (merits, benefits, rewards)

Another common type of question in this part of the test is a question about the merits of the topic you are discussing:

MODEL ANSWER

What are some of the advantages of being famous?

> **Clearly, there are a number of obvious merits.**
>
> **But I would probably say that the one thing that really stands out is that** it is easy to make money. **This is obviously favorable because** we can see the lavish* lifestyles that celebrities lead. You know they always seem to have cool cars and luxurious houses. [* lavish = luxurious]
>
> **Besides this, a second positive point could be that** famous people receive a lot of respect in society. **This can be seen in the way that** celebrities often receive special attention at hotels and restaurants.

USEFUL LANGUAGE

Opening:

Clearly, there are a number of obvious merits.

Obviously, there are a number of positive features.

The main advantage:

But I would probably say that the one thing that really stands out is.... This is obviously favorable because...

However, I guess that the greatest benefit would be that...This is surely a positive feature as...

The second advantage:

Besides this, a second positive point could be that... This is undoubtedly favorable because...

As well as this, a second merit might be that.... This can be seen

Practice Questions

1. What are the advantages of living in high-rise apartments?
2. What are the merits of living in big cities?
3. What are the benefits of owning an up-to-date mobile phone?
4. What benefits do companies get from advertising?
5. What are the rewards of studying abroad?
6. How does public transport benefit society?

5. Disadvantages (drawbacks, shortcomings)

Another common type of question in this part of the exam is to ask you about the disadvantages of a topic. Let's stick with the topic of being famous and see how we can answer the question regarding this topic.

MODEL ANSWER

Do you think there are any disadvantages of being famous?

For sure there are some drawbacks.

I suppose the most difficult aspect might be that famous people enjoy less privacy, because the paparazzi* try to follow them to find out everything about them including their relationships and anything that may be interesting to the public. **And this can be irritating because** they can't enjoy any quiet time alone with their loved ones and there is always a feeling of being in the public eye

At the same time, another stumbling block with fame might be that these celebrities always seem larger than life. **And the trouble with this is that** they must have a lot of pressure to meet people's expectations. **For instance**, at a party a comedian would be expected to be funny and this might be a kind of hassle when someone is just trying to relax and enjoy themselves.

[paparazzi* = aggressive media and reporters]

USEFUL LANGUAGE

Opening:

For sure there are some drawbacks.

Of course there are a couple of shortcomings.

The main disadvantage:

I suppose the most difficult aspect might be that... And this can be irritating because...

I guess the most disadvantageous characteristic would be that.... This is a clear limitation because...

The second disadvantage:

At the same time, another stumbling block with fame might be that ... And the trouble with this is that

Correspondingly, an additional drawback may be that ... This is obviously a problem as...

Practice Questions

1. What are the disadvantages of living in high-rise apartments?
2. What are the drawbacks of living in big cities?
3. What are the downsides of owning an up-to-date mobile phone?
4. What risks do companies get from spending a lot on advertising?
5. What are the pitfalls of studying abroad?
6. What are the drawbacks of today's fast-paced lifestyle?

6. Problems

Another common type of question in this part of the test is to ask you about problems that occur with the topic you are discussing. For this question you can think back to problem-solution essays. And if you're lucky, you might even get to discuss some of the points you wrote an essay about. You can also use language from problem and solution essays.

MODEL ANSWER

What do you think the consequences of global warming will be?

Obviously, we can see there are quite a few hazards with regard to this issue.

The most obvious effects are that many animals and plants are having trouble coping with the changing temperature. In some cases global warming may even lead to the extinction of some species.

The second detrimental effect is that the ocean levels are rising. **This is a major concern because** many cities around the world are already starting to flood due to their coastal locations and this is causing particular hardship for those who have built their houses by the sea.

Opening:

Obviously, we can see there are quite a few hazards with regard to this issue.

It seems likely that [topic] causes a number of issues.

The main problem:

The most obvious effects are that...In some cases [issue] even leads to...

Essentially, a fundamental issue is that ... This is clearly alarming as...

The second problem:

The second detrimental effect is that...This is a major concern because...

Equally worrying is the suggestion that... And the underlying repercussions of this are that.

Practice Questions

1. What problems are associated with eating fast food?
2. What issues are caused by a lack of physical exercise?
3. What problems does traffic congestion in big cities cause?
4. What problems are being caused by racial intolerance?
5. What problems does violence in the media cause?
6. What issues are caused by an over-dependence on technology?

7. Solutions:

If the examiner asks a question about a problem they are likely to follow this up with a question about how the problem could be solved. Try to give an answer that clearly addresses the problem or problems that you identified. It is also worth remembering that education and action by the government can be used to solve almost every problem.

MODEL ANSWER

Are there any ways to prevent global warming?

I believe there are a few ways to tackle this problem.

Perhaps the most effective solution is for governments to more quickly implement clean sources of energy. **Consequently,** carbon emissions would be drastically reduced which will solve the greenhouse effect and return the Earth back to its normal climate.

In addition, if schools were to educate young people about the need to preserve our environment **it would result in** an increased awareness of the need to take action at the grassroots level* to protect the environment. You know people should recycle things more and teachers should increase awareness amongst their students about this.

[* action at the grassroots level is action at the local level by ordinary citizens]

Opening:

I believe there are a few ways to tackle this problem.

I think that a few measures are available.

The first solution:

Perhaps the most effective solution is ... Consequently, ...

When dealing with [problem], the easiest way to solve it is to ... This will result in....

The second solution:

In addition, if [schools/the government] were to... it would result in...

I also think that we could ...This would enable...

Practice Questions

1. How could we prevent people from eating too much fast food?
2. How can we encourage people to do more physical exercise?
3. What are some measures to reduce traffic congestion in big cities?
4. What steps could be taken to tackle racial intolerance?
5. How could children be prevented from seeing violence on TV?
6. How can we avoid becoming over-dependent on technology?

8. Opinion (why) questions

It is highly likely that you'll be asked for your opinion on a topic in this section of the test. As with previous questions, don't ignore what you have learnt from studying IELTS writing. One of the common types of essays asks for your opinion. And, if you're lucky you might get asked a question in the speaking test that you have already written an essay on. In this case it should be easy to have ideas! As well as this, you may have learnt language that can be used in the speaking test. If you have learnt how to write concessions [counter arguments], then you can also use these in the speaking test.

MODEL ANSWER

Should schools focus on preparing students for their future careers?

Well, that's quite a controversial question, but I guess my opinion is that this should be the focal point of education.

The main reason I feel this way is because a person's career is so important for their life in terms of not only money but also experiencing job satisfaction.

As well as this, from a societal standpoint we need to have people who have the relevant skills to fill the jobs that are required. Like for instance, we need to have enough medical personnel to help out the sick and injured, and we need to have enough teachers to educate our adolescents.

However, it is sometimes argued that schools should fulfill some additional roles in addition to preparing youngsters for their working lives. The main argument here seem to be that young people should learn general life skills such as the ability to communicate and cooperate with others.

Opening:

Well, that's quite a controversial question, but I guess my opinion is...

As far as I'm concerned...

It seems to me that...

I tend to think that...

The first reason:

The main reason I feel this way is because...

The key basis for my opinion is...

The second reason:

As well as this, from a [societal/educational/environmental] standpoint...

At the same time, as far as I'm concerned...

Making a concession [counter-argument]

However, it is sometimes argued that...

Admittedly, in some circumstances it may not be the...

OTHER USEFUL EXPRESSIONS

Reckon: usually to express an opinion about what is likely to happen

I reckon students will learn social skills even if the focus is on preparing them for work.

If you ask me: to emphasize your own personal opinion

If you ask me, it's much better for teachers to prepare their students for their careers.

To be honest with you: to express a personal feeling

To be honest with you, I really think a person's career is the biggest part of their lives.

PRACTICE QUESTIONS

1. Do you think most people like travelling to foreign countries?
2. Why do so many people move from the countryside to cities?
3. Have people in your country become too dependent on technology?
4. Do you think young people spend too much time on the Internet?
5. Do you think there should be stricter controls on the advertising industry?
6. Do you support capital punishment [the death penalty]?

6.1 ASKING THE EXAMINER QUESTIONS

You can ask the IELTS examiner questions in the IELTS speaking exam. There are numerous ways to deal with problems by asking questions and it is a good idea to learn how to ask these before taking an exam.

FUNCTION	PHRASE
Repeat the question (Part 1 -3)	Could you please repeat that? Sorry, I didn't quite catch what you said?
Checking the meaning of a word (Part 1 -3)	Sorry, what does X mean? Could you please explain the meaning of X?
Checking the question (Part 3 only. You can try in Part 1 but the examiner may not respond. Look for body language, like nodding of the head)	Are you asking me....? Do you mean....?

6.2 USEFUL FUNCTIONAL PHRASES

FUNCTION	PHRASE
buying time	Let me see now, that really is quite a tricky question. Well, I suppose I would have to say that... Oh gosh! I'm really not sure about that, but probably...
getting to the key point	Let me cut to the chase, the key point is... Anyway, the thing I really want to say is... What I'm trying to say is...
repeating	Let me put it another way Or, in other words... To put it more succinctly...
restarting	Let me put it this way... Let me start over... Oh, I seem to have lost my train of thought a bit, let me see, oh yes, that's right, what I mean to say is...
conversation repair [when you realize that you've made a mistake in your response]	What I mean to say is... What I'm trying to say is... Another way to put it is...

Useful linking words and phrases

Linking words help increase your score for fluency and coherence because they help the examiner to see how ideas are sequenced and to catch the main ideas. They also help you to structure and extend your ideas.

SEQUENCING IDEAS

sequencing the first idea	adding supporting ideas	adding a contrasting idea
The main reason is...	Another reason is...	On the other hand,
First of all,	Furthermore,	Nevertheless,
The most important consideration is...	In the same vein,	Although,

GIVING OPINIONS

starting your opinion	giving your opinion	clarifying an opinion
From my perspective,	totally agree/disagree	To be more precise...
From my point of view,	somewhat agree/disagree	More specifically...
In my opinion,	agree/disagree to a certain degree	By this I mean...

GIVING EXPLANATIONS AND EXAMPLES

giving an explanation	giving examples
The reason for this is... This is because... This is due to...	This is clearly illustrated by... A clear example of this is...

EXPLAINING CAUSES AND EFFECTS

to express cause	to express effect	drawing a conclusion
Owing to... Due to the fact that... For the reason that...	As a consequence, As a result... For this reason...	All things considered, I firmly believe... Taking everything into account I am inclined to believe that...

EXPLAINING ADVANTAGES AND DISADVANTAGES

to give advantages	to give disadvantages
A major advantage of this is... Another important merit is... The final benefit is...	One major drawback is... Another disadvantage is... The final limitation is that...

6.3 IDIOMATIC LANGUAGE

Using idiomatic expressions is a way to show the examiner your talent with vocabulary and increase your score in the speaking exam. Using a few of the phrases below is a good way to get a score of 7 or higher. A 7 requires that you use advanced language such as idiomatic language.

	Idiomatic Expressions
1.	**on the go** = busy *I've been **on the go** all day and I'm really tired.*
2.	**work flat out** = work very hard *I have to **work flat out** all day to meet the deadline at 5 PM.*
3.	**up-market** = fashionable *She lives in an **up-market** neighborhood with lots of expensive houses.*
4.	**chill out** = relax *My favorite way to **chill out** is to put on some music and lie down on the sofa.*
5.	**the in thing** = fashionable, popular *Doing yoga has become **the in thing** as trying to be healthy is really popular now.*
6.	**at the height of fashion** = fashionable *Televisions were **at the height of fashion** in the 1980s.*
7.	**up-to-the-minute** = the most recent *Nowadays, the Internet includes **up-to-the-minute** news stories.*
8.	**off the top of my head** = without thinking ***Off the top of my head**, I will probably go shopping at the weekend.*

9.	**run of the mill** = average, typical *This is not your **run of the mill** computer. It has many advanced functions.*
10.	**mouth-watering** = delicious , appetizing *The pizza was so **mouth-watering**, I ate it as soon as I got home.*
11.	**eye-opening experience** = enlightening or unexpected experience *It was an eye-**opening experience** to see an actual robbery take place.*
12.	**in high spirits** = happy *When I passed the exam, I felt in **high spirits**.*
13.	**bump into** = meet *I usually **bump into** my old friends once a month at Starbucks.*
14.	**once in a blue moon** = not very often *You only get an opportunity this good once in a **blue moon.***
15.	**over the moon** = really happy *I felt **over the moon** when I opened the door to my surprise birthday party.*
16.	**have a chin-wag** = have a chat *Every Friday, I like to meet my mates at Starbucks for a **chin-wag**.*
17.	**give a hand** = help *The nurses are ready to **give a hand** to all those people who are sick.*
18.	**the wee hours** = after midnight, very early in the morning *My assignment was due at 9AM the next day, so I had to work until **the wee hours**.*
19.	**make a fuss over** = overly care for someone/something *Don't **make a fuss over** this, it is really quite trivial.*
20.	**early bird** = someone who gets up early *My father is an **early bird.** He gets up at 6AM every morning to go jogging.*

Using Idioms

I suggest you don't try to learn too many idiomatic phrases. The key point is to use them and also to use them correctly. Focus on learning a few well. Also you should try to avoid very common idioms and especially clichés. A cliché is an overused expression. These can be considered as "ugly" English. These do not help your score, and may possibly lower it.

Examples:

In this day and age,

At the end of the day,

Raining cats and dogs.

Just like every coin has two sides,

7. TOPICS FOR PARTS 1-3

You can use this section to build vocabulary and to practice doing complete IELTS speaking tests. It includes language for different topics and questions for PARTS 1-3 of the speaking test.

7.1 CLOTHING

Language

NOUNS	MEANING
accessory	something added to an outfit such as a belt or piece of jewelry
boutique	small shop that sells fashionable clothes
garment	item of clothing
fabric	the type of cloth used to make a piece of clothing
fitting room	a room in a clothes store to try on clothes
outfit	a complete set of clothing

VERBS	MEANING
accessorize	to add something to an outfit like a belt or jewelry
dress up	to make an effort to put on stylish clothes
flaunt	show off, especially to seek admiration
go out of style	to become unfashionable
try on clothes	to check whether clothing fits
in vogue	to become fashionable

ADJECTIVES	MEANING
casual	clothing suitable for relaxing in
formal	clothing suitable for formal social events or work
elegant	stylish
gorgeous	beautiful
outrageous	unusual and rather shocking
trendy	popular

IDIOMS
all dressed up = dressed in one's best clothes *We got all dressed up to attend the party.*
dressed to kill = wearing stylish clothes that will attract attention *Nicole Kidman turned up at the Oscars dressed to kill.*
fit like a glove = to fit perfectly *My new jeans fit like a glove.*
the in thing = fashionable *This summer, baggy jeans are the in thing.*

SAMPLE QUESTIONS

PART 1

Let's talk about clothing...

What types of clothes do you like wearing?

What color clothing do you prefer?

Did you wear a school uniform when you were younger?

Do you prefer clothes that are comfortable or stylish?

Let's talk about shoes...

What sort of shoes do you usually like to wear?

Do you have a favorite pair shoes?

How often do you buy shoes?

When was the last time you bought a pair of shoes?

Let move on to discuss shopping for clothes...

Where do you go shopping for clothes?

Do you try on clothes before you buy them?

Do you prefer to shop alone or with another person?

Have you ever bought clothing on the Internet?

PART 2

Describe an item of clothing you purchased that you didn't like

You should say:

what the clothing is

where and why you bought it

what color and style it is

and explain why you didn't like it.

PART 3

Let's talk about clothes...

What kind of clothes do people in your country usually wear?

How important is it to wear fashionable clothes in your country?

Do older people and younger people wear different colored clothes?

Now let's talk about spending money on clothes...

Are clothes expensive in your country?

Do people wear more expensive clothes to work in your country?

Do you think people spend too much money on clothes nowadays?

7.2 EDUCATION

Language

NOUNS	MEANING
the curriculum	the entire school program including course materials and testing of students. Everything that a school aims to teach students.
a graduate	a person who has graduated from a school
literacy	the ability to read and write
pedagogy	the way of teaching including the instructional methods that are used
qualification	what someone gets when they graduate from school. For instance, a diploma is a qualification.
student centered education	a philosophy of education where the student is the central focus
tuition	the fees for studying a course

VERBS	MEANING
graduate	to pass a course or level of study
concentrate	to focus attention towards a particular activity, subject or problem
revise	to review materials that have already been taught
enroll	to join a class
indoctrinate	to teach following a biased belief or point of view. For example: Hitler indoctrinated young Germans with a hatred for other races.
persevere	to not give up. To keep doing something until success is achieved.

ADJECTIVES	MEANING
academic	relating to education especially universities
co-educational	when male and female students are taught together in the same school
single sex	when only male or female students are taught in the same school
hands-on	to learn by actually doing. We can get hands-on experience by actually doing things
multi-disciplinary	involving several different subjects or areas of study
pedagogical	relating to teaching methods and principles
primary education	an elementary school or the first years of formal schooling
secondary education	high school
tertiary education	university or vocational school
vocational	concerning the skills necessary for a particular job. This includes trade schools. So if you are studying cooking or hairdressing then you are going to a vocational school

IDIOMS
bookworm = someone who reads a lot *My brother is a bit of a bookworm; he's always reading a book.*
drop out of school = to stop attending school *I dropped out of school and began to work for the family business.*
hit the books = study hard *I have to hit the books because I have a 5,000 word essay due tomorrow.*
pass with flying colors = to pass something with a high score *I got the highest score in the science test ...I passed with flying colors!*

SAMPLE QUESTIONS

PART 1

Now let's talk about schools

How many schools have you been to?

Which school was your favorite?

Did your parents choose your schools for you?

Would you send your children to the same schools?

Let move on to discuss high school

What was your favorite subject?

Did you like any of the teachers?

What sports or hobbies did you do at school?

Which were more important to you the teachers or your classmates?

Let's talk about handwriting and writing by hand

When did you last handwrite something?

Is your handwriting easy to read?

Do you like writing cards and letters by hand?

Do you receive many handwritten letters or cards?

PART 2

Describe a time when you learnt a useful skill

You should say:

what skill you learnt?

why you learnt it?

where you did it?

and explain how the skill is useful in your life.

PART 3

Let's talk about skills...

What kinds of skills are most important for young people to learn?

Do you think children learn more skills from their parents or their teachers?

What skills might become more important in the future?

Now let's talk about learning...

Why do you think some people enjoy learning new things?

Do you think people were more intelligent in the past?

Do you think people will be more knowledgeable in the future?

7.3 ENVIRONMENT

Language

NOUNS	MEANING
biodegradable	something that is able to decay naturally and harmlessly
biodiversity	refers to the variety of plant and animal species that exist in a particular environmental area or in the world generally
climate	the weather conditions of a region
climate change	the concept that change is occurring to the earth's climate. [Especially based on the influence of people].
fossil fuels	a natural fuel such as coal, gas, or oil formed over long periods of time from the remains of living organisms
extinction	the complete dying out of a species
habitat	a place where animals and plants live
natural resources	resources derived from the environment. For example, wood and oil.
renewable energy	describes a form of energy that can be produced as quickly as it is used, such as solar energy

VERBS	MEANING
conserve	to not waste something
deplete	to reduce the amount of something
discharge	to release something
contaminate	to make something become polluted
endanger	to put something or someone in danger
preserve	to keep something safe

ADJECTIVES	MEANING
critical	extremely important
disposable	something that can be thrown away
environmentally friendly	something that is good or not harmful to the environment
hazardous	something dangerous
renewable	able to be renewed or replenished
toxic	something poisonous

IDIOMS
a race against time = a need to finish something quickly *We are in <u>a race against time</u> to reverse the effects of global warming.*
no quick fix = no simple solution. *There seems to be <u>no quick fix</u> to solve our needs for energy consumption from fossil fuels.*
sweep under the carpet – to ignore or hide something *It seems politicians would rather <u>sweep</u> the problem of climate change <u>under the carpet</u> than deal with it.*
the tip of the iceberg = *a small part of something much bigger* *Rising oceans are only the <u>tip of the iceberg</u> of the problems being caused by climate change.*

PART 1

Let's talk about natural places

How often do you visit natural places?

Do you prefer to visit the ocean or mountains?

Have you ever gone camping?

Would you like to live in the countryside?

Now let's talk about the weather

What's the weather like in your country?

What kind of weather do you like the most?

Do you pay attention to weather forecasts?

Is the weather changing in your country?

Let move on to discuss parks

Do you like going to parks or, public gardens?

Who do you usually go there with?

When was the last time you went to a park?

Do you prefer to relax with your friends in a park or an indoor place?

PART 2

Describe a park you remember visiting

You should say:

where it s

what it looks like

what activities people do there

and explain why you still remember it.

PART 3

Let's talk about parks and green spaces...

Are there a lot of public parks in your country?

What are some of the different reasons people go to parks?

What sort of facilities do public parks need to have?

Now let's talk about the natural environment ...

Do you think the natural environment is getting worse?

What problems do you think this might cause?

What are some potential solutions to improve the environment?

7.4 FOOD

Language

NOUNS	MEANING
additives	substances added to food to preserve it or enhance its taste
chef	the chief cook
cuisine	a style of cooking; for example, Italian cuisine
fusion cuisine	mixing two or more styles of cooking together
ingredients	the different types of food that go into a recipe
obese	being extremely overweight
nutrition	the health value of food
recipe	a set of instructions for making a food dish

VERBS	MEANING
chop	to cut with a knife
diet	to attempt to lose weight by eating more carefully
mix	to combine ingredients together
garnish	add something to food to give it flavor, or decorative color
peel	to remove the skin from something.

ADJECTIVES	MEANING
aromatic	good smell
malodorous	bad smell
pungent	powerful smell
nutritious	used to describe food that is healthy. For example, fruit and vegetables are very nutritious.
delicious	good taste
unappetizing	bad taste

FLAVORS	EXAMPLE
sweet	candy
sour	lemons
salty	chips, bacon
bitter	medicine, coffee
fatty	deep fried food

IDIOMS
mouthwatering = *food that is delicious and appetizing* *Look at all the food! It is so mouthwatering. I can't wait to start eating it.*
not my cup of tea = *something you do not enjoy* *Steaks are simply not my cup of tea, I prefer chicken.*

SAMPLE QUESTIONS

PART 1

Cooking

Do you know how to cook?

Do you think all children should learn how to cook?

Is there anything you would like to learn how to cook?

Do you prefer to eat at home or to eat out?

Food

What types of food do you like to eat?

What kind of food is popular in your country?

What did you like to eat when you were a child?

Would you like to try any new type of food?

Healthy eating

Do you eat anything healthy?

Is there anything unhealthy you like to eat?

Did you eat a lot of vegetables when you were a child?

Is there any type of healthy food you would like to start eating in the future?

PART 2

Describe a restaurant you like

You should say:

where it is

how often you go there

what food it has

and explain why you like it.

PART 3

Let's talk about restaurants...

What types of restaurants are popular in your country?

Do people care more about the food or the service?

Do you think it's healthier to eat at home or at restaurants?

Now let's talk about cafes...

Are cafes popular in your country?

Do you think there will be more cafes in the future?

Is it better to have a business meeting at a cafe or a restaurant?

7.5 FRIENDS AND FAMILY

Language

NOUNS	MEANING
acquaintance	someone you know, but not as well as a friend
companion	friend, buddy
sibling	brother or sister
soul mate	very dear and close friend who you share your secrets and emotions with
social skills	the ability to communicate and interact well with others
spouse	husband or wife

VERBS	MEANING
admire	respect and think highly of
befriend	make friends with someone
help out	help [phrasal verb]
gossip	to talk idly, especially about the affairs of others
socialize	to be social or friendly towards others

ADJECTIVES	MEANING
amiable	friendly
casual	relaxed and not following strict rules
extrovert	out-going
introvert	shy
inspirational	motivating
passionate	intense or strong emotional feeling about something [positive]

IDIOMS
a chin wag = have a chat *Last night I met my best pal and had a bit of a* *chin wag.*
own flesh and blood *= family member or relative.* *We must always take good care of our own flesh and blood.*
sounding board = *a good person to talk to and seek advice from* *My soul mate is an excellent sounding board whenever I have a problem.*

PART 1

Let's talk about friends and friendship

How much time do you spend with your friends?

What do you usually do with your friends?

Is friendship important to you?

Do you prefer to have many friends or a few close ones?

Now let's talk about family

Do you have a large or small family?

How much time do you spend with your family?

Do you usually eat dinner with your family?

Are people in your country generally close to their family members?

Let's discuss politeness and being polite

Do you think you are a polite person?

Who taught you to be polite?

Do you think people should always be polite?

Is it more important to be polite to friends or family?

PART 2

Describe a friend that you often spend time with.

You should say:

when and how you met your friend

how often you see this friend

what kind of interests you share with your friend

and say why you like spending time with your friend.

PART 3

Let's talk about friends and friendships

How important is it to have friends?

Do you think teenagers rely more on their friends or family?

As people get older do they rely more on their friends or family?

Now let's talk about neighbors

Why is it important to have a good relationship with neighbors?

What do you think might cause neighbors to have arguments?

Why do neighbors often have difficulty getting to know each other?

7.6 HEALTH

Language

NOUNS	MEANING
addiction	the condition of not being unable to stop doing something. Especially something harmful like drinking alcohol or playing video games.
allergy	a strong reaction to something. For instance, an allergy to a certain food.
anxiety	stress
diagnosis	an opinion of a patient's health condition or illness
diet	1. everything that we eat 2. a plan to eat carefully to reduce weight
insomnia	inability or difficulty to get to sleep
physician	a doctor
treatment	a way of curing an illness or medical condition

VERBS	MEANING
cure	healing or restoring to health; provide a remedy
diagnose	to work-out what is wrong with a patient
eliminate	to get rid of something
prescribe	to recommend the use of a drug or other remedy
prevent	to stop something happening
remedy	cure
trigger	to cause something to happen. For example, certain foods may trigger an allergy

ADJECTIVES	MEANING
acute	very serious
chronic	long-lasting
hazardous	very dangerous
nutritious	used to describe food that is healthy such as fruit
vital	very important

IDIOMS
back on one's feet = physically healthy again My brother is <u>back on his feet</u> after being sick for two days.
burned out = to become very tired and almost sick from doing something for a long time or from working too hard After working long hours for many years the man finally <u>burned himself out</u>.
feel on top of the world = to feel very healthy I have been <u>feeling on top of the world</u> since I started exercising.
under the weather = not feeling well My brother has been <u>under the weather</u> all day and has not gone to work.

SAMPLE QUESTIONS

PART 1

Now let's talk about health

What do you do to keep in good health?

Do you have any unhealthy habits?

What could you do to be healthier?

Do you think you will be healthier in the future?

Let's move on to relaxation

What do you do to relax?

Do you do any healthy activities to help you relax?

Do you feel you have enough time to relax?

What did you do to relax when you were a child?

Now let's talk about bicycles

How popular are bicycles in your home town?

How often do you ride a bicycle?

Do you think that bicycles are suitable for all ages?

What are the advantages of a bicycle compared to a car?

PART 2

Describe something you did as a child to be healthier.

You should say:

what you did

why you did it

where you did it

and explain how it made you healthier

PART 3

Let's talk about healthy lifestyles...

Why do you think some people live unhealthy lifestyles?

Do you think people were healthier in the past?

Do you think people will be healthier in the future?

Now let's talk about fast food...

Why do you think fast food has become so popular?

What problems do you think fast food causes?

What are some ways to reduce the consumption of fast food?

7.7 HOBBIES

Language

NOUNS	MEANING
amusement	an enjoyable activity
hobby	frequent leisure activity
pastime	recreational activity
spare time	free time for recreation
tournament	competition

VERBS	MEANING
go sightseeing	visit tourist sites
nurture	to help grow or develop
take up	start doing an activity
take part in	participate in
unwind	relax

ADJECTIVES	MEANING
appealing	pleasing
fascinating	interesting
leisurely	unhurried
time-consuming	requiring a lot of time
thrilling	exciting

Idioms
get into = enjoy *Recently I've been getting into surfing.*
get a kick out of = really enjoy something *I really get a kick out of camping because it is so much fun to experience nature.*
kill time = spend time to avoid boredom *I like to kill time by surfing the Internet*

SAMPLE QUESTIONS

PART 1

Let's talk about your hobbies and interests

Do you have any hobbies or interests?

Did you have any hobbies or interests when you were a child?

What free-time activities are popular in your country?

Are there any outdoor activities you would like to try in the future?

Let move on to discuss free time

What do you do in your free time?

Do you have enough free time?

When do you usually get free time?

What free-time activities would you like to try if you had more free time?

Now let's talk about photos

Is it popular for people in your country to take photos?

Do you like to take photos?

What kind of photos do you like to take?

Will you take lots of photos in the future?

PART 2

Describe an outdoor activity you would like to do <u>for the first time.</u>

You should say:

what the activity would be

where you would do it

what preparations and equipment you would need

and explain why you would like to do this activity.

PART 3

Let's talk about outdoor activities...

What types of outdoor activities are most popular in your country?

Do people of different ages do different types of activities?

Do people spend more time outdoors than in the past?

Now let's talk about indoor activities...

What types of indoor activities are popular with children?

Do you think children spend too much time indoors?

What are some ways to encourage children to do outdoor activities?

7.8 MEDIA

Language

NOUNS	MEANING
a medium	a medium is the singular form of media [plural].
censorship	when certain types of messages are blocked. For instance, the government often uses censorship for movies that are violent or have sexual content.
genre	a style or category of art, music, movie, or literature.
mass media	mass media refers collectively to all the forms of media we have such as television, on-line services, magazines and newspapers.
paparazzi	aggressive media [negative]
scandal	dishonorable news story
social media	websites that enable people to create and share content with others

VERBS	MEANING
broadcast	to send messages. For instance, the TV broadcasts shows every night.
censor	to block or restrict information or content, especially when it includes violence or inappropriate content
exaggerate	when the truth is stretched or enlarged
manipulate	control or influence a person
publicize	to make public.

ADJECTIVES	MEANING
cultural	relating to culture. For example, cultural awareness is being aware of someone's culture.
eclectic	getting ideas, style, or taste from a wide range of sources
inspirational	motivating
monotonous	boring
passionate	intense or strong emotional feeling about something
vivid	clear and bright

IDIOMS
figure out = to try to understand someone or something *I can't <u>figure out</u> why the stock markets went down today as all the news seemed to be positive.*
word of mouth = information passed on through conversations *Before the scandal had hit newspapers the news had already spread by <u>word of mouth</u>.*
up-to-the-minute = the most recent *Nowadays, the Internet includes <u>up-to-the-minute</u> news stories.*

SAMPLE QUESTIONS

PART 1

Let's talk about the news

How do you find out about the news?

What type of news stories do you like to follow?

Do you think it's important to follow the news?

Do people in your country prefer to follow international news or local news?

Let's discuss the Internet

When did you first use the Internet?

What do you do on the Internet?

Have you ever brought anything online?

Do you always believe the information people post on their websites?

Now let's talk about reading...

How often do you read a book or magazine?

What types of books or magazines do you like to read?

Are there any types of things that you don't like to read?

What types of books or magazines did you like to read when you were a child?

PART 2

Describe a recent news story that interested you.

You should say:

how you heard about this news story

what the news was about

is this news positive or negative

and explain why this news story was interesting to you.

Let's talk about how people find out about the news ...

How do most people in your country find out about the news?

Are people more interested in local news or international news?

Are people these days more interested in the news than people were in the past?

Now let's talk about celebrities...

Why do people seem to be so fascinated to follow gossip about celebrities?

Do you think that most of the stories about celebrities' lives are true?

Do you think the media should respect celebrities' rights to privacy more?

7.9 SHOPPING

Language

NOUNS	MEANING
chain store	a store that has multiple locations such as Starbucks
family business	a shop that is run and managed by a family
luxury	an expensive and extravagant item
an essential	a necessary product like soap
market vendor	someone who sells products at a street market
street market	a street with outdoor stalls instead of shops
shopping complex	mall or places with multiple stores and maybe entertainment

VERBS	MEANING
browse	to look around for products of interest
discount	to sell for less than the usual price
haggle	to bargain over the price
pick out	to choose a product
window shopping	just looking at products without necessarily looking to buy something

ADJECTIVES	MEANING
exclusive	special and limited availability
extravagant	excessive and beyond what is necessary
fake	not real
genuine	real
sophisticated	stylish and complicated

IDIOMS
golden opportunity = an excellent opportunity *An internship at Google would be a golden opportunity.*
the in thing = fashionable, popular *Doing yoga has become the in thing as trying to be healthy is really popular now.*
up-market = fashionable *She lives in an up-market neighborhood with lots of expensive houses.*

SAMPLE QUESTIONS

PART 1

Let's talk about shopping.

Do you like to go shopping?

How often do you go shopping?

What kind of shops are there where you live?

What's the worst thing about going shopping?

Street Markets

Do you like visiting street markets?

Are street markets very common in your country?

Do you like to buy anything in particular at street markets?

Does your country have street markets open at night?

Let's talk about shopping on the Internet

Have you ever bought anything on the Internet?

Is it popular for people to shop on the Internet in your country?

Will you buy anything on the Internet in the future?

What are some disadvantages with buying products on the Internet?

PART 2

Describe a place that you like to visit for shopping. You should say: where this place is what it looks like what people buy there and explain why you like shopping in this place.

PART 3

Let's talk about places to go shopping...

What are some of the different types of places people shop in your country?

Do men and women prefer different types of shops?

Do you think people spend more time shopping these days?

Now let's talk about shopping on the Internet ...

What types of products are most suitable to buy on the Internet?

What are the advantages of shopping online?

What are some potential drawbacks of shopping online?

7.10 TECHNOLOGY

Language

NOUNS	MEANING
cyberspace	Internet
gadget	any small piece of equipment
revolution	major change in the way of doing something
social media	this usually refers to online tools for communication such as Facebook and Twitter
technophobe	someone who has a fear of using technology
technophile	someone who embraces technology and uses it often

VERBS	MEANING
develop	to make or create
engage in	get involved in
envisage	to conceive or imagine an idea
revolutionize	to make dramatic changes
surpass	to exceed or overtake. For example, technology is developing so fast that it will one day surpass our ability to use it.

ADJECTIVES	MEANING
computer literate	able to understand and communicate about how to use computers and computer applications
obsolete	something that is no longer used. For example, typewriters are now obsolete.
up-to-date	something that is still in fashion
virtual	almost, especially as in almost real. For example, when we play games using virtual reality they seem like they are almost real.

IDIOMS
state-of-the-art = the latest and most recently available version of a product *The latest smartphones incorporate the most state-of-the-art technology.*
user-friendly = easy to use *My new tablet is so user-friendly even my grandmother can use it.*

SAMPLE QUESTIONS

PART 1

Let's talk about computers

How often do you use a computer?

What do you use it for?

Do you play computer games?

Will you use a computer more in the future?

Now let's talk about cell phones

How often do you use a mobile phone?

Do you prefer to text people or call them?

In what situation is a mobile phone most useful?

Have you ever lost a cell phone?

Let's move on to discuss email and letters

Do you still write letters?

Do you think email will ever totally replace letters?

How do you feel if you receive a handwritten letter or card?

When did you last write a handwritten letter or card?

PART 2

> **Describe a website that you often use.**
>
> You should say:
>
> what type of website it is
>
> how you found out about it
>
> when you use it
>
> and why you find it useful.

PART 3

Let's talk about websites...

What types of websites are most popular in your country?

Is the Internet becoming more popular in your country?

Do you think most of the information on the net is reliable?

Now let's talk about social media...

Why has social media become so popular?

What are the benefits of social media?

What are some potential drawbacks of social media?

8. GRAMMAR

Grammar is a huge area with tons of books dedicated to it. If you are taking an IELTS exam in the near future you may not have a lot of time to work on grammar. The best ways to improve your grammar score are to reduce the number of errors you make and also use a variety of sentence types. Looking below at the grading criteria for grammar makes this clear.

Criteria for grammar

7	8
flexibly uses a range of complex structures	uses a wide range of structures
frequently produces error-free sentences,	most sentences are error-free with only very occasional inappropriacies that are not repeated

This section focuses on some ways to use complex sentence structures and then on explaining a few of the types of grammatical errors that commonly occur when people speak.

8.1 DEVELOP WAYS OF USING COMPLEX SENTENCES

Complex sentences are sentences that include an independent and dependent clause. Two excellent ways to form these are to use conditionals [phrases] and relative clauses [who, which, that, where]. To read about the rules and do some quizzes go here:

http://www.ieltsanswers.com/IELTS-Grammar.html

Conditional sentences

A conditional sentence is a complex sentence structure used to talk about something that occurs only if something else happens. The condition may be something real or imagined, and the result could be a definite result, or just a possible result. Conditionals are a useful way of forming complex sentences, which can boost your grammar score. Another reason why I teach candidates to use them is because they can be easily noticed by an examiner, due to the word *if*. If sends a signal to the examiner that a conditional is being used.

There are two clauses to a conditional sentence:

One part is the **if** clause. This is the event that needs to occur. It is a dependent clause because it is not a complete sentence and is dependent on the other part of the sentence.

The second part is the **result** or main clause, or what happens when the event in the **if** clause occurs. The result clause is an independent clause because it can stand on its own as a sentence. The dependent and independent clauses can be spoken in any order, as shown below:

If I have holidays, I go to Australia. [A comma as needed when the dependent clause comes first]

I go to Australia if I have holidays. [No comma]

Summary of conditions

	Usage	Example	
0	facts and opinions	If I have holidays, **present tense,**	I go to the UK. **present tense**
1	likely outcomes	If I have enough days off, **present tense**	I will go to the UK. **future tense**
2	unlikely outcomes or imagined situations	If I won the lottery, **past tense**	I would go to the UK. **would**
3	past situations that didn't occur	If I had had enough time, **past perfect tense**	I would have gone the UK. **would have**

Note: To read more about the rules about conditionals and do some quizzes go here:

http://www.ieltsanswers.com/IELTS-Grammar.html

Relative clauses

Another good way to increase your grammar score by using complex sentences, is to add relative clauses to your sentences. Relative clauses use relative pronouns (that, which, who,) and are dependent clauses, which means that they cannot stand on their own as a complete sentence.

Summary of relative pronouns

Relative pronoun	Use	Example
who	people	I like students who study hard.
which	things	I ive in a flat, which s in a high-rise building.
where	places	I like shopping at places where there is lots of parking.
whose	possession	Do you know the boy whose mother is a nurse?
that	for a specific person or thing	I don't like the table that is in the kitchen.

Note: To read more about the rules about relative clauses and do some quizzes go here: http://www.ieltsanswers.com/IELTS-Grammar.html

Passive Form

The passive begins with the object (receiver of the action) and is followed by an auxiliary verb and a main verb in the past participle form. The table below compares the passive to the active tense. When speaking, the passive tense is used when we want to emphasize the object of the sentence.

Tense	Receiver	Verb	Object
Present Active	Mike	writes	a book.
Present Passive	A book	is written	by Mike.
Past Active	Mike	wrote	a book.
Past Passive	A book	was written	by Mike

8.2 REDUCE ERRORS

The second way to increase your score is to reduce errors. To get to grade 7 and above you need to have frequent error-free sentences. If you do not have this you cannot get to 7 and above. If you want to get to 8 or 9 you need to decrease errors to a similar frequency as a native speaker. In order to achieve this you need to identify your areas of weakness and work on these by learning the rules, doing quizzes, and getting feedback on your speaking from a teacher.

Articles (a, an, the)

An article is a word that is used with a noun to indicate to the reader whether the noun is a particular and specific noun, or an instance of a noun in general., There are two types of articles the indefinite (a/an), which refers to the general usage of a noun; and the definite article (the) which refers to a specific noun.

An **indefinite** article indicates that its noun is not a specific one that can be identified by the listener. It may be something that the speaker is mentioning for the first time, or the speaker may be making a general statement about something. The indefinite articles are ***a*** and ***an***. The word ***a*** is *used* before words that begin with a consonant sound (even if the word starts with a vowel, as in *a unicorn*). ***An*** is used before words that begin with a vowel sound (even if the word starts with a consonant, as in *an hour*).

Example: *She had **a** house so large that **an** elephant would get lost.*

A **definite** article is used with a noun that refers to something specific the reader should be aware of. It may be used to refer back to something that the speaker has already mentioned, or it may be used with a noun that has only one possible instance such as the Internet.

Summary of the usage of articles

	Indefinite (*a* or *an*)	**Definite** (*the*)
Singular	a cat (any cat) an orange (any orange)	the dirtiest cat the orange on the table
	[None used]	**Definite** (*the*)
Plural	Plurals, languages, sports, subjects, cities, countries... with a few exceptions!	the best cats) the sweetest oranges

Note the following:

1. First versus subsequent mention of a noun

A or an is used to introduce a noun when it is used for the first time.

"Please give me a pen."

The is used afterward each time you mention that same noun.

"Where is the pen?"

There was a cat in my room. When my dog came in, the cat ran away.

2. Zero articles:

Some common types of nouns that don't take an article are:

a. Plurals usually have no articles: "please give me some apples," "I like apples.;" unless they are definite "these are <u>the</u> best apples.

b. Names of languages and nationalities: "I am Chinese."

c. Names of sports: "I like playing soccer."

d. Names of academic subjects: "I studied math for three years."

3. Places usually have no article:

Do not use *the* before names of streets, countries, lakes, and mountains.

There are a few exceptions such as: the USA, the UK, the EU [note that these are all areas that are made up of different regions]; likewise with groups of lakes like the Great Lakes, and ranges of mountains like the Himalayas.

Note: To read more about the rules about articles and do some quizzes go here: http://www.ieltsanswers.com/IELTS-Grammar.html

Errors with word endings and forms

"S" endings of words

Almost every non-native speaker makes this mistake. The speaker puts an "S" where it's not needed or else forgets to put one where it is needed. Examples below:

Student ~~are~~ always studying hard. ["s" is needed for students]

Students ~~goes~~ home tired every day. [The verb should be *go*]

The Internet ~~are~~ developing rapidly. [The Internet is uncountable, so it should be: The Internet *is* developing rapidly]

Other common errors are errors with word endings such as "ed" for past tense, and errors with word forms such as when a verb is incorrectly used as a noun. A couple of examples:

Last year my uncle ~~work~~ in America.
Last year my uncle worked in America

We need to ~~management~~ the environment better.
We need to manage the environment better

Prepositions

Prepositions are used to locate something in time and space, modify a noun; or tell when or where or under what conditions something happened. The following are guidelines for using prepositions correctly. This covers many common situations. However, you need to refer to my website or other sources for an exhaustive list: http://www.ieltsanswers.com/IELTS-Grammar.html

Prepositions of Time: at, in, on

Preposition	Usage	Example
at	**at** is for specific times	The exam is at 12:15 PM
in	**in** is for nonspecific times during a day/month/year.	The exam is in the morning
on	**on** for days and dates	The exam is on Monday. The exam is on Christmas Day.

Prepositions of Place: at, in, on

Preposition	Usage	Example
at	We use **at** for specific addresses.	I live at 50 Pong Lai Road.
in	We use **in** for the names of areas (cities and countries).	I live in Taipei.
on	We use **on** for the names of streets, avenues, etc.	I live on Pong Lai Road.

Prepositions for describing our work:

Preposition	Usage	Example
at	at company's	I work at Comtrend
in	in departments	in the marketing department, **as** a technical writer.
on	on projects	I am working on a new manual

9. FREQUENTLY ASKED QUESTIONS

What should I do if I didn't hear or understand the question?

In Part 1-3 you can ask the examiner to repeat the question (they can do this 1 time only for each question). It won't have a negative impact on your grade unless you do this often.

Can I ask the examiner what a word means?

In Part 1-3 you can ask the examiner the meaning of a WORD

In Part 3 you can ask the examiner to REPHRASE the entire question

What should I do if I don't know how to answer the question?

If you are really stuck about how to answer a question, do not sit there in silence! Say it: *"gosh that's a tricky question cf never thought about that before."* Then try to give some sort of answer. If you can't, then tell the examiner. Of course this is not ideal, but the worst thing is to sit there in silence. Additionally, even communicating that you don't understand the question is still producing language.

What should I do if I get an unfamiliar or difficult question in part two?

This is covered in the strategies section under Part Two of the speaking test. Essentially, start by directly answering the question and then try to drift off onto some part of the question that you can talk about. If you have pre-prepared some responses you may drift off onto one of these. For instance, if the question is about the gift you bought, you may drift off onto talking about the actual event [maybe it was a birthday party] or describing the person you bought the gift for [maybe this is your best friend]. Note that you do not need to stick to the sub-questions on the topic card; as long as

you are talking about the topic you can say anything about it. You also do not need to cover ALL of the sub-questions.

What should I do when I first walk into the room for the speaking test?

Just politely greet the examiner. Say something like: *"Hello it's nice to meet you."* Smile if you can and do your best to not look nervous! If you are in Australia you could start with something colloquial like *"Gidday, how's it going."*

What should I do when the examiner tells me the test is finished?

Thank the examiner for their time. Say something like: *"Thanks, I appreciate your time."* Or you could say: *"Thanks have a great day."*

Does the examiner really hold no bias on the candidate's opinion? Is this true even if the candidate express an unpleasant idea, for example, some sort of racial or sexual discrimination?

In theory there should be no bias, but remember that the examiner is human, so it's best to avoid anything that may upset them. Some things are just not appropriate anyway, like sexual discrimination.

Is there any difference in the marking scheme between different countries?

The grading criteria are the same for every country and every testing centre, and every examiner.

What can I say if the examiner asks me if I am studying or working and I am doing neither?

The above situation can make for a messy start. One choice is to tell a white lie and just talk about your previous job/studies as though you are still doing it. This also allows you to use the present tense. Otherwise, if you say you are doing neither the examiner will ask you to talk about your most recent study/work and you will need to use the past tense to talk about it.

Is my speaking score affected by my accent?

Accent comes under the pronunciation criterion. If you accent makes you difficult to understand your score will be lowered. If the examiner can easily understand what you are saying, despite an accent, your score should not be lowered. However, the more native-like you sound, the more the examiner is likely to have a positive feeling about your pronunciation. If you have lots of time before your exam, one way to improve in this area is to pick an accent of a county or even a particular person, such as a famous actor or actress, and try to copy their accent.

What bothers me is that I can`t come up with ideas quickly; so my question is how to cope with that problem?

My suggestion here is to look at lots of typical questions and think how you would answer them. Think about the ideas you have and also the language you would use to explain them.

Am I allowed to make notes in both the second and third part of the exam?

Only in the second part (you get one minute). Most examiners will take away the paper after part 2. As well as this and you don't have time to make notes in part 3, you must answer fairly quickly (no preparation time is given).

Can I ask the examiner about my performance at the end of the test?

No! You should not do this as the examiner is not allowed to tell you.

When will I get my results?

Usually, your results will be available two weeks after your test from your test centre.

Why is the test recorded?

The test is recorded because you are allowed to ask for a remark of your test. In this case a different examiner will listen to the recording and give your score. Note that you need to pay for a remark!

Which part of the test is the most important?

Your score is based off all three parts equally. However, for those needing to get to 7 and beyond I believe that part two and three are the most important. This is because in part two the examiner gets to listen to you without having to ask questions. This allows the examiner to start to form an opinion about the grade they are going to give to you. By the end of Part Two the examiner might have formed an opinion about your grade. Part Three is then used to confirm this opinion.

Thanks for buying my book.

Other books in this series available at:

http://www.ieltsanswers.com/IELTS-Books.html

IELTS Task 2 Essay Writing

IELTS Task 1 Writing Academic Test

IELTS Task 1 Writing General Test

Ways to follow me!

http://www.ieltsanswers.com/

http://www.youtube.com/user/IELTSanswers

https://www.facebook.com/IELTSanswers

17857896R00123

Printed in Great Britain
by Amazon